ESSENTIALS OF
*Athletic
Training*

ESSENTIALS OF
Athletic Training

Fourth Edition

Daniel D. Arnheim, D.P.E., A.T.C.
Fellow, American College of Sports Medicine

Professor Emeritus of Physical Education
California State University
Long Beach, California

William E. Prentice, Ph.D., P.T., A.T.C.
Professor, Coordinator of the Sports Medicine Specialization,
Department of Physical Education, Exercise, and Sports Science
Clinical Professor, Division of Physical Therapy,
Department of Medical Allied Health Professions,
Associate Professor, Department of Orthopaedics
School of Medicine
The University of North Carolina
Chapel Hill, North Carolina

Director, Sports Medicine Education and Fellowship Program
HEALTHSOUTH Corporation
Birmingham, Alabama

Boston   Burr Ridge, IL   Dubuque, IA   Madison, WI   New York   San Francisco   St. Louis
Bangkok   Bogotá   Caracas   Lisbon   London   Madrid
Mexico City   Milan   New Delhi   Seoul   Singapore   Sydney   Taipei   Toronto

WCB/McGraw-Hill

*A Division of The **McGraw·Hill** Companies*

ESSENTIALS OF ATHLETIC TRAINING, FOURTH EDITION

This book is printed on acid-free paper.

1 2 3 4 5 6 7 8 9 0 QPF/QPF 9 3 2 1 0 9 8

ISBN 0–07–092125–3 (softcover)
       0–07–232537–2 (hardcover)

Vice president and editorial director: *Kevin T. Kane*
Publisher: *Edward E. Bartell*
Executive editor: *Vicki Malinee*
Senior developmental editor: *Michelle Turenne*
Senior marketing manager: *Pamela S. Cooper*
Project manager: *Vicki Krug*
Production supervisor: *Sandy Ludovissy*
Coordinator of freelance design: *Michelle Whitaker*
Art editor: *Joyce Watters*
Supplement coordinator: *David A. Welsh*
Compositor: *ElectraGraphics, Inc.*
Typeface: *10/12 Meridien*
Printer: *Quebecor Printing Book Group/Fairfield, PA*

Freelance interior designer: *Jeanne M. Rivera*
Freelance cover designer: *Paul Uhl; Design Associates*
Cover image: *© Terje Rakke/Image Bank*

The credits section for this book begins on page C1 and is considered an extension of the copyright page.

This text was based on the most up-to-date research and suggestions made by individuals knowledgeable in the field of athletic training. The authors and publisher disclaim any responsibility for any adverse effects or consequences from the misapplication or injudicious use of information contained within this text. It is also accepted as judicious that the coach and/or athletic trainer performing his or her duties is, at all times, working under the guidance of a licensed physician.

Library of Congress Cataloging-in-Publication Data

Arnheim, Daniel D.
    Essentials of athletic training / Daniel D. Arnheim, William E.
Prentice. — 4th ed.
        p.   cm.
    Includes bibliographical reference and index.
    ISBN 0–07–092125–3
    1. Physical education and training.   I. Prentice, William E.
II. Title.
RC1210.A749   1999
617.1'027—dc21   98–35782
                                                          CIP

www.mhhe.com

Contents in Brief

Contents

Applications at a Glance

Preface

The majority of students who take courses dealing with prevention and management of injuries that typically occur in an athletic population have little or no intention of pursuing athletic training as a career. However, it is also true that a large percentage of those students who are taking these courses are doing so because they do intend to pursue careers in coaching, fitness, physical education, or other areas related to exercise and sport science. For these individuals, some knowledge and understanding of the many aspects of health care for both recreational and competitive athletes is "essential" for them to effectively perform the associated responsibilities of their job.

Other students who are personally into fitness or training and conditioning may be interested in taking a course that will provide them with guidelines and recommendations for preventing injuries; or they want to recognize what an injury is should one occur and learn at least a little about how to correctly manage it. *Consequently, the fourth edition of* Essentials of Athletic Training *is written for these students rather than only athletic trainers. Essentials of Athletic Training* has been designed to provide basic information on a variety of topics, all of which relate in one way or another to health care for the athlete.

Essentials of Athletic Training was created from the foundations established by another well-recognized textbook, *Principles of Athletic Training*, currently in its ninth edition. Whereas *Principles of Athletic Training* serves as a major text for professional athletic trainers and those individuals interested in sports medicine, *Essentials of Athletic Training* is written at a level more appropriate for the coach, fitness professional, or physical educator. It provides guidance, suggestions, and recommendations for proper athletic health care when an athletic trainer or physician are not available.

ORGANIZATION AND COVERAGE

This edition of *Essentials of Athletic Training* provides the reader with the most current information possible on the subject of prevention and basic care of sports injuries. The general philosophy of the text is that adverse effects of physical activity arising from participation in sport should be prevented to the greatest extent possible. However, the nature of participation in physical activity dictates that sooner or later injury may occur. In these situations, providing immediate and correct care can minimize the seriousness of an injury.

Overall, this text is designed to take the beginning student from general to more specific concepts. Each chapter focuses on promoting an understanding of the prevention and care of athletic injuries.

Essentials of Athletic Training is divided into three parts: Organizing and

Establishing an Effective Athletic Health Care System; Techniques for Preventing and Minimizing Sport-Related Injuries; and Recognition and Management of Specific Injuries and Conditions.

Part 1, Organizing and Establishing an Effective Athletic Health Care System, begins in Chapter 1 with a discussion of the roles and responsibilities of all the individuals on the sports medicine team who in some way impact on the delivery of health care to the athlete. Chapter 2 provides guidelines and recommendations for setting up a system that provides athletic health care in situations in which an athletic trainer is not available to oversee that process. For people in today's society in general, and in particular for anyone who is remotely related to providing athletic health care, the issues of legal responsibility and, perhaps more important, legal liability are of utmost concern. Chapter 3 discusses ways to minimize the chances of litigation and also to make certain that both the athlete and the coach are protected by appropriate insurance coverage. Chapter 4 emphasizes the importance of fitness in preventing injuries. Chapter 5 discusses the importance of eating a healthy diet and paying attention to sound nutritional practices.

Part 2, Techniques for Preventing and Minimizing Sport-Related Injuries, discusses a variety of topics that both individually and collectively can reduce the chances for injury to occur. Chapter 6 provides guidelines for selecting and using protective equipment. Chapter 7 explains in some detail how to assess the severity of an injury and then provides specific steps that should be taken to handle emergency situations. Chapter 8 provides guidelines and universal precautions that can help reduce the chances of spreading infectious diseases by preventing the transmission of bloodborne pathogens. Chapter 9 discusses the psychology of preparing to compete and proposes techniques for coping with injury when it does occur. Chapter 10 looks at ways to minimize the potentially negative threats of various environmental conditions on the health of the athlete. Chapter 11 discusses the more common taping techniques that can be used to prevent new injuries from occurring and old ones from becoming worse. Chapter 12 includes a brief discussion of the general techniques that may be used in rehabilitation following injury. Chapter 13 defines and classifies the various types of injuries that are most commonly seen in the physically active population.

Part 3, Recognition and Management of Specific Injuries and Conditions includes Chapters 14 through 22 which discuss injuries that occur in specific regions of the body: the foot; the ankle and lower leg; the knee; the hip, thigh, groin, and pelvis; the shoulder; the elbow, wrist, forearm, and hand; the spine; the thorax and abdomen; and the head and face. Injuries are discussed individually in terms of the most common causes, the recognizable signs, and a basic plan of care. Chapter 23 provides guidelines and suggestions for managing various illnesses and other health conditions that may effect athletes and their ability to play and compete. Chapter 24 provides special considerations for injuries that may occur in young athletes.

NEW TO THIS EDITION

- *Bloodborne pathogens:* A new Chapter 8 provides coverage of hepatitis B, HIV, and AIDS and the universal precautions necessary in the athletic environment. This chapter includes discussions of the symptoms and signs, prevention, and management of HBV and HIV as well as personal precautions, testing, and precautions from exposure.

- *Legal liability and insurance:* Chapter 3 provides greater detail about preventing litigation and about the different types of insurance available.

- *Young athletes:* Rather than being integrated as has been done in previous editions, this content is conveniently presented in one chapter, Chapter 24, which discusses young athletes from physical maturity to injury prevention.

- *Second-impact syndrome:* Chapter 22, The Head and Face, provides a timely discussion of this condition using the most current information available.

- *Critical thinking exercises:* Included in every chapter, these brief case studies correspond with the accompanying text and help students apply the content just learned. Solutions for each exercise are located at the end of the chapters.

- *Web sites:* Web sites are included at the end of appropriate chapters as an additional resource for students to obtain further information as well as to link to other web sites.

- *Pronunciation guides:* Selected margin definitions now provide pronunciation guides to reinforce learning of more difficult terms.

- *Bulleted chapter summaries:* New with this edition, chapter summaries are now bulleted to help reinforce content and to aid in test preparation.

PEDAGOGICAL FEATURES

A number of teaching devices are included in this text:

- *Chapter objectives:* Objectives are presented at the beginning of each chapter to reinforce learning goals.

- *Focus boxes:* Important information is highlighted to provide additional content that supplements the main text.

- *Margin information:* Key concepts, selected definitions, helpful training tips, and illustrations are placed in margins throughout the text for added emphasis and ease of reading and studying.

- *Photographs and line drawings:* These crucial tools are presented to facilitate the student's comprehension.

- *Color throughout the text:* A second color appears throughout the text to enhance the overall appearance and accentuate and clarify illustrations.

- *Chapter summaries:* Chapter content is summarized and bulleted to reinforce key concepts and aid in test preparation.
- *Review questions and class activities:* A list of questions and suggested class activities follows each chapter to offer review and application of the concepts learned.
- *References:* All chapters have a bibliography of pertinent references that includes the most complete and up-to-date resources available.
- *Annotated bibliography:* For students and instructors who want to expand on the information provided in each chapter, relevant and timely articles, books, and topics from the current literature have been annotated to provide additional resources.
- *Glossary:* A comprehensive list of key terms and their definitions are presented at the end of the text to reinforce information in one convenient location.
- *Appendices:* For those students interested in learning more about athletic training, Appendices A through C provide information about the profession, about certification, and about employment settings in the athletic training field. Appendix D contains helpful charts for metric and celsius conversions.

ANCILLARIES

Instructor's Manual and Test Bank

Developed for the fourth edition, the *Instructor's Manual and Test Bank* was prepared by Meredith Busby, M.A., A.T.C. Practical features include the following:

- Brief chapter overviews
- Learning objectives
- Key terminology
- Discussion questions
- Class activities
- Worksheets
- Worksheet answer keys
- Test bank
- Appendix of additional resources
- Twenty-four transparency masters
- Perforated format, ready for immediate use

Computerized Test Bank

A computerized version of the instructor's manual test bank for both IBM and Macintosh is available to qualified adopters. This software provides user-friendly aids and enables the instructor to select, edit, add, or delete questions as well as construct and print tests and answer keys.

ACKNOWLEDGMENTS

Special thanks are extended to Michelle Turenne, with whom we have enjoyed a long-standing relationship as our developmental editor on this and several other projects. She has provided invaluable guidance once again in the preparation of this fourth edition of *Essentials of Athletic Training*.

Our editor, Vicki Malinee, continues to be the "rock" that keeps us focused for all our projects. We both have benefited tremendously from our years of working with her. We look forward to continuing our rewarding relationship with her for many years to come.

Meredith Busby from the University of North Carolina has been responsible for preparing the *Instructor's Manual and Test Bank* that accompanies this text as well as for providing web site resources in this edition. Her efforts have provided a much-needed educational resource for individuals teaching a course in athletic injuries, and we certainly appreciate the manner in which she has completed her part of this project.

We would also like to thank the following individuals who served as reviewers for their input into the revision of this text:

Brad Brown
University of Nebraska Lincoln

Colleen Keenan
New Mexico State University

Mike Lester
Idaho State University

Ken Sarubbi
De Paul University

Julie K. Svec
College of DuPage

Donald W. Crane
Bowdoin College

Melissa Lachman
Morgan State University

Debra R. Runkle
Mankato State University

Stephanie Stout
Purdue University

Finally, Dan would like to extend a special thank you to Vicki Krug and her production staff at WCB/McGraw-Hill Higher Education, who helped make this edition possible. Bill would like to thank his wife, Tena, and their sons, Brian and Zachary, for always being an important part of everything he does.

Daniel D. Arnheim
William E. Prentice

ORGANIZING AND ESTABLISHING AN EFFECTIVE ATHLETIC HEALTH CARE SYSTEM

The Sports Medicine Team and Their Roles

When you finish this chapter you will be able to:

- Define the umbrella term *sports medicine*.
- Identify various sports medicine organizations.
- Explain how the sports medicine team should interact with the athlete.
- Describe the role of the coach in injury prevention, emergency care, and injury management.
- Identify the responsibilities of the athletic trainer in dealing with the injured athlete.
- Describe the role of the team physician and his or her interaction with the athletic trainer.
- Identify other members of the sports medicine team and describe their roles.

Millions of individuals participate on a regular basis in both organized and recreational sport activities. Ironically, participation in sports places the athlete in situations in which injury is likely to occur. Fortunately, most injuries are not serious and lend themselves to rapid rehabilitation. Athletes who engage in organized sports have every right to expect that their health and safety be kept as the highest of priorities. Both coaches and athletic trainers must be concerned with the well-being of the athlete and in those roles assume responsibility for overseeing the total health care of the athlete (Figure 1-1).

In an ideal world, specific responsibilities of both the coach and the athletic trainer would be clearly defined. Coaches could concentrate their efforts on coaching, and athletic trainers could assume total responsibility for the health needs of the athlete. Unfortunately, because of budget constraints at institutions or within organizations that offer organized athletic programs, every coach does not have access to an athletic trainer.[4] Even if your school or organization employs an athletic trainer, there is no chance that that single athletic trainer can be available to cover every practice and game of all the teams that compete at your school or within your organization. In these less-than-ideal situations,

Figure 1-1

The field of athletic training
is a major link between the
sports program and the
medical community.

coaches are forced not only to be coaches but also to assume more responsibility for providing health care to their athletes. This situation dictates that the coach have some knowledge about injury prevention,
emergency care, and injury management.

WHAT IS SPORTS MEDICINE?

The term *sports medicine* has many connotations, depending on which
group is using it. The term encompasses many different areas of sports related to both performance and injury. Among the areas of specialization
within sports medicine are athletic training, physical therapy, biomechanics, exercise physiology, the practice of medicine relative to the athlete, sports nutrition, and sports psychology.

Sports Medicine Organizations

A number of professional organizations are dedicated to athletic training
and sports medicine. Professional organizations have many goals: (1) to
upgrade the field by devising and maintaining a set of professional standards, including a code of ethics; (2) to bring together professionally competent individuals to exchange ideas, stimulate research, and promote
critical thinking; and (3) to give individuals an opportunity to work as a
group with a singleness of purpose, thereby making it possible for them
to achieve objectives that, separately, they could not accomplish. Addresses for these organizations are in the accompanying Focus Box.

Many of the national organizations that are interested in athletic
health and safety have state and local associations that are extensions of
the larger bodies. National, state, and local sports organizations have all
provided extensive support to the reduction of illness and injury risk to
the athlete.

Sports medicine encompasses
many different fields of study
related to sport, including:
• athletic training
• biomechanics
• exercise physiology
• the practice of medicine
  relative to the athlete
• physical therapy
• sports nutrition
• sports psychology

As a professional, the athletic
trainer must be a member of
and be active in professional
organizations.

1-1   *Focus Box*

List of Professional Sports Medicine Organizations

American Academy of Pediatrics, Sports Committee, 1801 Hinman Ave., Evanston IL 60204

American Board of Physical Therapy Specialists, American Physical Therapy Association, 1111 North Fairfax St., Alexandria VA 22314

American College of Sports Medicine, 401 W. Michigan St., Indianapolis IN 46202-3233

American Orthopaedic Society for Sports Medicine, Suite 202, 70 West Hubbard, Chicago IL 60610

National Athletic Trainers' Association, 2952 Stemmons Freeway, Dallas TX 75247

National Collegiate Athletic Association, Competitive Safeguards and Medical Aspects of Sports Committee, P.O. Box 1906, Mission KS 66201

The National Federation of State High School Athletic Associations, 11724 Plaza Circle, P.O. Box 20626, Kansas City, MO 64195

The National Athletic Trainers' Association

Many professional organizations are dedicated to achieving health and safety in sports.

The professional organization to which most athletic trainers belong is the National Athletic Trainers' Association (NATA). Before the formation of the NATA in 1950, athletic trainers occupied a somewhat insecure place in the athletic program. Since that time, as a result of the raising of professional standards and the establishment of a code of ethics, the field has experienced considerable professional advancement. The NATA accepts as members only those athletic trainers who are properly qualified and who are prepared to subscribe to a code of ethics and to uphold the standards of the association.[7] The NATA is constantly working to improve both the quality and the status of athletic training. Through the efforts of the membership of the NATA, the profession of athletic training is now recognized as an allied health profession and is accredited by the Commission on Accreditation of Allied Health Education Programs (CAAHEP)[10] (see Appendix A).

THE PLAYERS ON THE SPORTS MEDICINE TEAM

The primary athletic training team consists of the coach, the athletic trainer, and the team physician.

The provision of health care to the athlete requires a group effort to be most effective.[6,12] The sports medicine team involves a number of individuals, each of whom must perform specific functions relative to caring for the injured athlete. Those people having the closest relationship with the injured athlete are the coach, the athletic trainer, and the team physician.

The Sports Medicine Team and the Athlete

The major concern of everyone on the sports medicine team should always be the athlete. If not for the athlete, the coach, athletic trainer, and team physician would have nothing to do in sports. All decisions made by the physician, coach, and athletic trainer will ultimately affect the athlete. Athletes are frequently caught in the middle between the coaches, who tell them one thing, and the medical staff, who tells them something else. Thus the injured athlete must always be informed and made aware of the why, how, and when factors that collectively dictate the course of an injury rehabilitation program.

Both the coach and the athletic trainer should educate student-athletes about injury prevention and management. Athletes should learn about techniques of training and conditioning that may reduce the likelihood of injury. They should be well informed about their injuries and about listening to what their bodies are telling them in order to prevent reinjury.

In a high school setting, both the coach and the athletic trainer must take the time to explain to and inform the parents about injury management.[6,12] With an athlete of high school age, the parents' decisions regarding health care must be taken into consideration.

The Coach

The coach is directly responsible for preventing injuries by seeing that athletes have undergone a preventive injury conditioning program. The coach must ensure that sports equipment, especially protective equipment, is of the highest quality and is properly fitted. The coach must also make sure that protective equipment is properly maintained.[12] A coach must be keenly aware of what produces injuries in his or her particular sport and what measures must be taken to avoid them (Figure 1-2). A coach should be able, when called on to do so, to apply proper first aid.

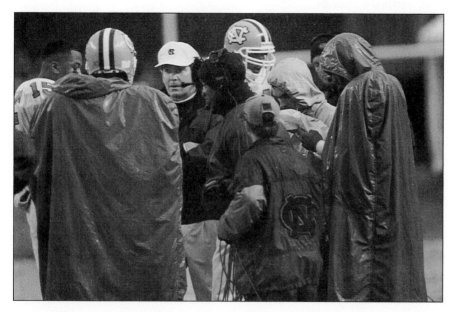

Figure 1-2

The coach is directly responsible for preventing injuries in his or her sport.

This knowledge is especially important in serious head and spinal injuries. *All coaches should be certified in cardiopulmonary resuscitation* by either the American Red Cross, the American Heart Association, or the National Safety Council. *Coaches should also be certified in first aid* by the American Red Cross or the National Safety Council.

It is essential that a coach have a thorough understanding of the skill techniques and environmental factors that may adversely affect the athlete. Poor biomechanics in skill areas such as throwing and running can lead to overuse injuries of the arms and legs, whereas overexposure to heat and humidity may cause death. Just because a coach is experienced in coaching does not mean that he or she knows proper skill techniques. Coaches must engage in a continual process of education to further their knowledge in their particular sport. When a sports program or specific sport is without an athletic trainer, the coach very often takes over this role.

Coaches work closely with athletic trainers; therefore both must develop an awareness and an insight into each other's problems so that they can function as effectively as possible. The athletic trainer must develop patience and must earn the respect of the coaches so that his or her judgment in all training matters is fully accepted. In turn, the athletic trainer must avoid questioning the abilities of the coaches in their particular fields and must restrict opinions to athletic training matters. To avoid frustration and hard feelings, the coach must coach, and the athletic trainer must conduct athletic training matters. In terms of the health and well-being of the athlete, the physician and the athletic trainer have the last word. This position must be backed at all times by the athletic director.

The Athletic Trainer

Employment settings for
athletic trainers:
• schools
• school systems
• colleges and universities
• professional teams
• clinics
• corporations

If no athletic trainer is
available, the coach should
assume the responsibility for
the health care of the athlete.

Of all the professionals charged with injury prevention and health care provision for the athlete, perhaps none is more intimately involved with the athlete than the athletic trainer.[12] The athletic trainer is the one individual who deals with the athlete from the time of the initial injury, throughout the period of rehabilitation, until the athlete's complete, unrestricted return to practice or competition.[12] The athletic trainer is most directly responsible for all phases of health care in an athletic environment, including preventing injuries from occurring, providing initial first aid and injury management, evaluating injuries, and designing and supervising a timely and effective program of rehabilitation that can facilitate the safe and expeditious return of the athlete to activity. Athletic trainers are employed by schools and school systems, colleges and universities, professional athletic teams, sports medicine clinics, and by corporations in industry (see Appendix B).

Qualifications for an Athletic Trainer

The athletic trainer must be knowledgeable and competent in a variety of sports medicine specialities if he or she is to be effective in preventing and treating injuries to the athlete.[2] The NATA has established specific requirements that must be met for an individual to become certified as an athletic trainer.[1] These requirements include a combination of both academic coursework and clinical experience in athletic training settings (see Appendix C). (In this text all references to athletic trainers imply that this individual has met the requirements for certification set forth by the NATA.) The specific roles and responsibilities of the athletic trainer will differ and, to a certain extent, will be defined by the situation in which he or she works.[11]

Roles and Responsibilities of the Athletic Trainer

Prevention of Athletic Injury

Participation in competitive sports places the athlete in a situation in which injuries are possible at any given time. One major responsibility of the athletic trainer is to make the competitive environment as safe as possible to reduce the likelihood of injury. Injuries that are prevented initially do not need first aid and subsequent rehabilitation.

Injury prevention includes (1) conducting physical examinations and preparticipation screenings to identify conditions that predispose an athlete to injury (see Chapter 2); (2) ensuring appropriate training and conditioning of the athlete (see Chapter 4); (3) monitoring environmental conditions to ensure safe participation (see Chapter 10); (4) selecting, properly fitting, and maintaining protective equipment (see Chapter 6); and (5) educating parents, coaches, and athletes about the risks inherent to sport participation.[11]

Recognition, Evaluation, and Immediate Care of Injuries

Frequently, the athletic trainer is the first person to see an athlete who has sustained an injury. The athletic trainer must be skilled in recognizing the nature and extent of an injury through competency in injury evaluation. The athletic trainer must be able to efficiently and accurately evaluate that injury (see Chapter 7). Information obtained in this initial evaluation may be critical later on when swelling, pain, and guarding mask some of the functional signs of this injury. Once the injury has been evaluated, the athletic trainer must be able to provide the appropriate first aid and then refer the athlete to appropriate medical personnel (see Chapter 7).

Rehabilitation and Reconditioning

An athletic trainer must work closely with and under the supervision of the team physician with respect to designing rehabilitation and reconditioning protocols that make use of appropriate rehabilitative equipment, manual therapy techniques, or therapeutic modalities. The athletic trainer should then assume the responsibility of overseeing the rehabilitative process and of ultimating returning the athlete to full activity (see Chapter 12).

Athletic training must be considered as a specialization under the broad field of sports medicine.

Roles and responsibilities of the athletic trainer:
(1) prevention of athletic injuries
(2) recognition, evaluation, and immediate care of injuries
(3) rehabilitation and reconditioning of athletic injuries
(4) health care administration
(5) professional development and responsibility

1-1

Critical Thinking Exercise

A basketball player suffers a grade 2 ankle sprain during midseason of the competitive schedule. After a three-week course of rehabilitation, most of the athlete's pain and swelling has been eliminated. The athlete is anxious to get back into practice and competitive games as soon as possible and subsequent injuries to other players have put pressure on the coach to force this player's return. Unfortunately the athlete is still unable to perform functional tasks (cutting and jumping) essential in basketball.

? Who is responsible for making the decision regarding when the athlete can fully return to practice and game situations?

Health Care Administration

The athletic trainer is responsible for the organization and administration of the athletic training program, including the maintenance of health and injury records for each athlete, the requisition and inventory of necessary supplies and equipment, the supervision of assistant or student trainers, and the establishment of policies and procedures for day-to-day operation of the athletic training program (see Chapter 2).

Professional Development and Responsibility

The athletic trainer must educate the general public, in addition to a large segment of the various allied medical health care professions, as to exactly what athletic trainers are and what their roles and responsibilities are. This education is perhaps best accomplished by holding professional seminars, publishing research in scholarly journals, meeting with local and community organizations, and most important, doing a good and professional job of providing health care to the injured athlete.

The athletic trainer must act at all times with the highest standards of conduct and integrity.[2,9] To ensure this behavior, the NATA has developed a Code of Ethics[9] that includes the following:

1. Athletic trainers shall respect the rights, welfare, and dignity of all individuals.
2. Athletic trainers shall comply with the laws and regulations governing the practice of athletic training.
3. Athletic trainers shall accept the responsibility for the exercise of sound judgment.
4. Athletic trainers shall maintain and promote high standards in the provision of services.
5. Athletic trainers shall not engage in conduct that constitutes a conflict of interest or that adversely reflects on the profession.

Athletic trainers who act in a manner that is unethical or unbecoming to the profession can ultimately lose their certification.

The Team Physician

The athletic trainer works primarily under the supervision of the team physician, who is ultimately responsible for directing the total health care of the athlete (Figure 1-3). In cooperation with the team physician, the athletic trainer must make decisions that ultimately have a direct effect on the athlete who has sustained an injury.

The team physician assumes a number of roles and responsibilities with regard to injury prevention and the health care of the athlete.[8,13]

The physician should be a supervisor and an advisor to the athletic trainer and coach. However, the athletic trainer must be given flexibility to function independently in the decision-making process and must often act without the advice or direction of the physician. Therefore it is critical

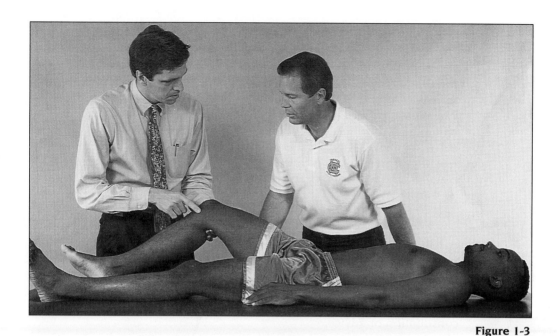

Figure 1-3

In treating the athlete, the athletic trainer carries out the directions of the physician.

that the team physician and the athletic trainer share philosophical opinions regarding injury management and rehabilitation programs so as to minimize any discrepancies or inconsistencies that may exist. Most athletic trainers would prefer to work with rather than for a team physician.

Compiling Medical Histories

The team physician should be responsible for compiling medical histories and conducting physical examinations for each athlete, both of which can provide critical information that may reduce the possibility of injury. Preparticipation screening done by both the athletic trainer and physician are important in establishing baseline information to be used for comparison should injury occur during the season.

Diagnosing Injury

The team physician should assume responsibility for diagnosing an injury and should be keenly aware of the program of rehabilitation as designed by the athletic trainer following the diagnosis. Athletic trainers should be capable of doing an accurate initial evaluation following acute injury. Input from that evaluation may be essential to the physician, who may not see the patient for several hours or perhaps days following the injury. However, the physician has been trained specifically to diagnose injuries and to make recommendations to the athletic trainer for treatment based on that diagnosis. The athletic trainer should have a sound background in injury rehabilitation and must be the one to design and supervise an effective rehabilitation scheme. These roles are closely related yet very distinct and require both cooperation and close communication if they are to be optimized.

Team physicians must have absolute authority in determining the health status of an athlete who wishes to participate in the sports program.

Organizing and Establishing
an Effective Athletic Health
Care System

Deciding on Disqualification

The physician should determine when an athlete should be disqualified from competition on medical grounds and must have the final say in when an injured athlete may return to activity. Any decision to allow an athlete to resume activity should be based on recommendations from the athletic trainer. An athletic trainer most often has an advantage in that he or she knows the injured athletes well, how they respond to injury, how they move, and how hard to push to return them safely to activity. The physician's judgment must be based not only on medical knowledge but also on knowledge of the psychophysiological demands of a particular sport.[5]

Attending Practices and Games

A team physician should make an effort to attend as many practices, scrimmages, and competitions as possible. This attendance obviously becomes very difficult at an institution with twenty or more athletic teams. Thus the physician must make himself or herself readily available should the athletic trainer (who generally is at most practices and games) require consultation or advice.

Commitment to Sports and the Athlete

Most important, the team physician must have a strong love of sports and must be generally interested in and concerned for the young people who compete. Colleges and universities typically employ a full-time team physician. But high schools most often rely on local physicians who volunteer their time. To serve as a team physician for the purpose of enhancing social standing in the community can be a frustrating and potentially dangerous situation for everyone involved in the athletic program.

It is essential that the team physician promote and maintain consistently high quality care for the athlete in all phases of the sports medicine program.

Other Members of the Sports Medicine Team

A number of support health services may be used by a sports program. Those people may include a nurse, team orthopedist, team dentist, team podiatrist, physician's assistants, strength and conditioning coaches, team nutritionist, sport psychologists, exercise physiologists, physical therapists, equipment personnel, and referees.

The Nurse

As a rule, the nurse is not usually responsible for the recognition of sports injuries. Education and background, however, render the nurse quite capable in the recognition of skin disease, infections, and minor irritations. The nurse works under the direction of the physician and in liaison with the athletic trainer and the school health services.

Support personnel concerned
with the athletes' health and
safety:
nurse
school health services
team orthopedist
team dentist
team podiatrist
physician's assistant
biomechanist
strength and conditioning
coach
sport psychologist
physical therapist
exercise physiologist
team nutritionist
equipment personnel
referees

Team Orthopedist

Often the team physician has a speciality in family medicine or is an internist. In such cases, serious musculoskeletal injuries are referred to an orthopedic surgeon who specializes in these disorders.

Team Dentist

The role of team dentist is somewhat analogous to that of team physician. He or she serves as a dental consultant for the team and should be available for first aid and emergency care. Good communication between the dentist and the coach or athletic trainer should ensure a good dental program. The team dentist has three areas of responsibility:

1. Organizing and performing the preseason dental examination
2. Being available to provide emergency care when needed
3. Conducting the fitting of mouth protectors

Team Podiatrist

Podiatry, the specialized field dealing with the study and care of the foot, has become an integral part of sports health care. Many podiatrists are trained in surgical procedures, foot biomechanics, and the fitting and construction of orthotic devices for the shoe. Like the team dentist, a podiatrist should be available on a consulting basis.

Physician's Assistants

Physician's assistants (PAs) are trained to assume some of the responsibilities for patient care traditionally done by the physician. They assist the physician by conducting preliminary patient evaluations, arranging for various hospital-based diagnostic tests, and dispensing appropriate medications. A number of athletic trainers have also become PAs in recent years.

Strength and Conditioning Coach

Many colleges and universities and some high schools employ full-time strength coaches to advise athletes on training and conditioning programs. Athletic trainers should routinely consult with these individuals to advise them about injuries to a particular athlete and exercises that should be avoided or modified relative to a specific injury.

Sports Psychologists

The sports psychologist can advise the athletic trainer on matters related to the psychological aspects of the rehabilitation process. The way the athlete feels about his or her injury and how it affects his or her social, emotional, intellectual, and physical dimensions can have a substantial effect on the course of a treatment program and how quickly the athlete may return to competition. The sports psychologist uses different intervention strategies to help the athlete cope with injury.

1-2

Critical Thinking Exercise

A new high school has hired a coach to establish and develop the football program. Unfortunately, the school did not have enough funds to also hire an athletic trainer. Thus the coach must assume the responsibility of creating a safe playing environment for the athletes.

? What considerations should the coach make to ensure that his athletes will be competing under the safest possible conditions?

Physical Therapists

Some athletic trainers use physical therapists to supervise the rehabilitation programs for injured athletes while the athletic trainer concentrates primarily on getting a player ready to practice or compete. A number of athletic trainers are also physical therapists.[3]

Exercise Physiologists

The exercise physiologist can significantly influence the athletic training program by giving input to the trainer regarding training and conditioning techniques, body composition analysis, and nutritional considerations.

Team Nutritionist

Increasingly, individuals in the field of nutrition are becoming interested in athletics. Some large athletic training programs engage a nutritionist as a consultant who plans eating programs that are geared to the needs of a particular sport. He or she also assists individual athletes who need special nutritional counseling.

Equipment Personnel

Sports equipment personnel are becoming specialists in the purchase and proper fitting of protective equipment. They work closely with the coach and the athletic trainer.

Referees

Referees must be highly knowledgeable regarding rules and regulations, especially those that relate to the health and welfare of the athlete. They work cooperatively with the coach and the athletic trainer. They must be capable of checking the playing facility for dangerous situations and equipment that may predispose the athlete to injury. They must routinely check athletes to ensure that they are wearing adequate protective pads.

SUMMARY

- The sports medicine team consists of the coach, the athletic trainer, and the team physician.
- The term *sports medicine* has many connotations, depending on which group is using it. The term encompasses many different areas of sports related to both performance and injury.
- The provision of health care to the athlete requires a group effort to be most effective.
- The coach must ensure that the environment and the equipment that is worn are the safest possible, that all injuries and illnesses are properly cared for, that skills are properly taught, and that conditioning is at the highest level.

- The athletic trainer is responsible for preventing injuries from occurring, for providing initial first aid and injury management, for evaluating injuries, and for designing and supervising a program of rehabilitation that can facilitate the safe return to activity.

- The team physician is responsible for preparticipation health examinations, for diagnosing and treating illnesses and injuries, for advising and teaching the athletic training staff, for attending games, scrimmages, and practices, and for counseling the athlete about health matters.

- Other members of the sports medicine team may include a nurse, team orthopedist, team dentist, team podiatrist, physician's assistants, strength and conditioning coaches, team nutritionist, sport psychologists, exercise physiologists, physical therapists, equipment personnel, and referees.

Solutions to Critical Thinking Exercises

1-1 Ultimately the team physician is responsible for making that decision. However, that decision must be based on collective input from the coach, the athletic trainer, and the athlete. Remember that everyone in the sports medicine team has the same ultimate goal—returning the athlete to full competitive levels as quickly and safely as possible.

1-2 The coach should be responsible for designing an effective conditioning program; be responsible for ensuring that protective equipment is of the highest quality, properly fitted, and properly maintained; be able to apply proper first aid; be certified in cardiopulmonary resuscitation and first aid; and be aware of the environmental factors that may adversely affect the athlete.

REVIEW QUESTIONS AND CLASS ACTIVITIES

1. What areas of specialization are encompassed under the general heading of sports medicine?
2. List some of the professional sports medicine organizations.
3. How should the sports medicine team work together to provide the most optimal health care for the athlete?
4. What are the responsibilities of a coach who must assume the role of a health care provider when an athletic trainer is not available?
5. What are the specific roles of the athletic trainer in overseeing the total health care of the athlete?
6. Discuss the role of the team physician as an important member of the sports medicine team.
7. What special impact can other members of the sports medicine team have in providing health care for the athlete?

REFERENCES

1. Committee on Allied Health Education and Accreditation: Essentials and guidelines for an accredited educational program for athletic trainers, Chicago, 1992, American Medical Association.

2. Cramer C: A preferred sequence of competencies for athletic training education programs, *J Ath Train* 25(2):123, 1990.
3. Knight K: Roles and relationships between sports PTs and ATCs, *Ath Train* 23(2):153, 1988.
4. Lephart S, Metz K: Financial and appointment trends of the athletic trainer clinician/educator, *J Ath Train* 25(2):118, 1990.
5. Loeffler RD: On being a team physician, *Sports Med Dig* 9(2):1, 1987.
6. Lombardo JA: Sports medicine: a team effort, *Phys Sportsmed* 13:72, April 1985.
7. Mangus, BC, Ingersoll, CD: Approaches to ethical decision making in athletic training, *J Ath Train* 25(4):340, 1990.
8. Mellion MB, Walsh WM: The team physician. In Mellion MB, Walsh WM: *The team physician's handbook,* Philadelphia, 1990, Hanley & Belfus.

9. National Athletic Trainers' Association: New NATA code of ethics approved, *NATA News,* 4(7):15, 1992.
10. National Athletic Trainers' Association Board of Certification: *Study guide for the NATABOC entry level athletic trainer certification examination,* Philadelphia, 1993, FA Davis.
11. National Athletic Trainers' Association Professional Education Committee: *Competencies in athletic training,* Dallas, 1992, National Athletic Trainers' Association.
12. Prentice W: *The athletic trainer.* In Mueller F, Ryan A: *Prevention of athletic injuries: the role of the sports medicine team,* Philadelphia, 1991, FA Davis.
13. Rich BS: All physicians are not created equal; understanding the educational background of the sports medicine physician, *J Ath Train* 28(2):177, 1993.

ANNOTATED BIBLIOGRAPHY

Arnheim D, Prentice W: *Principles of athletic training,* ed 9, Madison, Wis, 1997, Brown & Benchmark.
   Discusses the sports medicine team approach with particular attention to the role of the athletic trainer in providing health care to the athlete.
Bloomfield J et al, editors: *Text book of science and medicine in sports,* Champaign, Ill, 1992, Human Kinetics.
   A sports medicine text divided into five sections including basic sciences, athletic training, nutrition, and environmental stresses.
Cantu RC, Micheli LJ, editors: *ACSM's guidelines for the team physician,* Malvern, Pa, 1991, Lea & Febiger.

   Covers most aspects of the information needed for the team physician including precompetition, postcompetition, and medicolegal aspects as well as other health-related topics.
Mueller F, Ryan A: *Prevention of athletic injuries: the role of the sports medicine team,* Philadelphia, 1991, FA Davis.
   Provides an in-depth discussion of the various members of the sports medicine team.
Shahody EJ, Petrizzi MJ: *Sports medicine for coaches and trainers,* Chapel Hill, 1991, University of North Carolina Press.
   A general guide to the management of sports medicine.

WEB SITES

National Athletic Trainers' Association: http://www.nata.org
   Presents a description of the athletic *training profession, the role of an athletic trainer, and how to become involved in athletic training.*

American Sports Medicine Institute: http://www.asmi.org

The American Sports Medicine Institute's mission is to improve the understanding, prevention, and treatment of sports-related injuries through research and education. In addition to stating this mission, the site provides access to current research and journal articles.

American Academy of Orthopaedic Surgeons: http://www.aaos.org

Presents general public information as well as information to its members. The public information is in the form of patient education brochures as well as a description of the organization and a definition of orthopedics.

The American Orthopaedic Society for Sports Medicine: http://www.sports-med.org

Dedicated to educating health care professionals and the general public about sports medicine; access is provided to the American Journal of Sports Medicine and a wide variety of links to related sites.

Athletic Trainer.com: http://athletic-trainer.com

Specifically designed to give information to athletic trainers, including students and those interested in athletic training; provides access to interesting journal articles and links to several additional informative Web sites.

NCAA: http://www.ncaa.org

Provides general information about the NCAA and the publications that the NCAA circulates; is useful for those working in the collegiate setting.

Organizing and Administering an Athletic Training Program

When you finish this chapter you will be able to:

- Describe a well-designed athletic training facility.
- Identify the rules of operation that should be enforced in an athletic training program.
- Explain budgetary concerns for ordering supplies and equipment.
- Explain the importance of the preparticipation physical examination.
- Identify the necessary records that must be maintained by the athletic trainer.

Operating an effective athletic training program requires careful organization and administration regardless of whether the setting is in a high school, college or university, or at the professional level. In addition to taking care of the injured athlete, a coach must also be an administrator who performs both managerial and supervisory duties. This chapter looks at the administrative tasks required of the coach for successful operation of the program, including facility design, policies and procedures, budget considerations, administration of physical examinations, and record keeping.

PLANNING AN ATHLETIC TRAINING FACILITY

Essential to any sports program is the maximum use of facilities and the most effective use of equipment and supplies. The athletic training facility must be specially designed to meet the many requirements of the sports athletic training program (Figure 2-1). The size and the layout of the athletic training facility is dependent on the scope of the athletic training program, including the size and number of teams and athletes and what sports are offered. To accommodate the various functions of an athletic training program, it must serve as a health care center for athletes.[6]

An athletic training area of less than 1,000 square feet is impractical. An athletic training facility 1,000 to 1,200 square feet in size is satisfactory for most schools. The 1,200-square-foot area (40 by 30 feet) permits the handling of a sizable number of athletes at one time besides allowing ample room for the rather bulky equipment needed. A facility of this size is well suited for pregame preparation. Careful planning will determine whether a larger area is needed or is desirable.

The athletic training facility should be located immediately adjacent to the locker rooms. The facility should have an outside entrance from the field or court, making it unnecessary to bring injured athletes in through the building. This door also permits access when the rest of the building is not in use.

The training room should be organized to provide distinct areas for (1) taping and bandaging; (2) injury treatment using rehabilitative equipment and/or therapeutic modalities; and (3) a wet area for whirlpools, a refrigerator, and an ice machine.

Storage Facilities

Many athletic training facilities lack ample storage space (Figure 2-2). Often storage facilities are located a considerable distance away, which is extremely inconvenient. Each of the three special service areas should contain storage cabinets and shelves for storing general supplies as well

The training facility is a multipurpose area used for first aid, therapy and exercise rehabilitation, injury prevention, medical procedures such as the physical examination, and athletic training administration.

Figure 2-1

The ideal training room facility should be well designed to maximize its use.

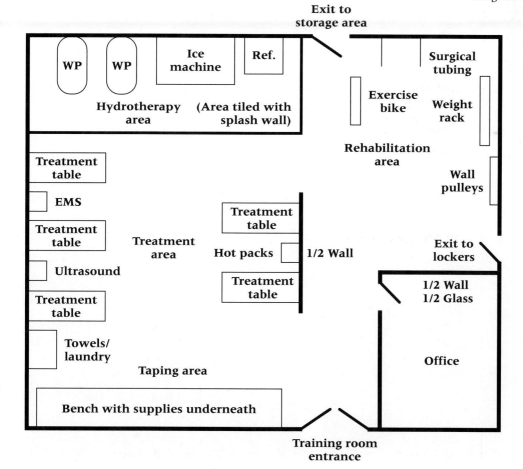

Organizing and Establishing an Effective Athletic Health Care System

It is essential to have sufficient storage space available for supplies and equipment.

Every athletic training program must develop policies and procedures that carefully delineate the daily routine of the program.

as the small specialized equipment used in the respective areas. A large walk-in closet is a necessity for storing bulky equipment, medical supplies, adhesive tape, bandages, and protective devices. Another important piece of equipment is a refrigerator for storing frozen water in styrofoam cups for ice massage and other necessities.

ESTABLISHING RULES OF OPERATION FOR AN ATHLETIC TRAINING PROGRAM

Every athletic training program must develop policies and procedures that carefully delineate the daily routine of the program. This is imperative for handling health problems and injuries.

It is first necessary to decide exactly who will be taken care of in the athletic training room. The coach must decide the extent to which the athlete will be served. For example, will prevention and care activities be extended to athletes for the entire year, including summer and other vacations, or only during the competitive season? A policy should clarify whether students other than athletes, athletes from other schools, faculty, and staff are to receive care. Often legal concerns and the school liability insurance dictate who, other than the athlete, is to be served.

Providing Coverage

A major concern of any athletic department is to try and provide the most qualified health care possible to the athlete. Unfortunately, as indicated in Chapter 1, budgetary limitations often dictate who will be responsible for overseeing the health care program for the athletes. Ideally an institution would hire a certified athletic trainer who would be primarily responsible. In some cases, schools rely on a nurse to provide care. And in other situations in which there are no athletic trainers or nurses, health care responsibility usually falls on the coach. Regardless of who is in charge of the health care program, policies must be established concerning how to best provide coverage to various athletic teams. High schools

Figure 2-2

An effective athletic training program must have appropriate storage facilities that are highly organized.

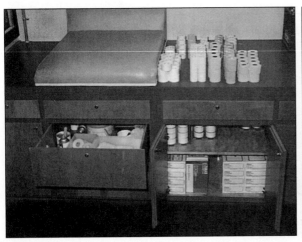 

with limited available supervision may only be able to provide athletic training facility coverage in the afternoons and during vacation periods. Ideally, high-risk sports should have a certified athletic trainer and physician present at all practices and contests.

Training Room Policies

The athletic training room should be used only for the prevention and care of sports injuries. Too often the athletic training facility becomes a meeting or club room for teams and athletes. Unless definite rules are established and practiced, room cleanliness and sanitation become an impossible chore. The following are some important athletic training room policies:

- *No cleated shoes are allowed.* Dirt and debris tend to cling to cleated shoes; therefore cleated shoes should be removed before athletes enter the athletic training facility.
- *Game equipment is kept outside.* Because game equipment such as balls and bats adds to the sanitation problem, it should be kept out of the athletic training room. Athletes must be continually reminded that the athletic training room is not a storage room for sports equipment.
- *Shoes must be kept off treatment tables.* Because shoes tend to contaminate treatment tables, they must be removed before any care is given to the athlete.
- *Athletes should shower before receiving treatment.* The athlete should make it a habit to shower before being treated if the treatment is not an emergency. This procedure helps keep tables and therapeutic modalities sanitary.
- *Roughhousing and profanity should not be allowed.* Athletes must be continually reminded that the athletic training facility is for injury care and prevention. Horseplay and foul language lower the basic purpose of the athletic training room.
- *No food or smokeless tobacco should be allowed.*

Keeping Facilities Clean

The practice of good hygiene and sanitation is of the utmost importance in an athletic training program. The prevention of infectious diseases is a direct responsibility of the coach, whose duty it is to see that all athletes are surrounded by as hygienic an environment as is possible and that each individual is practicing sound health habits. Chapter 8 discusses the management of bloodborne pathogens. The coach must be aware of and adhere to guidelines for the operation of an athletic care facility as dictated by the Occupational Safety and Health Administration (OSHA).

The following guidelines will help maintain a sanitary environment:

- Sweep the gymnasium floors daily.
- Clean and disinfect drinking fountains, showers, sinks, and urinals and toilets daily.

2-1

Critical Thinking
Exercise

The members of the school board at All-American High School voted to allocate $25,000 to renovate a 25 foot by 40 foot storage space and to purchase new equipment for an athletic training room. The coach has been asked to provide the school principal with a wish list of what should be included in this facility. It has been estimated that the physical renovation will cost approximately $17,000.

? How may this space be best utilized, and what type of equipment should be purchased to maximize the effectiveness of this new facility?

Good hygiene and sanitation are essential for an athletic training program.

- Air out and sanitize lockers frequently.
- Clean wrestling mats and wall mats daily.
- Provide clean dry towels each day for each individual athlete.
- Issue individual equipment and clothing to each athlete to avoid skin irritations.
- Do not allow swapping of equipment and clothing.
- Launder and change clothing frequently.
- Allow wet clothing to dry thoroughly before the athlete wears it again.

Cleaning responsibilities in most schools are divided between the athletic training or coaching staff and the maintenance crew. Care of permanent building structures and trash disposal are usually the responsibilities of maintenance, whereas upkeep of specialized equipment falls within the province of the coaches or athletic trainers. Division of routine cleaning responsibilities may be organized in the following manner.

The maintenance crew should:

- Sweep floors daily.
- Clean and disinfect sinks and built-in tubs daily.
- Mop and disinfect hydrotherapy area twice a week.
- Refill paper towel and drinking cup dispensers as needed.
- Empty wastebaskets and dispose of trash daily.

The athletic training staff should:

- Clean and disinfect treatment tables daily.
- Clean and disinfect hydrotherapy modalities daily.
- Clean and polish other therapeutic modalities weekly.

Establishing Rules for the Athlete

To promote good health among the athletes, the coach or the athletic trainer should encourage sound health habits. The following checklist may be a useful guide for coaches, athletic trainers, and athletes:

- Are the athletes medically cleared to participate?
- Is each athlete insured?
- Do the athletes promptly report injuries, illnesses, and skin disorders to the coach or the athletic trainer?
- Do the athletes practice good daily living habits of resting, sleeping, and proper nutrition?
- Do they shower after practice?
- Do they dry thoroughly and cool off before departing from the gymnasium?
- Do they avoid drinking from a common water dispenser?
- Do they avoid using a common towel?

- Do they avoid exchanging gym clothes with teammates?
- Do they practice good foot hygiene?
- Do they avoid contact with teammates who have a contagious disease or infection?

Providing Emergency Phones

The installation of an emergency phone adjacent to all major activity areas is a must. It should be possible to use this phone to call outside for emergency aid or to contact the athletic training facilities when additional assistance is required.

RECORD KEEPING

Record keeping is a major responsibility in an athletic training program. Some coaches and athletic trainers object to keeping records and filling out forms, stating they have neither the time nor the inclination to be bookkeepers. Nevertheless, in a time in which lawsuits are the rule rather than the exception, accurate and up-to-date records are an absolute necessity. In addition to keeping medical records, the coach or athletic trainer should maintain injury reports, treatment logs, personal information cards, injury evaluations and progress notes, supply and equipment inventories, and annual reports.

Keeping adequate records is of major importance in the athletic training program.

Administering Preparticipation Health Examinations

The primary purpose of the preseason health examination is to identify whether an athlete is at risk before he or she participates in a specific sport.[7] The preparticipation examination should consist of a medical history, a physical examination, and a brief orthopedic screening. Information obtained during this examination will establish a baseline to which comparisons may be made following injury. The examination may reveal conditions that could warrant disqualification from certain sports. The examination will also satisfy insurance and liability issues (see Chapter 3).

Preparticipation health examination:
Medical history
Physical examination
Maturity assessment
Orthopedic screening

The preparticipation physical may be administered on an individual basis by a personal physician, or it may be done using a station examination system with a team of examiners.[3] Examination by a personal physician has the advantage of yielding an in-depth history and an ideal physician-patient relationship. A disadvantage of this type of examination is that it may not be directed to detection of factors that predispose the athlete to a sports injury.[14]

The most thorough and sport-specific type of preparticipation examination is the station examination.[3] This method can provide the athlete with a detailed examination in a short period of time. A team of nine people is needed to examine thirty or more athletes. The team should include two physicians, two medically trained nonphysicians (nurse, athletic trainer, physical therapist, or physician's assistant), and five managers, student athletic trainers, or assistant coaches.

A preparticipation exam should include all of the following:

2-2

Critical Thinking Exercise

All-American High School offers
eighteen sports, which are
divided into six fall, six winter,
and six spring sports. The
school has a total of
approximately 500 athletes,
and approximately 200 of them
are involved in the fall sports.
The coach is charged with the
responsibility of arranging and
administering preparticipation
examinations so that each
athlete can be cleared for
competition.

? How can the coach most
efficiently set up the preparti-
pation exams to clear 200 athletes for competition in the fall
sports?

Medical History

A medical history form should be completed before the physical examination and orthopedic screening; its purpose is to identify any past or existing medical problems.[1] This form should be updated for each athlete
every year. Medical histories should be closely reviewed by both the
physician, the coach, and the athletic trainer so that they will be prepared
should some medical emergency arise. Necessary participation release
forms and insurance information should be collected along with the medical history[8] (Figure 2-3).

Physical Examination

The physical examination should include assessment of height, weight,
body composition, blood pressure, pulse, vision, skin, dental, ear, nose,
throat, heart and lung function, abdomen, lymphatics, genitalia, maturation index, urinalysis, and blood work[9] (Figure 2-4).

Maturity Assessment

Maturity assessment should be part of the physical examination as a
means of protecting the young athlete.[4] Most commonly used methods
are the circumpubertal (sexual maturity), skeletal, and dental assess-
ments. Of the three, Tanner's five stages of assessment, indicating maturity of secondary sexual characteristics, is the most expedient for use in
the station method of examination. The Tanner approach evaluates pubic hair and genitalia development in boys and pubic hair and breast development in girls. Other indicators that may be noted are facial and axillary hair. Stage one indicates that puberty is not evident, whereas stage
five indicates full development. The crucial stage in terms of collision and
high-intensity noncontact sports is stage three, in which there is the
fastest bone growth. In this stage, the growth plates are two to five times
weaker than the joint capsule and tendon attachments.[5] Young athletes
in grades seven to twelve must be matched by maturity, not age.[10]

Orthopedic Screening

Orthopedic screening may be done as part of the physical examination
or separately by the athletic trainer. An example of a very quick orthopedic screening examination appears in Table 2-1; it usually will take
about ninety seconds.[2] A more detailed orthopedic examination may be
conducted to assess strength, range of motion, and stability at various
joints.

Sport Disqualification

As discussed previously, sports participation involves risks. Most conditions that warrant a recommendation for disqualification would be identified during a preparticipation health evaluation and should be noted in
the medical history.[11] Because of the Americans with Disabilities Act, a
physician cannot legally disqualify athletes from competing because of an

existing medical problem. They can only recommend that the athlete voluntarily choose not to participate. In general, the athlete who has lost one of two paired organs such as eyes or kidneys is cautioned against playing a collision or contact sport.[5] Such an athlete should be counseled into participating in a noncontact sport. The athlete with one testicle, or one or both that are undescended, must be apprised that there is a small risk, which is substantially minimized with the use of an athletic supporter and a protective device.[11]

Injury Reports

An injury report serves as a record for future reference (Figure 2-5). If the emergency procedures followed are questioned at a later date, one's memory of the details may be somewhat hazy, but a report completed on the spot provides specific information. In a litigation situation, an athletic trainer may be asked questions about an injury that occurred three years in the past. All injury reports should be filed in the athletic trainer's office. The reports should be made out in triplicate, with one copy sent to the school health office, one to the physician, and one retained.

Figure 2-3

Sample medical history
examination form

MEDICAL HISTORY FORM

HEAD
1. Do you experience headaches? _____
   If yes, how frequently do they appear? _____
   Where are they located? _____
   Do you take any medicine to relieve them? _____
   If yes, what do you use? _____
2. Do you have any episodes of dizziness, seizures, or convulsions? _____
3. Have you ever fainted? _____
4. Have you ever had a head or neck injury? _____
   If yes, did you lose consciousness? _____
   If yes, how long? _____
   Were you under the care of a doctor? _____
   Were you hospitalized? _____
   Paralysis? _____ Numbness, tingling, or weakness of any extremity? _____
   How long before you resumed normal activity? _____

EYES
1. Have you ever had a problem with your eyes? Trauma? _____
   Loss of vision? _____ Pink eye? _____ Pain? _____

EARS
1. Have you ever had a problem with your ears? _____
   Infection? _____ Swimmer's ear? _____ Pain? _____
   Drainage? _____ Loss of hearing? _____

NOSE
1. Have you ever had a problem with your nose? _____
   Broken? _____ Sneezing? _____ Nosebleeds? _____

THROAT
1. How often do you have colds or sore throats? _____

SKIN
1. Do you ever have a skin rash? _____
   If yes, explain. _____

CHEST
1. Do you ever have chest pain? _____
   If yes, explain. _____
2. Do you have chronic cough? _____ Asthma? _____
   Hay fever? _____ Have you ever coughed up blood? _____

HEART
1. Have you ever been told you had a heart murmur? _____
   If yes, explain. _____
2. Have you ever been told you had elevated blood pressure? _____
   If yes, explain. _____
3. Is heart disease present in your family? _____
   If yes, explain. _____
4. Have you ever been told that a member of your family died suddenly or had a heart attack at a young age? _____

GI
1. Do you have trouble with heartburn? _____ Indigestion _____
   Nausea? _____ Vomiting? _____ Constipation? _____
   Diarrhea? _____ Have you ever vomited blood? _____
   If yes, explain. _____
2. Have you ever passed blood in your stools? _____
   If yes, explain. _____

GU
1. Have you ever noted burning on urination? _____
   Urgency? _____ Frequency? _____ Wake up at night to pass urine? _____ Penile discharge? _____ Passed blood on urination? _____ Kidney stone? _____

SKELETAL
1. Have you ever had arthritis? _____
   Sprained ankle? _____ If yes, explain. _____
   Knee injury? _____ If yes, explain. _____
   Shoulder injury? _____ If yes, explain. _____
   Broken bone? _____ If yes, explain. _____
   Neck injury? _____ If yes, explain. _____
   Back trouble? _____ If yes, explain. _____
   Have you ever had surgery? _____ If yes, explain. _____
   Have you ever had a dislocation? If yes, explain. _____
2. Does any joint feel as if it is slipping? _____
3. Do you have a pin, plate, screw, or anything metal in your body? _____ If yes, explain. _____

GENERAL
1. Do you have any drug allergies? _____
2. Are you allergic to insect bites? _____
3. Are you allergic to anything? _____
4. Have you ever had hepatitis? _____ Mononucleosis? _____
   Diabetes? _____ Does any family member have diabetes? _____
5. Have you ever had any serious disease? _____ If yes, explain. _____
6. Have you ever had heat exhaustion or heat stroke? _____
   If yes, explain. _____
7. Has any member of your family ever had head exhaustion or heat stroke? _____
8. Has any member of your family been told they were allergic to medication used as anesthesia? _____
9. Have you ever been allergic to local anesthetics used by doctors or dentists? _____
10. Has your weight changed in the last three months? _____
    If yes, explain. _____

Name _____ SS# _____ Date _____
Height _____ Weight _____ Percent body fat _____
                                                                Check if negative

1. Blood pressure _____ / _____
2. Pulse _____
3. Vision
        Without glasses R 20/_____ L 20/_____
        With glasses R 20/_____ L 20/_____
4. Skin _____
5. Dental/mouth _____
6. Ears _____
7. Nose _____
8. Throat _____
9. Chest
        Heart rhythm _____
        Lungs _____
        Breasts _____
10. Abdomen
        Liver _____
        Spleen _____
        Kidneys _____
        Stomach _____
        Bowel _____
11. Lymphatics
        Cervical _____
        Axillary _____
        Femoral _____
12. Genitalia _____
13. Maturation Index _____
14. Urinalysis
        Protein _____
        Sugar _____
15. Blood
        Hematocrit _____
16. Other _____
Disposition
        No participation
        Limited participation
        Clearance withheld
        Cleared for participation
Comments _____
_____
_____

_____

                                    Physician's signature
                                    _____
                                        Date

Figure 2-4

Sample physical examination
form

The Treatment Log

Each athletic facility should have a sign-in log available for the athlete
who receives any service. Emphasis is placed on recording treatments for
the athlete who is receiving daily therapy for an injury. As with injury
records, treatment logs often have the status of legal documents and are

TABLE 2-1 Orthopedic Screening Examination	
Activity and Instruction	**To Determine**
Stand facing examiner	Acromioclavicular joints; general habitus
Look at ceiling, floor, over both shoulders; touch ears to shoulders	Cervical spine motion
Shrug shoulders (examiner resists)	Trapezius strength
Abduct shoulders 90° (examiner resists at 90°)	Deltoid strength
Full external rotation of arms	Shoulder motion
Flex and extend elbows	Elbow motion
Arms at sides, elbows 90° flexed; pronate and supinate wrists	Elbow and wrist motion
Spread fingers; make fist	Hand or finger motion and deformities
Tighten (contract) quadriceps; relax quadriceps	Symmetry and knee effusion; ankle effusion
Duckwalk four steps (away from examiner with buttocks on heels)	Hip, knee, and ankle motion
Stand with back to examiner	Shoulder symmetry; scoliosis
Knees straight, touch toes	Scoliosis, hip motion, hamstring tightness
Raise up on toes, raise heels	Calf symmetry, leg strength

used to establish certain facts in a civil litigation, an insurance action, or a criminal action following injury.

Personal Information Card

The coach or athletic trainer should maintain on file an athlete's personal information card. This card is completed by the athlete at the time of the health examination and serves as a means of contacting the family, personal physician, and insurance company in case of emergency.

Injury Evaluation and Progress Notes

Injuries should be evaluated by the coach, who must record this information in some consistent format. The SOAP format is a concise method of recording the evaluation and the treatment plan for the injured athlete (see Chapter 7). The *subjective* portion of the SOAP note refers to what the athlete tells the athletic trainer about the injury relative to the history or what he or she felt. The *objective* portion documents information that the athletic trainer gathers during the evaluation, such as range of motion, strength levels, patterns of pain, and so forth. The *assessment* records the athletic trainer's professional opinion about the injury based on information obtained during the subjective and objective portions. The *plan* for treatment indicates how the injury will be managed and includes short- and long-term goals for rehabilitation.

Figure 2-5

Athletic injury record form

Name _____ Sport _____ Date: ___ / ___ / ___ Time: _____ Injury number: _____

Player I.D. _____ Age: _____ Location: _____ Intercollegiate-nonintercollegiate

Initial injury   Recheck   Reinjury   Preseason—Practice—Game   Incurred while participating in sport: yes ___ no ___

Description: How did it happen? _____

_____

Initial impression: _____

_____

_____

Site of injury	Body part		Structure	Treatment _____
1 Right	1 Head	25 MP joint	1 Skin	_____
2 Left	2 Face	26 PIP joint	2 Muscle	_____
3 Proximal	3 Eye	27 Abdomen	3 Fascia	_____
4 Distal	4 Nose	28 Hip	4 Bone	_____
5 Anterior	5 Ear	29 Thigh	5 Nerve	_____
6 Posterior	6 Mouth	30 Knee	6 Fat pad	_____
7 Medial	7 Neck	31 Patella	7 Tendon	_____
8 Lateral	8 Thorax	32 Lower leg	8 Ligament	_____
9 Other	9 Ribs	33 Ankle	9 Cartilage	_____
	10 Sternum	34 Achilles tendon	10 Capsule	_____
	11 Upper back	35 Foot	11 Compartment	_____
Site of evaluation	12 Lower back	36 Toes	12 Dental	_____
1 SHS	13 Shoulder	37 Other	13 _____	
2 Athletic Trn Rm.	14 Rotator cuff			Medication _____
3 Site-Competition	15 AC joint			
4 _____	16 Glenohumeral			_____
	17 Sternoclavicular	Nontraumatic	Nature of injury	_____
Procedures	18 Upper arm	1 Dermatological	1 Contusion	_____
1 Physical exam	19 Elbow	2 Allergy	2 Strain	_____
2 X-ray	20 Forearm	3 Influenza	3 Sprain	_____
3 Splint	21 Wrist	4 URI	4 Fracture	_____
4 Wrap	22 Hand	5 GU	5 Rupture	_____
5 Cast	23 Thumb	6 Systemic infect.	6 Tendonitis	_____
6 Aspiration	24 Finger	7 Local infect.	7 Bursitis	
7 Other		8 Other	8 Myositis	Prescription dispensed
			9 Laceration	1 Antibiotics 5 Muscle relaxant
			10 Concussion	2 Antiinflammatory 6 Enzyme
			11 Avulsion	3 Decongestant 7 _____
Disposition			12 Abrasion	4 Analgesic
	Referral	Disposition of injury	13 _____	
1 SHS	1 Arthrogram	1 No part.		Injections
2 Trainer	2 Neurological	2 Part part.		
3 Hospital	3 Int. Med.	3 Full part	Degree	1 Steroids
4 H.D.	4 Orthropedic		1° 2° 3°	2 Antibiotics
5 Other	5 EENT			3 Steriods-xylo
	6 Dentist			4 _____
	7 Other			
		Previous injury _____		

Supply and Equipment Inventory

A major responsibility of the coach is to manage a budget, most of which
is spent on equipment and supplies. Every year an inventory must be
conducted and recorded on such items as new equipment that is needed,
equipment that needs to be replaced or repaired, and expendable supplies
that need replenishing.

Annual Reports

Most athletic departments require an annual report on the functions of
the athletic training program. This report serves as a means for making
program changes and improvements. It commonly includes the number
of athletes served, a survey of the number and types of injuries, an analysis of the program, and recommendations for future improvements.

Release of Medical Records

The coach may not release an athlete's medical records to anyone without written consent. If the athlete wishes to have medical records
released to colleges or universities, professional sports organizations, insurance companies, the news media, or any other group or individual,
he, she, the parent, or the guardian must sign a waiver that specifies
which information is to be released.

DEVELOPING A BUDGET

One of the major problems faced by coaches is to obtain a budget of sufficient size to permit them to perform a creditable job of providing health
care to the athlete. Many high schools fail to make any budgetary provi-
sions for athletic training except for the purchase of tape, ankle wraps,
and a training bag that contains a minimum amount of equipment. Many
schools fail to provide a room and any of the special facilities that are
needed to establish an effective athletic training program. Some school
boards and administrators fail to recognize that the functions performed
in the athletic training facility are an essential component of the athletic
program and that even if no specialist is used, the facilities are nonethe-
less necessary. Colleges and universities do not usually face this problem
to the extent that high schools do. By and large, athletic training is recognized as an important aspect of the college athletic program.

A major problem often facing
athletic trainers is a budget of
sufficient size.

Budgetary needs vary considerably within programs; some require
only a few thousand dollars, whereas others spend hundreds of thousands of dollars. The amount spent on building and equipping a training
facility, of course, is entirely a matter of local option. In purchasing equipment, immediate needs as well as availability of personnel to operate specialized equipment should be kept in mind.

Budget records should be kept on file so that they are available for
use in projecting the following year's budgetary needs. They present a
picture of the distribution of current funds and serve to substantiate
future budgetary requests. Expenditures for individual items vary in

accordance with different training philosophies. Some coaches may spend much of their budget on expendable supplies such as adhesive tape. An annual inventory must be conducted at the end of the year or before replenishing supplies and equipment. Accurate records must be kept to justify future requests.

Ordering Supplies and Equipment

Equipment may be fixed or nonfixed.

Supplies are expendable and usually are for injury prevention, first aid, and management. Examples of supplies are athletic training tape, germicides, and massage lotion. The term *equipment* refers to those items that are not expendable. Equipment may be further divided into fixed and nonfixed. Fixed equipment does not necessarily mean that it cannot be moved but that it is not usually removed from the athletic training facility. Examples of fixed equipment are icemakers, weight equipment, and electrical therapeutic modalities. Nonfixed equipment refers to nonexpendable items that are less fixed, that may be part of an athletic trainer's kit, or that may be at the sport site. Examples are blankets, scissors, and training kits.

Purchasing may be done through direct buy or competitive bid.

Additional Budget Considerations

In addition to supplies and equipment, the coach must also consider other costs that may be included in the operation of an athletic training program; these costs include telephone and postage, contracts with physicians or clinics for services, professional liability insurance, memberships in professional organizations, the purchase of professional journals or textbooks, travel and expenses for attending professional meetings, and clothing to be worn in the training room.[12,13]

SUMMARY

- Organization of the athletic training program demands a significant portion of the coach's time and effort.
- The athletic training program can certainly be enhanced by designing or renovating a facility to maximize the potential use of the space available.
- The athletic training program best serves the athlete by establishing specific policies and regulations governing the use of available services.
- Preparticipation exams must be given to athletes and should include a medical history, a general physical examination, and an orthopedic screening.
- The coach must maintain accurate and up-to-date medical records in addition to the other paperwork necessary for the operation of the athletic training program.
- Budgets should allow for the purchase of equipment and supplies essential for providing appropriate preventive and rehabilitative care for the athlete.

Solutions to Critical Thinking Exercises

2-1 The training room should have specific areas designated for taping and preparation, treatment and rehabilitation, and hydrotherapy, and should have adequate storage facilities that are positioned within the space to allow for an efficient traffic flow. Equipment purchases might include four to five treatment tables and two to three taping tables (these could be made in-house if possible), a large-capacity ice machine, a combination ultrasound/electrical simulating unit, a whirlpool, and various free weights and exercise tubing.

2-2 The preparticipation examination should consist of a medical history, a physical examination, and a brief orthopedic screening. The preparticipation physical may be effectively administered using a station examination system with a team of examiners. A station examination can provide the athlete with a detailed examination in a short period of time. A team of people is needed to examine this many athletes. The team should include physicians, medically trained non-physicians (nurses, athletic trainers, physical therapists, or physician's assistants), and managers, student coaches, or assistant coaches.

REVIEW QUESTIONS AND CLASS ACTIVITIES

1. What major administrative functions must a coach in an athletic training setting perform?
2. Design two athletic training facilities—one for a medium-sized university and one for a large university.
3. Observe the activities in the athletic training facility. Pick both a slow time and a busy time to observe.
4. Why do hygiene and sanitation play an important role in athletic training? How should the athletic training facility be maintained?
5. Fully equip a new medium-sized high school or college athletic training facility or a clinical facility. Pick equipment from current catalogs.
6. Establish a reasonable health care budget for a small high school, a large high school, and a large college or university.
7. Identify the groups of individuals to be served in the athletic training facility.
8. Organize a preparticipation health examination for ninety football players.
9. Record keeping is a major function in athletic training. What records are necessary to keep?
10. Debate what conditions constitute good grounds for medical disqualification from a sport.

REFERENCES

1. Abdenour TE, Weir NJ: Medical assessment of the prospective student athlete, *Ath Train* 21:122, 1986.
2. American Academy of Pediatrics Policy Statement: Recommendations for participation in competitive sports, *Physician Sportsmed* 16(5):168, 1988.
3. Bonci CM, Ryan R: Preparticipation screening in intercollegiate athletics, *Postgrad Adv Sports Med* 3:3, 1988.
4. Caine DJ, Broekhoff J: Maturity

assessment: a viable preventive measure against physical and psychological insult to the young athlete? *Physician Sportsmed* 15(3):67, 1987.

5. Dorsen PJ: Should athletes with one eye, kidney, or testicle play contact sports? *Physician Sportsmed* 14(7):130, 1986.

6. Forseth EA: Consideration in planning small college athletic training facilities, *Ath Train* 21(1):22, 1986.

7. Herbert D: Professional considerations related to conduct of preparticipation exams, *Sports Med Stand Malpract Report* 6(4):49, 1994.

8. Jones R: The preparticipation, sport-specific athletic profile examination, *Semin Adolesc Med* 3:169, 1987.

9. Kibler, W: *The sports participation fitness examination*, Champaign, Ill, 1990, Human Kinetics.

10. McKeag DB: Preseason physical examination for the prevention of sports injuries, *Sports Med* 2:413, 1985.

11. Myers GC, Garrick JG: The preseason examination of school and college athletes. In Strauss RH, editor: *Sports medicine*, Philadelphia, 1984, WB Saunders.

12. Rankin J, Ingersoll C: *Athletic training management: concepts and applications*, St Louis, 1995, Mosby.

13. Ray R: *Management strategies in athletic training*, Champaign, Ill, 1994, Human Kinetics.

14. Swander H: *Preparticipation physical examination*, Kansas City, 1992, American Academy of Family Physicians, American Academy of Pediatrics, American Orthopaedic Society for Sports Medicine, American Osteopathic Academy for Sports Medicine.

ANNOTATED BIBLIOGRAPHY

Rankin J, Ingersoll C: *Athletic training management: concepts and applications*, St Louis, 1995, Mosby.

Designed for students interested in all aspects of organization and administration of an athletic training program; contains many examples and case studies.

Ray R: *Management strategies in athletic training*, Champaign, Ill, 1994, Human Kinetics.

The first text available to cover the principles of organization and administration as they apply to many different employment settings in athletic training; contains many examples and case studies based on principles of administration presented in the text.

Chapter 3

Legal Liability and Insurance

When you finish this chapter you will be able to:

- Explain legal considerations for the coach acting as a health care provider.
- Define the legal concepts of liability, negligence, torts, assumption of risks.
- Identify measures that can be taken by both the coach and athletic trainer to minimize chances of litigation.
- Describe product liability.
- Identify the essential insurance requirements for protection of the athlete.
- Describe the types of insurance necessary to protect the coach acting as a health care provider.

L EGAL CONCERNS OF THE COACH AND ATHLETIC TRAINER

In recent years negligence suits against teachers, coaches, athletic trainers, school officials, and physicians because of sports injuries have increased both in frequency and in the amount of damages awarded. An increasing awareness of the many risk factors present in physical activities has had a major effect on the coach in particular. A great deal of care must be taken in following coaching and athletic training procedures that conform to the legal guidelines governing liability.[12]

Liability

liability
The state of being legally responsible for the harm one causes another person.

Liability is the state of being legally responsible for the harm one causes another person.[9] Liability assumes that a coach would act according to the standards of care of any individual with similar educational background or training. In most cases in which someone has been charged with negligence, the actions of a hypothetical, reasonably prudent person have been compared with the actions of the defendant to ascertain whether the course of action followed by the defendant was in conformity with the judgment exercised by such a reasonably prudent person.[9] The key phrase has been "reasonable care." Individuals who have many years of experience, who are well educated in their field, and who are certified or licensed must act in accordance with this background (Figure 3-1).

Figure 3-1

The coach can minimize the
chances of litigation by
providing reasonable and
prudent care to an injured
athlete.

Negligence is the failure to use ordinary or reasonable care—care
that persons would normally exercise to avoid injury to themselves or to
others under similar circumstances.[9] **Injury** is an act that damages or
hurts. This standard assumes that the individual is neither an exception-
ally skillful individual nor an extraordinarily cautious one but is a person
of reasonable and ordinary prudence. Put another way, it is expected that
the individual will bring a commonsense approach to the situation at
hand and will exercise due care in its handling. An example of negligence
is when a coach, through improper or careless handling of a heat pack,
seriously burns an athlete. Another illustration, occurring all too often in
sports, is when a coach moves a possibly seriously injured athlete from
the field of play to permit competition or practice to continue and does
so either in an improper manner or before consulting those qualified to
know the proper course of action. Should a serious or disabling injury result, the coach is liable.

negligence
The failure to use ordinary
or reasonable care.

injury
An act that damages or
hurts.

Assumption of Risk

The courts generally acknowledge that hazards are present in sports
through the concept of **assumption of risk.** In other words, athletes, either by expressed or implied agreement, assume the danger and hence
relieve any other individual of legal responsibility to protect them; by so

assumption of risk
The individual, through
expressed or implied
agreement, assumes that
some risk or danger will be
involved in the particular
undertaking. In other
words, a person takes his or
her own chances.

---

accident

An act that occurs by
chance or without
intention.

torts

Legal wrongs committed
against a person.

3-1

Critical Thinking Exercise

A baseball batter was struck
with a pitched ball directly in
the orbit of the right eye and
fell immediately to the ground.
The coach ran to the player to
examine the eye. There was
some immediate swelling and
discoloration around the orbit;
however, the eye appeared to
be normal. The player insisted
that he was fine and told the
coach that he could continue to
bat. After the game, the coach
told the athlete to go back to
his room, put ice on his eye,
and check in tomorrow. That
night the baseball player began
to hemorrhage into the anterior
chamber of the eye and
suffered irreparable damage to
his eye.

? An ophthalmologist stated
that if the athlete's eye had
been examined immediately after injury, the bleeding could
have been controlled and the
athlete would not have suffered
any damage to his vision. If the
athlete brings a lawsuit against
the coach, what must he prove
to win a judgment?

doing, athletes agree to take their own chances.[10] This concept, however,
is subject to many and varied interpretations in the courts, especially
when minors are involved, because they are not considered able to render a mature judgment about the risks inherent in the situation. Although athletes participating in a sports program are considered to assume a normal risk, this assumption in no way exempts those in charge
from exercising reasonable care and prudence in the conduct of such activities or from foreseeing and taking precautionary measures against
accident-provoking circumstances.[11] **Accident** is an act that occurs by
chance or without intention. In general, the courts have been fairly consistent in upholding waivers and releases of liability for adults unless
there is evidence of fraud, misrepresentation, or duress.[9]

Torts

Torts are legal wrongs committed against the person or property of another.[9] Such wrongs may emanate from an *act of omission,* wherein the individual fails to perform a legal duty, or from an *act of commission,* wherein
he or she commits an act that is not legally his or hers to perform. In either instance, if injury results, the person can be held liable. In the case
of omission a coach may fail to refer a seriously injured athlete for the
proper medical attention. In the case of commission, the coach may perform a medical treatment not within his or her legal province and from
which serious medical complications develop.

Negligence

The tort concept of negligence is held by the courts when it is shown that
an individual (1) does something that a reasonably prudent person would
not do or (2) fails to do something that a reasonably prudent person
would do under circumstances similar to those shown by the evidence.[1]
Coaches employed by an institution have a duty to provide health care to
athletes at that institution. Once the coach assumes the duty of caring for
an athlete, the coach is also under the obligation to make sure that appropriate care is given.

It is expected that a person possessing more training in a given field
or area will possess a correspondingly higher level of competence than,
for example, a student. An individual will, therefore, be judged in terms
of his or her performance in any situation in which legal liability may be
assessed. Liability per se in all its various aspects is not assessed at the
same level nationally but varies in interpretation from state to state and
from area to area. Therefore, athletic trainers should know and acquire
the level of competence expected in their particular region. In essence,
negligence is conduct that results in the creation of an "unreasonable risk
of harm to others."[16]

A coach who fails to provide an acceptable standard of care has committed a breach of duty, and the athlete must then prove that this breach
caused the injury or made the injury worse.[7] If the coach or athletic
trainer breaches a duty but no harm was done, there is no negligence.

Statute of Limitations

Statutes of limitations set a specific length of time that individuals may sue for damages from negligence. These statutes vary from state to state but in general, in states in which coaches are covered by malpractice laws, the statute of limitation is between one and three years. In states in which there is no regulation, there may be no statute of limitations for coaches.

Avoiding Litigation

Coaches can significantly decrease risk of litigation by paying attention to several key points.[3,8] A coach must follow these guidelines:

- Warn the athlete of the potential dangers inherent in the sport.
- Supervise constantly and attentively.
- Properly prepare and condition the athlete.
- Properly instruct the athlete in the skills of the sport.
- Ensure that proper and safe equipment and facilities are used by the athlete at all times.
- Work to establish good personal relationships with the athletes, parents, and coworkers.
- Establish specific policies and guidelines for the operation of an athletic training facility and maintain qualified and adequate supervision of the training room, its environs, facilities, and equipment at all times.[4]
- Develop and carefully follow an emergency plan.
- Make it a point to become familiar with the health status and medical history of the athletes under his or her care so as to be aware of any problems that could present a need for additional care or caution.
- Keep good records that document all injuries and rehabilitation steps.
- Document efforts to create a safe playing environment.
- Have a detailed job description in writing.
- Obtain written consent for providing health care, particularly when minors are involved.
- Maintain confidentiality of medical records.
- Don't dispense prescription drugs, and if allowed by law, exercise extreme caution in the administration of nonprescription medications.
- Use only those therapeutic methods that he or she is qualified to use and that the law states may be used.
- Don't use or permit the presence of faulty or hazardous equipment.
- Work cooperatively with the team physician in the selection and use of sports protective equipment, and insist that the best equipment be obtained, properly fitted, and properly maintained.
- Don't permit injured players to participate unless cleared by the team

physician. Players suffering a head injury should not be permitted to reenter the game. In some states a player who has suffered a concussion may not continue in the sport for the balance of the season.

■ Develop an understanding that an injured athlete will not be allowed to reenter competition until, in the opinion of the team physician or the athletic trainer, he or she is psychologically and physically able. Coaches should not allow themselves to be pressured to clear an athlete until he or she is fully cleared by the physician.

■ Follow the express orders of the team physician at all times.

■ Purchase liability insurance to protect against litigation and be aware of the limitations of the policy.

■ Know the limitations of his or her expertise as well as the applicable state regulations and restrictions limiting his or her scope of practice.

■ Use common sense in making decisions about the athlete's health and safety.

   In the case of an injury, a coach must use reasonable care to prevent further injury until medical care is obtained.

Product Liability

Manufacturers of athletic equipment have a duty to design and produce equipment that will not cause injury as long as it is used as intended. An express warranty is the manufacturer's written guarantee that a product is safe. Warning labels placed on football helmets inform the player of possible dangers inherent in using the product. Athletes must read and sign a form indicating that they have read and understand the warning. The National Operating Committee on Standards for Athletic Equipment (NOCSAE) establishes minimum standards for equipment that must be met to ensure its safety.

WHAT TYPES OF INSURANCE ARE NECESSARY TO PROTECT THE ATHLETE?

Because of the high cost of medical care, every athlete should be covered by appropriate insurance policies that maximize the benefits should injury occur. Since 1971 there has been a significant increase in the number of lawsuits filed, caused in part by the steady increase in individuals who have become active in sports. The costs of insurance have also significantly increased during this period. More lawsuits and much higher medical costs are creating a crisis in the insurance industry.[5] Medical insurance is a contract between an insurance company and a policyholder in which the insurance company agrees to reimburse a portion of the total medical bill after some deductible has been paid by the policyholder. The major types of insurance that coaches should be familiar with are general health insurance, catastrophic insurance, accident insurance, and liability insurance as well as insurance for errors and omissions. All sports health and safety personnel need to be adequately protected.

General Health Insurance

Every athlete should have a general health insurance policy that covers illness, hospitalization, and emergency care. Some institutions offer primary insurance coverage in which all medical expenses are paid for by the athletic department. The institutions pay an extremely high premium for this type of coverage. Most institutions offer secondary insurance coverage that pays the athlete's remaining medical bills once the athlete's personal insurance company has made its payment. Secondary insurance always includes a deductible that will not be covered by the plan.

Many athletes are covered under some type of family health insurance policy. However, the school must make certain that personal health insurance is arranged for or purchased by athletes not covered under family policies.[14] A form letter directed to the parents of all athletes should be completed and returned to the institution to make certain that appropriate coverage is provided (Figure 3-2). Some so-called comprehensive plans do not cover every health need. For example, such plans may cover physicians' care but not hospital charges. Many of these plans require large prepayments before the insurance takes effect. Supplemental policies such as accident insurance and catastrophic insurance are designed to take over where general health insurance stops.

Every athlete should have a general health insurance policy that covers illness, hospitalization, and emergency care.

Third-Party Reimbursement

Third-party reimbursement is the primary mechanism of payment for medical services in the United States.[15] Health care professionals are reimbursed for services performed by the policyholder's insurance company. Medical insurance companies may provide group and individual

Third-party reimbursement involves reimbursement for services performed by the policyholder's insurance company.

Figure 3-2

Sample insurance information form

Insurance Information on Student Athletes
Student's Name _____ Date of Birth _____
Address _____
Social Security Number _____ Sex: M _____ F _____
Names of Insurance Companies _____
Address of Insurance Company _____
Certificate Number _____ Group _____ Type _____
Policy Holder _____ Relationship to Student _____
Employer or Policyholder _____
Should my son/daughter require services beyond those covered by the Sports Medicine Program, I give permission to the Division of Sports Medicine to file a claim for such services with the above health care insurer.
According to NCAA regulations, I understand that any insurance payments I receive must be returned to be placed on my child's account.
Date _____   _____
                                        Parent's Signature

Third-party payers: Private
insurance carriers, HMOs,
PPOs

coverage for employees and dependents. To cut payout costs, many insurance companies have begun to pay for preventive care (to reduce the need for hospitalization) and to limit where the individual can go for care. Managed care involves a prearranged system for delivering health care that is designed to control costs while continuing to provide quality care. A number of different health care systems have been developed to contain costs.

Health maintenance organizations   Health maintenance organizations (HMOs) provide both preventive measures and limit where the individual can receive care. With the exception of an emergency, permission must be obtained before the individual can go to another provider. HMOs generally pay 100 percent of the medical costs as long as care is rendered at an HMO facility. Many supplemental policies will not cover the medical costs that would normally be paid by the general policy. Therefore an athlete treated outside the HMO may be ineligible for any insurance benefits. Many HMOs determine fees using a capitation system that limits the amount that will be reimbursed for a specific service. Athletic trainers must understand the limits of and restrictions on coverage at their individual institutions.

Preferred provider organizations   Preferred provider organizations (PPOs) provide discount health care but also limit where a person can go for treatment of an illness. The coach and/or athletic trainer must be apprised in advance where the ill athlete should be sent. Athletes sent to a facility not on the approved list may be required to pay for care, but if they are sent to a preferred facility, all costs are paid.[6] Added services such as physical therapy may be more easily attained and at no cost or at a much lower cost than with other insurance policies. PPOs pay on a fee-for-service basis.

Point of service plan   The point of service plan is a combination of HMO and PPO plans. It is based on an HMO structure, yet it allows members to go outside the HMO to obtain services. This flexibility is allowed only with certain conditions and under special circumstances.

Fee for service   The fee for service is the most traditional form of billing for health care, in which the provider charges the patient or a third-party payer for services provided. Charges are based on a set fee schedule.

Capitation   Capitation is a form of reimbursement used by managed care providers in which members make a standard payment each month regardless of how much service is rendered to the member by the provider.

Third-Party Reimbursement for Athletic Trainers

Currently, unless an athletic trainer is also a licensed physical therapist, it is difficult if not impossible to obtain third-party reimbursement for health care services provided. Because the majority of athletic trainers are now employed in for-profit clinical or industrial settings, this lack of reimbursement has become a major concern for their future. State licensing or credentialing of the athletic trainer has, to date, not helped with obtaining reimbursement. Insurance companies have not been willing to cover services provided by the athletic trainer. Athletic trainers working in the clinical setting perform many of the same functions as do physical therapists in the clinic and are also responsible for obtaining referrals to the clinic through contacts in the local high schools. Securing third-party reimbursement for athletic training services should be a priority, especially for the clinical athletic trainer.[15]

Accident Insurance

Besides general health insurance, low-cost accident insurance is available to the student. This insurance covers accidents on school grounds while the student is in attendance. The purpose of this insurance is to protect the student against financial loss from medical and hospital bills, to encourage an injured student to receive prompt medical care, to encourage prompt reporting of injuries, and to relieve a school of financial responsibility.

The school's general insurance may be limited; thus accident insurance for a specific activity such as sports may be needed to provide additional protection.[5] This type of coverage is limited and does not require knowledge of fault, and the amount it pays is limited. For serious sport injuries requiring surgery and lengthy rehabilitation, accident insurance is usually not adequate. This inadequacy can put families with limited budgets into a real financial bind. Of particular concern is insurance that does not adequately cover catastrophic injuries.

INSURANCE TO PROTECT THE COACH

Personal Liability Insurance

Most individual schools and school districts have general liability insurance to protect against damages that may arise from injuries occurring on school property. Liability insurance covers claims of negligence on the part of individuals. Its major concern is whether supervision was reasonable and whether unreasonable risk of harm was perceived by the sports participant.[14]

Because of the amount of litigation based on alleged negligence, premiums have become almost prohibitive for some schools. Typically, when a victim sues, the lawsuit has been a shotgun approach, with the coach, athletic trainer, physician, school administrator, and school district all named. If a protective piece of equipment is involved, the product manufacturer is also sued.

All coaches should carry professional liability insurance and must clearly understand the limits of coverage. Liability insurance typically covers negligence in a civil case. If a criminal complaint is also filed, liability insurance will not cover the coach.

Because of the amount of litigation for alleged negligence, all professionals involved with the sports program must be fully protected by personal liability insurance.

Catastrophic Insurance

Although catastrophic injuries in sports participation are relatively uncommon, if they do occur, the consequences to the athlete, family, and
institution as well as society can be staggering.[2] In the past, when available funds had been completely diminished, the family was forced to seek
funding elsewhere, usually through a lawsuit. Organizations such as the
NCAA and NAIA provide plans that deal with the problem of a lifetime
that requires extensive medical and rehabilitative care because of a
permanent disability.[5,13] Benefits begin when expenses have reached
$25,000 and are then extended for a lifetime. At the secondary school
level, a program is offered to districts by the National Federation of State
High School Associations (NFSHSA). This plan provides medical, rehabilitation, and transportation costs in excess of $10,000 not covered by
other insurance benefits.[14] Costs for catastrophic insurance are based on
the number of sports and the number of hazardous sports offered by the
institution.

To offset this shotgun mentality and to cover what is not covered by
a general liability policy, errors and omissions liability insurance has
evolved. This insurance is designed to cover school employees, officers,
and the district against suits claiming malpractice, wrongful actions, errors and omissions, and acts of negligence.[14] Even when working in a
program that has good liability coverage, each person within that program who works directly with students must have his or her own personal liability insurance.

As indicated, insurance that covers the athlete's health and safety can
be very complex. Coaches must be concerned that every athlete is adequately covered by a good, reliable insurance company. In some athletic
programs the filing of claims becomes the responsibility of the athletic
trainer. This task can be highly time consuming, taking the athletic
trainer away from his or her major role of directly working with the athlete. Because of the intricacies and time involved with claim filing and
follow-up communications with parents, doctors, and vendors, a staff
person other than the coach should be assigned this responsibility.

INSURANCE BILLING

It is essential that the coach file insurance claims immediately and correctly.[15] The coach working in an educational setting can facilitate this
process by collecting insurance information on every athlete at the beginning of the year. A letter should also be drafted to the parents of the
athlete, explaining the limits of the school insurance policy and what the
parents must do to process a claim if injury does occur. Schools that have
secondary policies should stress to the parents that they must submit all
bills to their insurance company before submitting the remainder to the
school. In educational institutions, most claims will be filed with a single
insurance company, which will pay for medical services provided by individual health care providers.

SUMMARY

- A great deal of care must be taken in following coaching and athletic training procedures that conform to the legal guidelines governing liability.

- Liability is the state of being legally responsible for the harm one causes another person. Liability assumes that a coach would act according to the reasonable standards of care of any individual with similar educational background or training.

- A coach who fails to use ordinary or reasonable care—care that persons would normally exercise to avoid injury to themselves or to others under similar circumstances—would be deemed negligent.

- Although athletes participating in a sports program are considered to assume a normal risk, this assumption in no way exempts those in charge from exercising reasonable care.

- Coaches can significantly decrease risk of litigation by making certain that they have done everything possible to provide a reasonable degree of care to the injured athlete.

- The major types of insurance that coaches should be familiar with are general health insurance, catastrophic insurance, accident insurance, and liability insurance as well as insurance for errors and omissions.

- Third-party reimbursement is the primary mechanism of payment for medical services in the United States. A number of different health care systems—including health maintenance organizations, preferred provider organizations, point of service plans, fee-for-service plans, and capitation plans—have been developed to contain costs.

- It is essential that the coach or athletic trainer file insurance claims immediately and correctly.

Solutions to Critical Thinking Exercises

3-1 When a coach assumes the duty of caring for an athlete, that coach is also under the obligation to make sure that appropriate care is given. A coach who fails to provide an acceptable standard of care has committed a breach of duty, and the athlete must then prove that this breach caused the injury or made the injury worse.

3-2 Besides general health insurance, low-cost accident insurance often covers accidents on school grounds while the athlete is competing. The purpose of this insurance is to protect the athlete against financial loss from medical and hospital bills, to encourage an injured athlete to receive prompt medical care, to encourage prompt reporting of injuries, and to relieve a school of financial responsibility.

REVIEW QUESTIONS AND CLASS ACTIVITIES

1. What are the major legal concerns of the coach in terms of liability, negligence, assumption of risk, and torts?

2. What measures can a coach take to minimize the chances of litigation should an athlete be injured?
3. Invite an attorney who is familiar with sport litigation to class to discuss how you can protect yourself from a lawsuit.
4. Discuss how a coach provides reasonable and prudent care in dealing with an injured athlete.
5. Why is it necessary for an athlete to have both general health insurance and accident insurance?
6. Briefly discuss the various methods of third-party reimbursement.
7. Why should a coach carry individual liability insurance?
8. What are the critical considerations for filing insurance claims?

REFERENCES

1. Appenzeller H: *Sports and the law: contemporary issues,* Charlottesville, Va, 1985, Michie.
2. Berg R: Catastrophic injury insurance, an end to costly litigation, *Ath J* 8:10, 1987.
3. Borkowski RP: Coaches and the courts, *First Aider* 54:1, 1985.
4. Borkowski RP: Lawsuit less likely if safety comes first, *First Aider* 55:11, 1985.
5. Chambers RL: Insurance types and coverages: knowledge to plan for the future (with a focus on motor skill activities and athletics), *Phys Educ* 44:233, 1986.
6. Clement A: Patterns of litigation in physical education instruction. Paper presented at the American Association of Health, Physical Education, and Dance, National Convention and Exposition, Cincinnati, April 1986.
7. Drowatzky JN: Legal duties and liability in athletic training, *Ath Train* 20:11, 1985.
8. Graham L: Ten ways to dodge the malpractice bullet, *Ath Train* 20(2):117, 1985.
9. Hawkins J, Appenzeller H: Legal aspects of sports medicine. In Mueller F, Ryan A: *Prevention of athletic injuries: the role of the sports medicine team,* Philadelphia, 1991, FA Davis.
10. Herbert D: *Legal aspects of sports medicine,* Canton, Ohio, 1990, Professional Reports Corporation.
11. Herbert D: Professional considerations related to conduct of preparticipation exams, *Sports Med Stand Malpract Report* 6(4):49, 1994.
12. Leverenz L, Helms L: Suing athletic trainers, parts I and II, *Ath Train* 25(3):212, 1990.
13. Mueller F: Catastrophic sports injuries. In Mueller F, Ryan A: *Prevention of athletic injuries: the role of the sports medicine team,* Philadelphia, 1991, FA Davis.
14. Rankin J, Ingersoll C: *Athletic training management: concepts and applications,* St Louis, 1995, Mosby.
15. Ray R: *Management strategies in athletic training,* Champaign, Ill, 1994, Human Kinetics.
16. Yasser R: Calculating risk, *Sports Med Dig* 9(2):5, 1987.

ANNOTATED BIBLIOGRAPHY

Appenzeller H: *Sports and law: contemporary issues,* Charlottesville, Va, 1985, Michie.

Exposes sports litigation from the perspectives of the athletic director, athlete, athletic trainer, coach, officials, and products liability expert. A chapter on the athletic trainer emphasizes the use of modalities and how this use relates to the practice of physical therapy in different states.

Herbert D: *Legal aspects of sports medicine,* Canton, Ohio, 1990, Professional Reports Corporation.

A discussion of sports medicine, poli-

cies, procedures, responsibilities of the
sports medicine team, informed consent,
negligence, insurance and risk management, medication, drug testing, and other
topics.

Nygard G, Boone T: *Coaches guide to sport law*, Champaign, Ill, 1985, Human Kinetics.

Provides general information on the legal responsibilities of coaches and physical educators.

WEB SITES

Legal Information Institute at Cornell:
http://www.law.cornell.edu/topics/
sports.html

Part of a series of legal information, this site specifically addresses law in sport, but is rather technical in nature, the relevant area to sports medicine is addressed in the area titled torts.

Cramer First Aider: http://www.ccsd.
k12.wy.us/CCHS_web/sptmed/
fstaider.htm

The Cramer First Aider is a newsletter published by Cramer that provides information about current topics in sports medicine; see the Legal Issues section.

Preventing Injuries through Fitness Training

When you finish this chapter you will be able to:

- Identify the major conditioning seasons and the types of exercise that are performed in each season.
- Identify the principles of conditioning.
- Explain the importance of the warm-up and cooldown periods.
- Describe the importance of flexibility, strength, and cardiorespiratory endurance for both athletic performance and injury prevention.
- Identify specific techniques and principles for improving flexibility, muscular strength, and cardiorespiratory endurance.

Lack of fitness is one of the primary causes of sports injury.

To compete successfully at a high level, the athlete must be fit. An athlete who is not fit is more likely to sustain an injury. Coaches recognize that improper conditioning is one of the major causes of sports injuries. Thus coaches should work cooperatively to supervise training and conditioning programs that minimize the possibility of injury and maximize performance.[28]

Fitness does not develop overnight. It takes time and careful preparation to bring an athlete into competition at a level of fitness that will preclude early-season injury. Both the coach and the athlete must possess sound understanding of the principles of training and conditioning relative to flexibility, strength, and cardiorespiratory endurance.

CONDITIONING SEASONS AND PERIODIZATION

No longer do serious athletes engage in just preseason conditioning and in-season competition. Sports conditioning is a year-round endeavor. The concept of **periodization** is an approach to conditioning that attempts to bring about peak performance while reducing injuries and overtraining in the athlete by developing a training and conditioning program to be followed throughout the various seasons. Periodization takes into account athletes' different needs relative to training and conditioning during different seasons and modifies the program according to individual needs. For the athlete, the conditioning program often encompasses four training seasons: postseason, off-season, preseason, and in-season. This

periodization
Allows athletes to train year-round with less risk of injury and staleness.

Sports conditioning often falls into four seasons: postseason, off-season, preseason, and in-season.

plan is especially appropriate for collision sports such as football. This approach is referred to as the quadratic training cycle.[10]

Postseason Conditioning

Conditioning during the postseason is commonly dedicated to physical restoration. This application is particularly appropriate when the athlete has been injured during the in-season. Postsurgical rehabilitation takes place during this time, and detailed medical evaluations can be obtained.[14]

Off-Season Conditioning

It is essential that athletes continue with a conditioning program during the off-season. The coach should encourage athletes to participate in another sport during this period. Such an activity should make certain physical demands embodying strength, endurance, and flexibility by means of running and general all-around physical performance. This activity will assist athletes in maintaining their level of fitness. In other words, the sport must be sufficiently demanding and require a good level of fitness for effective participation. An excellent off-season sport for the football player would be wrestling or gymnastics. Track, especially cross-country, is a conditioner.

A weekly workout of moderate-to-strong intensity is usually all that is required, because physical fitness is retained for a considerable length of time after an active program of competition ends. The physically vigorous athlete tends to be quite active in the off-season too and, as a rule, will stay in reasonably good condition throughout the year.[14] Establishing regular training routines for the off-season enables the coach to keep a close check on athletes even if they are seen only at two-week or three-week intervals.

Preseason Conditioning

Coaches should impress on their athletes the need for maintaining a reasonably high level of physical fitness during the off-season. If such advice is followed, the athlete will find preseason work relatively rewarding and any proneness to potential injury considerably diminished. The athlete should experience no difficulty in reaching a state of athletic fitness suitable for competition within six to eight weeks. During this preliminary period flexibility, endurance, and strength should be emphasized in a carefully graded developmental program. Such a program must make wise and constant use of established physiological bases for improving physical condition and performance.

Many athletes, particularly in one-season sports, tend to reach their highest level of performance halfway through the season. As a result, they are truly efficient only half the time. Conference and federation restrictions often hamper or prohibit effective preseason training, especially in football, and therefore compel the athlete to come into early-season competition before being physically fit for it. At the high school level, six to eight weeks of preseason conditioning affords the best insurance against susceptibility to injury and permits the athlete to enter competition in a good state of physical fitness, provided a carefully graded program is established and adhered to conscientiously. Recently, physicians have been adding their voices to the demands for a realistic approach to proper conditioning, and school administrators and the general public may see the need for and effectiveness of permitting adequate and properly controlled preseason training.

In-Season Conditioning

Intensive preseason conditioning programs, which bring the athlete to the competitive season, may not be maintained by the sport itself. Unless strenuous conditioning is undergone throughout the season, a problem of deconditioning may occur. Athletes who do not undergo maintenance conditioning may lose their entry level of physiological fitness.[14]

Cross Training

The concept of cross training is an approach to training and conditioning for a specific sport that involves substitution of alternative activities that have some carryover value to that sport. For example, a swimmer could engage in jogging, running, or aerobic exercise to maintain levels of cardiorespiratory conditioning. Cross training is particularly useful in both the postseason and the off-season to help athletes maintain fitness levels and avoid the boredom that would typically occur from following the same training regimen and using the same techniques for conditioning as during the preseason and competitive season.

FOUNDATIONS OF CONDITIONING

The SAID principle indicates that the body will gradually adapt to the specific demands imposed on it.

The SAID principle relates to the process of training and conditioning.[19] SAID is an acronym for Specific Adaptation to Imposed Demands. The SAID principle states that when the body is subjected to stresses and overloads of varying intensities, it will gradually adapt over time to overcome whatever demands are placed on it.

Although overload is a critical factor in training and conditioning, the stress must not be great enough to produce damage or injury before the body has had a chance to adjust specifically to the increased demands. Therefore, to reduce the likelihood of injury, coaches should be aware of the principles of training and conditioning. See the accompanying Focus Box.

Warm-Up

A proper warm-up before exercise will reduce the tearing of muscle fibers and prevent muscle soreness.

A period of warm-up exercises should take place before a training session begins. The warm-up increases body temperature, stretches ligaments and muscles, and increases flexibility. Related warm-ups, those similar to the activity engaged in, are preferable to unrelated ones because of the rehearsal or practice effect that results.

4-1 ⟩ **Focus Box**

Principles of Conditioning

1. *Warm-up/cooldown.* Give the athletes time to do an appropriate warm-up before engaging in any activity. Do not neglect the cooldown period following a training bout.

2. *Motivation.* Athletes are generally highly motivated to work hard because they want to be successful in their sport. By varying the training program and incorporating different aspects of conditioning, the program can remain enjoyable rather than becoming routine and boring.

3. *Overload.* To see improvement in any physiological component, the system must work harder than it is accustomed to working. Gradually, that system will adapt to the imposed demands.

4. *Consistency.* The athlete must engage in a training and conditioning program on a consistent, regularly scheduled basis if the program is to be effective.

5. *Progression.* Increase the intensity of the conditioning program gradually and within the individual athlete's ability to adapt to increasing workloads.

6. *Intensity.* Stress the intensity of the work rather than the quantity. Coaches and athletic trainers too often confuse working hard with working for long periods of time. They make the mistake of prolonging the workout rather than increasing tempo or workload. The tired athlete is prone to injury.

7. *Specificity.* Specific goals for the training program must be identified. The program must be designed to address specific components of fitness (i.e., strength, flexibility, cardiorespiratory endurance) relative to the sport in which the athlete is competing.

8. *Individuality.* The needs of individual athletes vary considerably. The successful coach is one who recognizes these individual differences and adjusts or alters the training and conditioning program accordingly to best accommodate the athlete.

9. *Stress.* Expect that athletes will train as close to their physiological limits as possible. Push the athletes but consider other stressful aspects of their lives; allow them time to be away from the conditioning demands of their sport.

10. *Safety.* Make the training environment as safe as possible. Take time to educate athletes about proper techniques, how they should feel during the workout, and when they should push harder or back off.

4-1 ⟩

Critical Thinking Exercise

A track athlete constantly complains of tightness in her lower extremity during workouts. She states that she has a difficult time during her warm-up and cannot seem to "get loose" until her workout is almost complete. She feels that she is always on the verge of "pulling a muscle."

? What should the coach recommend as a specific warm-up routine that should consistently be done before this athlete begins her workout?

Warm-ups have been found to be important in preventing injury and muscle soreness.[24] Muscle injury can result when vigorous exercises are not preceded by a related warm-up. An effective, quick warm-up can also be an effective motivator. If athletes derive satisfaction from a warm-up, they probably will have a stronger desire to participate in the activity. By contrast, a poor warm-up can lead to fatigue and boredom, limiting athletes' attention and ultimately resulting in a poor program. A good warm-up may also improve certain aspects of performance.[20]

The function of the warm-up is to prepare the body physiologically for some upcoming physical work bout. Most coaches view the warm-up period as a precaution against unnecessary musculoskeletal injury and possible muscle soreness. The purpose is to very gradually stimulate the cardiorespiratory system to a moderate degree, thus producing an increased blood flow to working skeletal muscles and resulting in an increase in muscle temperature.

Moderate activity speeds up the metabolic processes that produce an increase in core body temperature. An increase in the temperature of skeletal muscle causes an increased speed of contraction and relaxation, probably because nerve impulse conduction velocity is increased. The elastic properties (the length of stretch) of the muscle are increased, whereas the viscous properties (the rate at which the muscle can change shape) are decreased.

Warming up involves general body warming and warming specific body areas for the demands of the sport.

Every workout should be preceded by a warm-up. This activity should include a general warm-up followed by a specific warm-up. The general warm-up elevates the core temperature through the use of static stretching exercises. The specific warm-up involves actions related to the activity to be performed. These actions are sport specific and should gradually increase in intensity. For example, soccer players use the upper extremity considerably less than the lower extremity, so their general warm-up should be directed more toward the lower extremity, perhaps by adding some stretching exercises for the lower extremity. The specific warm-up also relates to the sport: A basketball player should warm up by shooting layups and jump shots and by dribbling, for example, or a tennis player should hit forehand and backhand shots and serves.

The warm-up should last approximately ten to fifteen minutes. Athletes should not wait longer than fifteen minutes after the warm-up to get started in the activity, although the effects will generally last up to about forty-five minutes. Thus the third-string football player who warms up before the game and then does nothing more than stand around until he gets into the game during the fourth quarter is running a much higher risk of injury. This player should be encouraged to stay warmed up and ready to play throughout the course of a game. In general, sweating is a good indication that the body has been sufficiently warmed up and is ready for more strenuous activity.

Reduce injuries by
increasing:
Flexibility
Strength
Power
Endurance

The warm-up should begin with two or three minutes of light jogging to increase metabolic rate and core temperature. The jogging should be followed by flexibility exercises in which the muscles are stretched to take advantage of the increase in muscle elasticity. Finally, the intensity of the warm-up should be increased gradually by performing body movements and skills associated with the specific activity in which the athlete is going to participate.

Cooldown

After a vigorous workout, a cooldown is essential. This part of the training program helps in returning the blood to the heart for reoxygenation, thus preventing the blood from pooling in the muscles of the arms and the legs. Pooling of the blood in the extremities places additional unnecessary stress and strain on the heart. After vigorous activity, enough blood may not circulate back to the brain, heart, and intestines, and symptoms such as dizziness or faintness may occur without a cooldown period. The cooldown enables the body to cool and return to a resting state. Such a period should last about five to ten minutes.

Although the value of warm-up and workout periods is well accepted, the importance of a cooldown period afterward is often ignored. Persons who stretch during the cooldown period tend to have fewer problems with muscle soreness following strenuous activity.[24]

WHY IS IT IMPORTANT TO HAVE GOOD FLEXIBILITY?

Flexibility may best be defined as the range of motion possible about a given joint or series of joints.[23] Flexibility can be discussed in relation to movement involving only one joint, such as in the knees, or movement involving a whole series of joints, such as the spinal vertebral joints, which must all move together to allow smooth bending, or rotation, of the trunk. Flexibility is specific to a given joint or movement. A person may have good range of motion in the ankles, knees, hips, back, and one shoulder joint. However, if the other shoulder joint lacks normal movement, then this person has a problem that needs to be corrected before he or she can function normally.

For an athlete, good flexibility is considered essential for both successful performance and injury prevention. Lack of flexibility may result in uncoordinated or awkward movements and may predispose a person to muscle strain.

A lack of flexibility in an athlete will likely impair performance. For example, a sprinter with tight, inelastic hamstring muscles may have a problem sprinting at maximum speed because tight hamstrings restrict the ability to flex the hip joint, thus shortening stride length. Most activities in sport require relatively normal amounts of flexibility. However, some athletic activities, such as gymnastics, ballet, diving, karate, and yoga, require increased flexibility for superior performance (Figure 4-1). Increased flexibility may increase an athlete's performance through improved balance and reaction time. Experts in the field of training and conditioning generally agree that good flexibility is essential to successful physical performance.

Most coaches feel that maintaining good flexibility is important in prevention of injury to muscles and tendons, and they will generally insist that stretching exercises be included as part of the warm-up before engaging in strenuous activity.

Properly cooling down decreases blood and muscle lactic acid levels more rapidly.

Conditioning should be performed gradually, with work added in small increments.

The "tight" or inflexible athlete performs with a considerable handicap in terms of movement.

Figure 4-1

Certain athletic activities require extreme flexibility for successful performance.

What Structures in the Body Can Limit Flexibility?

A number of different anatomical structures may limit the ability of a joint to move through a full, unrestricted range of motion. Normal bone structure, fat, and skin or scar tissue may limit the ability to move through a full range of motion.[23]

Muscles and their tendons are most often responsible for limiting range of motion. Performing stretching exercises for the purpose of improving a particular joint's flexibility is an attempt to take advantage of the highly elastic properties of a muscle. Over time it is possible to increase the elasticity, or the length, that a given muscle can be stretched. Athletes who have a good range of motion at a particular joint tend to have highly elastic and flexible muscles.

Connective tissue surrounding the joint, such as ligaments or the joint capsule, may be subject to contractures. Ligaments and joint capsules do have some elasticity; however, if a joint is immobilized for a period of time, these structures tend to lose some elasticity and actually shorten. This condition is most commonly seen after surgical repair of an unstable joint, but it can also result from long periods of inactivity.

On the other hand, it is also possible for an athlete to have slack ligaments and joint capsules. These individuals are generally referred to as being loose-jointed. An example of this condition would be an elbow or knee that extends beyond being straight. Frequently the instability associated with loose-jointedness may present as great a problem in movement as a joint that is too tight.

Active and Passive Range of Motion

When a muscle actively contracts, it produces a joint movement through a specific range of motion. However, if passive pressure is applied to an extremity, it is capable of moving farther in the range of motion. *Active range of motion* refers to that portion of the total range of motion through which a joint can be moved by an active muscle contraction. The ability to move through the active range of motion is not necessarily a good indicator of the stiffness or looseness of a joint because it applies to the ability to move a joint efficiently, with little resistance to motion. *Passive range of motion* refers to the portion of the total range of motion through which a joint may be moved passively. No muscle contraction is needed to move a joint through a passive range of motion. Passive range of motion begins at the end of and continues beyond active range of motion.

It is essential in sport activities that an extremity be capable of moving through a nonrestricted range of motion.[1] For example, a hurdler who cannot fully extend the knee joint in a normal stride is at a considerable disadvantage because stride length and thus speed will be reduced significantly. Passive range of motion is important for injury prevention. Sports contain many situations in which a muscle is forced to stretch beyond its normal active limits. If the muscle does not have enough elasticity to compensate for this additional stretch, the muscle or its tendon will likely be injured.

Agonist versus Antagonist Muscles

Before discussing the three different stretching techniques, it is essential to define the terms *agonist muscle* and *antagonist muscle*. Most joints in the body are capable of more than one movement. The knee joint, for example, is capable of flexion and extension. Contraction of the quadriceps group of muscles on the front of the thigh causes knee extension, whereas contraction of the hamstring muscles on the back of the thigh produces knee flexion. The muscle that contracts to produce a movement, in this case the quadriceps, is referred to as the agonist muscle. Conversely, the muscle being stretched in response to contraction of the agonist muscle is called the antagonist muscle. In this example of knee extension, the antagonist muscle would be the hamstring group.

Some degree of balance in strength must exist between agonist and antagonist muscle groups. This balance is necessary for normal, smooth, coordinated movement as well as for reducing the likelihood of muscle strain due to the muscular imbalance. Understanding the relationship between agonist and antagonist muscles facilitates the following discussion of the three techniques of stretching (see the accompanying Focus Box).

What Are the Different Stretching Techniques?

Maintaining a full, nonrestricted range of motion has long been recognized as an essential component of being fit. Flexibility is important not only for successful physical performance but also in the prevention of injury. The goal of any effective flexibility program should be to improve the range of motion around a given joint by altering the extensibility of the muscles and tendons that produce movement at that joint. Exercises that stretch these muscles and tendons over a period of time will increase the range of movement possible about a given joint.

Stretching techniques for improving flexibility have evolved over the years. The oldest technique for stretching is called **ballistic stretching,** which makes use of repetitive bouncing motions. A second technique, known as **static stretching,** involves stretching a muscle to the point of discomfort and then holding it at that point for an extended time. This technique has been used for many years. Recently another group of stretching techniques known collectively as **proprioceptive neuromuscular facilitation (PNF),** involving alternating contractions and stretches, has also been recommended. Researchers have had considerable discussion about which of these techniques is most effective for improving range of motion.

Ballistic Stretching

On the track any spring or fall afternoon, runners can be seen warming up by stretching, using bouncing movements to stretch a particular

ballistic stretching
Older stretching technique that uses repetitive bouncing motions.

static stretching
Passively stretching an antagonist muscle by placing it in a maximal stretch and holding it there.

proprioceptive neuromuscular facilitation (PNF)
Stretching techniques that involve combinations of alternating contractions and stretches.

Guidelines and Precautions for Stretching

The following guidelines and precautions should be incorporated into a sound stretching program:

Warm up using a slow jog or fast walk before stretching vigorously.

To increase flexibility, the muscle must be overloaded or stretched beyond its normal range but not to the point of pain.

Stretch only to the point at which tightness or resistance to stretch or perhaps some discomfort is felt. Stretching should not be painful.

Increases in range of motion will be specific to whatever joint is being stretched.

Exercise caution when stretching muscles that surround painful joints. Pain is an indication that something is wrong; it should not be ignored.

Avoid overstretching the ligaments and capsules that surround joints.

Exercise caution when stretching the low back and neck. Exercises that compress the vertebrae and their discs may cause damage.

Stretching from a seated position rather than a standing position takes stress off the low back and decreases the chances of back injury.

Stretch those muscles that are tight and inflexible.

Strengthen those muscles that are weak and loose.

Always stretch slowly and with control.

Be sure to continue normal breathing during a stretch.

Static and PNF techniques are most often recommended for individuals who want to improve their range of motion.

Ballistic stretching should be done only by those who are already flexible and/or are accustomed to stretching and should be done only after static stretching.

Stretching should be done at least three times per week to see minimal improvement, between five and six times per week to see maximum results.

muscle. This bouncing technique is more appropriately known as ballistic stretching, in which repetitive contractions of the agonist muscle are used to produce quick stretches of the antagonist muscle. The ballistic stretching technique, although apparently effective in improving range of motion, should be used with some caution by sedentary, inactive people because increased range of motion is achieved through a series of jerks or pulls on the resistant muscle tissue. If the forces generated by the jerks are greater than the tissues' extensibility, muscle injury may result. For a conditioned athlete, ballistic stretching will not normally be detrimental and in fact is perhaps the most appropriate stretching technique for most sport activities that require dynamic movements.

Successive forceful contractions of the agonist that result in stretching of the antagonist may cause muscle soreness. For example, forcefully kicking a soccer ball fifty times may result in muscular soreness of the hamstrings (antagonist muscle) as a result of eccentric contraction of the hamstrings to control the dynamic movement of the quadriceps (agonist muscle). Ballistic stretching that is controlled usually does not cause muscle soreness.

Static Stretching

The static stretching technique is still an extremely effective and popular technique of stretching. This technique involves passively stretching a muscle by placing it in a maximal position of stretch and holding it there for an extended time. Recommendations for the optimal time for holding this stretched position vary, ranging from as short as three seconds to as long as sixty seconds. It appears that twenty to thirty seconds may be the best length of time to hold a stretch. The static stretch of each muscle should be repeated three or four times. Much research has been done comparing ballistic and static stretching techniques for the improvement of flexibility. Both static and ballistic stretching are effective in increasing flexibility, and there is no significant difference between the two. However, static stretching offers less danger of exceeding the extensibility limits of the involved joints because the stretch is more controlled. Ballistic stretching may cause muscular soreness (if the athlete is not fit), whereas static stretching generally does not and is commonly used in injury rehabilitation of sore or strained muscles.

Static stretching is certainly a much safer stretching technique, especially for unfit individuals. However, many physical activities involve dynamic movement. Thus, stretching as a warm-up for these types of activities should begin with static stretching followed by ballistic stretching, which more closely resembles the dynamic activity.

Proprioceptive Neuromuscular Facilitation (PNF) Techniques

PNF techniques were first used by physical therapists for treating patients who had various types of neuromuscular paralysis.[17] Only recently have PNF stretching exercises been used as a stretching technique for increasing flexibility. A number of different PNF techniques are currently being used for stretching, including *slow-reversal-hold-relax, contract-relax,* and *hold-relax* techniques. All involve some combination of alternating contraction and relaxation of both agonist and antagonist muscles (a ten-second pushing phase followed by a ten-second relaxing phase).

Using a hamstring stretching technique as an example (Figure 4-2), the slow-reversal-hold-relax technique would be done as follows. With the athlete lying supine with knee extended and the ankle flexed to 90 degrees, the athletic trainer passively flexes the leg at the hip joint to the point at which the athlete feels slight discomfort in the muscle. At this point the athlete begins pushing against the athletic trainer's resistance by contracting the hamstring muscle. After pushing for ten seconds, the athlete relaxes the hamstring muscles and contracts agonist quadriceps muscle while the athletic trainer applies passive pressure to further stretch the hamstrings. This pressure should move the leg so that the hip joint flexion is increased. The relaxing phase lasts for ten seconds, at which time the athlete again push against the trainer's resistance,

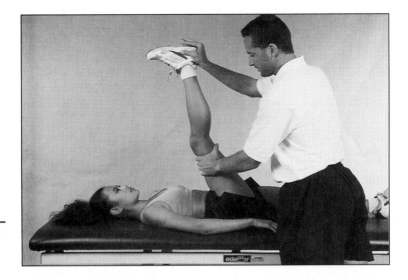

Figure 4-2

The slow-reversal-hold-relax
technique can be used to
stretch hamstring muscles.

beginning at this new joint angle. The push-relax sequence is repeated at least three times.[22]

The contract-relax and hold-relax techniques are variations on the slow-reversal-hold-relax method. In the contract-relax method, the hamstrings are isotonically contracted so that the leg actually moves toward the floor during the push phase. The hold-relax method involves an isometric hamstring contraction against immovable resistance during the push phase. During the relax phase, both techniques involve relax-

Figure 4-3

Arm hang exercise
Muscles stretched: Entire
shoulder girdle complex
Instructions: Using a
chinning bar, simply hang
with shoulders and arms
fully extended for thirty
seconds. Repeat five times.

ation of hamstrings and quadriceps while the hamstrings are passively stretched. This same basic PNF technique can be used to stretch any muscle in the body. PNF stretching techniques are perhaps best performed with a partner, although they may also be done using a wall as resistance.[22]

Practical Application

Although all three stretching techniques have been demonstrated to effectively improve flexibility, there is still considerable debate as to which technique produces the greatest increases in range of movement. The ballistic technique is seldom recommended because of the potential for causing muscle soreness. However, most sport activities are ballistic in nature (i.e., kicking, running). In highly trained individuals, it is unlikely that ballistic stretching will result in muscle soreness. Static stretching is perhaps the most widely used technique. It is a simple technique and does not require a partner. A fully nonrestricted range of motion can be attained through static stretching over time.

PNF stretching techniques are capable of producing dramatic increases in range of motion during one stretching session. Studies comparing static and PNF stretching suggest that PNF stretching is capable of producing greater improvement in flexibility over an extended training period.[22] The major disadvantage of PNF stretching is that a partner is required, although stretching with a partner may have some motivational

Figure 4-4

Shoulder towel stretch exercise
Muscles stretched: Internal and external rotators
Instructions: Begin by holding towel above head shoulder width apart. A, Try to pull towel down behind back, first with left hand then with right. B, you should end up in position C. Reverse order to get back to position A. Repeat five times on each side.

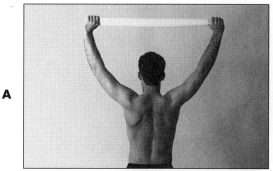
A

B

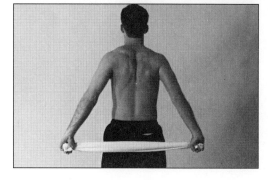
C

advantages. More and more athletic teams seem to be adopting the PNF technique as the method of choice for improving flexibility.

Stretching Exercises

Figures 4-3 to 4-14 illustrate stretching exercises that may be used to improve flexibility at specific joints throughout the body. The exercises described may be done statically or with slight modification; they may also be done with a partner using a PNF technique.

Each of these exercises has many possible variations. The exercises selected are those that seem to be the most effective for stretching various muscle groups.

Figure 4-5

Chest and shoulder stretch
exercise
Muscles stretched: Pectoralis
and deltoid
Instructions: Stand in a
corner, hands on walls, and
lean forward. Hold for thirty
seconds. Repeat three times.

Figure 4-6

Abdominal and anterior
chest wall stretch exercise
Muscles stretched: Muscles of
respiration in thorax and
abdominal muscles
Instructions: Extend upper
trunk, support weight on
elbows, keeping pelvis on the
floor. Hold for thirty seconds.
Repeat three times.

Assessment of Flexibility

Accurate measurement of the range of joint motion is difficult. Various devices have been designed to accommodate variations in the size of the joints as well as the complexity of movements in articulations that involve more than one joint. Of these devices, the simplest and most widely used is the goniometer (Figure 4-15). A goniometer is a large protractor with measurements in degrees. By aligning the two arms parallel to the longitudinal axis of the two segments involved in motion about a specific joint, it is possible to obtain relatively accurate measures of range of movement. The goniometer has its place in a rehabilitation setting, in which assessing improvement in joint flexibility is essential for modifying injury rehabilitation programs.

Is There a Relationship between Strength and Flexibility?

It is often said that strength training has negative effects on flexibility. For example, someone who develops large bulk through strength training is often referred to as muscle-bound. The expression "muscle-bound" has negative connotations in terms of the ability of that person to move. People who have highly developed muscles are thought to have lost much of their ability to move freely through a full range of motion.

Figure 4-7

William's flexion exercise
Muscles stretched: Low back and hip extensors
Instructions: A, Touch chin to right knee and hold, then to left knee and hold. B, Touch chin to both knees and hold. Hold each position for thirty seconds.

Figure 4-8

Low back twister exercise
Muscles stretched: Rotators of lower back and sacrum and hip abductors
Instructions: Lie on back on edge of bed or table. Keep shoulders and arms flat on surface. Cross leg farthest from edge over the top and let it hang off the side of bed, keeping knee straight; hold for thirty seconds. Repeat with other leg. Repeat three times with each leg.
Caution: If keeping the leg straight produces pain, this exercise may be done with the leg bent. Be sure to exercise caution in returning the leg to the starting position.

Organizing and Establishing
an Effective Athletic Health
Care System

Figure 4-9

Forward lunge exercise
Muscles stretched: Hip
flexors and quadriceps
Instructions: In a kneeling
position with one knee on
the ground, thrust pelvis
forward. Hold for thirty
seconds. Repeat three times.

Figure 4-10

Lateral trunk stretch exercise
Muscles stretched: Lateral
abdominals and intercostals
Instructions: Standing with
feet spread at shoulder
width, hands on hips, drop
head toward shoulder and
bend trunk in a lateral
direction. Hold for thirty
seconds. Repeat three times
on each side.

Figure 4-11

Trunk twister exercise
Muscles stretched: Trunk and
hip rotators
Instructions: Place one foot
over opposite knee. Rotate
trunk to bent knee side.

Figure 4-12

Hamstring stretch exercise
Muscles stretched: Hip extensors and knee flexors
Instructions: Lie flat on back. Raise one leg straight up with knee extended and ankle flexed to 90 degrees. Grasp leg around calf and pull toward head; hold for thirty seconds. Repeat with opposite leg. Repeat three times with each leg.

Figure 4-13

Groin stretch exercise
Muscles stretched: Hip adductors in groin
Instructions: Sit with knees flexed and soles of feet together. Try to press knees flat on the floor; if they are flat to begin with, try to touch face to floor. Hold for thirty seconds. Repeat three times.

Figure 4-14

Achilles heel cord stretch exercise
Muscles stretched: Foot plantar flexors. A, Gastrocnemius. B, Soleus. Instructions: A, Stand facing wall with toes pointing straight ahead and with the knee straight. Lean forward toward wall, keeping heels flat on floor. You should feel stretching high in calf. B, Stand facing wall with toes pointing straight ahead and with the knee flexed. Lean forward toward wall, keeping heels flat on floor. You should feel stretching low in calf. Hold each position for thirty seconds. Repeat each position three times for each leg.

Organizing and Establishing
an Effective Athletic Health
Care System

Figure 4-15

Goniometric measurement of
hip joint flexion

Occasionally a person develops so much bulk that the physical size of
the muscle prevents a normal range of motion. When strength training is
not properly done, movement can be impaired. However, weight training, if done properly through a full range of motion, will not impair flexibility. Proper strength training probably improves dynamic flexibility
and, if combined with a rigorous stretching program, can greatly enhance
powerful and coordinated movements that are essential for success in
many athletic activities.[12] In all cases a heavy weight-training program
should be accompanied by a strong flexibility program (Figure 4-16).

Figure 4-16

If strength training is
combined with flexibility
exercise, a full range of
motion may be maintained.

WHY ARE MUSCULAR STRENGTH, ENDURANCE, AND POWER IMPORTANT FOR ATHLETES?

The development of muscular strength is an essential component of a training program for every athlete. By definition, **muscular strength** is the ability of a muscle to generate force against some resistance. **Muscular endurance** is the ability to perform repetitive muscular contractions against some resistance for an extended period of time. As muscular strength increases, there tends to be a corresponding increase in endurance.[7] For example, an athlete can lift a weight twenty-five times. If muscular strength is increased by 10 percent through weight training, the maximal number of repetitions would be increased because it is easier for the athlete to lift the weight.

Most movements in sports are explosive and must include elements of both strength and speed if they are to be effective. If a large amount of force is generated quickly, the movement can be referred to as a *power* movement. Without the ability to generate power, an athlete will be limited in his or her performance capabilities.[18,23] It is difficult to hit a baseball, drive a golf ball, or kick a soccer ball without generating power. For most athletes, the ability to generate power is more critical for successful performance than simply having great strength or muscular endurance.

Types of Skeletal Muscle Contraction

Skeletal muscle is capable of three different types of contraction: (1) an *isometric contraction*, (2) a *concentric*, or positive, contraction, and (3) an *eccentric*, or negative, contraction. An isometric contraction occurs when the muscle contracts to produce tension, but there is no change in length of the muscle. Considerable force can be generated against some immovable resistance, even though no movement occurs. In a concentric contraction, the muscle shortens in length while tension is developed to overcome or move some resistance. In an eccentric contraction, the resistance is greater than the muscular force being produced, and the muscle lengthens while producing tension. For example, when lifting a weight in the hand the biceps muscle in the upper arm is shortening as it contracts, which is a concentric contraction. As the weight is lowered, the biceps muscle is still contracting but now it is lengthening. This movement is an eccentric contraction. Concentric and eccentric contractions must occur to allow most movements.

What Determines Amount of Strength?

Size of the Muscle

Muscular strength is proportional to the size of a muscle as determined by the cross-sectional diameter of the muscle fibers.[20] The greater the cross-sectional diameter or the bigger a particular muscle, the stronger it is, thus, the more force it is capable of generating. The size of a muscle tends to increase in cross-sectional diameter with weight training. This

muscular strength
The maximum force that can be applied by a muscle during a single maximum contraction.

muscular endurance
The ability to perform repetitive muscular contractions against some resistance.

4-2

Critical Thinking Exercise

A swimmer has been engaged in an off-season weight training program to increase her muscular strength and endurance. Although she has seen some improvement in her strength, she is concerned that she also seems to be losing flexibility in her shoulders, which she feels is critical to her performance as a swimmer. She has also noticed that her muscles are hypertrophying to some degree and is worried that that may be causing her to lose flexibility. She has just about decided to abandon her weight training program altogether.

? What can the coach recommend that will allow her to continue to improve her muscular strength and endurance while simultaneously maintaining or perhaps even improving her flexibility?

increase in muscle size is referred to as *hypertrophy*. Conversely, a decrease in the size of a muscle is referred to as *atrophy*.

Number of Muscle Fibers

Strength is a function of the number and diameter of muscle fibers composing a given muscle. The number of fibers is an inherited characteristic; a person with a large number of muscle fibers to begin with has the potential to hypertrophy to a much greater degree than does someone with relatively few fibers. But anyone can increase his or her strength through exercise.

Neuromuscular Efficiency

Strength is also directly related to the efficiency of both the nervous and muscular systems (or the neuromuscular system) and the function of the motor unit in producing muscular force. Initial increases in strength during a weight-training program can be attributed primarily to increased neuromuscular efficiency. For a muscle to contract, a nerve impulse must be transmitted from the nervous system to the muscle. Each muscle fiber is innervated by a specific *motor unit*. By overloading a particular muscle, as in weight training, the muscle is forced to work efficiently. Efficiency is achieved by getting more motor units to fire, causing a stronger contraction of the muscle.[25]

Biomechanical Factors

Strength in a given muscle is determined not only by the physical properties of the muscle but also by biomechanical factors. Bones along with muscles and their tendons form a system of levers and pulleys that collectively generate force to move an external object. The position of attachment of a particular muscle tendon on the bone will largely determine how much force this muscle is capable of generating.

Fast-Twitch versus Slow-Twitch Muscle Fibers

There are two basic types of muscle fibers:
Slow-twitch
Fast-twitch

The fibers that make up a muscle are either slow-twitch fibers or fast-twitch fibers.[9] Within a particular muscle, both types of fibers exist, and the ratio in an individual muscle varies with each person. Those muscles that have a primary function of maintaining posture against the pull of gravity require more endurance and have a higher percentage of slow-twitch fibers. Muscles that produce powerful, explosive, and strength movements tend to have a much greater percentage of fast-twitch fibers.

Because this ratio is genetically determined, it may play a large role in determining ability for a given sport activity. For example, sprinters and weight lifters have a large percentage of fast-twitch fibers in relation to slow-twitch ones. One study has shown that sprinters may have as many as 95 percent fast-twitch fibers in certain muscles. Conversely, marathon runners generally have a higher percentage of slow-twitch fibers. The question of whether fiber types can change as a result of training has not been completely resolved.[20] However, both types of fibers can improve their metabolic capabilities through specific strength and endurance training.

Level of Physical Activity

Loss in muscle strength is definitely related to individual levels of physical activity. Those people who are more active, or perhaps those who continue to strength train, considerably reduce this tendency toward declining muscle strength. In addition, exercise may also have an effect in slowing the decrease in cardiorespiratory endurance and flexibility as well as slowing increases in body fat that tend to occur with aging. Therefore, if total wellness and health is an ultimate goal, strength maintenance is important for all individuals regardless of age or the level of competition.

Overtraining

Overtraining can have a negative effect on the development of muscular strength. The statement "If you abuse it you will lose it" is very applicable. Overtraining can result in psychological breakdown (staleness) or physiological breakdown, which may involve musculoskeletal injury, fatigue, or sickness. Engaging in proper and efficient resistance training, eating a proper diet, and getting appropriate rest can all minimize the potential negative effects of overtraining.

Gains in muscular strength resulting from resistance training are reversible. Individuals who interrupt or stop resistance training altogether will see rapid decreases in strength gains. "If you don't use it, you'll lose it."

WHAT PHYSIOLOGIC CHANGES OCCUR TO CAUSE INCREASED STRENGTH?

Weight training to improve muscular strength unquestionably results in an increased size, or hypertrophy, of a muscle. What causes a muscle to hypertrophy? Over the years, a number of theories have been proposed to explain this increase in muscle size, the majority of which have been discounted.

The primary explanation for this hypertrophy is best attributed to an increase in the size and number of small contractile protein filaments within the muscle, called *myofilaments*. Increases in both size and number of the myofilaments as a result of strength training causes the individual muscle fibers to increase in cross-sectional diameter.[20] This increase is particularly true in men, although women will also see some increase in muscle size. More research is needed to further clarify and determine the specific causes of muscle hypertrophy.

WHAT ARE THE TECHNIQUES OF RESISTANCE TRAINING?

There are a number of different techniques of resistance training for strength improvement, including *isometric exercise, progressive resistance exercise, isokinetic training, circuit training, plyometric exercise,* and *calisthenic exercise.* Regardless of which technique is used, one basic principle of training is extremely important: *For a muscle to improve in strength, it must be forced to work at a higher level than that to which it is accustomed.* In other words, the muscle must be *overloaded.* Without overload the muscle will be able to *maintain* strength as long as training is continued against a level of resistance to which the muscle is accustomed. However, *no additional* strength gains will be realized. This maintenance of existing levels of muscular strength may be more important in weight-training programs that emphasize muscular endurance rather than strength gains. Many individuals can benefit more in terms of overall health by concentrating on improving muscular endurance. However, to most effectively build muscular strength, weight training requires a consistent, increasing effort against progressively increasing resistance. Progressive resistance exercise is based primarily on the principles of overload and progression although the principle of overload also applies to isometric and plyometric exercise. All three training techniques produce improvement of muscular strength over a period of time. Table 4-1 summarizes the six different techniques for improving muscular strength.

Isometric Exercise

An **isometric exercise** involves a muscle contraction in which the length of the muscle remains constant while tension develops toward a maximum force against an immovable resistance (Figure 4-17). To develop strength, the muscle should generate a maximum force for ten seconds at a time, and this contraction should be repeated five to ten times per day.

Isometric exercises are capable of increasing muscular strength; unfortunately, strength gains in a particular muscle will occur only in the position in which resistance is applied. At other positions in the range of

> **isometric exercise**
> Contracts the muscle statically without changing its length.

TABLE 4-1 Techniques for improving muscular strength

Technique	Action	Equipment/Activity
Isometric exercise	Force develops while muscle length remains constant	Any immovable resistance
Progressive resistance exercise	Force develops while the muscle shortens or lengthens	Free weights, Universal, Nautilus, Cybex, Eagle, Body Master
Isokinetic training	Force develops while muscle is contracting at a constant velocity	Cybex, Orthotron, Kincom, Biodex
Circuit training	Uses a combination of isometric, PRE, or isokinetic exercises organized into a series of stations	May use any of the equipment listed above
Plyometric exercise	Uses a rapid eccentric stretch of the muscle to facilitate an explosive concentric contraction	Hops, bounds, and depth jumping
Calisthenics	Uses body weight for resistance	No equipment needed (Sit-ups, push-ups, etc.)

Figure 4-17

An isometric exercise
involves a maximum force
against an immovable
resistance.

motion, the strength curve drops off dramatically because of a lack of motor activity at those angles, and there is no corresponding increase in strength.

Another major disadvantage of isometric exercises is that they tend to produce a spike in blood pressure that can result in potentially life-threatening cardiovascular accidents. This sharp increase in blood pressure results from holding the breath and increasing pressure within the chest cavity. Consequently, the heart experiences a significant increase in blood pressure. This spike has been referred to as the *Valsalva effect.* To avoid or minimize this effect, breathing should be done during the maximum contraction.

Isometric exercises certainly have a place in a conditioning program. In certain instances, an isometric contraction can greatly enhance a particular movement. A common use for isometric exercises would be for injury rehabilitation or reconditioning. Many conditions or ailments resulting either from trauma or overuse must be treated with strengthening exercises. Unfortunately, these problems may get worse with full range-of-motion strengthening exercises. It may be more desirable to make use of isometric exercises until the injury has healed to the point that full-range activities can be performed.

Progressive Resistance Exercise

Progressive resistance exercise is perhaps the most commonly used and most popular technique for improving muscular strength. Progressive resistance exercise training uses exercises that strengthen muscles through a contraction that overcomes some fixed resistance produced by equipment such as dumbbells, barbells, or various weight machines. Progressive resistance exercise uses isotonic contractions in which force is generated while the muscle is changing in length.[5]

Isotonic contractions may be either *concentric* or *eccentric.* Suppose an

Organizing and Establishing
an Effective Athletic Health
Care System

athlete is going to perform a biceps curl (see Figure 4-28). To lift the weight from the starting position, the biceps muscle must contract and shorten in length (**concentric,** or **positive, contraction**). If the biceps muscle does not remain contracted when the weight is being lowered, gravity would cause this weight to simply fall back to the starting position. Thus, to control the weight as it is being lowered, the biceps muscle must continue to contract while at the same time gradually lengthening (**eccentric,** or **negative, contraction**).

Various types of exercise equipment can be used with progressive resistance exercise including free weights (barbells and dumbbells) or weight machines such as Universal, Nautilus, Eagle, Cybex, and Body Master, to name a few (Figure 4-18A). Dumbbells and barbells require the use of iron plates of varying weights that can be easily changed by adding or subtracting equal amounts of weight to both sides of the bar.

Weight machines have a stack of weights that is lifted through a series of levers or pulleys. The stack of weights slides up and down on a pair of bars that restrict the movement to only one plane (Figure 4-18B). Weight can be increased or decreased simply by changing the position of a weight key.

There are advantages and disadvantages to both the free weights and the machines. The weight machines are safer to use than free weights are. For example, athletes who are doing a bench press with free weights

A

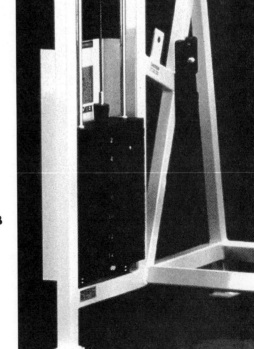

Figure 4-18

A, This Cybex equipment is isotonic. B, Resistance may be easily altered by changing the key in the stack of weights.

B

must have someone spot (help them lift the weights back onto the support racks if they don't have enough strength to complete the lift); otherwise the weights may be dropped on the chest. The weight machines allow an athlete to easily and safely drop the weight without fear of injury. It is also a simple process to increase or decrease the weight on the weight machines by moving a single weight key, although changes can generally be made only in increments of ten or fifteen pounds. With free weights, iron plates must be added or removed from each side of the barbell.

Athletes will find a difference in the amount of weight that can be lifted with free weights versus the weight machines. Unlike the weight machines, free weights have no restricted motion and can thus move in many different directions, depending on the forces applied. Also, with free weights, an element of muscular control on the part of the lifter is required to prevent the weight from moving in any direction other than vertical. This control will usually decrease the amount of weight that can be lifted. Regardless of which type of equipment is used, the same principles of **isotonic** training may be applied.

Progressive resistance exercise must incorporate both concentric and eccentric contractions.[15] It is possible to generate greater amounts of force against resistance with an eccentric contraction than with a concentric contraction. Eccentric contractions are less resistant to fatigue than are concentric contractions. The mechanical efficiency of eccentric exercise may be several times higher than that of concentric exercise. Research has clearly demonstrated that the muscle should be overloaded and fatigued both concentrically and eccentrically for the greatest strength improvement to occur.

For athletes training specifically for the development of muscular strength, the concentric, or positive, portion of the exercise should require one to two seconds, whereas the eccentric, or negative, portion of the lift should require two to four seconds. The ratio of negative to positive should be approximately one to two. Physiologically the muscle will fatigue much more rapidly concentrically than eccentrically.

One suggested disadvantage of any type of isotonic exercise is that the force required to move the resistance is constantly changing throughout the range of movement. Several years ago, Nautilus (refer to Figure 4-16) attempted to address this problem of changing force capabilities by using a cam in its pulley system (Figure 4-19). The cam has been individually designed for each piece of equipment so that the resistance is variable throughout the movement. This change in resistance at different points in the range has been labeled *accommodating resistance,* or **variable resistance.** Whether this design does what it claims to do is debatable. In real-life situations, it does not matter whether the resistance is changing.

Progressive Resistance Exercise Techniques

Perhaps the most confusing aspect of progressive resistance exercise is the terminology used to describe specific programs. Table 4-2 lists

> **isotonic exercise**
> Shortens and lengthens the muscle through a complete range of motion.

> **variable resistance**
> Resistance is varied throughout the range of motion.

Figure 4-19

The cam on Nautilus is
designed to equalize
resistance throughout the full
range of motion.

specific terms and their operational definitions, which may provide some clarification.

A considerable amount of research has been done in the area of resistance training to determine optimal techniques in terms of (1) the intensity or the amount of weight to be used, (2) the number of repetitions, (3) the number of sets, (4) the recovery period, and (5) the frequency of training.

There is no such thing as an optimal strength-training program. Achieving total agreement on a program of resistance training that includes specific recommendations relative to repetitions, sets, intensity, recovery time, and frequency among researchers and/or other experts in resistance training is impossible. However the following general recommendations will provide an effective resistance training program.

For any given exercise, the amount of weight selected should be sufficient to allow six to eight repetitions maximum (RM) in each of the three sets, with a recovery period of sixty to ninety seconds between sets. Initial selection of a starting weight may require some trial and error to achieve this 6 to 8 RM range. If at least three sets of six repetitions can-

TABLE 4-2 Progressive resistance exercise terminology

Terms	Definitions
Repetitions	Number of times a specific movement is repeated
Repetition maximum (RM)	Maximum number of repetitions at a given weight
Set	A particular number of repetitions
Intensity	The amount of weight or resistance lifted
Recovery period	The rest interval between sets
Frequency	The number of times an exercise is done in a week's period

not be completed, the weight is too heavy and should be reduced. If it is possible to do more than three sets of eight repetitions, the weight is too light and should be increased. Progression to heavier weights is determined by the ability to perform at least 8 RM in each of three sets. When progressing weight, an increase of about 10 percent of the current weight being lifted should still allow at least 6 RM in each of three sets.[3]

Muscular endurance is defined as the ability to perform repeated muscle contractions against resistance for an extended period of time. Most weight-training experts believe that muscular strength and muscular endurance are closely related. As one factor improves, the tendency is for the other factor to improve also. When weight training for strength, heavier weights with a lower number of repetitions should be used. Conversely, endurance training uses lighter weights with a greater number of repetitions.[3]

Endurance training should consist of three sets of ten to fifteen repetitions using the same criteria for weight selection progression and frequency as recommended for progressive resistance exercise. Thus, training regimens for both muscular strength and endurance are similar in terms of sets and numbers of repetitions. Athletes who possess great strength levels tend to also exhibit greater muscular endurance when asked to perform repeated contractions against resistance.[3]

A particular muscle or muscle group should be exercised consistently every other day. Thus, the frequency of weight training should be at least three times per week but no more than four times per week. Serious weight trainers commonly lift every day; however, they exercise different muscle groups on successive days. For example, Monday, Wednesday, and Friday may be used for upper body muscles, whereas Tuesday, Wednesday, and Saturday are used for lower body muscles.

Regardless of what technique is used, to improve strength in a muscle, it must be overloaded in a progressive manner. This criterion is the basis of progressive resistance exercise. The amount of weight used and the number of repetitions performed must be sufficient to make the muscle work at a higher intensity than it is used to. This factor is the single most critical factor in any strength-training program.

Figures 4-20 to 4-43 describe exercises for strength improvement of shoulder, hip, knee, and ankle joint movements. These exercises are demonstrated using free weights (barbells, dumbbells, weights, and some machine weights). Any of these exercises may be performed on various commercial weight machines such as Cybex or Body Master. Positions may differ slightly when different pieces of equipment are used. However, the joint motions that affect the various muscles are still the same.

Text continued on p. 79.

Organizing and Establishing
an Effective Athletic Health
Care System

Figure 4-20

Bench press
Joints affected: Shoulder,
elbow
Movement: Pushing away
Position: Supine, feet flat on
bench, back flat on bench
Primary muscles: Pectoralis
major, tricep

Figure 4-21

Incline press
Joints affected: Shoulder,
elbow
Movement: Pushing upward
and away
Position: Supine at an
inclined angle, feet flat on
floor, back flat against bench
Primary muscles: Pectoralis
major, triceps

Figure 4-22

Shoulder rotation
Joint affected: Shoulder
Movement: External rotation
Position: Supine, shoulder at
90-degree angle and elbow
flexed at 90-degree angle
Primary muscles:
infraspinatus, teres minor

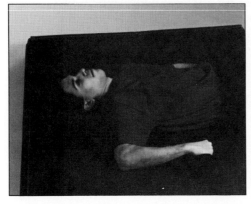

Figure 4-23

Military press
Joints affected: Shoulder, elbow
Movement: Pressing the weight overhead
Position: Standing, back straight
Primary muscles: Deltoid, trapezius, tricep

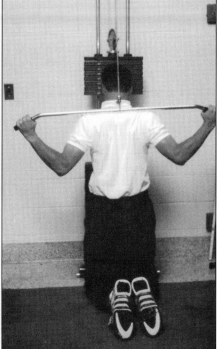

Figure 4-24

Lateral pull-downs
Joints affected: Shoulder, elbow
Movement: Pulling the bar down behind the neck
Position: Kneeling, back straight, head up
Primary muscles: Latissimus dorsi, biceps

Figure 4-25

Flys
Joint affected: Shoulder
Movement: Horizontal flexion, bringing arms together over head
Position: Lying on back, feet flat on floor, back flat on bench
Primary muscles: Deltoid, pectoralis major

Figure 4-26

Bent-over rows
Joint affected: Shoulder
Movement: Adduction of the scapula
Position: Standing bent over at waist, knee on bench
Primary muscles: Trapezius, rhomboids

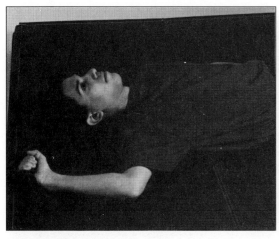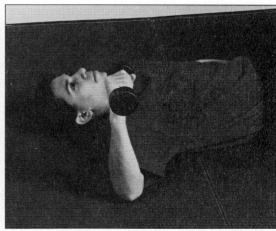

Figure 4-27

Shoulder medial rotation
Joint affected: Shoulder
Movement: Internal rotation, lifting weight off the floor
Position: Supine, shoulder abducted and elbow flexed
Primary muscles: Subscapularis

Figure 4-28

Bicep curls
Joint affected: Elbow
Movement: Elbow flexion, curling the weight up to the shoulder
Position: Standing feet front and back rather than side to side, back straight, arms extended
Primary muscles: Biceps

Figure 4-29

Tricep extensions
Joint affected: Elbow
Movement: Elbow extension,
pressing weight toward
ceiling
Position: Standing, elbows
pointing directly toward
ceiling beside ears
Primary muscles: Triceps

Figure 4-30

Wrist curls
Joint affected: Wrist
Movement: Wrist flexion,
curling weight upward
Position: Seated, forearms on
table, palms up
Primary muscles: Long
flexors of forearm

Figure 4-31

Wrist extensions
Joint affected: Wrist
Movement: Extension,
curling weight upward
Position: Seated, forearms on
table, palms down
Primary muscles: Long
extensors of forearm

Figure 4-32

Leg raises
Joint affected: Hip
Movement: Hip abduction, lifting leg up
Position: Lying on side, weight band strapped around ankle
Primary muscles: Hip abductors

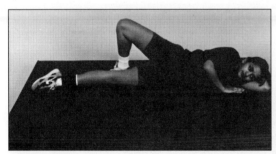

Figure 4-33

Leg lifts
Joint affected: Hip
Movement: Hip adduction, lifting bottom leg up
Position: Lying on side, one leg lifted upward, weight band around ankle
Primary muscles: Hip adductors

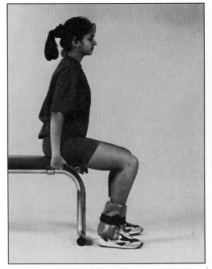 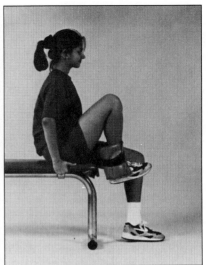

Figure 4-34

Bent-knee leg lifts
Joint affected: Hip
Movement: Hip flexion,
lifting knee up
Position: Sitting, knee flexed,
weight around ankle
Primary muscles: Iliopsoas

Figure 4-35

Reverse leg lifts
Joint affected: Hip
Movement: Hip extension,
lifting leg toward ceiling
Position: Prone, knee
extended, weight band
around ankle
Primary muscles: Gluteus
maximus, hamstrings

Figure 4-36

Hip medial rotation
Joint affected: Hip
Movement: Internal rotation, rotating lower
leg outward

Position: Sitting, knee flexed, weight on ankle
Primary muscles: Medial rotators

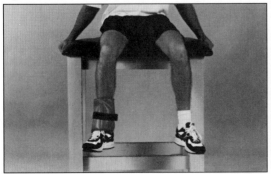 

Figure 4-37

Hip lateral rotation
Joint affected: Hip
Movement: Lateral rotation,
rotating lower leg inward
Position: Sitting, knee flexed,
weight on ankle
Primary muscles: Lateral
rotators

Figure 4-38

Quadricep extensions
Joint affected: Knee
Movement: Extension,
straightening knee
Position: Sitting, on knee
machine
Primary muscles: Quadriceps
group

Figure 4-39

Hamstring curls
Joint affected: Knee
Movement: Flexion, bending
knee and lifting weight up
Position: Prone, on knee
machine
Primary muscles: Hamstring
group

Organizing and Establishing
an Effective Athletic Health
Care System

Figure 4-40

Toe raises
Joint affected: Ankle
Movement: Plantar flexion,
pressing up on toes
Position: Standing on one leg
and lifting body weight
Primary muscles:
Gastrocnemius and soleus

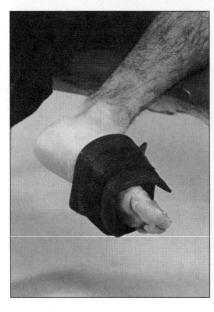

Figure 4-41

Ankle inversion
Joint affected: Ankle
Movement: Inversion, lifting
the sole of the foot up and in
Position: Sitting, knee flexed,
instep up, weight on foot
Primary muscles: Anterior
tibialis

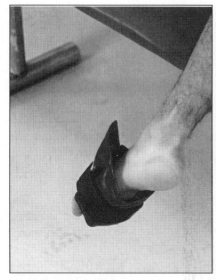

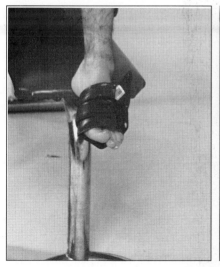

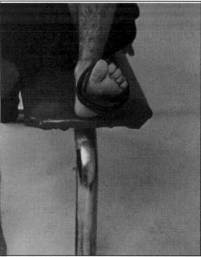

Figure 4-42

Ankle eversion
Joint affected: Ankle
Movement: Eversion, lifting
the sole of the foot up and
out
Position: Sitting, knee flexed,
instep down, weight on foot
Primary muscles: Peroneals

Figure 4-43

Ankle dorsiflexion
Joint affected: Ankle
Movement: Dorsiflexion,
lifting the toes upward
Position: Sitting, knee flexed,
heel on edge of table, weight
on foot
Primary muscles: Dorsiflexors
in shin

Isokinetic Exercise

An **isokinetic exercise** involves a muscle contraction in which the
length of the muscle is changing while the contraction is performed at a
constant velocity. In theory, maximum resistance is provided throughout
the range of motion by the machine. The resistance provided by the machine will move only at some preset speed, regardless of the force applied
to it by the individual. Thus, the key to isokinetic exercise is not the resistance but the speed at which resistance can be moved.[21]

    Several isokinetic devices are available commercially: Cybex, Biodex,
and KinCom are among the more common isokinetic devices (Figure

isokinetic exercise
Resistance is given at a
fixed velocity of movement
with accommodating
resistance.

4-44). In general, these devices rely on hydraulic, pneumatic, and mechanical pressure systems to produce this constant velocity of motion. The majority of isokinetic devices are capable of resisting both concentric and eccentric contractions at a fixed speed to exercise a muscle.

A major disadvantage of these units is their cost. Many of them come with a computer and printing device and are used primarily as diagnostic and rehabilitative tools in the treatment of various injuries.

Isokinetic devices are designed so that regardless of the amount of force applied against a resistance, the device can only be moved at a certain speed. That speed will be the same whether maximum force or only half the maximum force is applied. Consequently, when training isokinetically, it is absolutely necessary to exert as much force against the resistance as possible (maximum effort) for maximum strength gains to occur. This exertion is another major problem with an isokinetic strength-training program. Anyone who has been involved in a weight-training program knows that on some days it is difficult to find the motivation to work out. Because isokinetic training requires a maximum effort, it is very easy to cheat and not go through the workout at a high level of intensity. In a progressive resistance exercise program, the athlete knows how much weight has to be lifted with how many repetitions. Therefore isokinetic training is often more effective if a partner system is used as a means of motivation toward a maximum effort.

Assuming that a maximum effort is generated on each repetition, a general recommendation for isokinetic training is to use three sets of ten to fifteen repetitions at a selected speed of movement. If the athlete is exerting maximum effort, fatigue will usually occur at some point within each set.

Theoretically, maximum strength gains are best achieved through the isokinetic training method in which the velocity is equal throughout the range of motion if the exercise is done properly with a maximum effort. However, no conclusive research supports this theory.[2]

Figure 4-44

Cybex is one of the more widely used types of isokinetic exercise equipment.

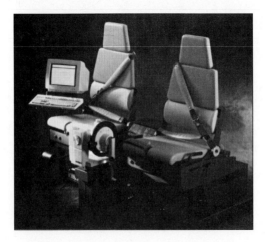

Circuit Training

Circuit training uses a series of exercise stations that consist of various combinations of weight training, flexibility, calisthenics, and brief aerobic exercises. Circuits may be designed to accomplish many different training goals. With circuit training, the athlete moves rapidly from one station to the next and performs whatever exercise is to be done at that station within a specified time period. A typical circuit would consist of eight to twelve stations, and the entire circuit would be repeated three times.

Circuit training is definitely an effective technique for improving strength and flexibility. Certainly, if the pace or the time interval between stations is rapid and if workload is maintained at a high level of intensity with heart rates at or above target training levels, the cardiorespiratory system benefits from this circuit. However, little research evidence shows that circuit training is very effective in improving cardiorespiratory endurance. It should be and is most often used as a technique for developing and improving muscular strength and endurance. Figure 4-45 provides an example of a simple circuit training setup.

> **circuit training**
> Exercise stations that consist of various combinations of weight training, flexibility, calisthenics, and aerobic exercises.

Plyometric Exercise

Plyometric exercise is a technique of exercise that involves a rapid eccentric (lengthening) stretch of a muscle, followed immediately by a rapid concentric contraction of that muscle for the purpose of producing a forceful explosive movement over a short period of time.[6] Plyometric exercises involve hops, bounds, and depth jumping for the lower extremity and the use of medicine balls and other types of weighted

> **plyometric exercise**
> Maximizes the myotatic or stretch reflex.

Figure 4-45

Sample circuit program. Station 1, squat thrusts, 75% maximum number of repetitions performed in 1 minute; Station 2, general flexion exercise, performed for 1 minute; Station 3, jump rope for 1 minute; Station 4, abdominal curls with weights, 75% maximum number of repetitions; Station 5, two-arm curls, 75% maximum number of repetitions; Station 6, vertical jump; (sargent), 75% maximum number of repetitions performed in one minute; Station 7, wrist curls with weight for 1 minute; Station 8, half squat, heels raised, exercise with weight, 75% maximum number of repetitions; Station 9, general flexion exercises.

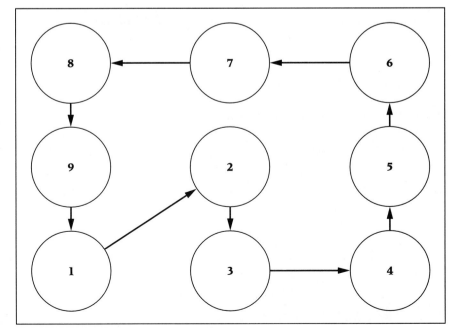

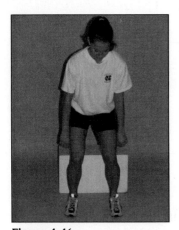

Figure 4-46

Depth jumping off a box or
platform is a form of
plyometric exercise.

Calisthenics, or free exercise,
use the force of gravity as
resistance.

equipment for the upper extremity. Depth jumping is an example of a plyometric exercise in which an individual jumps to the ground from a specified height and then quickly jumps again as soon as ground contact is made (Figure 4-46).

The greater the stretch put on the muscle from its resting length immediately before the concentric contraction, the greater the resistance the muscle can overcome. Plyometrics emphasize the speed of the stretch phase.[6] The rate of stretch is more critical than the magnitude of the stretch. An advantage to using plyometric exercise is that it can help develop eccentric control in dynamic movements. Plyometrics tend to place a great deal of stress on the musculoskeletal system. The learning and perfection of specific jumping skills and other plyometric exercises must be technically correct and specific to the athlete's age, activity, and physical and skill development.

Recommendations for plyometric exercise are variable, but the athlete should once again adhere to the three sets of six to eight repetitions rule discussed previously.

Calisthenic Strengthening Exercises

Calisthenics, or free exercise, is one of the more easily available means of developing strength. Isotonic movement exercises can be graded according to intensity by using gravity as an aid, ruling gravity out, moving against gravity, or using the body or body part as a resistance against gravity. Most calisthenics require the athlete to support the body or move the total body against the force of gravity. Push-ups are a good example of a vigorous antigravity free exercise. To be considered maximally effective, the isotonic calisthenic exercise, as in all types of exercise, must be performed in an exacting manner and in full range of motion. In most cases, ten or more repetitions are performed for each exercise and are repeated in sets of two or three.

Some free exercises use an isometric or holding phase instead of using a full range of motion. Examples of these exercises are back extensions and sit-ups. When the exercise produces maximum muscle tension, it is held between six and ten seconds and then repeated one to three times. The exercises illustrated in Figures 4-47 to 4-55 are recommended because they work on specific muscle groups and with a specific purpose. The athlete should work quickly and move from one exercise to the next without delay.

Text continued on p. 87.

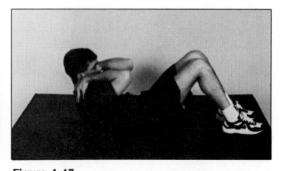

Figure 4-47

Curl-ups. A, Beginning. B, Intermediate. C, Advanced.
Joints affected: Spinal vertebral joints
Movement: Trunk flexion
Instructions: Lying on back, hands either on chest or behind back, knees flexed to 90-degree angle, feet on floor; curl trunk and head to approximately 45-degree angle.
Primary muscles: Rectus abdominis

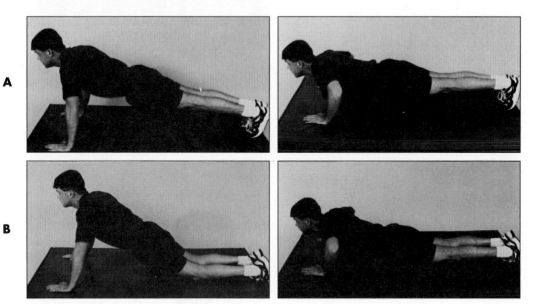

Figure 4-48

A, Push-ups. B, Modified push-ups.
Purpose: Strengthening
Muscles: Triceps and pectoralis major
Repetitions: Beginner, 10; intermediate, 20; advanced, 30
Instructions: Keep the upper trunk and legs extended in a straight line; touch floor with chest.
Caution: Avoid hyperextending the back, especially in modified push-ups.

Figure 4-49

Tricep extensions
Purpose: Strengthening and range of motion at shoulder joint
Muscles: Triceps and trapezius
Repetitions: Beginner, 7; intermediate, 12; advanced, 18
Instructions: Begin with arms extended and body straight; lower buttocks until they touch the ground, then press back up.

Figure 4-50

Trunk rotation. A, Beginner. B, Advanced.
Muscles: Internal and external obliques
Repetitions: Beginner, 10 each direction; intermediate, 15 each direction; advanced, 20 each direction
Instructions: Rotate trunk from side to side until knees touch the floor, keeping knees slightly bent.
Caution: This exercise should be done only by those who already have strong abdominals.

Figure 4-51

Sitting tucks
Purpose: Strengthen abdominals and stretch low back
Muscles: Rectus abdominis and erector muscles in low back
Repetitions: Beginner, 10; intermediate, 20; advanced, 30
Instructions: Keep legs and upper back off the ground and pull knees to chest.
Caution: This exercise should be done only by those who have strong abdominals.

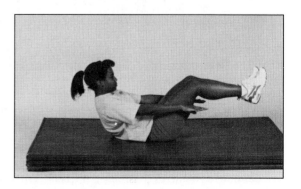

Figure 4-52

Bicycle
Purpose: Strengthen hip flexors and stretch lower back
Muscles: Iliopsoas
Repetitions: Beginner, 10 each side; intermediate, 20 each side; advanced, 30 each side
Instructions: Alternately flex and extend legs as if you were pedaling a bicycle.

A

B

C

D

Figure 4-53

Leg lifts. A, Front. B, Back. C, Side (leg up). D, Side (leg down).
Purpose: Strengthen A, hip flexors; B, hip extensors; C, hip abductors; D, hip adductors.
Muscles: A, Iliopsoas; B, gluteus maximus; C, gluteus medius; D, adductor group.
Repetitions: Beginner, 10 each leg; intermediate, 15 each leg; advanced, 20 each leg
Instructions: Raise the exercising leg up as far as possible in each position.

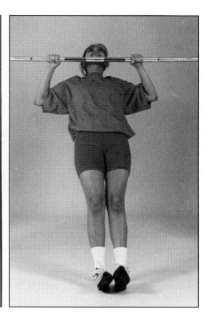

Figure 4-54

A, Chin-ups. B, Modified chin-ups.
Purpose: Strengthening and stretch of shoulder joint
Muscles: Biceps, brachiallis, and latissimus dorsi
Repetitions: Beginner, 7; intermediate, 10; advanced, 15
Instructions: Pull up until chin touches top of bar.

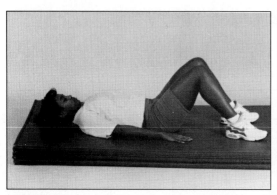

Figure 4-55

Buttock tucks
Purpose: Strengthen muscles of buttocks
Muscles: Gluteus maximus and hamstrings
Repetitions: Beginner, 10; intermediate, 15; advanced, 20
Instructions: Lying flat on back with knees bent, arch back and thrust the pelvis upward.

Strength Training Considerations for Female Athletes

Strength is just as important to women as it is to men.[27] The average female is incapable of building significant muscle bulk through weight training. Significant muscle hypertrophy is dependent on the presence of an anabolic steroidal hormone called *testosterone*. Testosterone is considered a male hormone, although all women possess some testosterone in their systems. Women with higher testosterone levels tend to have more masculine characteristics such as increased facial and body hair, a deeper voice, and the potential to develop a little more muscle bulk.

The average woman does not need to worry about developing large bulky muscles with strength building. What does happen is that muscle tone is improved. Muscle tone refers to the firmness, or tension, of the muscle during a resting state. For example, doing sit-ups increases the firmness of the abdominal muscles and makes them more resistant to fatigue.

A woman in weight training will probably see some remarkable gains in strength initially, even though her muscle bulk does not increase. How is this possible? These initial strength gains, which can be attributed to improved neuromuscular system efficiency, tend to plateau, and in the female, minimal improvement in muscular strength will be realized during a continuing strength-training program. These initial neuromuscular strength gains will also be seen in men, although their strength will continue to increase with appropriate training. Women who do possess higher testosterone levels have the potential to further increase their strength because of the development of greater muscle bulk.

Perhaps the most critical difference between men and women regarding physical performance is the ratio of strength to body weight. The reduced **strength/body weight ratio** in women is the result of their higher percentage of body fat.[20] The strength/body weight ratio may be significantly improved through weight training by decreasing the body fat percentage while increasing lean weight. Strength training programs for women should follow the same guidelines as those for men.

Perhaps the most critical
performance difference
between men and women is
the ratio of strength to
weight.

WHY IS CARDIORESPIRATORY FITNESS IMPORTANT FOR AN ATHLETE?

By definition, **cardiorespiratory endurance** is the ability to perform whole-body large muscle activities for extended periods of time. The cardiorespiratory system provides a means by which oxygen is supplied to the various tissues of the body. A healthy cardiorespiratory system is critical both for performance and for preventing undue fatigue that may predispose an athlete to injury.[13]

Aerobic exercise is great for building cardiorespiratory fitness. An aerobic activity is one in which the intensity of that activity is low enough that the cardiovascular system can supply enough oxygen to continue the activity for long periods. An activity in which the intensity is so great that the demand for oxygen is greater than the body's ability to deliver oxygen is called an *anaerobic* activity. Short bursts of muscle contraction, as

**cardiorespiratory
endurance**
Ability to perform activities
for extended periods of
time.

Cardiorespiratory endurance
refers to the body's ability to
transport and utilize oxygen
efficiently.

TABLE 4-3 Comparison of aerobic versus anaerobic activities

	Mode	Relative Intensity	Intensity	Frequency	Duration	Miscellaneous
Aerobic activities	Continuous, long-duration, sustained activities	Less intense	60%–90% of MHR	At least three but not more than six times per week	20–60 min	Less risk to sedentary or older individuals
Anaerobic activities	Explosive, short-duration, burst-type activities	More intense	90%–100% of MHR	Three to four times per week	10 sec–2 min	Used in sport and team activities

in running or swimming sprints or lifting weights, use predominantly the anaerobic system. However, endurance-type activities that last for a longer period of time depend a great deal on the aerobic system. In most activities both aerobic and anaerobic systems function simultaneously.[13] Table 4-3 provides a comparison summary between aerobic and anaerobic activities.

The capacity of the cardiorespiratory system to carry oxygen throughout the body depends on the coordinated function of four components: (1) the heart, (2) the blood vessels, (3) the blood, and (4) the lungs. Improvement of cardiorespiratory endurance through exercise occurs because of an increase in the capability of each of these four components in providing necessary oxygen to the working tissues.[8] A basic discussion of the training effects and responses to exercise that occur in the heart should make it easier to understand why the training techniques to be discussed later are effective in improving cardiorespiratory endurance.

How Does Exercise Affect the Function of the Heart?

The heart is the main pumping mechanism and circulates oxygenated blood throughout the body to the various tissues. The heart receives oxygen-poor blood from the venous system and pumps that blood through the pulmonary vessels to the lungs, where carbon dioxide is exchanged for oxygen. The oxygen-rich blood then returns to the heart, from which it exits through the aorta to the arterial system and is circulated throughout the body, supplying oxygen to the tissues (Figure 4-56).[4]

During exercise, muscles use the oxygen at a much higher rate, and thus the heart must pump more oxygenated blood to meet this increased demand. The heart is capable of adapting to this increased demand through several mechanisms:

1. *Increased heart rate.* As the intensity of the exercise increases, the heart rate will also increase, reaching a plateau at a given level after about two to three minutes. At rest the heart beats about seventy times per minute.[20]

2. *Increased stroke volume.* The volume of blood being pumped out of the heart with each beat is called the *stroke volume*. Stroke

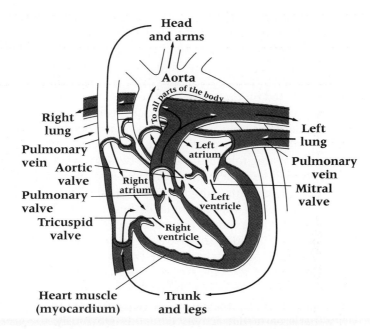

Figure 4-56

Anatomy of the heart

volume increases with exercise. At rest the heart pumps out approximately 70 ml of blood per beat. Stroke volume can continue to increase only to a point at which there is simply not enough time between beats for the heart to fill up.[8]

3. *Increased cardiac output. Cardiac output* indicates how much blood the heart is capable of pumping in exactly one minute. Approximately 5 l of blood are pumped through the heart during each minute at rest. Thus cardiac output is the primary determinant of the maximum rate at which oxygen can be used. During exercise, cardiac output increases to approximately four times that experienced during rest, about 20 l in the normal individual, and may increase as much as six times in the elite endurance athlete, to about 30 l. With endurance exercise, the heart becomes more efficient because it is capable of pumping more blood with each stroke.[20]

WHAT DETERMINES HOW EFFICIENTLY THE BODY IS USING OXYGEN?

The greatest rate at which oxygen can be taken in and used during exercise is referred to as *maximum aerobic capacity.* Maximum aerobic capacity determines how much oxygen can be used during one minute of maximal exercise. This rate is most often presented in terms of the volume of oxygen used relative to body weight per unit of time (ml/kg/min). Normal maximum oxygen utilization for most men and women aged fifteen to twenty-five years would fall in the range of 38 to 46 ml/kg/min. A world-class male marathon runner may have a maximum aerobic capacity in the 70 to 80 ml/kg/min range while a female marathoner will have a 60 to 70 ml/kg/min range.

Critical Thinking Exercise

A high school shot-putter has been working intensely on weight training to improve his muscular power. In particular he has been concentrating on lifting extremely heavy free weights using a low number of repetitions (3 sets of 6 to 8 reps). Although his strength has improved significantly over the last several months, he is not seeing the same degree of improvement in his throws even though his coach says that his technique is very good.

? The athlete is frustrated with his performance and wants to know if he can add anything to his training program that might enhance his performance.

The performance of any activity requires a certain rate of oxygen utilization that is about the same for everybody. Generally the greater the rate or intensity of the activity, the greater will be the oxygen demand. Each person has his or her own maximum rate of oxygen consumption, and the ability to perform an activity is closely related to the amount of oxygen required by that activity.

The maximum rate at which oxygen can be used is to a large extent a genetically determined characteristic. Each person's maximum aerobic capacity falls within a given range. The more active the athlete, the higher the existing maximum aerobic capacity will be within that range. The less active the athlete, the lower the maximum aerobic capacity will be in that range. Thus, athletes engaging in a serious training program can increase aerobic capacity to its highest limit within their range.

The range of maximum aerobic capacity inherited is to a large extent determined by the ratio of fast-twitch to slow-twitch muscle fibers. Athletes with a high percentage of slow-twitch muscle fibers are more resistant to fatigue and are able to use oxygen more efficiently; thus, maximum aerobic capacity will be higher.

Fatigue is closely related to the percentage of maximum aerobic capacity that a particular activity demands. Obviously, the greater the percentage of maximum aerobic capacity that is required during an activity, the less time the activity takes to perform. Fatigue occurs in part when insufficient oxygen is supplied to muscles. For example, Figure 4-57 presents two athletes, A and B. A has a maximum aerobic capacity of 50 ml/kg/min, whereas B has a maximum aerobic capacity of only 40 ml/kg/min. If both A and B are exercising at the same intensity, then A will be working at a much lower percentage of maximum aerobic capacity than B is. Consequently, A should be able to sustain his or her activity over a much longer period of time. Everyday activities such as walking up stairs or running to catch a bus may be adversely affected if a person's

Figure 4-57

Athlete A should be able to work longer than Athlete B as a result of using a lower percentage of maximum aerobic capacity.

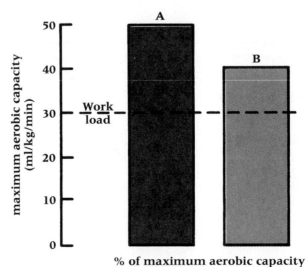

ability to use oxygen efficiently is impaired. Certainly, the ability to perform a sport activity is hindered if an athlete's level of cardiorespiratory
endurance is not what it should be. Thus improvement of cardiorespiratory endurance must be an essential component of any fitness program.

How Is Maximum Aerobic Capacity Determined?

The most accurate technique for measuring aerobic capacity must be
done in a laboratory. This technique involves exercising a subject on a
treadmill or bicycle ergometer at a specific intensity and then monitoring
heart rate and collecting samples of expired air using somewhat expensive and sophisticated equipment. Obviously for the typical person this
technique is somewhat impractical. Therefore, the technique used most
often is to monitor heart rate as a means of estimating a percentage of
maximum aerobic capacity.[13]

Monitoring heart rate is an indirect method of estimating maximum
aerobic capacity. In general, heart rate and aerobic capacity have a linear
relationship, although at very low intensities as well as at high intensities
this linear relationship breaks down (Figure 4-58). The greater the intensity of the exercise, the higher the heart rate. Because of this existing
relationship, the rate of oxygen utilization can be estimated by taking the
heart rate.

Monitoring Heart Rate

Heart rate can be determined by taking a pulse rate at specific sites. The
most accurate site for measuring the pulse rate is the radial artery located
on the thumb side of the wrist joint (Figure 4-59). An accurate heart rate
can be determined by counting the number of beats that occur in ten seconds and then multiply that number by six. Heart rate should be monitored within fifteen seconds after stopping exercise.

Critical Thinking Exercise

A female soccer player has a
grade I ankle sprain that is
likely to keep her out of
practice for about a week. She
has worked extremely hard on
her fitness levels and is very
concerned that not being able
to run for an entire week will
really hurt her cardiorespiratory
fitness.

? What activities should the
coach recommend during her
rehabilitation period that can
help her maintain her existing
level of cardiorespiratory
endurance?

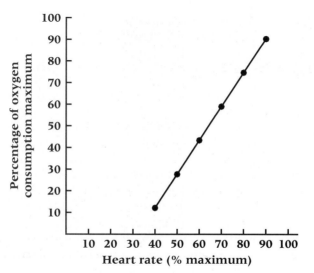

Figure 4-58

Maximum heart rate is
achieved at about the same
time as maximum aerobic
capacity.

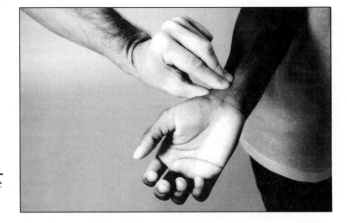

Figure 4-59

The radial artery provides the
most accurate estimation of
pulse rate.

WHAT TRAINING TECHNIQUES CAN IMPROVE CARDIORESPIRATORY ENDURANCE?

There are a number of different methods through which cardiorespiratory endurance may be improved, including (1) continuous training, (2) interval training, and (3) fartlek training. Regardless of the training technique used for the improvement of cardiorespiratory endurance, one principal goal remains the same: to increase the ability of the cardiorespiratory system to supply a sufficient amount of oxygen to working muscles. Without oxygen, the body is incapable of producing energy for an extended period of time.

Continuous Training

Continuous training is a technique that uses exercises performed at the same level of intensity for long periods of time. Continuous training has four considerations:

- The type of activity
- The frequency of the activity
- The intensity of the activity
- The duration of the activity

Type of Activity

The type of activity used in continuous training must be aerobic. Aerobic activities are any activities that use large amounts of oxygen, elevate the heart rate, and maintain it at that level for an extended time. Aerobic activities generally involve repetitive, whole body, large-muscle movements performed over an extended time. Examples of aerobic activities include walking, running, swimming, cycling, rowing, cross-country skiing, and so on. The advantage of these aerobic activities as opposed to more intermittent activities, such as racquetball, squash, basketball, or tennis, is that with aerobic activities it is easy to regulate intensity by either speeding up or slowing down the pace. Because it is already known that the given intensity of the workload elicits a given heart rate, these aerobic activities allow athletes to maintain heart rate at a specified *target level.* Intermittent activities involve variable speeds and intensities that cause the heart rate to fluctuate considerably. Although these intermittent activities will improve cardiorespiratory endurance, they are much more difficult to monitor in terms of intensity.

Frequency of Activity

To see at least minimal improvement in cardiorespiratory endurance, it is necessary for the average person to engage in no less than three exercise sessions per week. A competitive athlete should be prepared to train as often as six times per week. Everyone should take off at least one day per week to give damaged tissues a chance to repair themselves.

Intensity of Activity

The intensity of the exercise is also a critical factor even though recommendations regarding training intensities vary. This is particularly true in the early stages of training, when the body is forced to make a lot of adjustments to increased workload demands.

Determining exercise intensity by monitoring heart rate The objective of aerobic exercise is to elevate heart rate to a specified target rate and maintain it at that level during the entire workout. Because heart rate is directly related to the intensity of the exercise as well as to the rate of oxygen utilization, it becomes a relatively simple process to identify a specific workload (pace) that will make the heart rate plateau at the desired level. By monitoring heart rate, athletes know whether the pace is too fast or too slow to get the heart rate into a target range.

Heart rate can be increased or decreased by speeding up or slowing down pace. As mentioned, heart rate increases proportionately with the intensity of the workload and will plateau after two to three minutes of activity. Thus the athlete should be actively engaged in the workout for two to three minutes before measuring his or her pulse.

Several formulas can be used to identify a training *target heart rate.*[26] To calculate a specific target heart rate, maximum heart rate must first be calculated. Exact determination of maximum heart rate involves exercising an individual at a maximal level and monitoring the heart rate using an electrocardiogram. This process is difficult outside a laboratory. An approximate estimate of maximum heart rate for both males and females in the population is about 220 beats per minute. Maximum heart rate is related to age. As age increases, maximum heart rate decreases. A simple estimate of maximum heart rate (HR) would be Maximal HR = 220 − Age. For a 20-year-old individual, maximal heart rate would be about 200 beats per minute (220 − 20 = 200). Thus if training intensity is to be at 70 percent of maximal heart rate, the target heart rate can be calculated by multiplying 0.7 × (220 − Age).

Another commonly used formula that takes into account current levels of fitness is the Karvonen equation:[16]

Target HR = Resting HR* + (0.6 [Maximum HR − Resting HR]).

---

* True resting heart rate should be monitored with the subject lying down.

Organizing and Establishing
an Effective Athletic Health
Care System

---

training effect
Stroke volume increases
while heart rate is reduced
at a given exercise load.

TABLE 4-4 Rating of
perceived exertion

Scale	Verbal Rating
6	
7	Very, very light
8	
9	Very light
10	
11	Fairly light
12	
13	Somewhat hard
14	
15	Hard
16	
17	Very hard
18	
19	Very, very hard
20	

---

interval training
Alternating periods of work
with active recovery.

Resting heart rate generally falls between 60 and 80 beats per minute. A twenty-year-old athlete with a resting pulse of 70 beats per minute, according to the Karvonen equation, would have a target training heart rate of 148 beats per minute (70 + 0.6 [200 − 70] = 148).

Regardless of the formula used, the American College of Sports Medicine recommends that young healthy individuals train with a target heart rate in the 60 percent to 85 percent range when training continuously. Exercising at a 70 percent level is considered a moderate level because activity can be continued for a long period of time with little discomfort and still produce a **training effect.** A highly trained athlete will not find it difficult to sustain a heart rate at the 85 percent level.

Determining exercise intensity through rating of perceived exertion *Rating of perceived exertion* (RPE) can be used in addition to heart rate monitoring to indicate exercise intensity.[11] During exercise, individuals are asked to rate subjectively on a numerical scale from 6 to 20 exactly how they feel relative to their level of exertion (Table 4-4). More intense exercise that requires a higher level of oxygen consumption and energy expenditure is directly related to higher subjective ratings of perceived exertion. Over a period of time, individuals can be taught to exercise at a specific RPE that relates directly to more objective measures of exercise intensity.

Duration of Activity

For minimal improvement to occur, the American College of Sports Medicine recommends twenty to sixty minutes of workout/activity with the heart rate elevated to training levels. Generally, the greater the duration of the workout, the greater the improvement in cardiorespiratory endurance. The competitive athlete should train for at least forty-five minutes per session.

ADVANCED TRAINING METHODS

Interval Training

Unlike continuous training, **interval training** involves activities that are more intermittent. Interval training consists of alternating periods of relatively intense work and active recovery. It allows for performance of much more work at a more intense workload over a longer period of time than does working continuously. In continuous training, the athlete strives to work at an intensity of about 60 to 85 percent of maximal heart rate. Obviously, sustaining activity at this high intensity over a twenty-minute period would be extremely difficult. The advantage of interval training is that it allows work at this 80 percent or higher level for a short period of time followed by an active period of recovery during which the athlete may be working at only 30 to 45 percent of maximal heart rate. Thus the intensity of the workout and its duration can be greater than with continuous training.

Most sports are anaerobic, involving short bursts of intense activity followed by a sort of active recovery period (for example, football, basketball, soccer, or tennis). Training with the interval technique allows the athlete to be more sport specific during the workout. With interval training, the overload principle is applied by making the training period much more intense. There are several important considerations in interval training. The *training period* is the amount of time that continuous activity is actually being performed, and the *recovery period* is the time between training periods. A *set* is a group of combined training and recovery periods, and a *repetition* is the number of training/recovery periods per set. *Training time* or *distance* refers to the rate or distance of the training period. The training/recovery ratio indicates a time ratio for training versus recovery.

An example of interval training would be a soccer player running sprints. An interval workout would involve running ten 120-yard sprints in under twenty seconds each, with a one-minute walking recovery period between each sprint. During this training session, the soccer player's heart rate will probably increase to 85 to 90 percent of maximum level during the sprint and will probably fall to the 35 to 45 percent level during the recovery period.

Fartlek Training

Fartlek, a training technique that is a type of cross-country running, originated in Sweden. Fartlek literally means "speed play." It is similar to interval training in that the athlete must run for a specified period of time; however, specific pace and speed are not identified. The course for a fartlek workout should be a varied terrain with some level running, some uphill and downhill running, and some running through obstacles such as trees or rocks. The object is to put surges into a running workout, varying the length of the surges according to individual purposes. One big advantage of fartlek training is that because the pace and terrain are always changing, the training session is less regimented and allows for an effective alternative in the training routine. Most people who jog or walk around the community are really engaging in a fartlek-type workout.

Again, if fartlek training is going to improve cardiorespiratory endurance, it must elevate the heart rate to at least minimal training levels (60–85%). Fartlek may best be used as an off-season conditioning activity or as a change-of-pace activity to counteract the boredom of a training program that uses the same activity day after day.

SUMMARY

- Proper physical conditioning for sports participation should prepare the athlete for a high-level performance while helping to prevent injuries inherent to that sport.

- Year-round conditioning is essential in most sports to assist in preventing injuries. Postseason conditioning is used for injury rehabilitation, off-season conditioning provides a degree of physical maintenance, and preseason conditioning meets the demands of a particular sport.

- Physical conditioning must follow the SAID principle—an acronym for specific adaptation to imposed demands. It must work toward making the body as lean as possible, commensurate with the athlete's sport.

- A proper warm-up should precede conditioning, and a proper cooldown should follow. It takes at least fifteen to thirty minutes of gradual warm-up to bring the body to a state of readiness for vigorous sports training and participation. Warming up consists of general, unrelated activities followed by specific, related activities.

- Optimum flexibility is necessary for success in most sports. Too much flexibility can allow joint trauma to occur, whereas too little flexibility can result in muscle tears or strains. The safest and most effective means of increasing flexibility are static stretching and the PNF techniques.

- Strength is that capacity to exert a force or the ability to perform work against a resistance. There are numerous means to develop strength, including isometric exercise, progressive resistance exercise, isokinetic exercise, circuit training, plyometric exercise, and calisthenics.

- Cardiorespiratory endurance is the ability to perform whole-body, large-muscle activities repeatedly for long periods of time. Maximal aerobic capacity is the greatest determinant of the level of cardiorespiratory endurance. Improvement of cardiorespiratory endurance may be accomplished through continuous, interval, or fartlek training.

Solutions to Critical Thinking Exercises

4-1 The warmup should begin with a five- to seven-minute slow jog during which the athlete should break into a light sweat. At that point, she should engage in stretching (using either static or PNF techniques), concentrating on quadriceps, hamstrings, groin, and hip abductor muscles. She should repeat each specific stretch four times, holding the stretch for fifteen to twenty seconds. Once her workout begins, she should gradually and moderately increase the intensity of the activity. The coach should also stress the importance of stretching during the cooldown that follows the workout.

4-2 Weight training will not have a negative effect on flexibility as long as the lifting technique is done properly. Lifting the weight through a complete and full range of motion will improve strength and simultaneously maintain range of motion. This female swimmer is not likely to bulk up to the point at which range of motion will be effected by muscle size. The coach should also recommend that she continue to incorporate active stretching into her training regimen.

4-3 The shot put, like many other dynamic movements in sport, requires not only great strength, but also the ability to generate that strength very rapidly. To develop muscular power, the athlete must engage in dynamic, explosive training techniques that will help him develop his ability. Powerlifting techniques such as squats and power cleans should be helpful. In addition, plyometic exercises using weights for added resistance will help him learn to improve his speed of muscular contraction against some resistive force.

4-4 Alternative activities such as swimming or riding a stationary exercise bike should be incorporated into this athlete's rehabilitation program

immediately. If the pressure on the ankle when riding an exercise bike is initially too painful, she should use a bike
that incorporates upper extremity exercise. The coach should recommend
that the soccer player engage in a minimum of thirty minutes of continuous
training as well as some higher intensity interval training to maintain both
aerobic and anaerobic fitness.

REVIEW QUESTIONS AND CLASS ACTIVITIES

1. Why is year-round conditioning so important for injury prevention?
2. In terms of injury prevention, list as many advantages as you can for conditioning.
3. How does the SAID principle relate to sports conditioning and injury prevention?
4. What is the value of proper warm-ups and cooldowns to sports injury prevention?
5. Critically observe how a variety of sports use warm-up and cooldown procedures.
6. Compare ways to increase flexibility and how those ways may decrease or
   increase the athlete's susceptibility to injury.
7. How may increasing strength decrease susceptibility to injury?
8. Compare different techniques of increasing strength. How may each way be
   an advantage or a disadvantage to the athlete in terms of injury prevention?
9. Discuss the relationships between maximal oxygen consumption, heart rate,
   stroke volume, and cardiac output.
10. Differentiate between aerobic and anaerobic training methods.
11. How is continuous training different from interval training?

REFERENCES

1. Anderson B: *Stretching,* Bolinas,
   Calif, 1986, Shelter.
2. Baker D, Wilson G, Carlyon B:
   Generality vs. specificity: a comparison of dynamic and isometric
   measures of strength and speed-
   strength, *Eur J Appl Physiol* 68:350,
   1994.
3. Berger R: *Conditioning for men,*
   Boston, 1973, Allyn & Bacon.
4. Cox M: Exercise training programs
   and cardiorespiratory adaptation,
   Clin Sports Med 10(1):19, 1991.
5. De Lorme TL, Watkins AL: *Progressive resistance exercise,* New York,
   1951, Appleton-Century-Crofts.
6. Duda M: Plyometrics: a legitimate
   form of power training, *Physician
   Sportsmed,* 16:213, 1988.
7. Dudley GA, Fleck SJ: Strength and
   endurance training: are they mu-
   tually exclusive? *Sports Med*
   4(2):79, 1987 (review).
8. Durstein L, Pate R, Branch D: Cardiorespiratory responses to acute
   exercise. In American College of
   Sports Medicine: *Resource manual
   for guidelines for exercise testing and
   prescription,* Philadelphia, 1993,
   Lea & Febiger.
9. Faulkner J, Green H, White T: Response and adaptation of skeletal
   muscle to changes in physical activity. In Bouchard C, Shepard R,
   Stephens J, editors: *Physical activity,
   fitness, and health,* Champaign, Ill,
   1994, Human Kinetics.
10. Fleck SJ, Kramer WJ: Resistance
    training: Physiological responses
    and adaptations, *Physician Sports-
    med,* 16:108, 1988.
11. Glass S, Whaley M, Wegner M: A
    comparison between ratings of per-
    ceived exertion among standard
    protocols and steady state running,
    Int J Sports Med 12:77, 1991.

12. Graves JE, Pollack M, Jones A et al: Specificity of limited range of motion variable resistance training, *Med Sci Sports Exerc* 21:84, 1989.

13. Hawley J, Myburgh K, Noakes T: Maximal oxygen consumption: a contemporary perspective. In Fahey T, editor: *Encyclopedia of sports medicine and exercise physiology,* New York, 1995, Garland.

14. Hickson R, Hidaka C, Foster C: Skeletal muscle fiber type, resistance training, and strength-related performance, *Med Sci Sports Exerc* 26:593, 1994.

15. Hortobagyi T, Katch FI: Role of concentric force in limiting improvement in muscular strength, *J Appl Physiol* 68:650, 1990.

16. Karvonen MJ, Kentala E, Mustala O: The effects of training on heart rate: a longitudinal study, *Ann Med Exp Biol* 35:305, 1957.

17. Knott M, Voss P: *Proprioceptive neuromuscular facilitation,* ed 3, New York, 1985, Harper & Row.

18. Komi P: *Strength and power in sport,* London, 1992, Blackwell Scientific.

19. Logan GA, Wallis EL: Recent findings in learning and performance. Paper presented at the Southern Section Meeting, California Association for Health, Physical Education and Recreation, Pasadena, Calif, 1960.

20. McArdle W, Katch F, Katch V: *Exercise physiology, energy, nutrition, and human performance,* Philadelphia, 1994, Lea & Febiger.

21. Perrin DH: *Isokinetic exercise and assessment,* Champaign, Ill, 1993, Human Kinetics.

22. Prentice W: A comparison of static and PNF stretching for improvement of hip joint flexibility, *Ath Train* 18(1):56, 1983.

23. Prentice W: *Fitness and wellness for life,* Dubuque, 1998, WCB/MGraw-Hill.

24. Shellock F, Prentice WE: Warm-up and stretching for improved physical performance and prevention of sport related injury, *Sports Med* 2:267, 1985.

25. Strauss RH, editor: *Sports medicine,* Philadelphia, 1991, WB Saunders.

26. Swain D, Abernathy K, Smith C: Target heart rates for the development of cardiorespiratory fitness, *Med Sci Sports Exerc* 26:112, 1994.

27. Williford H, Scharff-Olson M, Blessing D: Exercise prescription for women: special considerations, *Sports Med* 15:299, 1993.

28. Wilmore JH: *Training for sport and activity,* Boston, 1985, Allyn & Bacon.

ANNOTATED BIBLIOGRAPHY

Alter J: *The Science of stretching,* Boston, 1988, Houghton Mifflin.

Explains the principles and techniques of stretching and details the anatomy and physiology of muscle and connective tissue; includes guidelines for developing a flexibility program and illustrated stretching exercises and warm-up drills.

Anderson B: *Stretching,* Bolinas, Calif, 1986, Shelter.

An extremely comprehensive best-selling text on stretching exercises for the entire body.

Baechle T, Groves B: *Weight training: steps to success,* Champaign, Ill, 1992, Leisure Press.

Explains the various concepts of exercise, identifies correct lifting techniques, corrects common weight-training errors, and lists personal goals for weight training.

Brooks G, Fahey T, White T: *Exercise physiology: human bioenergetics and its applications,* Mountain View, Calif, 1996, Mayfield.

An up-to-date advanced text in exercise physiology that contains a comprehensive listing of the most current journal articles relative to exercise physiology.

Chu, D: *Jumping into plyometrics,* Champaign, Ill, 1992, Human Kinetics.

Helps you develop a safe plyometric

training program with exercises designed to improve your quickness, speed, upper body strength, jumping ability, balance, and coordination; well illustrated.

Fahey T: *Basic weight training for men and women*, Mountain View, Calif, 1994, Mayfield.

Details specific weight-training principles and techniques for both males and females; well illustrated.

Fahey T: *Encyclopedia of sports medicine and exercise physiology*, New York, 1995, Garland.

Includes a wide range of topics relative to fitness; does a particularly good job of discussing cardiorespiratory endurance.

Prentice W: *Fitness and wellness for life*, Dubuque, 1998, WCB/McGraw-Hill.

A comprehensive fitness text that covers all aspects of a training and conditioning program.

Tobias M, Sullivan JP: *Complete stretching*, New York, 1992, Alfred Knopf.

A colorful and well-illustrated guide to maximum mental and physical energy, increased flexibility, improved body shape, and enhanced relaxation.

Wilmore J, Costill D: *Physiology of sport and exercise*, Champaign, Ill, 1994, Human Kinetics.

An excellent introductory text for undergraduate students; well illustrated with color photographs; explains difficult material in a clear and understandable manner.

Whitehead N: *Learn weight training in a weekend*, New York, 1992, Alfred A Knopf.

An extremely well-illustrated text that provides a handbook of weight-training exercises on all types of equipment for all muscle groups.

WEB SITES

Health and Fitness Worldguide Forum: http://www.worldguide.com/ Fitness/hf.html

Includes coverage of anatomy, strength, cardiovascular exercise, eating well, and sports medicine.

Stretching and Flexibility: Everything you never wanted to know: http:// www.cs.huji.ac.il/papers/rma/stretch ing_toc.html

Prepared by Brad Appleton, detailed information on stretching and stretching techniques is presented, including normal ranges of motion, flexibility, how to stretch, the physiology of stretching, and the types of stretching including PNF.

Tips on Fitness: http://www.geocities. com/HotSprings/2894

Provides information on exercise, flexibility, and nutritional guidelines in an easy-to-read and straightforward format.

Mesomorphosis Interactive: Cardiovascular exercise principles and guidelines: http://mesomorphosis.com/ tackett.cardiol.htm

Topics discussed include warm-up, stretching, cooldown, frequency of exercise, and duration of exercise; there are also links to related pages that may be informative.

Fitness World: http://www.fitness world.com

Presents information about fitness in general and includes access to Fitness Management magazine.

Kaiser Permanente Health Reference: http://www.scl.ncal.kaiperm.org/ healthinfo/index.html

Click on Cardiovascular Exercise and find several topics including how to start, target heart rate, and injuries.

Chapter 5

Nutritional Considerations

When you finish this chapter you will be able to:

- Identify the six classes of nutrients and describe their major functions.
- Explain the importance of good nutrition in enhancing performance and preventing injuries.
- Describe the advantages or disadvantages of supplementing various nutrients in the athlete's diet.
- Explain the advantages and disadvantages of a preevent meal.
- Explain the distinction between body weight and body composition.
- Explain the principle of caloric balance and how to assess it.
- Describe methods for losing and gaining weight.
- List the signs of bulimia and anorexia nervosa.

The relation of nutrition, diet, and weight control to overall health and fitness is an important aspect of any training and conditioning program for an athlete. Athletes who practice sound nutritional habits reduce the likelihood of injury by maintaining a higher standard of healthful living. Eating a well-balanced diet can positively contribute to the development of strength, flexibility and cardiorespiratory endurance. Unfortunately, misconceptions, fads, and in many cases, superstitions regarding nutrition affect dietary habits, particularly in the athletic population.

Many athletes associate successful performance with the consumption of special foods or supplements. An athlete who is performing well may be reluctant to change dietary habits regardless of whether the diet is physiologically beneficial to overall health. The psychological aspect of allowing the athlete to eat whatever he or she is most comfortable with can greatly affect performance. The problem is that these eating habits tend to become accepted as beneficial and may become traditional when in fact they may be physiologically detrimental to athletic performance. Thus, many nutrition "experts" may disseminate nutritional information based on traditional rather than experimental information. The coach must possess a strong knowledge base in nutrition so that he or she may serve as an informational resource for the athlete.

THE NUTRIENTS

People usually think of losing weight when they hear the word *diet*. Actually, diet refers to a person's usual food selections. What people choose

Six classes of nutrients:
CHO
fats
proteins
vitamins
minerals
water

to eat is their diet. Although people have different food likes and dislikes, everyone must eat to survive. Nutrition is the science of certain food substances, *nutrients,* and what they do in the body.[6] Nutrients perform three major roles:[18]

1. grow, repair, and maintain all body cells
2. regulate body processes
3. supply energy for cells

The various nutrients are categorized into six major classes: *carbohydrates, fats* (often called *lipids*), *proteins, water, vitamins,* and *minerals.* Most foods are actually mixtures of these nutrients. Some nutrients can be made by the body, but an *essential nutrient* must be supplied by the diet. Not all substances in food are considered nutrients. There is no such thing as the perfect food; that is, no single natural food contains all of the nutrients needed for health. A summary of current percentages and recommended percentages of calories from carbohydrates, fats, and proteins is shown in Figure 5-1.

Nutrient-dense foods supply adequate amounts of vitamins and minerals in relation to caloric value.

Carbohydrates (CHO)

Athletes have increased energy needs. *Carbohydrates* are the body's most efficient source of energy and should be relied on to fill that need.[5] Carbohydrates should account for at least 55 percent or more of total caloric intake and some recommendations go as high as 60 to 70 percent. Carbohydrates are classified as simple (sugars) or complex (starch and most forms of fiber). During digestion, complex carbohydrates are broken down into *glucose.* The glucose that is not needed for immediate energy is stored as glycogen in the liver and muscle cells. Glucose can be released from glycogen later if needed. The body, however, can store only a limited amount of glucose as glycogen. Any extra amount of glucose is

Carbohydrates are sugar, starches, or fiber.

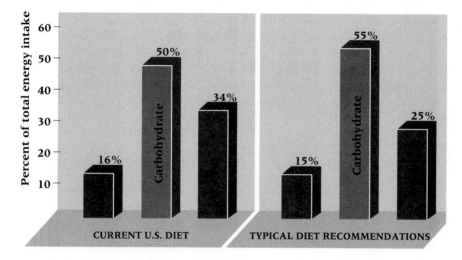

FIGURE 5-1

Comparison of calories from carbohydrates, fats, and proteins

Organizing and Establishing
an Effective Athletic Health
Care System

5-1

Critical Thinking Exercise

A female softball player has been told by her coach that she is slightly overweight and needs to lose a few pounds. The athlete has been watching television and reading about how important it is to limit the dietary intake of fat for losing weight. She has decided to go on a diet that is essentially fat free and is totally convinced that this diet will help her lose weight.

? What should the coach tell her about avoiding excessive intake of fat as a means of losing weight?

Fats may be saturated or unsaturated.

Dietary recommendations: CHO 55 percent, fats 30 percent, proteins 15 percent.

Proteins are made up of amino acids.

converted to body fat. An inadequate intake of dietary carbohydrate causes the body to use protein to make glucose. Therefore a supply of glucose must be kept available to prevent the use of protein for energy.

Fats

Fats are another essential component of the diet. They are the most concentrated source of energy, providing more than twice the calories per gram when compared to carbohydrates or proteins. Fat is used as a primary source of energy. Some dietary fat is needed to make food more flavorful and for sources of the fat-soluble vitamins. Also, a minimal amount of fat is essential for normal growth and development.[10]

In the United States, dietary fat represents a high percentage of the total caloric intake (see Figure 5-1). For many Americans, a substantial amount of the fat is from saturated fatty acids. This intake is believed to be too high and may contribute to the prevalence of obesity, certain cancers, and coronary artery disease. The recommended intake should be limited to less than 25 percent of total calories with saturated fat reduced to less than 10 percent of total calories.

Proteins

Proteins make up the major structural components of the body. They are needed for growth, maintenance, and repair of all body tissues. In addition, proteins are needed to make enzymes, many hormones, and antibodies that help fight infection. In general, the body prefers not to use much protein for energy; instead it relies on fats and carbohydrates. Protein intake should be around 12 to 15 percent of total calories.

The basic units that make up proteins are called *amino acids.* Most of the body's proteins are made up of about twenty amino acids. The majority of the amino acids can be produced as needed in the body. The others cannot be made to any significant degree and therefore must be supplied by the diet. These are referred to as the *essential* amino acids. A diet that contains large amounts of protein will not support growth, repair, and maintenance of tissues if the essential amino acids are not available in the proper proportions.[7] Most of the proteins from animal foods contain all the essential amino acids that humans require. Examples are the proteins found in meat, fish, poultry, eggs, milk, and other dairy products.

Vitamins

Although they are required in very small amounts when compared to carbohydrates, fats, proteins, and water, *vitamins* perform essential roles primarily as regulators of body processes. Over the years, researchers have identified thirteen vitamins and determined their specific roles in the body.

People mistakenly think that vitamins provide energy. In fact, the body cannot break them down to release energy. Table 5-1 provides information about vitamins, including rich food sources, deficiency symptoms, and toxicity potential from high doses.

TABLE 5-1 Vitamins

Vitamin	Major Function	Most Reliable Sources	Deficiency	Excess (Toxicity)
A	Maintains skin and other cells that line the inside of the body; bone and tooth development; growth; vision in dim light	Liver, milk, egg yolk, deep green and yellow fruits and vegetables	Night blindness, dry skin, growth failure	Headaches, nausea, loss of hair, dry skin, diarrhea
D	Normal bone growth and development	Exposure to sunlight; fortified dairy products; eggs and fish liver oils	Rickets in children—defective bone formation leading to deformed bones	Appetite loss, weight loss, failure to grow
E	Prevents destruction of polyunsaturated fats caused by exposure to oxidizing agents; protects cell membranes from destruction	Vegetable oils, some in fruits and vegetables, whole grains	Breakage of red blood cells leading to anemia	Nausea and diarrhea; interferes with vitamin K if vitamin D is also deficient. Not as toxic as other fat-soluble vitamins
K	Production of blood-clotting substances	Green leafy vegetables; normal bacteria that live in intestines produce K that is absorbed	Increased bleeding time	
B₁ (thiamin)	Needed for release of energy from carbohydrates, fats, and proteins	Cereal products, pork, peas, and dried beans	Lack of energy, nerve problems	
B₂ (riboflavin)	Energy from carbohydrates, fats, and proteins	Milk, liver, fruits and vegetables, enriched breads and cereals	Dry skin, cracked lips	
B₃ (niacin)	Energy from carbohydrates, fats, and proteins	Liver, meat, poultry, peanut butter, legumes, enriched breads and cereal	Skin problems, diarrhea, mental depression, and eventually death (rarely occurs in U.S.)	Skin flushing, intestinal upset, nervousness, intestinal ulcers
B₆	Metabolism of protein; production of hemoglobin	White meats, whole grains, liver, egg yolk, bananas	Poor growth, anemia	
B₁₂	Production of genetic material; maintains central nervous system	Foods of animal origin	Neurological problems, anemia	Severe loss of coordination from nerve damage
Folate (folic acid)	Production of genetic material	Wheat germ, liver, yeast, mushrooms, green leafy vegetables, fruits	Anemia	
C (ascorbic acid)	Formation and maintenance of connective tissue; tooth and bone formation; immune function	Fruits and vegetables	Scurvy (rare), swollen joints, bleeding gums, fatigue, bruising	Kidney stones, diarrhea
Pantothenic acid	Energy from carbohydrates, fats, and proteins	Widely found in foods	Not observed in humans under normal conditions	
Biotin	Use of fats	Widely found in foods	Rare under normal conditions	

Organizing and Establishing
an Effective Athletic Health
Care System

5-2

Critical Thinking Exercise

A volleyball player complains
that she constantly feels tired
and lethargic even though she
thinks that she is eating well
and getting a sufficient amount
of sleep. A teammate has
suggested that she begin taking
vitamin supplements, which,
the teammate claims, will give
her more energy and make her
more resistant to fatigue. The
athlete comes to the coach to
ask advice about what kind of
vitamins she needs to take.

? What facts should the coach
explain to the athlete about vitamin supplementation, and
what recommendations should
be made?

The fat-soluble vitamins are
A, D, E, and K.

The water-soluble vitamins
are C, thiamin, riboflavin,
niacin, folate, biotin, and
panothenic acid.

The antioxidants are vitamin
C, vitamin E, and beta
carotene.

Vitamins are classified into two groups: The *fat-soluble vitamins* are dissolved in fats and stored in the body; the *water-soluble vitamins* are dissolved in watery solutions and are not stored. The fat-soluble vitamins
that dissolve in fat rather than water are vitamins A, E, D, and K. Extra
amounts of the fat-soluble vitamins are not easy to eliminate from the
body in urine, which is mostly water. Instead they are stored in the liver
or body fat until needed, making them potentially toxic.

The water-soluble vitamins are vitamin C, known as *ascorbic acid,* and
the B-complex vitamins, including thiamin (B_1), riboflavin (B_2), niacin
(B_3), B_6, folate, B_{12}, biotin, and pantothenic acid. Vitamin C is used for
building bones and teeth, maintaining the tissues that hold muscles and
other tissues together (connective tissues), and strengthening the immune system. Unlike fat-soluble vitamins, the water-soluble ones cannot
be stored to any significant extent in the body and should be supplied in
the diet each day.

Antioxidant Nutrients

Certain nutrients, called antioxidants, may prevent premature aging, certain cancers, heart disease, and other health problems.[18] An antioxidant
protects vital cell components from the destructive effects of certain
agents, including oxygen. Vitamins C and E and beta carotene are antioxidants. Beta carotene is a plant pigment found in dark green, deep
yellow, or orange fruits and vegetables. The body can convert beta carotene to vitamin A. In the early 1980s, researchers reported that smokers
who ate large quantities of beta carotene–rich fruits and vegetables were
less likely to develop lung cancer than were other smokers. Since that
time, more evidence is accumulating about the benefits of a diet rich in
the antioxidant nutrients.

Some experts believe athletes should increase their intake of antioxidants, even if it means taking supplements. Others are more cautious.
Excess beta carotene pigments circulate throughout the body and may
turn the skin yellow. However, the pigment is not believed to be toxic like
its nutrient cousin, vitamin A. On the other hand, increasing intake of vitamins C and E is not without some risk. Excesses of vitamin C are not
well absorbed; the excess is irritating to the intestines and creates diarrhea. Although less toxic than vitamins A or D, too much vitamin E
causes health problems.

Minerals

More than twenty *mineral* elements need to be supplied by the diet. Some
of these minerals are listed in Table 5-2. Other mineral elements are
found in the body. The role of minerals is unclear. Minerals are needed
for a variety of jobs such as forming strong bones and teeth, generating
energy, activating enzymes, and maintaining water balance. Most minerals are stored in the body, especially in the bones and liver. Although
each of these minerals is important in its own way, two minerals, calcium
and iron, require special attention.

TABLE 5-2 Major minerals

Mineral	Major Role	Most Reliable Sources	Deficiency	Excess
Calcium	Bone and tooth formation; blood clotting; muscle contraction; nerve function	Dairy products	May lead to osteoporosis	Calcium deposits in soft tissues
Phosphorus	Skeletal development; tooth formation	Meats, dairy products, and other protein-rich foods	Rarely seen	
Sodium	Maintenance of fluid balance	Salt (sodium chloride) added to foods and sodium-containing preservatives		May contribute to the development of hypertension
Iron	Formation of hemoglobin; energy from carbohydrates, fats, and proteins	Liver and red meats, enriched breads and cereals	Iron-deficiency anemia	Can cause death in children from supplement overdose
Copper	Formation of hemoglobin	Liver, nuts, shellfish, cherries, mushrooms, whole grain breads and cereals	Anemia	Nausea and vomiting
Zinc	Normal growth and development	Seafood and meats	Skin problems, delayed development, growth problems	Interferes with copper use; may decrease HDL levels
Iodine	Production of the hormone thyroxin	Iodized salt, seafood	Mental and growth retardation; lack of energy	
Fluorine	Strengthens bones and teeth	Fluoridated water	Teeth are less resistant to decay	Damage to tooth enamel

Organizing and Establishing
an Effective Athletic Health
Care System

Water

Water is the most essential of all the nutrients and should be the nutrient of greatest concern to the athlete.[10] It is the most abundant nutrient of the body, accounting for approximately 60 percent of the body weight. Water is essential for all the chemical processes that occur in the body, and an adequate supply of water is necessary for energy production and normal digestion of other nutrients. Water is also necessary for temperature control and for elimination of waste products of nutrient and body metabolism. Too little water leads to dehydration, and severe dehydration frequently leads to death. The average adult requires a minimum of 2.5 liters of water per day.

The body has a number of mechanisms designed specifically to maintain body water at near-normal level. Too little water leads to accumulation of solutes in the blood. These solutes signal the brain that the body is thirsty while signaling the kidney to conserve water. Excessive water dilutes these solutes, which signals the brain to stop drinking and the kidneys to get rid of the excess water. A good indicator of adequate hydration is when the color of urine is reasonably clear.

Replacing fluid after heavy
sweating is far more
important than replacing
electrolytes.

Water is the only nutrient of greater importance to the athlete than to people who are more sedentary, especially during prolonged exercise carried out in a hot, humid environment. Such a situation may cause excessive sweating and subsequent loss of large amounts of water. Restriction of water during this time will result in dehydration. Dehydration's symptoms include fatigue, vomiting, nausea, exhaustion, fainting, and possibly death.

Electrolyte Requirements

Electrolytes: sodium,
chloride, potassium,
magnesium, and calcium.

Electrolytes, including sodium, chloride, potassium, magnesium, and calcium, are electrically charged ions. They maintain the balance of water outside the cell. Electrolyte replenishment may be needed when a person is not fit, suffers from extreme water loss, participates in a marathon, or has just completed an exercise period and is expected to perform at near-maximum effort within the next few hours. In most cases, electrolytes can be sufficiently replaced with a balanced diet. Free access to water (ad libitum) before, during, and after activity should be the rule. Electrolyte losses are primarily responsible for muscle cramping and intolerance to heat. Sweating results not only in a body water loss but in some electrolyte loss as well.[14]

Commercial sport drinks   In most cases, plain water is a very effective and inexpensive means of fluid replacement for most types of exercise. Commercial drinks, rather than adequately hydrating the athlete, may in fact hinder water absorption because of their high sugar content. Drinks containing too much glucose, fructose, or sucrose are hypertonic and may draw water from blood plasma into the intestinal tract, dehydrating the athlete even more. For most sports, electrolytes provided by commercial sports drinks are not needed unless the athlete is engaging in long-duration events lasting longer than one hour.[19]

A new generation of sports drinks that uses glucose **polymers** has been recently introduced. These drinks have the advantage of not causing the hypertonic problems of other commercial solutions. These drinks are most appropriate for highly intense and prolonged events that severely deplete glycogen stores.[19]

During cold weather, water is not as critical as in hot weather. Therefore, a stronger electrolyte solution that allows a slower, more steady release of fluid from the stomach should be used. As in hot weather, thirst is not an indicator of hydration.

polymers (pall ah mers) Natural or synthetic substances formed by the combination of two or more molecules of the same substance.

THE PRODUCTION OF ENERGY FROM FOODSTUFFS

Energy is produced when cells break down CHO, fats, or proteins to release energy stored from these compounds. As can be seen in Figure 5-2, carbohydrates provide the major proportion of energy for short-term, high-intensity muscular contractions. As the duration and the intensity of the activity increases, breathing also increases, supplying more oxygen for the cells and maximizing energy production. When the activity is prolonged, such as in an endurance sport, the percentage of fat and carbohydrate used for fuel is similar. Under usual conditions, proteins supply less than about 5 percent of energy. However, athletes engaged in endurance activities, receive as much as 10 to 15 percent of their energy needs from protein.[12]

WHAT IS A NUTRITIOUS DIET?

The Food Pyramid

The Basic Four Food Groups Plan, first introduced in the mid-1950s, has recently been redesigned into a food pyramid concept that is believed to do a better job of educating Americans about the relationship of food choices to health. Figure 5-3 illustrates the food groupings, the minimum number of servings that should be eaten daily, and examples of foods from this group. Carbohydrate-rich foods (the breads and cereals group) form the foundation of the diet, which reflects the recommendations in the Dietary Guidelines for Americans that suggest a need for people to consume a greater percentage of total calories from this group. The other food groups are shown according to their relative importance in a healthy diet. One major change from the Basic Four plan is that the fruits and vegetables are separated into two distinct groups, each with a specified number of servings. Note that fats and sugars form the small apex of the pyramid. This placement indicates that foods rich in fat and sugar should provide the smallest proportion of total calories; no minimum number of servings is suggested because many Americans consume far too much fat and sugar.

Nutrient Dense Foods versus Junk Foods

Foods that contain considerable amounts of vitamins, minerals, and proteins in relation to their caloric content are referred to being *nutrient dense*. Candy, chips, doughnuts, cakes, and cookies are often referred to

FIGURE 5-2

The relative portions of CHO, fat, and protein fuels used during physical activity

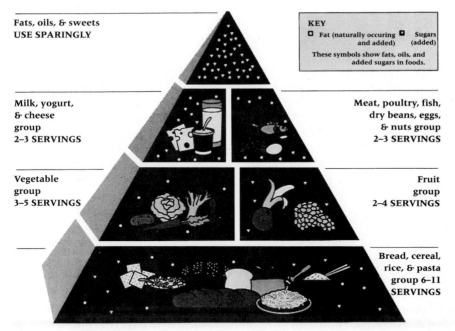

Fats, oils, & sweets
USE SPARINGLY

KEY
☐ Fat (naturally occuring ◼ Sugars
and added)   (added)
These symbols show fats, oils, and
added sugars in foods.

Milk, yogurt,
& cheese
group
2–3 SERVINGS

Meat, poultry, fish,
dry beans, eggs,
& nuts group
2–3 SERVINGS

Vegetable
group
3–5 SERVINGS

Fruit
group
2–4 SERVINGS

Bread, cereal,
rice, & pasta
group 6–11
SERVINGS

FIGURE 5-3

USDA food guide pyramid

as junk foods. These foods are not nutrient-dense because they provide
too many calories from fats and sugars in relation to vitamins and minerals. If an athlete's overall diet is nutritious, and he or she can afford the
extra calories, it's okay to eat occasional fatty or sugary foods. However,
many people who live on diets that are rich in these kinds of foods displace more nutritious food items in their diets. This behavior is not a
healthy one to practice in the long run.[8]

NUTRITION AND PHYSICAL ACTIVITY

Athletes often believe that exercise increases requirements for nutrients
such as proteins, vitamins, and minerals and that it is possible and desirable to saturate the body with these nutrients.[11] There is no scientific basis for ingesting levels of these nutrients above U.S. Recommended Dietary Allowances (RDA) levels. Exercise increases the need for energy,
not for proteins, vitamins, and minerals.[14] Thus it is necessary to explore
some of the more common myths that surround the subject of nutrition's
role in physical performance.

Vitamin requirements do not
increase during exercise.

U.S. RDA helps consumers
compare nutritional values of
foods.

Vitamin Supplementation

Many athletes believe that taking large amounts of vitamin supplements
can lead to superior health and performance. A megadose of a nutrient
supplement is essentially an overdose; the amount ingested far exceeds
the RDA levels. The rationale used for such excessive intakes is that if a
pill that contains the RDA for each vitamin and mineral makes an athlete
healthy, then taking a pill that has ten times the RDA should make that
athlete ten times healthier. There is no truth to this kind of logic. For an
athlete eating a balanced diet, vitamin supplementation is probably not

necessary. Supplementing with excessive amounts of fat-soluble vitamins can produce toxic effects.

Mineral Supplementation

Obtaining adequate levels of certain minerals can be a problem for some athletes. Calcium and iron intakes may be low for athletes whose diets do not include dairy products, red meats, or enriched breads and cereals. However, athletes must first determine whether they need extra minerals to prevent wasting their money and overdosing. The following sections explore some of the minerals that can be low in the diet as well as some suggestions for improving the quality of the diet so that supplements may not be necessary.

Calcium Deficiency

Calcium is the most abundant mineral in the body. It is essential for bones and teeth as well as for muscle contraction and conduction of nerve impulses. If calcium intake is too low to meet needs, the body can remove calcium from the bones. Over time, the bones become weakened and appear porous on x-ray films. These bones are brittle and often break spontaneously. This condition is called **osteoporosis** and is estimated to be eight times more common among women than men. Osteoporosis becomes a serious problem for women after menopause.

osteoporosis
A decrease in bone density.

Exercise causes calcium to be retained in bones, so physical activity is beneficial. However, younger females who exercise to extremes so that their normal hormonal balance is upset are prone to develop premature osteoporosis. For females who have a family history of osteoporosis, calcium supplementation, preferably as calcium carbonate or citrate rather than phosphate, may be advisable.

Milk products are the most reliable sources of calcium. Many athletes dislike milk or complain that it upsets their stomach. Those athletes may lack an enzyme called lactase that is needed to digest milk sugar, lactose. This condition is referred to as lactose intolerance, or **lactase deficiency.** The undigested lactose enters the large intestine, where the bacteria that normally reside there use it for energy. The bacteria produce large quantities of intestinal gas, which causes discomfort and cramps. Many lactose-intolerant people also suffer from diarrhea. Fortunately, scientists have produced the missing enzyme, lactase. Lactase is available without prescription in forms that can be added to foods before eating or taken along with meals.

lactase deficiency
Difficulty digesting dairy products.

Iron Deficiency

Iron deficiency is also a common problem, especially for young females. Lack of iron can result in iron-deficiency **anemia.** Iron is needed to properly form hemoglobin. In this condition, the oxygen-carrying ability of the red blood cells is reduced so that muscles cannot obtain enough oxygen to generate energy. An anemic person feels tired and weak. Obviously, athletes cannot compete at their peak level while suffering from an iron deficiency.

anemia
Lack of iron.

Sugar and Performance

Ingesting large quantities of glucose in the form of honey, candy bars, or pure sugar immediately before physical activity has a significant impact on performance. As carbohydrates are digested, large quantities of glucose enter the blood. This increase in blood sugar (glucose) levels stimulates the release of the hormone insulin. Insulin allows the cells to use the circulating glucose so that blood glucose levels soon return to normal. It was hypothesized that this decline in blood sugar levels was detrimental to performance and endurance. However, recent evidence indicates the effect of eating large quantities of carbohydrates is beneficial rather than negative.[15]

Nevertheless, some athletes are sensitive to high carbohydrate feedings and experience problems with increased levels of insulin. Also, some athletes cannot tolerate large amounts of the simple sugar fructose. For these individuals, too much fructose leads to intestinal upset and diarrhea. Athletes should test themselves with various high-carbohydrate foods to see if they are affected, but they should not try this test before a competitive event.[13]

Caffeine

Caffeine is a central nervous system stimulant. Most people who consume caffeine in coffee, tea, or carbonated beverages are aware of its effect of increasing alertness and decreasing fatigue. Chocolate contains compounds that are related to caffeine and have the same stimulating effects. However, large amounts of caffeine cause nervousness, irritability, increased heart rate, and headaches. Also, headaches are a withdrawal symptom experienced when a person tries to stop consuming caffeinated products.

Although small amounts of caffeine do not appear to harm physical performance, cases of nausea and lightheadedness have been reported. Caffeine may enhance the use of fat during endurance exercise, thus delaying the depletion of glycogen stores, which would help endurance performance. Caffeine also appears to help make calcium more available to the muscle during contraction, which would help the muscle work more efficiently. However, Olympic officials rightfully consider caffeine to be a drug. It should not be present in an Olympic competitor's blood in levels greater than that resulting from drinking five or six cups of coffee.

Alcohol

Alcohol provides energy for the body; each gram of pure alcohol (ethanol) supplies seven calories. However, sources of alcohol provide very little other nutritional value in regard to vitamins, minerals, and proteins. The depressant effects of alcohol on the central nervous system include decreased physical coordination, slowed reaction times, and decreased mental alertness. Also, this drug increases the production of urine, resulting in body water losses (diuretic effect). Therefore use of alcoholic beverages by the athlete cannot be recommended before, during, or after physical activity.

Organic, Natural, or Health Foods

Many athletes are concerned about the quality of the foods they eat—not just the nutritional value of the food but also its safety. Organic foods are foods grown without the use of synthetic fertilizers and pesticides. People who advocate the use of organic farming methods claim that these foods are nutritionally superior and safer than the same products grown using chemicals such as pesticides and synthetic fertilizers.

Technically, the description of organic food is meaningless. All foods (except water) are organic, that is, contain the element carbon. Organically produced foods are often quite expensive when compared to the same foods produced by conventional means. There is no advantage to consuming organic food products. They are not more nutritious than those foods produced by conventional methods. Nevertheless, for some, the psychological benefit of believing that they are doing something "good" for their bodies justifies the extra cost.

Natural foods have been subjected to very little processing and contain no additives such as preservatives or artificial flavors. Processing can protect nutritional value. Preservatives save food that would otherwise spoil and have to be destroyed. Furthermore, many foods in their natural form are quite poisonous. The green layer often found under the skin of potatoes is poisonous if eaten in large amounts. There are poisonous mushrooms, and molds in peanuts can cause liver cancer.

Both organic and natural foods could be described as health foods. However, there is no benefit derived from eating a diet consisting of health foods, even for the athlete.

Vegetarianism

Many athletes are health conscious and try to do things that are good for their bodies. *Vegetarianism* has emerged as an alternative to the usual American diet. All vegetarians use plant foods to form the foundation of their diet; animal foods are either totally excluded or included in a variety of eating patterns. Athletes who choose to become vegetarians do so for economic, philosophical, religious, cultural, or health reasons. Vegetarianism is no longer considered to be a fad if it is practiced intelligently. However, the vegetarian diet may create deficiencies if nutrient needs are not carefully considered. Athletes who follow this eating pattern need to plan their diet carefully so that their calorie needs are met.

Preevent Nutrition

The importance and content of the preevent meal has been heatedly debated among coaches, athletic trainers, and athletes. The trend has been to ignore logical thinking about what should be eaten before competition in favor of upholding the tradition of "rewarding" the athlete for hard work by serving foods that may hamper performance. For example, the traditional steak-and-eggs meal before football games is great for coaches and trainers; however, the athlete gains nothing from this meal. The important point is that too often people are concerned primarily with the preevent meal and fail to realize that those nutrients consumed over several days before competition are much more important than what is eaten three hours before an event. The purpose of the preevent meal should be to provide the competitor with sufficient nutrient energy and fluids for competition while taking into consideration the digestibility of the food and, most importantly, the eating preferences of the individual athlete. Figure 5-4 gives an example of a preevent meal.

The athlete should be encouraged to be conscious of his or her diet. However, no experimental evidence indicates that performance may be enhanced by altering a diet that is basically sound. A nutritious diet may be achieved in several ways, and the diet that is optimal for one athlete may not be the best for another. In many instances, the individual will be the best judge of what he or she should or should not eat in the preevent meal or before exercising. A person's best guide is to eat whatever he or she is most comfortable with.

Liquid Food Supplements

Recently, liquid meals have been recommended as extremely effective preevent meals and are being used by high school, college, university, and professional teams with some indications of success. These supplements supply from 225 to 400 calories per average serving. Athletes who have used these supplements report elimination of the usual pregame symptoms of dry mouth, abdominal cramps, leg cramps, nervous defecation, and nausea.

Under ordinary conditions it usually takes approximately four hours

FIGURE 5-4

Sample preevent meals

MEAL 1
3/4 c Orange juice
1/2 c Cereal with 1 tsp sugar
1 slice whole wheat toast with:
   1 tsp Margarine
   1 tsp Honey or jelly
8 oz Skim or lowfat milk
Water
(Approximately 450–500 kcal)

3/4 c Orange juice
1–2 Pancakes with:
   1 tsp Margarine
   2 tbsp Syrup
8 oz Skim or lowfat milk
Water
(Approximately 450–500 kcal)

MEAL 2
1 c Vegetable soup
1 Turkey sandwich with:
   2 Slices bread
   2 oz Turkey (white or dark)
   1 oz Cheese slice
   2 tsp Mayonnaise
8 oz Skim or lowfat milk
Water
(Approximately 550–600 kcal)

1 c Spaghetti with tomato sauce and cheese
1/2 c Sliced pears (canned) on 1/4 c cottage cheese
1–2 Slices (Italian) bread with 1–2 tsp margarine
(avoid garlic)
1/2 c Sherbet
1–2 Sugar cookies
4 oz Skim or lowfat milk
Water
(Approximately 700 kcal)

for a full meal to pass through the stomach and the small intestine. Pregame emotional tension often delays the emptying of the stomach; therefore the undigested food mass remains in the stomach and upper bowel for a prolonged time, even up to or through the actual period of competition, and frequently results in nausea, vomiting, and cramps. This unabsorbed food mass is of no value to the athlete. According to team physicians who have experimented with the liquid food supplements, one of their major advantages is that they do clear both the stomach and the upper bowel before game time, thus making available the caloric energy that would otherwise still be in an unassimilated state. There is merit in the use of such food supplements for pregame meals.

GLYCOGEN SUPERCOMPENSATION (LOADING)

For endurance events, maximizing the amount of glycogen that can be stored, especially in muscles, may make the difference between finishing first or at the "end of the pack." Glycogen supplies in muscle and liver can be increased by reducing the training program a few days before competing and by significantly increasing carbohydrate intake during the week before the event. Reducing training for at least forty-eight hours before the competition allows the body to eliminate any metabolic waste products that may hinder performance. The high-carbohydrate diet restores glycogen levels in muscle and the liver. This practice is called **glycogen supercompensation.** (In the past this practice has been called glycogen loading.) The basis for this practice is that the quantity of glycogen stored in muscle directly affects the endurance of that muscle.

> **glycogen supercompensation**
> High carbohydrate diet.

Glycogen supercompensation is accomplished over a six-day period divided into three phases. In phase 1 (days 1 to 2), training should be very hard and dietary intake of carbohydrates fairly normal, accounting for about 60 percent of total calorie intake. During phase 2 (days 3 to 5), training is cut back while the individual eats at least 70 percent or more of the diet in carbohydrates. Studies have indicated that glycogen stores may be increased from 50 to 100 percent, theoretically enhancing endurance during a long-term event. Phase 3 (day 6) is the day of the event, during which a normal diet must be consumed.

The effect of glycogen supercompensation in improving performance during endurance activities has not yet been clearly demonstrated. Glycogen supercompensation should not be done more than two to three times during the course of a year. Glycogen loading is only of value in long-duration events that produce glycogen depletion, such as in a marathon.

Fat Loading

Recently some endurance athletes have tried fat loading in place of carbohydrate loading. Their intent was to have a better source of energy at their disposal. The deleterious effects of this procedure outweigh any benefits that may be derived. Fat loading can lead to cardiac protein and potassium depletion, causing arrhythmias and increased levels of serum cholesterol as a result of the ingestion of butter, cheese, cream, and marbled beef.

WEIGHT CONTROL AND BODY COMPOSITION

Gain or loss of weight in an athlete often poses a problem because the individual's ingrained eating habits are difficult to change. The coach's inability to adequately supervise the athlete's meal program in terms of balance and quantity further complicates the problem. An intelligent and conscientious approach to weight control requires some knowledge of what is involved on the part of both the coach and the athlete. Such understanding allows athletes to better discipline themselves as to the quantity and kinds of foods they should eat.

Body Composition

Body composition refers to both the fat and nonfat components of the body. That portion of total body weight that is composed of fat tissue is referred to as the percent body fat. That portion of the total body weight that is composed of nonfat or lean tissue, which includes muscles, tendons, bones, connective tissue, and so on, is referred to as lean body weight. Body composition measurements are the most accurate way to determine precisely how much weight an athlete may gain or lose.[4]

> **body composition**
> Percent body fat plus lean body weight.

The average college-age female has between 20 and 25 percent of her total body weight made up of fat. The average college-age male has between 12 and 15 percent body fat. Male endurance athletes may get their fat percentage as low as 8 to 12 percent, and female endurance athletes may reach 10 to 18 percent. The recommendation is that body fat percentage not go below 3 percent in males and 12 percent in females, because below these percentages the internal organs tend to lose their protective padding of essential fat, potentially subjecting them to injury.[3]

Assessing Body Composition

Measuring the thickness of skin folds is based on the fact that about 50 percent of the fat in the body is contained in the subcutaneous fat layers and is closely related to total fat. The remainder of the fat in the body is found around organs and vessels and serves a shock-absorptive function. The skin-fold technique involves measurement of the thickness of the subcutaneous fat layer with a skin-fold caliper.

Assessing Caloric Balance

Changes in body weight are almost entirely the result of changes in caloric balance.

Caloric balance = Number of Calories Consumed – Number of Calories Expended

Calories may be expended by three different processes: (1) basal metabolism; (2) work (work may be defined as any activity that requires

Positive caloric balance = weight gain
Negative caloric balance = weight loss

more energy than sleeping); and (3) excretion. If more calories are consumed than expended, the positive caloric balance results in weight gain. Conversely, weight loss results from a negative caloric balance in which more calories are expended than are consumed.

Caloric balance is determined by the number of calories consumed regardless of whether the calories are contained in fat, carbohydrate, or protein. There are differences in the caloric content of these three foodstuffs:

Carbohydrate = 4 calories per gram

Protein = 4 calories per gram

Fat = 9 calories per gram

Alcohol = 7 calories per gram

(Alcohol should not be considered as a foodstuff, but cannot be classified under the other headings, but does contain seven calories per gram.)

Estimations of caloric intake for college athletes range between 2,000 and 5,000 calories per day. Estimations of caloric expenditure range between 2,200 and 4,400 calories on the average. Energy demands will be considerably higher in endurance-type athletes, who may require as many as 7,000 calories.[12]

Methods of Weight Loss

There are several ways to lose weight: (1) dieting, (2) increasing the amount of physical exercise, or (3) a combination of diet and exercise.

Weight loss through dieting alone is difficult, and in most cases, dieting is an ineffective means of weight control. Long-term weight control through dieting alone is successful only 20 percent of the time.[3] Through dieting, 35 to 45 percent of the weight decrease results from a loss of lean tissue. The minimum caloric intake for a female should not go below 1,000 to 1,200 calories per day, and for a male, not below 1,200 to 1,400 calories per day.[3]

Weight loss through exercise involves an 80 to 90 percent loss of fat tissue with almost no loss of lean tissue. Weight loss through exercise alone is almost as difficult as losing weight through dieting. However, exercise will not only result in weight reduction but may also enhance cardiorespiratory endurance, improve strength, and increase flexibility.[11] For this reason, exercise has some distinct advantages over dieting in any weight-loss program.

The most efficient method of decreasing body fat is through some combination of diet and exercise. A moderate caloric restriction combined with a moderate increase in caloric expenditure will result in a negative caloric balance. This method is relatively fast and easy compared with either of the other methods because habits are being moderately changed.

In any weight loss program, the goal should be to lose 1.5 to 2 pounds per week. Weight loss of more than 4 to 5 pounds during a week's time may be attributed to dehydration as opposed to a loss of body fat. The American College of Sports Medicine has established specific guidelines for losing weight.[1] See the accompanying Focus Box.

Methods of Weight Gain

The aim of a weight-gaining program should be to increase lean body mass, that is, increase muscle as opposed to body fat. Muscle mass should be increased only by muscle work combined with an appropriate increase in dietary intake. It cannot be increased by the intake of any special food or vitamin.

The recommended rate of weight gain is approximately one to two pounds per week. Each pound of lean body mass gained represents a positive caloric balance, which is an intake in excess of an expenditure of approximately 2,500 calories. One pound of fat represents the equivalent of 3,500 calories; lean body tissue contains less fat, more protein, and more water and represents approximately 2,500 calories. To gain one pound of muscle, an excess of approximately 2,500 calories is needed; to lose one pound of fat, approximately 3,500 calories must be expended in activities

5-3

Critical Thinking Exercise

An ice hockey attackman is at an excellent level of fitness and has superb skating ability and stick work. He is convinced that the only thing keeping him from moving to the next level is his body weight. In recent years he has engaged more in weight-training activities to improve his endurance and, to a lesser extent, to increase strength.

? What recommendations should the coach make for him to be successful in his weight-gaining efforts?

5-1 ***Focus Box***

Guidelines for Weight Loss

The American College of Sports Medicine has made the following statements and recommendations regarding weight loss:[2]

- Prolonged fasting and diet programs that severely restrict caloric intake are scientifically undesirable and can be medically dangerous.

- Fasting and diet programs that severely restrict caloric intake result in the loss of large amounts of water, electrolytes, minerals, glycogen stores, and other fat-free tissue (including proteins within fat-free tissues), with minimal amounts of fat loss.

- Mild calorie restriction (500 to 1,000 calories less than the usual daily intake) results in a smaller loss of water, electrolytes, minerals, and other fat-free tissue and is less likely to cause malnutrition.

- Dynamic exercise of large muscles helps to maintain fat-free tissue, including muscle mass and bone density, and results in losses of body weight. Weight loss resulting from an increase in energy expenditure is primarily in the form of fat weight.

- A nutritionally sound diet resulting in mild calorie restriction coupled with an endurance exercise program, along with behavioral modification of existing eating habits, is recommended for weight reduction. The rate of sustained weight loss should not exceed one kilogram (two pounds) per week.

- To maintain proper weight control and optimal body fat levels, a lifetime commitment to proper eating habits and regular physical activity is required.

in excess of intake. Adding 500 to 1,000 calories daily to the usual diet will provide the energy needs of gaining one to two pounds per week and fuel the increased energy expenditure of the weight training program. Weight training must be part of the program. Otherwise, the excess intake of energy will be converted to fat.

EATING DISORDERS

There is an epidemic in this society, especially in sports. This problem is the inordinate concern with being overweight. Out of this obsession has emerged the eating disorders bulimia and anorexia nervosa. Both these disorders are increasingly seen in athletes.[2] The accompanying Focus Box provides tips for identifying athletes with eating disorders.

Bulimia

The bulimic person is commonly female, ranging in age from adolescence to middle age. One out of every 200 American girls ages twelve to eighteen years (1 to 2 percent of the population) will develop patterns of bulimia and/or anorexia nervosa.[17] The bulimic individual typically gorges herself with thousands of calories after a period of starvation and then purges herself through induced vomiting and further fasting or through the use of laxatives or diuretics. This secretive binge-eating-and-purging cycle may go on for years.

Typically the bulimic athlete is white and belongs to a middle- or upper-middle-class family. She is perfectionistic, obedient, overcompliant, highly motivated, very successful academically, well-liked by her peers, and a good athlete.[9] She most commonly participates in gymnastics, track, and dance. Male wrestlers and gymnasts may also develop bulimia. The formal definition of bulimia is as follows: recurrent episodes of

---

(**5-2**)   ***Focus Box***

Recognizing the Athlete with an Eating Disorder

Signs to look for are when athletes display:

- Social isolation and withdrawal from friends and family
- A lack of confidence in athletic abilities
- Ritualistic eating behavior (e.g., organizing food on plate)
- An obsession with counting calories
- An obsession with constantly exercising, especially just before a meal
- An obsession with weighing self
- A constant overestimation of body size
- Patterns of leaving the table directly after eating to go into the restroom
- Problems related to eating disorders (e.g., malnutrition, menstrual irregularities, or chronic fatigue)
- Family history of eating disorders

rapid, uncontrollable ingestion of large amounts of food in a short period of time, usually followed by purging, either by forced vomiting and/or abuse of laxatives or diuretics.

Binge-purge patterns of eating can cause stomach rupture, disrupt heart rhythm, and cause liver damage. Stomach acids brought up by vomiting cause tooth decay and chronically inflame the mucous lining of the mouth and throat.[17]

Anorexia Nervosa

Thirty to 50 percent of all individuals diagnosed as having anorexia nervosa also develop some symptoms of bulimia. Anorexia nervosa is characterized by a distorted body image and a major concern about weight gain. As with bulimia, anorexia nervosa affects mostly females. It usually begins in adolescence and can be mild without major consequences or can become life threatening. As many as 15 to 21 percent of those individuals diagnosed as anorexic will ultimately die from this disorder. Despite being extremely thin, the athlete sees herself as too fat. These individuals deny hunger and are hyperactive, engaging in abnormal amounts of exercise such as aerobics or distance running.[9] In general, the anorexic individual is highly secretive and the coach and athletic trainer must be sensitive to eating problems. Early intervention is essential. Any athlete with signs of bulimia or anorexia nervosa must be confronted in a kind, sympathetic manner by the coach. When detected, individuals with eating disorders must be referred for psychological or psychiatric treatment. Unfortunately, simply referring an anorexic person to a health education clinic for help is not usually effective. The key to treatment of anorexia seems to be getting the patient to realize that a problem exists and that he or she could benefit from outside professional help. The individual must voluntarily accept such help if treatment is to be successful.[16]

SUMMARY

- The classes of nutrients are carbohydrates, fats, proteins, vitamins, minerals, and water.
- Carbohydrates, fats, and proteins provide the energy required for muscular work and also play a role in the function and maintenance of body tissues.
- Protein supplementation is not necessary.
- Vitamins are substances found in foods that have no caloric value but are necessary to regulate body processes.
- Antioxidants are nutrients that protect the body against various destructive agents.
- Minerals are also involved in regulation of bodily functions and are used to form important body structures.
- Water is the most essential nutrient and should be the drink of choice.
- A nutritious diet consists of eating a variety of foods in the amounts

recommended on the food pyramid. An athlete whose diet meets those recommendations may not need nutrient supplements.

- Some people need extra iron and calcium.

- The preevent meal should be (1) higher in carbohydrates, (2) easily digested, (3) eaten two to four hours before an event, and (4) acceptable to the athlete.

- Glycogen supercompensation involves maximizing the stores of carbohydrate in muscle and liver before a competitive event.

- Body composition analysis indicates the percentage of total body weight composed of fat tissue versus the percentage composed of lean tissue.

- Changes in body weight are caused almost entirely by a change in caloric balance, which is a function of the number of calories taken in and the number of calories expended.

- Weight can be lost by increasing caloric expenditure through exercise, by decreasing caloric intake through reducing food intake, or most effectively, by using a combination of moderate caloric restriction and a moderate increase in physical exercise during the course of each day.

- Bulimia is an eating disorder that involves periodic binging and subsequent purging.

- Anorexia nervosa is a form of mental illness in which a person reduces food intake and increases energy expenditure to the extent that the loss of body fat threatens health and life.

Solutions to Critical Thinking Exercises

5-1 In terms of weight control, the important consideration is the total number of calories that this athlete consumes relative to the total number of calories she expends. It makes no difference whether the calories consumed are CHO, fat, or protein. Because fat contains more than twice the number of calories as either CHO or protein, this athlete can eat significantly more food and still have about the same calorie intake if the diet is high in CHO. The coach should also stress the necessity of consuming at least some fat in the diet, which is necessary for the production of certain enzymes and hormones.

5-2 If this athlete is truly consuming anything close to a well-balanced diet, vitamin supplementa-tion is generally not necessary. However if taking a one-a-day vitamin supplement makes her feel better, no harm is done. The fact that she feels tired could be related to a number of medical conditions (e.g., mononucleosis). An iron deficiency anemia may be detected through a laboratory blood test. The coach should refer the athlete to a physician for blood work.

5-3 This athlete must understand the importance of adding lean tissue muscle mass rather than increasing his percent body fat. It is true that caloric intake must be increased so that he is in a positive caloric balance of about 500 calories per day. Additional calorie intake should consist primarily of CHO. Additional supplementation with protein is not necessary. It is ab-

solutely essential that this athlete incorporate a weight-training program
using heavy weights that will overload
the muscle, forcing it to hypertrophy
over a period of time.

REVIEW QUESTIONS AND CLASS ACTIVITIES

1. What is the value of good nutrition in terms of an athlete's performance and injury prevention?
2. Ask coaches of different sports about the type of diet they recommend for their athletes and their rationale for doing so.
3. Have a nutritionist talk to the class about food myths and fallacies.
4. Have each member of the class prepare a week's food diary; then compare it with other class members' diaries.
5. What are the daily dietary requirements according to the food pyramid? Should the requirements of the typical athlete's diet differ from those on the food pyramid? If so, in what ways?
6. Have the class debate the value of vitamin and mineral supplements.
7. Describe the advantages and disadvantages of supplementing iron and calcium.
8. Is there some advantage to preevent nutrition?
9. Are there advantages and/or disadvantages in the vegetarian diet for the athlete?
10. Discuss the importance of having an athlete monitor body composition.
11. Explain the most effective technique for losing weight.
12. Contrast the signs and symptoms of bulimia and anorexia nervosa. If a coach is aware of an athlete who may have an eating disorder, what should he or she do?

REFERENCES

1. American College of Sports Medicine: Proper and improper weight loss programs, *Med Sci Sports Exerc* 15:ix, 1983.
2. Black DR, Burckes-Miller ME: Male and female college athletes: use of anorexia and bulimia nervosa weight loss methods. *Res Q Exer Sport* 59:252, 1988.
3. Brownell KD, Steen SN, and Wilmore JH: Weight regulation practices in athletes: analysis of metabolic and health effects, *Med Sci Sports Exerc* 19(6):546, 1987 (review).
4. Champaign BN: Body fat distribution: metabolic consequences and implications for weight loss, *Med Sci Sports Exerc* 22:291, 1990.
5. Coyle EF, Coyle E: CHOs that speed recovery from training, *Physician Sportsmed* 21:111, 1993.
6. First International Conference on Nutrition and Fitness: Proceedings of a conference, Ancient Olympia, Greece, May 21–26, 1988, *Am J Clin Nutr* 49(5 suppl):909, 1989.
7. Hegarty V: *Decisions in nutrition,* St Louis, 1988, Mosby.
8. James WP: The role of nutrition and fitness in chronic diseases, *Am J Clin Nutr* 49(5 suppl):933, 1989.
9. Jones J: Bulimia: determining prevalence and examining intervention, *J Am College Health,* 37(5): 23, 1989.
10. Koszuta LE: Experts speak out on fitness and nutrition, *Physician Sportsmed* 16(6):42, 1988.
11. Liang MTC, McKeigue ME, Walker C: Nutrition for athletes and physically active adults, *J Osteopath Sports Med* 2(2):15, 1988.
12. McArdle W, Katch F, and Katch V:

Exercise physiology, energy, nutrition, and human performance, Philadelphia, 1994, Lea & Febiger.

13. Schlabach, G: Carbohydrate strategies for injury prevention, *J Ath Train* 29(3):244, 1994.

14. Sherman WM, Lamb DR: Nutrition and prolonged exercise. In Lamb DR, Murray R, editors: *Perspectives in exercise science and sports medicine,* vol 1, Indianapolis, 1988, Benchmark.

15. Sherman WM, Peden MC, Wright DA: Carbohydrate feedings 1 hour before exercise improves exercise performance, *Am J Clin Nutr* 54:866, 1991.

16. Thames K: Teaching nutrition: serve up a nutritional stew to fill students' appetite for health information, *Idea Today* 6(8):15, 1988.

17. Thornton JS: Feast or famine: eating disorders in athletes, *Physician Sportsmed* 18:116, 1990.

18. Wardlaw GM, Insel PM: *Perspectives in nutrition,* St Louis, 1993, Mosby.

19. Williams M: *Nutrition for fitness and sports,* Dubuque, Iowa, 1992, William C Brown.

ANNOTATED BIBLIOGRAPHY

Barrett S, Herbert V: *The vitamin pushers: how the "health food" industry is selling America a bill of goods,* Buffalo, 1994, Prometheus Books.

Outlines how the health-food companies have created a multi-billion dollar industry, mostly by preying on the fears of uninformed consumers.

Clark N: *Sport nutrition guidebook: eating to fuel your active lifestyle,* Champaign, Ill, 1990, Leisure Press.

Contains real-life case studies of nutritional advice given to athletes and provides recommendations for pregame meals.

Crayhorn R: *Nutrition made simple: a comprehensive guide to the latest findings in optimal nutrition,* New York, 1994, M Evans.

Discusses topics that include what constitutes a healthy diet, how energy can be increased, which healthy fats are essential for weight loss and disease prevention, and the role of antioxidants.

Gutherie H: *Human nutrition,* St Louis, 1995, Mosby.

A foundation text in all aspects of human nutrition.

Thompson R, Trattner-Sherman R: *Helping athletes with eating disorders,* Champaign, Ill, 1993, Human Kinetics.

Discusses the difficult issues of dealing with and treating individuals who have eating disorders.

Williams M: *Nutrition for fitness and sport,* Dubuque, Iowa, 1992, William C Brown.

An excellent and comprehensive guide to the concepts of sound nutrition for individuals engaging in sport or fitness activities.

WEB SITES

Food and Nutrition Information Center: http://www.nalusda.gov/fnic

Part of the information centers at the National Agricultural Library, this site provides access to information on healthy eating habits, food composition, and many additional resources.

Yahoo Health and Nutrition Information:

http://www.yahoo.com/Health/Nutrition

Includes diet analysis information, nutritional facts, and links to many informative sites.

Eating Disorders: http://www.something_fishy.com/ed.htm

Eating disorder information can be found here, including information about anorexia, bulimia, and overeating as well as information about how to access support groups.

Athletes and Eating Disorders: http://www.uq.net.au/~zzedainc/n3frames.html

Part of the Eating Disorders Resources web site; recent statistics of an NCAA study are provided including a section on the coach's responsibility; also includes

information about warning signs and the female athlete triad.

The American Dietetic Association: http://www.eatright.org

This site includes access to the journal published by the American Dietetic Association and provides informative nutritional tips as well as a section entitled "gateway to nutrition".

P A R T

2

TECHNIQUES FOR PREVENTING AND MINIMIZING SPORT-RELATED INJURIES

Protective Sports Equipment

When you finish this chapter you will be able to:

- Identify the major legal ramifications related to manufacturing, buying, and issuing commercial protective equipment.
- Fit selected protective equipment properly (e.g., football helmets, shoulder pads, running shoes).
- Differentiate between good and bad features of selected protective devices.
- Compare the advantages and disadvantages of customized versus commercial foot and ankle protective devices.
- Describe the controversies surrounding the use of certain protective devices—are they in fact weapons against opposing players, or do they really work?
- Rate the protective value of various materials used to make pads and orthotic devices.

prophylactic (pro fill **lack** tic)
Refers to prevention, preservation, or protection.

M odifications and improvements in sports equipment are continually being made, especially for sports in which injury is common. In this chapter, commercial and **prophylactic** techniques are discussed.

MANUFACTURED EQUIPMENT

The proper selection and fit of sports equipment are essential in the prevention of many sports injuries. This protection is particularly important in direct contact and collision sports such as football, hockey, and lacrosse, but it can also be important in indirect contact sports such as basketball and soccer. Whenever protective sports equipment is selected and purchased, a major decision is being made about the safeguarding of athletes' health and welfare.

Currently there is serious concern about the standards for protective sports equipment, particularly material durability standards—concerns that include who should set these standards, mass production of equipment, equipment testing methods, and requirements for wearing protective equipment. Some people are concerned that a piece of equipment that protects one athlete may be used as a weapon against another athlete.[2]

Standards are also needed for protective equipment maintenance,

Old, worn-out, ill-fitting equipment should never be passed down to younger, less-experienced players; it compounds their risk of injury.

both to keep it in good repair and to determine when to throw it away. Too often, old, worn-out, and ill-fitting equipment is passed down from the varsity players to the younger and often less-experienced players, compounding their risk of injury. Coaches must learn to be less concerned with the color, look, and style of a piece of equipment and more concerned with its ability to prevent injury. Many national organizations are addressing these issues. Engineering, chemistry, biomechanics, anatomy, physiology, physics, computer science, and other related disciplines are applied to solve problems inherent in safety standardization of sports equipment and facilities. (See the accompanying Focus Box.)

6-1

Critical Thinking Exercise

A student coach must acquire a basic understanding of protective sports equipment.

? What competencies in protective sports equipment must coaches have?

6-1 ▷ **Focus Box**

Equipment Regulatory Agencies

The following is a list of addresses and telephone numbers for protective sports equipment regulatory organizations:

Athletic Equipment Manager Association (AEMA)
723 Keil Court
Bowling Green OH 43402
(419) 352-1207

National Association of Intercollegiate Athletics (NAIA)
1221 Baltimore
Kansas City MO 64105
(816) 824-5050

National Collegiate Athletic Association (NCAA)
P.O. Box 1906
Nall at 63rd Street
Mission KS 66201
(913) 384-3220

National Federation of State High School Associations (NFSHSA)
P.O. Box 20626
11724 Plaza Circle
Kansas City MO 64195
(816) 464-5400

American National Standards Institute (ANSI)
1430 Broadway
New York NY 10018
(212) 354-3300

United States Olympic Committee (USOC)
1750 Boulder Street
Colorado Springs CO 80909
(719) 632-5551

Legal Concerns

As with other aspects of sports participation, there is increasing litigation related to equipment.[3] Manufacturers and purchasers of sports equipment must foresee all possible uses and misuses of the equipment and must warn the user of any potential risks inherent in the use or misuse of that equipment.

To decrease the possibilities of sports injuries and litigation stemming from equipment, the practitioner should do the following:

1. Buy sports equipment from reputable manufacturers.
2. Buy the safest equipment that resources will permit.
3. Make sure that all equipment is assembled correctly. The person who assembles equipment must be competent to do so and must follow the manufacturer's instructions to the letter.
4. Maintain all equipment properly, according to the manufacturer's guidelines.
5. Use equipment only for the purpose for which it was designed.
6. Warn athletes who use the equipment about all possible risks that using the equipment could entail.
7. Use great caution in the construction or customizing of any piece of equipment.
8. Use no defective equipment. All equipment must routinely be inspected for defects, and all defective equipment must be rendered unusable.

6-2

Critical Thinking Exercise

C- and B-level high school football players are issued their equipment. These athletes and their parents know very little about the equipment's potential for preventing injury.

? What is the responsibility of the coach in educating the team and their parents about equipment safety limits?

Commercial stock and custom protective devices differ considerably. Stock devices are premade and packaged and are for immediate use. Customized devices are constructed according to the individual characteristics of an athlete. Stock items may cause problems with sizing. In contrast, a custom device can be specifically sized and made to fit the protection and support needs of the individual.

HEAD PROTECTION

Direct-collision sports such as football and hockey require special protective equipment, especially for the head. Football involves more body contact than does hockey, but hockey players generally move faster and therefore create greater impact forces. Besides direct head contact stemming from hitting the boards, hockey has the added injury elements of swinging sticks and fast-moving pucks. Other sports using fast-moving projectiles are baseball, with its pitched ball and swinging bat, and track and field, with the javelin, discus, and heavy shot, which can also produce serious head injuries.[1]

Football Helmets

Football helmets must withstand repeated blows that are of high mass and low velocity.

The National Operating Committee on Standards for Athletic Equipment (NOCSAE) has developed standards for football helmet certification. An approved helmet must protect against concussive forces that may injure the brain.[6,8]

Schools must provide the athlete with quality equipment, especially the football helmet. All helmets must have a NOCSAE certification. The fact that a helmet is certified does not mean that it is completely fail-safe. Athletes as well as their parents must be apprised of the dangers that are inherent in any sport, particularly football. To make this point especially clear, the NOCSAE has adopted the following recommended warning to be placed on all football helmets:

> *Warning: Do not strike an opponent with any part of this helmet or face mask. This is a violation of football rules and may cause you to suffer severe brain or neck injury: including paralysis or death. Severe brain or neck injury may also occur accidentally while playing football.* NO HELMET CAN PREVENT ALL SUCH INJURIES. USE THIS HELMET AT YOUR OWN RISK.

Each player's helmet must have a visible exterior warning label ensuring that players have been made aware of the risks involved in the game of American football. The label must be attached to each helmet by both the manufacturer and the reconditioner.[6]

It is of major importance that each player read this warning, after which it is read aloud by the equipment manager. The athlete then signs a statement agreeing that he or she understands this warning (Figure 6-1).

When fitting helmets, always wet the player's hair to simulate playing conditions; this will make the initial fitting easier. Closely follow the manufacturer's directions for a proper fit (see the accompanying Focus Box).

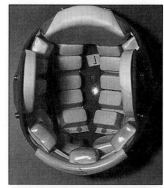

Figure 6-1

The air and fluid-filled football helmet

6-2 | ***Focus Box***

Proper Football Helmet Fit

To properly fit a football helmet:

- The helmet should fit snugly around all parts of the player's head (front, sides, and crown), and there should be no gaps between the pads and the head or face.
- It should cover the base of the skull. The pads placed at the back of the neck should be snug but not to the extent of discomfort.
- It should not come down over the eyes. It should sit (front edge) ¾ inch (1.91 cm) above the player's eyebrows.
- The ear holes should match.
- It should not shift when manual pressure is applied.
- It should not recoil on impact.
- The chin strap should be an equal distance from the center of the helmet.
- Straps must keep the helmet from moving up and down or side to side.
- The cheek pads should fit snugly against the sides of the face.
- The face mask should be attached securely to the helmet, allowing a complete field of vision.

6-3

Critical Thinking Exercise

The coach explains the helmet's limitations to a football team.

? Why does the football helmet have a warning label?

Techniques for Preventing
and Minimizing
Sport-Related Injuries

Even high-quality helmets
are of no use if not properly
fitted or maintained.

Figure 6-2

Fitting a football helmet: A,
Pull down on face mask;
helmet must not move. B,
Turn helmet to position on
the athlete's head. C, Push
down on helmet; there must
be no movement. D, Try to
rock helmet back and forth;
there must be no movement.
E, Check for a snug jaw pad
fit. F, Proper adjustment of
the chin strap is necessary to
ensure proper helmet fit.

The football helmet must be routinely checked for proper fit, especially in the first few days that it is worn (Figure 6-2). A check for snugness should be made by inserting a tongue depressor between the head and the liner. Fit is proper when the tongue depressor firmly resists being moved back and forth. If air bladder helmets are used by a team that travels to a different altitude and air pressure, the helmet fit must be routinely rechecked.

Chin straps are also important in maintaining the proper head and helmet relationship. Two basic types of chin straps are in use today—a two-snap and a four-snap strap. Many coaches prefer the four-snap chin strap because it keeps the helmet from tilting forward and backward.

Jaw pads are also essential to keep the helmet from rocking laterally. They should rest snugly against the player's cheekbones. Even if a helmet's ability to withstand the forces of the game is certified, it is of no avail if the helmet is not properly fitted or maintained.

Ice Hockey Helmets

As with football helmets, there has been a concerted effort to upgrade and standardize ice hockey helmets.[3] In contrast to football, blows to the head in ice hockey are usually singular rather than multiple. An ice hockey helmet must withstand both high-velocity impacts (e.g., being hit with a

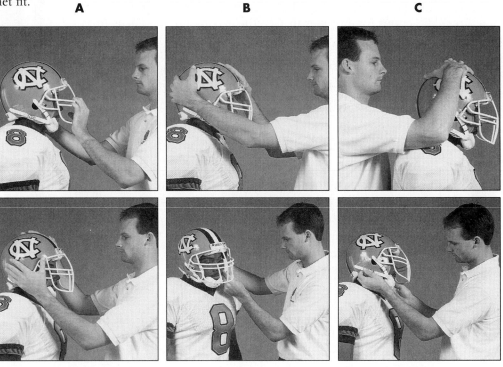

A   B   C

D   E   F

stick or a puck, which produces a force that has low mass and high velocity) and the high-mass–low-velocity forces produced by running into the sideboard or falling on the ice. In each instance, the hockey helmet, like the football helmet, must be able to spread the impact over a large surface area through a firm exterior shell and at the same time be able to decelerate forces that act on the head through a proper energy-absorbing liner. All hockey players must wear protective helmets that carry the stamp of approval from the Canadian Standards Association (CSA).

Ice hockey helmets must withstand the high-velocity impact of a stick or puck and the low-velocity forces of falling or hitting a sideboard.

Baseball/Softball Batting Helmets

Like ice hockey helmets, the baseball/softball helmet must withstand high-velocity impacts. Unlike football and ice hockey, baseball and softball have not produced a great deal of data on batting helmets.[3] It has been suggested, however, that baseball/softball helmets do not adequately dissipate the energy of the ball during impact (Figure 6-3). A possible answer is to add external padding or to improve the helmet's suspension. The use of a helmet with an ear flap can afford some additional protection to the batter. Each on-deck batter and runner is required to wear a baseball/softball head protector that carries a NOCSAE stamp similar to that on football helmets.

Figure 6-3

There is some question about how well baseball batting helmets protect against high-velocity impacts.

FACE PROTECTION

Devices that provide face protection fall into four categories: full face guards, mouth guards, ear guards, and eye protection devices.

Face Guards

Face guards are used in a variety of sports to protect the face from carried or flying objects during a collision with another player (Figure 6-4). Since the adoption of face guards and mouth guards for use in football, mouth injuries have been reduced more than 50 percent (Figure 6-5), but the

In sports, the face may be protected by:
Face guards
Mouth guards
Ear guards
Eye-protection devices

Figure 6-4

Sports such as fencing require complete face protection.

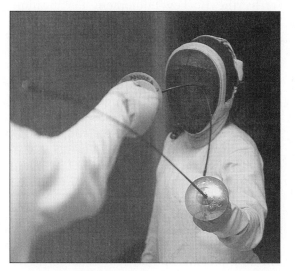

Figure 6-5

Face guards used in football

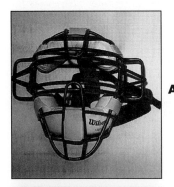

Figure 6-6

A, Baseball catcher's mask. B,
Lacrosse helmet and
faceguard

incidence of neck injuries has increased significantly. The catcher in baseball, hockey players, lacrosse players, and football players should all be adequately protected against facial injuries, particularly lacerations and fractures (Figure 6-6).

A great variety of face masks and bars is available to the player, depending on the position played and the protection needed. In football no face protection should have fewer than two bars. Proper mounting of the face mask and bars is imperative for maximum safety. All mountings should be made in such a way that the bar attachments are flush with the helmet. A 3-inch (7.62 cm) space should exist between the top of the face guard and the lower edge of the helmet. No helmet should be drilled more than one time on each side, and this drilling must be done by a factory-authorized reconditioner. Attachment of a bar or face mask not specifically designed for the helmet can invalidate the manufacturer's warranty.

Ice hockey face masks have been shown to reduce the incidence of facial injuries. In high school face masks are required for all players, not just the goalkeeper. The rule stipulates that helmets be equipped with commercial plastic-coated wire-mesh guards that must meet standards set by the Hockey Equipment Certification Council (HECC) and the American Society for Testing Materials (ASTM).[6] The openings in the guard must be small enough to prevent a hockey stick from penetrating. Plastic guards such as polycarbonate face shields have been approved by the HECC/ASTM and by the CSA Committee on Hockey Protective Equipment. The rule also requires that in addition to face protectors, goalkeepers must wear commercial throat protectors. The National Federation of High School Associations (NFSHSA) rule is similar to the National Collegiate Athletic Association (NCAA) rule requiring players to wear face guards. There should be a space of 1 to 1½ inches (3.81 cm) between the player's nose and the face guard. As with the helmet shell, pads, and chin strap, the face guard must be checked daily for defects.[7]

Laryngotracheal Protection

A laryngotracheal injury, though relatively uncommon, can be fatal. Baseball catchers, lacrosse goalies, and ice hockey goalies are most at risk. Throat protection should be mandatory in these sports.[8]

Mouth Protection

The majority of dental traumas can be prevented if the athlete wears a customized intraoral mouth guard, as compared with an extraoral type (Figure 6-7). In addition to protecting the teeth, the intraoral mouth guard absorbs the shock of chin blows and helps prevent cerebral concussion. Mouth guards serve also to prevent lacerations to the lips and cheeks and fractures to the lower jaw.[3]

The mouth protector should give the athlete proper and tight fit, comfort, unrestricted breathing, and unimpeded speech during competition. The athlete's air passages should not be obstructed in any way by the mouthpiece. It is best when the mouthpiece is retained on the upper jaw and projects backward only as far as the last molar, thus permitting speech.

Cutting down mouth guards to cover only the front four teeth should never be condoned. It invalidates the manufacturer's warranty against dental injuries, and a cut-down mouth guard can easily become dislodged and lead to an obstructed airway, which poses a serious life-threatening situation for the athlete. Maximum protection is afforded when the mouth guard is composed of a flexible, resilient material and is form fitted to the teeth and upper jaw.

Three types of mouth guards generally used in sports include the ready-made stock variety, a commercial mouth guard formed after submersion in boiling water, and the custom-fabricated type, which is formed over a model made from an impression of the athlete's maxillary arch.

Many high schools and colleges now require that mouth guards be worn at all times during competition and must be visible to the officials. To assist enforcement, official mouth guards are increasingly made in the most visible color, yellow.[3] The NCAA mandates that a time-out be charged a team if a player fails to wear the mouth guard.

It is important that coaches and athletic trainers measure the arch length of the mouth guards to ensure adequate protection for the athlete and to be in compliance with the NCAA rule. Other sport governing bodies also require the use of mouth guards to reduce dental injuries and concussions in their sports.

A properly fitted mouth guard protects the teeth, absorbs blows to the chin, and can prevent concussion.

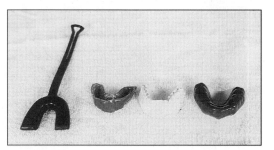

Figure 6-7

Moldable and customized mouth protectors

Ear Guards

With the exception of boxing and wrestling, most contact sports do not make a special practice of protecting the ears. Both boxing and wrestling can cause irritation of the ears to the point that permanent deformity can result. To avoid this problem special ear guards should be routinely worn. Recently a very effective ear protection has been developed for the water polo player (Figure 6-8).

Eye Protection Devices

The National Society to Prevent Blindness estimates that the highest percentage of eye injuries are sports related. Most serious eye injuries are from a blunt trauma. Eye protective devices must be sport specific.

Spectacles

For the athlete who must wear corrective lenses, spectacles can be both a blessing and a nuisance. They may slip on sweat, get bent when hit, fog from perspiration, detract from peripheral vision, and be difficult to wear with protective headgear. Even with all these disadvantages, properly fitted and designed spectacles can provide adequate protection and withstand the rigors of the sport. If the athlete has glass lenses, they must be case-hardened to prevent them from splintering on impact. When a case-hardened lens breaks, it crumbles, eliminating the sharp edges that may penetrate the eye. The cost of this process is relatively low. The only disadvantages involved are that the glasses are heavier than average and they may be scratched more easily than regular glasses.

Another possible sports advantage of glass-lensed spectacles is a process through which the lenses can become color tinted when exposed to ultraviolet rays from the sun and then return to a clear state when removed from the sun's rays. These lenses are known as *photochromic lenses.* Plastic lenses for spectacles are popular with athletes. They are much lighter in weight than glass lenses and they can be made scratch resistant with a special coating.

Figure 6-8

Ear protection: A, Wrestler's ear guard. B, Water polo player's ear protection

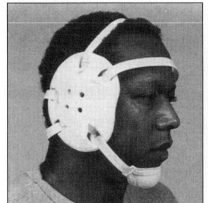
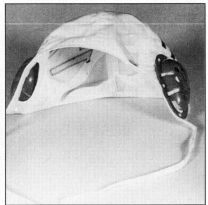

A

B

Contact Lenses

The athlete who is able to wear contact lenses without discomfort can avoid many of the inconveniences of spectacles. The greatest advantage to contact lenses is that they "become a part of the eye" and move with it.

Contact lenses come mainly in two types: the corneal type, a hard plastic lens that covers just the iris of the eye, and the scleral type, a soft plastic lens that covers the entire front of the eye, including the white. Peripheral vision, astigmatism, and corneal waviness are improved through the use of contact lenses. Unlike regular glasses, contact lenses do not normally cloud during temperature changes. They also can be tinted to reduce glare. For example, yellow lenses can be used against ice glare and blue ones against glare from snow. Currently, athletes prefer the soft, hydrophilic lenses to the hard type. The soft lenses require a shorter adjustment time than the hard lenses do, they can be more easily replaced, and they are more adaptable to the sports environment.

Eye and Glasses Guards

It is essential that athletes take special precautions to protect their eyes, especially in sports that use fast-moving projectiles and implements (Figure 6-9). Besides the more obvious sports of ice hockey, lacrosse, and baseball, the racquet sports also cause serious eye injury. Athletes not wearing spectacles should wear closed eye guards to protect the orbital cavity. Athletes who normally wear spectacles with plastic or case-hardened lenses are to some degree already protected against eye injury from an implement or projectile; however, greater safety is afforded if the athlete wears a metal-rimmed frame that surrounds and fits over the athlete's glasses. The protection that the guard offers is excellent, but it does hinder vision in some planes.

Eye protection must be worn by all athletes who play sports that use fast-moving projectiles.

Figure 6-9

Athletes playing sports that involve small, fast projectiles should wear the closed type of eye guards.

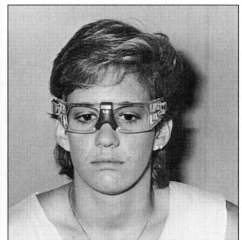

Figure 6-10

Full-body protection:
Baseball chest protector for
catchers

Polycarbonate eye shields that have recently been developed can be attached to football face masks, hockey helmets, and baseball/softball helmets.

Neck Protection

Restrictive neck straps are being used by some football teams. A semi-elastic strap 1½ inches (3.75 cm) wide is fixed to the back of the helmet and shoulder pad to restrict excessive flexion. Experts in cervical injuries consider the major value of commercial and customized cervical collars to be mostly a reminder to the athlete to be cautious rather than to provide a definitive restriction.[3]

TRUNK AND THORAX PROTECTION

Trunk and thorax protection is essential in many contact and collision sports. Areas that are most exposed to impact forces must be properly covered with some material that offers protection against soft-tissue compression. Of particular concern are the exposed bony protuberances of the body that have insufficient soft tissue for protection, such as shoulders, ribs, and spine as well as external genitalia (Figures 6-10, 6-11, 6-12, and 6-13).

As discussed earlier, the problem that arises in the wearing of protective equipment is that, although it is armor against injury to the athlete wearing it, it can also serve as a weapon against all opponents. Standards must become more stringent in determining what equipment is absolutely necessary for body protection without being itself a source of trauma.

Football Shoulder Pads

Manufacturers of shoulder pads have made great strides toward protecting the football player against direct force on the shoulder muscle complex (see Figure 6-12). There are two general types of pads, flat and cantilevered. The player who uses the shoulder a great deal in blocking and tackling requires the bulkier cantilevered type, whereas the quarterback and ball receiver would use the flat type. Over the years the shoulder pad's front and rear panels have been extended along with the cantilever. The following are rules for fitting the football shoulder pad:

- The width of the shoulder is measured to determine the proper size of pad.
- The inside shoulder pad should cover the tip of the shoulder in a direct line with the lateral aspect of the shoulder.
- The epaulets and cups should cover the deltoid muscle and allow movements required by the athlete's specific position.
- The neck opening must allow the athlete to raise the arm over the head without placing undue pressure on the neck yet must not allow the pad to slide back and forth.

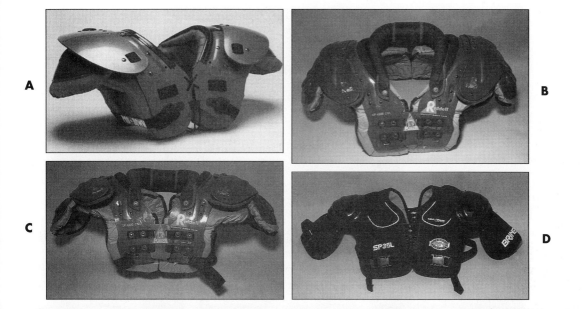

Figure 6-11

Football shoulder pads protect both the shoulder and thorax. A, B, C, Football shoulder pads. D, Lacrosse shoulder pad

- If a split-clavicle shoulder pad is used, the channel for the top of the shoulder must be in the proper position.
- Straps underneath the arm must hold the pads firmly in place, but not so they constrict soft tissue. A collar and drop-down pads may be added to provide additional protection.

Some coaches use a combination of football and ice hockey shoulder pads to prevent injuries high on the upper arm and shoulder. A pair of supplemental shoulder pads are placed under the regular football pads. The deltoid cap of the hockey pad is connected to the main body of the hockey pad by an adjustable lace (see Figure 6-13). The distal end of the deltoid cap is held in place by a Velcro strap. The chest pad is adjustable to ensure proper fit for any size athlete. The football shoulder pads are placed over the hockey pads. The coach should inspect the pads for a proper fit. Larger football pads may be needed.[1]

Breast Support

In the past the primary concern for female breast protection had focused on preventing contusions or bruising. With the continued increase in the number of physically active women, concern has been redirected to protecting the breasts against unwanted movement as the result of running and jumping. This movement is a particular problem for large-breasted women. Many girls and women in the past may have avoided vigorous physical activity, especially in public, because of the discomfort of uncontrolled movement of their breasts. Manufacturers have made a concerted effort to develop specialized bras for women who participate in all

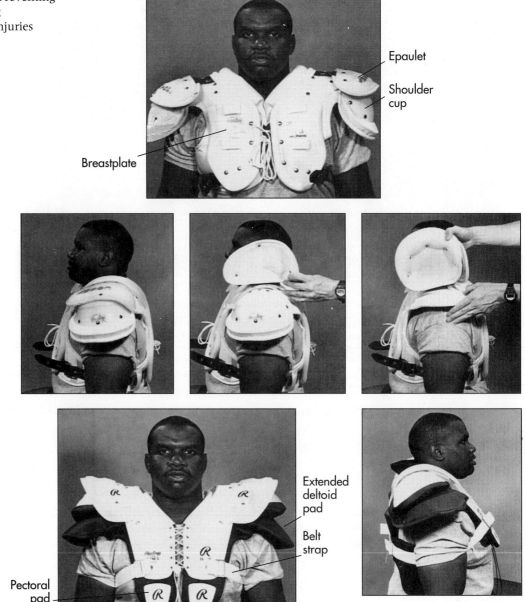

Figure 6-12

Football shoulder pads should be made to protect the player against direct force to the entire shoulder complex.

types of physical activity. The athletic clothing industry has produced an array of stylish, comfortable, and supportive sports bras. Women today have a variety of choices in their sport bras: style, support, fabric, and color. Some of the designs are stylish enough that the sports bras are sometimes worn as an outer garment.

Sport bras have the following characteristics:

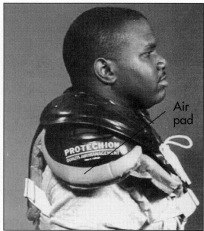

Air pad

1. Bras with good upward support with nonelastic material have wide bands under the breasts with wide shoulder straps that are attached close to the hooks in the back (Figure 6-14A).

2. Compressive bras are like wide elastic bandages binding the breasts to the chest wall (Figure 6-14B).

3. Hold the breasts to the chest and prevent stretching of the Cooper's ligament, which causes premature sagging (Figure 6-15).

4. Avoid metal parts (snaps, fastener, underwire support) that rub and abrade the skin.

5. Avoid seams over nipples which can lead to skin irritation.

For women with small breasts, no special type of bra is required except to protect the nipple area. Women with medium-sized breasts generally prefer the compressive bras, but women with a size C cup or larger should wear a firm supportive bra. Fabric, fabric weight, and firmness of construction depend on the intensity of activity, support needed,

Figure 6-13

Customized foam is placed on the underside of the shoulder pad to provide additional protection.

To be effective, a bra should hold the breasts tightly to the chest.

Figure 6-14

Female athletes should wear sports bras made of elastic material. A, Supportive bra. B, Compressive bra

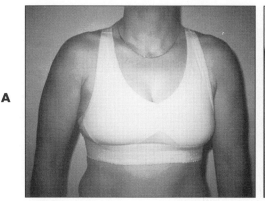

A

B

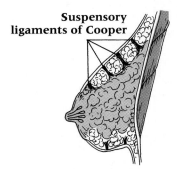

Figure 6-15

Going braless can cause a
stretching of the Cooper's
ligament, producing
premature sagging.

sensitivity to the fabric, and climate. In contact sports, additional padding may be placed inside the cup if needed. Women competing in ice hockey, for example, wear protective plastic chest pieces that attach to their shoulder pads to protect against contusions. Women should look for a bra with these features:

- No irritating seams or fasteners next to skin
- Nonslip straps
- Good support or compression that holds the breast close to the body
- Firm, durable construction

Thorax

Manufacturers such as Bike Company and Casco provide equipment for thorax protection. Many of the thorax protectors and rib belts can be modified, replacing stock pads with customized thermomoldable plastic protective devices[3] (Figure 6-16). Recently many lightweight pads have been developed to protect the athlete against external forces. A jacket for the protection of a rib injury incorporates a pad composed of air-inflated, interconnected cylinders that protect against severe external forces. This same principle has been used in the development of other protective pads.

Hips and Buttocks

Pads in the region of the hips and buttocks are often needed by athletes in collision and high-velocity sports such as hockey and football. Other athletes needing protection in this region are amateur boxers, snow skiers, equestrians, jockeys, and water skiers. Two popular commercial pads are the girdle and belt types (Figure 6-17).

Groin and Genitalia

Sports involving high-velocity projectiles (e.g., hockey, lacrosse, and baseball) require cup protection for male participants. The cup comes as a stock item that fits into place in a jockstrap, or athletic supporter (Figure 6-18).

Figure 6-16

Protective rib belt

LIMB PROTECTION

Limbs, like other areas of the body, can be exposed a great deal to sports injuries and can require protection or, where there is weakness, support. Compression and mild soft-tissue support can be provided by neoprene sleeves (Figure 6-19), and hard bony areas of the body can be protected by commercial pads. In contrast, the athlete with a history of injury that needs special protection and support may require a commercial brace.

Footwear

Footwear can mean the difference between success, failure, and injury in competition. It is essential that the coach and equipment personnel make every effort to fit their athletes with proper shoes and socks (Figure 6-20).

Socks

Poorly fitted socks can cause abnormal stresses on the foot. For example, socks that are too short crowd the toes, especially the fourth and fifth ones. Socks that are too long can cause skin irritation because of wrinkles. All athletic socks should be clean, dry, and without holes to avoid irritations. Manufacturers are now providing a double-knit tubular sock without heels that decreases friction considerably within the shoe. The heelless tubular sock is especially good for the basketball player. The sock's material also should be noted. Cotton socks can be too bulky; a combination of materials such as cotton and polyester is less bulky and dries faster.

Shoes

Even more damaging than improperly fitted socks are improperly fitted shoes. Chronic abnormal pressures to the foot often cause permanent structural deformities as well as potentially dangerous calluses and blisters. Besides these local problems, improperly fitted shoes result in mechanical disturbances that affect the body's total postural balance and may eventually lead to pathological conditions of the muscles and joints. It also should be noted that shoes that are worn and/or broken down predispose the athlete to injuries of the foot and leg. Badly worn shoes have also been known to create hip and low back problems.

Shoe composition   The bare human foot is designed to function on uneven surfaces. Shoes were created to protect against harmful surfaces, but they should never interfere with natural functioning. Sports shoes, like all shoes, are constructed of different parts, each of which is designed for function, protection, and durability. Each sport places unique stresses and performance demands on the foot. In general, all sport shoes, like street shoes, are made of similar parts—a sole, uppers, heel counter, and toe box. The sole, or bottom, of a shoe is divided into an outer, middle, and inner section, each of which must be sturdy and flexible and must provide a degree of cushioning, depending on the specific sport requirements. A heel counter should support and cushion the heel, and the toe

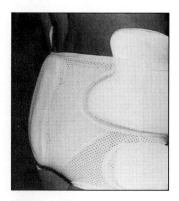

Figure 6-17

Girdle-style hip and coccygeal pad

All athletic socks should be clean and dry and without holes. Socks of the wrong size can irritate the skin.

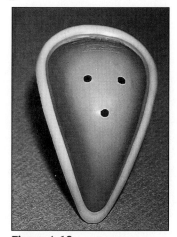

Figure 6-18

A cup, held in place by an athletic supporter, used for protecting the genitals against high-velocity projectiles

142

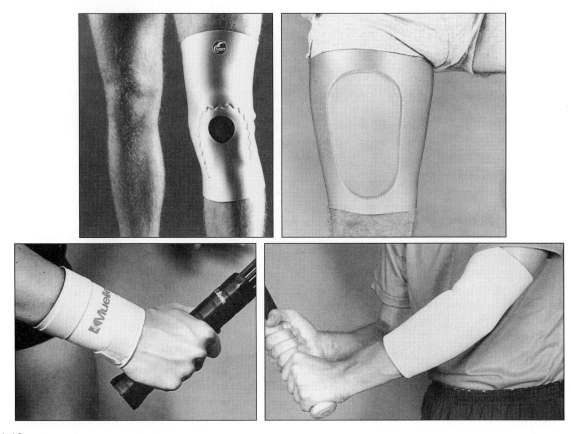

Figure 6-19

Types of neoprene sleeves

box should protect without crowding.[3] The uppers must give the foot support and freedom to withstand a high degree of stress[10] (Figure 6-20).

Sole   The sole, or bottom, of a shoe is divided into a center, middle, and inner section, each of which must be sturdy and flexible and must provide a degree of cushioning[10] Most shoes have three layers on the sole: a thick, spongy layer, which absorbs the force of the foot strike under the heel; a midsole, which cushions the midfoot and toes; and a hard rubber layer, which comes in contact with the ground. The average runner's feet strike the ground between 1,500 and 1,700 times per mile. Thus

Figure 6-20

Parts of a well-designed sports shoe

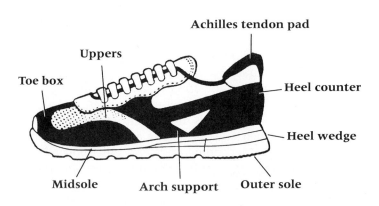

it is essential that the force of the heel strike be absorbed by the spongy layer to prevent overuse injuries from occurring in the ankles and knees. Heel wedges are sometimes inserted either on the inside or outside surface of the sole underneath the heel counter to accommodate and correct various structural deformities that alter biomechanics and the running gait.

Shoe uppers   The upper part of the shoe is made of some combination of nylon and leather. The uppers should be lightweight, capable of quick drying, and well ventilated. The uppers should have extra support in the saddle area and extra padding in the area of the heel cord just above the heel counter.

Heel counters   The heel counter is the portion of the shoe that prevents the foot from rolling from side to side at heel strike. The heel counter should be firm but well fitted to minimize movement of the heel up and down or side to side. A good heel counter may prevent ankle sprains and painful blisters.[10]

Toe Box   A good athletic shoe should allow plenty of room for the toes. Most experts recommend a ½-inch to ¾-inch, distance between the toes and the front of the shoe. Most shoe salespersons can recommend a specific shoe for the athlete's foot. The best way to ensure adequate room in the toe box is to have the foot measured and then try on the shoe.[10] (See Figure 6-20 and the accompanying Focus Box.)

Shoe fitting   Fitting sports footgear is always difficult, mainly because the individual's left foot varies in size and shape from the right foot. Therefore measuring both feet is imperative. To fit the sports shoe properly, the athlete should approximate the conditions under which he or she will perform, such as wearing athletic socks, jumping up and down, and running. It is also desirable to fit the athlete's shoes at the end of the day to accommodate the gradual increase in size that occurs from the time of awakening. The athlete must carefully consider this choice because he or she will be spending countless hours in those shoes[5] (Table 6-1).

6-3   *Focus Box*

Proper Running Shoe Design and Construction

- To avoid injury, the running shoe should:[8]
- Have a strong heel counter that fits well around the foot and locks the shoe around the foot.
- Always have good flexibility in the forefoot where toes bend.
- Have a high heel for the athlete with a tight heel cord.
- Have a midsole that is moderately soft but does not flatten easily.
- Have a heel counter that is high enough to surround the foot but still allows room for an orthotic insert, if needed.
- Have a counter that is attached to the sole to avoid the possibility of its coming loose from its attachment.
- Always be of quality construction.

A properly fitted shoe will
bend where the foot bends.

6-4

Critical Thinking E x e r c i s e

A high school basketball player
is given advice on purchasing a
pair of basketball shoes.

? What fitting factors must be
taken into consideration when
purchasing basketball shoes?

During performance conditions the new shoe should feel snug but not too tight.[3] The sports shoe should be long enough that all toes can be fully extended without being cramped. Its width should permit full movement of the toes, including flexion, extension, and some spreading. A good point to remember is that the wide part of the shoe should match the wide part of the foot to allow the shoe to crease evenly when the athlete is on the balls of the feet. The shoe should bend (or "break") at its widest part; when the break of the shoe and the ball joint coincide, the fit is correct. However, if the break of the shoe is in back or in front of the normal bend of the foot (metatarsophalangeal joint), the shoe and the foot will be opposing one another, causing abnormal skin and structural stresses to occur. Two measurements must be considered when fitting shoes: (1) the distance from the heel to the bend in the foot and (2) the distance from the heel to the end of the longest toe. An individual's feet may be equal in length from the heels to the balls of the feet but different between heels and toes. Shoes, therefore, should be selected for the longer of the two measurements. Other factors to consider when buying the sports shoe are the stiffness of the sole and the width of the shank, or narrowest part of the sole. A shoe with a too rigid, nonyielding sole places a great deal of extra strain on the foot tendons. A shoe with too narrow a shank also causes extra strain because it fails to adequately support the athlete's inner, longitudinal arches. Two other shoe features to consider are innersoles to reduce friction and built-in arch supports.

The speciality soled shoe The cleated or speciality soled sports shoe presents some additional problems in selection. For example, American football shoes use the multi-short-and-cleated polyurethane sole and often use five-in-front-and-two-in-back cleat arrangement that is common with the soccer-type sole. Both of which have cleats no longer than 1/2 inch (1.27 cm) (Figure 6-21). Special-soled shoes are also worn when playing on a synthetic surface. If cleated shoes are used, no matter what

TABLE 6-1 Shoe comparisons

	Tennis	Aerobic	Running
Flexibility	Firm sole, more rigid than running shoe	Sole between running and tennis shoe	Flexible ball of foot
Uppers	Leather or leather with nylon	Leather or leather with nylon	Nylon or nylon mesh
Heel flare	None	Very little	Flared for stability
Cushioning	Less than a running shoe	Between running and tennis shoe	Heel and sole well padded
Soles	Polyurethane	Rubber or polyurethane	Carbon-based material for greater durability
Tread	Flattened	Flat or pivot dot	Deep grooves for grip

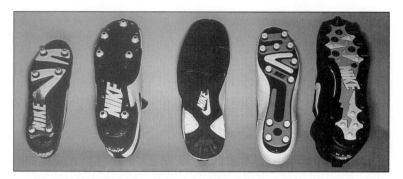

Figure 6-21

Variations in cleated shoes—
the longer the cleat, the
higher the incidence of
injury

the sport, the cleats must be properly positioned under the two major
weight-bearing joints and must not be felt through the soles of the
shoes.[10] (See Table 6-1 for shoe comparisons.)

Commercial Foot Pads

Commercial foot pads are intended for use by the general public and are
not usually designed to withstand the rigors of sports activities. Those
commercial pads that are suited for sports are generally not durable
enough for hard, extended use. If money is no object, the ready-made
commercial pad has the advantage of saving time. Commercial pads are
manufactured for almost every type of common structural foot condition,
from corns and bunions to fallen arches and pronated feet. In general,
excessive foot pronation often leads to overuse injuries. Available to the
athlete commercially are preorthotic and arch supports (Figure 6-22).

Figure 6-22

Commercially manufactured
orthotic devices

Techniques for Preventing
and Minimizing
Sport-Related Injuries

Indiscriminate use of
commercial foot orthotics
may give the athlete a false
sense of security.

Scholl 610.2, Spenco arch supports, Shea devices, and Foothotics Ready to Dispense orthotics are commonly used before more formal customized orthotic devices are made (see below). These commercial products offer a compromise to the custom-made foot orthotics, providing some biomechanical control. Indiscriminate use of these aids, however, may intensify the pathological condition and encourage the athlete to delay seeing the team physician or team podiatrist for evaluation.

For the most part, foot devices are fabricated and customized from a variety of materials such as foam, felt, plaster, aluminum, and spring steel. One item that began as a custom-fabricated device but now is commercial is the heel cup, designed to reduce tissue shearing and shock (Figure 6-23).

Commercial Ankle Supports

Currently, semirigid ankle braces such as the Air Stirrup are being used successfully to restrain ankle motion. Compared with ankle taping, these devices do not loosen significantly during exercise (Figure 6-24). Commercial ankle stabilizers, used either alone or in combination with ankle taping, are becoming increasingly popular in sports.[4]

Shin and Lower Leg

The shin is commonly neglected in contact and collision sports. Commercially marketed hard-shelled, molded shin guards are used in field hockey and soccer (Figure 6-25).

Thigh and Upper Leg

Thigh and upper leg protection is necessary in collision sports such as hockey and football. Generally, pads slip into ready-made pockets in the sports suit or uniform (Figure 6-26). To avoid abnormal slipping within the pocket or to protect from injury, customized pads are constructed.

Figure 6-23

Heel cups and pads, including lifts of orthotic felt

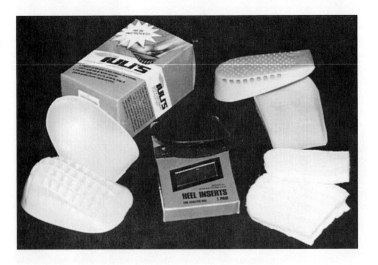

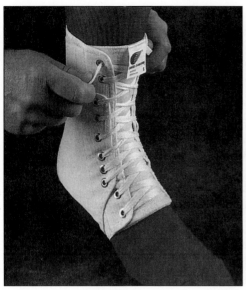
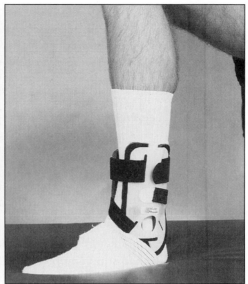

Figure 6-24

Commercial ankle supports
for an injured ankle

Knee Supports and Protective Devices

Knees are next in order to ankles and feet in terms of incidence of sports injury. As a result of the variety and rather high frequency of knee afflictions, many protective and supportive devices have been developed. The devices most frequently used in sports today are sleeves, pads, and braces.

Elastic knee pads or guards are extremely valuable in sports in which the athlete falls or receives a direct blow to the anterior aspect of the knee. An elastic sleeve containing a resilient pad may help dissipate an anterior striking force but fails to protect the knee against lateral, medial, or twisting forces.

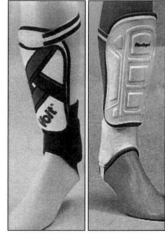

Figure 6-25

Soccer shin guards

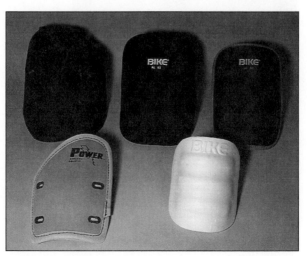

Figure 6-26

Protective thigh pads

A number of different knee braces are on the market. Some are vertical rigid strips held in an elastic sleeve; others consist of an elastic sleeve containing rigid hinges placed on either side of the knee joint. The protection by these braces against initial or recurrent injury is extremely questionable.[7] Wraparound braces with rigid strips contained in less elastic material hold the knee more firmly in place.

The Prophylactic Knee Brace

The American Academy of Orthopedic Surgeons (AAOS) and the American Orthopedic Society for Sports Medicine have voiced reservations about knee braces.[1] Knee braces are classified into three types: prophylactic, functional, and rehabilitative. The AAOS Committee on Sports Medicine indicates that the ideal prophylactic knee brace should have all the following criteria:[8]

- It should adapt to various anatomic shapes and sizes.
- It should supplement the stiffness of the knee, reducing loads from contact and noncontact forces.
- It should be cost effective and durable.
- It should not interfere with normal knee function.
- It should not harm other players.
- It should not increase injuries to the lower extremity.
- It should have documented efficacy in preventing injuries.

Currently no brace on the market fulfills all these criteria. Therefore, use of the prophylactic knee brace is controversial and should be employed on an individual basis[9,11] (see Figure 6-27).

Other popular knee devices are sleeves composed of elastic or neoprene material. Sleeves of this type provide mild soft-tissue support and,

Figure 6-27

A prophylactic knee brace designed to protect against a lateral force and to distribute load away from the joint

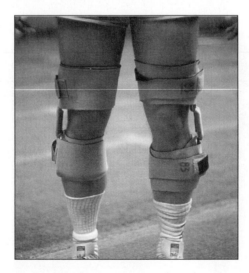

to some extent, retain body heat and help reduce edema caused by tissue compression.

Hand, Wrist, and Elbow Protection

As with the lower limbs, the upper limbs require initial protection from injury as well as prevention of further injury following a trauma. One of the finest physical instruments, the human hand, is perhaps one of the most neglected in terms of protection, especially in sports. Special attention must be paid to protecting the integrity of all aspects of the hand when encountering high-speed projectiles or receiving external forces that contuse or shear. Constant stress to the hand, as characterized by the force received by the hand of the baseball catcher, can lead to irreversible damage in later life (Figure 6-28). The wrist and the elbow are also vulnerable to sports trauma and often need compression or support for protection (Figure 6-29).

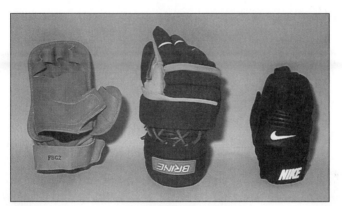

Figure 6-28

Hand protection is often neglected in sports.

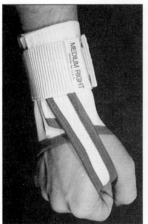

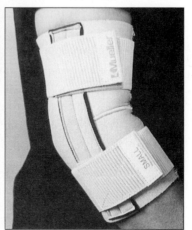

Figure 6-29

Commercial wrist and elbow pads and braces

SUMMARY

- The proper selection and fitting of sports equipment are essential in the prevention of many sports injuries.

- Due to the current number of litigations, both durability of material and fit and wear requirements must meet sports equipment standards.

- Manufacturers must foresee all the possible uses and misuses of their equipment and warn the user of any potential risks.

- Head protection in many collision and contact sports is of particular concern: The helmet must be used as intended and not as a weapon; proper fit is also a requirement.

- A warning label on the outside of the helmet must indicate that it is not fail-safe, and the helmet must be used as intended.

- Face protection is of major importance in sports that have fast-moving projectiles, that use implements that come in close proximity to other athletes, and that are characterized by body collisions.

- Protection of teeth and eyes is of particular significance.

- The customized mouth guard, fitted to individual requirements, provides the best protection for the teeth and also protects against concussions.

- Eyes must be protected against projectiles and sports implements.

- The safest eye guard for the athlete not wearing contact lenses or spectacles is the closed type that completely protects the orbital cavity.

- Many sports require protection of various parts of the athlete's body. American football players, ice hockey players, and baseball/softball catchers are examples of players who require body protection.

- The most common protection is for the shoulders, chest, thighs, ribs, hips, buttocks, groin, genitalia (male athletes), and breasts (female athletes).

- Quality sportswear, properly fitted, is essential to prevent injuries.

- Socks must be clean, without holes, and made of appropriate materials.

- Shoes must be suited to the sport and must be fitted to the larger foot, the wide part of the foot must match the wide part of the shoe, if the shoe has cleats, they must be positioned at the metatarsophalangeal joints.

- The hand, wrist, and elbow are also vulnerable to sports trauma and require special protective devices.

Solutions to Critical Thinking Exercises

6-1 The student coach must acquire the following protective equipment competencies:

- Identify good-quality and poor-quality commercial protective equipment.

- Properly fit commercial protective equipment.
- Construct protective and supportive devices.

6-2 The coach initiates the following steps:

1. A team meeting is called in which the risks entailed in the use and fitting of the equipment is fully explained.
2. A defective piece of equipment must be immediately reported and repaired.
3. A letter is sent out to each parent or guardian explaining equipment limitations. This letter is signed and returned to the athletic trainer.
4. A meeting of parents, team members, and coaches is called to further explain equipment limitations.

6-3 The coach explains that the helmet cannot prevent serious neck injuries. Striking an opponent with any part of the helmet or face mask can place abnormal stress on cervical structures. Most severe neck injuries occur from striking an opponent with the top of the helmet; this action is known as axial loading.

6-4 The coach advises the following:

- Purchase shoes to fit the large foot.
- Fit shoes wearing athletic socks.
- Purchase shoes at the end of the day.
- Each foot is measured from the heel to the end of the largest toe.
- Shoes feel snug but comfortable when jumping up and down and performing cutting motions.
- Shoe length and width allow full toe function.
- Wide part of foot matches the wide part of the shoe.
- Shoe bends at widest part of shoe.

REVIEW QUESTIONS AND CLASS ACTIVITIES

1. What are the legal responsibilities of the equipment manager, coach, and athletic trainer in terms of protective equipment?
2. Invite an attorney to class to discuss product liability and its impact on the athletic trainer, coach, and equipment manager.
3. What are the various sports with high-risk factors that require protective equipment?
4. How can the athletic trainer or coach select and use safety equipment so as to decrease the possibility of sports injuries and litigation?
5. Why is continual inspection and/or replacement of used equipment important?
6. What are the standards for fitting football helmets? Are there standards for any other helmets?
7. Invite your school equipment manager to class to demonstrate all the protective equipment and how to fit it to the athlete.
8. Why are mouth guards important, and what are the advantages of custom-made mouth guards over the stock type?
9. What are the advantages and disadvantages of glasses and contact lenses in athletic competition?
10. How do you fit shoulder pads for the different-sized players and their positions?
11. Why is breast protection necessary? Which types of sport bras are available and what should the athlete look for when purchasing one?
12. How do you properly fit shoes? What type of shoes should you use for the various sports and the different floor and field surfaces?

13. What types of commercial pads and braces are on the market today? Do they provide adequate support and protection from injury?

REFERENCES

1. American Academy of Orthopedic Surgeons: *Athletic training and sports medicine,* ed 2, Park Ridge, Ill, 1991, American Academy of Orthopedic Surgeons.
2. Arnheim DD, Prentice W: *Principles of athletic training,* ed 9, Dubuque, Iowa, 1997, McGraw-Hill.
3. American Society for Testing and Materials, Committee F-8 on Sports Equipment and Facilities: *Member information packet.* Philadelphia, 1978, American Society for Testing and Materials.
4. Davis PF, Trevino SG: Ankle injuries. In Baxter DE, editor: *The foot and ankle in sports,* St Louis, 1995, Mosby.
5. Frey C: The shoe in sports. In Baxter DE, editor: *The foot and ankle in sports,* St Louis, 1995, Mosby.
6. Hodgson VR, Thomas LM: Biomechanical study of football head impacts using a head model—condensed version. Final report prepared for National Operating Committee on Standards for Athletic Equipment, 1975.
7. Kramer, JF et al: Functional knee braces and dynamic performance: a review. *Clinics J Sports Med* 7:32, January 97.
8. Lord JL: Protective equipment in high risk sports. In Berrier RB, editor: *Sports medicine for primary care physicians,* ed 2, Boca Raton, Fla, 1994, CRC Press.
9. Montgomery DL: Prophylactic knee braces. In Torg JS, Shephard RJ, editors: *Current therapy in sports medicine,* St Louis, 1995, Mosby.
10. Prentice W: *Fitness for college life,* ed 5, St Louis, 1995, Mosby.
11. Wichmann S, Martin DR: Bracing for activity. *Physician Sportsmed* 24:88, 1996.

ANNOTATED BIBLIOGRAPHY

Baxter DE, editor: *The foot and ankle in sport,* St Louis, 1995, Mosby.

An in-depth medical text covering all aspects of foot and ankle conditions in sport.

Nicholas JA, Hershman EB, editors: *The upper extremity in sports medicine,* St Louis, 1990, Mosby–Year Book.

Includes a special chapter on protective equipment for the shoulder, elbow, wrist, and hand.

Nicholas JA, Hershman EB, editors: *The lower extremity and spine in sports medicine,* vol 1, St Louis, 1986, Mosby–Year Book.

Contains two excellent chapters on protective devices: Chapter 9, Athletic training techniques and protective equipment, and Chapter 20, Athletic footwear and modifications.

Segesser B, Pjorringer W, editors: *The shoe in sports,* St Louis, 1989, Mosby–Year Book.

An excellent, detailed text on different types of sport shoes and their unique features.

Wu K: *Foot orthoses: principles and clinical applications,* Baltimore, 1990, Williams & Wilkins.

A complete text on examination, fabrication, and application of foot orthoses.

WEB SITES

Riddell: http://riddell.com/index.htm
 Riddell is an equipment manufacturing company, and this site gives information about the safety of the products they sell and the necessary standards for safety equipment.

Red Cross Tips: http://www.redcross.org/tips/april/aprtip98.html
 The April tip for the American Red Cross is sports eye safety. This site gives tips on eye safety and safety equipment for the eyes.

Healthyway Sporting Protective Eyewear: http://www1.sympatico.ca/healthyway/HEALTHYWAY/feature_vis3c.html
 Emphasizes the importance of protective eyewear for young athletes and provides links to related informative sites.

Emergency Situations and Injury Assessment

When you finish this chapter you will be able to:

- Establish a plan for handling emergency situations at your institution.
- Explain the importance of knowing cardiopulmonary resuscitation (CPR) and how to manage an obstructed airway.
- Describe techniques for control of hemorrhage.
- Assess the types of shock and their management.
- Describe the various phases of injury assessment.
- Explain the importance of controlling swelling during initial injury management.
- Describe techniques for moving and transporting the injured athlete.
- Describe appropriate care for skin wounds.

Most sports injuries do not result in life-or-death emergency situations, but when such situations do arise, prompt care is essential. An emergency is defined as "an unforeseen combination of circumstances and the resulting state that calls for immediate action."[14] Time becomes the critical factor, and assistance to the injured athlete must be based on knowledge of what to do and how to do it—how to perform effective aid immediately. There is no room for uncertainty, indecision, or error. A mistake in the initial management of injury can prolong the length of time required for rehabilitation and can potentially create a life-threatening situation for the athlete.

In situations in which an athletic trainer may not be available to provide care, the responsibility falls on the shoulders of the coach. Therefore it is critical that the coach be well prepared to handle whatever emergency situation may arise.

THE EMERGENCY PLAN

Time becomes critical in an emergency situation.

The prime concern of emergency aid is to maintain cardiovascular function and, indirectly, central nervous system function, because failure of any of these systems may lead to death. The key to emergency aid in the sports setting is the initial evaluation of the injured athlete. Time is of the essence, so this evaluation must be done rapidly and accurately so that proper aid can be rendered without delay. In some instances these first steps not only will be lifesaving but also may determine the degree and extent of permanent disability.

As discussed in Chapter 1, the sports medicine team—the coach, the athletic trainer, and the team physician—must at all times act reasonably and prudently. This behavior is especially important during emergencies.

All sports programs must have a prearranged emergency plan that can be implemented immediately when necessary. The following issues must be addressed when developing the emergency system:

All sports programs must have an emergency plan.

1. Phones should be readily accessible. Cellular phones are best because they provide the coach with immediate access to either the emergency medical system or the athletic trainer, who may be with another team. If cellular phones are not available, the location of the telephone should be well known by coaches, athletes, managers, and athletic trainers. These phone locations should be clearly marked. (Use 911 if available.)

2. A specific person should be assigned to make an emergency phone call. The emergency medical system can usually be accessed by dialing 911. This number gets you a dispatcher who has access to the rescue squad and the police and fire departments. The person making the emergency phone call must provide the following information:
   a. Type of emergency situation
   b. Type of suspected injury
   c. Present condition of the athlete
   d. Current assistance being given (e.g., cardiopulmonary resuscitation)
   e. Location of telephone being used
   f. Exact location of emergency (give names of streets and cross streets) and how to enter facility

3. Keys to gates or padlocks must be easily accessible. Both coaches and athletic trainers should have the appropriate key.

4. There should be separate emergency plans for each sport's fields, courts, or gymnasiums.

5. All coaches, athletic trainers, athletic directors, school nurses, and maintenance personnel should be apprised of the emergency plan at a meeting held annually prior to the beginning of the school year. Each individual must know his or her responsibilities should an emergency occur.

6. A responsible adult should always be assigned to accompany the injured athlete to the hospital.

Individuals providing emergency care to the injured athlete must cooperate and act professionally. Too often, the rescue squad personnel, a physician, an athletic trainer, or a coach disagree over exactly how the injured athlete should be handled and transported. The coach or athletic trainer is usually the first individual to deal with the emergency situation. The athletic trainer has generally had more training and experience in moving and transporting an injured athlete than the physician has. If an athletic trainer or physician is not available, then the coach should not hesitate to dial 911 to let the rescue squad handle an emergency situation. If the rescue squad is called and responds, the EMTs should have the final say on how that athlete is to be transported while the coach and athletic trainer assume an assistive role.

To alleviate potential conflicts, it is a good idea for either the coach or the athletic trainer to establish procedures and guidelines and to arrange practice sessions at least once a year with all parties concerned for handling the injured athlete. The rescue squad may not be experienced in dealing with someone who is wearing a helmet or other protective equipment. The coach should make sure before an incident occurs that the EMTs understand how athletes wearing various types of athletic equipment should be managed. When dealing with the injured athlete, all egos should be put aside. Certainly the most important consideration is what is the best for the athlete.

Parent Notification

If the injured athlete is a minor, it is essential that actual consent to treat the athlete be obtained from the parent. Actual consent may be given in writing either before or during an emergency. Actual consent is notification that the parent has been informed about what the coach, athletic trainer, or other medical personnel thinks is wrong and what that person intends to do, and parental permission is granted to give treatment for a specific incident. If the athlete's parents cannot be contacted, then the predetermined wishes of the parent given at the beginning of a season or school year can be inacted. If there is no informed consent, then implied consent on the part of the athlete to save his or her life takes precedence.

PRINCIPLES OF ASSESSMENT

The coach cannot deliver appropriate medical care to the injured athlete until some systematic assessment of the situation has been made. This assessment (Figure 7-1) helps to determine the nature of the injury and provides direction in the decision-making process concerning the emergency care that must be rendered. The *primary survey* refers to assessment of potentially life-threatening problems including airway, breathing, circulation (ABC), severe bleeding, or shock. It takes precedence over all other aspects of victim assessment and should be used to correct life-threatening situations.[9] Once the condition of the victim is stabilized, the *secondary survey* is used to take a closer look at the injury sustained by the athlete. The secondary survey gathers specific information about the injury from the athlete, systematically assesses vital signs and symptoms, and allows for a more detailed evaluation of the injury. The secondary survey is done to uncover problems that do not pose an immediate threat to life but that may do so if they remain uncorrected.[9]

An injured athlete who is conscious and stable will not require a primary survey. However the unconscious athlete must be monitored for life-threatening problems throughout the assessment process.

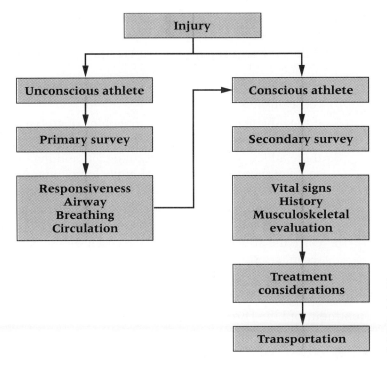

Figure 7-1

Flowchart showing
appropriate emergency
procedures for the injured
athlete

The Unconscious Athlete

The state of unconsciousness provides one of the greatest dilemmas in sports. *With an unconscious athlete, a coach acting alone without an athletic trainer should always call the rescue squad before attempting to move the athlete regardless of whether the situation is life threatening.* Unconsciousness may be defined as a state of insensibility in which there is a lack of conscious awareness. This condition can be brought about by a blow to either the head or the solar plexus, or it may result from general shock. It is often difficult to determine the exact cause of unconsciousness.

The unconscious athlete must always be considered to have a life-threatening injury, which requires an immediate primary survey. Here are guidelines that should be followed when dealing with the unconscious athlete:

1. The coach should immediately note the body position and determine the level of consciousness and unresponsiveness.
2. Airway, breathing, and circulation (ABC) should be established immediately.
3. Injury to the neck and spine is always a possibility in the unconscious athlete.
4. If the athlete is wearing a helmet, it should never be removed until neck and spine injury have been unequivocally ruled out.

However, the face mask must be cut away and removed to allow for CPR.

5. If the athlete is supine and not breathing, establish ABC immediately.

6. If the athlete is supine and breathing, do nothing until consciousness returns.

7. If the athlete is prone and not breathing, logroll him or her carefully to supine position and establish ABC immediately.

8. If the athlete is prone and breathing, do nothing until consciousness returns, then carefully logroll him or her onto a spine board because CPR could be necessary at any time.

9. Monitor and maintain life support for the unconscious athlete until emergency medical personnel arrive.

10. Once the athlete is stabilized, the coach should begin a secondary survey.

PRIMARY SURVEY

Treatment of Life-Threatening Injuries

Life-threatening injuries take precedence over all other injuries sustained by the athlete. Situations that are considered life threatening include those that will require cardiopulmonary resuscitation (i.e., obstruction of the airway, no breathing, no circulation), profuse bleeding, and shock. *Whenever there is a life-threatening situation, the coach should always call the rescue squad.*

Overview of Emergency CPR

All coaches should be currently certified in CPR so that if an athletic trainer is not available, the coach can perform the techniques correctly. It is essential that a careful evaluation of the injured athlete be made to determine whether CPR should be conducted. The following is an overview of adult CPR and is not intended to be used by persons who are not certified in CPR. It should also be noted that, because of the serious nature of CPR, updates should routinely be studied through courses offered by the American Red Cross, the American Heart Association, or the National Safety Council.

First, establish unresponsiveness of the athlete by tapping or gently shaking his or her shoulder and shouting, "Are you okay?" Note that shaking should be avoided if the athlete has a possible neck injury. If the athlete is unresponsive, the emergency medical system (EMS) should be activated immediately by dialing 911. Carefully position the athlete in the supine position. If the athlete is in a position other than supine, he or she must be carefully rolled over as a unit, avoiding any twisting of the body, because CPR can be administered only with the athlete lying flat on the back with knees straight or slightly flexed. In cases of suspected cervical spine injury, care must be taken to minimize cervical movement during logrolling. Then proceed with the ABCs of CPR.[14]

7-1

Critical Thinking Exercise

A football defensive back is making a tackle and on contact drops his head to tackle the ball carrier. He hits the ground and does not move. When the coach gets to him, the athlete is lying prone, is unconscious, but is breathing.

? How should the coach manage this situation?

Equipment Considerations

Protective equipment worn by an athlete may complicate life-saving CPR procedures. A great deal of controversy exists even among athletic trainers as to whether equipment should be removed or left in place. The presence of a football, ice hockey, or lacrosse helmet, with a face mask and various types of shoulder pads associated with each sport, will obviously make CPR more difficult if not impossible.

Removing the face mask should be the first step.[12] The face mask does not hinder the evaluation of the airway but it may hinder treatment.[3] A number of techniques using various instruments have been recommended to remove the face mask, including electric screwdrivers, which work well as long as the screws are not rusted; or wire cutters, bolt cutters, trainers' scissors, or scalpels, none of which work very well. Recently, two devices, the Anvil Pruner and the Trainer's Angel, have been effective in quickly cutting the plastic clips (Figure 7-2). The coach should be proficient in removing the face mask within 30 seconds.[10]

In 1992, the Occupational Safety and Health Administration (OSHA) mandated the use of barrier devices to protect the coach from transmission of bloodborne pathogens during CPR. It is possible to slip the barrier mask under the face mask, attach the one-way mouthpiece or valve through the bars of the face mask and begin CPR within five to ten seconds without removing the face mask.[13]

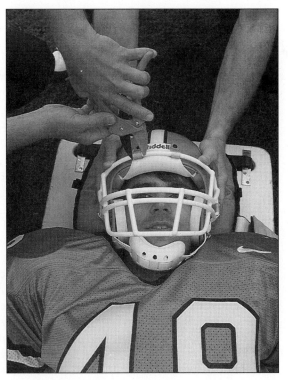

Figure 7-2

A Trainer's Angel is effective in quickly cutting the plastic clips on a face mask for easy removal.

Decisions to remove a helmet and shoulder pads prior to initiating CPR should be based on the potential of injury to the cervical spine. *A coach should never remove the helmet from an athlete with a suspected cervical spine injury.* If it is reasonably certain that no injury has occurred to the cervical spine, both the helmet and shoulder pads can be quickly removed before initiating CPR. If injury to the cervical spine is a possibility, care must be taken to minimize movement of the head and neck while permitting CPR to be performed. The face mask should be dealt with as recommended earlier, and the jersey and shoulder pad strings and/or straps should be cut and the shoulder pads spread apart so that the chest may be compressed according to CPR guidelines. Although removal of the helmet and shoulder pads has been recommended by some,[3] it seems that no matter how much care is taken, removal would create unnecessary movement of the cervical spine and would delay initiation of CPR, neither of which is best for the injured athlete.

If cervical neck injury is suspected yet the athlete is conscious and breathing and does not require CPR, the athlete should be transported with the helmet, chin strap, and shoulder pads in place. The face mask should be removed in case CPR becomes necessary.

ABCs

The ABCs of CPR are easily remembered and indicate the sequential steps used for basic life support:

A–Airway opened
B–Breathing restored
C–Circulation restored

Frequently, when A is restored, B and C will resume spontaneously, and it is then unnecessary to perform them. In some instances, the restoration of A and B obviates the necessity for step C. When performing CPR on an adult victim, the following sequence should be followed.

Opening the Airway

Open the airway by using the head-tilt/chin-lift method. Lift chin with one hand while pushing down on victim's forehead with the other, avoiding the use of excessive force. The tongue is the most common cause of respiratory obstruction; the forward lift of the jaw raises the tongue away from the back of the throat, thus clearing the airway. NOTE: On victims with suspected head or neck injuries, perform a modified jaw thrust maneuver by grasping each side of the lower jaw at the angles, thus displacing the lower mandible forward as the head is tilted backward. In executing this maneuver both elbows should rest on the same surface as that on which the victim is lying. Should the lips close, they can be opened by retracting the lower lip with a thumb. If breathing is still not restored, additional forward displacement of the jaw can be effected.

Establishing Breathing

1. To determine if the victim is breathing, maintain the open airway, place your ear over the mouth, observe the chest, and look, listen, and feel for breath sounds.

2. With the hand that is on the athlete's forehead, pinch the nose shut, keeping the heel of the hand in place to hold the head back (if there is no neck injury) (Figure 7-3). Taking a deep breath, place your mouth over the athlete's mouth to provide an airtight seal and give two slow full breaths at a rate of 1½ to 2 seconds per inflation. Observe the chest rise and fall. Remove your mouth and listen for the air to escape through passive exhalation. If the airway is obstructed, reposition the victim's head and try again to ventilate. If still obstructed, give up to 5 abdominal thrusts followed by a finger sweep with the index finger to clear objects from the mouth. Be careful not to push the object further into the throat. Continue to repeat this sequence until ventilation occurs. NOTE: OSHA has mandated the use of barrier shields by coaches and athletic trainers to minimize the risk of transmitting bloodborne pathogens (Figure 7-4). These shields have a plastic or silicone sheet that spreads over the face and separates the athletic trainer from the athlete. Some models have a tubelike mouthpiece, which may help in situations in which the athlete is wearing a face mask.

Establishing Circulation

1. To determine pulselessness, locate the Adam's apple with the index and middle fingers of the hand closest to the head. Then slide the fingers down into the groove on the side of the body on which you are kneeling to locate the carotid artery. Palpate the carotid pulse with one hand (allow five to ten seconds) while maintaining head tilt with the other.

2. Maintain open airway. Position yourself close to the side of the athlete's chest. With the middle and index fingers of the hand closest to the waist, locate the lower margin of the athlete's rib cage on the side next to you (Figure 7-5).

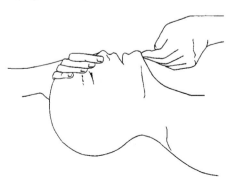

Figure 7-3

Head-tilt/chin lift technique for establishing an airway

Techniques for Preventing
and Minimizing
Sport-Related Injuries

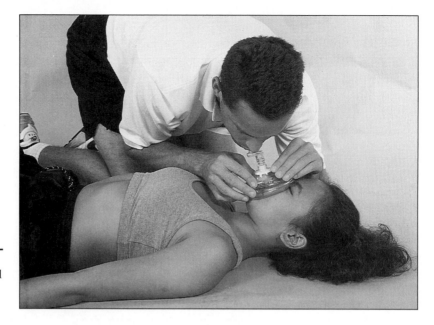

Figure 7-4

A barrier mask protects the
athletic trainer from potential
exposure to bloodborne
pathogens.

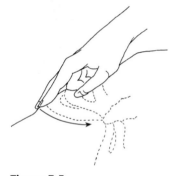

Figure 7-5

With the middle and index
fingers of the hand closest to
the waist, the lower margin
of the victim's rib cage is
located. The fingers are then
run along the rib cage to the
notch where the ribs meet
the sternum. The middle
finger is placed on the notch
with the index finger next to
it on the lower end of the
sternum.

3. Run the fingers up along the rib cage to the xiphoid notch
   where the ribs meet the sternum.
4. Place the middle finger on the notch and the index finger next
   to it on the lower end of the sternum.
5. Next, the hand closest to the athlete's head is positioned on the
   lower half of the sternum next to the index finger of the first
   hand that located the notch; the heel of that hand is placed on
   the long axis of the sternum.
6. The first hand is then removed from the notch and placed on
   top of the hand on the sternum so that the heels of both hands
   are parallel and the fingers are directed straight away from the
   coach (Figure 7-6).
7. Fingers can be extended or interlaced, but they must be kept
   off the chest wall.
8. Elbows are kept in a locked position with arms straight and
   shoulders positioned over the hands, enabling the thrust to be
   straight down.
9. In a normal-sized adult, enough force must be applied to
   depress the sternum 1½ to 2 inches (4 to 5 cm). After
   depression, there must be complete release of the sternum to
   allow the heart to refill. The time of release should equal the
   time of compression. For one rescuer, compression must be
   given at the rate of 80 to 100 times per minute, maintaining a
   rate of fifteen chest compressions to two full breaths.
10. After four cycles of fifteen compressions and two breaths (15:2)
    or about one minute, recheck the pulse at the carotid artery

(allow five seconds) while maintaining head tilt. If there is no pulse, continue the 15:2 cycle beginning with chest compressions.

Every coach should be certified in CPR and should take a refresher examination at least once a year. It is wise to have all assistants certified as well.

Obstructed Airway Management

An airway obstruction is a possibility in many sports activities; for example, an athlete may choke on a mouth guard, a broken bit of dental work, chewing gum, or even a chaw of tobacco. An unconscious athlete can have an obstructed airway when the tongue falls back in the throat, thus blocking the upper airway. Blood clots resulting from head, facial, or dental injuries may impede normal breathing, as may vomiting. When such emergencies arise, early recognition and prompt, knowledgeable action are necessary to avert a tragedy. When complete airway obstruction occurs, the individual is unable to speak, cough, or breathe. The athlete who is conscious will make a tremendous effort to breathe: The head is forced back, and the face initially is flushed and then becomes *cyanotic* (bluish color) as oxygen deprivation occurs. If partial airway obstruction is causing the choking, some air passage can be detected, but during a complete obstruction no air movement is discernible.

To relieve airway obstruction caused by foreign bodies, two maneuvers are recommended: (1) the Heimlich maneuver and (2) finger sweeps of the mouth and throat.

Heimlich maneuver   As with CPR, the Heimlich maneuver (subdiaphragmatic abdominal thrusts) requires practice before proficiency is acquired. The two methods of obstructed airway management depend on whether the victim is in an erect position or has collapsed and is either unconscious or too heavy to lift. For the conscious victim, the standing Heimlich maneuver is performed until he or she is relieved. In cases of unconsciousness, five abdominal thrusts are applied, followed by a finger sweep with an attempt at ventilation.

Method A   Stand behind and to one side of the athlete. Place both arms around the waist just above the belt line, and permit the athlete's head, arms, and upper trunk to hang forward (Figure 7-7A). Grasp one of your fists with the other, placing the thumb side of the grasped fist immediately below the xiphoid process of the sternum, clear of the rib cage. Now sharply and forcefully thrust the fists into the abdomen, inward and upward, several times. This "hug" pushes up on the diaphragm, compressing the air in the lungs, creating forceful pressure against the blockage, and thus usually causing the obstruction to be promptly expelled. Repeat the maneuver until he or she is relieved or becomes unconscious. If the athlete loses consciousness, activate the EMS system, perform a finger sweep, open the airway, and try to ventilate. If the airway is still obstructed, reposition the head and try again. Then give up to five abdominal thrusts. Repeat this sequence as long as necessary.

All coaches must have current CPR certification.

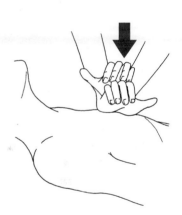

Figure 7-6

The heel of the headward hand is placed on the long axis of the lower half of the sternum next to the index finger of the first hand. The first hand is removed from the notch and placed on top of the hand on the sternum with fingers interlaced.

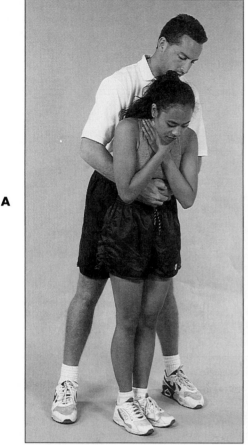

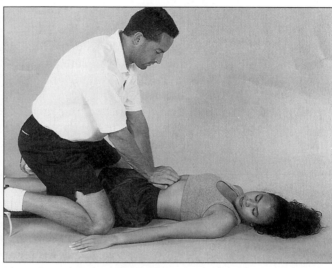

Figure 7-7

The Heimlich maneuver for an obstructed airway. A, Manual thrust maneuver for the conscious athlete. B, Manual thrust maneuver for the unconscious athlete.

Method B   If the athlete is on the ground or on the floor, place him or her on the back and straddle the victim's hips, keeping your weight centered over your knees. Place the heel of your left hand against the back of your right hand and push sharply into the abdomen just above the umbilicus (note the position, Figure 7-7B). Repeat this maneuver up to five times, then repeat the finger sweep. Care must be taken in either of these methods to avoid extreme force or applying force over the rib cage because fractures of the ribs and damage to the organs can result.

Finger sweeping   If a foreign object such as a mouth guard is lodged in the mouth or the throat and is visible, it may be possible to remove or release it with your fingers. Care must be taken that the probing does not drive the object deeper into the throat. It is usually impossible to open the mouth of a conscious victim who is in distress, so the Heimlich maneuver should be put to use immediately. In the unconscious athlete, turn the head either to the side or face up, open the mouth by grasping the tongue and the lower jaw, hold them firmly between your thumb and fingers, and lift—an action that pulls the tongue away from the back of

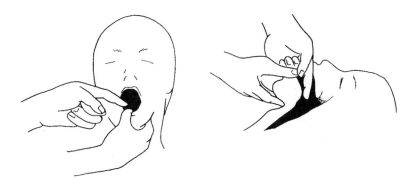

Figure 7-8

Finger sweeping of the
mouth is essential in
attempting to remove a
foreign object from a choking
victim.

the throat and from the impediment. If this action is difficult to do, the
crossed finger method can usually be used effectively. The index finger of
your free hand (or if both hands are used, an assistant can probe) should
be inserted into one side of the mouth along the cheek deeply into the
throat; using a hooking maneuver, attempt to free the impediment, moving it into a position from which it can be removed (Figure 7-8). Attempt
to ventilate after each sweep until the airway is open. Once the object is
removed, if the athlete is not already breathing, an attempt is made to
ventilate him or her.

Controlling Bleeding

An abnormal external or internal discharge of blood is called a *hemorrhage.* The hemorrhage may be venous, capillary, or arterial and may be
external or internal. Venous blood is characteristically dark red with a
continuous flow, capillary bleeding exudes from tissue and is a reddish
color, and arterial bleeding flows in spurts and is bright red. NOTE: The
coach must always be concerned with exposure to bloodborne pathogens
and other diseases when coming in contact with someone's blood or
other body fluids. It is essential to take *universal precautions* to minimize
this risk. Disposable latex gloves should be used routinely whenever the
athletic trainer comes in contact with blood or other body fluids. This
topic is discussed in detail in Chapter 8.

External bleeding can usually
be managed by using direct
pressure, elevation, or
pressure points.

Controlling External Bleeding

External bleeding stems from open skin wounds such as abrasions, incisions, lacerations, punctures, or avulsions. The control of external bleeding includes the use of direct pressure, elevation, and pressure points.

Direct pressure   Pressure is directly applied directly over a wound
with the hand over a sterile gauze pad. The pressure is applied firmly
against the resistance of a bone (Figure 7-9).

Elevation   Elevation, in combination with direct pressure, provides
an additional means for the reduction of external hemorrhage. Elevating
a hemorrhaging part against gravity reduces hydrostatic blood pressure
and facilitates venous and lymphatic drainage; consequently, elevating
slows bleeding.[16]

Figure 7-9

Direct pressure for the
control of bleeding is applied
with the hand over a sterile
gauze pad.

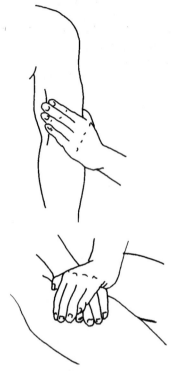

Figure 7-10

The two most common sites
for direct pressure are the
brachial artery and the
femoral artery.

Pressure points   When direct pressure combined with elevation fails to slow hemorrhage, the use of pressure points may be the method of choice. Eleven points on each side of the body have been identified for controlling external bleeding; the two most commonly used are the brachial artery in the upper limb and the femoral artery in the lower limb. The brachial artery is compressed against the medial aspect of the humerus, and the femoral artery is compressed as it is detected within the femoral triangle (Figure 7-10).

Internal Hemorrhage

Internal hemorrhage is invisible to the eye unless manifested through some body opening or identified through x-ray studies or other diagnostic techniques. Its danger lies in the difficulty of diagnosis. When internal hemorrhaging occurs, either subcutaneously such as in a bruise or contusion, intramuscularly, or in joints, the athlete may be moved without danger in most instances. However, the detection of bleeding within a body cavity such as the skull, thorax, or abdomen is of the utmost importance because it could mean the difference between life and death. Because the symptoms are obscure, internal hemorrhage is difficult to diagnose properly. As a result of this difficulty, *athletes with internal injuries require hospitalization under complete and constant observation by a medical staff to determine the nature and extent of the injuries.* All severe hemorrhaging will eventually result in shock and should therefore be treated on this premise. Even if there is no outward indication of shock, the athlete should be kept quiet and body heat should be maintained at a constant and suitable temperature (see the section on shock for the preferred body position).

Managing Shock

With any injury shock is a possibility. But when severe bleeding, fractures, or internal injuries are present, the potential for shock increases. Shock occurs when a diminished amount of blood is available to the circulatory system. As a result, not enough oxygen-carrying blood cells are available to the tissues, particularly those of the nervous system. This situation occurs when the vascular system loses its capacity to hold the fluid portion of the blood within its system because of dilation of the blood vessels within the body and disruption of the osmotic fluid balance. When shock occurs, a quantity of plasma is lost from the blood vessels to the tissue spaces of the body, leaving the blood cells within the vessels, thus causing stagnation and slowing the blood flow. With this general collapse of the vascular system is widespread tissue death, which will eventually cause the death of the individual unless treatment is given.[4]

Certain conditions such as extreme fatigue, extreme exposure to heat or cold, extreme dehydration of fluids and mineral loss, or illness predispose an athlete to shock. In a situation with potential for a shock condition, there are other signs by which the athletic trainer or coach should assess the possibility of the athlete's lapsing into a state of shock as an aftermath of the injury. The most important clue to potential shock is the recognition of a severe injury. It may happen that none of the usual signs of shock is present.

Symptoms and Signs

The major signs of shock are moist, pale, cool, clammy skin; the pulse becomes weak and rapid; the respiratory rate increased and shallow; blood pressure decreases; and in severe situations there is urinary retention and fecal incontinence. If conscious, the athlete may display a disinterest in his or her surroundings or may display irritability, restlessness, or excitement. There may also be extreme thirst.[16]

Management

Depending on the causative factor for the shock, the following emergency care should be given:

1. Maintain body temperature as close to normal as possible.
2. Elevate the feet and legs eight to twelve inches for most situations. However, shock positioning does vary according to the type of injury.[16] For example, for a neck injury, the athlete should be immobilized as found; for a head injury, his or her head and shoulders should be elevated; and for a leg fracture, his or her leg should be kept level and should be raised after splinting.

Shock can also be compounded or initially produced by the psychological reaction of the athlete to an injury situation. Fear or the sudden realization that a serious situation has occurred can result in shock. In the case of a psychological reaction to an injury, the athlete should be instructed to lie down and avoid viewing the injury. This athlete should be handled with patience and gentleness, but firmness as well. Spectators should be kept away from the injured athlete. Reassurance is of vital concern to the injured individual. The person should be given immediate comfort through the loosening of clothing. Nothing should be given by mouth until a physician has determined that no surgical procedures are indicated.

CONDUCTING A SECONDARY ASSESSMENT

If the athlete has no life-threatening injuries, the coach should conduct a secondary assessment to survey the existing injury more precisely.

Recognizing Vital Signs

Anyone providing emergency care has to be able to evaluate the existing physiological signs and symptoms of injury. Among these *vital signs* are heart rate, breathing rate, blood pressure, temperature, skin color, pupils of the eye, movement, the presence of pain, and level of consciousness. Although an athletic trainer must be able to assess in detail, and in some cases, accurately measure each of these vital signs, *it is perhaps more important for the coach to be able to recognize when one or more of the vital signs*

Signs of shock:
Blood pressure is low
Systolic pressure is usually
below 90 mm Hg
Pulse is rapid and very weak
Athlete may be drowsy and
appear sluggish
Respiration is shallow and
extremely rapid
Pale, cool, clammy skin

Secondary assessment
consists of:
History
Observation
Physical examination
Special tests

Vital signs to observe:
Pulse
Respiration
Blood pressure
Temperature
Skin color
Pupils
State of consciousness
Weakness of movement
Sensory changes

TABLE 7-1 Vital signs

Pulse	Normal pulse rate per minute for adults ranges between 60 and 80 beats and in children from 80 to 100 beats. Trained athletes usually have slower pulses. Pulse rate is measured at the carotid artery in the neck or the radial artery in the wrist (Figure 7-11).
Respiration	Normal breathing rate per minute is approximately twelve breaths in adults and twenty to twenty-five breaths in children. Breathing may be shallow (indicating shock), irregular, or gasping (indicating cardiac involvement).
Temperature	Normal body temperature is 98.6° F (37° C). Core temperature is most accurately measured in the rectum or at the tympanic membrane in the ear (Figure 7-12).
Skin Color	Red skin color may indicate heatstroke, high blood pressure, or elevated temperature. Pale, ashen, or white skin can mean insufficient circulation, shock, fright, hemorrhage, heat exhaustion, or insulin shock. Blue skin color (cyanotic), primarily noted in lips and fingernails, usually means an airway obstruction or respiratory insufficiency.
Pupils	Pupils should be of equal size. Pupil should respond to light, resulting in constriction or dilation. Response is more critical than pupil size.
State of Consciousness	Normally the athlete is alert, aware of the environment, and responds quickly to vocal stimulation.
Weakness of Movement	Weakness of one side of the body compared to the other is not normal and may indicate nerve damage.
Sensory Changes	Numbness, tingling, or complete loss of sensation is not normal.
Blood Pressure	Normal systolic pressure for fifteen- to twenty-year-old males ranges from 115 to 120 mm Hg. The diastolic pressure, on the other hand, usually ranges from 75 to 80 mm Hg. The normal blood pressure of females is usually 8 to 10 mm Hg lower than in males for both systolic and diastolic pressures. Blood pressure can only be measured using a blood pressure cuff (Figure 7-13).

Some athletes normally have irregular and unequal pupils. *does not appear to be normal.* Table 7-1 provides a list of what is considered to be normal with each of these vital signs.

On-Field Injury Inspection

Two phases of injury assessment take place during the secondary evaluation. The first involves the initial on-field injury inspection during which early decisions are made relative to (1) the seriousness of the injury and (2) how the injured athlete should be transported from the playing field.

Figure 7-11

Pulse rate taken at the A, carotid artery, and B, radial artery

A   B

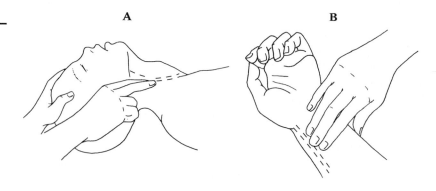

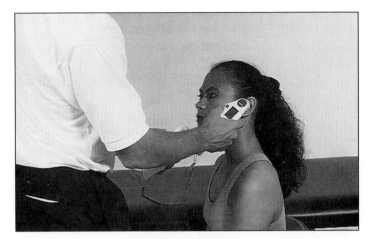

Figure 7-12

Thermometer for measuring
tympanic membrane
temperature

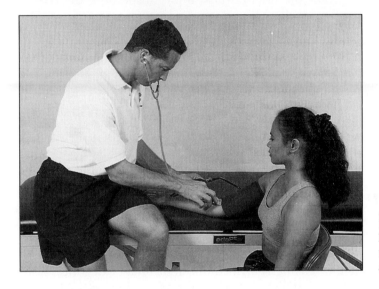

Figure 7-13

Blood pressure is measured
using a sphygmomanometer
and a stethoscope.

Quite often this on-field inspection must be done by the coach when an athletic trainer is not available. The more thorough off-field assessment is usually done by an athletic trainer or physician, if necessary.

A logical process must be used to evaluate accurately the extent of a musculoskeletal injury. Coaches must be aware of the major signs that reveal the site, nature, and above all, severity of the injury. Detection of these signs can be facilitated, as is true with all trauma, by understanding the mechanism or traumatic sequence and by methodically inspecting the injury. Knowledge of the mechanism of an injury is extremely important in determining which area of the body is most affected.

In an attempt to understand the mechanism of injury, a brief history of the complaint must be taken. The athlete is asked, if possible, about the events leading up to the injury and how it occurred. The athlete is further asked what was heard or felt when the injury took place. Such sounds as a snap, crack, or pop at the moment of injury often indicate bone fracture or injury to ligaments or tendons. The coach makes a visual observation of the injured site, comparing it to the uninjured body part. The initial visual examination can disclose obvious deformity, swelling, and skin discoloration.

Finally, the region of the injury is gently palpated. Feeling, or palpating, a part can, in conjunction with visual and audible signs, indicate the nature of the injury. Palpation is started away from the injury and gradually moved toward it. As the coach gently palpates the injury and surrounding structures, he or she can determine the extent of point tenderness, the extent of irritation (whether it is confined to soft tissue alone or extends to the bony tissue), and deformities that may not be detected by visual examination alone.

After the brief on-field injury inspection, the coach makes the following decisions regarding:

Decisions that can be made
from the secondary survey:
Seriousness of injury
Type of first aid required
Whether injury warrants
physical referral
Type of transportation
needed

1. The seriousness of the injury
2. The type of first aid and immobilization necessary
3. Whether the injury warrants immediate referral to a physician for further assessment
4. The manner of transportation from the injury site to the sidelines, training room, or hospital

Off-Field Assessment

The more thorough off-field evaluation is performed once the athlete has been removed from the site of initial injury to a place of comfort and safety. This detailed assessment may be performed on the sidelines, in an emergency room, in the training room, or in a sports medicine clinic. Further inspection and evaluation may be performed when the injury is still in an acute phase or has become chronic and/or recurrent. The evaluation scheme is divided into four broad categories: history, general observation, physical examination and special tests (HOPS). Numerous special tests can provide additional information about the extent of injuries. The following discussion provides a brief overview of some of the steps and techniques that can be used in an off-field assessment.

History

Obtaining as much information as possible about the injury is of major importance. Understanding how the injury may have occurred and listening to the complaints of the athlete and how key questions are answered can provide important clues to the exact nature of the injury. The examiner becomes a detective in pursuit of as much accurate information as possible, which will lead to a determination of the true nature of the injury. From the history, the examiner develops strategies for further examination and possible immediate and follow-up management.

When obtaining a history, the examiner should do the following:

1. Be calm and reassuring.
2. Express questions that are simple, not leading.
3. Listen carefully to the athlete's complaints.
4. Maintain eye contact to try and see what the athlete is feeling.
5. Record exactly what the athlete said without interpretation.

Questions might be stated under specific headings in an attempt to get as complete a historical picture as possible. In many cases, a history becomes very clear-cut because the mechanism, trauma, and pathology are obvious, whereas in other situations, symptoms and signs may be obscured.

The primary complaint If conscious and coherent, the athlete is encouraged to describe the injury in detail. The athletic trainer or coach who did not see the injury happen should have the athlete describe in detail the mechanism of the injury:

1. What is the problem?
2. How did it occur?
3. Did you fall and how did you land?
4. Which direction did your joint move?
5. When did it occur?
6. Has this happened before? If so, when?
7. Was something heard or felt when it occurred?

If the athlete is unable to describe accurately how the injury occurred, perhaps a teammate or someone who observed the event can do so.

The injury location Ask the athlete to locate the area of complaint by pointing to it with one finger only. If the athlete can point to a specific pain site, the injury is probably localized. On the other hand, if the exact pain site cannot be indicated, the injury may be generalized and nonspecific.

Pain characteristics Ask the athlete about the pain he or she is experiencing:

1. *What type of pain is it?* Nerve pain is sharp, bright, and/or burning. Bone pain tends to be localized and piercing. Pain in the vascular system tends to be poorly localized, aching, and referred from another area. Muscle pain is often dull, aching, and referred to another area.[8] Determining pain origin makes the evaluation of musculoskeletal injuries difficult. The deeper the injury site, the more difficult it is to match the pain with the site of trauma. This factor often causes treatment to be performed at the wrong site. Conversely, the closer the injury is to the body surface, the better the elicited pain corresponds with the site of pain stimulation.[15]

2. *Does the pain change at different times?* Pain that subsides during activity usually indicates a chronic inflammation. Pain that

7-2

Critical Thinking Exercise

A fencer comes into the training room complaining of pain in his shoulder that he has had for about a week. He indicates that he first hurt the shoulder when lifting weights but did not think it was a bad injury. During the past week he has not been able to lift because of pain. He has, however, continued to fence during practice but his shoulder seems to be getting worse instead of better.

? What evaluation scheme would a coach use?

increases in a joint throughout the day indicates a progressive increase in edema.

3. *Does the athlete feel sensations other than pain?* Pressure on nerve roots can produce pain and/or a sensation of pins and needles (paresthesia).

4. *What movement, if any, causes pain or other sensations?*

Joint responses Try to determine the extent of pain related to a joint:

1. If the injury is related to a joint, is there instability?
2. Does the joint feel as though it will give way?
3. Does the joint lock and unlock?

Positive responses may indicate that the joint has a loose body that is catching or that is inhibiting the normal muscular support in the area.

Determining whether the injury is acute or chronic Ask the athlete how long he or she has had the symptoms and how frequently they appear.

General Observation

Along with gaining knowledge and understanding of the athlete's major complaint from a history, general observation is also performed, often at the same time the history is taken. What is observed is commonly modified by the athlete's major complaints. The following are suggested as specific points to observe:

1. How does the athlete move? Is there a limp? Are movements abnormally slow, jerky, asynchronous, or is movement not allowed in a body part?
2. Is the body held stiffly to protect against pain? Does the athlete's facial expression indicate pain or lack of sleep?
3. Are there any obvious body asymmetries? Is there an obvious deformity? Does soft tissue appear swollen or wasted as a result of atrophy? Are there unnatural protrusions or lumps such as occur with a dislocation or a fracture? Is there a postural malalignment?
4. Are there abnormal sounds such as crepitus when the athlete moves?
5. Does a body area appear inflamed? Are there swelling, heat, and redness?

Physical Examination

In performing a more detailed examination of the musculoskeletal system, the coach engages in palpation, movement assessment, neurological assessment, and special tests of specific body areas, such as testing joint play and posture when called for. At certain times functional tests are also given.

Palpation   Some examiners use palpation in the beginning of the examination procedure, whereas others only use it when they believe they have identified the specific injury site by other assessment means.[5,8] In some cases, palpation would be beneficial at both the beginning and the end of the examination. The two areas of palpation are bony and soft tissue. As with all examination procedures, palpation must be performed systematically, starting with very light pressure followed by gradually deeper pressure and usually beginning away from the site of complaint, then gradually moving toward it.

Bony palpation   Both the injured and noninjured sites should be palpated and compared. The sense of touch might reveal an abnormal gap at a joint, swelling on a bone, joints that are misaligned, or abnormal protuberances associated with a joint or a bone.

Soft-tissue palpation   Through palpation, with the athlete as relaxed as possible, normal soft-tissue relationships can be ascertained. Tissue deviations such as swellings, lumps, gaps, and abnormal muscle tensions and temperature variations can be detected. The palpation of soft tissue can detect where ligaments or tendons have torn. Variations in the shape of structures, differences in tissue tightness and textures, differentiation of tissue that is pliable and soft from tissue that is more resilient, as well as pulsations, tremors, and other involuntary muscle twitching can be discerned. Excessive skin dryness and moisture can also be noted. Abnormal skin sensations such as diminished sensation (dysesthesia), numbness (anesthesia), or increased sensation (hyperesthesia) can be noted. Like bony palpation, soft-tissue palpation must be performed on both sides of the body for comparison.

Movement assessment   If a joint or soft-tissue lesion exists, the athlete is likely to complain of pain on movement. A muscle strain would cause pain both on active contraction and passive stretch. A sprain of a ligament will result in pain whenever that ligament is stretched, either through active contraction or passive stretching.

Active movement   Movement assessment should begin with active range of motion (AROM). The coach should evaluate the quality of movement, range of movement, motion in other planes, movement at varying speeds, and strength throughout the range but in particular at the endpoint. An athlete who seems to be pain free in each of these tests throughout a full range should be tested by applying passive pressure at the endpoint.

Passive movement   When passive range of motion (PROM) is being assessed, the athlete must relax completely and allow the coach to move the extremity in order to reduce the influence of the contractile elements. Particular attention should be directed toward the sensation of the athlete at the end of the passive range.

Throughout the passive range of movement, the coach is looking for limitation in movement and the presence of pain. If the athlete reports pain before the end of the available range, the probable indication is acute inflammation in which stretching and joint mobilization are both

 7-3

Critical Thinking E x e r c i s e

A coach is evaluating a volleyball player who complains of pain in her elbow. During the evaluation, manual muscle testing and active and passive range of motion tests reveal pain when the elbow is moved into extension both actively and passively. However, there is no pain when the elbow is moved actively into flexion.

? Is it likely that the injury involves a ligament of the musculotendinous unit?

Movement examination includes:
Active movement
Passive movement

Active movement refers to joint motion that occurs because of muscle contraction.

Passive movement refers to movement that is performed completely by the examiner.

contraindicated as treatments. Pain occurring synchronous with the end of the range indicates that the condition is subacute. If no pain occurs at the end of the range, the condition is chronic and contractures have replaced inflammation.[15]

Goniometric measurement of joint range   *Goniometry,* which measures joint range of motion, is an essential procedure during the early, intermediate, and late stages of injury. Full range of motion of an affected body part is a major criterion for the return of the athlete to participation. Active and passive joint range of motion can be measured using goniometry (Figure 7-14).

When measuring joint range of motion, the goniometer should generally be placed along the lateral surface of the extremity being measured. The zero degree, or starting position, for any movement is identical to the standard anatomical position. The athlete should move the joint either actively or passively through the available range to the endpoint. The stationary arm of the goniometer should be placed parallel with the longitudinal axis of the fixed reference part. The movable arm should be placed along the longitudinal axis of the movable segment. NOTE: The axis of rotation will change throughout the range as movement occurs. Thus the axis of rotation is located at the intersection of the stationary and movable arms.) A reading in degrees of motion should be taken and recorded as either active or passive range of motion for that specific movement. Accuracy and consistency in goniometric measurement may only be achieved through practice and repetition.

Manual muscle testing   Manual muscle testing is an integral part of the physical examination process.[5] The ability of the injured athlete to tolerate varying levels of resistance can indicate a great deal about the extent of the injury to the contractile units. For the athlete, the limitation in muscular strength is generally caused by pain. As pain diminishes and

Figure 7-14

Measurement of joint range
of motion using a
goniometer.

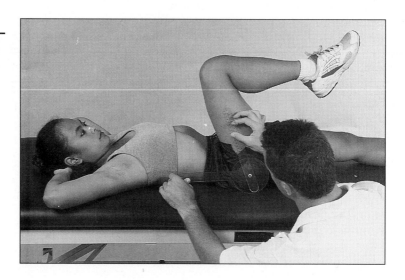

the healing process progresses, levels of muscular strength gradually return to normal.

Manual muscle testing is usually performed with the athlete positioned such that individual muscles or muscle groups can be isolated and tested through a full range of motion by the application of manual resistance. The ability of the athlete to move through a full range of motion or to offer resistance to movement is subjectively graded by the athletic trainer according to various classification systems and grading criteria that have been developed. Table 7-2 indicates a commonly used grading system for manual muscle testing.

Neurological examination   The neurological examination usually follows manual muscle testing. It consists of five major areas: cerebral function, cranial nerve function, cerebellar function, sensory testing, and reflex testing. Musculoskeletal injuries that do not involve head injury do not require an assessment of cerebral function, cranial nerve function, and cerebellar function. The coach should concentrate instead on sensation testing and reflex testing to determine involvement of the peripheral nervous system following injury.

Special Tests

Special tests have been designed for almost every body region as means for detecting specific pathologies. These tests are often used to substantiate what has been learned from other testing. For example, special tests are commonly used to determine ligament stability, impingement signs, tightness of specific structures, blood circulation, muscle imbalance, and body alignment discrepancies. Special tests for various joints will be discussed in Chapters 14 through 22.

Functional Evaluation

The functional evaluation of an athlete can be performed early in the initial examination or can be done to determine whether rehabilitation has

The functional examination determines if there is full strength, joint stability, and coordination and if the part is pain free.

TABLE 7-2 Manual muscle strength grading

Grade	Percentage (%)	Value of Concentration	Muscle Strength
5	100	Normal	Complete range of motion (ROM) against gravity, with full resistance
4	75	Good	Complete ROM against gravity, with some resistance
3	50	Fair	Complete ROM against gravity, with no resistance
2	25	Poor	Complete ROM, with gravity omitted
1	10	Trace	Evidence of slight contractility, with no joint motion
0	0	Zero	No evidence of muscle contractility

been successful. Functional evaluation is an important factor that precedes the return to full sports participation. A functional evaluation proceeds gradually from presenting little stress to mimicking the actual stress that comes from full sports participation. The major concern is whether the athlete has regained full strength, joint stability, and coordination and is pain free. A lack of any one of these three abilities may be a factor in excluding the athlete from his or her sport.

Recording and Documenting Injury Information

Documentation of acute athletic injury can be effectively accomplished through a system designed to record both subjective and objective findings and to document the immediate and future treatment plan for the athlete. The *SOAP Note* combines information provided by the athlete and the observations of the examiner.[6] Figure 7-15 presents a recommended injury report form that includes these components of documentation. This form also includes a provision to document findings arising from more definitive evaluation or from the examiner's subsequent day's evaluation.

SOAP Note:
Subjective
Objective
Assessment
Plan

S (subjective)   This component includes the subjective statements provided by the injured athlete. History taking is designed to elicit the subjective impressions of the athlete relative to time, mechanism, and site of injury. The type and course of the pain and the degree of disability experienced by the athlete are also noteworthy.

O (objective)   Objective findings result from the coach's visual in-

Figure 7-15

SOAP note form

INJURY REPORT FORM

ATHLETE'S NAME _____   DATE OF INJURY _____

INJURY SITE: R L _____   TODAY'S DATE _____

SPORT _____

Subjective findings (history):

Objective findings (inspection, palpation, mobility, and special tests):

Assessment (impression):

Plan (treatment administered and disposition):

Follow-up notes: Date _____

EVALUATED BY _____

RECORDED BY _____

spection, palpation, and assessment of active, passive, and resistive motion. Findings of special testing should also be noted here. Thus the objective report would include assessment of posture, presence of deformity or swelling, and location of point tenderness. Also, limitations of active motion and pain arising or disappearing during passive and resistive motion should be noted. Finally, the results of special tests relative to joint stability or apprehension are also included.

A (assessment) Assessment of the injury is the coach's professional judgment with regard to impression and nature of injury. Although the exact nature of the injury will not always be known initially, information pertaining to suspected site and anatomical structures involved is appropriate. A judgment of severity may be included but is not essential at the time of acute injury evaluation.

P (plan) The plan should include the first-aid treatment rendered to the athlete and the sports therapist's intentions relative to disposition. Disposition may include referral for more definitive evaluation or simply application of splint, wrap, or crutches and a request to report for reevaluation the next day. If the injury is of a more chronic nature, the examiner's plan for treatment and therapeutic exercise would be appropriate.

IMMEDIATE TREATMENT FOLLOWING ACUTE INJURY

Musculoskeletal injuries are extremely common in sports. The coach must be prepared to provide appropriate first aid immediately to control hemorrhage and associated swelling. *Every initial first-aid effort should be directed toward one primary goal—reducing the amount of swelling resulting from the injury.* If swelling can be controlled initially, the amount of time required for injury rehabilitation will be significantly reduced. Initial management of musculoskeletal injuries should include rest, ice, compression, and elevation (RICE). The accompanying Focus Box on page 178 summarizes the specific technique for initial management of the acute injuries.

RICE (rest, ice, compression, elevation) are essential in the emergency care of musculoskeletal injuries.

Rest

Rest after any type of injury is an extremely important component of any treatment program. Once a body part is injured, it immediately begins the healing process. If the injured part is not rested and is subjected to external stresses and strains, the healing process never really gets a chance to do what it is supposed to do. Consequently, the injured part does not heal, and the time required for rehabilitation is markedly increased. The number of days necessary for resting varies with the severity of the injury. Parts of the body that have experienced minor injury should rest for approximately forty-eight to seventy-two hours before a rehabilitation program is begun.

Ice (Cold Application)

The initial treatment of acute injuries should use cold.[7] Therefore ice is used for most conditions involving strains, sprains, and contusions.[17] Ice

---

7-1 ⟩ **Focus Box**

Initial Management of Acute Injuries

The appropriate technique for initial management of the acute musculoskeletal injury, regardless of where it occurs, is the following:

1. Apply a compression wrap directly over the injury. Wrapping should
   start distally and continue proximally. Tension should be firm and
   consistent. It may be helpful to wet the elastic wrap to facilitate the
   passage of cold from ice packs. A dry compression wrap should be left
   in place for at least seventy-two hours or until there is little chance of
   continued swelling.

2. Surround the injured area entirely with ice packs or bags, and secure
   them in place. The ice should be left on for twenty minutes initially
   and then one hour off and thirty minutes on as much as possible over
   the next twenty-four hours. During the following forty-eight-hour
   period, ice should again be applied as often as possible.

3. The injured part should be elevated for most of the initial seventy-
   two-hour period after injury. It is particularly important to keep the
   injury elevated while sleeping. This elevation also allows the damaged
   part to rest after the injury. The initial management of an injury is
   extremely important to reduce the length of time required for
   rehabilitation.

---

is most commonly used immediately after injury to decrease pain and
promote local constriction of the vessels (vasoconstriction), thus controlling hemorrhage and edema. Cold applied to an acute injury will lower
metabolism and the tissue demands for oxygen and will reduce hypoxia.
This benefit extends to uninjured tissue, preventing injury-related tissue
death from spreading to adjacent normal cellular structures. It is also
used in the acute phase of inflammatory conditions such as bursitis,
tenosynovitis, and tendinitis, conditions in which heat may cause additional pain and swelling. Cold is also used to reduce the reflex muscle
spasm and spastic conditions that accompany pain. Its pain-reducing
(analgesic) effect is probably one of its greatest benefits. One explanation
of the analgesic effect is that cold slows the speed of nerve transmission,
so the pain sensation is reduced. It is also possible that cold bombards
pain receptors with so many cold impulses that pain impulses are lost.
With ice treatments, the athlete usually reports an uncomfortable sensation of cold, followed by burning, then an aching sensation, and finally
complete numbness.

Because the subcutaneous (under the skin) fat slowly conducts the
cold temperature, applications of cold for short periods of time will be ineffective in cooling deeper tissues. For this reason, longer treatments of
at least twenty minutes are recommended. Prolonged application of cold,
however, can cause tissue damage.[7]

The temperature to which the deeper tissues can be lowered depends on (1) the type of cold that is applied to the skin, (2) the duration of its application, (3) the thickness of the subcutaneous fat, and (4) the region of the body to which it is applied. Ice packs should be applied to the area for at least seventy-two hours after an acute injury. With many injuries, regular ice treatments may be continued for several weeks.

For best results, ice packs (crushed ice and towel) should be applied over a compression wrap. Frozen gel packs should not be used directly against the skin, because they reach much lower temperatures than ice packs. A good rule of thumb is to apply a cold pack to a recent injury for a twenty-minute period and repeat every 1 to 1½ hours throughout the waking day. Depending on the severity and site of the injury, cold may be applied intermittently for one to seventy-two hours. For example, a mild strain will probably require one day of twenty-minute periods of cold application, whereas a severe knee or ankle sprain might need three to seven days of intermittent cold. If in doubt about the severity of an injury, it is best to extend the time that ice is applied.

Compression

In most cases immediate compression of an acute injury is considered an important adjunct to cold and elevation and in some cases may be superior to them.[18] Placing external pressure on an injury assists in decreasing hemorrhage and hematoma formation by mechanically reducing the space available for swelling to accumulate. Fluid seepage into interstitial spaces is retarded by compression, and absorption is facilitated. However, application of compression to an anterior compartment syndrome or to certain injuries involving the head and neck would be contraindicated.

Many types of compression are available. An elastic wrap that has been soaked in water and frozen in a refrigerator can provide both compression and cold when applied to a recent injury. Pads can be cut from felt or foam rubber to fit difficult-to-compress body areas. A horseshoe-shaped pad, for example, placed around the malleolus in combination with an elastic wrap and tape provides an excellent way to prevent or reduce ankle edema (Figure 7-16). Although cold is applied intermittently, compression should be maintained throughout the day and, if possible, throughout the night. Pressure buildup in the tissues may make it painful to leave a compression wrap in place for a long time. However, the wrap must be left in place even though there may be significant pain, because compression is so important in the control of swelling. The compression wrap should be left in place for at least seventy-two hours after an acute injury. In many chronic overuse problems, such as tendinitis, tenosynovitis, and particularly bursitis, the compression wrap should be worn until all swelling is almost entirely gone.

Elevation

Along with cold and compression, elevation reduces internal bleeding. The injured part, particularly an extremity, should be elevated to eliminate the effects of gravity on blood pooling in the extremities. Elevation

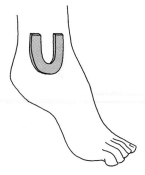

Figure 7-16

A horseshoe-shaped pad can be placed around the malleolus to reduce edema.

Critical Thinking Exercise

A field hockey player trips over an opponent's stick, turning her ankle inward, and falls to the turf, sustaining a grade 2 ankle sprain. She has immediate swelling and significant pain, and on examination, there appears to be some laxity in the ankle joint.

? What specifically should the coach do to most effectively control the initial swelling associated with this injury?

assists the veins, which drain blood and other fluids from the injured area and return them to the central circulatory system. The greater the degree of elevation, the more effective the reduction in swelling. For example, in an ankle sprain the leg should be placed in a position so that the ankle is virtually straight up in the air. The injured part should be elevated as much as possible during the first seventy-two hours.

Emergency Splinting

A suspected fracture must be splinted before the athlete is moved.

Any suspected fracture should be splinted before the athlete is moved. Transporting a person with a fracture without proper immobilization can result in increased tissue damage, hemorrhage, and shock. Conceivably a mishandled fracture could cause death. Therefore, a thorough knowledge of splinting techniques is important.The application of splints should be a simple process through the use of commercial emergency splints. In most instances the coach does not have to improvise a splint because such devices are readily available in most sports settings.

Regardless of the type of splint used, the principles of good splinting remain the same. Two major concepts of splinting are (1) to splint from one joint above the fracture to one joint below the fracture and (2) to splint where the athlete lies. If at all possible, do not move the athlete until he or she has been splinted.

Rapid Form Vacuum Immobilizers

The rapid form vacuum immobilizer is a new type of splint that is widely used by both EMTs and athletic trainers. It consists of styrofoam chips contained inside an airtight cloth sleeve that is pliable. It can be molded to the shape of any joint or angulated fracture using Velcro straps. A handheld pump sucks the air out of the sleeve, giving it a cardboardlike rigidity. This splint is most useful for injuries that are angulated and must be splinted in the position in which they are found (Figure 7-17A).

Air Splints

An air splint is a clear plastic splint that is inflated with air around the affected part; it can be used for extremity splinting, but its use requires some special training. This splint provides support and moderate pressure to the body part and affords a clear view of the site for x-ray examination. The inflatable splint should not be used if it will alter a fracture deformity (Figure 7-17B).

Half-Ring Splint

For fractures of the femur, the half-ring traction splint offers the best support and immobilization but takes considerable practice to master. An open fracture must be carefully dressed to avoid additional contamination.

Splinting of Lower-Limb Fractures

Fractures of the ankle or leg require immobilization of the foot and knee. Any fracture involving the knee, thigh, or hip needs splinting of all the lower-limb joints and one side of the trunk.

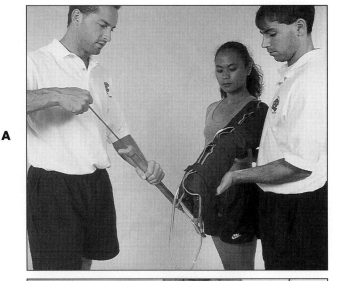

Figure 7-17

A, Rapid form vacuum
immobilizer. B, Air splint

Splinting of Upper-Limb Fractures

Fractures around the shoulder complex are immobilized by a sling and
swathe bandage, with the upper limb bound to the body securely. Upper-
arm and elbow fractures must be splinted, with immobilization effected
in a straight-arm position to lessen bone override. Lower-arm and wrist
fractures should be splinted in a position of forearm flexion and should
be supported by a sling. Hand and finger dislocations and fractures should
be splinted with tongue depressors, gauze rolls, or aluminum splints.

Splinting of the Spine and Pelvis

Injuries involving a possible spine or pelvic fracture are best splinted and
moved using a spine board. Recently, a total body rapid form vacuum
immobilizer has been developed for dealing with spinal injuries (Figure
7-18). The effectiveness of this piece of equipment as an immobilization
device has yet to be determined.

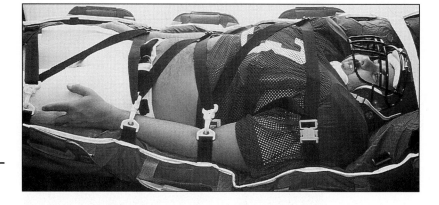

Figure 7-18

Rapid form total body
immobilizer

MOVING AND TRANSPORTING THE INJURED ATHLETE

Great caution must be taken
when transporting the
injured athlete.

Moving, lifting, and transporting the injured athlete must be executed
using techniques that will prevent further injury. Moving or transporting
the athlete improperly may cause more additional injuries than does any
other emergency procedure.[1,11] There is no excuse for poor handling of
the injured athlete. Planning should take into consideration all the possible transportation methods and the necessary equipment to execute
them. Capable and well-trained personnel, spine boards, stretchers, and
a rescue vehicle may be needed to transport the injured athlete. Special
consideration must be also given to extracting the injured athlete from a
pool.

Suspected Spinal Injury

*When spinal injuries are suspected, the coach should immediately access the EMS
and wait until the rescue squad arrives before attempting to move the athlete.* The
only exception would be in cases in which the athlete is not breathing
and logrolling the athlete onto the back is required for CPR.

A suspected spinal injury requires extremely careful handling and is
best left to properly trained paramedics, EMTs, or athletic trainers who
are more skilled and have the proper equipment for such transport. If
such personnel are not available, moving should be done under the express direction of a physician, and a spine board should be used (Figure
7-19). One danger inherent in moving an athlete with a suspected spinal
injury, in particular a cervical injury, is the tendency of the neck and head
to turn because of the victim's inability to control his or her movements.
Torque so induced creates considerable possibility of spinal cord or root
damage when small fractures are present. The most important principle
in transporting an individual on a spine board is to keep the head and
neck in alignment with the long axis of the body. In such cases it is best
to have one individual whose sole responsibility is to ensure and maintain proper positioning of the head and neck until the head is secured to
a spine board.

A

B

C

Figure 7-19

A, When moving an unconscious athlete, first establish whether the athlete is breathing and has a pulse. An unconscious athlete must always be treated as having a serious neck injury. If lying prone, the athlete must be turned over for CPR or be secured to a spine board for possible cervical fracture. All the athlete's extremities are placed in axial alignment, with one coach stabilizing the athlete's neck and head. B, The spine board is placed as close to the athlete as possible. C, Each assistant is responsible for one of the athlete's segments. When the coach (captain) gives the command "roll," the athlete is moved as a unit onto the spine board.

Placing the Athlete on a Spine Board

Once an injury to the neck has been recognized as severe, a physician and a rescue squad should be summoned immediately. Primary emergency care involves maintaining normal breathing, treating for shock,

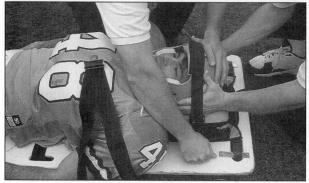

Figure 7-19—cont'd

D, At all times, the captain
continues to stabilize the
athlete's neck. E, The head
and neck are stabilized onto
the spine board by means of
a chin strap secured to metal
loops, and finally the trunk
and lower limbs are secured
to the spine board by straps.

and keeping the athlete quiet and in the position found until medical assistance arrives. Ideally, transportation should not be attempted until the physician has examined the athlete and has given permission to move him or her. The athlete should be transported while lying on the back with the curve of the neck supported by a rolled-up towel or pad or encased in a stabilization collar. Neck stabilization must be maintained throughout transportation, first to the emergency vehicle, then to the hospital, and throughout the hospital procedure. If stabilization is not continued, additional cord damage and paralysis may ensue.

These steps should be followed when moving an athlete with suspected neck injury:

1. Establish whether the athlete is breathing and has a pulse.
2. Plan to move the athlete on a spine board.
3. If the athlete is lying prone, he or she must be logrolled onto the back for CPR or to be secured to the spine board. An athlete with a possible cervical fracture is transported face up. An athlete with a spinal fracture in the lower trunk area may be transported face down.[2]

    a. Place all extremities in an axial alignment (see Figure 7-19A).
    b. To roll the athlete over requires four or five persons, with the

captain of the team protecting the athlete's head and neck. The neck must be stabilized and must not be moved from its original position, no matter how distorted it may appear.

   c. The spine board is placed close to the side of the athlete (see Figure 7-19B).

   d. Each assistant is responsible for one of the athlete's body segments. One assistant is responsible for turning the trunk, another the hips, another the thighs, and the last the lower legs.

4. With the spine board close to the athlete's side, the captain gives the command to logroll him or her onto the board as one unit (see Figure 7-19C).

5. On the board, the athlete's head and neck continue to be stabilized by the captain (see Figure 7-19D).

6. If the athlete is a football player, the helmet is not removed; however, the face guard is removed or lifted away from the face for possible CPR. NOTE: Remove the face guard by cutting the plastic fasteners holding it to the helmet.

7. The head and neck are next stabilized on the spine board by a chin strap secured to metal loops. Finally, the trunk and lower limbs are secured to the spine board by straps (see Figure 7-19E).

An alternate method of moving the athlete onto a spine board, if he or she is face up, is the straddle slide method. Four persons are used—a captain stationed at the athlete's head and three or four assistants. One assistant is in charge of lifting the athlete's trunk, one the hips, and one the legs. On the command "lift" by the captain, the athlete is lifted while the fourth assistant slides a spine board under the athlete between the feet of the captain and assistants (Figure 7-20).

Figure 7-20

An alternate method of placing the athlete on a spine board is the straddle slide method.

Ambulatory Aid

Ambulatory aid (Figure 7-21) is that support or assistance given to an injured athlete who is able to walk. Before the athlete is allowed to walk, he or she should be carefully scrutinized to make sure that the injuries are minor. Whenever serious injuries are suspected, walking should be prohibited. Complete support should be given on both sides of the athlete by two individuals who are approximately the same height. The athlete's arms are draped over the assistants' shoulders, and their arms encircle his or her back.

Manual Conveyance

Manual conveyance (Figure 7-22) may be used to move a mildly injured individual a greater distance than could be walked with ease. As with the use of ambulatory aid, any decision to carry the athlete must be made only after a complete examination to determine the existence of potentially serious conditions. The most convenient carry is performed by two assistants.

Figure 7-21

The ambulatory aid method of transporting a mildly injured athlete

Figure 7-22

Manual conveyance method
for transporting a mildly
injured athlete

Stretcher Carrying

Whenever a serious injury is suspected, the best and safest mode of transportation for a short distance is by stretcher. With each segment of the body supported, the athlete is gently lifted and placed on the stretcher, which is carried adequately by four assistants, two supporting the ends of the stretcher and two supporting either side (Figure 7-23). Any person with an injury serious enough to require the use of a stretcher must be carefully examined before being moved.

When transporting a person with a limb injury, be certain the injury is splinted properly before transport. Athletes with shoulder injuries are more comfortably moved in a semi-sitting position, unless other injuries preclude such positioning. If injury to the upper extremity is such that flexion of the elbow is not possible, the individual should be transported on a stretcher with the limb properly splinted and carried at the side and with adequate padding placed between the arm and the body.

Pool Extraction

Removing an injured athlete from a swimming pool requires some special consideration on the part of the coach.

Techniques for Preventing
and Minimizing
Sport-Related Injuries

Figure 7-23

Whenever a serious injury is
suspected, a stretcher is the
safest method for
transporting the athlete.

1. The injured athlete who has not sustained a head or neck injury
   should be told to roll onto their back in the water and then
   towed to the edge of the pool using a cross chest technique.

2. If the athlete is not breathing, a single rescuer should get the
   athlete out of the water and onto the deck as quickly as possible
   to perform CPR. If two rescuers are present, resuscitation should
   begin immediately while still in the water. With the athlete
   supine in the water, one rescuer supports the shoulders and
   head while the other performs a jaw thrust to open the airway
   and begins rescue breathing if necessary. The athlete should be
   moved onto the deck, where CPR is continued as rapidly as
   possible (Figure 7-24).

Figure 7-24

Rescue breathing should
begin in the water.

3. Athletes with a suspected head or cervical neck injury and who are unconscious require special precaution. The coach should approach the athlete in the water carefully, thus minimizing wave action that causes unnecessary movement of the head and neck. Using a head/chin support technique that uses the forearms to splint the chest and upper back and the hands to stabilize the head and neck, the athlete should be rolled onto the back and maintained in a horizontal position until help arrives (Figure 7-25A). NOTE: If necessary, a second rescuer can provide CPR in this position. The athlete should be secured to the spine board while still in the water. The spine board should be placed diagonally under the victim from the side with the foot end of

A

B

Figure 7-25

For a suspected head or cervical neck injury: A, Place the spine board under the athlete. B, Lift the spine board out of the water.

the board going down into the water first. Slide the board under the victim and allow it to rise directly under the victim. Once on the spine board the athlete's head should be stabilized by one rescuer while the others strap the athlete onto the board, ultimately securing the victim's head. When lifting the spine board out of the water, the rescuer at the head should be in charge and the spine board should be removed head first (Figure 7-25B).

FITTING AND USING THE CRUTCH OR CANE

When an athlete has a lower-limb injury, weight bearing may be contraindicated. Situations of this type call for the use of a crutch or cane. Very often, the athlete is assigned one of these aids without proper fitting or instruction in its use. An improper fit and usage can place abnormal stresses on various body parts. Constant pressure of the body weight on the crutch's axillary pads can cause crutch palsy. This pressure on the axillary radial nerves and blood vessels can lead to temporary or even permanent numbness in the hands. Faulty mechanics in the use of crutches or canes could produce chronic low back and/or hip strain.

Fitting the Athlete

Properly fitting a crutch or cane is essential to avoid placing abnormal stresses on the body.

The adjustable, wooden crutch is well suited to the athlete (Figure 7-26). For a correct fit the athlete should wear low-heeled shoes and stand with good posture and the feet close together. The crutch length is determined

Figure 7-26

The crutch must be properly fitted to the athlete. A, The crutch tips are placed six inches [15 cm] from the outer margin of the shoe and two inches [5 cm] in front of the shoe. B, The underarm crutch brace is positioned one inch [2.5 cm] below the anterior fold of the axilla. C, The hand brace is placed even with the athlete's hand, with the elbow flexed approximately 30 degrees.

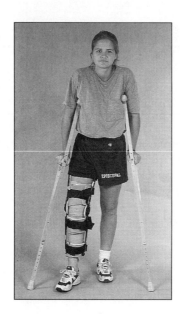
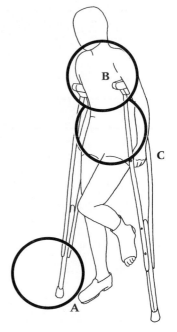

first by placing the tip six inches (15 cm) from the outer margin of the shoe and two inches (5 cm) in front of the shoe. The underarm crutch brace is positioned one inch (2.5 cm) below the anterior fold of the axilla. Next, the hand brace is adjusted so that it is even with the athlete's hand and the elbow is flexed at approximately a 30-degree angle (Figure 7-26). Fitting a cane to the athlete is relatively easy. Measurement is taken from the superior aspect of the greater trochanter of the femur to the floor while the athlete is wearing street shoes.

Walking with the Crutch or Cane

Many elements of crutch walking correspond with walking. The technique commonly used in sports injuries is the tripod method. In this method, the athlete swings through the crutches without making any surface contact with the injured limb or by partially bearing weight with the injured limb. The following sequence is performed:

1. The athlete stands on one foot with the affected foot completely elevated or partially bearing weight.
2. Placing the crutch tips twelve to fifteen inches (30 to 37.5 cm) ahead of the feet, the athlete leans forward, straightens the elbows, pulls the upper crosspiece firmly against the side of the chest, and swings or steps between the stationary crutches (Figure 7-27). The athlete should avoid placing the major support in the axilla.

Figure 7-27

Crutch gait. A, Tripod method. B, Four-point gait

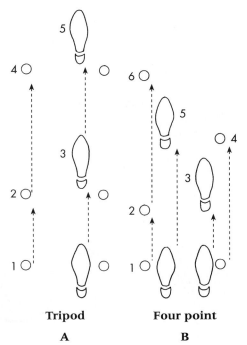

Tripod

A

Four point

B

3. After moving through, the athlete recovers the crutches and again places the tips forward.

An alternate method is the four-point crutch gait. In this method, the athlete stands on both feet. One crutch is moved forward and the opposite foot is stepped forward. The crutch on the same side as the foot that moved forward moves just ahead of the foot. The opposite foot steps forward, followed by the crutch on the same side, and so on.

Once the athlete is able to move effectively on a level surface, negotiating stairs should be taught. As with level crutch walking, a tripod is maintained on stairs. In going upstairs, the unaffected support leg moves up one step while the body weight is supported by the hands. The full weight of the body is transferred to the support leg, followed by moving the crutch tips and affected leg to the step. In going downstairs, the crutch tips and the affected leg move down one step followed by the support leg. If a handrail is available, both crutches are held by the outside hand, and a similar pattern is followed as with the crutch on each side.

CARING FOR SKIN WOUNDS

Skin wounds are extremely common in sports. A wound is defined as trauma to tissues that causes a break in the continuity of that tissue. The skin consists of two layers, the epidermis and the dermis. Because of the soft, pliable nature of skin, it can be easily traumatized. Numerous mechanical forces can injure soft tissue (Figure 7-28). These forces produce friction or rubbing, scraping, compression or pressure, tearing, cutting, and penetration, each of which can adversely affect the skin's integrity. Wounds are classified according to the mechanical force that causes them.

It is of the utmost importance to the well-being of the athlete that open wounds be cared for immediately. All wounds, even those that are relatively superficial, must be considered to be contaminated by microorganisms and therefore must be cleaned, medicated (when called for), and dressed. Dressing wounds requires a sterile environment to prevent infections.[1]

Various types of wounds may be classified as follows (Figure 7-29):

Abrasions are common conditions in which the skin is scraped against a rough surface such as grass, artificial playing surface, floor, or mat. The top layer of skin wears away, exposing numerous blood capillaries. This

Figure 7-28

Mechanical forces that can injure soft tissue: A, Compression. B, Tension. C, Shear

A   B   C

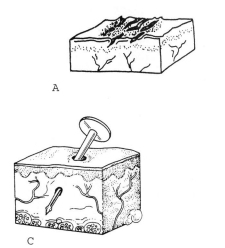

A

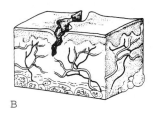

B

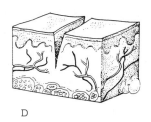

C   D

E

Figure 7-29

Wounds occurring in sports can present a serious problem of infection. A, Abrasion. B, Laceration. C, Puncture. D, Incision. E, Avulsion.

general exposure, with dirt and foreign materials scraping and penetrating the skin, increases the probability of infection unless the wound is properly debrided and cleansed.

Lacerations, also common in sports, occur when a sharp or pointed object tears the tissues, giving a wound the appearance of a jagged-edge cavity. As with abrasions, lacerations present an environment conducive to severe infections. The same mechanism that causes a laceration also can lead to a skin avulsion, in which a piece of skin is ripped off.

Incisions are clean wounds that often appear where a blow has been delivered over a sharp bone or a bone that is poorly padded. They are not as serious as the other types of exposed wounds.

Puncture wounds can easily occur during physical activities and can be fatal. Direct penetration of tissues by a pointed object such as a track shoe spike can introduce the tetanus bacillus into the bloodstream, possibly making the athlete a victim of lockjaw. All puncture wounds and severe lacerations should be referred immediately to a physician.

Avulsion wounds occur when skin is torn from the body and are frequently associated with major bleeding. The avulsed tissue should be placed on moist gauze, preferably saturated with saline solution.[3] It is then put into a plastic bag, immersed in cold water, and taken along with the athlete to the hospital for reattachment.[4]

Wound Infection

Tetanus is a bacterial infection that causes fever and convulsions. Tonic spasm of skeletal muscles is always a possibility for any nonimmunized athlete. The tetanus bacillus enters a wound as a spore and, depending on individual susceptibility, acts on the motor end plate of the central nervous system. After initial childhood immunization by tetanus vaccine, boosters should be given every ten years.[9] An athlete not immunized should receive an injection of tetanus immune globulin (Hyper-Tet) immediately after sustaining a skin wound. Also see the accompanying Focus Box to help reduce wound infections and Table 7-3 for the care of wounds.

SUMMARY

- An emergency is defined as "an unforeseen combination of circumstances and the resulting state that calls for immediate action." The prime concern of emergency aid is to maintain cardiovascular function

TABLE 7-3 Care of skin wounds

Type of Wound	Action of Coach	Initial Care	Follow-up Care
Abrasion	1. Provide initial care. 2. Wound seldom requires medical attention unless infected.	1. Cleanse abraded area with soap and water; debride with brush. 2. Apply an antibiotic ointment to keep abraded surface moist. In sports it is not desirable for abrasions to acquire a scab. Place a nonadherent sterile pad (Telfa pad) over the ointment.	1. Change dressing daily and look for signs of infection.
Laceration	1. Cleanse around the wound. Avoid wiping more contaminating agents into the area. 2. Apply dry, sterile compress pad and refer to physician.	1. Complete cleansing and suturing are accomplished by a physician; injections of tetanus vaccine may be required.	1. Change dressing daily and look for signs of infection.
Puncture	1. Cleanse around the wound. Avoid wiping more contaminating agents into the area. 2. Apply dry, sterile compress pad and refer to physician.	1. Complete cleansing and injections of tetanus vaccine, if needed, are managed by a physician.	1. Change dressing daily and look for signs of infection.
Incision	1. Clean around wound. 2. Apply dry, sterile compress pad to control bleeding and refer to physician.	1. Cleanse wound. 2. Suturing arid injections of tetanus vaccine are managed by a physician, it needed.	1. Change dressing daily and look for signs of infection.
Avulsion	1. Clean around wound; save avulsed tissue. 2. Apply dry, sterile compress pad to control bleeding and refer to physician.	1. Wound is cleansed thoroughly; avulsed skin is replaced and sutured by a physician; tetanus vaccine injection may be required.	1. Change dressing daily and look for signs of infection.

7-2   *Focus Box*

Suggested Practices in Wound Care

The following are suggested procedures to reduce the possibility of wound infections.

1. Make sure all instruments used, such as scissors, tweezers, and swabs, are sterilized.
2. Wash hands thoroughly and put on latex gloves.
3. Clean a skin lesion using soap and water.
4. Place a nonmedicated dressing on a lesion if the athlete is to be sent for medical attention.
5. Avoid touching any parts of a sterile dressing that will come in contact with a wound.
6. Place medication on a pad rather than directly on a lesion.
7. Secure the dressing with tape or a wrap.
8. If necessary, follow the procedures described in this chapter for control of bleeding.

and, indirectly, central nervous system function. All sports programs should have an emergency system that is activated any time an athlete is seriously injured.

- The coach must make a systematic assessment of the injured athlete to determine appropriate emergency care. A primary survey assesses and deals with life-threatening situations. Once stabilized, the secondary survey makes a more detailed assessment of the injury.

- The mnemonic for cardiopulmonary resuscitation is ABC: A—airway opened; B—breathing restored; C—circulation restored. To relieve an obstructed airway, the Heimlich maneuver and/or a finger sweep of the throat should be performed.

- Hemorrhage can occur externally and internally. External bleeding can be controlled by direct pressure, applying pressure at pressure points, and by elevation. Internal hemorrhage can occur subcutaneously, intramuscularly, or within a body cavity.

- Secondary assessment consists of four major areas: history, general observation, physical examination, and special tests. The physical examination includes palpation, movement assessment, and the neurological examination. Special tests may also be warranted, depending on the body site.

- Rest, ice, compression, and elevation (RICE) should be used for the immediate care of a musculoskeletal injury. Ice should be applied for at least twenty minutes every 1 to 1½ hours, while compression and elevation should be continuous for at least seventy-two hours following injury.

- Any suspected fracture should be splinted before the athlete is moved. Commercial rapid form vacuum immobilizers and air splints are most often used in an athletic training setting.

- Great care must be taken in moving the seriously injured athlete. The unconscious athlete must be handled as though he or she has a cervical fracture. Moving an athlete with a suspected serious neck injury must be performed only by persons specifically trained to do so. A spine board should be used, avoiding any movement of the cervical region.

- When removing an injured athlete from a swimming pool, the coach should make every effort to minimize movement of the head and cervical spine while placing them on a spine board in the water.

- The coach should be responsible for the proper fitting and instruction in the use of crutches or a cane by an athlete with an injury to the lower extremity.

- The biggest concern when treating a skin wound is cleaning the wound and preventing infection.

Solutions to Critical Thinking Exercises

7-1 Because of the mechanism of injury, it should be suspected that the athlete has a cervical neck injury. The head should be stabilized throughout. If the athlete is prone and breathing, do nothing until consciousness returns. An on-field exam should determine the athlete's neurological status. Then the athlete should be carefully log-rolled onto a spine board because CPR could be necessary at any time. The face mask should be removed in case CPR is required. The helmet and shoulder pads should be left in place. The athlete should then be transported to the emergency facility. Remember, in this situation the worst mistake the coach can make is not exercising enough caution.

7-2 The coach should first take a subjective history from the injured athlete, followed by an objective examination that includes observation, palpation, range of motion testing, manual muscle testing, special tests, tests for joint stability, and a functional performance evaluation.

7-3 In this case a ligamentous injury is more likely. A injury to a ligament will elicit pain on active and passive movement in the same direction. If an injury is present in muscle tissue, pain will occur on active motion in one direction as well as on passive motion in the opposite direction. A sprain of a ligament will result in pain whenever that ligament is stretched either through active contraction or passive stretching.

7-4 The ankle should be wrapped with a wet elastic compression wrap. Ice should be applied to both sides of the joint over the compression wrap and secured. The ankle should be elevated such that the leg is above 45 degrees at a minimum. The compression wrap, ice, and elevation should be maintained initially for at least thirty minutes but not longer than an hour. The coach should also make some determination as to whether a fracture is suspected and make the appropriate referral.

REVIEW QUESTIONS AND CLASS ACTIVITIES

1. What considerations are important in a well-planned system for handling emergency situations?
2. Discuss the rules for managing and moving an unconscious athlete.
3. What are the life-threatening conditions that should be evaluated in the primary survey?
4. What are the ABCs of life support?
5. Identify the major steps in giving CPR and managing an obstructed airway. When may these procedures be used in a sports setting?
6. List the basic steps in assessing a musculoskeletal injury.
7. What techniques should be used to stop external hemorrhage?
8. What are the signs and symptoms of shock and how do you treat it?
9. What first-aid procedures are used to decrease hemorrhage, inflammation, muscle spasm, and pain from a musculoskeletal injury?
10. Discuss the process for assessing an injury.
11. Describe the basic concepts of emergency splinting.
12. How should an athlete with a suspected spinal injury be transported?
13. What techniques can be used when transporting an athlete with a suspected musculoskeletal injury?
14. Discuss the methods for extracting an injured athlete from a swimming pool.
15. Explain how to properly fit crutches.
16. Discuss the techniques for correctly caring for a wound.

REFERENCES

1. American Red Cross: *First aid; responding to emergencies,* St Louis, 1991, Mosby–Year Book.
2. American Academy of Orthopaedic Surgeons: *Athletic training and sports medicine,* Park Ridge Ill, 1991, American Academy of Orthopaedic Surgeons.
3. Feld F: Management of the critically injured football player, *J Ath Train* 28(3):206, 1993.
4. Hafen BQ, Karren KJ: *First aid for colleges and universities,* Needham Heights, Mass, 1996, Allyn & Bacon.
5. Hoppenfeld S: *Physical examination of the spine and extremities,* New York, 1976, Appleton-Century-Crofts.
6. Kettenbach G: *Writing SOAP notes,* Philadelphia, 1990, FA Davis.
7. Knight K: *Cryotherapy in sport injury management,* Champaign, Ill, 1995, Human Kinetics.
8. Magee DL: *Orthopedic physical assessment,* Philadelphia, 1996, WB Saunders.
9. National Safety Council: *First aid and CPR,* Boston, 1997, Jones & Bartlett.
10. Ortolani A: Letter to the editor: Helmets and face masks, *J Ath Train* 27(4):294, 1992.
11. Parcel GS: *Basic emergency care of the sick and injured,* ed 4, St Louis, 1990, Mosby–Year Book.
12. Putman L: Alternative methods for football helmet face mask removal, *J Ath Train* 27(2):107, 1992.
13. Ray R: Letter to the editor: Helmets and face masks, *J Ath Train* 27(4):294, 1992.
14. Standards and guidelines for cardiopulmonary resuscitation (CPR) and emergency cardiac care (ECC), *JAMA* 255:2841, 1986.
15. Starkey C, Ryan J: *Evaluation of orthopedic and athletic injuries,* Philadelphia, 1996, FA Davis.
16. Thygerson AL: *First aid and emergency care workbook,* Boston, 1989, National Safety Council and Jones & Bartlett.

17. Walton M et al: Effects of ice packs on tissue temperatures at various depths before and after quadriceps hematoma: studies using sheep, *J Orthop Sports Phys Ther* 8:294, 1986.

18. Wilkerson GB: External compression for controlling traumatic edema, *Physician Sportsmed* 13:96, 1985.

ANNOTATED BIBLIOGRAPHY

American Red Cross: *First aid; responding to emergencies,* St Louis, 1996, Mosby–Year Book.

A well-illustrated, simple approach to the treatment of emergency illness and injury.

Hoppenfeld S: *Physical examination of the spine and extremities,* New York, 1976, Appleton-Century-Crofts.

Presents an easy-to-follow, methodical, and in-depth procedure for examining musculoskeletal conditions.

Magee DJ: *Orthopedic physical assessment,* Philadelphia, 1996, WB Saunders.

An extremely well-illustrated book, with excellent depth of coverage. Its strength lies in its coverage of injuries commonly found during athletic training.

National Safety Council, *First aid and CPR,* Boston, 1997, Jones & Bartlett.

A complete and widely used first-aid text that addresses all aspects of first aid and CPR.

Parcel GS: *Basic emergency care of the sick and injured,* ed 4, St Louis, 1990, Mosby–Year Book.

Presents wide coverage of emergency care. Of special interest are Chapter 2, Legal Considerations Involved in Emergency Care by Nonmedical Personnel, and Section 3, Trauma Emergencies.

Starkey C, Ryan J: *Evaluation of orthopedic and athletic injuries,* Philadelphia, 1996, FA Davis.

A detailed, well-illustrated text that addresses all aspects of injury assessment for the athletic trainer.

WEB SITES

American Red Cross: http://redcross.org/what.html

The American Red Cross offers many emergency services and training. This site describes those services as well as introduces information about various training opportunities.

American Heart Association: http://www.amhrt.org

World Wide Wounds: The Electronic Journal of Wound Management Practice: http://www.smtl.co.uk/World-Wide-Wounds

Lists interesting and informative information for health care professionals on the current management of wounds.

Cervical Spine Stabilization: http://www.trauma.org/spine/cspine-stab.html

Bloodborne Pathogens

When you finish you will be able to:

- Explain what bloodborne pathogens are and how they can infect coaches and athletes.
- Describe the transmission, symptoms and signs, and treatment of hepatitis B (HBV).
- Describe the transmission, symptoms, and signs of Human Immunodeficiency Virus (HIV) infection.
- Describe how HIV is most often transmitted.
- List the pros and cons of sports participation of athletes with an HBV or HIV infection.
- Identify universal precautions as mandated by the Occupational Safety and Health Administration and how they apply to the coach.

I t has always been important for any health care provider to be concerned with maintaining an environment that is as clean and sterile as possible.[1,9] In our 1990s society, it has become critical for everyone in the population to take measures to prevent the spread of infectious diseases.[8] Failure to do so may predispose any individual to potentially life-threatening situations.

Because of the close physical contact that occurs through athletic participation, the potential for spread of infectious disease among coaches, athletes, and sports medicine personnel is of major concern. The coach must be aware of the potential dangers of exposure to blood or other infectious materials and take whatever measures are necessary to prevent contamination (Figure 8-1).

WHAT ARE BLOODBORNE PATHOGENS?

Bloodborne pathogens are pathogenic microorganisms that can potentially cause disease. They may be present in human blood and other bodily fluids including semen, vaginal secretions, cerebrospinal fluid, synovial fluid, and any other fluid contaminated with blood. The two most significant bloodborne pathogens include the hepatitis B virus (HBV) and the human immunodeficiency virus (HIV). A number of other bloodborne diseases exist, including hepatitis C, hepatitis D, and syphilis. Although HIV has been more widely addressed in the media, HBV has a higher possibility for spread.[12] HBV is stronger and more durable than HIV.[9] HBV

Bloodborne pathogens:
Hepatitis B (HBV)
Human immunodeficiency virus (HIV)

Mode of transmission:
Human blood
Semen
Vaginal secretions
Cerebrospinal fluid
Synovial fluid

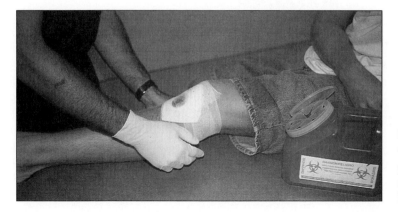

Figure 8-1

The coach must take
precautions to prevent
exposure and transmission of
bloodborne pathogens.

can be spread more easily via sharp objects, open wounds, or bodily fluids when compared to HIV.

Hepatitis B Virus

HBV is a major cause of viral infection that results in swelling, soreness, and loss of normal function in the liver. The number of cases of HBV has risen dramatically during the last ten years.[16]

Signs of HBV

The signs in a person infected with HBV include flulike symptoms such as fatigue, weakness, nausea, abdominal pain, headache, fever, and possible jaundice. It is possible that an individual infected with HBV will exhibit no signs or symptoms and may go undetected. In these individuals, the HBV antigen will always be present and thus the disease may be unknowingly transmitted to others through exposure to blood or other bodily fluids or by intimate contact.

An infected person's blood may test positive for the HBV antigen within two to six weeks after the symptoms develop. Approximately 85 percent of those infected recover within six to eight weeks.

Prevention

Good personal hygiene and avoiding high-risk activities is the best way to avoid HBV.[9] HBV can survive for at least one week in dried blood or on contaminated surfaces and may be transmitted through contact with these surfaces. Caution must be taken to avoid contact with any blood or other fluid that potentially contains a bloodborne pathogen.

A vaccine is now available that can prevent contraction of HBV. The vaccine requires a series of three innoculations spread over a six-month period. In 1991 the Occupational Safety and Health Administration OSHA mandated that vaccination against HBV must be made available by an employer at no cost to any individual who may be exposed to blood or other bodily fluids and may thus be at risk of contacting hepatitis B.[17] *All coaches,*

OSHA: Occupational Health
and Safety Administration

as well as any individual working in an allied health care profession who may potentially come in contact with blood, should receive HBV immunization.

Human Immunodeficiency Virus

HIV infection is caused by a family of complex viruses that invade normal healthy cells, thus decreasing the effectiveness of the host cell in preventing disease. HIV is a viral infection that has the potential to eventually destroy the immune system. The rapid increase in the number of known individuals who are HIV positive is alarming. The World Health Organization estimates that worldwide there are more than ten to twelve million adult carriers of the virus, with forty million estimated by the year 2000.[19]

Symptoms and Signs

As is the case with HBV, HIV is transmitted by exposure to infected blood or other bodily fluids or by intimate sexual contact. Symptoms of HIV include fatigue, weight loss, muscle or joint pain, painful or swollen glands, night sweats, and fever. HIV antibodies can be detected in a blood test within a year following exposure. Like people with HBV, people with HIV may be unaware that they have contracted the virus and may go as long as eight to ten years before developing any signs or symptoms. Unfortunately most individuals who test positive for HIV have a high probability of eventually developing AIDS. Table 8-1 summarizes information on HBV and HIV.

AIDS: Acquired
immunodeficiency syndrome

Acquired Immunodeficiency Syndrome

AIDS is an acronym for acquired immunodeficiency syndrome. A syndrome is a collection of signs and symptoms that are recognized as the effects of an infection. A person who has AIDS has no protection against even the simplest infections and thus is extremely vulnerable to developing a variety of illnesses, opportunistic infections, and/or cancers that cannot be stopped.[4] A positive HIV test cannot predict when the individ-

TABLE 8-1 HBV and HIV transmission

Disease	Symptoms & Signs	Mode of Transmission	Infectious Material
Hepatitis B	Flulike, jaundice	Direct & Indirect contact	Blood, saliva, semen, feces, and food, water, and other products
HIV	Fever, night sweats, weight loss, diarrhea, severe fatigue, swollen lymph nodes, lesions	Direct & Indirect contact	Blood, semen, vaginal fluid

ual might show the symptoms of AIDS. Those individuals who develop AIDS generally die within two years after the symptoms appear.

Management

Unlike HBV, there is no vaccine for HIV. Much research is being done to find a preventive vaccine and an effective treatment. Presently, it appears that certain combinations of various antiviral drugs, which have been labeled "cocktails," can slow replication of the virus and improve prospects for survival.

Prevention

The best means for prevention is through education.[11] Coaches should take the responsibility of educating their athletes about HIV. Athletes must be made to understand that their greatest risk for contracting HIV is through intimate sexual contact with an infected partner and not through contact that occurs during athletic participation. Practicing safe sex is of major importance. (See the accompanying Focus Box.) The athlete must choose nonpromiscuous sex partners and use condoms for vaginal or anal intercourse. Latex condoms provide a barrier against both HBV and HIV. Male condoms should have reservoir tips to reduce the chance of ejaculate being released from the sides of the condom. Condoms that are prelubricated are less likely to tear. Water-based, greaseless spermicides or lubricants should be avoided. If the condom tears, a vaginal spermicide should be used immediately. The condom should carefully be removed and discarded.[19]

> HIV is most often transmitted through intimate sexual contact.

> The use of latex condoms can reduce the chances of contracting HIV.

DEALING WITH BLOODBORNE PATHOGENS IN ATHLETICS

In general the chances of transmitting HIV among athletes is low. There is minimal risk of on-field transmission of HIV from one player to another in sports.[18] One study involving professional football estimated the risk of transmission from player to player was less than one per one million

---

8-1 > *Focus Box*

HIV Risk Reduction

- Avoid contact with others' bodily fluids, feces, and semen.
- Avoid sharing needles (e.g., injecting anabolic steroids or human growth hormones).
- Choose nonpromiscuous sex partners.
- Limit sex partners.
- Consistently use condoms.
- Avoid drugs that alter good judgment.
- Avoid sex with known HIV carriers.
- Get regular tests for sexually transmitted diseases (STDs).
- Practice good hygiene before and after sex.

games. In fact, at this writing there have been no validated reports of HIV transmission in sports.[15]

Sports that have a potentially higher risk for transmission are ones that involve close physical contact and possible direct contact with the blood of another person.[10] Sports such as the martial arts, wrestling, and boxing have more theoretical potential for transmission.[15] (See the accompanying Focus Box.)

Policy Regulation

Athletes participating in organized sports are subject to procedures and policies relative to transmission of bloodborne pathogens.[13] The United States Olympic Committee (USOC), the National Collegiate Athletic Association (NCAA), the National Federation of State High School Athletic Associations, the National Basketball Association, the National Hockey League, the National Football League, and Major League Baseball have established policies to help prevent the transmission of bloodborne pathogens. They have also initiated programs to help educate athletes under their control.

All institutions should take the responsibility for educating their student-athletes about how bloodborne pathogens are transmitted. Efforts should also be made to educate the parents of high-school athletes.[6] Professional, collegiate, and high-school athletes should be made to understand that the real risk of contracting HBV or HIV is through their off-the-field activities, which may include unsafe sexual practices and sharing needles, particularly in the use of steroids. Athletes, perhaps more than other individuals in the population, think that they are immune and that infection will always happen to someone else.

Each institution should implement policies and procedures concerning bloodborne pathogens.[18] A recent survey of NCAA institutions found that a large number of health care providers at many colleges and universities demonstrated significant deficits in following the universal guidelines mandated by OSHA. In a sports medicine or other health care

8-1

Critical Thinking Exercise

A wrestler comes to his coach with concern about the possibility of contracting HIV from wrestling with a sweaty partner.

? What can the coach tell this athlete to help him ease his fear?

> 8-2 > **Focus Box**

Risk Categories for Sports[10]

- Greatest risk: Boxing, tae kwon do, wrestling, rugby
- Moderate risk: Basketball, field hockey, football, ice hockey, judo, soccer, team handball
- Lowest risk: Archery, badminton, baseball, bowling, canoeing/kayaking, cycling, diving, equestrian sports, fencing, figure skating, gymnastics, modern pentathalon, raquetball, rhythmic gymnastics, roller skating, rowing, shooting, softball, speed skating, skiing, swimming, synchronized swimming, table tennis, volleyball, water polo, weightlifting, yachting

setting, following these universal precautions would protect the athlete, the coach, and the health care providers.[14]

HIV and Athletic Participation

There is no definitive answer as to whether asymptomatic HIV carriers should participate in sports. Bodily fluid contact should obviously be avoided, and the participant should also avoid engaging in exhaustive exercise that may lead to an increased susceptibility to infection.[12]

The Americans with Disabilities Act of 1991 states that athletes infected with HIV cannot be discriminated against and may be excluded from participation only on a medically sound basis. Exclusion must be based on objective medical evidence that takes into consideration the risk of infection to others and of potential harm to self and what means can be taken to reduce this risk.[15]

Testing Athletes for HIV

HIV testing should not be used as a screening tool to determine if an athlete can participate in sports. Mandatory testing for HIV may not be allowed for legal reasons related to the Americans with Disabilities Act. In terms of importance, mandatory testing should be secondary to education to prevent transmission of HIV. Neither the NCAA nor the Centers for Disease Control and Prevention (CDC) recommends mandatory HIV testing for athletes.[18]

Athletes who engage in high-risk activities should be encouraged to seek voluntary anonymous testing for HIV. A blood test may be able to detect the presence of the HIV virus within three months to one year following exposure. Testing therefore should occur at six weeks, at three months, and at one year.[19]

Many states have enacted laws that protect the confidentiality of the HIV-infected person. Coaches should be familiar with the laws of their state and make every effort to guard the confidentiality and anonymity of HIV testing for their athletes.

UNIVERSAL PRECAUTIONS IN AN ATHLETIC ENVIRONMENT

The guidelines instituted by OSHA were developed to protect the health care provider and the patient against bloodborne pathogens.[16] It is essential that every sports program develop and carry out a bloodborne pathogen exposure control plan. This plan should include counseling, education, volunteer testing, and the management of bodily fluids.[18]

OSHA's guidelines should be followed by anyone coming in contact with blood or other bodily fluids. Following are considerations specific to the sports arena.

For additional information on HIV and AIDS care, contact the Centers for Disease Control and Prevention (CDC) National AIDS Hotline: 1-800-342-2437.

Preparing the Athlete

Before an athlete participates in practice or competition, all open skin wounds or lesions must be covered with a dressing that is fixed in place and does not allow for transmission to or from an athlete. An occlusive

Critical Thinking Exercise

A soccer player jumps to win a head ball and an opponent's head smashes the right eyebrow, creating a significant laceration. The athlete is conscious but is bleeding profusely from the wound.

? What techniques are most effective to control the bleeding, and what should be done to close the wound?

Latex gloves should be worn whenever the athletic trainer deals with blood or bodily fluids.

dressing lessens the chances of cross-contamination and also reduces chances of the wound reopening by keeping it moist and pliable.[16]

When Bleeding Occurs

As mandated by the NCAA and the USOC, open wounds or other skin lesions considered a risk for disease transmission should be provided with aggressive treatment.[10] Athletes with active bleeding must be removed from participation as soon as possible and only returned when it is deemed safe by the medical staff.[7] Uniforms containing blood must be evaluated for infectivity. A uniform that is saturated with blood must be removed and changed before the athlete can return to competition. All personnel managing potential infective wound exposures must follow universal precautions.[16]

Personal Precautions

The coach or health care personnel working directly with bodily fluids on the field must make use of the appropriate protective equipment in all cases in which there is potential contact with bloodborne pathogens. Protective equipment includes disposable latex gloves, gowns, or aprons; masks and shields; eye protection; nonabsorbant gowns; and disposable mouthpieces for resuscitation devices.[5] *One-time use latex gloves must be used when handling any potentially infectious material.* Double gloving is suggested when there is heavy bleeding or when sharp instruments are used. Gloves are always carefully removed following their use (see the accompanying Focus Box). In cases of emergency, heavy toweling may be used until gloves can be obtained.[1]

Hands and all skin surfaces that come in contact with blood or other bodily fluids should be washed immediately with soap and water or other antigermicidal agents.

First-aid kits must have protection for hands, face, and eyes as well as resuscitation mouthpieces. Kits should also make towelettes available for cleaning skin surface.[3]

8-3 > **Focus Box**

Glove Removal and Use

1. Avoid touching personal items when wearing contaminated gloves.
2. Remove first glove and turn inside out, beginning at the wrist and peeling off without touching skin.
3. Remove second glove making sure not to touch ungloved hand to soiled surfaces.
4. Discard gloves that have been used, discolored, torn, or punctured.
5. Wash hands immediately after glove removal.

Availability of Supplies and Equipment

In keeping with universal precautions, the sports program must also have available chlorine bleach, antiseptics, proper receptacles for soiled equipment and uniforms, wound care bandages, and a designated container for sharps disposal such as needles, syringes, or scalpels.[7]

Biohazard warning labels should be fixed to regulated wastes, refrigerators containing blood, and other containers used to store or ship potentially infectious materials (Figure 8-2). The labels are fluorescent orange or red and should be affixed to containers. Red bags or containers should be used for disposal of potentially infected materials.

Universal precautions minimize the risk of exposure and transmission.

Disinfectants

All contaminated surfaces, such as the field or court, should be cleaned immediately with a solution consisting of one part bleach to ten parts water (1:10) or with a disinfectant approved by the Environmental Protection Agency.[6] Disinfectants should inactivate the virus. Towels or other linens that have been contaminated should be bagged and separated from other laundry. Soiled linen is to be transported in red containers or bags that prevent soaking or leaking and are labeled with the biohazard warn-

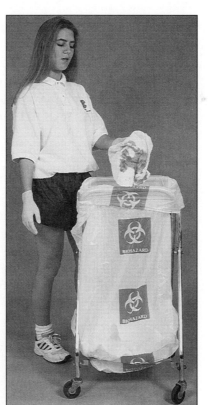

Figure 8-2

Soiled linens should be placed in a leakproof bag marked as a biohazard.

Sharps:
Scalpels
Razor blades
Needles

ing labels (Figure 8-2). Contaminated laundry should be washed in hot water (71°C for twenty-five minutes) using a detergent that deactivates the virus. Laundry done outside the institution should be taken to a facility that follows OSHA standards. Gloves must be worn during bagging and cleaning of contaminated laundry.

Sharps

Sharps refers to sharp objects such as needles, razor blades, and scalpels. Extreme care should be taken when handling and disposing of sharps to minimize risk of puncturing or cutting the skin. OSHA mandates that sharps should be disposed of in a leakproof and puncture-resistant container.[6] The container should be red in color and labeled as a biohazard (Figure 8-3).

Protecting the Athlete from Exposure

Several additional recommendations may further help protect the athlete. The USOC supports the required use of mouthpieces in those high-risk sports listed in the Focus Box on page 204. All athletes should shower immediately after practice or competition. Athletes who may be exposed to HIV or HBV should be evaluated for immunization against HBV.

POSTEXPOSURE PROCEDURES

Following a report of an exposure incident, the exposed individual should have a confidential medical evaluation that includes documentation of the exposure route, identification of the source individual, a blood test, counseling, and an evaluation of reported illness.[2] Again, the laws that pertain to reporting and notification of the test results relative to confidentiality vary from state to state.[17]

Figure 8-3

Sharps should be disposed of in a red, puncture-resistant, plastic container marked as a biohazard.

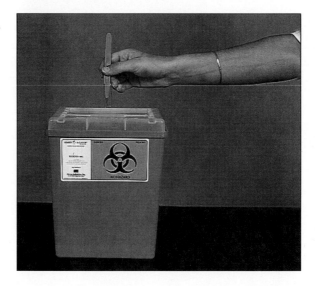

SUMMARY

- Bloodborne pathogens are microorganisms that can potentially cause disease and are present in human blood and other bodily fluids, including semen, vaginal secretions, synovial fluid, and any other fluid contaminated with blood. Hepatitis B (HBV) and human immunodeficiency virus (HIV) are bloodborne pathogens.

- A vaccine is available to prevent HBV. Currently no effective vaccine exists for treating HIV.

- An individual infected with HIV may develop acquired immunodeficiency syndrome (AIDS), which is fatal.

- The risks of contracting HBV or HIV may be minimized by avoiding exposure to blood and other bodily fluids and by practicing safe sex.

- The risk of an athlete being exposed to bloodborne pathogens on the field is minimal. Off-the-field activities involving risky sexual behaviors pose the greatest threat for transmission.

- Various national medical and sports organizations have established policies and procedures for dealing with bloodborne pathogens in the athletic population.

- The Occupational Health and Safety Administration (OSHA) has established rules and regulations that protect the health care employee.

- Universal precautions must be taken to avoid bloodborne pathogen exposure. All sports programs must carry out a plan for counseling, education, volunteer testing, and the management of exposure.

Solutions to Critical Thinking Exercises

8-1 Athletes must be made to understand that their greatest risk for contracting HIV is through intimate sexual contact with an infected partner and not through contact that occurs during athletic participation. It is highly unlikely that sweat carries HIV. However, this athlete should become concerned if his opponent begins bleeding; he should wait until the bleeding has been controlled and the wound securely covered before resuming physical contact.

8-2 The coach must first take precautions to protect against the transmission of bloodborne pathogens. The wound should be cleaned with soap and water. Direct pressure using a gauze pad should be applied along with cold. The athlete, if not dizzy, should remain in a sitting position and should be referred to a physician for suturing. Sterile strips or a butterfly bandage may also be applied, although sutures will generally leave a smaller scar. All blood-contaminated supplies should be disposed of in a clearly marked biohazard bag.

REVIEW QUESTIONS AND CLASS ACTIVITIES

1. Define and identify the bloodborne pathogens.
2. Discuss HBV transmission, symptoms and signs, prevention, and treatment.

3. Discuss the pros and cons of allowing the participation of an athlete who is an HBV carrier.
4. Discuss HIV transmission, symptoms and signs, prevention, and treatment.
5. How is HIV transmitted and why is it eventually fatal at this time?
6. Should an athlete who tests positive for HBV or HIV be allowed to participate in sports?
7. How can an athlete avoid the risk of HIV infection?
8. Define OSHA and discuss its universal precautions for preventing exposure to bloodborne pathogens.
9. What precautions would a coach take when caring for a bleeding athlete on the field?

REFERENCES

1. American Academy of Pediatrics: Human immunodeficiency virus [acquired immunodeficiency syndrome (AIDS) virus] in athletic settings, *Pediatrics* 88:640, 1991.
2. American College Health Association: *General statement of institutional response to AIDS.* Rockville, Md, 1988, Task Force on AIDS, American College Health Association.
3. American Medical Association Department of HIV, Division of Health Science: *Digest of HIV/AIDS policy,* Chicago, Ill, 1993, Department of HIV, American Medical Association.
4. American Medical Society for Sports Medicine and the American Academy for Sports Medicine: Human immunodeficiency virus (HIV) and bloodborne pathogens in sport: joint position statement, *Am J Sports Med,* 23:510, 1995.
5. American Red Cross: *First aid: responding to emergencies.* St Louis, 1995, Mosby–Year Book.
6. Arnold BL: A review of selected blood-borne pathogen position statements and federal regulations, *J Ath Train* 30 (2):171, 1995.
7. Benson M: *1994–1995 NCAA sports medicine handbook,* Overland Park, Kan, 1994, NCAA.
8. Brown L, Dortman P: What is the risk of HIV infection in athletic competition? International Conference on AIDS 19939:PO-C21-3102, 1993.
9. Buxton BP et al: Prevention of hepatitis B virus in athletic training. *J Ath Train* 29 (2):107, 1994.
10. Garl T, Hrisomalos T, Rink R: *Transmission of infectious agents during athletic competition,* 1991, USOC Sports Medicine and Science Committee.
11. Hamann B: *Disease: identification, prevention, and control,* St Louis, 1994, Mosby.
12. Howe WB: The athlete with chronic illness. In Birrer RB, editor: *Sports medicine for the primary care physician,* ed 2, Boca Raton, Fla 1994, CRC Press.
13. Landry GL: HIV infection and athletes. *Sports Med Digest* 15 (4):1, 1993.
14. McGrew C, Dick R, Schneidewind K: Survey of NCAA institutions concerning HIV/AIDS policies and universal precautions, *Med Sci Sports Exerc* 25:917, 1993.
15. Mitten MJ: HIV-positive athletes, *Physician Sportsmed* 22 (10):63, 1994.
16. National Safety Council: *Bloodborne pathogens,* Boston, Mass, 1993, Jones & Bartlett.
17. OSHA: The OSHA bloodborne pathogens standard, *Federal Register* 55(235):64175, 1991.
18. Rogers KJ: Human immunodeficiency virus in sports. In Torg JS, Shephard RJ, editors: *Current therapy in sports medicine,* St Louis, 1995, Mosby.
19. Seltzer DG: Educating athletes on HIV disease and AIDS, *Physician Sportmed* 21 (1):109, 1993.

ANNOTATED BIBLIOGRAPHY

Benson MA, editor: *National Collegiate Athletic Association 1994–95 sports medicine handbook,* Overland Park, Kan, 1994.

   A complete discussion of bloodborne pathogens and Intercollegiate athletic policies and administration.

Hall K et al, eds: *Bloodborne pathogens,* National Safety Council, Boston, Mass, 1993, Jones & Bartlett.

   A manual that presents OSHA's regulations specific to bloodborne pathogens.

Hamann B: *Disease: identification, prevention, and control,* St Louis, 1994, Mosby.

   Designed for health educators; detailed coverage of AIDS and hepatitis.

WEB SITES

Occupational Safety and Health Administration (OSHA): http://www.osha.gov

Department of Health and Human Services: http://www.os.dhhs.gov

HIV/AIDS Prevention: http://cdc.gov/nchstp/hiv_aids/dhap.htm

Centers for Disease Control and Prevention: http://www.cdc.gov

National Institute of Health: http://www.nib.gov

Chapter 9

Psychological Aspects of Sports Injury

When you finish this chapter you will be able to:

- Describe the athlete's psychological responses to stressors imposed by competition.
- Define the psychology of loss.
- Describe personality factors that can lead to sports injuries.
- Identify the psychological reactions that can be experienced by the ill or injured athlete.
- Identify attitudes in an athlete that can be of assistance rehabilitation and reconditioning.
- Describe how a coach can assist a seriously injured athlete to safely reenter competition.

M*ens sana in corpore sano,* or "a sound mind in a sound body," is the concept of mind-body relationship that we have accepted since the time of the early Greeks. The injured or ill athlete experiences not only physical disability but also, in many cases, adverse psychological reactions. The coach must understand how feelings and emotions enter into an athlete's response to a serious injury or illness.

STRESS IN SPORT

stress
The positive and negative forces that can disrupt the body's equilibrium.

Sports participation is both a physical and an emotional stressor.

Stress is not something that an athlete can do to his or her body, but it is something that the brain tells the athlete is happening.[12] When change occurs, the brain interprets that change and tells the body how to react to it. In other words, stress does not necessarily imply negative responses but can be a reaction to intense pleasure (Figure 9-1).

Sports participation serves as both a physical and an emotional stressor. Stress can be a positive or negative influence. All living organisms are endowed with the ability to cope effectively with stressful situations. Pelletier[12] stated: "Without stress, there would be very little constructive activity or positive change." Negative stress can contribute to poor health, whereas positive stress produces growth and development. A healthy life must have a balance of stress; too little causes a "rusting out," and too much stress can cause "burnout."

Athletes place their bodies in countless daily stress situations. Their

Figure 9-1

Sports participation offers the
athlete many negative and
positive stressors.

bodies undergo numerous "fight-or-flight" reactions to avoid injury or
other threatening situations. Inappropriate adjustment to fight-or-flight
responses can eventually lead to emotional or physical illness.

Physiological Responses to Stress

Stress is a **psychophysiological** phenomenon. A serious injury or illness
are major stressors for the athlete. Three stages characterize a stressor:
the alarm stage, the resistance stage, and the exhaustion stage.[14]

| psychophysiological |
| Involving the mind and the body. |

Alarm

In the alarm stage, secretions from the adrenal glands sharply increase,
creating the well-known flight-or-fight response. With adrenaline in the
blood stream, pupils dilate, hearing becomes more acute, muscles become
more responsive, and blood pressure increases to facilitate the absorption
of oxygen. In addition to these responses, respiration and heart rate increase to further prepare the body for action.

Resistance

After the alarm stage, the body gradually changes to the resistance stage.
The body prepares itself for coping by diminishing the adrenocortical secretions and directing stress to a particular body site. This stage is the
body's way of resisting the stressor. The physiological response may remain high and could eventually lead to the final stage, exhaustion.

Stress can be acute or
chronic.

Critical Thinking Exercise

A world-class sprinter tears his
left hamstring muscle, which
eliminates him from the
Olympic trials.

? What could be the psychological ramifications to this
athlete?

Psychological reactions to a
serious sport injury may
include:
Denial or disbelief
Anger
Bargaining
Depression
Acceptance

Exhaustion

The exhaustion stage refers to a single organ or to an entire organ system that succumbs to chronic stress and eventually to disease. Chronic stress can adversely affect brain function, the autonomic nervous system, the endocrine system, and the immune system, eventually leading to a psychosomatic illness.[3]

An athlete who is removed from a sport because of an injury or illness reacts in a very personal way. The athlete who has trained diligently, who has looked forward to a successful competitive season, and who is suddenly thwarted in that goal by injury or illness may become emotionally devastated.[10]

The Psychology of Loss

Athletes who have suddenly sustained an injury or illness that keep them from performing in their sport for a long period of time will usually develop psychological reactions of loss. They will experience some or all of the following reactions: denial or disbelief, anger, bargaining, depression, and acceptance of the situation[7] (see the accompanying Focus Box). These athletes may feel numb and unable to grasp the full consequences of the situation.[14] They might have thought that they were impervious to injury or serious illness. When these athletes realize that they are no longer able to participate, they may experience low self-esteem, worthlessness, and self-reproach.[8]

Although some athletes experience minimal mood disturbances after

---

 Focus Box

Psychological Reactions to Loss

Denial or disbelief
Soon after becoming disabled and unable to perform, the athlete will commonly deny the seriousness of the condition.

Anger
Anger often follows disbelief. As the athlete slowly becomes aware of the seriousness of the injury, a sense of anger develops.

Bargaining
As the anger becomes less intense, the athlete gradually realizes the true nature and extent of the injury or illness and, with this awareness, begins to have doubts and fears about the ability to fully recover, which leads to a need to bargain. Bargaining may be a prayer for help or putting pressure on the medical team to speed their healing process.

Depression
As the athlete becomes increasingly aware of the nature of the injury and of the time that will be needed for healing, depression can set in.

Acceptance
Hopefully the athlete eventually begins to feel less dejected and isolated and becomes resigned to the situation.

a serious injury or illness, others may experience a major depression.[15] Athletes with deep depression may be at risk for suicide.[16] The profile for an at-risk athlete is as follows:

- The athlete belongs to the high-risk group between fifteen and twenty-four years of age.
- The athlete sustains a serious injury requiring surgery.
- The athlete faces a long rehabilitation period.
- The athlete is replaced by a teammate.

Athletes with a painful injury requiring surgery may express other behavioral signs, such as exaggerated pain, complaints of sleep disturbances, feelings of fatigue, and moodiness.[13]

PERSONALITY FACTORS LEADING TO INJURY

Even when high-risk situations are ruled out, some athletes seem to receive more than their share of injuries.[6] A number of psychological factors can predispose an athlete to be accident prone: high **anxiety,** abnormal physical tension, restlessness and/or nervousness, insecurity, poor self-esteem, and low level of confidence. Chronically depressed individuals are more injury prone. Athletes who are undisciplined in developing good sports skills and who lack structure in their personal and social life can be accident prone.[6]

Accident-prone athletes are most likely to suffer an injury toward the end of a long, intense, sustained period of work. Fatigue always plays an integral part in sports injuries.

Overtraining and Staleness

An imbalance between the physical load placed on an athlete and the athlete's coping capacity can lead to overtraining and **staleness.**[1,5] This condition is also known as burnout, overreaching, overwork, or an overtraining syndrome.[6] Both physiological and psychological factors underlie overtraining and staleness.

Staleness

There are countless reasons why athletes become stale in their sport. They may be training too hard without proper rest, or they may have emotional problems stemming from daily worries, fears, and anxieties. An overzealous coach who acts like a drill sergeant can cause athletes to develop symptoms of overstress (Figure 9-2). Coaches must provide their athletes with positive reinforcements while avoiding negative statements. A losing season commonly produces stale athletes.[2] Worries about school, outside work, or family can increase the probability for staleness. Coaches should be aware that the athlete who shows signs of staleness is prone to acute and overuse injuries as well as infections.[6] Stress fractures and tendinitus are typical injuries that can occur during a time of staleness. (See the accompanying Focus Box.)

9-2

Critical Thinking Exercise

A seventeen-year-old world-class gymnast sustains a major knee injury after a horizontal bar dismount. The injury may end the athlete's career. As a result of this injury the athlete becomes very depressed.

? What should the coach be concerned with in terms of this athlete's emotional stability?

---

anxiety
A feeling of uncertainty or apprehension.

Accident-prone athletes are most likely to suffer an injury at the end of a long, hard practice or the end of a losing season.

Staleness refers to a loss of vigor, initiative, and successful performance.

A coach who is stingy with praise and overcritical can produce overstressed athletes.

Figure 9-2

A coach with a negative attitude can cause the athlete to become stressed and to even become burned out over time.

Overtraining

It is generally accepted that sports are stressors to the athlete. There is often a fine line between the athlete's reaching and maintaining peak performance and overtraining. Besides the actual demands of a sport, peripheral stressors can be imposed, such as unreasonable expectations by the athlete, by the coach, and/or by the parents.

The Coach

The coach is often the first person to identify an athlete who is becoming burned out.

The coach is often the first person to notice that an athlete is overstressed. The athlete whose performance is declining and whose personality is changing may need a training program that is less demanding. A serious talk with the athlete by the coach might reveal underlying emotional problems for which the athlete should be referred to a counselor or psychotherapist.

The Athletic Trainer

Injury prevention is both psychological and physiological. The athlete who enters a contest while angry, frustrated, or discouraged or while un-

| 9-2 | *Focus Box*

Recognizing Staleness in Athletes

An athlete who is becoming stale will often display some or most of the following signs. He or she may

- Show a decrease in performance level.
- Have difficulty falling asleep.
- Be awakened from sleep for no apparent reason.
- Experience a loss of appetite or weight loss because of anxiety.
- Have indigestion.
- Have difficulty concentrating.
- Have difficulty enjoying sex.
- Experience nausea for no apparent reason.
- Be prone to colds or allergic reactions.
- Be restless, irritable, anxious, or depressed.
- Have an elevated resting heart rate and elevated blood pressure.
- Display psychosomatic episodes of perceiving bodily pains, especially before competing.

dergoing some other disturbing emotional state is more prone to injury. The angry player, for example, who wants to vent ire in some way loses perspective of desirable and approved conduct. An athlete in the grip of uncontrolled anger will lose skill and coordination, which could result in an injury.

The Physician

The team physician, like the coach and the athletic trainer, plays an integral part with the athlete who is overstressed. Many emotional responses thought to be from stress may, in reality, stem from an undetected physical problem that requires medical attention.[16]

REACTING TO ATHLETES WITH INJURIES

No matter what reactions the athlete displays, he or she must be responded to as a person, not as an injury. An injured athlete may be difficult to be around, especially in the early stages of the condition. Part of this reaction is that the athlete is suddenly forced to be dependent and helpless.[16] While in this state the athlete may regress to childlike behaviors and may direct displaced anger toward the coach or person(s) administering first aid (Table 9-1). Comfort, care, and communication must be given freely during this time.[16]

Those persons who work directly with the athlete need to be honest, supportive, and respectful while he or she is disabled. Coaches should make a major effort to understand the athlete at a deeper level and to observe how he or she is coping.[13]

A number of questions should be asked: Is there a good doctor-

TABLE 9-1 Emotional first aid

Type of Emotional Reaction	Outward Signs	Trainer's Reactions	
		Yes	No
Normal	Weakness, trembling Nausea, vomiting Perspiration Diarrhea Fear, anxiety Heart pounding	Be calm and reassuring	Avoid pity
Overreaction	Excessive talking Argumentativeness Inappropriate joke telling Hyperactivity	Allow athlete to vent emotions	Avoid telling athlete he or she is acting abnormally
Underreaction	Depression; sitting or standing numbly Little talking if any Emotionless Confusion Failure to respond to questions	Be empathetic; encourage talking to express feelings	Avoid being abrupt; avoid pity

patient relationship stemming from confidence, trust, and optimism?[11] Does the athlete have a fear of pending surgery? How long is the recovery period? What is the possibility of reinjury? Is forced retirement a possibility, and if so, how good is the athlete's potential for healthy adjustment? What are the athlete's attitudes toward engaging in a program of rehabilitation and reconditioning?[11]

ATTITUDES TOWARD REHABILITATION AND RECONDITIONING

The athlete's psyche is a large factor in any program of rehabilitation and reconditioning exercise. Success in treatment of the athlete depends on the cooperation of the athlete with the athletic trainer and the physician. The coach can play an integral role in helping the injured athlete maximize his or her efforts in the rehabilitation and reconditioning process.[4]

The coach must be supportive of the athlete's efforts. The coach must encourage the athlete to feel a major responsibility toward recovery. The athlete must not miss or even arrive late for training room appointments. The athlete must have the attitude that performing all exercises correctly and doing assigned home exercises is essential for getting back into action as soon as possible.

Many injured athletes lack patience. Nevertheless, the coach must convince the athlete that patience and desire are necessary in securing the maximum rate of recovery.

Rehabilitation and Reconditioning Overcompliance and Undercompliance

Athletic trainers and therapists are often faced with injured athletes who engage in rehabilitation and reconditioning overcompliance or under-compliance. Both factors can produce treatment setbacks (Table 9-2).

REENTERING SPORTS PARTICIPATION FOLLOWING SERIOUS ILLNESS OR INJURY

Often, a seriously ill or injured athlete returns to participation physically ready but psychologically ill prepared. Although few athletes will admit it, when returning to participation they feel anxious about getting hurt again. This feeling may become a self-fulfilling prophecy. In other words, anxiety can lead to muscle tension and incoordination that may predispose the athlete to reinjury. Coaches can help the athlete safely reenter competition and return to a full performance level by following these steps:

1. Have the athlete perform all the necessary skills away from the team until the athlete feels confident.
2. Instruct the athlete to engage in highly controlled, small-group practices with no physical contact until the athlete feels confident.
3. Set up participation in full-team noncontact practices until the athlete feels confident.
4. Allow the athlete to participate in limited contact with a few team members until the athlete feels confident.
5. Have the athlete participate in full-team contact with a gradual increase in exposure time and intensity of play. *The athlete should be encouraged to express freely and honestly any anxiety that may be felt. Only when anxiety is no longer present should the athlete engage in full contact.*

Two techniques that can help the athlete reduce levels of competition anxiety are Jacobson's progressive relaxation and systematic

---

TABLE 9-2 Rehabilitation overcompliance and undercompliance

Overcompliance	Undercompliance
• Mild degree of denial	• Scheduling problems
• Obsessive-compulsive behavior and impulsivity	• School, financial, or family concerns
• Excessive risk taking	• Unclear on treatment rationale
• Behavior that masks an underlying fear of unworthiness	• Mistrust of treatment professionals
	• Fear of pain or reinjury

desensitization.[9] The athlete first learns to consciously relax as much as possible through Jacobson's progressive relaxation method.[13] When the athlete can relax completely at will, he or she moves on to systematic desensitization.

Jacobson's Progressive Relaxation Method

Jacobson's progressive muscle relaxation (PMR) method[9] is probably the most extensively used technique for relaxation today.[13] With PMR, athletes are trained to develop awareness and to control residual muscle tension.

PMR may be practiced in a reclining position or while seated in a chair. Each muscle group is tensed from five to seven seconds, then relaxed for twenty to thirty seconds. In most cases, one repetition is sufficient; however, if tension remains in the muscle or muscles, repeated contraction and relaxation is permitted. The sequence of tensing and releasing is systematically applied to the following body areas:

1. dominant hand and forearm
2. dominant upper arm
3. nondominant hand and forearm
4. nondominant upper arm
5. forehead
6. eyes and nose
7. cheeks and mouth
8. neck and throat
9. chest
10. back
11. respiratory muscles
12. abdomen
13. dominant upper leg, calf, and foot
14. nondominant upper leg, calf, and foot

Throughout the session, the athlete can repeat affirming expressions: "Let the tension dissolve. Let go of the tension. I am bringing my muscles to zero. Let the tension flow out of my body."

Eventually the athlete concentrates on only one area of the body and decreases contraction of that area until he or she reaches the point that only thinking about tensing the area will release the tension. This process helps the athlete become acutely aware of muscle tension and how to mentally will relaxation.

Systematic Desensitization

Once relaxation can be achieved at will, the athlete, with help from the coach, athletic trainer, or sports partner, uses systematic desensitization[3] to develop a fear hierarchy related to returning to the sport and going "all out." Each fear-related step is imagined while the athlete is fully relaxed.

Progressive steps are imagined, and as anxiety is experienced during a specific step, the thought processes are halted while the athlete restores total relaxation and holds it until the feeling of anxiety passes. The athlete continues to the next step and repeats the relaxation process. An athlete who completes the entire list of events without anxiety and who is physically rehabilitated is ready for competition.

Exercise Abstinence Syndrome

The coach should be aware of the possibility of the sudden exercise abstinence syndrome. In this syndrome the athlete may experience heart palpitations, irregular heartbeat, chest pain, problems with appetite and digestion, sleep disorders, increased sweating, depression, and in some cases emotional instability.

SUMMARY

- Sports participation can be both a physical and an emotional stressor and can be both a negative and a positive stressor.
- The pregame response is normal. In this response, the body and mind speed up to meet the anticipated demands of competition.
- An overstressed athlete may respond in a number of physiological and psychological ways, such as higher blood pressure, increased pulse rate, and increased catecholamine excretions. The athlete who continues at the reactive phase of stress eventually will become exhausted.
- Overstress can lead to adrenal exhaustion, causing a variety of psychoemotional problems.
- Discounting high-risk situations, some athletes seem to receive more than their share of injuries and are considered accident prone.
- High anxiety, abnormal muscle tension, restlessness, insecurity, and poor self-esteem coupled with a low level of confidence can lead an athlete to being accident prone.
- Injuries and illness can cause chronic stress in the athlete.
- An athlete who is removed from sports participation for an extended period of time can experience the psychological reaction of loss.
- The five phases of loss are denial or disbelief, anger, bargaining, depression, and acceptance.
- The coach is usually the first person to recognize that an athlete is overtraining or becoming stale.
- Staleness can result when the athlete has overtrained or when the coach teaches through negative reinforcement.
- The athletic trainer and the physician may also become aware of an athlete who is pushing too hard or for other reasons is becoming stressed out.
- The coach must be supportive of the athlete's efforts while the athlete is engaged in rehabilitation and reconditioning.

- An athlete's successful rehabilitation depends on cooperation with the athletic trainer and physician.

- Setbacks to recovery can occur when an athlete overcomplies or undercomplies with the treatment program.

- Reentering competition depends on both physical and psychological recovery.

- Often an athlete may be physically ready to return to competition but is psychologically unprepared.

- Because athletes may experience fear and anxiety about the possibility of reinjury, they should engage in a relaxation technique such as Jacobson's followed by a program of desensitization.

Solutions to Critical Thinking Exercises

9-1 This athlete experiences the psychological reaction to a sudden loss: disbelief, anger, bargaining, depression, and finally, resignation.

9-2 This athlete has the profile that may be a risk for suicide. He is in a high-risk age group. He has been a successful athlete who now faces surgery and a period of long rehabilitation. He is also faced with the possible ending of his career or, if he is able to return, being replaced by another athlete.

REVIEW QUESTIONS AND CLASS ACTIVITIES

1. What is the importance of psychology to sports injuries?
2. How does stress relate to serious illness and injury?
3. Discuss the psychology of loss when related to a sudden serious athletic injury.
4. Describe the emotional, social, and self-concept factors that are inherent in a serious sports injury.
5. How would you as a coach psychologically assist the athlete about to undergo knee surgery?
6. Discuss overtraining and staleness as they relate to overuse injuries.
7. How would you as a coach approach an athlete who is not complying with the athletic trainer's treatment program?
8. What mental training techniques might be used to assist the injured athlete who is anxious and fearful?

REFERENCES

1. Anderson MB, Williams JM: Psychological risk factors and injury prevention. In Heil J, editor: *Psychology of sport injury,* Champaign, Ill, 1993, Human Kinetics.
2. Benson HH: *Beyond the relaxation response,* New York, 1984, Times-Mirror.
3. Ellis A: *A new guide to rational living,* North Hollywood, Calif, 1975, Wilshire.
4. Fisher AC: Athletic trainer's attitudes and judgments of injured athletes' rehabilitation adherence, *J Ath Train* 28(1):43, 1993.
5. Froehlich J: Overtraining, In Heil

J, editor: *Psychology of sport injury,* Champaign, Ill, 1993, Human Kinetics.

6. Graham DJ: Personality traits relevant to the cause and treatment of athletic injuries, *Sports Med Digest* 15(2):1, 1993.

7. Heil J: A psychologist's view of the personal challenge of injury. In Heil J, editor: *Psychology of sport injury,* Champaign, Ill, 1993, Human Kinetics.

8. Heil J: Specialized treatment approaches: severe injury. In Heil J, editor: *Psychology of sport injury,* Champaign, Ill, 1993, Human Kinetics.

9. Jacobson E: *Progressive relaxation,* ed 2, Chicago, 1938, University of Chicago Press.

10. Mary JR: Psychological sequelae and rehabilitation of the injured athlete, *Sports Med Digest* 12(11):1, 1990.

11. McGuire R: Emotional healing, training, and conditioning. *J Ath Train* 4(4):4, 1994.

12. Pellitier KR: *Mind as healer, mind as slayer,* New York, 1977, Dell.

13. Petrie G: Injuries from the athlete's point of view. In Heil J, editor: *Psychology of sport injury,* Champaign, Ill, 1993, Human Kinetics.

14. Selye H: *Stress without distress,* New York, 1974, Lippincott.

15. Smith AM, Milliner EK: Injured athletes and the risk of suicide, *J Ath Train* 29(4):337, 1994.

16. Steadman J: A physician's approach to the psychology of injury. In Heil J, editor: *Psychology of sport injury,* Champaign, Ill, 1993, Human Kinetics.

ANNOTATED BIBLIOGRAPHY

Heil J, editor: *Psychology of sport injury,* Champaign, Ill, 1996, Human Kinetics.

> *An in-depth look at the psychology of sport injury for sports psychologists.*

Martins R: *Coaches guide to sport psychology,* Champaign, Ill, 1987, Human Kinetics.

> *A guide for helping students understand the key concepts of sport psychology.*

Pelletier KR: *Mind as healer, mind as slayer,* New York, 1977, Dell Publishing.

> *Provides an in-depth discussion of the relationship of the mind to the cause and healing of disease.*

Selye H: *Stress without distress,* New York, 1974, Lippincott.

> *A practical guide to understanding the role of stress in life.*

WEB SITES

Health and Sports Psychology: http://www.cmhc.com/guide/pro07.htm

> *Explores sport psychology and provides links to many health related sites.*

Sports Psychology General Information Page: http://www.mc.maricopa.edu/users/estabrook/html/sport_psychology.html

> *Go to the bottom of this page to access specific topics in sports psychology.*

Exercise and Sport Psychology: http://www.psyc.unt.edu/apadiv47

> *The sports and exercise division of the American Psychological Association.*

Chapter 10

Environmental Factors

When you finish this chapter you will be able to:

- Describe the physiology of hyperthermia and the clinical signs of heat stress and how they can be prevented.
- Identify the causes of hypothermia and the major cold disorders and how they may be prevented.
- Explain how an athlete should be protected from exposure to the sun.
- Describe precautions that should be taken in an electrical storm.

E nvironmental stress can adversely affect an athlete's performance and, in some instances, can pose a serious health threat. The environmental categories that coaches, athletic trainers, and sports physicians need to pay attention to are hyperthermia, hypothermia, exposure to the sun, and electrical storms.

HYPERTHERMIA

A major concern in sports is the problem of hyperthermia. Over the years, particularly among football players, there have been a number of deaths caused by hyperthermia.[1] It is vitally important that the coaching staff and athletic trainer have knowledge about temperature and humidity factors to assist them in planning practice. The coach must clearly understand when environmental heat and humidity are at a dangerous level and act accordingly. In addition, the clinical signs of heat stress must be recognized and managed properly.

Heat Stress

Regardless of the level of physical conditioning, extreme caution must be taken when exercising in hot, humid weather. Prolonged exposure to extreme heat can result in heat illness.[6] Heat stress is certainly preventable, but each year many athletes suffer illness and, occasionally, death from some heat-related cause.[12] Athletes who exercise in hot, humid environments are particularly vulnerable to heat stress. The physiological

Heat can be gained or lost through:
Metabolic heat production
Conductive heat exchange
Convective heat exchange
Radiant heat exchange
Evaporative heat loss

processes in the body can continue to function only as long as body temperature is maintained within a normal range.[7] Maintenance of normal temperature in a hot environment depends on the ability of the body to dissipate heat. Body temperature can be affected by five factors: metabolic heat production, conductive heat exchange, convective heat exchnage, radiant heat exchange, and evaporative heat loss.

Metabolic Heat Production

Normal metabolic function in the body results in the production and radiation of heat. Consequently, metabolism will always cause an increase in body heat depending on the intensity of the physical activity. The higher the metabolic rate, the more the heat produced.

Conductive Heat Exchange

Physical contact with other objects can result in either a heat loss or heat gain. A football player competing on astroturf on a sunny August afternoon will experience an increase in body temperature simply by standing on the turf.

Convective Heat Exchange

Body heat can be either lost or gained depending on the temperature of the circulating medium. A cool breeze will always tend to cool the body by removing heat from the body surface. Conversely, if the temperature of the circulating air is higher than the temperature of the skin, there will be a gain in body heat.

Radiant Heat Exchange

Radiant heat from sunshine will most definitely cause an increase in body temperature. Obviously, the effects of radiation are much greater in the sunshine than in the shade. However, on a cloudy day a person's body also emits radiant heat energy, and this radiation may also result in either heat loss or heat gain. During exercise the body attempts to dissipate heat produced by metabolism by dilating superficial arterial and venous vessels, thus channeling blood to the superficial capillaries in the skin.

Evaporative Heat Loss

Sweat glands in the skin allow water to be transported to the surface where it evaporates, taking large quantities of heat with it. When the temperature and radiant heat of the environment become higher than body temperature, loss of body heat becomes highly dependent on the process of sweat evaporation.The sweat must evaporate for heat to be dissipated. But the air must be relatively free of water for evaporation to occur. Heat loss through evaporation is severely impaired when the relative humidity reaches 65 percent and virtually stops when the humidity reaches 75 percent.

Heat Illnesses

It should be obvious that heat-related problems have the greatest chance of occurring on days when the sun is bright and the temperature and relative humidity are high. But it is certainly true that various forms of heat illness, including heat cramps, heat exhaustion, or heatstroke, can occur whenever the body's ability to dissipate heat is impaired.

Heat Cramps

Heat cramps occur because of some imbalance between water and electrolytes.

Heat cramps are extremely painful muscle spasms that occur most commonly in the calf and abdomen, although any muscle can be involved (Table 10-1). *The occurrence of heat cramps is related primarily to excessive loss of water and, to a lesser extent, loss of electrolytes. Electrolytes* are ions (sodium, chloride, potassium, magnesium, and calcium) that are each an essential element in muscle contraction.

Profuse sweating involves losses of large amounts of water and small quantities of the electrolytes, thus destroying the balance in concentration of these elements within the body. This imbalance will ultimately result in painful muscle contractions and cramps. The person most likely to get heat cramps is one who is in fairly good condition but who simply overexerts in the heat.

Treatment Heat cramps may be prevented by adequate replacement of water. Ingestion of salt tablets is not recommended. The immediate treatment for heat cramps is ingestion of large quantities of water and mild stretching with ice massage of the muscle in spasm. An athlete who experiences heat cramps will generally not be able to return to practice or competition for the remainder of the day because cramping is likely to reoccur.

Heat Exhaustion

Heat exhaustion results from dehydration.

Heat exhaustion results from inadequate replacement of fluids lost through sweating (Table 10-1). Clinically, the victim of heat exhaustion will collapse and manifest profuse sweating, flushed skin, mildly elevated temperature (102°), dizziness, hyperventilation, and rapid pulse.

It is sometimes possible to spot athletes who are having problems with heat exhaustion. They may begin to develop heat cramps. They may become disoriented and light-headed, and their physical performance will not be up to their usual standards when fluid replacement has not been adequate. In general, persons in poor physical condition who attempt to exercise in the heat are most likely to get heat exhaustion.

Treatment Immediate treatment of heat exhaustion requires ingestion and eventually intravenous replacement of large quantities of water. It is essential for the athletic trainer to obtain a rectal temperature to differentiate heat exhaustion from heatstroke. In heat exhaustion the rectal temperature will be around 102° F. If possible, the athlete should be placed in a cool environment, although it is more critical to replace fluids.

TABLE 10-1 Heat disorders: treatment and prevention

Disorders	Cause	Clinical Features and Diagnosis	Treatment	Prevention
Heat cramps	Hard work in heat; sweating heavily; imbalance between water and electrolytes	Muscle twitching and cramps, usually after midday; spasms in arms, legs, abdomen	Ingesting large amounts of water, mild stretching, and ice massage of affected muscle	Acclimatize athlete properly; provide large quantities of water; increase intake of calcium, sodium, and potassium slightly
Heat exhaustion	Prolonged sweating; inadequate replacement of body fluid losses; diarrhea; intestinal infection	Excessive thirst, dry tongue and mouth; weight loss; fatigue; weakness; incoordination; mental dullness; small urine volume; slightly elevated body temperature; high serum protein and sodium; reduced swelling	Bed rest in cool room, IV fluids if drinking is impaired; increase fluid intake to 6 to 8 l/day; sponge with cool water; keep record of body weight; keep fluid balance record; provide semiliquid food until salination is normal	Supply adequate water and other liquids. Provide adequate rest and opportunity for cooling
Heatstroke	Thermoregulatory failure of sudden onset	Abrupt onset, preceded by headache, vertigo, and fatigue, flushed skin; relatively less sweating than seen with heat exhaustion; pulse rate increases rapidly and may reach 160 to 180; respiration increases; blood pressure seldom rises; temperature rises rapidly to 105° or 106° F (40° to 41° C); athlete feels as if he or she is burning up; diarrhea, vomiting; circulatory collapse may produce death; could lead to permanent brain damage	Heroic measures to reduce temperature must be taken immediately (e.g., sponge cool water and air fan over body, massage limbs); remove to hospital as soon as possible	Ensure proper acclimatization, proper hydration. Educate those supervising activities conducted in the heat. Adapt activities to environment. Screen participants with past history of heat illness for malignant hyperthermia

Techniques for Preventing
and Minimizing
Sport-Related Injuries

Heatstroke is a life-
threatening emergency.

Heatstroke

Unlike heat cramps and heat exhaustion, heatstroke is a serious, life-threatening emergency (Table 10-1). The specific cause of heatstroke is unknown; however, it is clinically characterized by sudden collapse with loss of consciousness; flushed, hot skin; less sweating than would be seen with heat exhaustion; shallow breathing; a rapid, strong pulse; and most important, a core temperature of 106° F or higher. Basically heatstroke is a breakdown of the thermoregulatory mechanism caused by excessively high body temperature; the body loses the ability to dissipate heat through sweating.

Heatstroke can occur suddenly and without warning. The athlete will not usually experience signs of heat cramps or heat exhaustion. The possibility of death from heatstroke can be significantly reduced if body temperature is lowered to normal within forty-five minutes. The longer that the body temperature is elevated to 106° F or higher, the higher the mortality rate.

Treatment   *It is imperative that the victim be transported to a hospital as quickly as possible.* Every first-aid effort should be directed to lowering body temperature. Get the athlete into a cool environment. Strip all clothing off the athlete, sponge him or her down with cool water, and fan with a towel. Do not immerse the athlete in cold water. The replacement of fluid is not critical in initial first aid.

Preventing Heat Illness

The coach needs to understand that heat illness is preventable. Exercising common sense and caution will keep heat illnesses from occurring. The following suggestions should be considered when planning a practice or competitive program during hot weather.

Fluid Replacement

During hot weather athletes need to continually rehydrate by replacing fluids lost through evaporation of sweat (Figure 10-1). Unfortunately dehydration occurs frequently during physical activity because athletes do not ingest enough fluid to match sweat loss even though unlimited fluids are readily available.[7] In fact, seldom is more than 50 percent of this fluid loss replaced. Ideally, fluid replacement should match sweat loss. Fluid is most effectively replaced at regular intervals of about fifteen minutes.[7]

The problem in fluid replacement is how rapidly the fluid can be eliminated from the stomach into the intestine, from which it can enter the bloodstream. Water is absorbed rapidly from the intestine. Beverages containing 6 percent carbohydrate (glucose) are absorbed at about the same rate as water as long as there is normal hydration.[3] Cold drinks (45° to 55° F [7.2° to 12.8° C]) tend to empty more rapidly from the stomach than do warmer drinks; they are not more likely to induce cramps, nor do they offer any particular threat to a normal heart.

10-1

Critical Thinking Exercise

A high school football coach in southern Louisiana is concerned about the likelihood that several of his players will suffer heat-related illness during preseason football practice the first two weeks of August.

? What intervention strategies can the coach implement to help the athletes avoid heat-related illnesses?

The prevention of hyperthermia involves:
Gradual acclimatization
Identification of susceptible individuals
Lightweight uniforms
Routine weight record keeping
Unrestricted fluid replacement

Figure 10-1

Athletes must have unlimited access to water, especially in hot weather.

Athletes can tell if they are appropriately hydrated by paying attention to the color and volume of their urine. Within sixty minutes of exercise, a nearly clear urine of normal to above-normal output would indicate that the athlete is appropriately hydrated.

Commercially prepared drinks A number of commercially prepared drinks are available that may be used in fluid replacement. The new generation of manufactured drinks has reduced the negative effects of simple sugar solutions on gastric emptying by using a polymerized form of glucose. This process maximizes carbohydrate content while making the solution less hypertonic. Thus, a drink containing a 6 percent solution of polymerized glucose provides the athlete with more water and carbohydrate than does a drink containing simple sugars.[8]

Ingestion of drinks containing 6 percent glucose and electrolytes is most useful for replenishing fluids and electrolytes before and after activity in the heat.[8] The drinks are also beneficial for replacing glucose in activities lasting longer than one hour.

Gradual Acclimatization

Gradual acclimatization is probably the single most effective method of avoiding heat stress. Acclimatization should involve not only becoming accustomed to heat but also becoming acclimatized to exercising in hot temperatures.[6] A good preseason conditioning program—started well before the advent of the competitive season and carefully graded as to intensity—is recommended. During the first five or six days, an 80 percent acclimatization can be achieved on the basis of a two-hour practice period in the morning and a two-hour practice period in the afternoon. Each practice should be broken down into twenty minutes of work alternated with twenty minutes of rest in the shade.

Identifying Susceptible Individuals

Athletes with a large muscle mass are particularly prone to heat illness.[10] Heat victims also tend to be overweight. In addition, a considerable loss of fluid makes the athlete highly susceptible to heat illness (see the next section). Although slight differences exist, the same precautionary measures apply to both males and females.

Keeping Weight Records

Careful weight records of all players must be kept. Weights should be measured both before and after practice for at least the first two weeks of practice. If a sudden increase in temperature and/or humidity occurs during the season, weight should be recorded again for a period of time. A loss of 3 to 5 percent of body weight will reduce blood volume and could lead to a health threat.[13] The athlete should be held out of practice until normal body weight has been regained.

Uniforms

Uniforms should be selected on the basis of temperature and humidity. Initial practices should be conducted in light-colored, short-sleeved T-shirts, shorts, and socks, moving gradually into short-sleeved net jerseys, lightweight pants, and socks as acclimatization proceeds. All early-season practices and games should be conducted in lightweight uniforms. Because of the specialized equipment worn by the players, football requires particular consideration. In hot, humid environments, the helmet should be removed as often as possible.

HYPOTHERMIA

Many sports played in cold weather do not require heavy protective clothing; thus, weather becomes a factor in injury susceptibility.

Cold weather is a frequent adjunct to many outdoor sports in which the sport itself does not require heavy protective clothing; consequently, the weather becomes a pertinent factor in injury susceptibility.[14] In most instances, the activity itself enables the athlete to increase the metabolic rate sufficiently for normal physiological functioning and to dissipate the resulting heat and perspiration through the usual physiological mechanisms. An athlete may fail to warm up sufficiently or may become chilled because of relative inactivity for varying periods of time demanded by the particular sport, either during competition or training. Consequently, the athlete is predisposed to hypothermia.

Low temperatures accentuated by wind and dampness can pose major problems for athletes.

Low temperatures alone can pose some problems, but when such temperatures are further accentuated by wind, the chill factor becomes critical.[11] (See Figure 10-2.) A third factor, dampness or wetness, further increases the risk of hypothermia. Air at a temperature of 50° F is relatively comfortable, but water at the same temperature is intolerable. Certainly the combination of cold, wind, and dampness creates an environment that easily predisposes the athlete to hypothermia.

As muscular fatigue builds up during strenuous physical activity in cold weather, the rate of exercise begins to drop and may reach a level

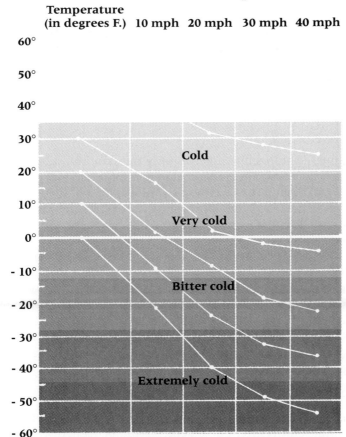

Wind speed

Temperature
(in degrees F.)   10 mph   20 mph   30 mph   40 mph

Figure 10-2

Low temperatures can pose
serious problems for the
athlete, but windchill could
be a critical factor.

wherein the body heat loss to the environment exceeds the metabolic heat protection, resulting in definite impairment of neuromuscular responses and exhaustion. A relatively small drop in body core temperature can induce shivering sufficient to materially affect the athlete's neuromuscular coordination. Shivering ceases below a body temperature of 85° to 90° F (29.4° to 32.2° C). Death is imminent if the core temperature rises to 107° F (41.6° C) or drops to between 77° and 85° F (25° and 29° C).

Cold Disorders

Athletes need to replace fluids when working out in a cold environment as much as they do in a hot environment.[2] Because dehydration reduces blood volume, less fluid is available for warming the tissues. Athletes performing in a cold environment should be weighed before and after practice, especially in the first two weeks of the season.[6] Severe overexposure to a cold climate occurs less often than hyperthermia does in a warm climate; however, it is still a major risk of winter sports, long-distance running in cold weather, and swimming in cold water.[2]

Cold injuries in sports
include:
Frostnip
Frostbite

Frostnip

Frostnip involves ears, nose, cheeks, chin, fingers, and toes. It commonly occurs during a high wind, severe cold, or both. The skin initially appears very firm, with cold, painless areas that may peel or blister in twenty-four to seventy-two hours. Affected areas can be treated early by firm, sustained pressure of the hand (without rubbing), by blowing hot breath on the spot, or if the injury is to the fingertips, by placing them in the armpits.

Frostbite

Superficial frostbite involves only the skin and subcutaneous tissue. The skin appears pale, hard, cold, and waxy. Palpating the injured area will reveal a sense of hardness but with yielding of the underlying deeper tissue structures. When rewarming, the superficial frostbite will at first feel numb, then will sting and burn. Later the area may produce blisters and be painful for a number of weeks.[9]

Deep frostbite is a serious injury indicating that tissues are frozen. This medical emergency requires immediate hospitalization. As with frostnip and superficial frostbite, the tissue is initially cold, hard, pale or white, and numb. Rapid rewarming is required, including hot drinks, heating pads, or hot water bottles that are 100° to 110° F (38° to 43° C).[9] During rewarming, the tissue will become blotchy, red, swollen, and extremely painful. Later the injury may become gangrenous, causing a loss of tissue.

Prevention

Apparel for competitors must be geared to the weather. The clothing should not restrict movement, should be as lightweight as possible, and should consist of material that will permit the free passage of body heat and sweat that would otherwise accumulate on the skin or the clothing and provide a chilling effect when activity ceases. The athlete should routinely dress in thin layers of clothing that can easily be added or removed to prevent sweating as the temperature decreases or increases. To prevent chilling, warm-up suits should be worn before exercise, during activity breaks or rest periods, and at the termination of exercise.[5]

OVEREXPOSURE TO SUN

Athletes, along with coaches, athletic trainers, and other support staff, frequently spend a great deal of time outdoors in direct sunlight. Applying sunscreens to protect these individuals from overexposure to ultraviolet radiation (UVR) is seldom done.

Long-Term Effects on Skin

The most serious effects of long-term UVR exposure are premature aging of the skin and skin cancer.[4] Lightly pigmented individuals are more susceptible. Premature aging of the skin is characterized by dryness, cracking, and a decrease in the elasticity of the skin. Skin cancer is the most common malignant tumor found in humans and has been epidemiologically and clinically associated with exposure to UVR. Fortunately the rate of cure exceeds 95 percent with early detection and treatment.[4]

Using Sunscreens

Sunscreens applied to the skin can help prevent many of the damaging effects of UVR. A sunscreen's effectiveness in absorbing the sunburn-inducing radiation is expressed as the sun protection factor (SPF). An SPF of 6 indicates that an athlete can be exposed to UVR six times longer than without a sunscreen before the skin will begin to turn red. Higher numbers provide greater protection. However, athletes who have a family or personal history of skin cancer may experience significant damage to the skin even when wearing an SPF 15 sunscreen. Therefore, these individuals should wear an SPF 30 sunscreen.

Sunscreen should be worn regularly by athletes, coaches, and athletic trainers who spend time outside. This caution is particularly relevant for individuals with fair complexions, light hair, or blue eyes or those whose skin burns easily. People with dark complexions should also wear sunscreens to prevent sun damage.

Sunscreens are needed most between the months of March and November but should be used year-round. Sunscreens are needed most between 10 A.M. and 4 P.M. and should be applied fifteen to thirty minutes before sun exposure. Although clothing and hats will provide some protection from the sun, they are not a substitute for sunscreens (a typical white cotton T-shirt provides an SPF of only 5). Reflected sunlight from water, sand, and snow may effectively increase sun exposure and risk of burning.

ELECTRICAL STORMS

Lightning is the number two cause of death by weather phenomena, accounting for 110 deaths per year.[16] Persons who hear thunder and/or see lightning are in immediate danger and should seek protective shelter in an indoor facility at once.[15]

The most dangerous storms give little or no warning; thunder and lightning are not heard or seen. All lightning is accompanied by thunder, and 20 to 40 percent of thunder cannot be heard because of atmospheric disturbances. At times, the only natural forewarning that might precede a strike is when a person feels the hair stand on end and the skin tingle. At this point, the person is in imminent danger of being struck by lightning and should drop to the ground and assume a crouched position immediately (see the accompanying Focus Box). A person should not lie flat. Should a ground strike occur nearby, lying flat increases the body's surface area that is exposed to the current traveling through the ground.[16]

The National Severe Storms Laboratory recommends that *thirty minutes should pass after the last sound of thunder is heard and/or lightning strike is seen before resuming play.* This time is sufficient to allow the storm to move

SPF stands for sun protection factor.

(10-2)
Critical Thinking Exercise

A track athlete is competing in a day-long outdoor track meet. She is extremely concerned about getting sunburned and has liberally applied sunscreen with an SPF of 30 during the early morning. It is a very hot, sunny day and she is sweating heavily. She is worried that her sunscreen has worn off and asks the coach for more sunscreen. The coach hands her sunscreen with an SPF of 15, and the athlete complains that it is not strong enough to protect her.

? What can the coach tell the athlete to assure her that she will be well protected by the sunscreen she has been given?

The most dangerous storms give little or no warning.

(10-1)   *Focus Box*

Guidelines for Electrical Storms

These basic guidelines should be followed during an electrical storm:[16]

- In situations in which thunder or lightning may or may not be present yet you feel your hair stand on end and skin tingle, immediately assume a crouched position: Drop to your knees, place your hands and arms on your legs, and lower your head. Do not lie flat.

- If thunder and/or lightning can be heard or seen, stop activity and seek protective shelter immediately. An indoor facility is recommended as the safest protective shelter. However, if an indoor facility is not available, an automobile is a relatively safe alternative. If neither of these options is available, you should avoid standing under large trees and telephone poles. If the only alternative is a tree, choose a small tree in a wooded area that is not on a hill. As a last alternative, find a ravine or valley. In all instances outdoors, assume the aforementioned crouched position.

- Avoid standing water and metal objects at all times (e.g., metal bleachers, metal cleats, umbrellas, etc.).

- Allow thirty minutes to pass after the last sound of thunder or lightning strike before resuming play.

(10-3)

Critical Thinking Exercise

A lacrosse team is practicing on a remote field with no indoor facility in close proximity. The weather is rapidly worsening, with the sky becoming dark and the wind blowing harder. Twenty minutes are left in the practice session and the coach is hoping to finish practice before it begins to rain. Suddenly, there is a bolt of lightning and an immediate burst of thunder.

? How should the coach manage this extremely dangerous situation?

out of lightning strike range. A perilous misconception that it is possible to see lightning coming and have time to act before it strikes could prove to be fatal. In reality, the lightning that is seen flashing is actually the return stroke flashing upward from the ground to the cloud, not downward. Seeing lightning strike means it already has hit.[16]

SUMMARY

- Environmental stress can adversely affect an athlete's performance as well as pose a serious health problem.

- Regardless of the athletes' level of physical conditioning, coaches must take extreme caution when conducting exercises in hot, humid weather. Prolonged exposure to extreme heat can result in heat cramps, heat exhaustion, or heatstroke.

- Heat illness is preventable. Exercising common sense and caution will keep heat illnesses from occurring. Coaches can prevent heat illness by encouraging adequate fluid replacement, acclimatizing athletes gradually, identifying susceptible individuals, keeping weight records, and selecting appropriate uniforms.

- Hypothermia is most likely to occur in a cool, damp, windy environment. Extreme cold exposure can cause conditions such as frostnip and frostbite.

- Athletes, coaches, and athletic trainers should be protected from overexposure to ultraviolet radiation (UVR) by the routine application of sunscreens.

- Thirty minutes should be allowed to pass after the last sound of thunder is heard or last lightning strike is seen before play is resumed.

Solutions to Critical Thinking Exercises

10-1 The coach should understand that heat-related illnesses are preventable. The athletes should come into preseason practice at least partially acclimatized to working in a hot, humid environment and during the first week of practice should become fully acclimatized. Temperature and humidity readings should be monitored and practice should be modified according to conditions. Practice uniforms should maximize evaporation and minimize heat absorption to the greatest extent possible. Weight records should be maintained to identify individuals who are becoming dehydrated. Most important, the athletes must keep themselves hydrated by constantly drinking large quantities of water both during and between practice sessions.

10-2 The sun protection factor (SPF) indicates the sunscreen's effectiveness in absorbing the sunburn-inducing radiation. An SPF of 15 indicates that an athlete can be exposed to UVR fifteen times longer than without a sunscreen before the skin will begin to turn red. Therefore the athlete needs to understand that a higher SPF doesn't indicate a greater degree of protection. She must simply apply the SPF 15 sunscreen twice as often as would be necessary with an SPF of 30 sunscreen.

10-3 As soon as lightning is observed, the coach should immediately end practice and get the athletes under cover. If an indoor facility is not available, an automobile is a relatively safe alternative. The athletes should avoid standing under large trees or telephone poles. As a last alternative, athletes should assume a crouched position in a ditch or ravine. If possible, athletes should avoid any standing water or metal objects around the fields.

REVIEW QUESTIONS AND CLASS ACTIVITIES

1. How do temperature and humidity cause heat illnesses?
2. Describe the symptoms and signs of the most common heat disorders.
3. What steps should be taken to avoid heat illnesses?
4. How is heat lost from the body to produce hypothermia?
5. Identify the physiological basis for the body's susceptibility to a cold disorder.
6. What should athletes do to prevent heat loss?
7. How should athletes protect themselves from the effects of ultraviolet radiation?
8. What precautions can be taken to minimize injury during an electrical storm?

REFERENCES

1. ACSM: Position statement on prevention of thermal injuries during distance running, *Med Sci Sports Exerc* 19(5):529, 1987.
2. Casey MJ, Foster C, Hixon E: *Winter sports medicine,* Philadelphia, 1990, F A Davis.
3. Coyle E: Fluid and carbohydrate replacement during exercise: how much and why? *Sports Science Exchange* 7(50):1, 1994.
4. Davis M: Ultraviolet therapy. In Prentice W: *Therapeutic modalities in sports medicine,* Dubuque, 1998, WCB/McGraw-Hill.
5. Fritz R, Perrin D: Cold exposure

injuries: prevention and treatment. In Ray R: *Clinics in sports medicine,* Philadelphia, 1989, WB Saunders.

6. Inbar O: Exercise and heat. In Welsh RP, Shephard RJ, editors: *Current therapy in sports medicine 1985–1986,* Philadelphia, 1985, BC Decker.

7. Murray R: Dehydration, hyperthermia, and athletes: Science and practice, *J Ath Train* 31(3):223, 1996.

8. Nadel ER: *Sports science exchange— new ideas for rehydration during and after exercise in hot weather,* Chicago, 1988, Gatorade Sports Science Institute.

9. Nelson WE, Gieck J, Kolb P: Treatment and prevention of hypothermia and frostbite, *Ath Train* 18:330, 1983.

10. Pandolf K: Avoiding heat illness during exercise. In Torg J, Shepard R: *Current therapy in sports medicine,* St Louis, 1995, Mosby.

11. Pate RR: *Sports science exchange— special considerations for exercise in cold weather,* Chicago, 1988, Gatorade Sports Science Institute.

12. Ryan A: Heat stress. In Mueller F, Ryan A: *Prevention of athletic injuries: the role of the sports medicine team,* Philadelphia, 1991, FA Davis.

13. Thein L: Environmental conditions affecting the athlete, *JOSPT* 21(3):158, 1995.

14. Vellerand A: Exercise in the cold. In Torg J, Shepard R: *Current therapy in sports medicine,* St Louis, 1995, Mosby.

15. Walsh K, Hanley M, Graner S: A survey of lightning policy in selected Division I colleges, *J Ath Train* 32(3):206, 1997.

16. Walters F: Position stand on lightning and thunder: the Athletic Health Care Services of the District of Columbia Public Schools, *J Ath Train* 28(3):201, 1993.

ANNOTATED BIBLIOGRAPHY

Casey MJ, Foster C, Hixon E: *Winter sports medicine,* Philadelphia, 1990, FA Davis.
  Provides a nontechnical approach to hypothermia; explains the importance of preparing for cold and how to recognize and manage cold injuries.

Haymes EM, Wells CL: *Environment and human performance,* Champaign, Ill, 1986, Human Kinetics.
  Examines sports performance during a variety of environmental conditions; 250 references are reported.

Strauss RH, editor: *Sports medicine,* Philadelphia, 1994, WB Saunders.
  Provides four pertinent chapters on the subject of environmental disorders that could affect the athlete.

WEB SITES

Sports Medicine: Dressing for the cold: http://www.olympic-usa.org/inside/in_1_3_5_4.html

Cramer First Aider: http://www.ccsd.k12.wy.us/CCHS_web/sptmed/fstaider.htm

Heat Stroke and Heat Exhaustion: http://www.city.swift-current.sk.ca/info/heat.htm

Physiology of Heat Exhaustion and Heat Stroke: http://www.uwrf.edu/~cg04/physiology/WELCOME.htm

Hypothermia and Cold Weather Injuries: http://www.princeton.edu/~oa/hypocold.html

Bandaging and Taping Techniques

When you finish this chapter you will be able to:

- Explain the need for and demonstrate the application of roller bandages.
- Explain the need for and demonstrate the application of triangular and cravat bandages.
- Demonstrate site preparation for taping.
- Demonstrate basic skills in the use of taping in sports.
- Demonstrate the skillful application of tape for a variety of musculoskeletal problems.

Eight basic uses for dressings and bandages:
Protect wounds from infection
Protect wounds from further insult and contamination
Control external and internal hemorrhage
Act as a compress over exposed or unexposed injuries
Immobilize an injured part
Protect an unexposed injury
Support an injured part
Hold protective equipment in place

bandage
A strip of cloth or other material used to hold a dressing in place.

B andaging and taping are major skills used in the protection and management of the injured athlete.[1] Each of these skill areas requires a development of these techniques:

BANDAGING

A **bandage,** when properly applied, can contribute to the healing of a sports injury. Bandages carelessly or improperly applied can cause discomfort, allow wound contamination, and hamper repair and healing. In every situation bandages must be firmly applied—neither so tight that circulation is impaired nor so loose that the **dressing** slips.

Bandage Materials

Bandages used on sports injuries are made of gauze, cotton cloth, or elastic wrapping. Plastics are also being used more frequently.

Gauze

Gauze materials are used in three forms: as sterile pads for wounds, as padding in the prevention of blisters on a taped ankle, and as a roller bandage for holding dressings and compresses in place.

Cotton Cloth

Cotton is used primarily for cloth ankle wraps and for triangular and cravat bandages. It is soft, is easily obtained, and can be washed many times without deterioration.

Elastic Roller Bandage

The elastic bandage is extremely popular in sports because of its extensibility, which allows it to conform to most parts of the body. Elastic wraps are active bandages that let the athlete move without restriction. They also act as a controlled compression bandage in which the regulation of pressure is graded according to the athlete's specific needs; however, they can cause dangerous constriction if not properly applied.

Elastic bandages allow the athlete to move without restriction.

Cohesive Elastic Bandage

A cohesive elastic bandage exerts constant, even pressure. It is lightweight and contours easily to the body part. The bandage is composed of two layers of nonwoven rayon, which are separated by strands of Spandex material. The cohesive elastic bandage is coated with a substance that makes the material adhere to itself, eliminating the need for metal clips or adhesive tape for holding it in place.

> **dressing**
> A material, such as gauze, applied to a wound.

COMMON TYPES OF BANDAGES USED IN SPORTS MEDICINE

Two common bandages used in sports are the roller bandage and the triangular bandage.

Roller Bandages

Roller bandages are made of many materials; gauze, cotton cloth, and elastic wrapping are predominantly used in the training room. The width and length vary according to the body part to be bandaged. The sizes most frequently used are the 2-inch (5 cm) width by 6-yard (5.5 m) length for hand, finger, toe, and head bandages; the 3-inch (7.5 cm) width by 10-yard (9 m) length for the extremities; and the 4-inch (10 cm) or 6-inch (15 cm) width by 10-yard length for thigh, groin, and trunk. For ease and convenience in the application of the roller bandage, the strips of material are first rolled into a cylinder. When a bandage is selected, it should be a single piece that is free from wrinkles, seams, and any other imperfections that may cause skin irritation.[4,7]

Wrinkles or seams in roller bandages may irritate skin.

Application

Application of the roller bandage must be executed in a specific manner to achieve the purpose of the wrap. When a roller bandage is about to be placed on a body part, the roll should be held in the preferred hand with the loose end extending from the bottom of the roll. The back surface of the loose end is placed on the part and held in position by the other hand. The bandage cylinder is then unrolled and passed around the injured area. As the hand pulls the material from the roll, it also standardizes the bandage pressure and guides the bandage in the proper direction. To anchor and stabilize the bandage, a number of turns, one on top of the other, are made. Circling a body part requires the operator to alternate the bandage roll from one hand to the other and back again.

To apply a roller bandage, hold it in the preferred hand with the loose end extending from the bottom of the roll.

For a roller bandage to provide maximum benefits, it should be applied uniformly and firmly but not too tightly. Excessive or unequal pressure can hinder the normal blood flow within the part. The following points should be considered when using the roller bandage:

1. A body part should be wrapped in its position of maximum muscle contraction to ensure unhampered movement or circulation.
2. It is better to use a large number of turns with moderate tension than a limited number of turns applied too tightly.
3. Each turn of the bandage should be overlapped by at least one half of the overlying wrap to prevent the separation of the material while the athlete is engaged in activity. Separation of the bandage turns tends to pinch and irritate the skin.
4. When limbs are wrapped, fingers and toes should be scrutinized often for signs of circulation impairment. Abnormally cold or cyanotic phalanges are signs of excessive bandage pressure.

Begin anchoring bandages at the smallest part of the limb.

The usual anchoring of roller bandages consists of several circular wraps directly overlying each other. Whenever possible, anchoring is commenced at the smallest circumference of a limb and is then moved upward. Wrists and ankles are the usual sites for anchoring bandages of the limbs. Bandages are applied to these areas in the following manner:

1. The loose end of the roller bandage is laid obliquely on the anterior aspects of the wrist or ankle and held in this position. The roll is then carried posteriorly under and completely around the limb and back to the starting point.
2. The triangular portion of the uncovered oblique end is folded over the second turn.
3. The folded triangle is covered by a third turn, which finishes a secure anchor.

After a roller bandage has been applied, it is held in place by a locking technique. The method most often used to finish a wrap is that of firmly tying or pinning the bandage or placing adhesive tape over several overlying turns.

Once a bandage has been put on and has served its purpose, removal can be performed either by unwrapping or by carefully cutting with bandage scissors. Whatever method of bandage removal is used, extreme caution must be taken to avoid additional injury.

CLOTH ANKLE WRAP

Because tape is so expensive, the ankle wrap is an inexpensive and expedient means of mildly protecting ankles (Figure 11-1).

MATERIALS NEEDED: Each muslin wrap should be 1½ to 2 inches (3.8 to 5 cm) wide and 72 to 96 inches (180 to 240 cm) long to ensure complete coverage and protection. The purpose of this wrap is to give mild support

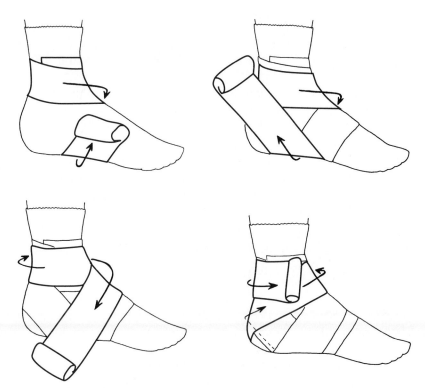

Figure 11-1

Ankle wrap

against lateral and medial motion of the ankle. It is applied over a sock.

POSITION OF THE ATHLETE: The athlete sits on a table, extending the leg and positioning the foot at a 90-degree angle. To avoid any distortion, it is important that the ankle be neither overflexed nor overextended.

PROCEDURE:

1. Start the wrap above the instep around the ankle, circle the ankle, and move the wrap at an acute angle to the inside of the foot.
2. From the inside of the foot move the wrap under the arch, coming up on the outside and crossing at the beginning point, where it continues around the ankle, hooking the heel.
3. Then move the wrap up, inside, over the instep, and around the ankle, hooking the opposite side of the heel. This completes one series of the ankle wrap.
4. Complete a second series with the remaining material.
5. For additional support, two heel locks with adhesive tape may be applied over the ankle wrap.

Elastic Wrap Techniques

Any time an elastic wrap is applied to the athlete, always check for and avoid decreased circulation and blueness of the extremity and check for a blood capillary refill.

Check circulation after applying an elastic wrap.

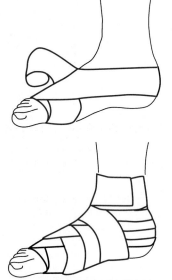

Figure 11-2

Ankle and foot spica

---

spica (spy ka)
A figure-eight bandage,
with one of the two loops
being larger.

Figure 11-3

Spiral bandage

ANKLE AND FOOT SPICA

The ankle and foot **spica** bandage (Figure 11-2) is used in sports for the compression of new injuries as well as for holding wound dressings in place.

MATERIALS NEEDED: Depending on the size of the ankle and foot, a 2- or 3-inch (5 to 7.5 cm) wrap is used.

POSITION OF THE ATHLETE: The athlete sits with ankle and foot extended over a table.

PROCEDURE:

1. An anchor is placed around the foot near the metatarsal arch.
2. The elastic bandage is brought across the instep and around the heel and returned to the starting point.
3. The procedure is repeated several times, with each succeeding revolution progressing upward on the foot and the ankle.
4. Each spica overlaps approximately three fourths of the preceding layer.

SPIRAL BANDAGE

The spiral bandage (Figure 11-3) is widely used in sports for covering a large area of a cylindrical part.

MATERIALS NEEDED: Depending on the size of the area, a 3- or 4-inch (7.5 to 10 cm) wrap is required.

POSITION OF THE ATHLETE: If the wrap is for the lower limb, the athlete bears weight on the opposite leg.

PROCEDURE:

1. The elastic spiral bandage is anchored at the smallest circumference of the limb and is wrapped upward in a spiral against gravity.

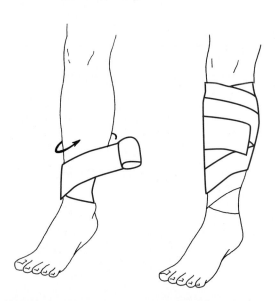

2. To prevent the bandage from slipping down on a moving extremity, two pieces of tape should be folded lengthwise and placed on the bandage at either side of the limb or tape adherent can be sprayed on the part.

3. After the bandage is anchored, it is carried upward in consecutive spiral turns, each overlapping the other by at least 0.5 inch.

4. The bandage is terminated by locking it with circular turns, which are then firmly secured by tape.

GROIN SUPPORT

The following procedure is used to support a groin strain and hip adductor strains (Figure 11-4).

MATERIALS NEEDED: One roll of extra-long 6-inch (15 cm) elastic bandage, a roll of 1½-inch (3.8 cm) adhesive tape, and nonsterile cotton.

POSITION OF THE ATHLETE: The athlete stands on a table with weight placed on the uninjured leg. The affected limb is relaxed and internally rotated.

PROCEDURE:

1. A piece of nonsterile cotton or a felt pad may be placed over the injured site to provide additional compression and support.

2. The end of the elastic bandage is started at the upper part of the inner aspect of the thigh and is carried posteriorly around the thigh. Then it is brought across the lower abdomen and over the crest of the ilium on the opposite side of the body.

3. The wrap is continued around the back, repeating the same pattern and securing the wrap end with 1½-inch (3.8 cm) adhesive tape.

NOTE: Variations of this method can be seen in Figure 11-5, used to support injured hip flexors, and Figure 11-6, used to limit the movement of the buttocks.

11-1

Critical Thinking Exercise

A baseball player strains his right groin while running the bases.

? Which elastic wrap should be applied when the athlete returns to his sport and why?

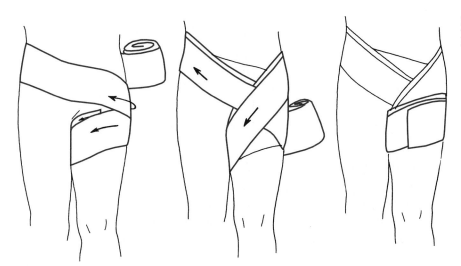

Figure 11-4

Elastic groin support

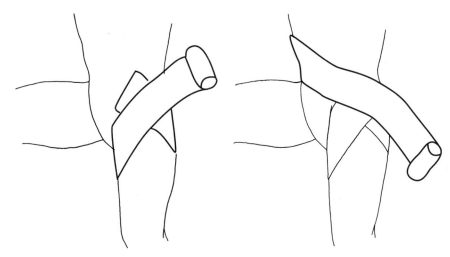

Figure 11-5

Hip spica for hip flexors

Figure 11-6

Method used to limit
movement of buttocks

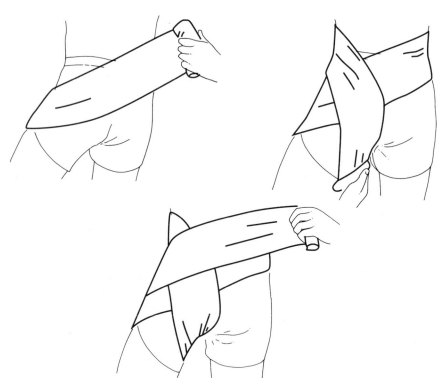

11-2

Critical Thinking Exercise

A wrestler sustains a left
shoulder point injury.

? The athletic trainer cuts a
sponge rubber doughnut to
protect the shoulder point from
further injury. How is the
doughnut held in place?

SHOULDER SPICA

The shoulder spica (Figure 11-7) is used mainly for the retention of
wound dressings and for moderate muscular support.

MATERIALS NEEDED: One roll of extra-length 4- to 6-inch (10 to 15 cm)
elastic wrap, 1½-inch adhesive tape, and padding for axilla.

POSITION OF THE ATHLETE: Athlete stands with side toward the operator.

PROCEDURE:

1. The axilla must be well padded to prevent skin irritation and constriction of blood vessels.
2. The bandage is anchored by one turn around the affected upper arm.
3. After anchoring the bandage around the arm on the injured side, the wrap is carried around the back under the unaffected arm and across the chest to the injured shoulder.
4. The affected arm is again encircled by the bandage, which continues around the back. Every figure-eight pattern moves progressively upward with an overlap of at least half of the previous underlying wrap.

ELBOW FIGURE EIGHT

The elbow figure-eight bandage (Figure 11-8) can be used to secure a dressing in the antecubital fossa or to restrain full extension in hyperextension injuries. When it is reversed, it can be used on the posterior aspect of the elbow.

MATERIALS NEEDED: One 3-inch elastic roll and 1½-inch adhesive tape.

POSITION OF THE ATHLETE: Athlete flexes elbow between 45 degrees and 90 degrees, depending on the restriction of movement required.

PROCEDURE:

1. Anchor the bandage by encircling the lower arm.
2. Bring the roll obliquely upward over the posterior aspect of the elbow.
3. Carry the roll obliquely upward, crossing the antecubital fossa; then pass once again completely around the upper arm and return to the beginning position by again crossing the antecubital fossa.
4. Continue the procedure as described, but for every new sequence move upward toward the elbow one half the width of the underlying wrap.

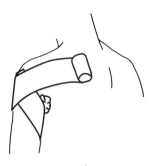

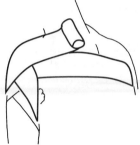

Figure 11-7

Elastic shoulder spica

Figure 11-8

Elastic elbow figure-eight bandage

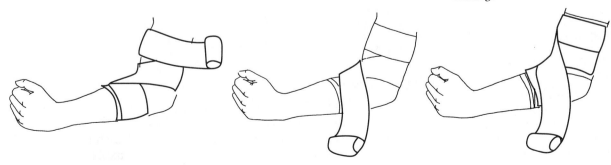

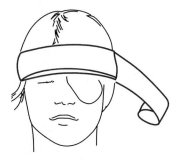

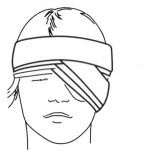

Figure 11-9

Eye bandage

EYE BANDAGE

When a bandage is needed to hold a dressing on an eye, the following procedure is suggested (Figure 11-9).

MATERIALS NEEDED: 2-inch (5 cm) gauge bandage roll, scissors, and ½- or 1-inch tape.

POSITION OF THE ATHLETE: Athlete sits in chair or on edge of table.

PROCEDURE:

1. The bandage is started with three circular turns around the head and then is brought obliquely down the back of the head.
2. From behind the head the bandage is carried forward underneath the earlobe and upward, crossing, respectively, the cheek bone, the injured eye, and the bridge of the nose; it is then returned to the original circular turns.
3. The head is encircled by the bandage, and the procedure is repeated, with each wrap overlapping at least two thirds of the underlying material over the injured eye.
4. When at least three series have been applied over the injured eye, the bandage is locked after completion of a circular turn around the head.

JAW BANDAGE

Bandages properly applied can be used to hold dressings and to stabilize dislocated or fractured jaws (Figure 11-10).

MATERIALS NEEDED: 2- or 3-inch (5 or 7.5 cm) gauze bandage roll, scissors, and 1½- or 2-inch tape.

POSITION OF THE ATHLETE: Athlete sits in chair or on edge of table.

PROCEDURE:

1. The bandage is started by encircling the jaw and head in front of both ears several times.
2. The bandage is locked by a number of turns around the head.
3. Each of the two sets of turns is fastened with tape strips.

Figure 11-10

Jaw bandage

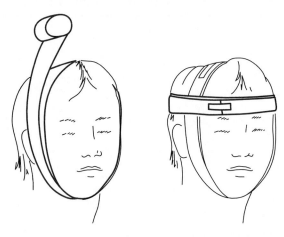

GAUZE CIRCULAR WRIST BANDAGE

In training procedures, the circular bandage (Figure 11-11) is used to cover a cylindrical area and to anchor other types of bandages.

MATERIALS NEEDED: One roll of 1- or 1½-inch (2.5 or 3.8 cm) gauze, 1-inch (2.5 cm) tape, and scissors.

POSITION OF THE ATHLETE: Athlete positions elbow at a 45-degree angle.

PROCEDURE:

1. A turn is executed around the part at an oblique angle.
2. A small triangle of material is exposed by the oblique turn.
3. The triangle is bent over the first turn, with succeeding turns made over the turned-down material, locking it in place.
4. After several turns have been made, the bandage is fastened at a point away from the injury.

GAUZE RECURRENT FINGER BANDAGE

This technique (Figure 11-12) is designed to hold a wound dressing on a finger.

MATERIALS NEEDED: One roll of ½-inch (1.25 cm) gauze, ½-inch (1.25 cm) tape, and scissors.

POSITION OF THE ATHLETE: Athlete positions elbow at a 45-degree angle.

PROCEDURE:

1. The gauze roll starts at the base of the finger dorsally and is extended up the full length of the finger and back down on the volar aspect. This procedure can be performed several times, depending on the thickness required.

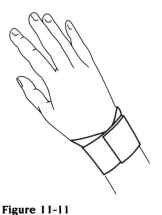

Figure 11-11

Circular wrist bandage

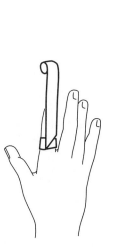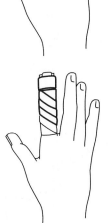

Figure 11-12

Recurrent finger bandage

2. After the finger has been covered vertically, a spiral pattern is started at the base, initially moved up to the distal aspect of the finger, and then moved proximally down, continuing several times.

3. The spiral pattern is completed at the finger's distal end and is secured by a piece of tape.

GAUZE HAND AND WRIST FIGURE EIGHT

A figure-eight bandage (Figure 11-13) can be used for mild wrist and hand support as well as for holding dressings in place.

MATERIALS NEEDED: One roll of ½-inch (1.25 cm) gauze, ½-inch (1.25 cm) tape, and scissors.

POSITION OF THE ATHLETE: Athlete positions elbow at a 45-degree angle.

PROCEDURE:

1. The anchor is executed with one or two turns around the palm of the hand.

2. The roll is carried obliquely across the anterior or posterior portion of the hand, depending on the position of the wound, to the wrist, which it circles once, then it is returned to the primary anchor.

3. As many figures as needed are applied.

GAUZE FINGER BANDAGE

The finger bandage can be used to hold dressings or tongue depressor splints in place.

MATERIALS NEEDED: One roll of 1-inch (2.5 cm) gauze, ½-inch (1.25 cm) tape, and scissors.

POSITION OF THE ATHLETE: Athlete positions elbow at a 45-degree angle.

PROCEDURE: The gauze finger bandage is applied in a fashion similar to the gauze hand and wrist figure eight, with the exception that a spiral is carried downward to the tip of the finger and then back up to finish around the wrist.

Figure 11-13

Hand and wrist figure-eight

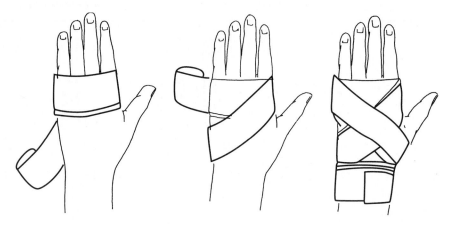

Triangular and Cravat Bandages

Triangular and cravat bandages, usually made of cotton cloth, may be used when roller bandages are not applicable or available.

The triangular and cravat bandages are primarily used as first-aid devices. They are valuable in emergency bandaging because of their ease and speed of application. In sports the more diversified roller bandages are usually available and lend themselves more to the needs of the athlete. The principal use of the triangular bandage in athletic training is for arm slings. There are two basic kinds of slings, the cervical arm sling and the shoulder arm sling, and each has a specific purpose.

CERVICAL ARM SLING

The cervical arm sling (Figure 11-14) is designed to support the forearm, wrist, and hand. A triangular bandage is placed around the neck and under the bent arm that is to be supported.

MATERIALS NEEDED: One triangular bandage.

POSITION OF THE ATHLETE: The athlete stands with the affected arm bent at approximately a 70-degree angle.

PROCEDURE:

1. The triangular bandage is positioned by the operator under the injured arm with the apex facing the elbow.
2. The end of the triangle nearest the body is carried over the shoulder of the uninjured arm; the other end is allowed to hang down loosely.
3. The loose end is pulled over the shoulder of the injured side.
4. The two ends of the bandage are tied in a square knot behind the neck. For the sake of comfort, the knot should be on either side of the neck, not directly in the middle.
5. The apex of the triangle is brought around to the front of the elbow and fastened by twisting the end, then tying in a knot.

NOTE: In cases in which greater arm stabilization is required than that afforded by a sling, an additional bandage can be swathed about the upper arm and body.

Triangular and cravat bandages allow ease and speed of application.

Figure 11-14

Cervical arm sling

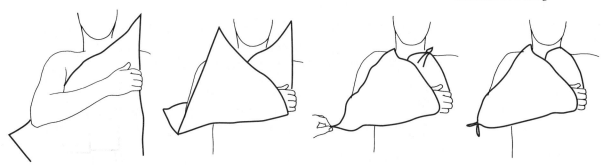

Figure 11-15

Shoulder arm sling

11-3

Critical Thinking Exercise

An athlete falls and sustains a dislocated right shoulder.

? How should the athlete be transported safely to the hospital?

SHOULDER ARM SLING

The shoulder arm sling (Figure 11-15) is suggested for forearm support when there is an injury to the shoulder girdle or when the cervical arm sling is irritating to the athlete.

MATERIALS NEEDED: One triangle bandage and one safety pin.

POSITION OF THE ATHLETE: The athlete stands with the injured arm bent at approximately a 70-degree angle.

PROCEDURE:

1. The upper end of the shoulder sling is placed over the *uninjured* shoulder side.
2. The lower end of the triangle is brought over the forearm and drawn between the upper arm and the body, then is swung around the athlete's back and upward to meet the other end, where a square knot is tied.
3. The apex end of the triangle is brought around to the front of the elbow and fastened with a safety pin.

SLING AND SWATHE

The sling and swathe combination is designed to stabilize the arm securely in cases of shoulder dislocation or fracture (Figure 11-16).

Figure 11-16

Sling and swathe

INJURY PROTECTION

Protecting against acute injuries is another major use of tape support. This protection can be achieved by limiting the motion of a body part or by securing some special device (see Chapter 6).

LINEN ADHESIVE TAPE

When purchasing linen tape, consider:
Grade of backing
Quality of adhesive mass
Winding tension

Modern adhesive tape has great adaptability for use in sports because of its uniform adhesive mass, adhering qualities, and lightness as well as the relative strength of the backing materials. All these qualities are of value in holding wound dressings in place and in supporting and protecting injured areas. This tape comes in a variety of sizes; 1-, 1½-, and 2-inch (2.5,

3.8, and 5 cm) widths are commonly used in sports medicine. The tape also comes in tubes or special packs. Some popular packs provide greater tape length on each spool. When linen tape is purchased, factors such as cost, grade of backing, quality of adhesive mass, and properties of unwinding should be considered.

Tape Grade

Linen-backed tape is most often graded according to the number of longitudinal and vertical fibers per inch of backing material. The heavier and more costly backing contains eighty-five or more longitudinal fibers and sixty-five vertical fibers per square inch. The lighter, less expensive grade has sixty-five or fewer longitudinal fibers and forty-five vertical fibers.

Adhesive Mass

As a result of improvements in adhesive mass, certain essentials should be expected from tape. It should adhere readily when applied and should maintain this adherence in the presence of profuse perspiration and activity. Besides sticking well, the mass must contain as few skin irritants as possible and must remove easily without leaving a mass residue or pulling away the superficial skin.

Winding Tension

The winding tension of a tape roll is quite important to the operator. Sports taping places a unique demand on the unwinding quality of tape; tape applied for protection and support must provide even and constant unwinding tension. In most cases a proper wind needs little additional tension to provide sufficient tightness.

STRETCH TAPE

Increasingly, tape with varying elasticity is being used in sports medicine, often in combination with linen tape. Because of its conforming qualities, stretch tape is used for the small, angular body parts, such as the feet, wrist, hands, and fingers. As with linen tape, stretch tape comes in a variety of widths.

Increasingly, tape with varying elasticity is being used in sports medicine.

TAPE STORAGE

When storing tape, take the following steps:

1. Store in a cool place such as in a low cupboard.
2. Stack so that the tape rests on its flat top or bottom to avoid distortion.

Store tape in a cool place, and stack it flat.

USING ADHESIVE TAPE IN SPORTS

Preparation for Taping

Special attention must be given when applying tape directly to the skin. Perspiration and dirt collected during sport activities will prevent tape from properly sticking to the skin. Whenever tape is used, the skin surface should be cleansed with soap and water to remove all dirt and oil.

Skin surface should be cleansed and hair should be shaved before applying tape.

Also, hair should be shaved to prevent irritation when the tape is removed. If additional adherence or protection from irritation is needed, a solution containing rosin and a skin-toughening preparation should be applied. Commercial benzoin and skin toughener offer astringent action and dry readily, leaving a tacky residue to which tape will adhere firmly.

Taping directly on skin provides maximum support. However, applying tape day after day can lead to skin irritation. To overcome this problem, many athletic trainers sacrifice some support by using a protective covering to the skin. The most popular is a moderately elastic commercial underwrap material that is extremely thin and fits snugly to the contours of the part to be taped. One commonly used underwrap material is polyester and urethane foam, which is fine, porous, extremely lightweight, and resilient. Proper use of an underwrap requires the part to be shaved and sprayed with a tape adherent. Underwrap material should be applied only one layer thick. It is also desirable to place a protective greased pad anterior and posterior to the ankle to prevent tape cuts and secondary infection.

Proper Taping Technique

The correct tape width depends on the area to be covered. The more acute the angles, the narrower the tape must be to fit the many contours. For example, the fingers and toes usually require ½- or 1-inch (1.25 or 2.5 cm) tape; the ankles require 1½-inch (3.75 cm) tape; and the larger skin areas such as thighs and back can accommodate 2- to 3-inch (5 to 7.5 cm) tape with ease. NOTE: *Supportive tape improperly applied can aggravate an existing injury or disrupt the mechanics of a body part, causing an initial injury to occur.*

Tearing Tape

Coaches and athletic trainers use various techniques in tearing tape (Figure 11-17). The method used should permit the operator to keep the tape roll in hand most of the time. The following is a suggested procedure:

1. Hold the tape roll in the preferred hand, with the index finger hooked through the center of the tape roll and the thumb pressing its outer edge.
2. With the other hand, grasp the loose end between the thumb and index finger.
3. With both hands in place, pull both ends of the tape so that it is tight. Next, make a quick, scissorslike move to tear the tape. In tearing tape, the movement of one hand is away from the body and the other hand toward the body. Do not try to bend or twist the tape to tear it.

To tear tape, move hands quickly in opposite directions.

When tearing is properly executed, the torn edges of the linen-backed tape are relatively straight, without curves, twists, or loose threads sticking out. Once the first thread is torn, the rest of the tape tears

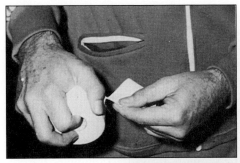
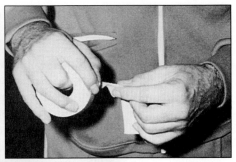
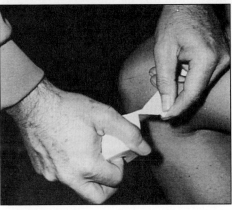

Figure 11-17

Methods of tearing linen-backed tape

easily. Learning to tear tape effectively from many different positions is essential for speed and efficiency. Many tapes other than the linen-backed type cannot be torn manually but require a knife, scissors, or razor blade.

Rules for Tape Application

Included here are a few of the important rules to be observed in the use of adhesive tape. With practice, the athletic trainer will become aware of other rules.

1. *If the part to be taped is a joint, place it in the position in which it is to be stabilized.* If the part is musculature, make the necessary allowance for contraction and expansion.

2. *Overlap the tape at least half the width of the tape below.* Unless tape is overlapped sufficiently, the active athlete will separate it, exposing the underlying skin to irritation.

3. *Avoid continuous taping.* Tape continuously wrapped around a part may cause constriction. One turn should be made at a time, and each encirclement should be torn to overlap the starting end by approximately 1 inch. This rule is particularly true of the nonyielding linen-backed tape.

4. *Keep the tape roll in hand whenever possible.* By learning to keep the

tape roll in the hand, seldom laying it down, and by learning to tear the tape, an operator can develop taping speed and accuracy.

5. *Smooth and mold the tape as it is laid on the skin.* To save additional time, tape strips should be smoothed and molded to the body part as they are put in place; this is done by stroking the top with the fingers, palms, and heels of both hands.

6. *Allow tape to fit the natural contour of the skin.* Each strip of tape must be placed with a particular purpose in mind. Linen-backed tape is not sufficiently elastic to bend around acute angles but must be allowed to fall as it may, fitting naturally to the body contours. Failing to allow this fit creates wrinkles and gaps that can result in skin irritations.

7. *Start taping with an anchor piece and finish by applying a lock strip.* Commence taping, if possible, by sticking the tape to an anchor piece that encircles the part. This placement affords a good medium for the stabilization of succeeding tape strips so that they will not be affected by the movement of the part.

8. *Where maximum support is desired, tape directly over skin.* In cases of sensitive skin, other mediums may be used as tape bases. With artificial bases, some movement can be expected between the skin and the base.

9. *Do not apply tape if skin is hot or cold from a therapeutic treatment.*

Removing Adhesive Tape

Tape usually can be removed from the skin by hand, by tape scissors or tape cutters, or by chemical solvents.

Manual Removal

Peel the skin from the tape, not the tape from the skin.

When pulling tape from the body, be careful not to tear or irritate the skin. Tape must not be wrenched in an outward direction from the skin but should be pulled in a direct line with the body (Figure 11-18). Remove the skin carefully from the tape; do not peel the tape from the skin. One hand gently pulls the tape in one direction, and the opposite hand gently presses the skin away from the tape.

Use of Tape Scissors or Cutters

The characteristic tape scissors have a blunt nose that slips underneath the tape smoothly without gouging the skin. Take care to avoid cutting the tape too near the site of the injury, lest the scissors aggravate the condition. Cut on the uninjured side.

Use of Chemical Solvents

When an adhesive mass is left on the skin after taping, a chemical agent may have to be used. Commercial cleaning solvents often contain a highly flammable agent. Take extreme care to store solvent in a cool place

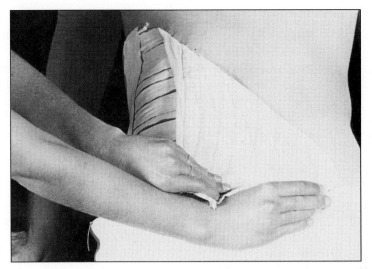

Figure 11-18

To remove tape from the
body by hand, pull in a direct
line with the body.

and in a tightly covered metal container. Extensive inhalation of benzene
fumes has a toxic effect. Adequate ventilation should be maintained
when using a solvent.

COMMON TAPING PROCEDURES

The Foot

The Arch

ARCH TECHNIQUE NO. 1: WITH PAD SUPPORT

Arch taping with pad support uses the following procedures to
strengthen weakened arches (Figure 11-19). NOTE: The longitudinal arch
should be lifted.

MATERIALS NEEDED: One roll of 1½-inch (3.8 cm) tape, tape adherent,
and a ⅛- or ¼-inch (0.3 or 0.6 cm) adhesive foam rubber pad or wool felt
pad, cut to fit the longitudinal arch.

POSITION OF THE ATHLETE: The athlete lies face downward on the table
with the foot that is to be taped extending approximately 6 inches (15 cm)
over the edge of the table. To ensure proper position, allow the foot to
hang in a relaxed position.

PROCEDURE:

1. Place a series of strips of tape directly around the arch or, if
   added support is required, around an arch pad and the arch. The
   first strip should go just above the metatarsal arch (1).
2. Each successive strip overlaps the preceding piece by about half
   the width of the tape (2 through 4).

CAUTION: Avoid putting on so many strips of tape that the action of the
ankle is hampered.

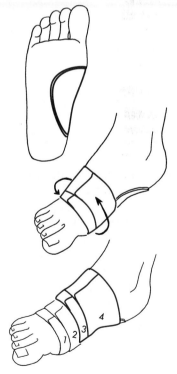

Figure 11-19

Arch taping technique no. 1,
including an arch pad and
circular tape strips

Techniques for Preventing
and Minimizing
Sport-Related Injuries

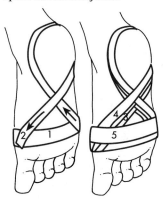

Figure 11-20

Arch taping technique no. 2
(X taping)

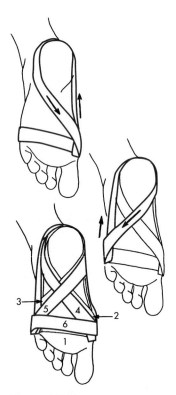

Figure 11-21

Arch taping technique no. 3,
with double X and forefoot
support

ARCH TECHNIQUE NO. 2: THE X FOR THE LONGITUDINAL ARCH

When using the figure-eight method for taping the longitudinal arch, execute the following steps (Figure 11-20).

MATERIALS NEEDED: One roll of 1-inch (2.5 cm) tape and tape adherent.

POSITION OF THE ATHLETE: The athlete lies face downward on a table, with the affected foot extending approximately 6 inches (15 cm) over the edge of the table. To ensure proper position, allow the foot to hang in a relaxed, natural position.

PROCEDURE:

1. Lightly place an anchor strip around the ball of the foot, making certain not to constrict the action of the toes (1).
2. Start tape strip 2 from the lateral edge of the anchor. Move it upward at an acute angle, cross the center of the longitudinal arch, encircle the heel, and descend, crossing the arch again and ending at the medial aspect of the anchor (2). Repeat three or four times (3 and 4).
3. Lock the taped Xs with a single piece of tape placed around the ball of foot (5).

After the X strips are applied, cover entire arch with 1.5-inch circular tape strips.

ARCH TECHNIQUE NO. 3: THE X TEAR DROP AND FOREFOOT SUPPORT

As its name implies, this taping both supports the longitudinal arch and stabilizes the forefoot into good alignment (Figure 11-21).

MATERIALS NEEDED: One roll of 1-inch (2.5 cm) tape and tape adherent.

POSITION OF THE ATHLETE: The athlete lies face down on a table, with the foot to be taped extending approximately 6 inches (15 cm) over the edge of the table.

PROCEDURE:

1. Place an anchor strip around the ball of the foot (1).
2. Start tape strip 2 on the side of the foot, beginning at the base of the great toe. Take the tape around the heel, crossing the arch and returning to the starting point (2).
3. The pattern of the third strip of tape is the same as the second strip except that it is started on the little toe side of the foot (3). Repeat pattern two or three times (4 and 5).
4. Lock each series of strips by placing tape around the ball joint (6). A completed procedure usually consists of a series of three strips.

ARCH TECHNIQUE NO. 4: FAN ARCH SUPPORT

Fan arch technique no. 4 supports the entire plantar aspect of the foot (Figure 11-22).

MATERIALS NEEDED: One roll of 1-inch (2.5 cm) and one roll of 1½-inch (3.8 cm) tape and tape adherent.

POSITION OF THE ATHLETE: The athlete lies face down on a table, with the

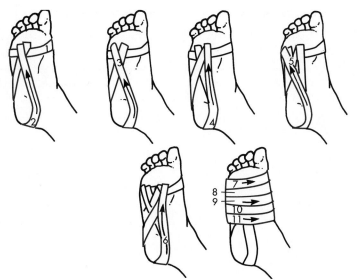

Figure 11-22

Fan arch taping technique

foot to be taped extending approximately 6 inches (15 cm) over the edge of the table.

PROCEDURE:

1. Place an anchor strip around the ball of the foot (1).

2. Starting at the third metatarsal head, take the tape around the heel from the lateral side and meet the strip where it began (2 and 3).

3. The next strip starts near the second metatarsal head and finishes on the fourth metatarsal head (4).

4. The last strip begins on the fourth metatarsal head and finishes on the fifth (5). The technique, when completed, forms a fan-shaped pattern covering the metatarsal region (6).

5. Lock strips (7 through 11) using 1½-inch (3.8 cm) tape and encircling the complete arch.

LOWDYE TECHNIQUE

The LowDye technique is an excellent method for managing the fallen medial longitudinal arch, foot pronation, arch strains, and plantar fasciitis. Moleskin is cut in 3-inch (7.5 cm) strips to the shape of the sole of the foot. It should cover the head of the metatarsal bones and the calcaneus bone (Figure 11-23).

MATERIALS NEEDED: One roll of 1-inch (2.5 cm) and one roll of 2-inch (5 cm) tape and moleskin.

POSITION OF THE ATHLETE: The athlete sits with the foot in a neutral position with the great toe and medial aspect of the foot in plantar flexion.

PROCEDURE:

1. Apply the moleskin to the sole of the foot, pulling it slightly downward before attaching it to the calcaneus.

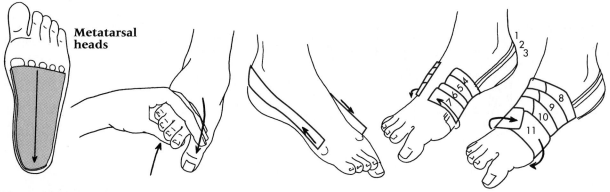

Figure 11-23

LowDye taping technique for fallen medial longitudinal arch, foot pronation, arch strains, and plantar fasciitis

2. Grasp the forefoot with the thumb under the distal 2 to 5 metatarsal heads, pushing slightly upward, with the tips of the second and third fingers pushing downward on the first metatarsal head. Apply two or three 1-inch (2.5 cm) tape strips laterally, starting from the distal head of the fifth metatarsal bone and ending at the distal head of the first metatarsal bone (1 through 3). Keep these lateral strips below the outer malleolus.

3. Secure the moleskin and lateral tape strips by circling the forefoot with four 2-inch (5 cm) strips (4 through 7): Start at the lateral dorsum of the foot, circle under the plantar aspect, and finish at the medial dorsum of the foot. Apply four 2-inch (5 cm) stretch-tape strips that encircle the arch (8 through 11).

NOTE: A variation of this method is to use two 2-inch (5 cm) moleskin strips, one at the ball of the foot and the other at the base of the fifth metatarsal. Cross the strips and extend them along the plantar surface of the foot; angle them over the center of the heel and 2 inches (5 cm) up the back of the foot. For anchors, apply 2-inch (5 cm) elastic tape around the forefoot, lateral to medial, giving additional support.

The Toes

THE SPRAINED GREAT TOE

This procedure is used for taping a sprained great toe (Figure 11-24).
MATERIALS NEEDED: One roll of 1-inch (2.5 cm) tape and tape adherent.
POSITION OF THE ATHLETE: The athlete assumes a sitting position.
PROCEDURE:

1. The greatest support is given to the joint by a half-figure-eight taping (1 through 3). Start the series at an acute angle on the top of the foot and swing down between the great and first toes, first encircling the great toe and then coming up, over, and across the starting point. Repeat this process, starting each series separately.

2. After the required number of half-figure-eight strips are in position, place one lock piece around the ball of the foot (4).

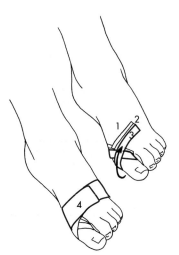

Figure 11-24

Taping for a sprained great toe

HAMMER, OR CLAWED, TOES

This technique is designed to reduce the pressure of the bent toes against the shoe (Figure 11-25).

MATERIALS NEEDED: One roll of ½- or 1-inch (1.25 or 2.5 cm) adhesive tape and tape adherent.

POSITION OF THE ATHLETE: The athlete sits on a table with the affected leg extended over the edge.

PROCEDURE:

1. Tape one affected toe; then lace under the adjacent toe and over the next toe.
2. Tape can be attached to the next toe or can be continued and attached to the fifth toe.

FRACTURED TOES

MATERIALS NEEDED: One roll of ½- to 1-inch (1.25 to 2.5 cm) tape, ⅛-inch (0.3 cm) sponge rubber, and tape adherent.

POSITION OF THE ATHLETE: The athlete assumes a sitting position.

PROCEDURE:

1. Cut a ⅛-inch (0.3 cm) sponge rubber wedge and place it between the affected toe and a healthy one.
2. Wrap two or three strips of tape around the toes (Figure 11-26). This technique splints the fractured toe with a nonfractured one.

BUNIONS

MATERIALS NEEDED: One roll of 1-inch (2.5 cm) tape, tape adherent, and ¼-inch (0.6 cm) sponge rubber or felt.

POSITION OF THE ATHLETE: The athlete assumes a sitting position.

PROCEDURE:

1. Cut the ¼-inch (0.6 cm) sponge rubber to form a wedge between the great and second toes.
2. Place anchor strips to encircle the midfoot and distal aspect of the great toe (Figure 11-27, 1 and 2).

Figure 11-25

Taping for hammer, or clawed, toes

Figure 11-26

Taping for fracture of a toe

Figure 11-27

Taping for a bunion

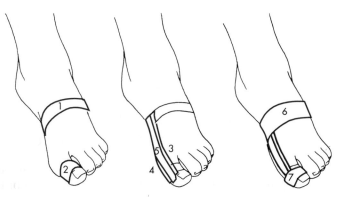

3. Place two or three strips on the medial aspect of the great toe to hold the toe in proper alignment (3 through 5).

4. Lock the ends of the strips with tape (6 and 7).

The Ankle Joint

ROUTINE NONINJURY

Ankle taping applied directly to the athlete's skin affords the greatest support; however, when applied and removed daily, skin irritation will occur. To avoid this problem, apply an underwrap material. Before taping, follow these procedures:

If the athlete has sensitive skin, thoroughly clean the area to be wrapped.

1. Shave all the hair off the foot and ankle.
2. Apply a coating of tape adherent to protect the skin and offer an adhering base. NOTE: It may be advisable to avoid the use of a tape adherent, especially if the athlete has a history of developing tape blisters. In cases of skin sensitivity, the ankle surface should be thoroughly cleansed of dirt and oil and an underwrap material applied; or tape directly to the skin.
3. Apply a gauze pad coated with friction-proofing material such as grease over the instep and to the back of the heel.
4. If underwrap is used, apply a single layer. The tape anchors extend beyond the underwrap and adhere directly to the skin.
5. Do not apply tape if skin is cold or hot from a therapeutic treatment.

MATERIALS NEEDED: One roll of 1½-inch (3.8 cm) tape and tape adherent.

POSITION OF THE ATHLETE: The athlete sits on a table with the leg extended and the foot held at a 90-degree angle.

PROCEDURE:

1. Place an anchor around the ankle approximately 5 or 6 inches (12.5 to 15 cm) above the malleolus (Figure 11-28, 1).
2. Apply two strips in consecutive order, starting behind the outer malleolus, taking care that each one overlaps half the width of the piece of tape it adjoins (2 and 3).
3. After applying the strips, wrap seven or eight circular strips around the ankle, from the point of the anchor downward until the malleolus is completely covered (4 through 12).
4. Apply two or three arch strips from lateral to medial, giving additional support to the arch (13 through 15).
5. Additional support is given by a heel lock. Starting high on the instep, bring the tape along the ankle at a slight angle, hooking the heel, leading under the arch, then coming up on the opposite side, and finishing at the starting point. Tear the tape to complete half of the heel lock (16). Repeat on the opposite side of the ankle. Finish with a band of tape around the ankle(17).

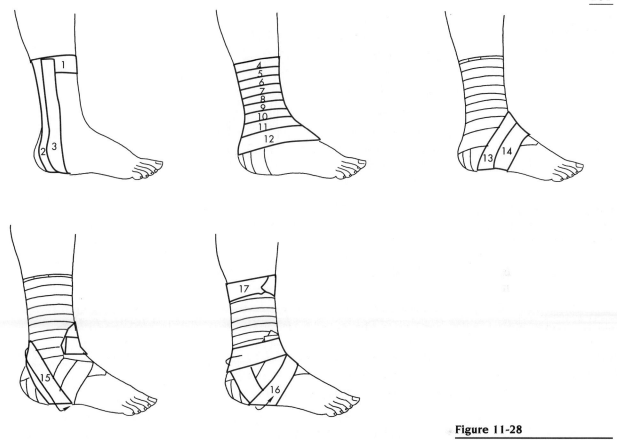

Figure 11-28

Routine noninjury ankle taping

CLOSED BASKET WEAVE (GIBNEY)

The closed basket weave, or Gibney, technique (Figure 11-29) offers strong tape support and is primarily used in athletic training for newly sprained or chronically weak ankles.

MATERIALS NEEDED: One roll of 1½-inch (3.8 cm) tape and tape adherent.

POSITION OF THE ATHLETE: The athlete sits on a table with the leg extended and the foot at a 90-degree angle.

PROCEDURE:

1. Place one anchor piece around the ankle approximately 5 or 6 inches (12.5 or 15 cm) above the malleolus, just below the belly of the gastrocnemius muscle, and a second anchor around the instep directly over the styloid process of the fifth metatarsal (1 and 2).

2. Apply the first strip posteriorly to the malleolus and attach it to the ankle strips (3). NOTE: When applying strips, pull the foot into eversion for an inversion strain and into a neutral position for an eversion strain.

Techniques for Preventing
and Minimizing
Sport-Related Injuries

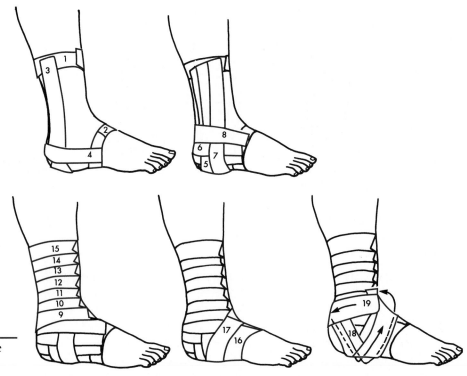

Figure 11-29

Closed basket weave ankle
taping

3. Start the first Gibney directly under the malleolus and attach it to the foot anchor (4).

4. In an alternating series, place three strips and three Gibneys on the ankle with each piece of tape overlapping at least half of the preceding strip (5 through 8).

5. After applying the basket weave series, continue the Gibney strips up the ankle, thus giving circular support (9 through 15).

6. For arch support, apply two or three circular strips lateral to medial (16 and 17).

7. After completing the conventional basket weave, apply two or three heel locks to ensure maximum stability (18 and 19).

OPEN BASKET WEAVE

This modification of the closed basket weave, or Gibney, technique is designed to give freedom of movement in dorsiflexion and plantar flexion while providing lateral and medial support and giving swelling room. Taping in this pattern (Figure 11-30) may be used immediately after an acute sprain in conjunction with a pressure bandage and cold applications, because it allows for swelling.

MATERIALS NEEDED: One roll of 1½-inch (3.8 cm) tape and tape adherent.

11-4

Critical Thinking Exercise

A cross-country runner steps in a hole and suffers a lateral sprain to the right ankle.

? What taping technique should be selected to provide ankle joint support while still allowing for swelling?

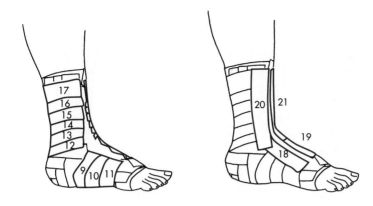

Figure 11-30

Open basket weave ankle
taping

POSITION OF THE ATHLETE: The athlete sits on a table with the leg extended and the foot held at a 90-degree angle.

PROCEDURE:

1. The procedures are the same as for the closed basket weave (Figure 11-29) with the exception of incomplete closures of the Gibney strips (11 through 17).

2. Lock the gap between the Gibney ends with two pieces of tape running on either side of the instep (18 through 21). NOTE: Application of a 1½-inch (3.8 cm) elastic bandage over the open basket weave affords added control of swelling; however, the athlete should remove it before retiring. Apply the elastic bandage distal to proximal to assist in preventing the swelling from moving into the toes.

Of the many ankle-taping techniques in vogue today, those using combinations of strips, basket weave patterns, and heel locks offer the best support.

CONTINUOUS STRETCH TAPE TECHNIQUE

This technique provides a fast alternative to other taping methods for the ankle (Figure 11-31).[8]

MATERIALS NEEDED: One roll of 1½-inch (3.8 cm) linen tape, one roll of 2-inch (5 cm) stretch tape, and tape adherent.

POSITION OF THE ATHLETE: The athlete sits on a table with the leg extended and the foot at a 90-degree angle.

PROCEDURE:

1. Place one anchor strip around the ankle approximately 5 to 6 inches (12.5 to 15 cm) above the malleolus (1).

2. Apply three strips, covering the malleoli (2 through 4).

3. Start the stretch tape in a medial-to-lateral direction around the midfoot and continue it in a figure-eight pattern to above the lateral malleolus (5).

4. Continue to stretch tape across the midfoot, then across the heel.

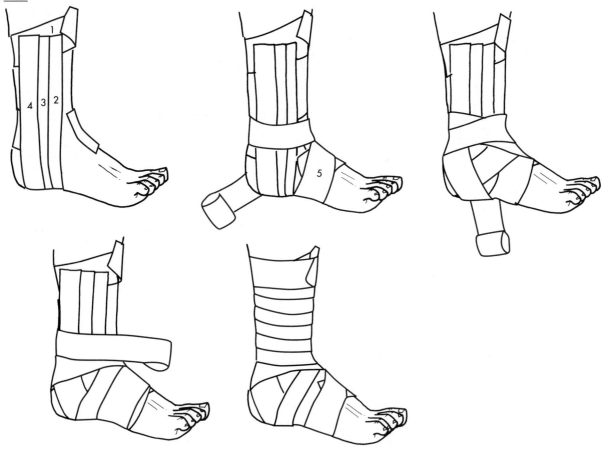

Figure 11-31

Continuous stretch tape technique for the ankle

5. Apply two heel locks, one in one direction and one in the reverse direction.
6. Next, repeat a figure-eight pattern followed by a spiral pattern, filling the space up to the anchor.
7. Use the lock technique at the top with a linen tape strip.

The Lower Leg

ACHILLES TENDON

Achilles tendon taping (Figure 11-32) is designed to prevent the Achilles tendon from overstretching.

MATERIALS NEEDED: One roll of 3-inch (7.5 cm) elastic tape, one roll of 1½-inch (3.8 cm) linen tape, and tape adherent.

POSITION OF THE ATHLETE: The athlete kneels or lies face down, with the affected foot hanging relaxed over the edge of the table.

PROCEDURE:

1. Apply two anchors with 1½-inch (3.8 cm) tape, one circling the leg loosely approximately 7 to 9 inches (17.5 to 22.5 cm)

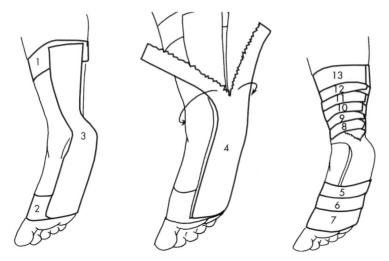

Figure 11-32

Achilles tendon taping

above the malleoli and the other encircling the ball of the foot (1 and 2).

2. Cut two strips of 3-inch (7.5 cm) elastic tape approximately 8 to 10 inches (20 to 25 cm) long. Moderately stretch the first strip from the ball of the athlete's foot along its plantar aspect up to the leg anchor (3). The second elastic strip (4) follows the course of the first, but cut it and split it down the middle lengthwise. Wrap the cut ends around the lower leg to form a lock. CAUTION: Keep the wrapped ends above the level of the strain.

3. Complete the series by placing two or three lock strips of elastic tape (5 through 7) loosely around the arch and five or six strips (8 through 13) around the athlete's lower leg.

NOTES:

1. Locking too tightly around the lower leg and foot will tend to restrict the normal action of the Achilles tendon and create more tissue irritation.

2. A variation to this method is to use three 2-inch-wide (5 cm) elastic strips in place of strips 3 and 4. Apply the first strip at the plantar surface of the first metatarsal head and end it on the lateral side of the leg anchor. Apply the second strip at the plantar surface of the fifth metatarsal head and end it on the medial side of the leg anchor. Center the third strip between the other two strips and end it at the posterior aspect of the calf. Wrap strips of 3-inch (7.5 cm) elastic tape around the forefoot and lower calf to close them off.[3]

MEDIAL SHINSPLINTS

Proper taping can afford some relief of the symptoms of shinsplints (Figure 11-33).

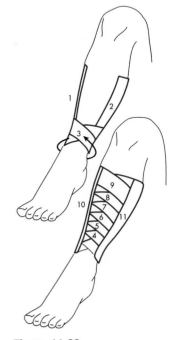

Figure 11-33

Taping for shinsplints

Techniques for Preventing
and Minimizing
Sport-Related Injuries

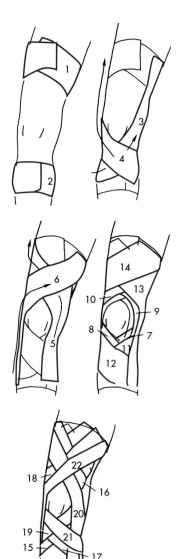

Figure 11-34

Taping for injuries to the
medial collateral ligament of
the knee

MATERIALS NEEDED: One roll of 1½-inch (3.8 cm) linen or elastic tape
and adherent.

POSITION OF THE ATHLETE: The athlete sits on a table with the knee bent
and the foot flat on the table. The purpose of this position is to fully relax the muscles of the lower leg.

PROCEDURE:

1. Apply two anchor tape strips, the first to the anterolateral aspect
   of the ankle and lower leg and the second to the posterolateral
   aspect of the midcalf (1 and 2).

2. Starting at the lowest end of the first anchor, run a strip of tape
   to the back of the lower leg, spiraling it over the shin to attach
   on the lower end of the second anchor strip. Apply three strips
   of tape in this manner, with each progressively moving upward
   on the leg. As each strip comes across the previous strip, make
   an effort to pull the muscle toward the tibia (3 strips).

3. After applying seven pieces of tape, lock their ends with one or
   two cross-strips (10 and 11).

4. After completing the procedure, you may apply an elastic wrap
   in a spiral fashion.

NOTE: A variation to this method is to place a ½-inch(1.25 cm) thickness
of felt 1 inch wide by 6 inches long (2.5 by 15 cm) on the medial border
of the tibia secured by underwrap. Beginning distally, use 6-inch (15 cm)
strips of white tape to hold the pad in place and provide support. The
strips do not encircle the leg but are completely covered by elastic tape or
a 3-inch (7.5 cm) elastic bandage.[2]

The Knee

MEDIAL COLLATERAL LIGAMENT

Like those with ankle instabilities, athletes with unstable knees should
never use tape and bracing as a replacement for proper exercise rehabilitation. If properly applied, taping can help protect the knee and aid in
the rehabilitation process (Figure 11-34).[5]

MATERIALS NEEDED: One roll of 2-inch (5 cm) linen tape, one roll of 3-
inch (7.5 cm) elastic tape, a 1-inch (2.5 cm) heel lift, and skin adherent.

POSITION OF THE ATHLETE: The athlete stands on a 3-foot (90 cm) table
with the injured knee held in a moderately relaxed position by a 1-inch
(2.5 cm) heel lift. The hair is completely removed from an area 6 inches
(15 cm) above to 6 inches (15 cm) below the patella.

PROCEDURE:

1. Lightly encircle the thigh and leg at the hairline with a 3-inch
   (7.5 cm) elastic anchor strip (1 and 2).

2. Precut 12 elastic tape strips, each approximately 9 inches
   (22.5 cm) long. Stretching them to their utmost, apply them to
   the knee as indicated in Figure 11-34 (3 through 14).

3. Apply a series of three strips of 2-inch (5 cm) linen tape (15 through 22). Some individuals find it advantageous to complete a knee taping by wrapping loosely with an elastic wrap, thus providing an added precaution against the tape's coming loose from perspiration.

CAUTION: Tape must not constrict patella.

ROTARY TAPING FOR INSTABILITY OF AN INJURED KNEE

The rotary taping method is designed to provide the knee with support when it is unstable from injury to the medial collateral and anterior cruciate ligaments (Figure 11-35).

MATERIALS NEEDED: One roll of 3-inch (7.5 cm) elastic tape, skin adherent, 4-inch (10 cm) gauze pad, and scissors.

POSITION OF THE ATHLETE: The athlete sits on a table with the affected knee flexed 15 degrees.

PROCEDURE:

1. Cut a 10-inch (25 cm) piece of elastic tape with both the ends snipped. Place the gauze pad in the center of the 10-inch (25 cm) piece of elastic tape to limit skin irritation and protect the popliteal nerves and blood vessels.
2. Put the gauze with the elastic tape backing on the popliteal fossa of the athlete's knee. Stretch both ends of the tape to the fullest extent and tear them. Place the divided ends firmly around the patella and interlock them (1).
3. Starting at a midpoint on the gastrocnemius muscle, spiral a 3-inch (7.5 cm) elastic tape strip to the front of the leg, then behind, crossing the popliteal fossa, and around the thigh, finishing anteriorly (2).
4. Repeat procedure 3 on the opposite side (3).
5. You may apply two or three more spiral strips for added strength (4 and 5).

Figure 11-35

Rotary taping for instability in an injured knee

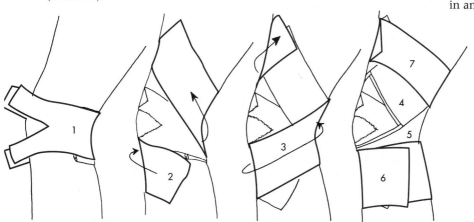

6. Lock the spiral strips by applying two strips around the thigh and two around the calf (6 and 7).

NOTE: Tracing the spiral pattern with linen tape yields more rigidity.

HYPEREXTENSION

Hyperextension taping (Figure 11-36) is designed to prevent the knee from hyperextending and also may be used for strained hamstring muscles or slackened cruciate ligaments.

MATERIALS NEEDED: One roll of 2½-inch (6.25 cm) tape or 2-inch (5 cm) elastic tape, cotton or a 4-inch (10 cm) gauze pad, tape adherent, underwrap, and a 2-inch (5 cm) heel lift.

POSITION OF THE ATHLETE: The athlete's leg should be completely shaved above midthigh and below midcalf. The athlete stands on a 3-foot (90 cm) table with the injured knee flexed by a 2-inch (5 cm) heel lift.

Figure 11-36

Hyperextension taping

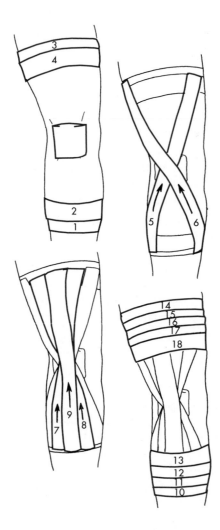

PROCEDURE:

1. Place four anchor strips at the hairlines, two around the thigh and two around the leg (1 through 4). They should be loose enough to allow for muscle expansion during exercise.

2. Place a gauze pad at the popliteal space to protect the popliteal nerves and blood vessels from constriction by the tape.

3. Start the supporting tape strips by forming an X over the popliteal space (5 and 6).

4. Cross the tape again with two more strips and one up the middle of the leg (7 through 9).

5. Complete the technique by applying four or five locking strips around the thigh and calf (10 through 18).

6. Apply an additional series of strips if the athlete is heavily muscled.

7. Lock the supporting strips in place by applying two or three overlapping circles around the thigh and leg.

PATELLOFEMORAL TAPING (MCCONNELL TECHNIQUE)

Patellofemoral orientation may be corrected to some degree by using tape. The McConnell technique evaluates four components of patellar orientation: glide, tilt, rotation, and anteroposterior (AP) alignment.[6] The glide component looks at side-to-side movement of the patella in the groove. The tilt component assesses the height of the lateral patellar border relative to the medial border. Patellar rotation is determined by looking for deviation of the long axis of the patella from the long axis of the femur. Anteroposterior alignment evaluates whether the inferior pole of the patella is tilted either anteriorly or posteriorly relative to the superior pole. Correction of patellar position and tracking is accomplished by passive taping of the patella in a more biomechanically correct position. In addition to correcting the orientation of the patella, the tape provides a prolonged gentle stretch to soft-tissue structures that affect patellar movement.[6]

MATERIALS NEEDED: Two special types of extremely sticky tape are required. Fixomull and Leuko Sportape are manufactured by Biersdorf Australia, Ltd.

POSITION OF THE ATHLETE: The athlete should be seated with the knee in full extension.

PROCEDURE:

1. Two strips of Fixomull are extended from the lateral femoral condyle just posterior to the medial femoral condyle around the front of the knee. This tape is used as a base to which the other tape may be adhered. Leuko Sportape is used from this point on to correct patellar alignment (Figure 11-37).

2. To correct a lateral glide, attach a short strip of tape one thumb's width from the lateral patellar border, pushing the patella

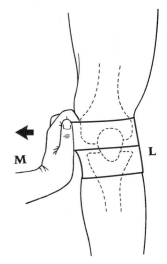

Figure 11-37

The first two strips of tape in the McConnell technique serve as the base to which additional tape is adhered.

Techniques for Preventing
and Minimizing
Sport-Related Injuries

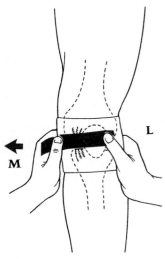

medially in the frontal plane. Crease the skin between the lateral patellar border and the medial femoral condyle and secure the tape on the medial side of the joint (Figure 11-38).

3. To correct a lateral tilt, flex the knee to 30 degrees, adhere a short strip of tape beginning at the middle of the patella, and pull medially to lift the lateral border. Again, crease the skin underneath and adhere it to the medial side of the knee (Figure 11-39).

4. To correct an external rotation of the inferior pole relative to the superior pole, adhere a strip of tape to the middle of the inferior pole, pulling upward and medially while internally rotating the patella with the free hand. The tape is attached to the medial side of the knee (Figure 11-40).

5. For correcting AP alignment in which there is an inferior tilt, take a 6-inch (15 cm) piece of tape, place the middle of the strip over the upper one-half of the patella and attach it equally on both sides to lift the inferior pole (Figure 11-41).

6. Once patellar taping is completed, the athlete should be instructed to wear the tape all day during all activities. The athlete should periodically tighten the strips as they loosen.

NOTE: The McConnell technique for treating patellofemoral pain also stresses the importance of more symmetrical loading of the patella through reeducation and strengthening of the vastus medialis.[3]

Figure 11-38

Taping technique to correct a lateral glide of the patella

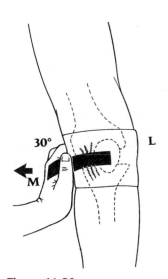

Figure 11-39

Taping technique to correct a lateral tilt of the patella

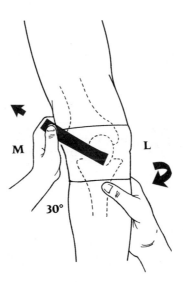

Figure 11-40

Taping technique to correct external rotation of the inferior pole of the patella

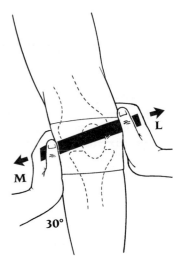

Figure 11-41

Taping technique to correct AP alignment with an inferior tilt

The Thigh

QUADRICEPS SUPPORT

The taping of the quadriceps muscle group (Figure 11-42) is designed to give support against the pull of gravity. In cases of moderate or severe contusions or strains, taping may afford protection or mild support and give confidence to the athlete. Various techniques fitted to the individual needs of the athletes can be used.

MATERIALS NEEDED: One roll of 1½- or 2-inch (3.75 or 5 cm) tape, skin toughener, and a 6-inch (15 cm) elastic bandage.

POSITION OF THE ATHLETE: The athlete stands on the massage table with leg extended.

PROCEDURE:

1. Apply two anchor strips, each approximately 9 inches (22.5 cm) long, one each on the lateral and medial aspects of the thigh, half the distance between the anterior and posterior aspects (1 and 2).

2. Apply strips of tape to the thigh, crossing one another to form an X. Begin the crisscrosses 2 or 3 inches (5 or 7.5 cm) above the kneecap and carry them upward, overlapping one another. It is important to start each tape strip at the anchor piece and carry it upward and diagonally over the quadriceps, lifting against gravity. Continue this procedure until the quadriceps is completely covered (3 through 9).

3. After applying the diagonal series, place a lock strip longitudinally over the medial and lateral borders of the series (11 and 12).

4. To ensure more effective stability of the quadriceps taping, encircle the entire thigh with either a 3-inch (7.5 cm) elastic tape or a 6-inch (15 cm) elastic bandage, paying special attention to lift against gravity for additional support.

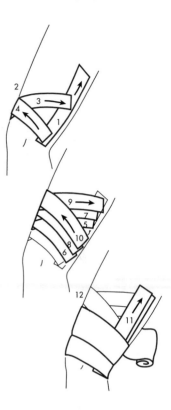

Figure 11-42

Quadriceps tape support

HAMSTRING SUPPORT

It is extremely difficult to relieve the injured hamstring muscles completely by any wrapping or taping technique, but some stabilization can be afforded by each. The hamstring taping technique (Figure 11-43) is designed to stabilize the moderately to severely contused or torn hamstring muscles, enabling the athlete to continue to compete.

MATERIALS NEEDED: One roll of 2- or 1½-inch (5 or 3.8 cm) tape, skin toughener, and a roll of 3-inch (7.5 cm) elastic tape or a 6-inch (15 cm) elastic wrap.

POSITION OF THE ATHLETE: The athlete lies face downward or may stand on the table, with the affected limb flexed at approximately a 15-degree angle at the knee, so the hamstring muscle is relaxed and shortened.

PROCEDURE:

1. Apply this taping similarly to the quadriceps technique. Place an anchor strip on either side of the thigh (1 and 2), and then crisscross strips, approximately 9 inches (22.5 cm) in length,

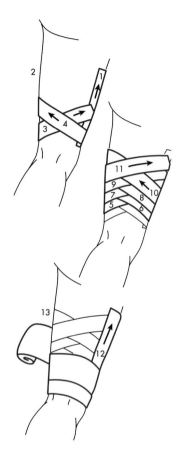

Figure 11-43

Hamstring taping

diagonally upward on the posterior aspect of the thigh, forming an X (3 through 11).

2. After the hamstring area is covered with a series of crisscrosses, apply a longitudinal lock on either side of the thigh (12 and 13).

3. Place 3-inch (7.5 cm) elastic tape or a 6-inch (15 cm) elastic wrap around the thigh if needed to hold the crisscross taping in place.

ILIAC SUPPORT

Iliac crest adhesive taping (Figure 11-44) is designed to support, protect, and immobilize the soft tissue surrounding the iliac crest.

MATERIALS NEEDED: One roll of 2-inch (5 cm) adhesive tape, 6-inch (15 cm) bandage, skin toughener, and tape adherent.

POSITION OF THE ATHLETE: The athlete stands on the floor, bending slightly laterally toward the injured side.

PROCEDURE:

1. Apply two anchor strips, each approximately 9 inches (22.5 cm) long, one longitudinally just lateral to the sacrum and lumbar spine and the other lateral to the umbilicus (1 and 2).

2. Commencing 2 to 3 inches (5 to 7.5 cm) below the crest of the ilium, tape crisscrosses from one anchor to the other, lifting the tissue against the pull of gravity. Carry the crisscrosses upward to a point just below the floating rib (3 through 8).

3. If additional support is desired, lay horizontal strips on alternately in posteroanterior and anteroposterior directions (9 through 14).

4. Put lock strips over approximately the same positions as the anchor strips (15 and 16).

5. Apply a 6-inch (15 cm) elastic bandage to secure the tape and to prevent perspiration from loosening the taping.

The Shoulder

STERNOCLAVICULAR IMMOBILIZATION

MATERIALS NEEDED: A felt pad ¼-inch (0.6 cm) thick, cut to a circumference of 4 inches (10 cm); 3-inch (7.5 cm) roll of elastic tape; two gauze pads; and tape adherent.

POSITION OF THE ATHLETE: Reduction of the most common sternoclavicular dislocation is performed by traction, with the athlete's arm abducted. Traction and abduction are maintained by an assistant while the immobilization taping is applied.

PROCEDURE:

1. Apply an anchor strip around the chest at the level of the tenth rib while the chest is expanded (Figure 11-45, 1).

2. Lay a felt pad over the sternoclavicular joint and apply gauze pads over the athlete's nipples.

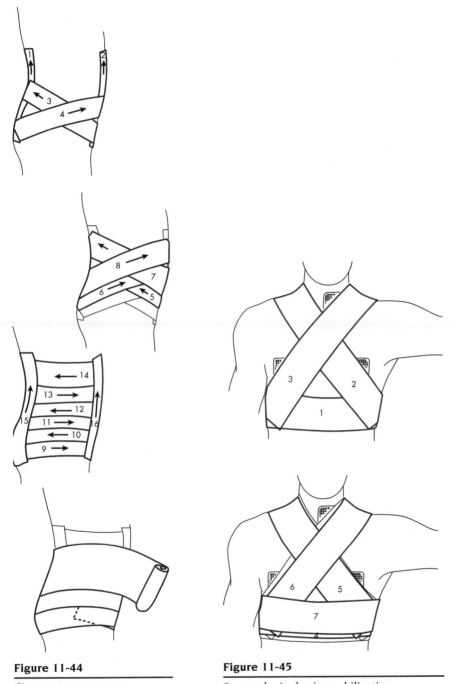

Figure 11-44

Iliac tape support

Figure 11-45

Sternoclavicular immobilization

3. Depending on the direction of displacement, apply tape pressure
   over the felt pad. With the most common dislocation (upward,
   forward, and anterior), taping starts from the back and moves
   forward over the shoulder. The first pressure strip runs from the

anchor tape on the unaffected side over the injured site to the
front anchor strip (2).

4. A second strip goes from the anchor strip on the affected side
   over the unaffected side to finish on the front anchor strip (3).

5. Apply as many series of strips as are needed to give complete
   immobilization (4 through 6). Lock all series in place with a tape
   strip placed over the ends (7).

ACROMIOCLAVICULAR SUPPORT

Protective acromioclavicular taping (Figure 11-46) is designed to stabilize
the acromioclavicular articulation in proper alignment and still allow
normal movement of the shoulder complex.

MATERIALS NEEDED: One ¼-inch (0.6 cm) thick felt pad, roll of 2-inch
(5 cm) adhesive tape, tape adherent, 2-inch (5 cm) gauze pad, and 3-inch
(7.5 cm) elastic bandage.

POSITION OF THE ATHLETE: The athlete sits in a chair with the affected
arm resting in a position of abduction.

PROCEDURE:

1. Apply three anchor strips: the first in a three-quarter circle just
   below the deltoid muscle (1); the second just below the (gauze-
   covered) nipple, encircling half the chest (2); and the third over
   the trapezius muscle near the neck, attaching to the second
   anchor in front and back (3).

2. Apply the first and second strips of tape from the front and back
   of the first anchor, crossing them at the acromioclavicular
   articulation and attaching them to the third anchor strip (4).

3. Place the third support over the ends of the first and second
   pieces, following the line of the third anchor strip (5).

4. Lay a fourth support strip over the second anchor strip (6).

5. Continue this basket weave pattern until the entire shoulder
   complex is covered. Follow it with the application of a shoulder
   spica with an elastic bandage (7 through 13).

Figure 11-46

Protective acromioclavicular
taping

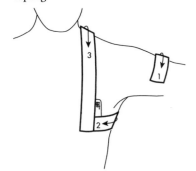
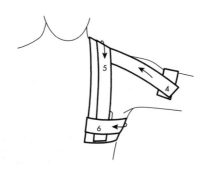
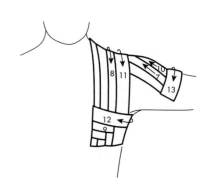

SHOULDER SUPPORT AND RESTRAINT

This taping supports the soft tissues of the shoulder complex and restrains the arm from abducting more than 90 degrees (Figure 11-47).

MATERIALS NEEDED: One roll of 2-inch (5 cm) tape, 2-inch (5 cm) gauze pad, cotton pad, tape adherent, and 3-inch (7.5 cm) elastic bandage.

POSITION OF THE ATHLETE: The athlete stands with the affected arm flexed at the elbow and the shoulder internally rotated and slightly abducted.

PROCEDURE:

1. The first phase is designed to support the capsule of the shoulder joint. After placing a cotton pad in the axilla, run a series of three loops around the shoulder joint (1 through 3). Start the first loop at the top of the athlete's scapula, pull it forward across the acromion process, around the front of the shoulder, back underneath the axilla, and over the back of the shoulder, crossing the acromion process again. Terminate it at the clavicle. Begin each of the subsequent strips down the shoulder half the width of the preceding strip.

2. Run strips of tape upward from a point just below the insertion of the deltoid muscle and cross them over the acromion process, completely covering the outer surface of the shoulder joint (4 through 9).

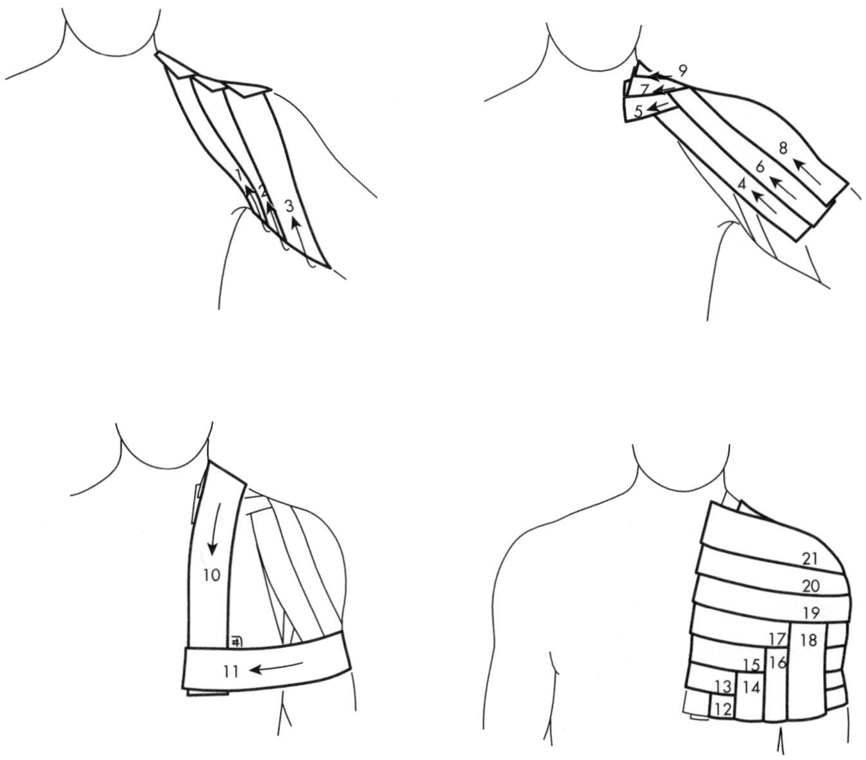

Figure 11-47

Taping for shoulder support and restraint

Techniques for Preventing
and Minimizing
Sport-Related Injuries

3. Before the final application of a basket weave shoulder taping, place a gauze pad over the nipple area and bring the arm back to the side of the thorax. Lay a strip of tape over the shoulder near the neck and carry it to the nipple line in front and to the scapular line in back (10).

4. Take a second strip from the end of the first strip, pass it around the middle of the upper arm, and end it at the back end of the first strip (11).

5. Continue the above alternation with an overlapping of each preceding strip by at least half its width until the shoulder has been completely capped (12 through 21).

6. Apply a shoulder spica to keep the taping in place.

ELBOW RESTRICTION

Tape the elbow as follows to prevent hyperextension (Figure 11-48).

MATERIALS NEEDED: One roll of 1½-inch (3.8 cm) tape, tape adherent, and 2-inch (5 cm) elastic bandage.

POSITION OF THE ATHLETE: The athlete stands with the affected elbow flexed at 90 degrees.

PROCEDURE:

1. Apply two anchor strips loosely around the arm, approximately 2 inches (25 cm) to each side of the curve of the elbow (antecubital fossa) (1 and 2).

2. Construct a checkrein by cutting a 10-inch (25 cm) and a 4-inch (10 cm) strip of tape and laying the 4-inch (10 cm) strip against the center of the 10-inch (25 cm) strip, blanking out that portion. Next place the checkrein so that it spans the two anchor strips with the blanked-out side facing downward. Leave checkrein extended 1 to 2 inches past anchor strips on both ends. This allows anchoring of the checkreins with circular strips to secure against slippage (3 and 4).

3. Place five additional 10-inch (25 cm) strips of tape over the basic checkrein.

4. Finish the procedure by securing the checkrein with three lock strips on each end (5 through 10). A figure-eight elastic wrap applied over the taping will prevent the tape from slipping because of perspiration.

NOTE: A variation to this method is to fan the checkreins, dispersing the force over a wider area (Figure 11-49).

The Wrist and Hand

WRIST TECHNIQUE NO. 1

This wrist taping (Figure 11-50) is designed for mild wrist strains and sprains.

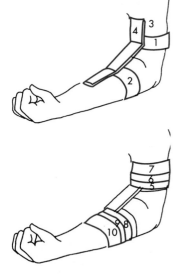

Figure 11-48

Taping to restrict elbow tension

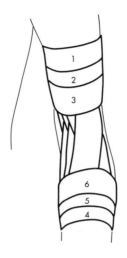

Figure 11-49

Fanned checkrein technique

MATERIALS NEEDED: One roll of 1-inch (2.5 cm) tape and tape adherent.

POSITION OF THE ATHLETE: The athlete stands with the affected hand flexed toward the injured side and the fingers moderately spread to increase the breadth of the wrist for the protection of nerves and blood vessels.

PROCEDURE:

1. Starting at the base of the wrist, bring a strip of 1-inch (2.5 cm) tape from the palmar side upward and around both sides of the wrist (1).

2. In the same pattern, with each strip overlapping the preceding one by at least half its width, lay two additional strips in place (2 and 3).

WRIST TECHNIQUE NO. 2

This wrist taping (Figure 11-51) stabilizes and protects badly injured wrists. The materials and positioning are the same as in technique no. 1.

MATERIALS NEEDED: One roll of 1-inch (2.5 cm) tape and tape adherent.

POSITION OF THE ATHLETE: The athlete stands with the affected hand flexed toward the injured side and the fingers moderately spread to increase the breadth of the wrist for the protection of nerves and blood vessels.

PROCEDURE:

1. Apply one anchor strip around the wrist approximately 3 inches (7.5 cm) from the hand (1); wrap another anchor strip around the spread hand (2).

2. With the wrist bent toward the side of the injury, run a strip of tape from the anchor strip near the little finger obliquely across the wrist joint to the wrist anchor strip. Run another strip from the anchor strip on the index finger side across the wrist joint to

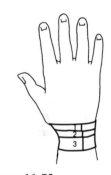

Figure 11-50

Wrist taping technique no. 1

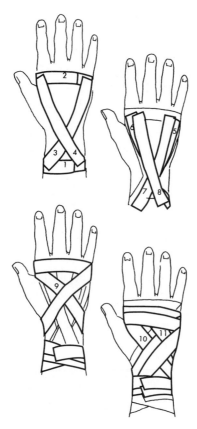

Figure 11-51

Wrist taping technique no. 2

the wrist anchor. This forms a crisscross over the wrist joint (3 and 4). Apply a series of four or five crisscrosses, depending on the extent of splinting needed (5 through 8).

3. Apply two or three series of figure-eight tapings over the crisscross taping (9 through 11). Start by encircling the wrist once, carry a strip over the back of the hand obliquely, encircling the hand twice, and then carry another strip obliquely upward across the back of the hand to where the figure-eight started. Repeat this procedure to ensure a strong, stabilizing taping.

BRUISED HAND

The following method is used to tape a bruised hand (Figure 11-52).

MATERIALS NEEDED: One roll of 1-inch (2.5 cm) adhesive tape, one roll of ½-inch (1.25 cm) tape, ¼-inch (0.6 cm) thick sponge rubber pad, and tape adherent.

POSITION OF THE ATHLETE: The fingers are spread moderately.

PROCEDURE:

1. Lay the protective pad over the bruise and hold it in place with three strips of ½-inch (1.25 cm) tape laced through the webbing of the fingers.

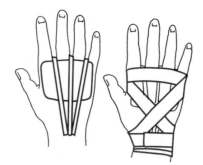

Figure 11-52

Taping for a bruised hand

2. Apply a basic figure-eight made of 1-inch (2.5 cm) tape.

SPRAINED THUMB

Sprained thumb taping (Figure 11-53) is designed to give both protection
for the muscle and joint and support to the thumb.

MATERIALS NEEDED: One roll of 1-inch (2.5 cm) tape and tape adherent.

POSITION OF THE ATHLETE: The athlete should hold the injured thumb in
a relaxed neutral position.

PROCEDURE:

1. Place an anchor strip loosely around the wrist and another
   around the distal end of the thumb (1 and 2).
2. From the anchor at the tip of the thumb to the anchor around
   the wrist, apply four splint strips in a series on the side of greater
   injury (dorsal or palmar side) (3 through 5) and hold them in
   place with one lock strip around the wrist and one encircling the
   tip of the thumb (6 and 7).
3. Add three thumb spicas. Start the first spica on the radial side at
   the base of the thumb and carry it under the thumb, completely
   encircling it, and then cross the starting point. The strip should
   continue around the wrist and finish at the starting point. Each
   of the subsequent spica strips should overlap the preceding
   strip by at least ⅔ inch (1.7 cm) and move downward on the
   thumb (8 and 9). The thumb spica with tape provides an
   excellent means of protection during recovery from an injury
   (Figure 11-54).

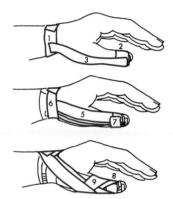

Figure 11-53

Taping for a sprained thumb

Figure 11-54

Thumb spica

FINGER AND THUMB CHECKREINS

The sprained finger or thumb may require the additional protection afforded by a restraining checkrein (Figure 11-55).

MATERIALS NEEDED: One roll of 1-inch (2.5 cm) tape.

POSITION OF THE ATHLETE: The athlete spreads the injured fingers widely
but within a range that is free of pain.

PROCEDURE:

1. Bring a strip of 1-inch (2.5 cm) tape around the middle phalanx
   of the injured finger over to the adjacent finger and around it

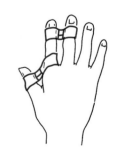

Figure 11-55

Finger and thumb checkreins

also. The tape left between the two fingers, which are spread apart, is called the checkrein.

2. Add strength with a lock strip around the center of the checkrein.

SUMMARY

- Bandages, when properly applied, can contribute to recovery from sport injuries.
- Cleanliness is of major importance at all times in the training room and on the field.
- Materials commonly used for bandages and dressings in sports are gauze, cotton cloth, elastic material, and plastics.
- Wound contamination can lead to the potentially fatal disease tetanus (lockjaw) if the athlete has not received a tetanus toxoid inoculation.
- Skin wounds are categorized as abrasions, puncture wounds, lacerations, incisions, and avulsion wounds.
- Common types of bandages used in sports are roller, triangular, and cravat for first aid and arm slings, of which the cervical and shoulder types are the most common.
- Common roller bandages are gauze for wounds, cotton cloth ankle wraps, and elastic wraps.
- As with taping, roller bandages must be applied uniformly, firmly but not so tightly as to impede circulation.
- Historically, taping has been an important aspect of athletic training. Sports tape is used in a variety of ways—as a means of holding a wound dressing in place, as support, and as protection against musculoskeletal injuries.
- For supporting and protecting musculoskeletal injuries, two types of tape are currently used—linen and stretch.
- Sports tape must be stored in a cool place and must be stacked on the flat side of each roll.
- The skin of the athlete must be carefully prepared before tape is applied.
- The skin should first be carefully cleaned; then all hair should be removed.
- An adherent may be applied, followed by an underwrap material, if need be, to help avoid skin irritation.

- When tape is applied, it must be done in a manner that provides the least amount of irritation and the maximum support.

- All tape applications require great care that the proper materials are used, that the proper position of the athlete is ensured, and that procedures are carefully followed.

Solutions to Critical Thinking Exercises

11-1 The coach applies a 6-inch (15 cm) elastic wrap as a hip adductor restraint. This technique is designed to prevent the groin from being overstretched and the hip adductors reinjured.

11-2 The coach applies tape and a 4-inch (10 cm) elastic shoulder spica to hold the doughnut in place.

11-3 The coach applies a sling and swathe combination. This combination stabilizes the shoulder joint and upper arm.

11-4 Initially the open basket weave taping technique is selected for a sprained ankle. This technique in conjunction with a pressure bandage and cold application can also control swelling.

REVIEW QUESTIONS AND CLASS ACTIVITIES

1. What is the difference between a dressing and a bandage? What are the uses of each?
2. What are some common types of bandages used in sports medicine today? What are these bandages used for? How do you apply them?
3. Observe the athletic trainer dressing wounds in the training room.
4. Demonstrate proper use of the roller, triangular, and cravat bandages.
5. What types of tape are available? What is the purpose of each type? What qualities should you look for in selecting tape?
6. How should you prepare an area to be taped?
7. How should you tear tape?
8. How should you remove tape from an area? Demonstrate the various methods and cutters that can be used to remove tape.
9. What are some general rules for tape application and why should you follow them?
10. What are some common taping procedures?
11. Bring the different types of tape to class. Discuss their uses and the qualities to look for in purchasing tape. Have the class practice tearing tape and preparing an area for taping.
12. Take each joint or body part and demonstrate the common taping procedures used to give support to that area. Have the students pair up and practice these taping jobs on each other. Discuss the advantages and disadvantages of using tape as a supportive device.

REFERENCES

1. Arnheim DD: *Modern principles of athletic training,* ed 8, St Louis, 1993, Times Mirror/Mosby College Publishing.
2. Bisek AM: Shin splint taping: something extra, *Ath Train* 22:216, 1987.
3. Ellison AE, editor: *Athletic training and sports medicine,* Chicago, 1984, American Academy of Orthopaedic Surgeons.
4. Hafen BQ: *First aid for health emergencies,* ed 4, St Paul, Minn, 1989, West Publishing.
5. Handling KA: Taping procedure for an unstable knee, *Ath Train* 16:371, 1984.
6. McConnell J: The management of chondro-malacia patella: a long term solution, *Aust J Physiother* 32:215, 1986.
7. Parcel GS: *Basic emergency care of the sick and injured,* ed 4, St Louis, 1990, Times Mirror/Mosby College Publishing.
8. The continuous technique of ankle support, *Sports Med Guide* 3:14, 1984.

ANNOTATED BIBLIOGRAPHY

Athletic Training, National Athletic Training Association, PO Box 1865, Greenville NC 27835-1865.
   Each volume of this quarterly journal contains practical procedures for bandaging and taping as well as for orthotic application.
Athletic Training, National Athletic Training Association, Dallas, Texas.
   Each volume of this quarterly journal contains practical procedures for taping.
Beuersdorf's medical program: manuals of taping and strapping technique, Agoura, Calif, 1988, Macmillan.
   A complete detailed guide to various taping and strapping techniques.
First aider, Gardner, Kan, Cramer Products.

   Published seven times throughout the school year, this periodical contains useful taping and bandaging techniques that have been submitted by readers.
National Safety Council: *First aid and CPR,* Boston, 1993, Jones & Bartlett.
   Chapter 5 provides an excellent discussion on wound care.
Sports Medicine Digest, PO Box 2160, Van Nuys CA 91404-2160.
Sports Medicine Guide, Mueller Sports Medicine, 1 Quench Dr, Prairie du Sac WI 53578.
   Published four times a year, this quarterly often presents, along with discussions on specific injuries, many innovative taping and bandaging techniques.

WEB SITE

Cramer First Aider: http://www.ccsd.k12.wy.us/CCHS_web/sptmed/fstaider.htm

Basics of Injury Rehabilitation

When you finish this chapter you will be able to:

- Explain the philosophy of the rehabilitative process in a sports medicine environment.
- Identify the individual short-term and long-term goals of a rehabilitation program.
- Describe the criteria and the decision-making process for determining when the injured athlete may return to full activity.

The athletic trainer is responsible for design, implementation, and supervision of the rehabilitation program.

The long-term goal is to return the injured athlete to practice or competition as quickly and safety as possible.

Sports medicine rehabilitation = aggressiveness.

PHILOSOPHY OF ATHLETIC INJURY REHABILITATION

Even though coaches make every effort to create a safe playing environment and prevent injuries, the nature of athletic participation dictates that injuries will eventually occur. Fortunately, few of the injuries that occur in an athletic setting are life threatening. The majority of the injuries are not serious and lend themselves to rapid rehabilitation. Long-term rehabilitation programs require the supervision of a highly trained professional if they are going to be safe and effective. In an athletic setting, the coach should rely on the athletic trainer to assume the primary responsibility for design, implementation, and supervision of the rehabilitation program for the injured athlete. The coach, in the absence of an athletic trainer, is responsible for design, implementation, and supervision of the rehabilitation program for the injured athlete.

The competitive nature of athletics necessitates an aggressive approach to rehabilitation. Because of the short competitive season in most sports, the injured athlete does not have the luxury of simply sitting around and doing nothing until the injury heals. *The goal of the injured athlete is to return to activity as soon as safely possible.*[9] Consequently, the tendency is to try and push the athlete to return. Unfortunately there is a thin line between not pushing the athlete hard enough or fast enough and being overly aggressive. In either case, a mistake in judgment on the part of the person overseeing the rehabilitation program may hinder the athlete's return to activity.

GOALS OF A REHABILITATION PROGRAM

Designing an effective rehabilitation program is simple if several basic components are addressed. These basic components may also be considered as the short-term goals of a rehabilitation program and should include: (1) providing correct immediate first aid and management following injury to limit or control swelling; (2) reducing or minimizing pain; (3) restoring full range of motion; (4) restoring or increasing muscular strength, endurance, and power; (5) reestablishing neuromuscular control; (6) improving balance; (7) maintaining cardiorespiratory fitness; and (8) incorporating appropriate functional progressions.[8] *The long-term goal is almost invariably to return the injured athlete to practice or competition as quickly and safely as possible.*

Providing Correct First Aid and Controlling Swelling

As discussed in detail in Chapter 7, the process of rehabilitation begins immediately after injury. Initial first-aid and management techniques are perhaps the most critical part of any rehabilitation program. How the injury is managed initially has a significant impact on the course of the rehabilitative process.[2] Everything that is done in first-aid management of any injury should be directed toward controlling the swelling.[1] To control and significantly limit the amount of swelling, the RICE principle—rest, ice, compression, and elevation—should be applied (Figure 12-1). Each factor plays a critical role in limiting swelling, and all these elements should be used simultaneously (see Chapter 7).

Controlling Pain

When an injury occurs, the athlete will experience some degree of pain. The extent of the pain will be determined in part by the severity of the injury, by the athlete's individual response to and perception of pain, and by the circumstances under which the injury occurred. The coach can effectively control acute pain by using the RICE technique immediately after injury.[7] In addition, using appropriate therapeutic modalities such

12-1

Critical Thinking Exercise

A soccer player has been diagnosed as having a grade 2 sprain of the MCL in her knee. The team physician has referred the athlete to the coach, who is charged with the responsibility of overseeing the rehabilitation program.

? What are the short-term goals of a rehabilitation program, and how can the coach best achieve these goals?

12-2

Critical Thinking Exercise

A runner complains of anterior knee pain. She has greatly cut back on the distance of her training runs and indicates that she has been taking antiinflammatory medication to help her continue to train. However, she is frustrated because her knee seems to be getting worse instead of better.

? What can the coach recommend to most effectively help her deal with her knee pain?

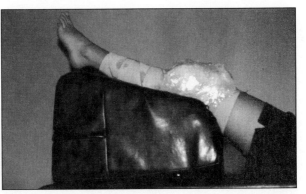

Figure 12-1

The RICE technique should be used immediately following injury to limit swelling.

Techniques for Preventing and Minimizing Sport-Related Injuries

Components of a rehabilitation program:
Controlling swelling
Reducing pain
Restoring full range of motion
Restoring muscle strength, endurance, power
Reestablishing neuromuscular control
Regaining balance
Maintaining cardiorespiratory fitness
Incorporating functional progressions

Controlling swelling:
Rest
Ice
Compression
Elevation

Limited range of movement = stretching.

Strengthening exercises:
Isometrics
Progressive resistance exercise
Isokinetics
Plyometrics

as ice, heat, or electrical stimulating currents can help modulate pain throughout the rehabilitation process.[10]

Restoring Range of Motion

Injury to a joint will always be followed by some associated loss of motion. That loss of movement may be caused by resistance of the muscle and its tendon to stretch, by contracture of the ligaments and capsule around a joint, or by some combination of the two. The athlete should engage in stretching activities designed to improve flexibility (Figure 12-2).

Restoring Muscular Strength, Endurance, and Power

Muscular strength, endurance, and power are among the most essential factors in restoring the function of a body part to preinjury status (see Chapter 4). Isometric, progressive resistance (isotonic), isokinetic, and plyometric exercises can benefit rehabilitation.[5] A major goal in performing strengthening exercises is to work through a full, pain-free range of motion.

Isometric Exercise

Isometric exercises are commonly performed in the early phase of rehabilitation when a joint is immobilized for a period of time. They are useful in cases in which using resistance training through a full range of motion may make the injury worse. Isometrics increase static strength and assist in decreasing the amount of atrophy. Isometrics also can lessen swelling by causing a muscle pumping action to remove fluid and edema.

Progressive Resistance Exercise

Progressive resistance exercise (PRE) is the most commonly used strengthening technique in a rehabilitation program. PRE may be done with free weights, exercise machines, or rubber tubing (Figure 12-3). Progressive resistance exercise uses isotonic contractions in which force is generated against resistance while the muscle is changing in length. In a rehabilitation program, both eccentric (shortening) and concentric (lengthening) strengthening exercises should be used.

Figure 12-2

Stretching techniques are used with tight musculotendinous structures to improve range of motion.

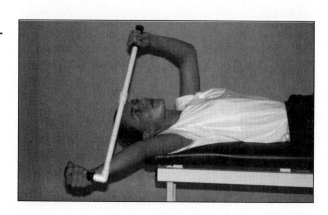

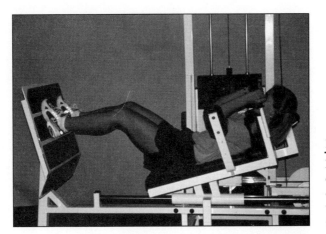

Figure 12-3

Progressive resistance
exercise using isotonic
contractions is the most
widely used rehabilitative
strengthening technique.

Isokinetic Exercise

Isokinetic exercise is commonly used in the rehabilitative process.[8] It is most often incorporated during the later phases of a rehabilitation program. Isokinetics uses a fixed speed with accommodating resistance to provide maximal resistance throughout the range of motion (Figure 12-4). The speed of movement can be altered in isokinetic exercise. Isokinetic measures are commonly used as criteria for return of the athlete to functional activity following injury.

Plyometric Exercise

Plyometric exercises are most often incorporated into the later stages of a rehabilitation program. Plyometrics use a quick stretch of a muscle to facilitate a subsequent concentric contraction. Plyometric exercises are useful in restoring or developing the athlete's ability to produce dynamic movements associated with muscular power (Figure 12-5). The ability to generate force very rapidly is a key to successful performance in many sport activities. It is critical to address the element of muscular power in rehabilitation programs for the injured athlete.

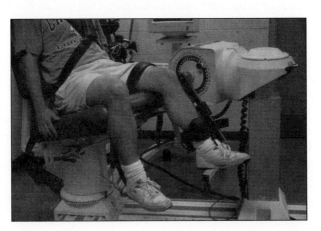

Figure 12-4

Isokinetic exercise is most
often used in the later stages
of rehabilitation.

Figure 12-5

Plyometric exercise focuses
on improving dynamic,
power movements.

Neuromuscular control
produces coordinated
movements.

Balance = postural stability.

All exercise rehabilitation
must be conducted as part of
a carefully designed plan.

 12-3

Critical Thinking Exercise

Following an ankle sprain, a
basketball player is placed in
an ankle immobilizer and given
crutches with instructions to
begin with totally non-weight-
bearing movement and
progress to full weight-bearing
movement without crutches as
soon as possible. After four
days the athlete is out of the
immobilizer and can walk
without crutches but still has a
significant limp.

? What should the coach do
to help the athlete regain a normal gait pattern, and why is it
important to do so as soon as
possible?

Reestablishing Neuromuscular Control

Neuromuscular control is the mind's attempt to teach the body conscious
control of a specific movement. Neuromuscular control relies on the central nervous system to interpret and integrate propriceptive and kinesthetic information and then to control individual muscles and joints
to produce coordinated movement.[11] Following injury and subsequent
rest and immobilization, the central nervous system "forgets" how to put
this information together. Regaining neuromuscular control means regaining the ability to follow some previously established sensory pattern.
Strengthening exercises, particularly those that tend to be more functional, are essential for reestablishing neuromuscular control.[11]

Regaining Balance

The ability to balance and maintain postural stability is essential to reac-
quiring athletic skills.[3] A rehabilitation program must include functional
exercises that incorporate balance training to prepare the athlete for return to activity (Figure 12-6). Failure to address balance problems may
predispose the athlete to reinjury.[4]

Maintaining Cardiorespiratory Fitness

Maintaining cardiorespiratory fitness is perhaps the single most neglected
component of a rehabilitation program. An athlete spends a considerable
amount of time preparing the cardiorespiratory system to handle the increased demands made upon it during a competitive season. When injury
occurs and the athlete is forced to miss training time, levels of cardiorespiratory fitness may decrease rapidly. Thus the coach must design or substitute alternative activities that allow the athlete to maintain existing
levels of cardiorespiratory fitness as early as possible in the rehabilitation
period[6] (Figure 12-7).

Depending on the nature of the injury, several possible activities can help the athlete maintain fitness levels. A lower extremity injury necessitates non-weight-bearing activities. Pool activities provide an excellent means for injury rehabilitation. Cycling also can positively stress the cardiorespiratory system.

Functional Progressions

The purpose of any rehabilitation program is to restore normal function following injury. Functional progressions involve a series of gradually progressive activities designed to prepare the individual for return to a specific sport.[11] Those skills necessary for successful participation in a given sport are broken down into component parts, and the athlete gradually reacquires those skills within the limitations of his or her individual progress.[12] Every new activity introduced must be carefully monitored by the coach to determine the athlete's ability to perform as well as his or her physical tolerance. If an activity does not produce additional pain or swelling, the level should be advanced; new activities should be introduced as quickly as possible.

Functional progressions will gradually assist the injured athlete in achieving normal pain-free range of motion, in restoring adequate

Figure 12-6

Reestablishing neuromuscular control and balance are critical components in regaining functional performance capabilities.

Figure 12-7

Every rehabilitation program must include some exercise designed to maintain cardiorespiratory fitness.

Functional progressions
incorporate sport-specific
skills into the rehabilitation
program.

strength levels, and in regaining neuromuscular control throughout the rehabilitation program.

Functional Testing

Functional testing uses functional progression drills for the purpose of assessing the athlete's ability to perform a specific activity (Figure 12-8). Functional testing involves the performance of a single maximal effort to give the coach some idea of how close the athlete is to a full return to activity. For years coaches have used a variety of functional tests to assess the athlete's progress, including agility runs (e.g., Figure eights, shuttle runs, cariocas), side stepping, vertical jumps, hopping for time or distance, and co-contraction tests.[11]

Criteria for Full Recovery

All exercise rehabilitation plans must determine what is meant by complete recovery from an injury. Often it means that the athlete is fully reconditioned and has achieved full range of movement, strength, neuromuscular control, cardiovascular fitness, and sport-specific functional skills. Besides physical well-being, the athlete must also have regained full confidence to return to his or her sport. Specific criteria for a return to full activity after rehabilitation is determined to a large extent by the nature and severity of the specific injury, but it also depends on the philosophy and judgment of both the physician and the coach.[7]

The decision to release an athlete recovering from injury to a full return to athletic activity is the final stage of the rehabilitation/recovery process. The decision should be carefully considered by each member of the sports medicine team involved in the rehabilitation process.The team physician should be ultimately responsible for deciding that the athlete is ready to return to practice and/or competition. That decision should

Figure 12-8

Performance on functional
tests can determine the
capability of the athlete to
return to full activity.

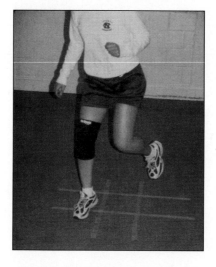

be based on collective input from the coach, the athletic trainer, and the athlete.

In considering the athlete's return to activity, the following concerns should be addressed:

- *Physiological healing constraints.* Has rehabilitation progressed to the later stages of the healing process?
- *Pain status.* Has pain disappeared, or is the athlete able to play within his or her own levels of pain tolerance?
- *Swelling.* Is there still a chance that swelling may be exacerbated by a return to activity?
- *Range of motion.* Is range of motion adequate to allow the athlete to perform both effectively and with minimized risk of reinjury?
- *Strength.* Is strength, endurance, or power great enough to protect the injured structure from reinjury?
- *Neuromuscular control/proprioception/kinesthetia.* Has the athlete "relearned" how to use the injured body part?
- *Cardiorespiratory fitness.* Has the athlete been able to maintain cardiorespiratory fitness at or near the level necessary for competition?
- *Sport-specific demands.* Are the demands of the sport or a specific position such that the athlete will not be at risk of reinjury?
- *Functional testing.* Does performance on appropriate functional tests indicate that the extent of recovery is sufficient to allow successful performance?
- *Prophylactic strapping, bracing, padding.* Are any additional supports necessary for the injured athlete to return to activity?
- *Responsibility of the athlete.* Is the athlete capable of listening to his or her body and of knowing enough not to put himself or herself in a potential reinjury situation?
- *Predisposition to injury.* Is this athlete prone to reinjury or a new injury when not 100 percent?
- *Psychological factors.* Is the athlete capable of returning to activity and competing at a high level without fear of reinjury?
- *Athlete education and preventive maintenance program.* Does the athlete understand the importance of continuing to engage in conditioning exercises that can greatly reduce the chances of reinjury?

SUMMARY

- The rehabilitation philosophy in sports medicine is an aggressive one, with the ultimate goal being to return the injured athlete to full activity as quickly and safely as possible.
- Short-term goals of a rehabilitation program: (1) providing correct immediate first aid and management following injury to limit or control swelling; (2) reducing or minimizing pain; (3) restoring full range of

motion; (4) restoring or increasing muscular strength, endurance, and power; (5) reestablishing neuromuscular control; (6) improving balance; (7) maintaining cardiorespiratory fitness; and (8) incorporating appropriate functional progressions.

- Permitting the athlete to fully return to activity should occur when the athlete is fully reconditioned and has achieved full range of movement, strength, neuromuscular control, cardiovascular fitness, and sport-specific functional skills. Besides physical well-being, the athlete must also have regained full confidence to return to his or her sport.

Solutions to Critical Thinking Exercises

12-1 In sports medicine, the short-term goals in any rehabilitation program should include controlling pain, regaining range of motion, regaining strength, reestablishing neuromuscular control, and maintaining levels of cardiorespiratory fitness. The approach to rehabilitation should be aggressive, and decisions as to when and how to alter and progress specific components within a rehabilitation program should be based on, and are limited by, the healing process. The long-term goal is to return the athlete to full activity as soon as safely possible.

12-2 Anterior knee pain can result from many different causes. However, strengthening of the quadriceps can often be quite helpful. If full-range-of-motion strengthening exercises increase pain, the athlete should begin with isometric exercises done at different points in the range and should progress to full-range concentric and eccentric resistance exercise as tolerated. Exercises such as minisquats,

stepping exercises, or leg presses are excellent exercises for strengthening quadriceps and tend to be more functional in nature than are exercises done on an exercise machine.

12-3 Following injury and subsequent rest and immobilization, it is not unusual for the athlete to "forget" how to walk. The coach must help the athlete relearn neuromuscular control, which means regaining the ability to follow some previously established motor and sensory pattern by regaining conscious control of a specific movement until that movement becomes automatic. Strengthening exercises, particularly those that tend to be more functional, are essential for reestablishing neuromuscular control. Addressing neuromuscular control is critical throughout the recovery process but may be most critical during the early stages of rehabilitation to avoid reinjury or even overuse injuries to additional structures.

REVIEW QUESTIONS AND CLASS ACTIVITIES

1. Explain the role of the coach in a rehabilitation program.
2. Describe the techniques for controlling swelling following injury.
3. Why it is important to modulate pain during a rehabilitation program?
4. How is range of motion restored after an injury?
5. Compare the use of isometric, progressive resistance, isokinetic, and plyometric exercises in rehabilitation.
6. How is neuromuscular control related to movement?
7. Why must an athlete condition the body generally while an injury heals?

8. How and when should functional progressions be incorporated into the rehabilitation program?
9. Describe how to determine if an athlete is ready to return to activity following injury.

REFERENCES

1. Arnheim D, Prentice W: *Principles of athletic training,* ed 9, Madison, Wis, 1997, Brown & Benchmark.
2. Buschbacher R, Braddom R: *Sports medicine and rehabilitation; a sport specific approach,* Philadelphia, 1994, Hanley & Belfus.
3. Guskiewicz K, Perrin D: Research and clinical applications of assessing balance, *J Sport Rehab* 5(1):45, 1996.
4. Irrgang J, Whitney S, Cox E: Balance and proprioceptive training for rehabilitation of the lower extremity, *J Sport Rehab* 3(1):68, 1994.
5. Kisner C, Colby A: *Therapeutic exercise: foundations and techniques,* Philadelphia, 1996, FA Davis.
6. Magnusson P, McHugh M: Current concepts on rehabilitation in sports medicine. In Nicholas J, Hirschman E: *The lower extremity and spine in sports medicine,* St Louis, 1995, Mosby.
7. Malone T, editor: *Orthopedic and sports physical therapy,* St Louis, 1996, Mosby–Year Book.
8. Perrin D: *Isokinetic exercise and assessment,* Champaign, Ill, 1993, Human Kinetics.
9. Prentice W: *Rehabilitation techniques in sports medicine,* Dubuque, Iowa, 1999, WC Brown/McGraw-Hill.
10. Prentice W: *Therapeutic modalities in sports medicine,* Dubuque, Iowa, 1999, WC Brown/McGraw-Hill.
11. Tippett S, Voight M: *Functional progressions for sport rehabilitation,* Champaign, Ill, 1995, Human Kinetics.
12. Zachazewski J, Magee D, Quillen S: *Athletic injuries and rehabilitation,* Philadelphia, 1996, WB Saunders.

ANNOTATED BIBLIOGRAPHY

Buschbacher R, Braddom R: *Sports medicine and rehabilitation; a sport specific approach,* Philadelphia, 1994, Hanley & Belfus.
   Discusses the rehabilitation of injuries that occur in specific sports.
Prentice W: *Rehabilitation techniques in sports medicine,* ed 3, Dubuque, Iowa, 1999, WC Brown/McGraw-Hill.
   A comprehensive text dealing with all aspects of rehabilitation used in a sports medicine setting.
Tippett S, Voight M: *Functional progressions for sport rehabilitation,* Champaign, Ill, 1995, Human Kinetics.
   Presents scientific principles and practical applications for using functional exercise to rehabilitate athletic injuries.

WEB SITES

Cramer First Aider: http://www.ccsd.k12.wy.us/CCHS_web/sptmed/fstaider.htm

National Athletic Trainers' Association: http://www.nata.org
   Accesses rehabilitation in the athletic training journals.

The Physician and Sportsmedicine: http://www.physsportmed.com
   Search back issues and access the ones specifically geared toward weight training and rehabilitation.

Chapter 13

Recognizing Different Sports Injuries

When you finish this chapter you will be able to:

- Differentiate between acute and chronic/injury.
- Describe acute traumatic injuries, including fractures, dislocations and subluxations, contusions, ligament sprains, muscle strains, muscle soreness, and nerve injuries.
- Describe chronic overuse injuries involving tendinitis, tenosynovitis, bursitis, osteoarthritis, and myofascial trigger points.
- Explain the various phases of the healing process.

N o matter how much attention is directed toward the general principles of injury prevention, the nature of participation in sports dictates that sooner or later injury will occur. Generally injuries that occur in an athletic setting may be classified as either acute or chronic. Acute injuries are caused by trauma; chronic injuries can result from overuse as would occur with the repetitive dynamics of running, throwing, or jumping. In this chapter we discuss the more common traumatic and overuse injuries that are likely be seen by the coach.

ACUTE (TRAUMATIC) INJURIES

Fractures

Fractures (broken bones) occur as a result of extreme stresses and strains placed on bones. Before discussing fractures, a brief discussion of bone anatomy is necessary.[9] The gross structure of the long bones includes the diaphysis, epiphysis, articular cartilage, and periosteum (Figure 13-1). The *diaphysis* is the main shaft of the bone. It is hollow, cylindrical, and covered by compact bone. The *epiphysis* is located at the ends of long bones. It is the growth area of the bone in adolescents. The ends of long bones are covered with a layer of *articular cartilage* that covers the joint surfaces of the epiphysis. This cartilage provides protection during movement and cushions jars and blows to the joint. A dense, white, fibrous membrane, the *periosteum,* covers long bones except at joint surfaces. In-

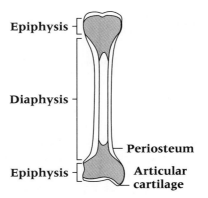

Epiphysis

Diaphysis

Periosteum

Epiphysis

Articular
cartilage

Figure 13-1

The gross structure of the
long bones includes the
diaphysis, epiphysis, articular
cartilage, and periosteum.

terlacing with the periosteum are fibers from the muscle tendons. Throughout the periosteum on its inner layer exist countless blood vessels and **osteoblasts** (bone-forming cells). The blood vessels provide nutrition to the bone, and the osteoblasts provide bone growth and repair.

Fractures generally can be classified as being either closed or open.[9] A **closed fracture** is one in which there is little or no movement or displacement of the broken bones. Conversely, in an **open fracture** there is enough displacement of the fractured ends that the bone actually breaks through surrounding tissues, including the skin. An open fracture increases the possibility of infection. Both types of fractures can be serious if not managed properly. Signs and symptoms of a fracture include obvious deformity, point tenderness, swelling, and pain on active and passive movement. The only definitive technique for determining if a fracture exists is to have it x-rayed.

Several different kinds of fractures can occur (Figure 13-2). Long bones can be stressed or forced to fail by tension, compression, bending, twisting (torsion), and shear.[7] These forces, either singly or in combination, can cause a variety of fractures. For example, spiral fractures are caused by twisting, whereas oblique fractures are caused by the combined forces of axial compression, bending, and torsion. Transverse fractures occur because of bending (Figure 13-3). Along with the type of stress, the amount of force must be considered. The more complex the fracture, the more energy is required. External energy can be used to deform and then actually fracture bone. Some energy can be dispersed to soft tissue adjacent to the bone.[3]

Healing of a Fracture

In most instances the fracture of a bone requires immobilization for some period of time in a cast. In general, fractures of the long bones of the arm and leg require approximately six weeks of casting, and the smaller bones in the hands and feet may require as little as three weeks of either casting or splinting. In some instances, immobilization may not be required for healing. For example, breaks of the four small toes are difficult to

osteoblasts (os tee oh blasts)
Bone-forming cells.

closed fracture
Fracture does not penetrate superficial tissue.

open fracture
Overlying skin has been lacerated by protruding bone fragments.

Long bones can be stressed by tension, compression, bending, torsion, and shearing.

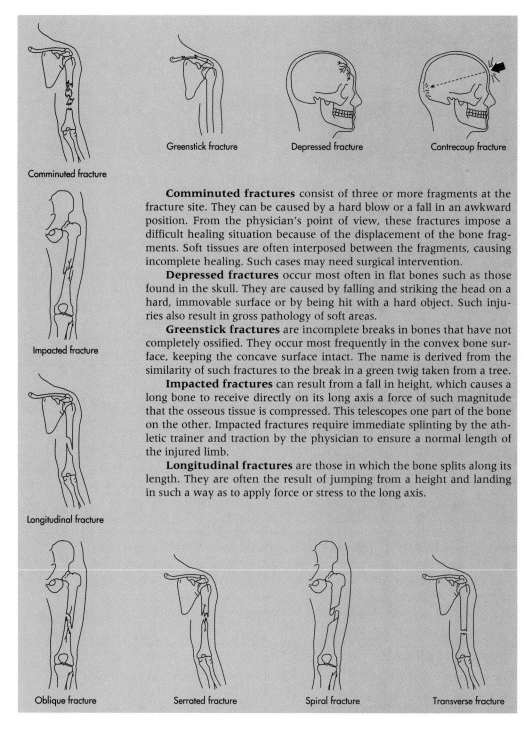

Comminuted fracture

Greenstick fracture

Depressed fracture

Contrecoup fracture

Impacted fracture

Longitudinal fracture

Oblique fracture

Serrated fracture

Spiral fracture

Transverse fracture

Comminuted fractures consist of three or more fragments at the fracture site. They can be caused by a hard blow or a fall in an awkward position. From the physician's point of view, these fractures impose a difficult healing situation because of the displacement of the bone fragments. Soft tissues are often interposed between the fragments, causing incomplete healing. Such cases may need surgical intervention.

Depressed fractures occur most often in flat bones such as those found in the skull. They are caused by falling and striking the head on a hard, immovable surface or by being hit with a hard object. Such injuries also result in gross pathology of soft areas.

Greenstick fractures are incomplete breaks in bones that have not completely ossified. They occur most frequently in the convex bone surface, keeping the concave surface intact. The name is derived from the similarity of such fractures to the break in a green twig taken from a tree.

Impacted fractures can result from a fall in height, which causes a long bone to receive directly on its long axis a force of such magnitude that the osseous tissue is compressed. This telescopes one part of the bone on the other. Impacted fractures require immediate splinting by the athletic trainer and traction by the physician to ensure a normal length of the injured limb.

Longitudinal fractures are those in which the bone splits along its length. They are often the result of jumping from a height and landing in such a way as to apply force or stress to the long axis.

Figure 13-2

Various types of fractures

Oblique fractures are similar to spiral fractures. They occur when one end receives sudden torsion or twisting and the other end is fixed or stabilized.

Serrated fractures are sawtooth, sharp-edged fracture lines of the two bony fragments. They are usually caused by a direct blow. Because of the sharp and jagged edges, extensive internal damage such as the serverance of vital blood vessels and nerves often occurs.

Spiral fractures have an S-shaped separation. They are fairly common in football and skiing, in which the foot is firmly planted and the body is suddenly rotated.

Transverse fractures occur in a straight line, more or less at right angles to the bone shaft. A direct outside blow usually causes this injury.

Contrecoup fractures occur on the side opposite to the part where trauma was initiated. Fracture of the skull is at times an example of the contrecoup. An athlete may be hit on one side of the head with such force that the brain and internal structures compress against the opposite side of the skull, causing a fracture.

Avulsion fracture An avulsion fracture is the separation of a bone fragment from its cortex at an attachment of a ligament or tendon. This fracture usually occurs as a result of a sudden, powerful twist or stretch of a body part. An example of a ligamentous episode is the sudden eversion of the foot that causes the deltoid ligament to avulse bone from the medial malleolus. An example of a tendinous avulsion is one that causes a patellar fracture, which occurs when an athlete falls forward while suddenly bending a knee. The stretch of the patellar tendon pulls a portion of the inferior patellar pole apart (Figure 6-15).

Blow-out fracture Blow-out fracture occurs to the wall of the eye orbit as the result of a blow to the eye.

Figure 13-2—cont'd

splint or cast. Of course, complications such as infections may lengthen the time required for both casting and rehabilitation.

For a fracture to heal, osteoblasts, the bone-producing cells, must lay down extra bone formation, called a **callus,** over the fracture site during the immobilization period. Once the cast is removed, the bone must be subjected to normal stresses and strains so that tensile strength may be regained before the healing process is complete. Cells called **osteoclasts** function to reshape the bone in response to normally applied stresses and strains.[9]

callus
New bone formation over a fracture.

osteoclasts (os tee oh klasts**)**
Cells that absorb and remove osseous tissue.

Stress Fractures

Perhaps the most common fracture that results from physical activity is a **stress fracture.** Unlike the other types of fractures that have been discussed, the stress fracture results from overuse rather than acute trauma.[2] Common sites for stress fractures include the weight-bearing bones of the leg or foot. In either case, repetitive forces transmitted through the bones produce irritations at specific spots on the bone. The pain usually begins as a dull ache, which becomes progressively painful day after day. Initially, pain is most severe during activity. However, when a stress fracture develops, pain becomes worse after the activity is stopped.

stress fracture
Spot of irritation on the bone.

MECHANISM	PATTERN	APPEARANCE
Bending	Transverse	
Torsion	Spiral	
Compression plus bending	Oblique-transverse or butterfly	
Compression plus bending plus torsion	Oblique	
Variable	Comminuted	
Compression	Metaphyseal compression	

Figure 13-3

Mechanisms, patterns, and
appearance of bone fractures

13-1

Critical Thinking Exercise

A track athlete training for a
marathon is complaining of
pain in the lower leg. She
consults with her physician,
who determines that she has a
stress fracture. When she
returns to practice, she is
confused about how a stress
fracture is different from a real
fracture.

? How should the coach explain the difference between
the two, and what is the course
of management?

The biggest problem with a stress fracture is that often it will not
show up on an x ray until the bone-producing cells begin laying down
bone. At that point, a small white line appears on the x ray. If a stress
fracture is suspected, it is best to stop the activity for a period of at least
fourteen days. Stress fractures do not usually require casting; however, if
they are not handled correctly, they may become true fractures that must
be immobilized (see the accompanying Focus Box).

13-1   ***Focus Box***

Differentiating between Injuries to a Muscle or Joint

Here is a simple procedure to help the coach determine whether an injury
is to the muscle or joint:

1. To rule out the possibility of fracture, the coach has the athlete move
   the part through a full range of motion. Pain may indicate muscle
   injury.
2. The coach passively moves the relaxed part through a range of
   motion. Pain may indicate a joint condition.
3. The coach applies a resistance against the moving extremity. Pain may
   suggest a muscle injury.

Dislocations and Subluxations

A **dislocation** occurs when at least one bone in an articulation is forced out of its normal and proper alignment and stays out until it is either manually or surgically put back into place or reduced. Dislocations most commonly occur in the shoulder joint, elbow, and fingers, but they can occur wherever two bones articulate (Figure 13-4A). A **subluxation** is like a dislocation except that in this situation a bone pops out of its normal articulation but then goes right back into place.[4] Subluxations most commonly occur in the shoulder joint and, in females, in the knee cap (Figure 13-4B).

In dislocations, deformity is almost always apparent; however, it may be obscured by heavy musculature, making it important for the examiner to routinely palpate, or feel, the injured site to determine the loss of normal contour. Comparison of the injured side with the uninjured side often reveals asymmetry.

Dislocations or subluxations may result in a rupture of the stabilizing ligaments and tendons surrounding the joint. Occasionally an avulsion fracture occurs in which an attached tendon or ligament pulls a small piece of bone away from the rest of the bone. In other cases, the force may separate growth plates or cause a complete fracture of a long bone. These possibilities indicate the importance of administering complete and thorough medical attention to first-time dislocations. It has often been said, "Once a dislocation, always a dislocation." In most cases this statement is true, because once a joint has been either subluxated or completely dislocated, the connective tissues that bind and hold it in its correct alignment are stretched to such an extent that the joint will be extremely vulnerable to subsequent dislocations.

A first-time dislocation should always be considered and treated as a possible fracture. Once it has been ascertained that the injury is a dislocation, a physician should be consulted for further evaluation. However, before the athlete is taken to the physician, the injury should be properly splinted and supported to prevent any further damage.

Dislocations should never be reduced immediately, regardless of where they occur. The coach should take the athlete to an x-ray facility and rule out fractures or other problems before reduction. Inappropriate techniques of reduction may only exacerbate the problem. Return to

---

dislocation
A bone is forced out and stays out until surgically or manually replaced or reduced.

---

subluxation (sub **lucks** ashun)
A bone is forced out but goes back into place.

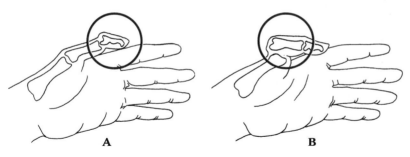

Figure 13-4

A joint that is forced beyond its anatomical limits can become partially dislocated (subluxated; A) or completely dislocated (luxated; B).

A   B

sprain
Injury to a ligament that
connects bone to bone.

synovia (sin **oh** vee ah**)**
A transparent lubricating
fluid forced in joints,
bursae, and tendons.

mechanoreceptors
Located in muscles,
tendons, ligaments, and
joints; provide information
on position of a joint.

Figure 13-5

Structure of a synovial joint

activity after dislocation or subluxation is largely dependent on the degree of soft tissue damage.

Ligament Sprains

A **sprain** involves damage to a ligament that provides support to a joint.[5] A ligament is a tough, relatively inelastic band of tissue that connects one bone to another. Before discussing injuries to ligaments, a review of joint structure is necessary (Figure 13-5). All **synovial** joints are composed of two or more bones that articulate with one another to allow motion in one or more planes. The articulating surfaces of the bone are lined with a very thin, smooth, cartilaginous covering called an articular, or *hyaline, cartilage*. All joints are entirely surrounded by a thick, ligamentous *joint capsule*. The inner surface of this joint capsule is lined by a very thin *synovial membrane* that is highly vascularized and innervated. The synovial membrane produces *synovial fluid*, the functions of which include lubrication, shock absorption, and nutrition of the joint.[9]

The articular capsule, ligaments, outer aspects of the synovial membrane, and fat pads of the synovial joint are well supplied with nerves. The inner aspect of the synovial membrane, cartilage, and articular disks, if present, have nerves as well. These nerves, called **mechanoreceptors,** provide information about the relative position of the joint and are found in the fibrous capsule and ligaments.[9]

Some joints contain a thick fibrocartilage called a *meniscus*. The knee joint, for example, contains two wedge-shaped menisci that deepen the

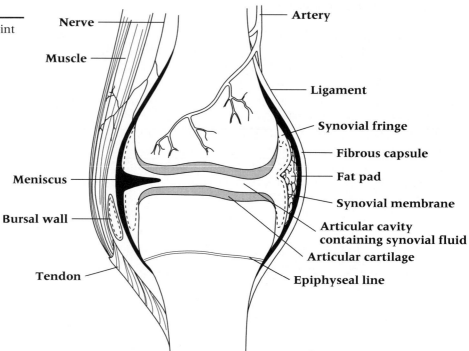

articulation and provide shock absorption in that joint. Finally, the main structural support and joint stability is provided by the ligaments, which may be either thickened portions of a joint capsule or totally separate bands. The anatomical position of the ligaments partly determines what motions a joint is capable of making.[9]

If a joint is forced to move beyond normal limits or planes of movement, injury to the ligament is likely to occur (Figure 13-6). The severity of the damage is subject to many different classifications; however, the most commonly used system involves three grades of sprain.

- *Grade 1 sprain.* There is some stretching and separation of the ligamentous fibers, with moderate instability of the joint. Mild to moderate pain, localized swelling, and joint stiffness should be expected.
- *Grade 2 sprain.* There is some tearing and separation of the ligament fibers, with moderate instability of the joint. Moderate to severe pain, swelling, and joint stiffness should be expected.
- *Grade 3 sprain.* There is total tearing of the ligament, which leads to major instability of the joint. Initially, severe pain may be present, followed by little or no pain as a result of total disruption of nerve fibers. Swelling may be great, and the joint tends to become very stiff some hours after the injury. In some cases, a grade 3 sprain with marked instability requires surgical repair. Frequently, the force producing the ligament injury is so great that other ligaments or structures surrounding the joint may also be injured. Rehabilitation of grade 3 sprains involving surgery is a long-term process.

The greatest problem in the rehabilitation of grade 1 and grade 2 sprains is restoring stability to the joint.[9] Once a ligament has been stretched or partially torn, inelastic scar tissue forms, preventing the ligament from regaining its original tension. To restore stability to the joint, the other structures surrounding that joint, primarily muscles and their tendons, must be strengthened. The increased muscle tension provided by strength training can improve stability of the injured joint.

13-2

Critical Thinking Exercise

A volleyball player has sprained her ankle just two days prior to the beginning of the conference tournament. The athlete, her parents, and her coach are extremely concerned that she is going to miss the tournament and want to know if anything can be done to make her get well more quickly.

? What can this athlete be told about the process of healing?

Figure 13-6

A ligament sprain in the knee joint

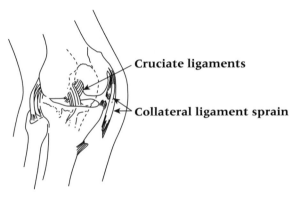

Cruciate ligaments

Collateral ligament sprain

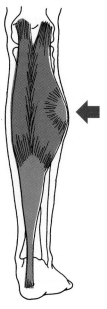

Figure 13-7

A contusion occurs when soft
tissues are compressed
between bone and some
external force.

---

myositis ossificans (my
oh **sigh** tis ah **sif** ah cans)
Calcium deposits that result
from repeated trauma.

Skin wounds:
Blister
Abrasion
Laceration
Incision
Puncture
Avulsion

---

strain
A stretch, tear, or rip in the
muscle or its tendon.

Contusions

A contusion is another word for a bruise. We are all very familiar with
the mechanism that produces a bruise. A blow from some external object
causes soft tissues (i.e., skin, fat, and muscle) to be compressed against
the hard bone underneath[2] (Figure 13-7). If the blow is hard enough,
capillaries will be torn, which allows bleeding into the tissues. Minor
bleeding often causes a bluish-purple discoloration of the skin that persists for several days. The contusion may be very sore to the touch, and
if damage has occurred to muscle, pain may be experienced on active
movement. In most cases the pain will cease within a few days and discoloration will disappear usually in a few weeks.[6]

The major problem with contusions occurs in an area that is subjected to repeated blows. If the same area, or more specifically, a muscle,
is bruised over and over again, small calcium deposits may begin to accumulate in the injured area. These pieces of calcium may be found between several fibers in the muscle belly, or calcium may build up to form
a spur, which projects from the underlying bone. These calcium formations may significantly impair movement and are referred to as **myositis
ossificans.**[4]

The key to preventing the occurrence of myositis ossificans from repeated contusions is to protect the injured area with padding. If the area
is properly protected after the first contusion, myositis may never develop. Protection and rest may allow the calcium to be reabsorbed, eliminating any need for surgery.

The two areas that seem to be the most vulnerable to repeated contusions during physical activity are the quadriceps muscle group on the
front of the thigh and the biceps muscle on the front of the upper arm.
The formation of myositis ossificans in these or any other areas may be
detected by x rays.

Muscle Strains

The muscle is composed of separate fibers that are capable of simultaneous contraction when stimulated by the central nervous system. Each
muscle is attached to bone at both ends by strong, relatively inelastic tendons that cross over joints.

If a muscle is overstretched or forced to contract against too much
resistance, separation or tearing of the muscle fibers occurs. This damage
is referred to as a **strain**[4] (Figure 13-8). Muscle strains, like ligament
sprains, are subject to various classification systems. The following is a
simple system of strain classification:

- *Grade 1 strain.* Some muscle fibers have been stretched or actually
  torn. There is some tenderness and pain on active motion. Movement
  is painful, but full range of motion is usually possible.
- *Grade 2 strain.* A number of muscle fibers have been torn, and active
  contraction of the muscle is extremely painful. Usually a depression
  or divot can be felt somewhere in the muscle belly at the place at

**Strained hamstring
muscles**

Figure 13-8

A muscle strain results in
separation or tearing of
fibers.

which the muscle fibers have been torn. Some swelling may occur
because of capillary bleeding; therefore, some discoloration is
possible.

- *Grade 3 strain.* A complete rupture of a muscle has occurred in the
area of the muscle belly at the point at which muscle becomes tendon
or at the tendinous attachment to the bone. There will be significant
impairment to or perhaps total loss of movement. Initially, pain is
intense but quickly diminishes because of complete nerve fiber
separation.

Muscle strains can occur in any muscle and usually result from some
uncoordinated activity between muscle groups. Grade 3 strains are most
common in the biceps tendon of the upper arm or in the Achilles heel
cord in the back of the calf. When either of these tendons tears, the muscle tends to bunch toward its attachment at the bone site. Grade 3 strains
involving large tendons that produce great amounts of force must be surgically repaired. Smaller musculotendinous ruptures such as those that
occur in the fingers may heal by immobilization with a splint.

Regardless of the severity of the strain, the time required for rehabilitation is lengthy.[9] In many instances muscle strains are incapacitating,
making rehabilitation time for a muscle strain even longer than for a ligament sprain. Incapacitating muscle strains occur most frequently in the
large, force-producing hamstring and quadriceps muscles of the lower
extremity. The treatment of hamstring strains requires a healing period of
six to eight weeks and a considerable amount of patience. Trying to return to activity too soon often causes reinjury to the area of the muscle
that has been strained, and the healing process must begin again.

Muscle Cramps

Muscle cramps are extremely painful involuntary muscle contractions
that occur most commonly in the calf, abdomen, or hamstrings, although
any muscle can be involved.[3] The occurrence of heat cramps is related to
excessive loss of water and, to some extent, several electrolytes or ions

13-3

Critical Thinking Exercise

A football player sustains
repeated contusions to the left
quadriceps muscle.

? What should he be most
concerned about?

muscle cramps
Involuntary muscle
contraction.

(sodium, chloride, potassium, magnesium, and calcium), which are each essential elements in muscle contraction (see Chapter 10).

Muscle Guarding

Following injury, the muscles that surround the injured area contract to, in effect, splint that area, thus minimizing pain by limiting movement. Quite often this "splinting" is incorrectly referred to as a muscle spasm. The terms *spasm* and *spasticity* are more correctly associated with increased tone or contractions of muscle that occur because of some upper motor neuron lesion in the brain. Thus **muscle guarding** is a more appropriate term for the involuntary muscle contractions that occur in response to pain following musculoskeletal injury.[9]

> **muscle guarding**
> Muscle contraction in response to pain.

Muscle Soreness

Overexertion in strenuous muscular exercise often results in muscular pain. All active people at one time or another have experienced muscle soreness, usually resulting from some physical activity to which they are unaccustomed. The older a person gets, the more easily muscle soreness seems to develop.

There are two types of muscle soreness. The first type of muscle pain is *acute-onset muscle* soreness, which accompanies fatigue. It is transient and occurs during and immediately after exercise. The second type of soreness involves delayed muscle pain that appears approximately twelve hours after injury. This *delayed-onset muscle soreness* (*DOMS*) becomes most intense after twenty-four to forty-eight hours and then gradually subsides so that the muscle becomes symptom-free after three or four days. DOMS is described as a syndrome of delayed muscle pain leading to increased muscle tension, swelling, and stiffness and to resistance to stretching.[3]

DOMS is thought to result from several possible causes. It may occur from very small tears in the muscle tissue, which seems to be more likely with eccentric or isometric contractions. It may also occur because of disruption of the connective tissue that holds muscle tendon fibers together.

Muscle soreness may be prevented by beginning exercise at a moderate level and gradually progressing the intensity of the exercise over a period of time. Treatment of muscle soreness usually also involves static or PNF stretching activity. Another important treatment for muscle soreness, as for other conditions discussed in this chapter, is ice applied within the first forty-eight to seventy-two hours.[9]

Nerve Injuries

In athletics, nerve injuries usually involve either compression or tension. Nerve injuries, as with injuries to other tissues in the body, can be acute or chronic. Trauma directly affecting nerves can produce a variety of sensory responses, including hypoesthesia (diminished sense of feeling), hyperesthesia (increased sense of feelings such as pain or touch), or paresthesia (numbness, prickling, or tingling, which may occur from a direct blow or stretch to an area). For example, a sudden nerve stretch or pinch can produce both a sharp burning pain that radiates down a limb and muscle weakness. **Neuritis,** a chronic nerve problem, can be caused by a variety of forces that usually have been repeated or continued for a long period of time. Symptoms of neuritis can range from minor nerve problems to paralysis. More serious injuries involve the crushing of a nerve or complete division (severing). This type of injury may produce a lifelong physical disability, such as paraplegia or quadriplegia, and should therefore not be overlooked in any circumstance.

Specialized tissue, such as nerve cells, cannot regenerate once the nerve cell dies. In an injured peripheral nerve, however, the nerve fiber can regenerate significantly if the injury does not affect the cell body. For regeneration to occur, an optimal environment for healing must exist.

Regeneration is slow, at a rate of only three to four millimeters per day. Damaged nerves within the central nervous system regenerate very poorly compared to nerves in the peripheral nervous system.[9]

neuritis
Chronic nerve irritation.

CHRONIC OVERUSE INJURIES

The Importance of Inflammation in Healing

For most people, the word *inflammation* has negative connotations. However, inflammation is an essential part of the healing process. Once a structure is damaged or irritated, inflammation must occur to initiate the healing process. Symptoms of inflammation include pain, swelling, warmth, and perhaps redness.[6] Inflammation is supposed to be an acute process that ends when its role in the healing process has been accomplished. However, if the source of irritation (e.g., the repetitive movements that cause stress to the tendon) is not removed, then the inflammatory process becomes chronic rather than acute. When this situation occurs, an acute condition may become a chronic disabling problem.

Tendinitis

Of all the overuse problems associated with sport activity, **tendinitis** is probably the most common. Any term ending in the suffix *itis* means inflammation is present. Tendinitis means inflammation of a **tendon.** During muscle activity, a tendon must move or slide on other structures around it whenever the muscle contracts. If a particular movement is performed repeatedly, the tendon becomes irritated and inflamed.[5] This inflammation is manifested by pain on movement, swelling, possibly some warmth, and usually crepitus. **Crepitus** is a crackling sound. It is usually caused by the tendon's tendency to stick to the surrounding structure while it slides back and forth. This sticking is caused primarily by the chemical products of inflammation that accumulate on the irritated tendon.

The key to the treatment of tendinitis is rest.[9] If the repetitive motion causing irritation to the tendon is eliminated, the inflammatory process will allow the tendon to heal. Unfortunately, athletes find it difficult to totally stop activity and rest for two or more weeks while the tendinitis subsides. The athlete should substitute some form of activity, such as

tendinitis
Inflammation of a tendon.

The suffix *itis* means "inflammation of"

tendon
Tough band of connective tissue that attaches muscle to bone.

crepitus
A crackling feel or sound.

bicycling or swimming, to maintain present fitness levels while avoiding continued irritation of the inflamed tendon. In runners, tendinitis most commonly occurs in the Achilles tendon in the back of the lower leg; in swimmers, it often occurs in the muscle tendons of the shoulder joint. However, tendinitis can flare up in any activity in which overuse and repetitive movements occur.

Tenosynovitis

Tenosynovitis is very similar to tendinitis in that the muscle tendons are involved in inflammation. However, many tendons are subject to an increased amount of friction because of the tightness of the space through which they must move. In these areas of high friction, tendons are usually surrounded by synovial sheaths that reduce friction on movement. If the tendon sliding through a synovial sheath is subjected to overuse, inflammation is likely to occur (Figure 13-9).[4] The inflammatory process produces by-products that are "sticky" and tend to cause the sliding tendon to adhere to the synovial sheath surrounding it.

Tenosynovitis occurs most commonly in the long flexor tendons of the fingers as they cross over the wrist joint and in the biceps tendon around the shoulder joint. Treatment for tenosynovitis is the same as for tendinitis. Because both conditions involve inflammation, antiinflammatory drugs may be helpful in chronic cases.

Bursitis

Bursitis occurs around joints, where there is friction between tendon and bone, skin and bone, or muscle and other muscles. Without some mechanism of protection in these high-friction areas, chronic irritation would exist.

Bursae are pieces of synovial membrane that contain a small amount of fluid (synovial fluid). Just as oil lubricates a hinge, these small pieces of synovium permit motion of these structures without friction.

---

tenosynovitis (ten oh sin oh **vie** tis)
Inflammation of a tendon and its synovial sheath.

---

bursae
Pieces of synovial membrane that contain a small amount of fluid.

Figure 13-9

Tenosynovitis is an inflammation of the sheath covering a tendon. A, Normal. B, Inflamed.

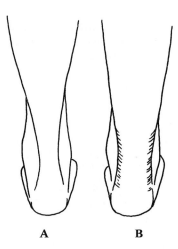

A   B

If excessive movement or perhaps some acute trauma occurs around the bursae, they become irritated and inflamed and begin producing large amounts of synovial fluid.[8] The longer the irritation continues or the more severe the acute trauma, the more fluid is produced. As fluid continues to accumulate in the limited space available, pressure increases causing pain in the area. Bursitis can be an extremely painful condition that has the capability of severely restricting movement, especially if it occurs around a joint. Synovial fluid will continue to be produced until the movement or trauma producing the irritation is eliminated.

Occasionally, a bursa or synovial sheath completely surrounds a tendon, allowing more freedom of movement in a tight area. Irritation of this synovial sheath may restrict tendon motion. All joints have many bursae surrounding them. The three bursae that are most commonly irritated as a result of various types of physical activity are the subacromial bursa in the shoulder joint under the clavicle; the olecranon bursa on the tip of the elbow; and the prepatellar bursa on the front surface of the patella. All three of these bursae produce large amounts of synovial fluid, affecting motion at their respective joints.

Osteoarthritis

Any mechanical system wears out with time. The joints in the body are mechanical systems, and wear and tear, even from normal activity, is inevitable. The most common result of this wear and tear, a degeneration of the articular or hyaline cartilage, is referred to as **osteoarthritis**.[10] The cartilage may be worn away to the point of exposing, eroding, and polishing the underlying bone.

Any process that changes the mechanics of the joint eventually leads to degeneration of that joint. Degeneration is a result of repeated trauma to the joint and to tendons, ligaments, and fasciae surrounding the joint. Such injuries may be caused by a direct blow or fall, by pressure of carrying or lifting heavy loads, or by repeated trauma to the joint as in running or cycling.

Osteoarthritis most often affects the weight-bearing joints: the knees, hips, and lumbar spine. Also affected are the shoulders and cervical spine. Although many other joints may show pathological degenerative change, clinically the disease only occasionally produces symptoms in them. Any joint that is subjected to acute or chronic trauma may develop osteoarthritis.[9]

The symptoms of osteoarthritis are relatively local in character. Osteoarthritis may be localized to one side of the joint or may be generalized about the joint. One of the most distinctive symptoms is pain, which is brought about by friction that occurs with use and which is relieved by rest. Stiffness is a common complaint that occurs with rest and is quickly loosened with activity. This symptom is prominent upon rising in the morning. Joints may also show localized tenderness, crepitus, creaking, or grating that may be heard and felt.[6]

> **osteoarthritis**
> A wearing down of hyaline cartilage.

trigger point
Area of tenderness in a
tight band of muscle.

Phases of the healing process:
Inflammatory response phase
Fibroblastic repair phase
Maturation-remodeling
phase

Myofascial Trigger Points

A **trigger point** is an area of tenderness in a tight band of muscle. In the athlete, painful or active trigger points most often develop because of some mechanical stress to the muscle.[9] This stress could involve either an acute muscle strain or static postural positions that produce constant tension in the muscle. Trigger points occur most typically in the neck, upper back, and lower back. Palpation of the trigger point produces pain in a predictable distribution of referred pain. The pain may also cause some restricted range of motion. Pressure on the trigger point produces a twitch or a jump response from the pain. Pain can be increased by passive or active stretching of the involved muscle.

THE IMPORTANCE OF THE HEALING PROCESS FOLLOWING INJURY

The coach must possess some understanding of both the sequence and time frames for the various phases of healing, realizing that certain physiological events must occur during each of the phases. Any interference with the healing process during a rehabilitation program will likely slow return to full activity. The healing process must have an opportunity to accomplish what it is supposed to. At best, the coach can only try to create an environment that is conducive to the healing process. Little can be done to speed up the process physiologically, but many things may be done during rehabilitation to impede healing.

The healing process consists of three phases: the inflammatory response phase, the fibroblastic repair phase, and the maturation-remodeling phase.[1] Although the phases of healing are often discussed as three separate entities, the healing process is a continuum. Phases of the healing process overlap one another and have no definitive beginning or end points.[9]

Inflammatory Response Phase

The inflammatory response phase begins immediately following injury. The inflammatory response phase is perhaps the most critical phase of the healing process. Without the physiological changes that take place during the inflammatory process, the later stages of healing cannot occur. The destruction of tissue produces direct injury to the cells of the various soft tissues. During this phase, phagocytic cells clean up the mess created by the injury. Injured cells release chemicals that facilitate the healing process. It is characterized symptomatically by redness, swelling, tenderness, increased temperature, and loss of function. This initial inflammatory response lasts for approximately two to four days following initial injury.

Fibroblastic Repair Phase

During the fibroblastic phase of healing, proliferative and regenerative activity leading to scar formation and repair of the injured tissue occurs. The period of scar formation, referred to as *fibroplasia,* begins within the first few hours following injury and may last for as long as four to six weeks. During this period many of the signs and symptoms associated with the inflammatory response subside. The athlete may still indicate some tenderness to touch and will usually complain of pain when particular movements stress the injured structure. As scar formation progresses, complaints of tenderness or pain will gradually disappear.

Maturation-Remodeling Phase

The maturation-remodeling phase of healing is a long-term process. This phase features a realignment or remodeling of the scar tissue according to the tensile forces to which that scar is subjected. With increased stress and strain, the collagen fibers that make up the scar realign in a position of maximum efficiency parallel to the lines of tension. The tissue gradually assumes normal appearance and function, although a scar is rarely as strong as the normal uninjured tissue. Usually after about three weeks, a firm, strong, contracted, nonvascular scar exists. The maturation phase of healing may require several years to be totally complete.

SUMMARY

- Fractures may be classified as either greenstick, transverse, oblique, spiral, comminuted, impacted, avulsive, or stress.

- Dislocations and subluxations are disruptions of the joint capsule and ligamentous structures surrounding the joint.

- Ligament sprains involve stretching or tearing the fibers that provide stability at the joint.

- Repeated contusions may lead to the development of myositis ossificans.

- Muscle strains involve a stretching or tearing of muscle fibers and their tendons and cause impairment to active movement.

- Muscle soreness may be caused by spasm, connective tissue damage, muscle tissue damage, or some combination of these factors.

- Tendinitis, an inflammation of a muscle tendon that causes pain on movement, usually occurs because of overuse.

- Tenosynovitis is an inflammation of the synovial sheath through which a tendon must slide during motion.

- Bursitis is an inflammation of the synovial membranes located in areas in which friction occurs between various anatomical structures.

- Osteoarthritis involves degeneration of the articular cartilage or subchondral bone.

- A trigger point is an area of tenderness in a tight band of muscle that develops from some mechanical stress to the muscle.

- The three phases of the healing process, the inflammatory response phase, the fibroblastic repair phase, and the maturation-remodeling phase, occur in sequence but overlap one another in a continuum.

Solutions to Critical Thinking Exercises

13-1 A stress fracture is not an actual break of the bone, it is simply an irritation of the bone. Treatment of a stress fracture requires about fourteen days of rest. However, the coach should point out that a stress fracture can become a true fracture if it is not rested; if that happens, four to six weeks of immobilization in a cast is necessary. Thus, it is critical that this athlete rest for the required amount of time.

13-2 Little can be done to speed up the healing process physiologically. This athlete must realize that certain physi-

ological events must occur during each phase of the healing process. Any interference with this healing process during a rehabilitation program will likely slow return to full activity. The healing process must have an opportunity to accomplish what it is supposed to.

13-3 Repeated contusion of any muscle may lead to the development of myositis ossificans. The key to treating myositis ossificans is prevention. An initial contusion to any muscle should be immediately protected with padding to prevent reinjury.

REVIEW QUESTIONS AND CLASS ACTIVITIES

1. What is the difference between an acute injury and a chronic injury? Give examples of each.
2. Describe various types of fractures and the mechanisms that cause fractures to occur.
3. How does a stress fracture differ from a regular fracture?
4. Differentiate between a subluxation and a dislocation.
5. What structures are found at a joint? What are their functions?
6. How do the three grades of ligament sprains differ?
7. What is myositis ossificans and how can it be prevented?
8. Differentiate between muscle strains, muscle cramps, muscle guarding, and muscle soreness.
9. How does a damaged nerve heal?
10. How are tendinitis, tenosynovitis, and bursitis related to one another?
11. Explain how osteoarthritis develops.
12. What are myofascial trigger points, where are they most likely to occur, and what are the signs and symptoms?
13. Discuss the physiological events that occur during each of the different phases of the healing process.
14. Invite an orthopedist to class to discuss common injuries to the musculoskeletal system.

REFERENCES

1. American Orthopaedic Society for Sports Medicine: *Sports-induced inflammation*, Park Ridge, Ill, 1990, American Academy of Orthopaedic Surgeons.
2. Armstrong R, Warren G, Warren J: Mechanisms of exercise induced muscle fiber injury, *Sports Med* 12:184, 1991.
3. Arnheim D, Prentice WE: *Principles of athletic training*, Madison, Wis, 1997, Brown & Benchmark.
4. Blauvelt CT, Nelson FRT: *A manual of orthopaedic terminology*, ed 4, St Louis, 1990, Mosby–Year Book.
5. Cailliet R: *Soft tissue pain and disability*, Philadelphia, 1988, FA Davis.

6. Gallaspie J, May D: *Signs and symptoms of athletic injuries,* St Louis, 1996, Mosby.

7. Malone T, McPhoil T, Nitz A: *Orthopedic and sports physical therapy,* St Louis, 1997, Mosby.

8. Morris A: *Sports medicine: prevention of athletic injuries,* Dubuque, Iowa, 1992, WC Brown.

9. Prentice W: *Rehabilitation techniques in sports medicine,* Dubuque, Iowa, 1998, WC Brown/McGraw-Hill.

10. Strauss R: *Sports medicine,* Philadelphia, 1992, WB Saunders.

ANNOTATED BIBLIOGRAPHY

Blauvelt CT, Nelson FRT: *A manual of orthopaedic terminology,* ed 4, St Louis, 1990, Mosby–Year Book.

A resource book for all individuals who need to identify medical words or their acronyms.

Booher JM, Thibodeau GA: *Athletic injury assessment,* St Louis, 1994, Mosby.

An excellent guide to the recognition, assessment, classification, and evaluation of athletic injuries.

Garrick JG, Webb DR: *Sports injuries: diagnosis and management,* Philadelphia, 1990, WB Saunders.

An overview of musculoskeletal injuries that are unique to sports and exercise.

Micheli L: *The sports medicine bible,* New York, 1995, Harper Perennial.

A clearly written basic text that explains how to recognize and prevent injuries from occurring. Also discusses principles and management of injuries that do occur.

Peacinn M, Bojanic I: *Overuse injuries of musculoskeletal system,* Boca Raton, Fla, 1993, CRC Press.

A comprehensive text describing overuse injuries of the tendon, tendon sheath, bursae, muscle, muscle-tendon function, cartilage, and nerve.

Williams JGP: *Color atlas of injury in sport,* Chicago, 1990, Mosby–Year Book.

An excellent visual guide to the area of sports injuries, covering the nature and incidence of sport injury, types of tissue damage, and regional injuries caused by a variety of sports activities.

WEB SITE

Cramer First Aider: http://www.ccsd.k12.wy.us/CCHS_web/sptmed/fstaider.htm

PART

3

RECOGNITION AND MANAGEMENT OF SPECIFIC INJURIES AND CONDITIONS

14

The Foot

When you finish this chapter you will be able to:

- Briefly describe the anatomy of the foot.
- Explain the process of injury assessment for the foot.
- Identify steps that can be taken to minimize foot injuries.
- Explain the causes of various foot injuries commonly seen in athletes.
- Describe the appropriate care for injuries incurred in the foot.

FOOT ANATOMY

Bones

The human foot must function both to absorb forces and to provide a stable base of support during walking, running, and jumping. It contains twenty-six bones, (seven tarsal, five metatarsal, and fourteen phalangeal) that are held together by an intricate network of ligaments and fascia and moved by a complicated group of muscles (Figure 14-1). The tarsal bones that form the ankle include the talus and calcaneous. The navicular, cuboid, and three cuneiform bones form the instep of the foot.

Ligaments

Arches of the Foot

The foot is structured, by means of ligamentous and bony arrangements, to form several arches. The arches assist the foot in supporting the body weight and in absorbing the shock of weight bearing. There are four arches: the medial longitudinal, the lateral longitudinal, the anterior metatarsal, and the transverse (Figure 14-2).

The *metatarsal arch* is shaped by the distal heads of the metatarsals. The arch stretches from the first to the fifth metatarsal. The *transverse arch* extends across the transverse tarsal bones and forms a half dome.The *medial longitudinal arch* originates along the medial border of the calcaneus and extends forward to the distal head of the first metatarsal. The main

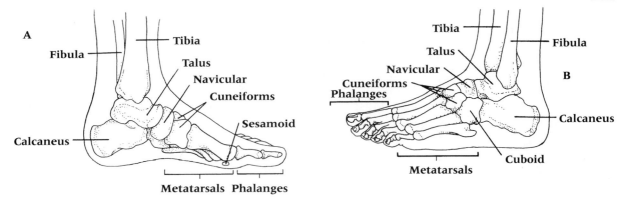

Figure 14-1

Bones of the foot: A, Medial; B, Lateral

supporting ligament of the longitudinal arch is the plantar calcaneonavicular ligament, which acts as a spring by returning the arch to its normal position after it has been stretched. The *outer longitudinal arch* is on the lateral aspect of the foot and follows the same pattern as that of the inner longitudinal arch. It is formed by the calcaneus, cuboic, and fifth metatarsal bones.

Plantar Fascia (Plantar Aponeurosis)

The plantar fascia is a thick white band of fibrous tissue originating from the medial aspect of the calcaneus and ending at the proximal heads of the metatarsals. Along with ligaments, the plantar fascia supports the foot against downward forces (Figure 14-3).

Muscles

The medial movements include adduction (medial movement of the forefoot), and supination (a combination of inversion and adduction). Muscles that produce these movements pass behind and in front of the

Figure 14-2

Arches of the foot: A, Metatarsal and transverse arches; B, Medial longitudinal arch; C, lateral longitudinal arch

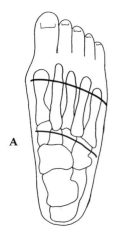
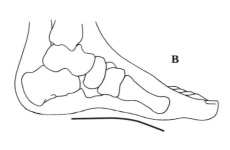
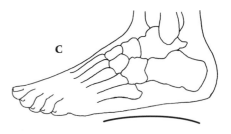

medial malleolus. Muscles passing behind are the tibialis posterior, flexor digitorum longus, and flexor hallucis longus. Muscles passing in front of the medial malleolus are the tibialis anterior and the extensor hallucis longus (Figure 14-4).

The lateral movements of the foot include abduction (lateral movement of the forefoot), and pronation (a combination of eversion and abduction). Muscles passing behind the lateral malleolus are the peroneus longus and the peroneus brevis. Muscles passing in front of the lateral malleolus are the peroneus tertius and extensor digitorum longus (Figure 14-5).

In general the small intrinsic muscles on the plantar surface of the foot cause toe flexion while those muscles on the dorsum of the foot cause toe extension.

PREVENTION OF FOOT INJURIES

Of major importance in preventing foot injuries is the understanding of the foot's structure and mechanics, types of footwear, and surface concerns. Coaches must pay particular attention to athletes who may be predisposed to injuries caused by muscular or tendinous tightness or, conversely, weakness or hypermobility. Such situations, when recognized early, can usually be remediated by exercise, by the use of appropriate shoe inserts, or *orthotics*, or by selecting appropriate shoes. Strengthening, stretching, and mobility exercises should be performed routinely by athletes in sports that place a great deal of stress and strain on the feet.

The foot must continually adapt to the contact surface. Training on surfaces that are irregular and variable in resilience can ultimately serve to strengthen the foot over time. However, a nonyielding surface may in some cases overstress joints and soft tissue, eventually leading to an acute or chronic pathological condition in the foot or somewhere in the kinetic chain. In contrast, a surface that is too resilient and absorbs too much of

Figure 14-3

Plantar fascia

Figure 14-4

Muscles and tendons of the
dorsum (top) of the foot

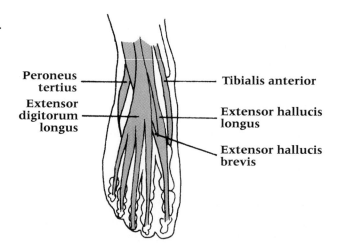

Peroneus tertius

Extensor digitorum longus

Tibialis anterior

Extensor hallucis longus

Extensor hallucis brevis

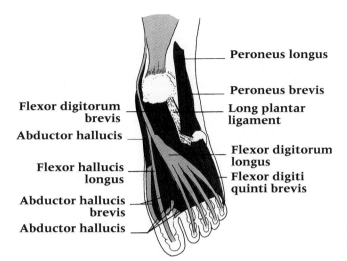

Peroneus longus

Peroneus brevis

Flexor digitorum
brevis

Abductor hallucis

Long plantar
ligament

Flexor hallucis
longus

Flexor digitorum
longus

Flexor digiti
quinti brevis

Abductor hallucis
brevis

Abductor hallucis

Figure 14-5

Muscles on the plantar
(bottom) surface of the foot

the impact energy may lead to early fatigue in sports such as basketball and indoor tennis.

The majority of foot skin conditions are preventable. The athlete should be instructed on proper foot hygiene, which includes proper washing and drying of the feet following activity and changing to clean socks daily. The coach should emphasize wearing properly fitting shoes and socks. Athletes who have abnormal foot stresses due to faulty mechanics may find the use of custom orthotics to be helpful.

Nearly all blisters, calluses, corns, and ingrown toenails are preventable.

FOOT ASSESSMENT

History

A coach who is deciding how to manage a foot injury must make an assessment to determine the type of injury and its history.[11] The following questions should be asked:

- How did the injury occur?
- Did it occur suddenly or come on slowly?
- Was the mechanism a sudden strain, twist, or blow to the foot?
- What type of pain is there? Is there muscle weakness? Are there noises such as crepitation during movement? Is there any alteration in sensation?
- Can the athlete point to the exact site of pain? When is the pain or other symptoms more or less severe?
- On what type of surface has the athlete been training? What type of footwear was being used during training? Is it appropriate for the type of training? Is discomfort increased when footwear is worn?
- Is this the first time this condition has occurred, or has it happened before? If so, when, how often, and under what circumstances?

Observation

The athlete should be observed to determine the following:

- Whether he or she is favoring the foot, is walking with a limp, or is unable to bear weight.
- Whether the injured part is deformed, swollen, or discolored.
- Whether the foot changes color when bearing weight and not bearing weight (changing rapidly from a darker to a lighter pink when not bearing weight).
- Whether the foot is well aligned and whether it maintains its shape when bearing weight.
- What do the wear patterns look like on the sole of the shoe? Is there symmetry between the two shoes?

Palpation

Palpation of the bony structures should be done first for deformities or areas of point tenderness. Palpation of the muscles and their tendons in the foot is essential to detect **point tenderness,** abnormal swelling or lumps, muscle spasm, or muscle guarding.[11]

> **point tenderness**
> Pain is produced when the site of injury is palpated.

> **exostoses** (ek **sosto** ses)
> Callus formations.

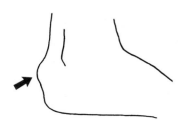

Figure 14-6

A pump bump that develops from retrocalcaneal bursitis can be protected using a doughnut-type pad.

The athlete who is prone to heel bruises should routinely wear a padded heel cup.

RECOGNITION AND MANAGEMENT OF SPECIFIC INJURIES

Retrocalcaneal Bursitis (Pump Bump)

Cause of injury   The retrocalcaneal bursa lies between the calcaneous and the Achilles tendon on the back of the heel. This bursa can become chronically irritated and inflamed due to constant rubbing or pressure from the heel counter of a shoe.[9] If inflammation continues for many months, a bone callus, or **exostoses,** is likely to form on the back of the heel (Figure 14-6). This exostoses has been referred to as a pump bump (A pump is a type of woman's shoe with a heel counter that tends to cross right over the retrocalcaneal bursa).

Signs of injury   All the signs of bursitis—tenderness, swelling, warmth, and redness—will be present and will progress eventually to a palpable and tender bony bump on the back of the calcaneous.

Care   A doughnut-type pad should be constructed and placed around the area of tenderness to disperse pressure created by the heel counter. Also, a heel lift can help to change the site of pressure. The athlete may also want to choose a shoe with a heel counter that is either a little higher or lower than the one presently being worn.

Heel Bruise

Cause of injury   Of the many contusions and bruises that an athlete may receive, none is more disabling than the heel bruise on the bottom of the calcaneous.[13] Sport activities that demand a sudden stop-and-go response or a sudden change from a horizontal to a vertical movement, such as basketball jumping, high jumping, and long horse vaulting, are particularly likely to cause heel bruises.[3] The heel has a thick, cornified skin layer and a heavy fat pad covering, but even this thick padding cannot protect against a sudden abnormal force directed to this area.

Signs of injury   When injury occurs, the athlete complains of severe pain in the heel and is unable to tolerate the stress of weight bearing. An acute bruise of the heel may progress to chronic inflammation of the bone covering (periosteum).

Care   Initially, cold is applied to the heel bruise, and if possible, the athlete should not step on the heel for at least twenty-four hours. If pain when walking has subsided by the third day, the athlete may resume moderate activity—with the protection of a heel cup, or protective doughnut (Figure 14-7). The coach should be aware that an athlete who is prone to or who needs protection from a heel bruise should routinely wear a heel cup with a foam rubber pad as a preventive aid. Surrounding the heel with a firm heel cup diffuses traumatic forces.[10]

Plantar Fasciitis

Cause of condition   Heel pain is a very common problem in both the athletic and nonathletic populations. The plantar fascia runs the length of the sole of the foot (see Figure 14-3). It assists in maintaining the stability of the foot and in supporting the longitudinal arch.[14] A number of conditions have been studied as possible causes of plantar fasciitis. They include leg length discrepancy, inflexibility of the longitudinal arch, tightness of the gastrocnemius-soleus unit, wearing shoes without sufficient arch support, a lengthened stride during running, and running on soft surfaces.[15]

Signs of condition   The athlete complains of pain in the anterior medial heel, usually at the attachment of the plantar fascia to the calcaneus that eventually moves more centrally into the middle of the plantar fascia. This pain is particularly troublesome when the athlete rises in the morning or bears weight on the foot after sitting for a long period. However, the pain lessens after a few steps. Pain also will be intensified when the toes and forefoot are forcibly dorsiflexed.

Care   Management of plantar fasciitis generally requires an extended period of treatment. It is not uncommon for symptoms to persist

Critical Thinking Exercise

A distance runner is complaining of pain that started on the bottom of her heel and now seems to also be bothering the long arch. She states that pain seems to be the worst in the morning when she first gets out of bed.

? What condition usually results in these complaints and how should this problem be managed?

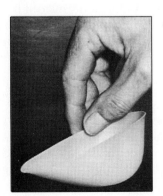
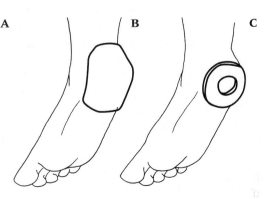

A   B   C

Figure 14-7

Protection of a heel bruise using, A & B, A heel cup; C, A doughnut pad

for as long as eight to twelve weeks. Vigorous heel cord stretching should be done, along with an exercise to stretch the plantar fascia in the arch. Use of a heel cup compresses the fat pad under the calcaneous and provides a cushion under the area of irritation (See Figure 14-7). A simple arch taping often allows pain-free ambulation (see Figure 11-23). Orthotic therapy is very useful in the treatment of this problem. In some cases, particularly during a competitive season, the athlete may continue to train and compete if symptoms and associated pain are not prohibitive.

Fractures of the metatarsals

Cause of injury   Fractures of the metatarsals can be caused by direct force, such as having the foot stepped on by another player, by being kicked or kicking another object, or by twisting or torsional stresses.[3] The most common acute fracture is to the base of the fifth metatarsal (Jones fracture).

Signs of injury   It is very difficult to differentiate a fracture from a sprain of the metatarsal ligaments. Fractures of the metatarsals are characterized by swelling and pain. A fracture may be more point tender and occasionally it may be possible to palpate a deformity. The most definitive way to distinguish a fracture from a sprain is to get an x ray.

Care   Treatment is usually symptomatic, with RICE used to control swelling. Once swelling has subsided, a short leg walking cast is applied for three to six weeks. Ambulation is usually possible by the second week. A shoe with a large toe box should be worn.

Jones Fracture

Cause of injury   A Jones fracture involves a fracture at the neck of the fifth metatarsal that can occur from overuse, acute inversion, or high-velocity rotational forces[5] (Figure 14-8). A Jones fracture occurs most often as a sequala of a stress fracture.

Signs of injury   The athlete will complain of a sharp pain on the lateral border of the foot and will usually report hearing a "pop." Because of a history of poor blood supply and delayed healing, a Jones fracture may result in nonunion, requiring an extended period of rehabilitation.[7]

Care   A Jones fracture of the fifth metatarsal usually requires a non-weight-bearing short leg cast for six to eight weeks for nondisplaced fractures. With cases of delayed union, nonunion, or especially displaced fractures, the Jones fracture requires internal fixation, with or without bone grafting. In the highly competitive athlete, immediate surgical internal fixation should be recommended.

Second Metatarsal Stress Fractures

Cause of injury   Second metatarsal stress fractures, also referred to as *march fractures*, occur most often in running and jumping sports. As with other overuse injuries in the foot, the most common causes include structural deformities in the foot, training errors, changes in training surfaces, and wearing inappropriate shoes.[5]

Morton's Toe is a condition in which the first metatarsal is abnormally

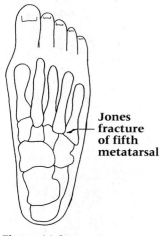

Jones fracture of fifth metatarsal

Figure 14-8

A Jones fracture occurs at the neck of the fifth metatarsal.

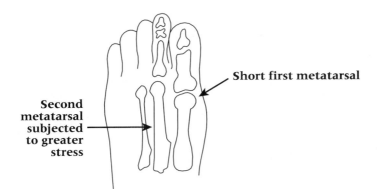

Short first metatarsal

Second metatarsal subjected to greater stress

Figure 14-9

In a Morton's Toe, the first metatarsal is abnormally short.

short in length, making the second toe appear longer than the great toe (Figure 14-9). In a normal walking gait, the first metatarsal bears most of the weight. However, because the first metatarsal in a Morton's Toe is short, the second metatarsal must bear a greater percentage of the forces during walking and even greater forces in a running gait. Thus, a Morton's Toe increases the chance of a stress fracture of the second metatarsal.[3]

Signs of injury The athlete will usually complain of pain and point tenderness along the second metatarsal. Commonly the athlete will indicate the presence of pain during running and perhaps also during walking. The athlete may also feel ongoing pain and aching during non-weight-bearing movements as well.

Care Treatment for stress fractures should focus on determining the precipitating cause or causes and alleviating those that created the problem. Athletes with second metatarsal stress fractures tend to do well with modified rest and non-weight-bearing exercises such as pool running or using an upper body ergometer or stationary bike to maintain cardiorespiratory fitness for two to four weeks. These exercises are followed by the athlete's progressive return to running and jumping sports over a two- to three-week period using appropriate shoes.

Metatarsal Arch Strain

Cause of injury Athletes with hypermobility of the metatarsals caused by laxity in the ligaments are prone to sprain of the metatarsal arch.[2] Hypermobility allows the metatarsals in the foot to spread apart (splayed foot), giving the appearance of a fallen metatarsal arch[8] (Figure 14-10).

Signs of injury The athlete has pain or cramping in the metatarsal region. There is point tenderness, with signs of inflammation and weakness in the area. Pain in this region is called **metatarsalgia**.[17] Although metatarsalgia is a general term to describe pain or cramping in the ball of the foot, it is more commonly associated with pain under the second and sometimes the third metatarsal head. A heavy callus often forms in the area of pain.

Care Treatment of acute metatarsalgia usually consists of applying a pad to elevate the depressed metatarsal heads. The pad is placed in

Fatigue, poor posture, overuse, excessive weight, or improperly fitting shoes may damage the supporting tissue of the arch.

metatarsalgia (metah tar **sal** gee ah)
Pain on the bottom of the foot.

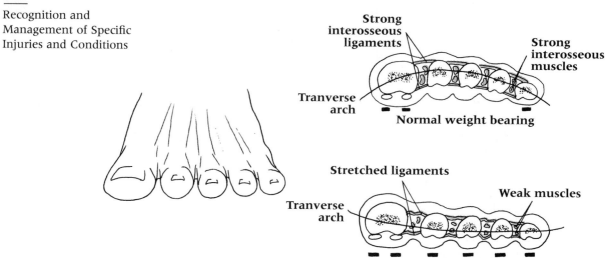

Figure 14-10

In hypermobility the
metatarsals splay apart.

pes planus (pees plan is)
Flat feet.

As long as an existing
condition in the foot is *not*
causing pain, don't try to fix
it.

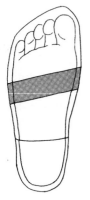

Figure 14-11

A metatarsal bar placed just
behind the metatarsal heads
is used to reduce
metatarsalgia.

the center and just behind the ball of the foot (metatarsal heads) (Figure
14-11). A daily regimen of exercise should concentrate on strengthening
foot muscles and stretching the heel cord.

Longitudinal Arch Strain

Cause of injury   Longitudinal arch strain is usually caused by subjecting the musculature on the plantar surface of the foot to unaccustomed stresses and forces when coming in contact with hard playing
surfaces. In this condition, there is a flattening or depression of the longitudinal arch (**pes planus**) while the foot is in the midsupport phase,
resulting in a strain to the arch.[16] Such a strain may appear suddenly, or
it may develop slowly over a considerable length of time.

Signs of injury   As a rule, pain is experienced only when running is
attempted and usually appears just below the medial malleolus and the
posterior tibial tendon, accompanied by swelling and tenderness along
the medial aspects of the foot. Prolonged strain will also involve the calcaneonavicular ligament and first cuneiform with the navicular. The
flexor muscle of the great toe (flexor hallucis longus) often develops
tenderness as a result of overuse in compensating for the stress on the
ligaments.

Many people have what appears to be a flat foot or a fallen longitudinal arch with no associated symptoms or pain whatsoever. In these
cases the rule that should always be followed is "If it's not broken, don't
try to fix it" (Figure 14-12).

Care   The management of a longitudinal arch strain involves immediate care consisting of RICE followed by appropriate therapy and reduction of weight bearing. Weight bearing must be performed pain-free.
Arch taping technique no. 1 or 2 might be used to allow earlier pain-free
weight bearing (see Figures 11-19 through 11-20).

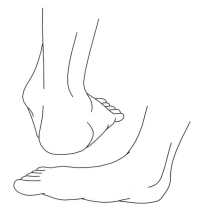

Figure 14-12

The approach to take with athletes who appear to have a flat foot or a fallen longitudinal arch but have no associated symptoms: "If it's not broken, don't try to fix it."

Hammer Toes

Cause of condition Hammer, or clawed, toes may be congenital, but more often the condition is caused by long-term wearing of shoes that are too short and that cramp the toes[9] (Figure 14-13). Hammer toe usually involves the second or third toe, whereas clawed toes involve more than one toe. In both conditions the toe joints become malaligned, and the foot develops overly contracted flexor tendons and overly stretched extensor tendons. This deformity eventually results in the formation of hard corns or calluses on the exposed joints.

Care Quite often surgery is the only cure. However, wearing properly fitting shoes and protective taping (see Figure 11-25) can help prevent irritation.

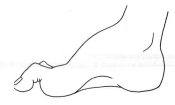

Figure 14-13

Hammer toes

Fractures and Dislocations of the Toes (Phalanges)

Cause of injury Fractures of the phalanges may be incurred by kicking an object or stubbing a toe or dropping a heavy object on the toes.

Signs of injury Generally fractures and dislocations of the phalanges are accompanied by swelling and discoloration. If the fracture is to the proximal phalanx of the great toe or to the distal phalanx and also involves the interphalangeal joint, the injury should be referred to a physician.

Care If the break is in the bone shaft, adhesive tape is applied. However, if more than one toe is involved, a cast may be applied for a few days. As a rule, three or four weeks of inactivity permit healing, although tenderness may persist for some time. A shoe with a wide toe box should be worn; in cases of great toe fracture, a stiff sole should be worn.

Dislocations of the phalanges are less common than fractures. If one occurs, it is usually a dislocation of the proximal joint of the middle phalanx. The mechanism of injury is the same as for fractures. Reduction is usually performed easily without anesthesia by a physician.

Fracture and dislocations of the toes can be caused by kicking an object or stubbing a toe.

Bunions (Hallux Valgus Deformity)

Cause of injury A bunion, also referred to as an exostoses, is a painful deformity of the head of the first metatarsal. A bunion involves

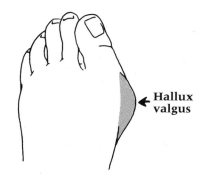

Figure 14-14

A bunion with a hallux
valgus deformity

14-2

Critical Thinking Exercise

A soccer player complains of
intermittent pain in the region
between the third and fourth
toes of the left foot. Pain along
with tingling and numbness
seems to radiate from the base
to the tip of the toes during
weight bearing.

? What condition usually
causes these symptoms and
how can it be managed?

neuroma
Enlargement of a nerve.

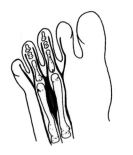

Figure 14-15

A Morton's Neuroma usually
occurs between the third and
fourth metatarsal heads.

bony enlargement of the head of the first metatarsal that progresses to
the point at which the great toe becomes malaligned and moves laterally
toward the second toe, sometimes to such an extent that it eventually
overlaps the second toe, creating what is called a hallux valgus deformity[4]
(Figure 14-14). This type of bunion may also be associated with a depressed or flattened transverse arch. Often the bunion occurs from wearing shoes that are pointed, too narrow, too short, or have high heels.

Signs of injury A bunion is one of the most frequent painful deformities of the great toe. As the bunion is developing, there is tenderness,
swelling, and enlargement with calcification of the head of the first
metatarsal. Poorly fitting shoes increase the irritation and pain.

Care Shoe selection plays an important role in the treatment of
bunions. Shoes of the proper width cause less irritation to the bunion.
Protective devices such as some type of doughnut pad over the bunion
helps disperse pressure, and tape can also be used. If the condition progresses, a special orthotic device may help normalize foot mechanics and
significantly reduce the symptoms and progression of a bunion. Surgery
to correct the hallux valgus deformity is very common during the later
stages of this condition.

Morton's Neuroma

Cause of condition A **neuroma** is a mass occurring in the common
plantar nerve. It occurs most commonly between the third and fourth
metatarsal heads, where the nerve is the thickest because it is receiving
both branches from the medial and lateral plantar nerves (Figure 14-15).

Signs of condition The athlete complains of severe intermittent
pain radiating from the distal metatarsal heads to the tips of the toes; the
pain is often relieved when the foot is not bearing weight. The athlete
complains of a burning numbness in the forefoot that is often localized to
the third web space and radiating to the toes. Hyperextension of the toes
on weight bearing, as in squatting, stair climbing, or running, can increase the symptoms. Wearing shoes with a narrow toe box or high heels
can increase the symptoms.

Care Either a metatarsal bar is placed just proximal to the metatarsal heads or a teardrop-shaped pad is placed between the heads of the
third and fourth metatarsals in an attempt to have these toes splay apart
with weight bearing (Figure 14-16). Shoe selection also plays an impor-

tant role in treatment of neuromas. A shoe that is wide in the toe box area should be selected.

Turf Toe

Cause of injury   Turf toe is a hyperextension injury resulting in a sprain of the great toe, either from repetitive overuse or trauma.[6] Typically, these injuries occur on unyielding synthetic turf, although they can occur on grass also. Many of these injuries occur because artificial turf shoes often are more flexible and allow more dorsiflexion of the great toe. Some shoe companies have addressed this problem by adding steel or other materials to the forefoot of their turf shoes to stiffen them. A sprain of the great toe can also occur from kicking some nonyielding object.

Care   Flat insoles that have thin sheets of steel under the forefoot are available. When commercially made products are not available, a thin, flat piece of thermoplastic material may be placed under the shoe insole or may be molded to the foot. Taping the toe to prevent dorsiflexion may be done separately or with one of the shoe-stiffening suggestions. In less severe cases, the athlete can continue to play with the addition of a rigid insole. With more severe sprains, three to four weeks may be required for pain to reduce to the point at which the athlete can push off on the great toe.

Calluses

Cause of condition   Foot calluses may be caused by shoes that are too narrow or too short. Calluses that develop from friction can be painful because the fatty layer loses its elasticity and cushioning effect. The excess callus moves as a gross mass, becoming highly vulnerable to tears, cracks, and ultimately, infections.

Care   Athletes who are prone to excess calluses should be encouraged to use an emery callus file after each shower. Massaging small amounts of lanolin into devitalized calluses once or twice a week after practice may help maintain some tissue elasticity. The coach may have the athlete decrease the calluses' thickness and increase their smoothness by sanding or pumicing. NOTE: *Great care should be taken not to remove the callus totally and the protection it affords at a given pressure point.*

Athletes whose shoes are properly fitted but who still develop heavy calluses commonly have faulty foot mechanics that may require special orthotics. Special cushioning devices such as wedges, doughnuts, and arch supports may help to distribute the weight on the feet more evenly and thus reduce skin stress. Excessive callus accumulation can be prevented by (1) wearing at least one layer of socks; (2) wearing shoes that are the correct size and in good condition; and (3) routinely applying materials such as petroleum jelly to reduce friction.

Blisters

Cause of injury   As a result of shearing forces acting on the skin, blisters develop in which fluid accumulates below the outer skin layer.

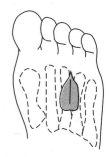

Figure 14-16

A teardrop-shaped pad will spread the metatarsal heads apart during weight bearing.

Critical Thinking Exercise

A football player who both practices and plays on artificial turf complains of pain in his right great toe.

? What type of injury frequently occurs to the great toe when competing on artificial turf?

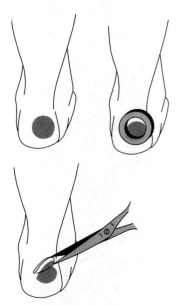

Figure 14-17

In some cases a blister should
be opened and padded to
allow that athlete to continue
to play.

This fluid may be clear, bloody, or infected. Soft feet coupled with this
shearing skin stress can produce severe blisters. It has been found that the
application of petroleum jelly can protect the skin against abnormal friction. Wearing socks with no folds or wrinkles can protect the athlete with
sensitive skin or the one who perspires excessively.[1] Wearing the correct-
size shoe is essential. Shoes should be broken in before being used for
long periods of time.

Care   If a blister or hot spot arises, the athlete has several options:
(1) cover the irritated skin with a friction-proofing material, such as petroleum jelly, (2) cover the blister with an adhesive bandage, or (3) apply a doughnut pad that surrounds the blister.

When caring for a blister, the coach must be aware at all times of the
possibility of infection from contamination. Any blister that appears to be
infected requires medical attention. In sports, two approaches are generally used to care for blisters. The conservative approach is that a blister
should not be contaminated by cutting or puncturing but should be protected from further insult by a small doughnut until the initial irritation
has subsided (Figure 14-17). However, the pressure of the fluid inside the
blister can often be extremely painful and in some cases debilitating.
Puncturing may be necessary to allow the athlete to continue to play or
practice. The accompanying Focus Box details the technique for opening
a blister. Conservative care of blisters is preferred when there is little danger of tearing or aggravation through activity. A product called Second
Skin by Spenco is widely used on blisters to provide a protective coating.

Corns

Cause of condition   The hard corn is the most serious type of corn.
It is caused by the pressure of improperly fitting shoes, the same mechanism that causes calluses. Hammer toes and hard corns are usually associated; the hard corns form on the tops of the deformed toes. The soft

---

14-1   *Focus Box*

Caring for a Torn Blister

1. Cleanse the blister and surrounding tissue with soap and water; rinse
   with an antiseptic.
2. Using sterile scissors, make a small cut along the perimeter of the
   blister.
3. Drain the fluid using a sterile gauze pad.
4. Apply antibiotic ointment under and around the loose skin; cover the
   area with a sterile dressing.
5. Apply a doughnut pad around blister.
6. Change dressing daily and check for signs of infection.
7. Within two or three days, or when the underlying tissue has
   hardened sufficiently, remove the dead skin by trimming the skin on a
   bevel and as close as possible to the perimeter of the blister.

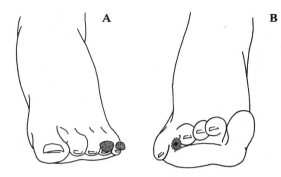

Figure 14-18

A, Hard corns appear on the top of a toe and are usually associated with hammer toes. B, Soft corns usually appear between the fourth and fifth toes.

corn is the result of a combination of wearing narrow shoes and having excessive foot perspiration (Figure 14-18).

Signs of condition   The corn usually forms between the fourth and fifth toes. A circular area of thickened, white, macerated skin appears between and at the base of the toes. There also appears to be a black dot in the center of the corn. Both pain and inflammation are likely to be present. Symptoms are local pain and disability, with inflammation and thickening of soft tissue.

Care   When caring for a soft corn, the best procedure is to have the athlete wear properly fitting shoes, keep the skin between the toes clean and dry, and decrease pressure by keeping the toes separated with cotton or lamb's wool. The athlete should soak feet daily in warm, soapy water to soften the corn. To alleviate further irritation, the corn should be protected by a small felt or sponge rubber doughnut.

Ingrown Toenails

Cause of condition   An ingrown toenail is a condition in which the leading side edge of the toenail has grown into the soft tissue nearby, usually resulting in a severe inflammation and infection.[12]

Care   It is important that the athlete's shoes be of the proper length and width, because continued pressure on a toenail can lead to serious irritation or cause it to become ingrown. In most cases ingrown toenails can be prevented by knowing how to trim the nails correctly. The nail must be trimmed so that its margins do not penetrate the tissue on the sides. Also, the nail should be left sufficiently long that it is clear of the underlying tissue and still should be cut short enough that it is not irritated by either shoes or socks. The accompanying Focus Box details the care for an ingrown toenail.

Toenail Hematoma

Cause of injury   Blood can accumulate under a toenail as a result of the toe being stepped on, of dropping an object on the toe, or of kicking another object. Nails subjected to repetitive shearing forces, as may occur in the shoe of a long-distance runner, may also cause bleeding into the nail bed. In any case, blood that accumulates in a confined space underneath the nail is likely to produce extreme pain and can ultimately cause loss of the nail.[12]

⟨14-2⟩   *Focus Box*

Managing the Ingrown Toenail

1. Soak the toe in hot water (110° to 120° F) [43.3° to 48.8° C]) for approximately twenty minutes, two or three times daily.

2. When the nail is soft and pliable, use forceps to insert a wisp of cotton under the edge of the nail and lift it from the soft tissue (see Figure 14-18).

3. Continue this procedure until the nail has grown out sufficiently that it can be trimmed straight across. The correct trimming of nails is shown in Figure 14-18.

An ingrown toenail can easily become infected. If this occurs, it should be immediately referred to a physician for treatment.

Signs of injury   Bleeding into the nail bed may be either immediate or slow, producing considerable pain. The area under the toenail assumes a bluish-purple color and gentle pressure on the nail greatly exacerbates pain.

Care   An ice pack should be applied immediately, and the foot should be elevated to decrease bleeding. Within the next twelve to twenty-four hours, the pressure of the blood under the nail should be released by drilling a small hole though the nail into the nail bed. This drilling must be done under sterile conditions and is best done by either a physician or an athletic trainer. It is not uncommon to have to drill the nail a second time because more blood is likely to accumulate.

SUMMARY

- The human foot must function both to absorb forces and to provide a stable base of support during walking, running, and jumping.

- The twenty-six bones in the foot are held together by an intricate network of ligaments and fascia and are moved by a complicated group of muscles.

- Foot injuries may be prevented by selecting appropriate footwear and using various orthotic devices inserted into the shoe to protect the foot from abnormal forces, stresses, and strains.

- A pump bump develops from chronic retrocalcaneal bursitis on the back of the heel.

- Plantar fasciitis is pain in the anterior medial heel, usually at the attachment of the plantar fascia to the calcaneus. Orthotics in combination with stretching exercises can significantly reduce pain.

- A Jones fracture is a fracture of the neck of the fifth metatarsal that often results in delayed healing.

- The most common stress fracture in the foot involves the second metatarsal (march fracture).

- Metatarsal and longitudinal arch sprains are best treated by inserting appropriate support pads into the shoes.

- A bunion is a deformity of the head of the first metatarsal in which the large toe assumes a hallux valgus position.

- To treat a Morton's Neuroma, a metatarsal bar is placed just proximal to the metatarsal heads or a teardrop-shaped pad is placed between the heads of the third and fourth metatarsals in an attempt to have these toes splay apart with weight bearing.

- Turf toe is a hyperextension injury resulting in a sprain of the great toe.

- The foot within the shoe can sustain forces that produce calluses, blisters, corns, or ingrown toenails.

Solutions to Critical Thinking Exercises

14-1 These complaints are most typically associated with plantar fasciitis, which can be treated with a combination of vigorous heel cord stretching, stretching the plantar fascia in the arch, using a heel cup, arch taping, and using an orthotic with increased arch support.

14-2 Most likely the athlete has a Morton's Neuroma. A metatarsal bar or a teardrop-shaped pad applied in the correct position on the sole of the foot can help to spread the metatarsal heads apart and take pressure off the neuroma, reducing the symptoms.

14-3 A sprain of the great toe is often referred to as turf toe. It results from a hyperextension of the great toe and usually occurs to athletes playing on artificial turf.

REVIEW QUESTIONS AND CLASS ACTIVITIES

1. Briefly describe the anatomy of the foot.
2. In evaluating an acute condition in the foot region, what general observations can be made?
3. What measures can be taken to prevent foot injuries?
4. What is the relationship between a pump bump and retrocalcaneal bursitis?
5. What is a Jones fracture, and why does it take so long to heal?
6. How is it possible for a heel bruise to lead to plantar fasciitis?
7. How are stress fractures of the second metatarsal managed?
8. Discuss how various arch sprains can be treated.
9. What injuries may potentially result from wearing shoes that are too tight?
10. How does a Morton's Toe differ from a Morton's Neuroma?
11. How would you care for a chronic case of turf toe?
12. What is the recommended procedure in caring for a blister on the foot?

REFERENCES

1. Benda C: Stepping in the right sock, *Physician Sportsmed* 19(12): 125, 1991.
2. Coughlin MJ: Forefoot disorders. In Baxter DE, editor: *The foot and ankle in sport*, St Louis, 1995, Mosby.
3. Crosby LA, McMullen ST: Heel pain in an active adolescent? *Physician Sportsmed* 21:125, 1993.
4. Hunter S, Prentice W: Rehabilitation of ankle and foot injuries. In Prentice WE, editor: *Rehabilitation techniques in sports medicine*, ed 3,

Dubuque, Iowa, 1999, WCB/
McGraw-Hill.

5. Irvine WO: Feet under force, *Physician Sportsmed* 20:137, 1992.

6. Mann RA: Great toe disorders. In Baxter DE, editor: *The foot and ankle in sport,* St Louis, 1995, Mosby.

7. McDermott EP: Basketball injuries of the foot and ankle, *Clin Sports Med* 12:373, 1993.

8. Myerson M: Tarsometatarsal joint injury, *Physician Sportsmed* 21:97, 1993.

9. Petrizzi MJ: Foot injuries. In Birrer RB, editor: *Sports medicine for the primary care physician,* ed 2, Boca Raton, Fla, 1994, CRC Press.

10. Pfeffer GB: Plantar heel pain. In Baxter DE, editor: *The foot and ankle in sport,* St Louis, 1995, Mosby.

11. Reynolds JC: Functional examination of the foot and ankle. In Sam-marco GJ, editor: *Rehabilitation of the foot and ankle,* St Louis, 1995, Mosby.

12. Scioli M: Managing toenail trauma, *Physician Sportsmed* 20:107, 1992.

13. Stephens MM: Heel pain. *Physician Sportsmed* 20:87, 1992.

14. Tanner SM: Plantar fasciitis: healing heel pain, *Sports Med Digest* 14:2, 1992.

15. Torg JS: Plantar fasciitis. In Torg JS, Shephard RJ, editors: *Current therapy in sports medicine,* ed 3, St Louis, 1995, Mosby.

16. Trevino S et al: Tendon injuries of the foot and ankle, *Clin Sports Med* 11:727, 1992.

17. Welsh RP: Metatarsalgia problems. In Torg JS, Shephard RJ, editors: *Current therapy in sports medicine,* ed 3, St Louis, 1995, Mosby.

ANNOTATED BIBLIOGRAPHY

Baxter DE: *The foot and ankle in sport,* St Louis, 1995, Mosby.

A complete medical text on all aspects of the foot and ankle; covers common sports syndromes, anatomical disorders in sports, unique problems, shoes, orthoses, and rehabilitation.

Donatelli R: *The biomechanics of the foot and ankle,* Philadelphia, 1990, FA Davis.

A practical book on the basic mechanics of the foot and ankle.

WEB SITES

Foot and Ankle Web Index: http://www.footandankle.com

The foot and ankle link library at this site is very helpful.

Premiere Medical Search Engine: http://www.medsite.com

Type in any medical condition at this site and it will search the Net to find relevant articles.

Dr. Pribut's Running Injuries Page: http://www.clarknet/pub/pribut/sp-sport.html

Wheeless' Textbook of Orthopaedics: http://www.medmedia.com/med.htm

An excellent page for injuries, anatomy, and x rays.

North Shore Podiatry Foot Care Center: http://www.BUNIONBUSTERS.com

The Ankle and Lower Leg

When you finish this chapter you will be able to:

- Describe the bony, ligamentous, and muscular anatomy of the ankle and lower leg.
- List considerations for preventing injuries to the ankle and lower leg.
- Explain how to assess common ankle and lower leg injuries.
- Identify the possible causes and signs of various injuries that can occur in the the ankle and lower leg.
- Explain the procedures that can be taken in caring for ankle and lower leg injuries.

The ankle joint is composed of:
Tibia
Fibula
Talus

The talocrural joint allows two motions: plantarflexion and dorsiflexion.

The subtalar joint allows two motions: inversion and eversion.

Medial ligament includes:
Deltoid

ANATOMY

Bones

The portion of the anatomy below the knee and above the ankle is the lower leg. It is composed of the thicker tibia, which is more medial, and the thinner fibula, which is more lateral. The ankle joint or *talocrural joint* (sometimes called the ankle mortise) is formed by the thickened distal portion of the fibula, called the lateral malleolus; the thickened distal portion of the tibia, called the medial malleolus; and the more-or-less cube-shaped tarsal bone, called the talus, that fits between the two malleoli. The ankle joint allows two motions: plantarflexion and dorsiflexion. The joint between the talus and the calcaneous is called the *subtalar joint*. Inversion and eversion take place at the *subtalar joint* (Figure 15-1).

Ligaments

The tibia and fibula are held together by the interosseous membrane, which extends the entire length of the two bones. The anterior and posterior tibiofibular ligaments bridge the tibia and fibula and form the distal portion of the interosseous membrane. The medial aspect of the ankle is relatively stable because of the thick deltoid ligament. The presence of this strong deltoid ligament combined with the fact that the lateral malleolus of the fibula extends further distally than the medial malleolus limits the ability of the ankle to evert. Thus eversion ankle sprains are con-

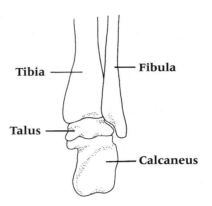

Figure 15-1

The ankle joint is formed by
the tibia, fibula, and talus.
The subtalar joint is formed
by the talus and calcaneus.

siderably less common than inversion sprains. The three lateral ligaments
include the anterior talofibular, the posterior talofibular, and the calcaneofibular. The lateral ligaments collectively limit inversion and are
much more susceptible to injury (Figure 15-2).

Lateral ligaments include:
Anterior talofibular
Posterior talofibular
Calcaneofibular

Musculature

Contraction of the muscles in the lower leg produce movement at the ankle joint. The muscles of the lower leg are divided into four distinct
groups. Each of the four muscle groups is contained separately within a
compartment by thick sheets of fascia (connective tissue) that surround
them. The muscles in the anterior compartment dorsiflex the ankle, the
muscles in the superficial posterior compartment plantarflex the ankle,
the muscles in the lateral compartment evert the ankle, and the muscles
in the deep posterior compartment invert the ankle (Figure 15-3).

Muscle actions by
compartment:
Anterior compartment—
dorsiflex the ankle
Superficial posterior
compartment—plantarflex
the ankle
Lateral compartment—evert
the ankle
Deep posterior
compartment—invert the
ankle

PREVENTION OF LOWER LEG AND ANKLE INJURIES

Many lower leg and ankle injuries, especially sprains, can be reduced by
heel cord (Achilles tendon) stretching, strengthening of key muscles, improving neuromuscular control, choosing appropriate footwear, and
when necessary, proper taping or bracing.[10,11]

Figure 15-2

Major ligaments of the ankle:
A, Lateral aspect. B, Medial
aspect

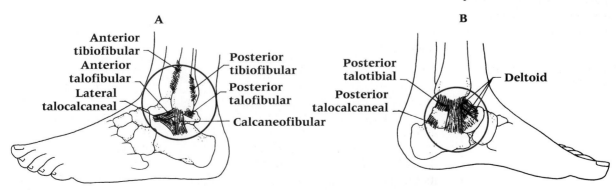

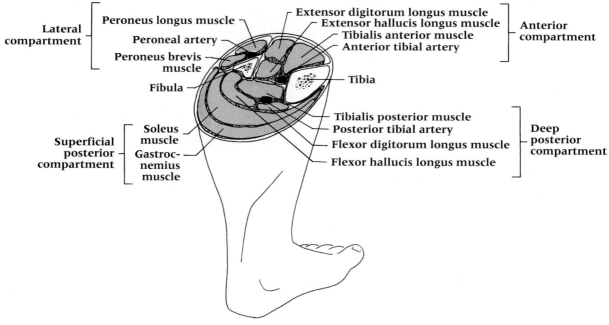

Lateral compartment
- Peroneus longus muscle
- Peroneal artery
- Peroneus brevis muscle
- Fibula

Anterior compartment
- Extensor digitorum longus muscle
- Extensor hallucis longus muscle
- Tibialis anterior muscle
- Anterior tibial artery
- Tibia

Superficial posterior compartment
- Soleus muscle
- Gastrocnemius muscle

Deep posterior compartment
- Tibialis posterior muscle
- Posterior tibial artery
- Flexor digitorum longus muscle
- Flexor hallucis longus muscle

Figure 15-3

The muscles of the lower leg are divided into four distinct groups contained separately within individual compartments: the anterior compartment, superficial posterior compartment, lateral compartment, and deep posterior compartment.

Preventing lower leg and ankle injuries:
Heel cord stretching
Strength training
Neuromuscular control
Appropriate footwear
Ankle taping and bracing

Heel Cord Stretching

The athlete with a tight heel cord should routinely stretch before and after practice. To properly stretch the heel cord, the ankle should be dorsiflexed and the knee fully extended to stretch the gastrocnemius muscle, and then the knee should be flexed to about 30 degrees to stretch the soleus muscle (Figure 15-4). There should be at least 10 degrees of dorsiflexion for normal ankle motion to occur.

Strength Training

Achieving both static and dynamic joint stability through strength training is critical in preventing ankle injury (Figure 15-5). A balance in strength throughout the full range of motion must be developed and maintained in each of the four muscle groups that surround the ankle joint.

Neuromuscular Control

As is the case with strength training, maintaining neuromuscular control is critical to prevention of injury to the ankle joint. Neuromuscular control relies on the central nervous system to interpret and integrate proprioceptive and kinesthetic information and then to control individual muscles and joints to produce coordinated movements that collectively protect the joint from injury. Thus, the foot and ankle must respond quickly to any uneven surface condition. Ankle joint position sense can be enhanced by training on uneven surfaces or by spending time each day on a balance board, or wobble board (Figure 15-6).

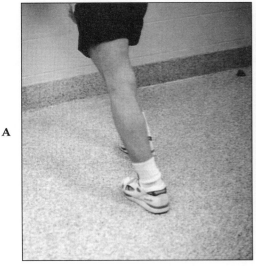

A

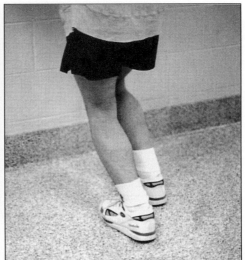

B

Figure 15-4

Stretching techniques for the heel cord complex: A, Stretching position for the gastrocnemius muscle. B, Stretching position for the soleus muscle

Footwear

As discussed in Chapters 6 and 14, proper footwear can be an important factor in reducing injuries to both the foot and the ankle. Shoes should not be used in activities for which they were not intended—for example, running shoes, which are designed for straight-ahead activity, should not be worn to play basketball, a sport demanding a great deal of lateral movement.

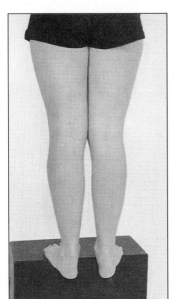

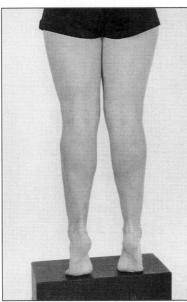

Figure 15-5

Strength training is essential for the prevention of ankle sprains.

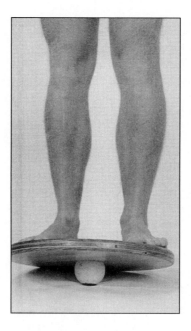

Figure 15-6

The wobble board is an
excellent device for
reestablishing neuromuscular
control.

Preventive Ankle Wrapping, Taping, and Bracing

As discussed in Chapter 11, there is some doubt about whether it is beneficial to routinely tape ankles that have no history of sprain. Tape, properly applied, can provide some prophylactic protection. Poorly applied tape will do more harm than good. Tape that constricts soft tissue and blood circulation or disrupts normal biomechanical function can, in time, create unnecessary problems.

Ankle bracing can also offer protection to the ankle joint (Figure 15-7). Braces may be effective in preventing lateral and inversion movement of the foot without inhibiting plantar flexion (see Chapter 6).

ASSESSING THE LOWER LEG

History

An athlete who complains of discomfort in the lower leg region should be asked the following questions:

- How long has it been hurting?
- Where is the pain or discomfort?
- Has the feeling changed or is there numbness?
- Is there a feeling of warmth?
- Is there any sense of muscle weakness or difficulty in walking?
- How did the problem occur?

Observation

The athlete is generally observed for the following:

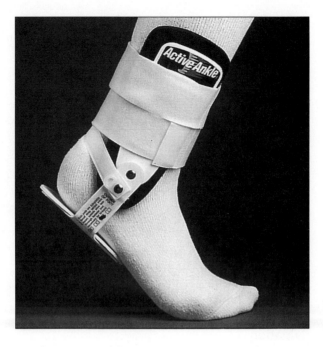

Figure 15-7

Ankle braces may be used to
support weakened ankles.

- Any postural deviations, such as toeing in, should be noted.
- Any walking difficulty should be noted, along with leg deformities or swellings.

Palpation

Palpation should be done over the musculature in each of the four compartments. When fracture is suspected, a gentle percussive blow can be given to the tibia or fibula below or above the suspected site. Percussion can also be applied upward on the bottom of the heel. Such blows set up a vibratory force that resonates at the fracture, causing pain.

ASSESSING THE ANKLE JOINT

The injured or painful ankle should be carefully evaluated to determine the possibility of fracture and whether medical referral is necessary.

History

The athlete's history may vary, depending on whether the problem is the result of sudden trauma or is chronic. The athlete with an acute sudden trauma to the ankle should be asked the following questions:

- What trauma or mechanism occurred?
- What was heard when the injury occurred—a crack, snap, or pop?
- What were the duration and intensity of pain?
- How disabling was the occurrence? Could the athlete walk right away, or was he or she unable to bear weight for a period of time?

- Has a similar injury occurred before?
- Was there immediate swelling, or did the swelling occur later (or at all)? Where did the swelling occur?
- What past ankle injuries have occurred?

Observation

In an initial look at the ankle, the athletic trainer determines the following:

- Is there an obvious deformity?
- Are the bony contours of the ankle normal and symmetrical, or is there a deviation such as a bony deformity?
- Is there any discoloration?
- Is there crepitus or abnormal sound in the ankle joint?
- Is heat, swelling, or redness present?
- Is the athlete in obvious pain?
- Does the athlete have a normal ankle range of motion?
- If the athlete is able to walk, is there a normal walking pattern?

Palpation

Palpation in the ankle region should start with key bony landmarks and ligaments and progress to the musculature, especially the major tendons that surround the ankle. The purpose of palpation in this region is to detect obvious structural deformities, swelling, and localized tenderness.

Functional Examination

Muscle function is important in evaluating the ankle injury. If the athlete cannot execute or has difficulty performing the following functional activities, the athlete is not ready to return to activity.

- Walk on toes
- Walk on heels
- Hop on affected foot without heel touching surface
- Start or stop the running motion
- Change direction rapidly
- Run figure eights

INJURIES TO THE ANKLE

Ankle Sprains

Cause Of injury   Ankle sprains are among the more common injuries seen in athletics[3] (Figure 15-8). Injuries to the ligaments of the ankle may be classified by the mechanism of injury.

Inversion sprains   An inversion ankle sprain is most common and often results in injury to the lateral ligaments. The anterior talofibular ligament is the weakest of the three lateral ligaments. It is injured in an

15-1

Critical Thinking Exercise

A basketball player sustains a grade 1 inversion sprain of her left ankle during a game. There is immediate pain and swelling, and she is unable to bear weight.

? What is the most important first-aid goal immediately following injury, and how may that first-aid goal best be accomplished?

Ankle sprain classifications:
Inversion
Eversion
Dorsiflexion

Figure 15-8

Ankle sprains are very
common in athletics.

inverted and plantarflexed position. The calcaneofibular and posterior talofibular ligaments are also likely to be injured in inversion sprains as the force of inversion is increased. Increased inversion force is needed to tear the calcaneofibular ligament[11] (Figure 15-9).

Eversion sprains As mentioned previously, eversion ankle sprains are less common than inversion ankle sprains largely because of the bony and ligamentous anatomy. Eversion injuries may involve an avulsion fracture of the tibia before the deltoid ligament tears. The deltoid ligament may also be contused in inversion sprains due to impingement between the lateral malleolus and the calcaneous. Despite the fact that eversion sprains are less common, the severity is such that these sprains may take longer to heal than do inversion sprains[11] (Figure 15-10).

Dorsiflexion sprains The anterior and posterior tibiofibular ligaments are torn with forced dorsiflexion and are often injured in conjunction with a severe sprain of the medial and lateral ligament complexes. Sprains of these ligaments are extremely hard to treat and often take

The most important factor in rehabilitation of an ankle sprain is controlling initial swelling with RICE.

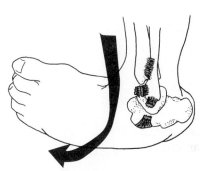

Figure 15-9

Mechanism of an inversion
ankle sprain

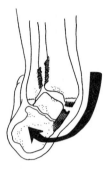

Figure 15-10

Mechanism of an eversion
ankle sprain

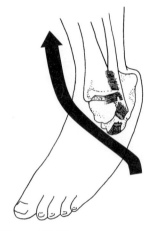

Figure 15-11

Mechanism of dorsiflexion
ankle sprain

Figure 15-12

A horseshoe-shaped pad
provides an excellent
compression when held in
place by an elastic wrap.

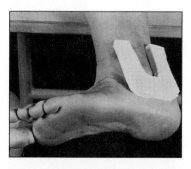

months to heal. Return to sport may be delayed for a longer period of
time than for inversion or eversion sprains[11] (Figure 15-11).

Signs of injury   In a grade 1 sprain, there is some stretching or perhaps tearing of the ligamentous fibers with little or no joint instability.
Mild pain, little swelling, and joint stiffness may be apparent.

With a grade 2 sprain, there is some tearing and separation of the ligamentous fibers and moderate instability of the joint. Moderate-to-severe
pain, swelling, and joint stiffness should be expected.

Grade 3 sprains involve total rupture of the ligament, manifested primarily by gross instability of the joint. Severe pain may be present initially, followed by little or no pain due to total disruption of nerve fibers.
Swelling may be profuse, and thus the joint tends to become very stiff
some hours after the injury. A grade 3 sprain with marked instability usually requires some form of immobilization lasting several weeks. Surgical
repair or reconstruction may be necessary to correct an instability.

Care   For ankle sprains, as for all acute musculoskeletal injuries, initial treatment efforts should be directed toward limiting the amount of
swelling. This treatment is more essential for ankle sprains than for any
other injury. Controlling initial swelling is the single most important
treatment measure that can be taken during the entire rehabilitation
process. Limiting the amount of acute swelling can significantly reduce
the time required for rehabilitation. Initial management includes ice,
compression, elevation, rest, and protection.[11]

Coaches should follow exactly the technique described here to be
maximally effective in controlling swelling following ankle sprain:

- As soon as possible following the injury, cut out a horseshoe-shaped
  pad made of felt or foam and fit it around the malleolus on the side
  of injury[16] (Figure 15-12).

- Apply a wet compression wrap over this pad. Wetting the elastic wrap
  helps facilitate the passage of cold from ice packs. Wrapping should
  begin covering the toes and progress proximally, completely
  compressing the ankle joint and ending just below the level of the
  gastrocnemius muscle (Figure 15-13A).

- Surround the ankle joint entirely with ice bags and secure them in
  place with a second, dry, elastic wrap. Ice bags should be left on for
  forty-five minutes initially and then one hour off and thirty minutes
  on as much as possible over the next twenty-four hours. During the

A

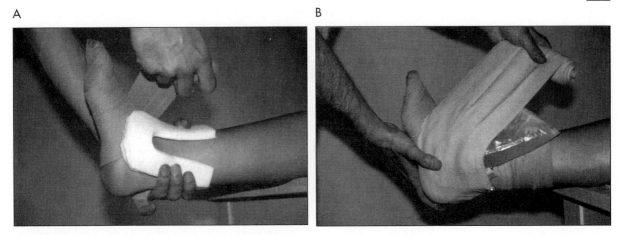

B

C

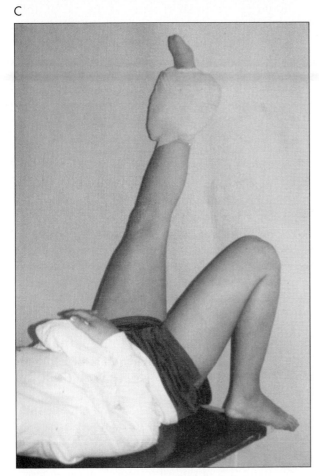

Figure 15-13

RICE technique: A, A wet
compression wrap should be
applied over the horseshoe
pad; B, Ice bags should be
secured in place by a dry
compression wrap; and C,
The leg should be elevated
during the initial treatment
period.

following forty-eight-hour period, ice should be applied as often as
possible (Figure 15-13B).

■ The foot and ankle should be elevated to a minimum of 45 degrees while icing. The ankle should be elevated as much as possible during the seventy-two-hour period after injury. Keeping the injured part elevated while sleeping is particularly important (Figure 15-13C).

- The athlete should be placed on crutches to avoid weight bearing for a minimum of twenty-four hours following injury to allow the healing process to accomplish what it needs to. After twenty-four hours the athlete should be encouraged to begin weight bearing as soon as tolerated.

In the past, athletes were simply returned to sports once the pain was low enough to tolerate the activity. Returning to full activity should include a gradual progression of functional activities (i.e., walking, jogging, running, cutting, etc.) that slowly increase the stress on the ligament. The specific demands of each individual sport dictate the individual drills of this progression.

Ideally, the athlete should return to sport without the aid of ankle support. However, it is common practice that some type of ankle support be worn initially. Ankle taping does have a stabilizing effect on unstable ankles without interfering with motor performance. Taping the ankle and also taping the shoe onto the foot to make the shoe and ankle function as one unit has been recommended. High-topped footwear may further stabilize the ankle. If cleated shoes are worn, cleats should be outset along the periphery of the shoe to provide stability. A protective ankle brace can also be worn for support as a substitute for taping.[11]

Ankle Fractures

Cause of injury   When assessing an ankle injury, the coach must always be cautious about suspecting an ankle sprain when a fracture actually exists. Ankle fractures can occur from several mechanisms that are similar to those that cause ankle sprains. In an inversion injury, medial malleolus fractures often occur along with a sprain of the lateral ligaments of the ankle (Figure 15-14). A fracture of the lateral malleolus is often more likely to occur than a sprain if an eversion force is applied to the ankle. With a fracture of the lateral malleolus, however, there may also be a sprain of the deltoid ligament. With avulsion injuries it is often the injured ligaments rather than the fracture that prolong the rehabilitation period.

Signs of injury   A fracture of the malleoli will generally result in immediate swelling. There will be point tenderness over the bone and apprehensiveness by the athlete to bear weight.

Care   If the possibility of a fracture exists, the coach should splint the ankle and refer the athlete to the physician for x-ray examination and immobilization. Usually a physician will treat fractures by casting the leg in a short walking cast for six weeks with early weight bearing. The course of rehabilitation following this period of immobilization is generally the same as for ankle sprains. Once near-normal levels of strength flexibility and neuromuscular control have been regained and the injured athlete can perform functional activities, full activity may be resumed.[11]

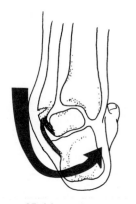

Figure 15-14

The mechanism that produces an ankle sprain can also cause an avulsion fracture.

Tendinitis

Cause of injury   Inflammation of the tendons surrounding the ankle joint is a common problem in athletes. The tendons most often involved are the posterior tibialis tendon behind the medial malleolus, the anterior tibialis on the dorsal surface of the ankle, and the peroneal tendons behind the lateral malleolus (Figure 5-15). Tendinitis in these tendons may result from one specific cause or from a collection of mechanisms including faulty foot mechanics, inappropriate or poor footwear that can create faulty foot mechanics, acute trauma to the tendon, tightness in the heel cord complex, or training errors.[8]

Signs of injury   Athletes who develop tendinitis are likely to complain of pain with both active movement and passive stretching; swelling around the area of the tendon due to inflammation of the tendon; crepitus on movement; and stiffness and pain following periods of inactivity but particularly in the morning.[8]

Care   Techniques that act to reduce or eliminate inflammation, including rest, therapeutic modalities (ice), and antiinflammatory medications, should be used. The use of an orthotic device to correct the biomechanics or taping the foot may also be helpful in reducing stress on the tendons.

In many instances, if the mechanism that is causing the irritation and inflammation of the tendon is removed and the inflammatory process is allowed to run its normal course, the tendinitis will resolve within ten days to two weeks. It is better to allow the athlete to rest for a sufficient period of time so that tendon healing can take place.

> Common sites for tendinitis:
> Anterior tibialis
> Posterior tibialis
> Peroneals

INJURIES TO THE LOWER LEG

Tibial and Fibular Fractures

Cause of injury   The tibia and fibula constitute the bony components of the lower leg and are primarily responsible for weight bearing and muscle attachment. The tibia is the most commonly fractured long

> The tibia is more commonly
> fractured than the fibula.

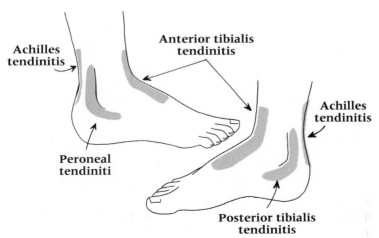

Figure 15-15

Common sites of tendinitis
around the ankle

bone in the body; this injury is usually the result either of direct trauma to the area or of indirect trauma, such as a combination rotatory/compressive force. Fractures of the fibula are usually seen in combination with a tibial fracture or as a result of direct trauma to the area[10] (Figure 15-16).

Signs of injury Tibial fractures will present with immediate pain, swelling, and possible deformity and may be open or closed in nature. Fibular fractures alone are usually closed and present with pain and point tenderness on palpation and with ambulation.

Care Treatment of these fractures is immediate medical referral and most likely a period of immobilization and restricted weight bearing for weeks to possibly months, depending on the severity and involvement of the injury.

Tibial and Fibular Stress Fractures

Cause of injury Stress fractures of the tibia and fibula are common in sports. Studies indicate that tibial stress fractures occur at a higher rate than those of the fibula. Stress fractures in the lower leg are usually the result of repetitive loading during training and conditioning (Figure 15-17). Tibial stress fractures are prevalent in athletes involved with jumping.[1]

Signs of injury The athlete will complain of pain with activity that sometimes becomes worse when activity is stopped. Focal point tenderness on the bone will help differentiate a stress fracture from medial tibial stress syndrome, which is located in the same area but is more diffuse. Tibial stress fractures usually occur in the middle of the shaft whereas fibular stress fractures are more likely to occur in the distal part of the bone.[13]

Care An athlete with a suspected stress fracture should be referred to a physician for diagnosis. The physician will most likely do a bone

Figure 15-16

Fractures of the lower leg can be serious injuries.

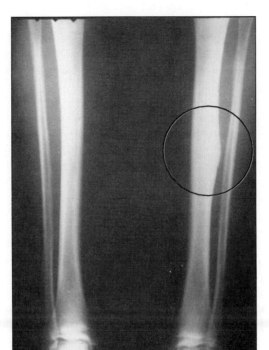

Figure 15-17

X ray of a stress fracture in
the tibia

scan, looking for signs of inflammation. Immediate elimination of the of-
fending activity is most important. Generally recuperation will require
about a two-week period during which the athlete can continue to be
weight bearing but must not engage in the activity that caused the problem in the first place. The athlete must be educated on the importance of
adhering to this advice in order to prevent further damage to the bone.
Progressively increasing stresses and strains can be placed on the bone so
the athlete can gradually return to normal training.[1,13]

Shinsplints (Medial Tibial Stress Syndrome)

Cause of injury   The term **shinsplints** is a catchall term that has traditionally referred to any type of pain in the anterior aspect of the lower
leg. Medial tibial stress syndrome, as it is more correctly called, is a condition that involves increasing pain specifically at the distal two-thirds of
the posterior medial aspect of the tibia. A strain of the posterior tibialis
muscle and its fascial sheath at its attachment to the periosteum of the
distal tibia during running activities is the most likely mechanism for this
injury.[2] Pain can arise secondary to a combination of faulty foot mechanics, tightness of the heel cord, muscle weakness, improper shoeware,
and training errors usually involving running on changing surfaces.[10]

Signs of injury   Pain is usually diffuse about the distal medial tibia
and the surrounding soft tissues. Initially, the area may only hurt after an
intense workout. As the condition worsens, daily ambulation may be

> **shinsplints**
> Medial tibial stress
> syndrome; anterior lower
> leg pain.

Compartment syndrome
classifications:
Acute compartment
syndrome
Acute exertional
compartment syndrome
Chronic compartment
syndrome

painful and morning pain and stiffness may be present. Medial tibial stress syndrome can progress to a stress fracture if not treated appropriately.[5]

Care Management of this condition should include physician referral to rule out the possibility of stress fracture via the use of bone scan and plain films. Activity modification along with measures to maintain cardiovascular fitness are set in place immediately. Correction of abnormal foot mechanics during walking and running must also be addressed with shoes and, if needed, custom foot orthotics. Ice massage to the area may be helpful in the reduction of localized pain and inflammation. A stretching program for the heel cord should be initiated (See Figure 15-4). Occasionally, supportive taping to the longitudinal arch might be helpful[10] (see Figure 11-33).

Compartment Syndromes

Cause of injury Compartment syndromes are conditions in which increased pressure within one of the four compartments of the lower leg causes compression of muscular and neurovascular structures within that compartment (see Figure 15-3). The anterior and deep posterior compartments are usually involved.[15]

Compartment syndromes can be divided into three categories: acute compartment syndrome, acute exertional compartment syndrome, and chronic compartment syndrome. *Acute compartment syndrome* occurs secondary to direct trauma to the area, such as being kicked in the anterior aspect of the lower leg. Acute compartment syndrome is considered to be a medical emergency. *Acute exertional compartment syndrome* occurs without any precipitating trauma and can evolve with minimal to moderate activity. *Chronic compartment syndrome* is activity related in that the symptoms arise rather consistently at a certain point in the activity. Chronic compartment syndrome usually occurs during running and jumping activities, and symptoms cease when activity stops.[4,17]

Signs of injury Because of increased intracompartmental pressure associated with compartment syndromes, the athlete will complain of a deep aching pain, tightness and swelling of the involved compartment, and pain with passive stretching of the involved muscles. Reduced circulation and sensory changes can be detected in the foot. Intracompartmental pressure measurements will further define the severity of the condition. A compartment syndrome that is not recognized, diagnosed, and treated properly can lead to a poor functional outcome for the athlete.[14]

Care Immediate first aid for acute compartment syndrome should include the application of ice and elevation. However, in this situation, a compression wrap should not be used to control swelling because there is already a problem with increased pressure in the compartment. Using a compression wrap will only act to increase the pressure.

In the case of both acute compartment syndrome and acute exertional compartment syndrome, measurement of intracompartmental pressures by a physician will confirm the diagnosis with emergency fas-

15-2

Critical Thinking Exercise

A soccer player who is not wearing shin guards is kicked on the outside shin of his right leg. After several minutes the pain begins to increase and he feels some tingling and numbness in his foot.

? What is the primary concern with this injury, and what steps should be taken to manage this situation?

15-3

Critical Thinking Exercise

A thirty-five-year old racquetball player feels a pop and severe immediate pain in the back of his left lower leg. He actually felt like someone kicked him, but when he turned around no one was there. Then he realized he could not push off on his foot.

? What injury does he most likely have, and how should it be managed?

ciotomy to release the pressure within that compartment being the definitive treatment. Athletes undergoing anterior or deep posterior compartment fasciotomy may not return to full activity for two to four months post surgery.[12]

Management of chronic compartment syndrome is initially conservative, with activity modification, icing, and stretching of the anterior compartment musculature and heel cord complex. If conservative measures fail, fasciotomy of the affected compartments has shown favorable results in an athlete's return to higher levels of activity.

Achilles Tendon Rupture

Cause of injury The Achilles tendon is the largest tendon in the human body. It serves as a common tendon for the gastrocnemius and soleus muscles and inserts on the calcaneus. This heel cord complex produces plantarflexion of the ankle. The resulting injury may range from a grade 1 strain of the muscle to complete rupture of the tendon. A tight heel cord is prone to strain, particularly of the gastrocnemius muscle, which is sometimes referred to as a **tennis leg**[7] (Figure 15-18). Achilles tendon rupture is usually caused by a sudden, forceful plantarflexion of the ankle. A rupture of the Achilles tendon is more common in athletes above the age of thirty years and occurs in activities requiring ballistic movement, such as tennis and basketball[9] (Figure 15-19).

Signs of injury The athlete may feel or hear a pop and feel as if they have been kicked in the back of the leg. The ability to plantarflex the ankle will be painful and limited but still possible with the assistance of the tibialis posterior and the peroneals. A palpable defect will be noted along the length of the tendon. The athlete will require the use of crutches to continue ambulation without an obvious limp.[9]

Care After an Achilles tendon rupture, the question of surgical repair versus cast immobilization will arise. Surgical repair of the tendon is recommended in allowing the athlete to return to previous levels of activity.[8] Surgical repair of the Achilles tendon may require a period of immobilization for six to eight weeks to allow for proper tendon healing. It is important that the athlete not only regain full range of motion without harming the repair, but also regain normal muscle function through controlled progressive strengthening exercises.[10]

Achilles Tendinitis

Cause of injury Achilles tendinitis is an inflammatory condition that occurs because of repetitive stresses and strains placed on the tendon such as with running or jumping activities.[6] Repetitive weight-bearing activities such as running or early season conditioning in which the duration and intensity are increased too quickly with insufficient recovery time will worsen the condition. Uphill running or hill workouts will usually aggravate the condition. The athlete may experience reduced gastrocnemius and soleus muscle flexibility in general that may worsen as the condition progresses and adaptive shortening occurs.

Figure 15-18

Strain of the gastrocnemius muscle

Figure 15-19

Achilles tendon rupture

tennis leg
Strain of gastrocnemius
muscle.

Achilles tendinitis generally
takes a long time to resolve.

A ruptured Achilles tendon
can occur following chronic
inflammation.

Severe blows to an
unprotected shin can lead to
a chronic inflammation.

Signs of injury   The athlete often complains of generalized pain and stiffness about the Achilles tendon just proximal to the calcaneal insertion. Achilles tendinitis will often begin with a gradual onset over a period of time. Symptoms may progress to morning stiffness and discomfort with walking after periods of prolonged sitting. The tendon may be warm and painful to palpation, and if the inflammation persists, the tendon may thicken (Figure 15-20).

Care   Achilles tendinitis generally takes a long time to resolve. It is important to create a proper healing environment by limiting or restricting the activity that caused the inflammation. Aggressive stretching of the heel cord complex (see Figure 15-4), inserting a heel lift under the calcaneus, using taping techniques to provide support to the Achilles tendon (see Figure 11-32), and using antiinflammatory medication have all been recommended as treatments.[10] Chronic Achilles tendinitis may eventually predispose the athlete to rupture of the Achilles tendon.

Shin Contusions

Cause of injury   The shin (tibia), lying just under the skin, is exceedingly vulnerable and sensitive to blows or bumps. Because of the absence of muscular or adipose padding, force is not dissipated and the periosteum receives the impact delivered to the shin. Shin contusions occur frequently in soccer, and the incidence can be minimized by wearing appropriate shin guards (see Figure 6-25).

Signs of injury   The athlete complains of intense pain, swelling, and increased warmth. A bulging hematoma with a jellylike consistency develops rapidly. In some instances the hematoma may increase to the size of a golf ball (Figure 15-21).

Figure 15-20

Diffuse swelling and tendon
thickening in Achilles
tendinitis

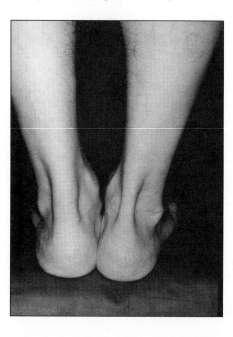

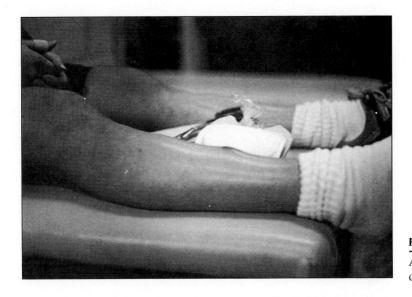

Figure 15-21

A serious shin bruise can
destroy bony tissue.

Care A compressive wrap along with ice and elevation should be applied immediately to minimize swelling. Occasionally a physician may decide to aspirate the hematoma. A protective doughnut pad constructed to disperse pressure away from the contusion should be worn to protect the area from additional injury.

SUMMARY

- The movements that take place at the talocrural joint are ankle plantarflexion and dorsiflexion. Inversion and eversion occur at the subtalar joint.

- Many lower leg and ankle injuries, especially sprains, can be reduced by heel cord (Achilles tendon) stretching, strengthening of key muscles, improving neuromuscular control, choosing appropriate footwear, and when necessary, proper taping or bracing.

- Ankle sprains are very common. Inversion sprains usually involve the lateral ligaments of the ankle, and eversion sprains frequently involve the medial ligaments of the ankle. Dorsiflexion injuries often involve the tibiofibular ligaments and may be very severe.

- The early phase of treatment following ankle sprain uses ice, compression, elevation, rest, and protection, all of which are critical components in preventing swelling.

- Tendinitis in the posterior tibialis, anterior tibialis, and the peroneal tendons may result from one specific cause or from a collection of mechanisms. Techniques that act to reduce or eliminate inflammation, including rest, ice, and antiinflammatory medications, should be incorporated into rehabilitation.

- Although some injuries that occur in the region of the lower leg are acute, the majority of injuries seen in an athletic population result from overuse, most often from running.

- Tibial fractures can create long-term problems for the athlete if inappropriately managed, whereas fibular fractures generally require much shorter periods for immobilization. Treatment of these fractures is immediate medical referral and most likely a period of immobilization and restricted weight bearing.

- Stress fractures in the lower leg are usually the result of the bone's inability to adapt to the repetitive loading response during training and conditioning of the athlete and are more likely to occur in the tibia.

- Chronic compartment syndromes can occur from acute trauma or from repetitive trauma or overuse They can occur in any of the four compartments but are most likely to occur in the anterior compartment or deep posterior compartment.

- Care for medial tibial stress syndrome must be comprehensive and must address several factors, including musculoskeletal training and conditioning as well as proper shoeware and orthotics intervention.

- Perhaps the greatest question after an Achilles tendon rupture is whether surgical repair or cast immobilization is the best method of treatment. Regardless, the time required for rehabilitation is significant.

- Achilles tendinitis will often present with a gradual onset over a period of time and may be resistant to a quick resolution.

Solutions to Critical Thinking Exercises

15-1 The most important care that can be given immediately following ankle sprain is to control or minimize the swelling. This goal is accomplished by using a combination of ice, compression, elevation, and rest beginning immediately and continuing for at least the next seventy-two hours.

15-2 This athlete may be developing an acute compartment syndrome in the anterior compartment. If so, this condition should be handled as an emergency. The coach should immediately elevate the leg and apply ice but no compression wrap, and the athlete should be given medical attention as soon as possible.

15-3 This scenario is a classic description of a ruptured Achilles tendon. In cases of a complete rupture, surgery is necessary to repair the tendon, followed by a reasonably long period of rehabilitation.

REVIEW QUESTIONS AND CLASS ACTIVITIES

1. Describe the anatomy of the ankle and lower leg.
2. How can ankle and lower leg injuries be prevented?
3. What questions should be asked when assessing injuries to the lower leg or ankle?
4. Describe the common mechanisms of injury for acute ankle sprains. What structures are damaged?

5. How can the coach rule out fractures in the lower leg and ankle?

6. What is the appropriate care for stress fractures of the tibia and fibula?

7. Which of the tendons surrounding the ankle joint can potentially develop tendinitis?

8. What are some indications of a heel cord rupture? How is a heel cord rupture cared for?

9. How does Achilles tendinitis develop? How should it be cared for?

10. Contrast acute compartment syndrome with chronic compartment syndrome.

11. What exactly are shinsplints and what measures can be taken to eliminate this problem?

12. What is the most important thing that can be done in caring for a shin contusion?

REFERENCES

1. Bennell K, Malcolm S, Thomas S et al: Risk factors for stress fractures in track and field athletes: a twelve-month prospective study, *Am J Spts Med* 24(6):810, 1996.

2. Case W: Relieving the pain of shinsplints, *Physician Sportsmed* 22(4):31, 1994.

3. Case WS: Recovering from ankle sprains, *Physician Sportsmed* 21(11): 43, 1993.

4. Fehlandt A, Micheli L: Acute exertional anterior compartment syndrome in an adolescent female, *Med Sci Spts Exerc* 27(1):3, 1995.

5. Fick D, Albright J, Murray B: Relieving painful shinsplints, *Physician Sportsmed* 20(12):105, 1992.

6. Galloway M, Jokl P, Dayton W: Achilles tendon overuse injuries, *Clin Sports Med* 11(4):771, 1992.

7. Garrick J, Couzens G: Tennis leg: how I manage gastrocnemius strains, *Physician Sportsmed* 20(5): 203, 1992.

8. Gross M: Chronic tendinitis: Pathomechanics of injury factors affecting the healing response, and treatment, *J Ortho Spts Phys Ther* 16(6):248, 1992.

9. Hamel R: Achilles tendon ruptures: making the diagnosis, *Physician Sportsmed* 20(9):189, 1992.

10. Hirth C: Rehabilitation of lower leg injuries. In Prentice WE, editor: *Rehabilitation techniques in sports medicine,* ed 3, Dubuque, Iowa, 1998, WCB/McGraw-Hill.

11. Hunter S, Prentice W: Rehabilitation of foot and ankle injuries. In Prentice WE, editor: *Rehabilitation techniques in sports medicine,* ed 3, Dubuque, Iowa, 1998, WCB/McGraw-Hill.

12. Kohn H: Shin pain and compartment syndromes in running. In Guten G, editor: *Running injuries,* Philadelphia, 1997, WB Saunders.

13. Reeder M, Dick B, Atkins J et al: Stress fractures: current concepts of diagnosis and treatment, *Sports Med* 22(3):198, 1996.

14. Stuart M, Karaharju T: Acute compartment syndrome: recognizing the progressive signs and symptoms, *Physician Sportsmed* 22(3): 91, 1994.

15. Vincent N: Compartment syndromes. In Harries M, Williams C, Stanish W, Micheli, L, editor: *Oxford textbook of sports medicine,* New York, 1994, Oxford University Press.

16. Wilkerson GB: Treatment of the inversion ankle sprain through synchronous application of focal compression and cold, *J Ath Train* 26(3):220, 1991.

17. Willy C, Becker B, Evers H: Unusual development of acute exertional compartment syndrome due to delayed diagnosis: a case report, *Int J Sports Med,* 17(6):458, 1996.

ANNOTATED BIBLIOGRAPHY

Baxter D: *The foot and ankle in sport,* St Louis, 1995, Mosby.

Discusses all aspects of dealing with foot and ankle injuries as they occur in an athletic population.

Brown DE, Neumann RD, editors: *Orthopedic secrets,* Philadelphia, 1995, Hanley & Belfus.

Presents an overview of orthopedics in a question-and-answer format. The ankle and lower leg are well presented.*

Kwong PK, editor: Foot and ankle injuries. *Clinics in sports medicine,* vol 13, no 4, Philadelphia, 1994, Saunders.

An up-to-date monograph for the practitioner on assessing and managing foot and ankle injuries.

WEB SITES

Cramer First Aider: http://www.ccsd.k12.wy.us/CCHS_web/sptmed/fstaider.htm

Ankle and lower leg anatomy cross section: http://rpiwww.mdacc.tmc.edu/cgibin/ankle_engine

The University of Texas Anatomy of The Human Body: http://rpiwww.mdacc.tmc.edu/mmlearn/anatomy.html

American Othopaedic Foot and Ankle Society: http://aofas.org

World Ortho: http://www.worldortho.com

Use the search engine in this site to locate relevant information.

Chapter 16

The Knee and Related Structures

When you finish this chapter you will be able to:

- Describe the anatomical relationships of the bones, ligaments, and muscles that surround the knee joint.
- Explain how to prevent knee injuries.
- Briefly describe how to assess an injury of the knee joint.
- Describe injuries to the stabilizing structures of the knee.
- Identify injuries to the knee that can occur either from acute trauma or from overuse.
- Identify injuries that can occur to the patella.
- Describe injuries that can occur to the extensor mechanism.

T he knee is considered one of the most complex joints in the human body. Because so many sports place extreme stress on the knee, it is also one of the most frequently injured joints. The knee is commonly considered a hinge joint because its two principal movements are flexion and extension. However, because rotation of the tibia is an essential component of knee movement, the knee is not a true hinge joint. The stability of the knee joint depends primarily on the ligaments, the joint capsule, and the muscles that surround the joint. The knee functions to provide stability in weight bearing and mobility in locomotion.

ANATOMY

Bones

The knee joint consists of four bones: the femur, the tibia, the fibula, and the patella (Figure 16-1). These four bones form several articulations between the femur and the tibia; the femur and the patella; the femur and the fibula; and the tibia and fibula. The articular surfaces of the knee joint are completely enveloped by the largest joint capsule in the body. Synovial membrane lines the inner surface of the joint capsule.

The distal end of the femur expands into the lateral and medial femoral condyles, which are designed to articulate with the tibia and the patella. The patella, or kneecap, is located in the tendon of the quadriceps muscle group on the front of the knee and moves up and down in a groove between the two femoral condyles as the quadriceps muscle group

Muscles and ligaments provide the main source of stability in the knee.

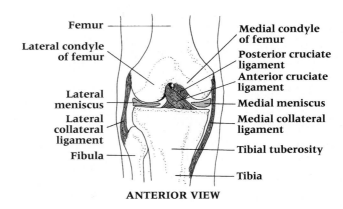

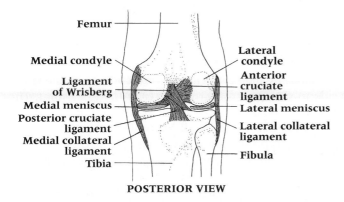

contracts and relaxes. The proximal end of the tibia, or the tibial plateau, is very flat and must articulate with the round condyles of the femur.

The medial meniscus and lateral meniscus are fibrocartilage disks that are shaped like bowls, thicker on the outside border and thinner on the inside (Figure 16-2). They lie on top of the flat tibial plateau and function to make the rounded femoral condyles fit better on the flat tibial plateau, thus increasing the stability of the joint. They also help cushion any stresses placed on the knee joint by keeping the bony surface of the femur separated from the tibial plateau.

Stabilizing Ligaments

The major stabilizing ligaments of the knee include the cruciate ligaments and the collateral ligaments (see Figure 16-1).

The anterior and posterior cruciate ligaments account for a considerable amount of stability in the knee. In general, the anterior cruciate ligament (ACL) prevents the femur from moving posteriorly during weight bearing. It also stabilizes the tibia against excessive internal rotation and serves as a secondary stabilizer when there is injury to the collateral ligaments. The posterior cruciate ligament (PCL) prevents the femur from sliding forward during weight bearing.

Figure 16-1

The bony and ligamentous arrangement of the knee

Generally the meniscus has a poor blood supply.

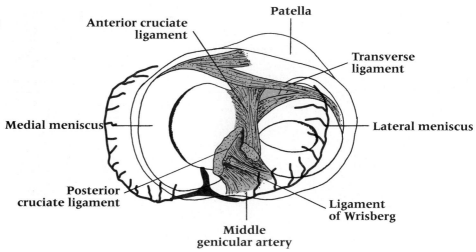

Figure 16-2

Menisci of the knee

The medial and lateral collateral ligaments function to stabilize the knee against the side to side (valgus/varus) forces at the knee joint. The medial collateral ligament (MCL) attaches above the joint line on the medial condyle of the femur and inserts well below the joint line on the tibia. Its major purpose is to protect the knee from valgus forces that are applied to the lateral surface of the joint and to resist external tibial rotation. There are two parts of the MCL: the superficial portion and the deep portion, which is actually a thickened part of the medial joint capsule. The medial meniscus is attached to the deep portion of the medial collateral ligament.

The lateral collateral ligament (LCL) is attached to the lateral condyle of the femur and to the head of the fibula. The lateral collateral ligament resists varus forces that are applied to the medial surface of the knee. Both the medial and lateral collateral ligaments are tightest during knee extension but relaxed during flexion.

Knee Musculature

Major movements of the
knee:
Flexion
Extension
Rotation

For the knee to function properly, a number of muscles must work together in a highly complex fashion (Figure 16-3). In general, contraction of the quadriceps muscle group on the front of the thigh causes knee extension, while contraction of the hamstring muscle group on the back of the thigh causes knee flexion. Table 16-1 summarizes all the muscles that produce various movements at the knee joint.

PREVENTION OF KNEE INJURIES

Preventing knee injuries in sports is a complex problem. Of major importance are effective physical conditioning, rehabilitation, and skill development as well as shoe type. A questionable practice may be the routine use of protective bracing.

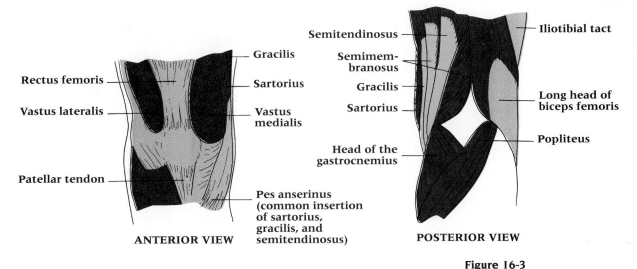

Figure 16-3

Musculature of the knee

Physical Conditioning and Rehabilitation

To avoid knee injuries, the athlete must be as highly conditioned as possible, meaning total body conditioning that includes strength, flexibility, cardiovascular and muscle endurance, agility, speed, and balance.[15] Specifically, the muscles surrounding the knee joint must be as strong as possible. Depending on the requirements of a sport, some balance in strength should exist between the quadriceps and hamstring muscle

TABLE 16-1 Muscles of the knee joint	
Knee flexion	Hamstring group
	biceps femoris
	semitendinosus
	semimembranosus
	gracilis
	sartorius
	gastrocnemius
	popliteus
	plantaris
Knee extension	Quadriceps muscle group
	vastus medialis
	vastus lateralis
	vastus intermedius
	rectus femoris
External tibial rotation	biceps femoris
Internal tibial rotation	popliteus
	semitendinosus
	semimembranosus
	sartorius
	gracilis

groups. For example, in football players the hamstring muscles should have about 60 percent of the strength of the quadriceps muscles.[16] The gastrocnemius muscle should also be strengthened to help stabilize the knee. Although maximizing muscle strength may prevent some injuries, it fails to prevent rotational injuries.

Knees that have been injured must be properly rehabilitated. Once the ligaments that stabilize the knee have been injured, the knee will rely to a great extent on the strength of all the muscles that surround the joint to provide the inherent stability that was lost with the injury. Thus strengthening exercises are essential in preventing reinjury. Repeated minor injuries to a knee make it susceptible to a major injury.

Shoe Type

During recent years, collision sports such as football have been using soccer-style shoes. The change from a few long conical cleats to a large number of cleats that are short and broad has significantly reduced knee injuries in football. The higher number and shorter cleats are better because the foot does not become fixed to the surface and the shoe still allows controlled running and cutting.

Functional and Prophylactic Knee Braces

Functional and prophylactic knee braces were discussed in Chapter 6. These braces have been designed to prevent or reduce the severity of knee injuries.[12] Prophylactic knee braces are worn on the lateral surface of the knee to protect the medial collateral ligament (Figure 16-4A).[6]

Functional knee braces are worn to provide some degree of support

Figure 16-4

A, Prophylactic knee brace.
B, Functional knee brace

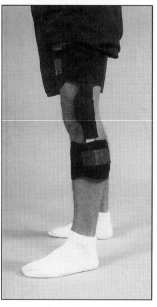

A   B

to the unstable knee once an athlete returns to activity following injury.[8] All functional braces are custom fitted to some degree and use hinges and posts for support. Some braces use custom-molded thigh and calf enclosures to hold the brace in place, whereas others rely on straps for suspension (Figure 16-4B). These braces are custom molded and are designed to control excessive rotational stress or tibial translation. The effectiveness of protective knee braces is at best controversial.[8,15] However, if combined with an appropriate rehabilitation program, these braces have been shown to restrict anterior/posterior translation of the tibia at low loads.[8]

ASSESSING THE KNEE JOINT

The coach is usually the first person to observe the injury and thus assumes responsibility for initial evaluation and immediate care. Unquestionably, the most important aspect of understanding what pathological process has taken place is to become familiar with the traumatic sequence and mechanisms of injury, either through having seen the injury occur or through learning its history. If an athletic trainer is not present when the injury occurs, the coach must relate the pertinent information[7] and then provide the appropriate first aid measures as discussed in Chapter 7.

History

To determine the history and major complaints involved in a knee injury, the following questions should be asked.

Current Injury

- What were you doing when the knee was hurt?
- What position was your body in?
- Did the knee collapse?
- Did you hear a noise or feel any sensation at the time of injury, such as a pop or crunch? (A pop could indicate an anterior cruciate tear, a crunch could be a sign of a torn meniscus, and a tearing sensation might indicate a capsule tear.)
- Could you move the knee immediately after the injury? If not, was it locked in a bent or extended position? (Locking could mean a meniscal tear.) After being locked, how did it become unlocked?
- Did swelling occur? If yes, was it immediate, or did it occur later? (Immediate swelling could indicate a cruciate or tibial fracture, whereas later swelling could indicate a capsular, synovial, or meniscal tear.)
- Where was the pain? Was it local, all over, or did it move from one side of the knee to the other?
- Have you hurt the knee before?

When first assessing the injury, the athletic trainer or coach should observe whether the athlete is able to support body weight flat-footed on the injured leg or whether the athlete finds it necessary to stand and walk on the toes. Toe walking is an indication that the athlete is holding the knee in a splinted position to avoid pain or that the knee is being held in a flexed position by a wedge of dislocated meniscus.

In first-time acute knee sprains, fluid and blood effusion is not usually apparent until after a twenty-four-hour period. However, in an anterior cruciate ligament sprain, blood may accumulate in the joint (hemarthrosis) during the first hour after injury. Swelling and discoloration (ecchymosis) will occur unless the swelling is controlled through the use of compression, elevation, and ice.

Recurrent or Chronic Injury

- What is your major complaint?
- When did you first notice the condition?
- Is there recurrent swelling?
- Does the knee ever lock or catch? (If yes, it may be a torn meniscus or a loose body in the knee joint.)
- Is there severe pain? Is it constant, or does it come and go?
- Do you feel any grinding or grating sensations? (If yes, it could indicate chondromalacia or traumatic arthritis.)
- Does your knee ever feel like it is going to give way or has it actually done so? (If yes and often, it may be a capsular, cruciate, or meniscal tear, a loose body, or a subluxating patella.)
- What does it feel like to go up and down stairs? (Pain may indicate a patellar irritation or meniscal tear.)
- What past treatment, if any, have you received for this condition?

Observation

If possible, the athlete with an injured knee should be observed in the following actions:
Walking
Half-squatting
Going up and down stairs

A visual examination should be performed after the major complaints have been determined. The athlete should be observed in a number of situations: walking, half-squatting, and going up and down stairs. The leg also should be observed for asymmetry. The coach must establish whether both the athlete's knees look the same:

- Do the knees appear symmetrical?
- Is one knee obviously swollen?
- Is muscle atrophy apparent?

Walking

- Does the athlete walk with a limp, or is the walk free and easy? Is the athlete able to fully extend the knee during heel strike?
- Can the athlete fully bear weight on the affected leg?
- Is the athlete able to perform a half-squat to extension?
- Can the athlete go up and down stairs with ease? (If stairs are unavailable, stepping up on a box or stool will suffice.)

Palpation

For palpation to yield any valuable information as to the nature of the injury, the coach must know at least a little about the anatomy of the bones, ligaments, and the muscles as described previously. The athlete should either be lying on the back (supine) or sitting on the edge of the training table or a bench with the knee flexed to 90 degrees.

The bone structures of the knee are palpated for areas of tenderness or pain or for deformities, which might indicate a fracture or dislocation.

After palpation of the bony structures, the lateral collateral ligament and medial collateral ligament should be palpated for areas of tenderness. Because the anterior and posterior cruciate ligaments are inside the joint capsule they cannot be palpated. However the *joint line,* which is the articulation between the femoral condyles and the flat tibial plateau, should be palpated all around the knee joint. Tenderness at the joint line may indicate injury to either the medial or lateral menisci or the joint capsule.

Special Tests

Both acute and chronic injury to the knee can produce ligamentous instability.[19] It is critical that the injured knee's stability be evaluated as soon after injury as possible. To be able to correctly conduct a series of stability tests and then determine the exact nature of the injury takes a considerable amount of training. However, because the coach will almost always be on the field when the athlete is injured, a quick initial assessment of knee stability may give important information about the extent of the injury.

Perhaps the simplest test is to compare the injured knee with the uninjured knee to determine any differences in stability. Determination of the degree of instability is made by the endpoint feel during stability testing. As stress is applied to a joint, some motion will be limited by an intact ligament. In a normal joint, the endpoint will be abrupt with little or no give and no reported pain. With a grade 1 sprain, the endpoint will still be firm with little or no instability and some pain will be indicated. With a grade 2 sprain, the endpoint will be soft with some instability present as well as a moderate amount of pain. In a grade 3 complete rupture, the endpoint will be very soft with marked instability, and pain will be severe initially, then mild.

There are many different tests that should be performed by a trained individual to accurately assess ligament stability. However, the valgus/varus stress test, the drawer test, and the McMurray's test may be easily done to determine the degree of instability in the knee due to ligament or meniscal injury.

Valgus/Varus Stress Tests

Valgus and varus stress tests are intended to reveal laxity of the medial and lateral collateral ligaments. The athlete lies supine with the leg extended. To test the medial collateral ligament, valgus stress is applied with the knee fully extended and at 30 degrees of flexion (Figure 16-5).

To test the lateral collateral ligament, the examiner holds the ankle firmly with one hand while placing the other over the medial joint line. The examiner then places a varus force laterally in an attempt to open the lateral side of the knee (Figure 16-6).

Drawer Test

The drawer test is used to test the stability of the anterior and posterior cruciate ligaments. To perform this test, the athlete lies on the back with the injured knee flexed to 90 degrees. The examiner faces the anterior aspect of the athlete's leg and encircles the tibia immediately below the knee joint with both hands. The fingers of the examiners' hands are positioned on the back of the knee with the thumbs on the medial and lateral joint lines (Figure 16-7).

An anterior drawer test assesses the stability of the anterior cruciate ligament. The examiner's hands pull the tibia forward. If a positive anterior drawer sign occurs, the test should be repeated with the athlete's leg rotated internally 30 degrees and externally 15 degrees to see if the degree of instability changes.

Figure 16-5

Valgus knee stress test

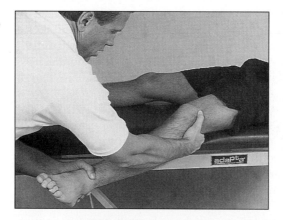

Figure 16-6

Varus knee stress test

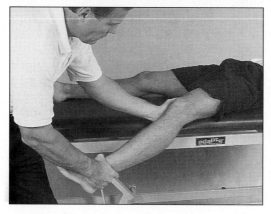

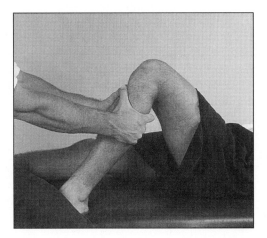

Figure 16-7

Drawer test for cruciate laxity

A posterior drawer test is performed to assess the stability of the posterior cruciate ligament. Force is exerted in a posterior direction at the proximal tibial plateau. A tibia that slides backward excessively from under the femur is considered a positive posterior drawer sign (see Figure 16-5).

The McMurray Test

The McMurray test (Figure 16-8) is used to determine the presence of a meniscus tear within the knee. The athlete is positioned supine on the table with the injured leg fully flexed. The examiner places one hand on the foot and one hand over the top of the knee, fingers touching the joint line. The hand on the foot scribes a small circle and pulls the leg into extension. As this movement occurs, the hand on the knee feels for a clicking response. Medial meniscal tears can be detected at the medial joint line when the tibia is externally rotated, whereas lateral meniscal tears can be detected at the lateral joint line when the tibia is internally rotated.

Figure 16-8

The McMurray meniscal test

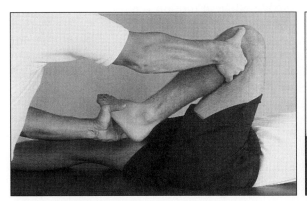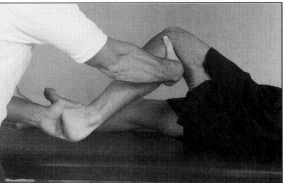

Functional Tests

It is important that the athlete's knee also be tested for function. The athlete should begin with walking (forward, backward, straight line, curve) and progress to jogging (straight, curve, uphill, downhill), running (forward, backward), and then sprinting (straight, curve, large figure eight, small figure eight, zig-zag, carioca).

INJURIES TO THE KNEE

Ligament Injuries

The major ligaments of the knee can be torn in isolation or in combination.[1] Depending on the application of forces, injury can occur from a direct straight-line or single-plane force, from a rotary force, or from a combination of the two.

Medial Collateral Ligament Sprain

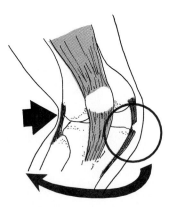

Figure 16-9

A valgus force with the tibia in external rotation injures the medial collateral and capsular ligaments, the medial meniscus, and sometimes the anterior cruciate ligaments.

Cause of injury   Injury to the MCL most often occurs either as a result of a medially directed valgus force from the lateral side or from external rotation of the tibia (Figure 16-9). MCL tears resulting from rotation combined with valgus stress with the foot fixed frequently result in ACL and occasionally PCL tears.[1]

More significant injury usually occurs with medial sprains than from lateral sprains because of the increased potential of injury to the joint capsule and the medial meniscus. Many mild-to-moderate sprains leave the knee unstable and thus vulnerable to additional internal derangements.

Signs of injury   The force and angle of the trauma usually determine the extent of injury that takes place. Even after witnessing the occurrence of a knee injury, coaches have difficulty predicting the extent of tissue damage. The most revealing time for testing joint stability is immediately after injury before effusion masks the extent of derangement.

In a *Grade 1* medial collateral ligament sprain, a few ligament fibers are torn or stretched; the joint is stable during valgus stress tests; there is little or no joint effusion; there may be some joint stiffness and point tenderness just below the medial joint line; even with minor stiffness, there is almost full passive and active range of motion (Figure 16-10A).

A *Grade 2* medial collateral ligament sprain involves moderate tearing or partial separation of ligament fibers; no gross instability, but minimum or slight laxity during full extension; slight or absent swelling unless the meniscus or ACL has been torn; moderate-to-severe joint tightness with an inability to fully, actively extend the knee (the athlete is unable to place the heel flat on the ground); definite loss of passive range of motion; and pain in the medial aspect with general weakness and instability (Figure 16-10B).

A *Grade 3* medial collateral ligament sprain means a complete tear of the ligament; complete loss of medial stability; minimum-to-moderate swelling; immediate severe pain followed by a dull ache; loss of motion

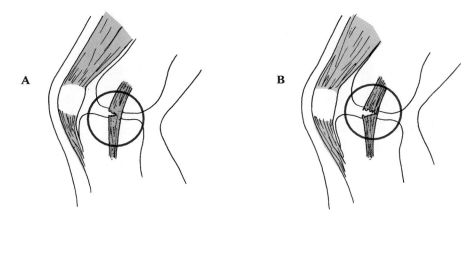

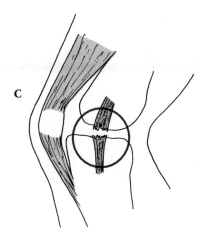

Figure 16-10

A, Grade 1 MCL sprain; B,
Grade 2 MCL sprain; C,
Grade 3 MCL sprain

because of effusion and hamstring guarding; a valgus stress test that reveals some joint opening in full extension and significant opening at 30
degrees of flexion (Figure 16-10C).

   Care   Immediate care consists of RICE for at least twenty-four
hours. Crutches may be used if the athlete is unable to walk without a
limp. Depending on the severity and possible complications, a full-leg cast
or postoperative knee immobilizer may be applied by the physician (Figure 16-11) for two to five days, after which range-of-motion exercises are
begun. Isometric exercise emphasizing quadriceps strengthening (quad
sets, straight leg lifts) should progress to active, resisted, full-range exercise as soon as possible. The athlete then graduates to stationary biking,
stair climbing, and resisted flexion/extension exercises as soon as possible. Use of tape or perhaps a hinged brace when attempting to return to
running activities is encouraged.

Recognition and
Management of Specific
Injuries and Conditions

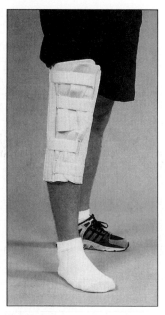

Figure 16-11

Knee immobilizer used after
a ligament injury

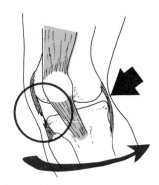

Figure 16-12

A varus force with the tibia
internally rotated injures the
lateral collateral ligament; in
some cases both the cruciate
ligaments and the
attachments of the iliotibial
band and biceps muscle of
the thigh may be torn.

Conservative nonoperative treatment is recommended for isolated
Grade 2 and even Grade 3 MCL sprains. Conservative treatment usually
involves limited immobilization with range of motion and progressive
weight bearing for two weeks followed by protection with a functional
hinged brace for another two to three weeks.

The athlete is allowed to return to full participation when the knee
has regained normal strength, power, flexibility, endurance, and coordination. Usually one to three weeks is necessary for recovery. When returning to activity, the athlete may require tape support for a short
period.

Lateral Collateral Ligament Sprain

Cause of injury   Injury to the LCL most often occurs either as a result of a laterally directed varus force from the medial side or from internal rotation of the tibia (Figure 16-12). If the force is great enough, bony
fragments can be avulsed from the femur or tibia. Sprain of the LCL is
much less prevalent than sprain of the MCL.

Signs of injury   An LCL sprain exhibits pain and tenderness over the
ligament; swelling and effusion; some joint laxity with a varus stress test
at 30 degrees (if laxity exists in full extension, ACL and possibly PCL injury should be evaluated); and pain will be greatest with Grade 1 and
Grade 2 sprains. In Grade 3 sprains, pain will be intense initially, then
subside to a dull ache.

Care   Management of the LCL injury should follow the same procedures as MCL injuries.

Anterior Cruciate Ligament Sprain

Cause of injury   The ACL is usually injured when the foot is on the
ground, the femur is externally rotated, and the knee is in a valgus position (Figure 16-13). In this position, the ACL becomes taut and vulnerable to sprain. Hyperextension from a force to the front of the knee with
the foot planted can tear the ACL (Figure 16-14) and, if severe enough,
can also sprain the MCL. Tears of the anterior cruciate are often associated
with injury to other supporting structures in the knee.

Signs of injury   The athlete with a torn ACL will experience a pop
followed by immediate disability and will complain that the knee feels
like it is coming apart. ACL tears produce rapid swelling at the joint line.
Usually the athlete will experience intense pain initially. However, within
minutes the athlete will begin to feel that the knee is not badly hurt and
will profess to an ability to get up and walk. The athlete with an isolated
ACL tear will exhibit a positive anterior drawer sign.

Care   Even with application of proper first aid and immediate RICE,
swelling begins within one to two hours and peaks within four to six
hours.[2] The athlete typically cannot walk without help.

Anterior cruciate ligamentous injury could lead to serious knee instability; an intact ACL is necessary for a knee to function in high-
performance situations. Controversy exists among physicians about how
best to treat an acute ACL rupture and when surgery is warranted.

Figure 16-13

A major mechanism causing
an anterior cruciate tear
occurs when a running
athlete suddenly decelerates
and makes a sharp cutting
motion.

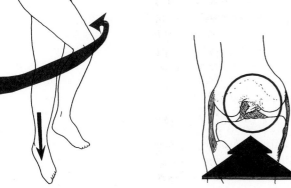

Figure 16-14

An anterior force with the
foot planted can tear the
anterior cruciate ligament.

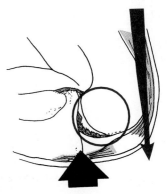

Figure 16-15

A fall or a hit on the anterior
aspect of the bent knee can
tear the PCL.

Surgery may involve joint reconstruction to replace the lost anterior cruciate support. This type of surgery involves a brief hospital stay, three to five weeks in braces, and four to six months of rehabilitation.[18] Little scientific evidence exists to support the use of functional knee braces following ACL injury, yet many physicians feel that the braces can provide some protection during activity.[3,4]

Posterior Cruciate Ligament Sprain

Cause of injury   The PCL is most likely to be injured when the knee is hyperflexed from falling with full weight on the anterior aspect of the bent knee with the foot in plantar flexion. A posteriorly directed force to the front of the bent knee can tear the PCL (Figure 16-15). In addition, it can be injured by a rotational force, which also affects the medial or lateral side of the knee.[18]

Signs of injury   The athlete will report feeling a pop in the back of the knee; tenderness and relatively little swelling will be evident in the popliteal fossa; laxity will be demonstrated in a posterior drawer test.

Care   RICE should be initiated immediately. Nonoperative rehabilitation of Grade 1 and 2 injuries should focus on quadriceps strengthening. Controversy exists as to whether a Grade 3 PCL tear should be treated nonoperatively or with surgical intervention. Unlike the situation faced by athletes with ACL tears, many high-level athletes can do very well without the PCL. Rehabilitation following surgery generally involves six weeks of immobilization in extension with full weight bearing on crutches. Range of motion exercises are begun at six weeks, progressing to the use of progressive resistance exercise at four months.

A lateral knee sprain can be caused by a varus force when the tibia is internally rotated.

16-1
Critical Thinking Exercise

A lacrosse player carrying the ball attempts to avoid a defender by planting his right foot firmly on the ground and cutting hard to his left. His knee immediately gives way, and he hears a loud pop. He has intense pain immediately but after a few minutes he feels as if he can get up and walk.

? What ligament has most likely been injured? What stability tests should be done by the coach to determine the extent of the injury to this ligament?

Meniscus Injuries

Cause of injury   A tear of the meniscus most often results from weight bearing combined with a rotational force while extending or flexing the knee (Figure 16-16). The medial meniscus has a much higher incidence of injury than does the lateral meniscus. Because of its attachment to the deep portion of the MCL, the medial meniscus is prone to disruption from valgus and rotational forces. The lateral meniscus does not attach to the capsule and is more mobile during knee movement.

A large number of medial meniscus lesions are the outcome of a sudden, strong, internal rotation of the femur with a partially flexed knee while the foot is firmly planted.[10] As a result of the force of this action, the meniscus is pulled out of its normal bed and pinched between the femoral condyles. Tears within the cartilage fail to heal because of inadequate blood supply. However, some peripheral meniscus tears do heal when an adequate supply of blood is available.

Signs of injury   An absolute diagnosis of meniscal injury is difficult. A meniscal tear may or may not result in the following: effusion developing gradually over forty-eight to seventy-two hours; joint-line pain and loss of motion; intermittent locking and giving way; and pain when squatting.[10] Chronic meniscal lesions may also display recurrent swelling and obvious muscle atrophy around the knee. Often the athlete complains of an inability to perform a full squat or to change direction quickly when running without experiencing pain, a sense of the knee collapsing, or a popping sensation.

Care   Immediate care involves RICE. Even if the knee is not locked but shows indications of a tear, the athlete should be sent to a physician for diagnosis. The knee that is locked by a displaced meniscus may require unlocking with the athlete under anesthesia so that a detailed examination can be conducted. Management of the nonlocking acute meniscus tear should follow a course similar to that for MCL injuries and does not necessarily require surgery.

If discomfort, disability, and locking of the knee continue, arthroscopic surgery may be required to remove a portion of the meniscus. Surgical management of meniscal tears should make every effort to minimize loss of any portion of the meniscus.

Figure 16-16

Common mechanisms of injury to the meniscus. Forced flexion produces a peripheral tear, whereas cutting with the foot fixed is likely to produce a "bucket handle" tear.

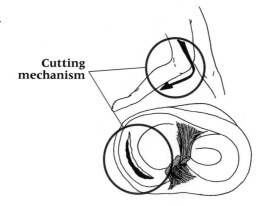

Cutting
mechanism

Joint Contusions (Bruises)

Cause of injury   A blow struck against the muscles crossing the knee joint can result in a handicapping condition. One of the muscles frequently involved is the vastus medialis of the quadriceps group, which is primarily involved in locking the knee in a position of full extension.

Signs of injury   Bruises of the vastus medialis produce all the appearances of a knee sprain, including severe pain, loss of movement, and signs of acute inflammation. Such bruising is often manifested by swelling and discoloration caused by the tearing of muscle tissue and blood vessels. If adequate first aid is given immediately, the knee will usually return to functional use twenty-four to forty-eight hours after the trauma.

Care   Care of a bruised knee depends on many factors. However, management principally depends on the location and severity of the contusion. The following procedures are suggested. Apply compression bandages and cold until resolution has occurred. Recommend inactivity and rest for twenty-four hours. If swelling occurs, continue cold application for seventy-two hours. If swelling and pain are intense, refer the athlete to the physician. Once the acute stage has ended and the swelling has diminished to little or none, cold application with active range-of-motion exercises should be conducted within a pain-free range. Allow the athlete to return to normal activity with protective padding when pain and the initial irritation have subsided. If swelling is not resolved within a week, a chronic condition of either synovitis or bursitis may exist, indicating the need for rest and medical attention.

Bursitis

Cause of injury   Bursitis in the knee can be acute, chronic, or recurrent. Although any one of the numerous knee bursae can become inflamed, the prepatellar and the deep infrapatellar bursae on the front of the knee have the highest incidence of irritation in sports (Figure 16-17). The prepatellar bursa often becomes inflamed from continued kneeling

The knee has many bursae; the prepatellar and deep infrapatellar bursae are most often irritated.

Figure 16-17

Common bursae of the knee

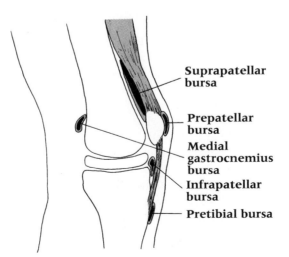

Suprapatellar
bursa

Prepatellar
bursa

Medial
gastrocnemius
bursa

Infrapatellar
bursa

Pretibial bursa

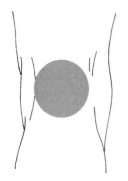

Figure 16-18

A Baker's cyst causes very
little or no pain in the
popliteal fossa.

A knee that locks and
unlocks during activity may
indicate a torn meniscus.

---

iliotibial band friction
syndrome
(**eel** e oh **tib** ee ul)
Runner's knee.

---

or falling directly on the knee, while the deep infrapatellar becomes irritated from overuse of the patellar tendon.

Signs of injury Prepatellar bursitis results in localized swelling above the knee that is similar to a balloon. Swelling occurs outside the joint, and there may be some redness and increased temperature. Swelling in the back of the knee does not necessarily indicate bursitis but could instead be a sign of Baker's cyst (Figure 16-18). A Baker's cyst is connected to the joint, which swells because of a problem in the joint and not because of bursitis. A Baker's cyst is commonly painless, causing no discomfort or disability. Some inflamed bursae may be painful and disabling because of the swelling and should be treated accordingly.

Care Management usually follows a pattern of eliminating the cause, prescribing rest, and reducing inflammation. Perhaps the two most important techniques for controlling bursitis are the use of elastic compression wraps and antiinflammatory medication. When the bursitis is chronic or recurrent and the synovial lining of the joint capsule has thickened, a physician may cautiously use aspiration and a steroid injection.

Loose Bodies within the Knee

Cause of condition Because of repeated trauma to the knee during sports activities, loose bodies, sometimes called *joint mice*, can develop within the joint cavity. Loose bodies can result from osteochondritis dissecans (fragments of bone and cartilage), fragments from the menisci, pieces of torn synovial tissue, or a torn cruciate ligament.

Signs of condition The loose bodies may move in the joint space and become lodged to cause locking and popping. The athlete will complain of pain, instability, and a feeling that the knee is giving way.

Care When the loose body becomes wedged between articulating surfaces, irritation can occur. If not surgically removed, the loose body can create conditions that lead to joint degeneration.

Iliotibial Band Friction Syndrome (Runner's Knee)

Cause of injury **Iliotibial band friction syndrome** is an overuse condition commonly occurring in runners or cyclists that can be attributed to malalignment and structural asymmetries of the foot and lower leg. Irritation develops over the lateral femoral condyle or at the band's insertion on the lateral side of the knee where friction is created.[11]

Signs of injury There may be tenderness, some mild swelling, increased warmth, and possibly some redness over the lateral femoral condyle. Pain increases during running or cycling activities.

Care Treatment includes stretching the iliotibial band and performing techniques for reducing inflammation.[9] Management of runner's or cyclist's knee involves correction of foot and leg alignment problems. Therapy includes cold packs or ice massage before and after activity, proper warm-up and stretching, and avoiding activities that aggravate the problem, such as running on inclines. Other procedures may include administering antiinflammatory medications.

INJURIES AND CONDITIONS OF THE PATELLA

Fracture of the Patella

Cause of injury Fractures of the patella can be caused by either direct or indirect trauma. Most patellar fractures are the result of indirect trauma in which a severe pull of the patellar tendon occurs against the femur when the knee is semiflexed. This position subjects the patella to maximum stress from the quadriceps tendon and the patellar ligament. Forcible muscle contraction may then fracture the patella at its lower half. Direct injury most often produces fragmentation with little displacement. Falls, jumping, or running may result in a fracture of the patella.

Signs of injury The fracture causes hemorrhage, resulting in generalized swelling. An indirect fracture causes tearing of the joint capsule, separation of bone fragments, and possible tearing of the quadriceps tendon. Direct fracture involves little bone separation.

Care Diagnosis usually requires x-ray confirmation. As soon as the examiner suspects a patellar fracture, a cold wrap should be applied, followed by an elastic compression wrap and splinting. The athlete should then be referred to the team physician. The athlete will normally be immobilized for two to three months.

Acute Patellar Subluxation or Dislocation

Cause of injury When an athlete plants the foot, decelerates, and simultaneously cuts in an opposite direction from the weight-bearing foot, the thigh rotates internally while the lower leg rotates externally, causing a medially directed valgus force at the knee.[5] The quadriceps muscle attempts to pull in a straight line and as a result pulls the patella laterally—a force that may dislocate the patella. As a rule, displacement takes place outwardly, with the patella resting on the lateral condyle.

Signs of injury The athlete experiences a complete loss of knee function along with pain and swelling; the patella rests in an abnormal position. A first-time patellar dislocation should always be suspected of being associated with a fracture.

Care The knee should be immobilized in the position it is in (do not try to straighten the knee). Ice should be applied around the joint. The athlete should be taken to the physician, who will reduce the kneecap (put it back into place). After reduction, the knee is immobilized in extension for four weeks or longer, and the athlete is instructed to use crutches when walking. Muscle rehabilitation should involve strengthening all the muscles of the knee, thigh, and hip.

The athlete may find it helpful to wear a neoprene brace that has a horseshoe-shaped felt pad designed to push the patella medially; the brace is worn while running or performing in sports (Figure 16-19).

Knees that give way or catch have a number of possible pathological conditions:
Subluxating patella
Meniscal tear
Anterior cruciate ligamentous tear

Figure 16-19

A special pad for the dislocated patella

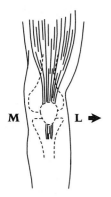

Figure 16-20

Lateral patellar tracking

Chondromalacia Patella

Cause of condition   Chondromalacia patella is a softening and deterioration of the articular cartilage on the back of the patella. The exact cause of chondromalacia is unknown but it is often related to either abnormal movement of the patella within the femoral groove or to overuse. Normally the patella moves up and down in the femoral groove between the femoral condyles as the knee flexes and extends. In some athletes the patella has a tendency to move or track in a lateral direction as the quadriceps group contracts (Figure 16-20).[17] This tracking most often occurs in athletes with weakness in the quadriceps muscle group or in female athletes who have a wider pelvis.

Signs of condition   The athlete may experience pain in the anterior aspect of the knee while walking, running, ascending and descending stairs, or squatting. There may be recurrent swelling around the kneecap and a grating sensation when flexing and extending the knee. The athlete may experience pain on the back of the patella or when the patella is compressed within the femoral groove while the knee is passively flexed and extended.

Care   Conservative treatment includes avoiding irritating activities such as stair climbing and squatting; doing pain-free isometric exercises that concentrate primarily on strengthening the quadriceps muscles; and wearing a neoprene knee sleeve (Figure 16-21). If conservative measures fail to help, surgery may be the only alternative.

INJURIES AND CONDITIONS OF THE EXTENSOR MECHANISM

The extensor mechanism of the knee consists of the quadriceps muscle group, the patellar tendon, the patella located within that tendon, and the tibial tubercle, which is the site of attachment for the patellar tendon.

Figure 16-21

Neoprene sleeve

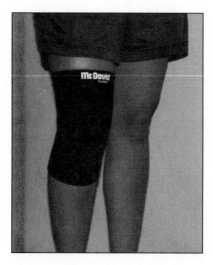

Jumper's Knee (Patellar Tendinitis)

Cause of injury   Jumping, kicking, or running may place extreme tension on the knee extensor muscle complex. As a result of either a single acute injury or, more commonly, repetitive injuries, **patellar tendinitis** occurs in the patellar or quadriceps tendon. On rare occasions, a patellar tendon may completely fail and rupture. Sudden or repetitive forceful extension of the knee may begin an inflammatory process that will eventually lead to tendon degeneration.[13]

Signs of injury   The athlete indicates vague pain and tenderness generally around the bottom of the patella on the posterior aspect that worsens when engaging in jumping or running activities. Quite often athletes will say that if they could take their finger and reach under the kneecap at the bottom, the pain would be there.[14]

Care   Any pain in the patellar tendon must preclude sudden explosive movement such as that characterized by heavy plyometric-type exercising. Several approaches to treating athletes with inflammation associated with jumper's knee have been reported, including rest, the use of ice, and antiinflammatory medications. A patellar tendon tenodesis brace or strap may also be used (Figure 16-22).

Osgood-Schlatter Disease

Cause of condition   Osgood-Schlatter disease is a condition common to the immature adolescent's knee. The most commonly accepted cause is the repeated pull of the patellar tendon at the tibial tubercle on the front of the femur. The tibial tubercle is an important bony landmark because it is the site of attachment for the tendon of the entire quadriceps muscle group. Osgood-Schlatter disease is characterized by ongoing pain at the attachment of the patellar tendon at the tibial tubercle. Over a period of time, a bony callus forms and the tubercle enlarges. This condition usually resolves when the athlete reaches the age of eighteen or nineteen. The only remnant is an enlarged tibial tubercle.

Signs of condition   Repeated irritation causes swelling, hemorrhage, and gradual degeneration at the tibial tubercle. The athlete complains of severe pain when kneeling, jumping, and running. There is point tenderness over the anterior proximal tibial tubercle.

Care   Treatment is usually conservative and includes the following: Stressful activities are decreased for approximately six months to one year; severe cases may require a cylindrical cast; ice is applied to the knee before and after activities; and isometric strengthening of quadriceps and hamstring muscles is performed.

SUMMARY

- The knee is one of the most complex joints in the human body. Stability of the knee depends primarily on the bony articulations, ligaments, joint capsule, and muscles that surround the joint.

- Prevention of knee injuries involves maximizing muscle strength and

---

> **patellar tendinitis**
> (pa **teller**)
> Jumper's knee.

Critical Thinking Exercise

A high jumper has been diagnosed as having patellar tendinitis, or jumper's knee. He has two important track meets in three weeks and wants to know what he can do to get over this injury as soon as possible.

? What options does the coach have in treating the athlete with patellar tendinitis?

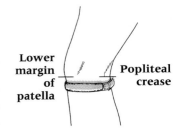

Figure 16-22

The chondromalacia brace

wearing appropriate shoes. Use of protective knee bracing may be questionable.

- Assessing an injury to the knee joint requires taking a history, observing both the appearance of the injured part and how the athlete moves, palpating the injured structures around the joint, and using special tests, including valgus/varus stress tests, drawer tests, and the McMurray's test to determine the existing stability of the joint.

- The stabilizing structures most often injured are the medial and lateral collateral ligaments, the anterior and posterior cruciate ligaments, and the menisci.

- Other knee joint injuries that can occur either from acute trauma or from overuse are contusions, bursitis, joint mice, and iliotibial band friction syndrome.

- The patella and its surrounding area can develop a variety of injuries from sports activities, including fractures, subluxation and dislocation, and chondromalacia patella.

- The extensor mechanism of the knee consists of the quadriceps muscle group, the patellar tendon, the patella located within that tendon, and the tibial tubercle. Jumper's knee and Osgood-Schlatter's disease are conditions associated with the extensor mechanism.

Solutions to Critical Thinking Exercises

16-1 This mechanism is typical for a sprain of the anterior cruciate ligament, although other ligamentous, capsular, and meniscal structures may be injured as well. An appropriate stability test for determining an injury to the ACL would be the anterior drawer test.

16-2 A conservative approach would be to use normal techniques—reduce inflammation, rest, ice, ultra-sound, antiinflammatory medications, and so on. An alternative and more aggressive approach would be to use a deep friction massage technique to increase the inflammatory response, which will ultimately facilitate healing. If successful, the more aggressive treatment may allow a quicker return to full activity.

REVIEW QUESTIONS AND CLASS ACTIVITIES

1. What are the various structures that give the knee stability? What movements do these various structures prevent?
2. What motions can occur at the knee? Which muscles produce these movements?
3. Explain how a knee injury can best be prevented. What injuries are most difficult to prevent?
4. Demonstrate the steps that should be taken when assessing the knee.
5. Describe the mechanisms of injury for the collateral ligaments, the cruciate ligaments, and the menisci.
6. Contrast the signs and characteristics of Grades 1, 2, and 3 medial collateral ligament sprains.

7. How might a contusion of the knee joint be related to bursitis of the knee?
8. How does a patellar subluxation or dislocation usually occur?
9. What factors can contribute to the development of chondromalacia?
10. What types of conditions can develop in the extensor mechanism? How are they cared for?
11. Invite an orthopedic physician to discuss the latest treatment and rehabilitation techniques for treating an injured knee.

REFERENCES

1. Arnosky P: Physiologic principles of ligament injuries and healing. In Scott N: *Ligament and extensor mechanism injuries of the knee: diagnosis and treatment*, St Louis, 1991, Mosby–Year Book.
2. Boland AL Jr: Soft tissue injuries of the knee. In Nicholas JA, Hershman EB, editors: *The lower extremity and spine in sports medicine*, St Louis, 1995, Mosby.
3. Colville MR et al: The Lenox Hill brace: an evaluation of effectiveness in treating knee instability, *Am J Sports Med* 14:257, 1986.
4. Coughlin L et al: Knee bracing and anterolateral rotary instability, *Am J Sports Med* 15:161, 1987.
5. DeStefano V: Skeletal injuries of the knee. In Nicholas JA, Hershman EB, editors: *The lower extremity and spine in sports medicine*, St Louis, 1995, Mosby.
6. Fujiwara L et al: Effect of three lateral knee braces on speed and agility in experienced and nonexperienced wearers, *Ath Train* 25(2):160, 1990.
7. Jensen K: Manual laxity tests for anterior cruciate ligament injuries, *J Orthop Sports Phys Ther* 11(10): 474, 1990.
8. Johnson C, Bach B: Use of knee braces in athletic injuries. In Scott N: *Ligament and extensor mechanism injuries of the knee: diagnosis and treatment*, St Louis, 1991, Mosby–Year Book.
9. Lebsack D et al: Iliotibial band friction syndrome, *Ath Train* 25(4): 356, 1990.
10. Lutz G, Warren R: Meniscal injuries. In Griffin L: *Rehabilitation of the injured knee*, St. Louis, 1995, Mosby.
11. Martens M: Iliotibial band friction syndrome. In Torg J, Shepard R: *Current therapy in sports medicine*, St Louis, 1995, Mosby.
12. Montgomery D: Prophylactic knee braces. In Torg J, Shepard R: *Current therapy in sports medicine*, St Louis, 1995, Mosby.
13. Pellecchia G, Hame H, Behnke P: Treatment of infrapatellar tendinitis: a combination of modalities and transverse friction massage, *J Sport Rehab* 3(2):125, 1994.
14. Prentice W, Davis M: Rehabilitation of the knee. In Prentice W: *Rehabilitation techniques in sports medicine*, Dubuque, Iowa, 1999, WCB/ McGraw-Hill.
15. Prentice W, Toriscelli T: The effects of lateral knee stabilizing braces on running speed and agility, *Ath Train* 21(2):112, 1986.
16. Scriber K, Matheny M: Knee injuries in college football: an 18-year report, *Ath Train* 25(3):233, 1990.
17. Shea K, Fulkerson J: Patellofemoral joint injuries. In Griffin L: *Rehabilitation of the injured knee*, St Louis, 1995, Mosby.
18. Shelbourne D, Klootwyk T, De Carlo M: Ligamentous injuries. In Griffin L: *Rehabilitation of the injured knee*, St Louis, 1995, Mosby.
19. Zarins B, Boyle J: Knee ligament injuries. In Nicholas JA, Hershman EB, editors: *The lower extremity and spine in sports medicine*, St Louis, 1995, Mosby.

ANNOTATED BIBLIOGRAPHY

Griffin L: *Rehabilitation of the knee*, St Louis, 1995, Mosby.

Incorporates new advances in rehabilitation techniques and equipment and gives emphasis to sport-specific functional rehabilitation programs.

Scott N: *Ligament and extensor mechanism injuries of the knee,* St Louis, 1991, Mosby.

A totally comprehensive text that looks at all aspects of the knee joint, including anatomy, biomechanics, ligamentous stability testing, injuries, surgical procedures, bracing, and rehabilitation. Provides an outstanding review of the existing literature on all topics.

Tria AJ, Klein K: *An illustrated guide to the knee,* New York, 1992, Churchill-Livingstone.

A basic, concise, easy-to-read guide to the knee.

WEB SITES

Cramer First Aider: http://www.ccsd.k12.wy.us/CCHS_web/sptmed/fstaider.htm

World Ortho: http://www.worldortho.com

Use the search engine in this site to locate relevant information.

Wheeless' Textbook of Orthopaedics: http://www.medmedia.com/med/htm

An excellent page for injuries, anatomy, and x rays.

Karolinska Institute Library: Musculoskeletal Disease: http://www.mic.ki.se/Disease/c5.htm

Anatomy of the Knee Tutorial: http://ncl.ac.uk/~nccc/tutorials/knee

Knee Surgery Information: http://www.arthroscopy.com/sp04000.htm

The Thigh, Hip, Groin, and Pelvis

When you finish this chapter you will be able to:

- Describe the major anatomical features of the thigh, hip, groin, and pelvis as they relate to sports injuries.
- Identify the major sports injuries to the thigh, hip, groin, and pelvis.
- Demonstrate appropriate emergency procedures for injuries to the thigh, groin, and pelvis.

Although the thigh, hip, groin, and pelvis have lower incidences of injury than do the knee and lower limb, they receive considerable trauma from a variety of sports activities. Of major concern are thigh strains and contusions and chronic and overuse stresses affecting the thigh and hip.

THE THIGH REGION

Anatomy

The thigh is generally considered that part of the leg between the hip and the knee. Several important anatomical units must be considered in relationship to sports injuries: the shaft of the femur, musculature, nerves and blood vessels, and the fascia that envelops the thigh (Figures 17-1 through 17-6).

The Femur

The femur (see Figure 17-1) is the longest and strongest bone in the body and is designed to permit maximum mobility and support during weight bearing.

Musculature

The muscles of the thigh (see Figures 17-2 through 17-6) are complex and categorized according to their location: anterior, posterior, and medial.

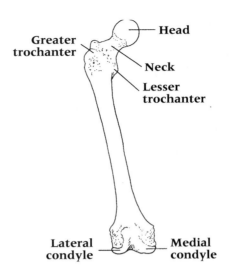

Greater
trochanter

Head

Neck

Lesser
trochanter

Lateral
condyle

Medial
condyle

Figure 17-1

Femur (or femoris)

Assessing Thigh Injuries

Thigh injury evaluation is concerned with the femur and the soft tissue
that surrounds it.

History

The coach should ask the following questions:

- Was the onset of injury fast or slow?
- Has this injury occurred before?
- How was the thigh injured?
- Can you describe the intensity or duration of the pain?
- Is the pain constant? If not, when does it occur?
- Can you point to the pain site?

Figure 17-2

Sartorius

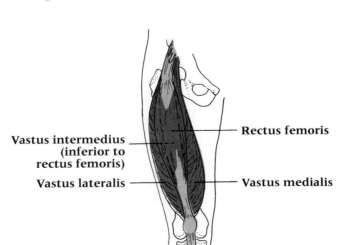

Vastus intermedius
(inferior to
rectus femoris)

Vastus lateralis

Rectus femoris

Vastus medialis

Figure 17-3

Quadriceps femoris

The coach should recognize that muscle pain is hard to localize, dull, and achy. Bone pain is described as feeling deep, penetrating, and localized.

Observation

The coach observes the thigh as to:

- being symmetrical with the noninjured thigh.
- displaying swelling.
- normal skin coloration and texture.
- displaying the obvious presence of pain.

Is the athlete willing to move the thigh?

Prevention of Thigh Injuries

As with all muscles in sports, the thigh must have maximum strength, endurance and extensibility to withstand strain. In collision sports such

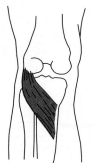

Figure 17-4

Popliteus

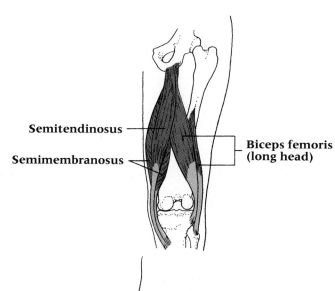

Figure 17-5

Hamstring muscles

Semitendinosus

Semimembranosus

Biceps femoris
(long head)

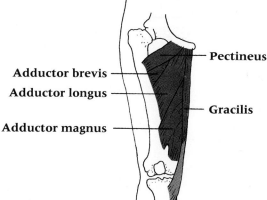

Figure 17-6

Hip adductors

Pectineus

Adductor brevis

Adductor longus

Gracilis

Adductor magnus

as football, the thigh must be protected against contusion by the wearing of thigh guards.

Soft-Tissue Thigh Injuries

Injuries to the thigh muscles are among the most common in sports. Contusions and strains occur often to the thigh, with the former having the highest incidence.

Quadriceps Contusions

Cause of injury The quadriceps group is continually exposed to traumatic blows in a variety of rigorous sports. Contusions of the quadriceps display all the classic symptoms of most muscle bruises.

Signs of injury Quadriceps contusions usually develop as the result of a severe impact on the relaxed thigh, compressing the muscle against the hard surface of the femur. At the instant of trauma, pain, a temporary loss of function, and the immediate bleeding of the effective muscles usually occur. The extent of the force and the degree of thigh relaxation determine the depth of the injury and the amount of structural and functional disruption that take place.[10]

Early detection and avoidance of profuse internal bleeding are vital, both in effecting a fast recovery by the athlete and in the prevention of widespread scarring of the muscle tissue. The athlete usually describes having been hit by a sharp blow to the thigh, which produced intense pain and weakness. The coach observes that the athlete is limping and holding the thigh. Palpation by the coach may reveal a swollen area that is painful to the touch. The seriousness or extent of injury is determined by the amount of weakness and decreased range of motion.

Grade 1 (mild) contusions The Grade 1 quadriceps contusions can have either a very superficial intramuscular bruise or a slightly deeper one. The very superficial contusion (Figure 17-7A) creates a mild hemorrhage, little pain, no swelling, and a mild point tenderness with no restriction of the range of motion. In contrast, a deeper first-degree contusion (Figure 17-7B) produces pain, mild swelling, point tenderness, and a knee flexion of no more than 90 degrees.

Grade 2 (moderate) contusions The Grade 2 quadriceps contusion is of moderate intensity, causing pain, swelling, and a range of knee flexion that is less than 90 degrees with an obvious limp present (Figure 17-7C).

Grade 3 (severe) contusions The severe quadriceps, or grade 3, contusion represents a major disability. A blow may have been so intense as to split the fasciae, allowing the muscle to protrude (muscle herniation) (Figure 17-7D). A characteristically deep intramuscular hematoma with an intermuscular spread is present. Pain is severe, and swelling may lead to hematoma. Movement of the knee is severely restricted, and the athlete has a decided limp.

Care On-site action by the coach includes compression by elastic bandage; the application of a cold medium can help control superficial hemorrhage (Figure 17-8). The thigh contusion should be handled

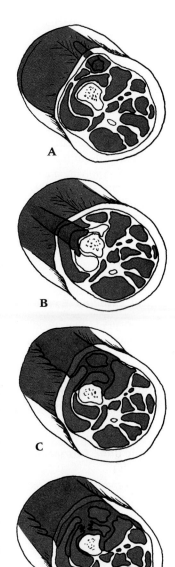

Figure 17-7

Quadriceps contusion: A, Grade 1 mild internal bleeding; B, Grade 1 mild pain and point tenderness; C, Grade 2 moderate pain and swelling; D, Grade 3 deep muscle bleeding.

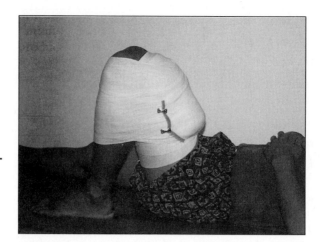

Figure 17-8

Immediate care of the thigh
contusion: Applying a cold
pack and pressure bandage
along with a mild stretch
may provide some relief.

conservatively with RICE followed by a very gentle static stretch and
crutch walking when a limp is present.

Once an athlete has sustained a Grade 2 or 3 thigh contusion, great
care must be taken to avoid the occurrence of another one. The athlete
should routinely wear a protective pad held in place by an elastic wrap
while engaged in sports activity.

Note: With Grade 3, there is between 45 and 90 degrees of restriction
flexion. With Grade 4, there is a restriction of less than 45 degrees of
flexion.

Muscle Ossification

Cause of injury   A severe blow or repeated blows to the thigh, usually the quadriceps muscle, can cause **ectopic bone formation** within
the muscle, known as myositis ossificans traumatica.

Signs of injury   Ectopic bone formation commonly follows bleeding
into the quadriceps muscle and formation of a blood tumorous formation. The contusion causes a disruption of muscle fibers, blood vessels,
connective tissue, and periosteum of the femur. Acute inflammation follows resolution of hemorrhage. The irritated tissue may produce tissue
formations resembling cartilage or bone. In two to four weeks, particles
of bone may be noted under x-ray examination. If the injury is to a muscle belly, complete absorption or a decrease in size of the formation may
occur. This absorption is less likely if calcification is at a muscle origin or
insertion. Some formations are completely free of the femur, whereas another may be stalklike and yet another broadly attached (Figure 17-9).

Improper care of a thigh contusion can lead to ossification in muscle.
The following can cause the condition or, once present, aggravate it,
causing it to become more pronounced:

- Attempting to run off a quadriceps contusion
- Too vigorous treatment of a contusion—for example, massage directly
  over the contusion, ultrasound therapy, or superficial heat to the
  thigh.

Critical Thinking Exercise

A basketball player performing
a layup shot receives a sharp
blow to his right quadriceps
muscle.

?   How may the grade of this
contusion be determined?

ectopic bone formation
(ek **topic**)

Bone formation occurring
in an abnormal place.

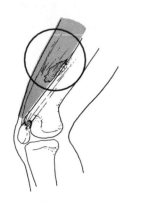

Figure 17-9

Myositis ossificans

Care   Once myositis ossificans traumatica is apparent, treatment should be extremely conservative. If the condition is painful and restricts motion, the formation may be surgically removed after one year with much less likelihood of its return. Too early removal of the formation may cause it to return. Recurrent myositis ossificans may indicate a problem with blood clotting.[6]

Myositis ossificans traumatica
can occur following:
A single severe blow
Many blows to a muscle area
Improper care of a contusion

Quadriceps Muscle Strain

Cause of injury   The rectus femoris muscle of the quadriceps muscle group occasionally becomes strained by a sudden stretch (for example, falling on a bent knee) or a sudden contraction (for example, jumping in volleyball or kicking in soccer). Usually this muscle strain is associated with a muscle that is weakened or overly constricted.[9]

A tear in the region of the rectus femoris may cause partial or complete disruption of muscle fibers (Figure 17-10). The incomplete tear may be located centrally within the muscle or more peripheral to the muscle.

Signs of injury   A peripheral quadriceps rectus femoris tear causes fewer symptoms than the deeper tear. In general, there is less point tenderness and little bleeding. A more centered partial muscle tear causes more pain and discomfort than does the peripheral tear. The deep tear causes a great deal of pain, point tenderness, spasm, and loss of function, but little discoloration from internal bleeding. In contrast, complete muscle tear of the rectus femoris may leave the athlete with little disability and discomfort but with some deformity of the anterior thigh.

Care   On-site care of the quadriceps strain by the coach includes rest, cold application, and pressure to control internal bleeding.[8] The extent of the tear should be ascertained as soon as possible before swelling masks the extent of injury (see Figure 17-10). To stabilize the muscle, the coach might consider having the athlete wear a neoprene sleeve as healing occurs (Figure 17-11).

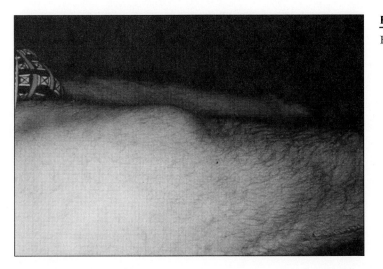

Figure 17-10

Rupture of the rectus femoris

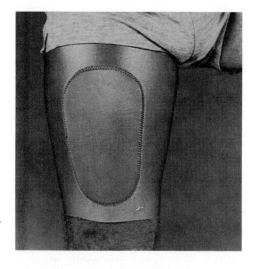

Figure 17-11

A neoprene sleeve may be
worn for soft tissue support.

In order of incidence of
sports injury to the thigh,
Quadriceps contusions rank
first and hamstring strains
rank second

Hamstring Muscle Strains

Of all the thigh muscles subject to strain, the hamstring group has the
highest incidence of strain.

Cause of injury　The exact cause of hamstring strain is not known.
It is speculated that a quick change of the hamstring muscle from knee
stabilization to extension of the hip when running may be a major cause
of this strain (Figure 17-12). What leads to this muscle failure and deficiency in the complementary action of opposing muscles is not clearly
understood. Some possible reasons are muscle fatigue, sciatic nerve irritation, faulty posture, leg-length discrepancy, tight hamstrings, improper
form, and imbalance of strength between hamstring muscle groups.

In most athletes, the hamstring muscle group should have 60 to 70
percent of the strength of the opposing quadriceps group. Stretching after exercise is imperative to avoid muscle contraction.

Figure 17-12

In many sports, severe
stretching of the hip region
can cause a groin strain.

Hamstring strain can involve the muscle belly or bony attachment. The extent of injury can vary from the pulling apart of a few muscle fibers to a complete rupture or an avulsion fracture (Figure 17-13).

Signs of injury   Internal bleeding, pain, and immediate loss of function vary according to the degree of trauma. Discoloration may occur one or two days after injury.

Grade 1 hamstring strain   A Grade 1 hamstring strain is usually evidenced by muscle soreness on movement and is accompanied by point tenderness. These strains are often difficult to detect when they occur. Irritation and stiffness do not become apparent until the athlete has cooled down after activity. The soreness of the mild hamstring strain in most instances can be attributed to muscle spasm rather than to the tearing of tissue.[1]

Grade 2 hamstring strain   A Grade 2 muscle strain represents partial tearing of muscle fibers and can be identified by a sudden snap or tear of the muscle accompanied by severe pain and a loss of function of knee flexion.

Grade 3 hamstring strain   A Grade 3 hamstring strain is the rupturing of tendinous or muscular tissue, involving major hemorrhage and disability.

Care   Initially an ice pack with crushed ice and compression by an elastic wrap should be employed. Activity should be cut down until soreness has been completely alleviated. Ballistic stretching and explosive sprinting must be avoided.

Strains are always a problem to the athlete; they tend to recur because they sometimes heal with inelastic fibrous scar tissue. The higher the incidence of strains at a particular muscle site, the greater the amount of scar tissue and the greater the likelihood of further injury. The fear of another pulled muscle becomes to some individuals almost a neurotic obsession, often more handicapping than the injury itself.

17-2

Critical Thinking Exercise

A sprinter competing in a 100-yard dash experiences a sudden snap, severe pain, and weakness in the left hamstring muscle.

?   What kind of injury can be expected by the coach?

Figure 17-13

Hamstring tear

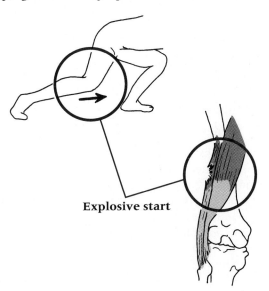

Explosive start

Femoral Fractures

Acute Femoral Fracture

Cause of injury In sports, fractures of the femur occur most often in the shaft rather than at the bone ends and are almost always caused by a great force, such as falling from a height or being hit directly by another participant. A fracture of the shaft most often takes place in the middle third of the bone because of the anatomical curve at this point and because the majority of direct blows are sustained in this area.

Signs of injury Shock generally accompanies a fracture of the femur as a result of the extreme amount of pathology and pain associated with this injury. Bone displacement is usually present as a result of the great strength of the quadriceps muscle, which causes overriding of the bone fragments. Direct violence produces extensive soft-tissue injury with muscle lacerations, major internal bleeding, and muscle spasms.

An acute fractured femur is recognized by these classic signs:

- Deformity, with the thigh rotated outward
- A shortened thigh, caused by bone displacement
- Loss of thigh function
- Pain and point tenderness
- Swelling of the soft tissues

To prevent danger to the athlete's life, the coach must secure immediate emergency assistance and medical referral.[6]

Stress Fracture of the Femur

Cause of injury The popularity of jogging and the increased mileage covered by serious runners has increased the incidence of stress fractures to the femur bone.

Femoral stress fractures are becoming more prevalent because of the increased popularity of repetitive, sustained activities such as distance running.

Signs of injury Stress fracture must be considered when the athlete complains of constant pain. It occurs most often at the neck of the femur. Rest and limited weight bearing is the treatment of choice.[7]

THE HIP, GROIN, AND PELVIC REGION

Normal function of the hip and pelvis is necessary for sports performance.

Anatomy

Bones

The pelvis is a bony ring formed by the two innominate bones (ossa coxae), the sacrum, and the coccyx (Figure 17-14). The two innominate bones are each made up of an ilium, ischium, and pubis. The functions of the pelvis are to support the spine and trunk and to transfer their weight to the lower limbs. In addition to providing skeletal support, the pelvis serves as a place of attachment for the trunk and thigh muscles and a protection for the pelvic viscera.

The hip and pelvis form the body's major power source for full body

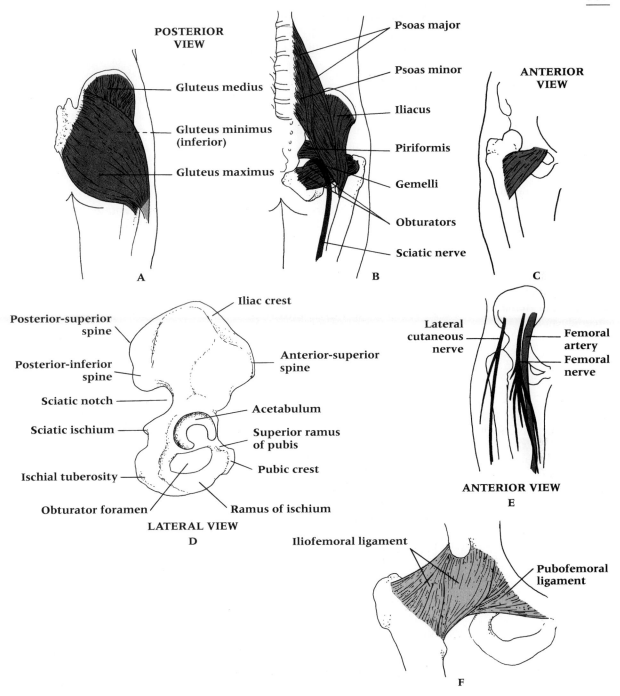

Figure 17-14

Anatomy of the hip: Gluteal muscles (A, B, and C); pelvis (D); blood and nerve supply of the hip region (E); and ligaments of the hip (F).

movement. The body's center of gravity is just in front of the upper part of the sacrum. Injuries to the hip or pelvis cause the athlete major disability in the lower limb or trunk or both.[2]

Joints

The sacrum's sacroiliac joint is joined to other parts of the pelvis by strong ligaments. The coccyx bone also articulates with the sacrum. The hip joint is formed by articulation of the femur with the innominate, or hipbone. Joint capsules and ligaments are associated with these joints.

Hip Musculature

Major movements of the hip and groin:
Internal and external rotation
Adduction
Abduction
Extension
Flexion
Internal and external circumduction

The muscles of the hip can be divided into anterior and posterior groups. The anterior muscles flex the thigh at the hip joint, rotate the thigh outwardly, and adduct the thigh when it's free to move. Muscles in this region also serve to bend the trunk and hip.

The posterior muscles bend, inwardly rotate, and outwardly rotate the hip and abduct the thigh. Muscles of the posterior hip also help bend the knee and extend the thigh.

Assessing the Pelvis and Hip

History

The coach should ask the following questions:

- What does the injury feel like (e.g., weakness, pain, etc.)?
- When did you first notice this problem with your hip or pelvis?
- Describe the type of pain you have (e.g., sharp, dull, pulsating, etc.)
- Does your pain radiate to the back or front of your thigh or to your buttocks area?
- When does the pain occur most intensely (e.g., during activity, at rest, or at night in bed)?

Observation

The coach observes the athlete to see if pain is causing him or her to favor the injury when standing, walking, or sitting.

Groin Strain

The groin is the depression between the thigh and the abdomen. The muscles in the groin region are responsible for all the major bending and internal rotation of the thigh.

Cause of injury Any one of the muscles in the groin region can be torn in sports activity and elicit a groin strain (Figure 17-15). In addition, overextension of the groin musculature may result in a strain. Running, jumping, and twisting with external rotation can produce such injuries.[4]

Signs of injury The strain can appear as a sudden twinge or feeling of tearing during a movement, or it may not be noticed until after termination of activity. As is characteristic of most tears, the groin strain also produces pain, weakness, and internal bleeding.

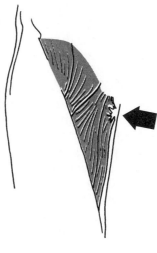

Figure 17-15

Contact and collision sports
can produce serious pelvic
injuries.

Care If it is detected immediately after it occurs, the strain should
be treated by intermittent ice, pressure, and rest for forty-eight to
seventy-two hours.[5]

Rest has been found to be the best treatment for groin strains. Until
normal flexibility and strength are developed, a protective spica bandage
should be applied. Commercial restraints are also available to protect the
injured groin (Figure 17-16). Note that a pelvic stress fracture may

Figure 17-16

Commercial restraints such
as the Sowa groin and thigh
braces are increasingly being
used in athletic training.

produce groin pain. Any athlete complaining of severe groin pain should be referred for medical attention.

Problems of the Hip Joint

The hip joint, the strongest and best-protected joint in the human body, is seldom seriously injured during sports activities.

Sprains of the Hip Joint

The hip joint is substantially supported by the ligamentous tissues and muscles that surround it, so any unusual movement that exceeds the normal range of motion may tear tissue. Such an injury may follow a violent twist, either produced through an impact force delivered by another participant or by forceful contact with another object, or a situation in which the foot is firmly planted and the trunk forced in an opposing direction. A hip sprain displays all the signs of a major acute injury but is best revealed through the athlete's *inability to circumduct* the thigh.[2]

Dislocated Hip Joint

Dislocation of the hip joint rarely occurs in sports.

Cause of injury   The dislocated hip is caused by traumatic force along the long axis of the femur or by the athlete falling on his or her side. Such dislocations are produced when the knee is bent.

Signs of injury   The incomplete dislocation or luxation presents a picture of a flexed, adducted, and internally rotated thigh. Palpation will reveal that the head of the femur has moved to a position posterior to the acetabulum. A hip dislocation causes serious pathology by tearing capsular and ligamentous tissue. A fracture is often associated with this injury, accompanied by possible damage to the sciatic nerve and the nutrient artery, causing **atrophic necrosis.**

Care   Medical attention must be secured immediately after displacement, or muscle contractures may complicate the initial treatment. Immobilization usually consists of two weeks of bed rest and the use of a crutch for walking for a month or longer.

Complications   Complication of the posterior hip dislocation is likely. Such complications include muscle paralysis as a result of nerve injury in the area and later development of degeneration of the femoral head.

Immature Hip Joint Problems

The coach working with a child or adolescent should understand two major problems stemming from the immature hip joint. They are coxa plana, or Legg-Perthes disease, which is caused by a death of the articular cartilage due to a disruption of blood circulation; and a slipping of the femoral head's growth center, or epiphysis.[11]

Coxa Plana or Legg-Perthes Disease

Cause of Condition   Coxa plana is due to a loss of blood circulation to the articular head of the femur (Figure 17-17). It occurs in children

---

atrophic necrosis (ah **tro** fick **necro** sis)
Death of an area due to lack of circulation.

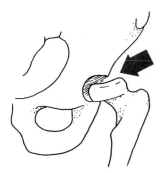

Figure 17-17

Coxa plana (Legg-Perthes disease); arrow indicates the avascular necrosis of the femoral head.

ages three to twelve and in boys more often than in girls. The reason for this condition is not clearly understood. Because of a disruption of circulation to the head of the femur, the articular cartilage dies and becomes flattened.

Signs of Condition The young athlete commonly complains of pain in the groin that sometimes is referred to the abdomen or knee. Limping is also typical. The condition can have a rapid onset, but more often it comes on slowly over a number of months. Examination may show limited hip movement and pain.[3]

Care This condition could warrant complete bed rest to reduce the chances of a chronic hip condition. A special brace to avoid direct weight bearing on the hip may have to be worn. If treated in time, the head of the femur will revascularize and regain its original shape.

Complications If the condition is not treated early enough, the head of the femur will become ill shaped, producing osteoarthritis in later life.

A young athlete who complains of pain in the groin, abdomen, or knee and who walks with a limp may display signs of coxa plana or a slipped femoral epiphysis.

Slipped Growth Site of the Femoral Head

The slipped femoral epiphysis (Figure 17-18) is found mostly in boys between the ages of ten and seventeen who are very tall and thin or are obese.

Cause of condition Although the cause is unknown, the slipped femoral epiphysis may be related to the effects of a growth hormone. In one quarter of the cases, both hips are affected.[8]

Signs of condition Symptoms of this condition are similar to those for Legg-Perthes disease. The athlete has a pain in the groin that arises suddenly as a result of trauma or over weeks or months as a result of prolonged stress. In the early stages of this condition, signs may be minimal; however, in its most advanced stage there is hip and knee pain and major limitations on movement together with a limp.

Care In cases of minor slippage, rest and no weight bearing may prevent further slipping. Major displacement usually requires corrective surgery.

Complications If the slippage goes undetected or if surgery fails to restore normal hip mechanics, severe hip problems may occur in later life.

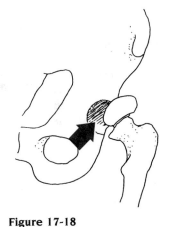

Figure 17-18

Slipped femoral epiphysis

Pelvic Conditions

Athletes who perform activities involving violent jumping, running, and collisions can sustain serious acute and overuse injuries to the pelvic region (Figure 17-19).

Iliac Crest Contusion (Hip Pointer)

Iliac crest contusion, commonly known as *hip pointer*, occurs most often in contact sports.

Cause of injury The hip pointer results from a blow to the inadequately protected iliac crest (Figure 17-20). The hip pointer is one of the

Figure 17-19

Athletes who perform
activities involving violent
jumping, running, and
collisions can sustain serious
acute and overuse injuries to
the pelvic region.

most handicapping injuries in sports. A direct force to the unprotected iliac crest causes a severe pinching action to the soft tissue of that region.

Signs of injury   The hip pointer produces immediate pain, spasms,
and transitory paralysis of the soft structures. As a result, the athlete is
unable to rotate the trunk or to flex the thigh without pain.[13]

Care   Cold and pressure should be applied immediately after injury
and should be maintained intermittently for at least forty-eight hours. In

Figure 17-20

A blow to the pelvic rim can
cause a bruise and hematoma
known as hip pointer.

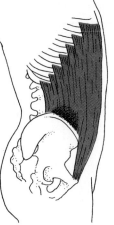

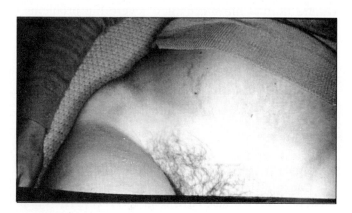

severe cases bed rest for one to two days will speed recovery. Referral to a physician must be made and an x-ray examination given. *Note that the reasons for the hip pointer are the same as those for an iliac crest fracture or epiphyseal separation.*

Osteitis Pubis

Since the popularity of distance running has increased, a condition known as *osteitis pubis* has become more prevalent. It is also caused by soccer, football, and wrestling. Repetitive stress on the *pubic symphysis* and adjacent bony structures by the pull of muscles in the area creates a chronic inflammatory condition (Figure 17-21). The athlete has pain in the groin region and in the bony projection under the pubic hair called the sympthesis pubis. There is point tenderness on the pubic tubercle and pain when movements such as running, sit-ups, and squats are performed.[12]

Care   Follow-up care usually consists of rest and an oral antiinflammatory agent. A return to activity should be gradual.

Fracture of the Pelvis

Acute Fractures

The pelvis is an extremely strong structure, and fractures stemming from sports are rare.

Cause of injury   The acute pelvic fracture usually occurs as the result of a direct trauma.

Signs of injury   The athlete responds to this injury with severe pain, loss of function, and shock.

Care   If a pelvic fracture is suspected, the athlete should be immediately treated for shock and referred to a physician. The seriousness of this injury depends on the extent of shock and the possibility of internal injury.

Stress Fractures

As with other stress fractures, pelvic and femur stress fractures can be produced by repetitive abnormal overuse forces. Pelvic stress fractures tend to occur during intensive internal training or competitive racing.

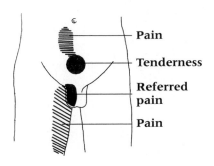

Figure 17-21

Osteitis pubis and other pain sites in the region of the pelvis

Signs of injury   Commonly the athlete complains of groin pain along with an aching sensation in the thigh that increases with activity and decreases with rest.

Care   The coach must listen to the athlete who complains of pelvic pain following intense exercise. Referral to a physician for a detailed examination with an x-ray is a must. Once this injury is verified, rest is the treatment of choice for two to five months.

Avulsion Fractures

The pelvis has a number of sites at which major muscles attach. Pain at these sites could mean that a muscle has begun to pull away from its attachment.

Cause of injury   Avulsion fractures in the pelvic region occur during sudden acceleration or deceleration such as in football, soccer, and basketball.

Signs of injury   The athlete complains of a sudden localized pain with limited movement. On inspection the coach observes swelling and a point tenderness.

Care   Early conditions require rest, limited activity, and graduated exercise.

SUMMARY

- The thigh is composed of the femoral shaft, musculature, nerves and blood vessels, and the fascia that envelops the soft tissue. It is the part of the leg between the hip and the knee.

- The quadriceps contusion and hamstring strain are the most common sports injuries to the thigh, with the quadriceps contusion having the highest incidence.

- Of major importance in acute thigh contusion is early detection and the avoidance of internal bleeding.

- One major complication to repeated contusions is myositis ossificans.

- It is not clearly known why hamstring muscles become strained. Strain occurs most often to the short head of the biceps femoris.

- The groin is the depression between the thigh and abdominal region. Groin strain can occur to any one of a number of muscles in this region. Running, jumping, or twisting can produce a groin strain.

- The hip joint, the strongest and best-protected joint in the human body, has a low incidence of acute sports injuries.

- Some athletes develop conditions that stem from an immature hip joint. These conditions are coxa plana, or Legg-Perthes disease, and the slipped femoral epiphysis.

- A common problem in the pelvic region is the hip pointer, which results from a blow to the inadequately protected iliac crest. The contusion causes pain, spasm, and malfunction of the muscles in the area.

Solutions to Critical Thinking Exercises

17-1 One of the best ways to determine the grade of a contusion to the quadriceps muscle is through the degree of restriction of knee flexion. With grade 1 there is a knee flexion of no more than 90 degrees; with grade 2, more than 90 degrees; with grade 3, between 45 and 90 degrees; and with grade 4, less than 45 degrees.

17-2 The coach can expect a moderate to severe hamstring strain.

REVIEW QUESTIONS AND CLASS ACTIVITIES

1. What signs and symptoms are seen in each of the three degrees of quadriceps contusions? How are they managed?
2. What complications can occur if a thigh contusion is mishandled?
3. Why do hamstring strains often become recurrent?
4. Where do fractures occur most often in the femur? How are they recognized? What emergency care must be given?
5. What muscles are most often injured in a groin strain? How is this type of injury managed?
6. What type of hip problems occur in the young athlete?
7. Describe hip pointer prevention and care.

REFERENCES

1. Best TM, Garrett WE Jr: Hamstring strains: expediting return to play, *Physician Sportsmed* 24(8), 1996.
2. Bielak JM, Henderson JM: Injuries of the pelvis and hip. In Birrer RB, editor: *Sports medicine for the primary care physician,* ed 2, Boca Raton, Fla, 1994, CRC Press.
3. Gerberg LF, Micheli LJ: Nontraumatic hip pain in active children, *Physician Sportsmed* 24:69, 1996.
4. Hagerstown MT: Groin pain, *Sports Med* 18:133, 1996.
5. Hasselman CT et al: When groin pain signals an adductor strain, *Physician Sportsmed* 18(2):54, 1990.
6. Hacutt JE: General types of injuries. In Birrer RB, editor: *Sports medicine for the primary care physician,* ed 2, Boca Raton, Fla, 1994, CRC Press.
7. Jackson DL: Stress fracture of the femur, *Physician Sportsmed* 19:39, 1991.
8. Johnson DL, Klabunde LA: The elusive slipped capital femoral epiphysis, *J Ath Train* 20(2):124, 1995.
9. Kaeding CC: Quadriceps strains and contusions, *Physician Sportsmed* 23 (1):59, 1995.
10. Levandowski R, Difliori JP: Thigh injuries. In Birrer RB, editor: *Sports medicine for the primary care physician,* ed 2, Boca Raton, Fla, 1994, CRC Press.
11. Paletta GA et al: Injuries about the hip and pelvis in the young athlete. In Michile LJ, editor: *The young athlete. Clinics in sports medicine,* vol 14, no 3, Philadelphia, 1995, Saunders.
12. Sing R et al: Osteitis pubis in the active patient, *Physician Sportsmed* 23:66, 1995.
13. Weicker GG, Munnings F: How to manage hip and pelvis injuries in adolescents, *Physician Sportsmed* 21:72, 1993.

ANNOTATED BIBLIOGRAPHY

Sim FH, Scott SG: Injuries of the pelvis and hip in athletics: anatomy and function. In Nicholas JA, Hershman EB, editors: *The lower extremity and spine in sports medicine,* ed 2, St Louis, 1986, Mosby–Year Book.

Provides a detailed discussion of hip and pelvic anatomy and sports injuries.

Torg JS, Shephard RJ, editors: *Current therapy in sports medicine,* ed 3, St Louis, 1995, Mosby.

A detailed sports medicine text with extensive coverage of thigh, hip, and pelvic injuries.

WEB SITES

Cramer First Aider: http://www.ccsd. k12.wy.us/CCHS_web/sptmed/ fstaider.htm

World Ortho: http://www.worldortho. com

Use the search engine in this site to locate relevant information.

Wheeless' Textbook of Orthopaedics: http://www.medmedia.com/med. htm

An excellent page for injuries, anatomy, and x rays.

Karolinska Institute Library: Musculoskeletal Disease: http://www.mic. ki.se/Disease/c5.htm

American Orthopaedic Society for Sports Medicine: http://www. sportsmed.org

The Shoulder Complex

When you finish this chapter you will be able to:

- Identify the bones, articulations, stabilizing ligaments, and musculature of the shoulder complex.
- Explain how shoulder injuries may be prevented.
- Describe the process for assessing injuries to the shoulder.
- Identify specific injuries that occur around the shoulder joint and describe plans for management.

T he anatomy of the shoulder complex allows for a great degree of mobility. To achieve this mobility, stability of the complex is sometimes compromised and instability of the shoulder frequently leads to injury, particularly in those sports that involve overhead activity.[1] Sport activities, such as throwing, swimming, or serving in tennis or volleyball, place a great deal of stress on the supporting structures (Figure 18-1). Consequently, injuries related to overuse in the shoulder are commonplace in the athlete.

Dynamic movement as well as stabilization of the shoulder complex requires integrated function of the rotator cuff muscles, the joint capsule, and the muscles that stabilize and position the scapula.

ANATOMY

Bones

The bones that comprise the shoulder complex and shoulder joint are the clavicle, scapula, and humerus (Figure 18-2). These three bones form the four major articulations associated with the shoulder complex: the sternoclavicular joint, the acromioclavicular joint, the glenohumeral joint, and the scapulothoracic joint.

Stabilizing Ligaments

A series of ligaments at each of the four articulations act collectively to provide stability to the shoulder complex (Figure 18-3).

Shoulder complex
articulations:
Sternoclavicular
Acromioclavicular
Glenohumeral
Scapulothoracic

The clavicle articulates with the sternum to form the sternoclavicular joint, the only direct connection between the upper extremity and the trunk. The sternoclavicular joint is extremely weak because of its bony arrangement, but it is held securely by the sternoclavicular ligament that pulls the clavicle downward and toward the sternum, in effect anchoring it. The clavicle is permitted to move up and down, forward and backward, in combination, and in rotation.

The acromioclavicular joint is a gliding articulation of the lateral end of the clavicle with the acromion process of the scapula. This junction is rather weak. The acromioclavicular ligament along with the coracoclavicular ligament helps to maintain the position of the clavicle relative to the acromion. The coracoacromial ligament connects the coracoid to the acromion. This ligament along with the acromion forms the coracoacromial arch.

At the glenohumeral joint (the true shoulder joint), the round head of the humerus articulates with the shallow glenoid cavity of the scapula. The position of the glenohumeral joint is maintained by the surrounding glenohumeral ligaments that form the joint capsule and by the rotator cuff muscles.

The scapulothoracic joint is not a true joint; however, the movement of the scapula on the wall of the thoracic cage is critical to shoulder joint motion. Contraction of the scapular muscles that attach the scapula, to the axial skeleton is critical in stabilizing the scapula thus providing a base on which a highly mobile joint can function.

Shoulder Musculature

The muscles that cross the glenohumeral joint produce dynamic motion and establish stability to compensate for a bony and ligamentous

Figure 18-1

Overhead throwing activities can produce a number of shoulder problems.

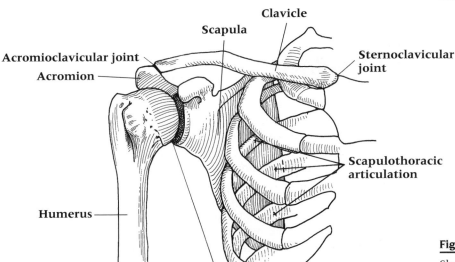

Figure 18-2

Skeletal anatomy of the shoulder complex

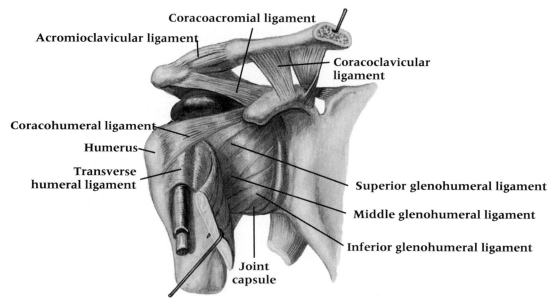

Coracoacromial ligament

Acromioclavicular ligament

Coracoclavicular ligament

Coracohumeral ligament

Humerus

Transverse humeral ligament

Superior glenohumeral ligament

Middle glenohumeral ligament

Inferior glenohumeral ligament

Joint capsule

Figure 18-3

Shoulder complex articulations and ligaments

Glenohumeral joint movements:
Flexion
Extension
Abduction
Adduction
External rotation
Internal rotation

arrangement that allows for a great deal of mobility (Figure 18-4). Movements at the glenohumeral joint include flexion, extension, abduction, adduction, and rotation. The muscles acting on the glenohumeral joint can be separated into three groups. The first group consists of muscles that originate on the axial skeleton and attach to the humerus, including the latissimus dorsi and the pectoralis major. The second group originates on the scapula and attaches to the humerus, including the deltoid, the teres major, the coracobrachialis, and the rotator cuff (subscapularis, supraspinatus, infraspinatus, teres minor). A third group of muscles attaches the axial skeleton to the scapula and includes the levator scapula, the trapezius, the rhomboids, and the serratus anterior and posterior. The scapular muscles are important in providing dynamic stability to the shoulder complex.

PREVENTION OF SHOULDER INJURIES

Proper physical conditioning is of major importance in preventing many shoulder injuries. As with all preventive conditioning, the program should be directed toward general body development and development of specific body areas for a given sport. If a sport places extreme, sustained demands on the arms and shoulders or if the shoulder is at risk for sudden traumatic injury, extensive conditioning must be used. All the muscles involved in movement of the shoulder complex should be strengthened through a full range of motion.

Proper warm-up must be performed gradually before dynamic arm movements are attempted. This warm-up causes a general increase in body temperature and is followed by sport-specific stretching of selected muscles.

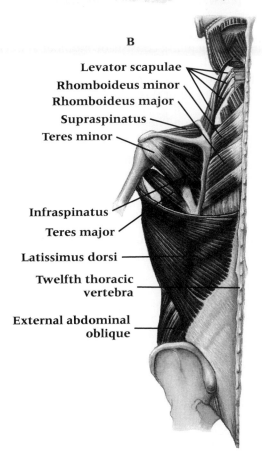

A

Deltoid (cut)

Coracobrachialis

Biceps brachii

Deltoid

Pectoralis major

Serratus anterior

B

Levator scapulae
Rhomboideus minor
Rhomboideus major
Supraspinatus
Teres minor

Infraspinatus
Teres major

Latissimus dorsi

Twelfth thoracic
vertebra

External abdominal
oblique

Figure 18-4

Shoulder musculature: A,
Anterior; B, Posterior

All athletes in collision and contact sports should be instructed and drilled on how to fall properly. They must be taught not to try to catch themselves with an outstretched arm. Performing a shoulder roll is a safer way to absorb the shock of the fall. Specialized protective equipment such as shoulder pads must be properly fitted to avoid some shoulder injuries in tackle football.

Using Correct Throwing Technique

To prevent overuse shoulder injuries, it is essential that athletes be correctly taught the appropriate techniques of throwing a baseball or football, throwing a javelin, serving or spiking a volleyball, and serving or hitting an overhead smash in tennis. If the thrower uses faulty technique, the joints are affected by atypical stresses that result in trauma to the joint and its surrounding tissues.[5]

Relative to the shoulder complex, throwing or pitching involves three distinct phases: a preparatory or cocking phase, the delivery or acceleration phase, and the follow-through or terminal phase[5] (Figure 18-5).

Throwing phases:
Cocking phase
Acceleration phase
Follow-through

Cocking Phase

The cocking phase consists of shoulder abduction/extension and external rotation. This phase can cause anterior shoulder pain as a result of strain of the pectoralis major muscle insertion and the origin of the anterior deltoid, long head of the biceps, or internal rotator muscles.

Acceleration Phase

In the acceleration phase, the humerus moves into abduction and internal rotation along with forward flexion, causing some tension on the posterior capsule. The anterior capsule relaxes, the posterior and inferior capsule tightens.

Follow-through and Deceleration Phase

In the follow-through, the humerus adducts and internally rotates, placing the middle and inferior posterior capsule and the anterior superior

Figure 18-5

Phases of throwing from left to right: wind-up, early cocking, late cocking, acceleration, follow-through

glenohumeral ligament under tension. In this phase, an eccentric load from throwing causes stress to the external rotators and capsule.

ASSESSING THE SHOULDER COMPLEX

The shoulder complex is one of the most difficult regions of the body to evaluate.[10] One reason for this difficulty is that the biomechanical demands placed on these structures during overhand accelerations and decelerations are not yet clearly understood. It is essential that the coach understands the athlete's major complaints and the possible mechanisms of the injury.

History

The following questions in regard to the athlete's complaints can help the coach determine the nature of the injury:

- What happened to cause this pain?
- Have you ever had this problem before?
- What is the duration and intensity of the pain?
- Where is the pain located?
- Is there crepitus during movement or numbness or distortion in temperature such as a cold or warm feeling?
- Is there a feeling of weakness or a sense of fatigue?
- What shoulder movements or positions seem to aggravate or relieve the pain?
- If therapy has been given before, what, if anything, offered pain relief (e.g., cold, heat, massage, or analgesic medication)?

Observation

The athlete should be generally observed while walking and standing. Observation during walking can reveal asymmetry of arm swing or a lean toward the painful shoulder. The athlete is next observed from the front, side, and back while in a standing position. The coach looks for postural asymmetries, bony or joint deformities, or muscle spasm or guarding patterns.

Anterior Observation

- Are both shoulder tips even with one another, or is one depressed?
- Is one shoulder held higher due to muscle spasm or guarding?
- Is the lateral end of the clavicle prominent (indicating acromioclavicular sprain or dislocation)?
- Is one lateral acromion process more prominent than the other (indicating a possible glenohumeral dislocation)?
- Does the clavicular shaft appear deformed (indicating possible fracture)?
- Is there loss of the normal lateral deltoid muscle contour (indicating glenohumeral dislocation)?

- Is there an indentation in the upper biceps region (indicating rupture of biceps tendon)?

Lateral Observation

- Is there thoracic kyphosis or are the shoulders slumped forward (indicating weakness of the erector muscles of the spine and tightness in the pectoral region)?
- Is there forward or backward arm hang (indicating possible scoliosis)?

Posterior Observation

- Is there asymmetry such as a low shoulder, uneven scapulae, or winging of one scapular wing and not the other (indicating postural scoliosis)?
- Is the scapula protracted because of constricted pectoral muscles?
- Is there a distracted or winged scapula on one or both sides? (A winged scapula on both sides could indicate a general weakness of the serratus anterior muscles; if only one side is winged, the long thoracic nerve may be injured.)

Palpation

Palpation of the bony structures should be done with the coach standing in front of and then behind the athlete. Both shoulders are palpated at the same time for pain sites and deformities. Palpation of the muscles around the shoulder detects point tenderness, abnormal swelling or lumps, muscle spasm or guarding, and trigger points. The shoulder is then also palpated anteriorly and posteriorly.

Special Tests

A number of special tests can help to determine the nature of an injury to the shoulder complex.[10] The shoulder's active and passive range of motion should be noted and compared to the opposite side. Strength of the shoulder musculature should be assessed by resisted manual muscle testing. Both the muscles that act on the glenohumeral joint and those that act on the scapula should be tested.

Following are descriptions of other tests used to assess shoulder instability, shoulder impingement, and muscle weakness.

Apprehension Test (Crank Test)

With the arm abducted 90 degrees, the shoulder is slowly and gently externally rotated as far as the athlete will allow. The athlete with a history of anterior glenohumeral instability will show great apprehension that is reflected by a facial grimace before an endpoint can be reached. At no time should the coach force this movement (Figure 18-6).

Tests for Shoulder Impingement

Forced flexion of the humerus in the overhead position may cause impingement of soft tissue structures between the humeral head and the

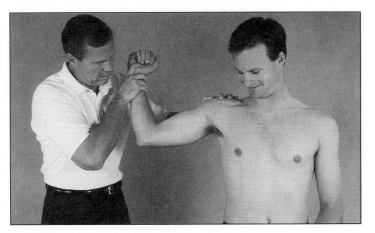

Figure 18-6

Shoulder apprehension test

coracoacromial ligament. A second test involves horizontal adduction with forced internal rotation of the humerus that also produces impingement (Figure 18-7). A positive sign is indicated if the athlete feels pain and reacts with a grimace.[8]

Test for Supraspinatus Muscle Weakness

The empty can test for supraspinatus muscle strength has the athlete bring both arms into 90 degrees of forward flexion and 30 degrees of horizontal abduction (Figure 18-8). In this position the arms are internally rotated as far as possible, thumbs pointing downward. A downward pressure is then applied by the coach. Weakness and pain can be detected as well as comparative strength between the two arms.

One test for supraspinatus weakness is the empty can test.

RECOGNITION AND MANAGEMENT OF SPECIFIC INJURIES

Clavicle Fractures

Cause of injury   Clavicular fractures (Figure 18-9) are one of the most frequent fractures in sports. Fractures of the clavicle result from a fall on the outstretched arm, a fall on the tip of the shoulder, or a direct impact.

Figure 18-7

Shoulder impingement tests

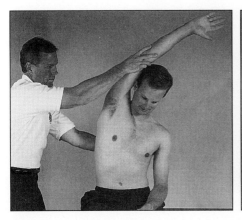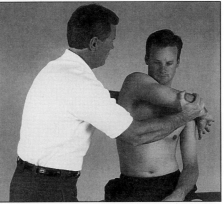

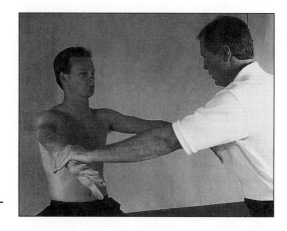

Figure 18-8

Empty can test

Figure 18-9

Clavicular fracture

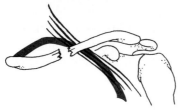

Signs of injury   The athlete with a fractured clavicle usually supports the arm on the injured side and tilts his or her head toward that side, with the chin turned to the opposite side. During inspection the injured clavicle appears a little lower than the unaffected side. Palpation may also reveal swelling, point tenderness, and mild deformity.

Care   The clavicular fracture is cared for immediately by applying a shoulder immobilizer and by treating the athlete for shock, if necessary (Figure 18-10). If x-ray examination reveals a fracture, a closed reduction should be attempted by the physician followed by immobilization with a

Figure 18-10

Shoulder immobilizer

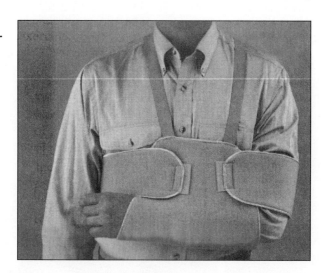

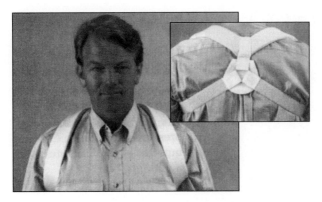

Figure 18-11

Figure 8 sling

figure 8 clavicle strap (Figure 18-11). Immobilization should be maintained for six to eight weeks. Following this period of immobilization, gentle isometric and mobilization exercises should begin with the athlete placed in a sling for an additional three to four weeks to provide protection. Occasionally, clavicle fractures may require operative management.[4]

Fractures of the Humerus

Cause of injury   Fractures of the humerus (Figure 18-12) happen occasionally in sports, usually as the result of a direct blow, a dislocation, or the impact received by falling onto the outstretched arm.

Signs of injury   A fracture of the humerus is difficult to recognize by visual inspection alone; x-ray examination gives the only positive proof. Some of the more prevalent signs that may be present are pain, inability to move the arm, swelling, point tenderness, and discoloration of the superficial tissue.

Care   Recognition of humeral shaft fractures requires immediate application of a splint or immediate support with a sling, treatment for shock, and referral to a physician. The athlete with a fracture to the humerus will be out of competition for approximately two to six months depending on the location and severity of the fracture.[1]

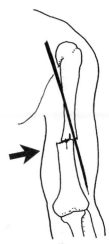

Figure 18-12

Humeral fractures

Sternoclavicular Joint Sprain

Cause of injury   A sternoclavicular sprain (Figure 18-13) is a relatively uncommon occurrence in sports. The mechanism of the injury is either an indirect force transmitted through the humerus, the shoulder joint, and the clavicle, or a direct impact to the clavicle. Usually the clavicle will be displaced upward and forward.

Signs of injury   Sprain to the sternoclavicular joint can be described in three degrees. A Grade 1 sprain is characterized by little pain and disability, with some point tenderness but no joint deformity. A Grade 2 sprain displays subluxation of the sternoclavicular joint with visible deformity, pain, swelling, point tenderness, and an inability to abduct the shoulder in full range or to bring the arm across the chest, indicating disruption of stabilizing ligaments. The Grade 3 sprain, which is the most

18-1

Critical Thinking Exercise

A soccer player is tripped to the ground on a hard tackle and lands on the tip of her left shoulder. She complains of pain both in the tip of her shoulder and in her chest. She has difficulty lifting her arm above her shoulder because of the pain.

? What injury diagnosis might result from this mechanism of injury?

Recognition and
Management of Specific
Injuries and Conditions

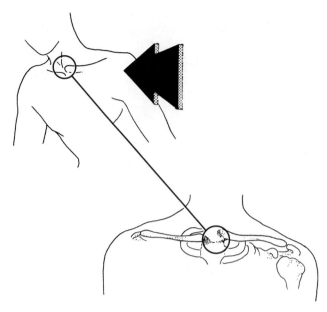

Figure 18-13

Sternoclavicular sprain and
dislocation

severe, presents a picture of complete dislocation with gross displacement
of the clavicle at its sternal junction, swelling, and disability, indicating
complete rupture of the sternoclavicular ligament.

Care RICE should be used immediately, followed by immobilization (see Figure 18-11). Immobilization is usually maintained for three to
five weeks, followed by graded reconditioning exercises. There is a high
incidence of recurrence of sternoclavicular sprains.

Acromioclavicular Joint Sprain

Cause of injury The acromioclavicular joint is extremely vulnerable
to sprains, especially in collision sports.[2] The primary mechanisms are a
fall on an outstretched arm or a direct impact to the tip of the shoulder
that forces the acromion process downward, backward, and inward while
the clavicle is pushed down against the rib cage (Figure 18-14).

Signs of injury In a Grade 1 acromioclavicular sprain, there is point
tenderness and discomfort during movement at the junction between the
acromion process and the outer end of the clavicle. There is no deformity,
indicating only mild stretching of the acromioclavicular ligaments.

A Grade 2 sprain shows definite displacement and prominence of the
lateral end of the clavicle when compared to the unaffected side. There is
point tenderness during palpation of the injury site, and the athlete is unable to fully abduct through a full range of motion or to bring the arm
completely across the chest.

A Grade 3 sprain involves rupture of the acromioclavicular and coracoclavicular ligaments with dislocation of the clavicle. Such an injury has
gross deformity and prominence of the distal clavicle, severe pain, loss of
movement, and instability of the shoulder complex.

Care Immediate care of the acromioclavicular sprain involves three
basic procedures: (1) application of cold and pressure to control local

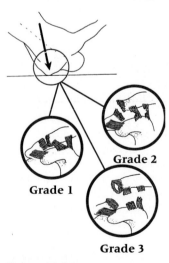

Figure 18-14

Mechanism of
acromioclavicular joint sprain

hemorrhage, (2) stabilization of the joint by a shoulder immobilizer (see Figure 18-10), and (3) referral to a physician for definitive diagnosis and treatment.[2] Immobilization ranges from three to four days with a Grade 1 to approximately two weeks with a Grade 3. With all grades, an aggressive rehabilitation program involving joint mobilization, flexibility exercises, and strengthening exercises should begin immediately following the recommended period of protection.[2] Progression should be as rapid as the athlete can tolerate without increased pain or swelling.

Glenohumeral Dislocations

Cause of injury   The most common glenohumeral dislocation is one in which the head of the humerus is forced out of its joint capsule in an anterior direction past the glenoid labrum and then downward to rest under the coracoid process. The mechanism for an anterior dislocation is abduction, external rotation, and extension that forces the humeral head out of the glenoid cavity[12] (Figure 18-15). An arm tackle in football or rugby or abnormal forces created in executing a throw can produce a sequence of events resulting in dislocation. On a rare occasion the humerus will dislocate in an inferior direction.

Once an athlete has suffered a glenohumeral dislocation, he or she risks a high probability of recurrence due to chronic instability.[11]

Signs of injury   The athlete with an anterior dislocation displays a flattened deltoid contour. Palpation of the axilla will reveal prominence of the humeral head. The athlete carries the affected arm in slight abduction and external rotation and is unable to touch the opposite shoulder with the hand of the affected arm. There is often moderate pain and disability.

Care   Initial management of the shoulder dislocation requires

Critical Thinking Exercise

A gymnast has a recurrent anterior dislocation of the glenohumeral joint. He is extremely worried that his shoulder will dislocate again.

?   What types of activities should the coach concentrate on during rehabilitation to help reduce the likelihood of a subsequent dislocation?

One test for glenohumeral instability is the apprehension test.

Figure 18-15

Anterior shoulder dislocation

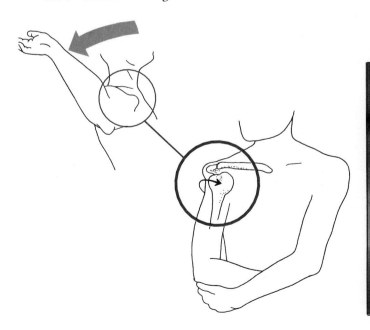

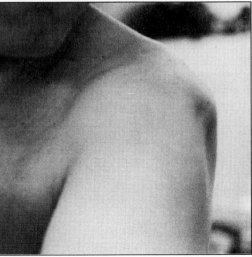

18-3

Critical Thinking Exercise

A volleyball player consistently experiences pain when serving the ball overhead. She also indicates that most of the time when she spikes a ball at the net she experiences pain. During an evaluation the coach observes that when the humerus is flexed and internally rotated, the pain is worse.

? What is most likely causing the pain when the athlete's shoulder is placed in this overhead position?

Shoulder impingement involves a mechanical compression of the supraspinatus tendon, the subacromial bursa, and the long head of the biceps tendon under the coracoacromial arch.

immediate immobilization in a position of comfort using a sling; immediate reduction by a physician; and control of the hemorrhage by cold packs. After the dislocation has been reduced and immobilized, muscle reconditioning should be initiated as soon as possible.[12] Protective sling immobilization should continue for approximately one week after reduction (see Figure 18-10). The athlete is instructed to begin a strengthening program, progressing as quickly as pain will allow. Protective shoulder braces may help limit shoulder motion (Figure 18-16).

Shoulder Impingement Syndrome

Cause of injury Shoulder impingement involves a mechanical compression of the supraspinatus tendon, the subacromial bursa, and the long head of the biceps tendon, all of which are located under the coracoacromial arch[9] (Figure 18-17). Repetitive compression eventually leads to irritation and inflammation of these structures. Impingement most often occurs in repetitive overhead activities such as throwing, swimming, serving a tennis ball, or spiking a volleyball.[13]

Signs of injury The athlete complains of diffuse pain around the acromion whenever the arm is in an overhead position. The external rotators are generally weaker than the internal rotators. There may be some tightness in the posterior and inferior joint capsule. There will usually be a positive impingement test, and the empty can test may increase pain.[14]

Care Management of impingement involves restoring normal biomechanics to the shoulder joint in an effort to maintain space under the coracoacromial arch during overhead activities. RICE can be used to modulate pain initially. Exercises should concentrate on strengthening the rotator cuff muscles, on strengthening those muscles that produce movement of the scapula, and on stretching posterior and inferior joint capsule. The activity that caused the problem in the first place should be modified so that the athlete has initial control over the frequency and the level of the activity with a gradual and progressive increase in intensity.[6]

Figure 18-16

Protective braces for the shoulder prevent overhead motion

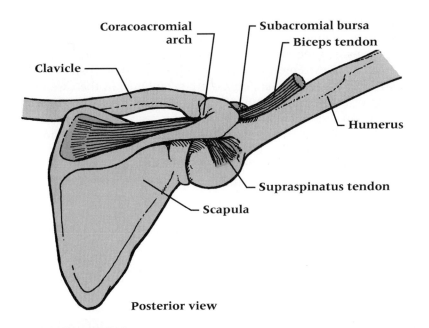

Coracoacromial arch

Subacromial bursa

Biceps tendon

Clavicle

Humerus

Supraspinatus tendon

Scapula

Posterior view

Figure 18-17

Shoulder impingement
compresses soft tissue
structures under the
coracoacromial arch.

Rotator Cuff Strains

Cause of injury   The most common rotator cuff tendon strain involves the supraspinatus muscle, although any of the rotator cuff tendons are subject to injury (Figure 18-18). The mechanism of rotator cuff strains involves dynamic rotation of the arm at a high velocity as occurs during overhead throwing or any other activity in which there is rotation of the humerus.[7] Most rotator cuff tears occur in the supraspinatus in individuals with a long history of shoulder impingement or instability and are relatively uncommon under the age of forty years. Tears of the rotator cuff muscles are almost always near their insertion on the humerus.

Rotator cuff muscles:
Subscapularis
Supraspinatus
Infraspinatus
Teres minor

Figure 18-18

Rotator cuff muscles

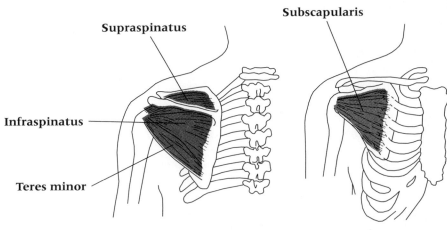

Supraspinatus

Subscapularis

Infraspinatus

Teres minor

POSTERIOR　　　　**ANTERIOR**

Signs of injury   Like other muscle strains, rotator cuff strains present pain with muscle contraction, some tenderness on palpation, and loss of strength due to pain. A tear or complete rupture of one of the rotator cuff tendons produces an extremely disabling condition in which pain, loss of function, swelling, and point tenderness are symptoms. In the case of a complete tear of the supraspinatus tendon, both the impingement test and the empty can test will be positive.[7]

Care   RICE can be used to modulate pain initially. Exercises should concentrate on progressive strengthening of the rotator cuff muscles. The frequency and level of the activity should be reduced initially with a gradual and progressive increase in intensity.

Shoulder Bursitis

Cause of injury   The shoulder joint is subject to chronic inflammatory conditions resulting from trauma or from overuse.[3] Bursitis may develop from a direct impact, from a fall on the tip of the shoulder, or as a result of shoulder impingement. The bursa that is most often inflamed is the subacromial bursa (Figure 18-19).

Signs of injury   The athlete has pain when trying to move the shoulder, especially in abduction or with flexion, adduction, and internal rotation. There will also be tenderness to palpation in the area just under the acromion. Impingement tests will be positive.

Care   The use of cold packs and antiinflammatory medications to reduce inflammation is necessary. If impingement is the primary mechanism precipitating bursitis, then, as previously discussed, measures should be taken to correct this activity.[3] The athlete must maintain a consistent program of exercise, with emphasis placed on maintaining a full range of motion, so that muscle contractures and adhesions do not immobilize the joint.

Biceps Tenosynovitis

Cause of injury   Tenosynovitis of the biceps muscle is common among athletes engaged in overhead activities. Biceps tenosynovitis is more prevalent among pitchers, tennis players, volleyball players, and javelin throwers. The repeated stretching of the biceps in these highly ballistic activities may eventually cause an inflammation of both the tendon and its synovial sheath.[1]

Signs of injury   There will be tenderness in the anterior upper arm. There may also be some swelling, increased warmth, and crepitus due to the inflammation. The athlete may complain of pain when performing dynamic overhead throwing activities.

Care   Biceps tenosynovitis is best cared for by complete rest for several days, combined with daily applications of cold to reduce inflammation. Antiinflammatory medications are also beneficial in reducing inflammation. After the inflammation is controlled, a gradual program of strengthening and stretching the biceps muscle should be initiated.

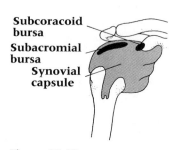

Subcoracoid bursa
Subacromial bursa
Synovial capsule

Figure 18-19

Synovial capsule and bursae of the shoulder

Contusions of the Upper Arm

Cause of injury   Contusions of the upper arm are frequent in contact sports. Although any muscle of the upper arm is subject to bruising, the area most often affected is the lateral aspect, primarily the brachialis muscle and portions of the triceps and biceps muscles. Repeated contusions to the lateral aspect of the upper arm can lead to myositis ossificans, more commonly known as linebacker's arm or blocker's exostosis. Myositis ossificans are calcifications or bone fragments that occur in a muscle or in soft tissues adjacent to bone.[11]

Signs of injury   Bruises to the upper arm area can be particularly handicapping, causing pain and tenderness, increased warmth, discoloration, and difficulty in achieving full extension and flexion of the elbow.

Care   RICE should be applied for a minimum of twenty-four hours after injury. In most cases this condition responds rapidly to treatment, usually within a few days. The key to treatment is to provide protection to the contused area to prevent repeated episodes that increase the likelihood of myositis ossificans. It is also important for the athlete to maintain a full range of motion through stretching of the contused muscle.

SUMMARY

- For the shoulder complex to have such a great degree of mobility, some compromise in stability had to be made; thus, the shoulder is highly susceptible to injury. Many sport activities that involve repetitive overhead movements place a great deal of stress on the shoulder joint.

- Four major articulations are associated with the shoulder complex: the sternoclavicular joint and ligament, the acromioclavicular joint and ligament, the glenohumeral joint and ligament, and the scapulothoracic joint.

- The muscles acting on the shoulder joint consist of those that originate on the axial skeleton and attach to the humerus, those that originate on the scapula and attach to the humerus, and a third group that attaches the axial skeleton to the scapula.

- When evaluating injuries to the shoulder complex, the coach must take into consideration all four joints. A number of special tests can provide insight relative to the nature of a particular injury.

- Fractures may occur to the clavicle or humerus, whereas sprains may occur at the sternoclavicular, acromioclavicular, or glenohumeral joints.

- Shoulder dislocations are relatively common, with an anterior dislocation being the most likely to occur. After a dislocation has been reduced and immobilized, muscle reconditioning should be initiated as soon as possible.

- Shoulder impingement most often occurs in athletes involved with overhead activities. Shoulder impingement involves a mechanical compression of the supraspinatus tendon, the subacromial bursa, and the long head of the biceps tendon under the coracoacromial ligament.
- A number of injuries, including rotator cuff strain, bursitis, contusions, and biceps tenosynovitis, are all common injuries to the shoulder complex in athletes.

Solutions to Critical Thinking Exercises

18-1 Falling on the tip of the shoulder is a typical mechanism of injury for a sprain of the acromioclavicular joint, the sternoclavicular joint, or both. It is also possible that a clavicular fracture has occurred.

18-2 Exercises should be designed to strengthen the muscles of the rotator cuff in particular as well as the muscles that allow the scapula to provide a stable base of support. Exercises that stress neuromuscular control should begin immediately in the rehabilitation program.

18-3 This athlete's pain is likely due to mechanical impingement or compression of the supraspinatus tendon, the subacromial bursa, or the long head of the biceps under the coracoacromial arch as the arm moves into a fully abducted or flexed position. The space under the arch becomes even more compressed as the humerus is internally rotated, which would occur during the follow-through.

REVIEW QUESTIONS AND CLASS ACTIVITIES

1. What are the bony and soft-tissue structures associated with the shoulder complex?
2. What four major joints make up the shoulder complex?
3. How can shoulder injuries be prevented?
4. Discuss the throwing motion and the injuries that can occur in each phase.
5. What causes clavicular fractures? How are they cared for?
6. Discuss the mechanism of injury of sternoclavicular and acromioclavicular ligament sprains.
7. What is the common mechanism of an anterior glenohumeral dislocation? How is it cared for?
8. What structural anatomic problems need to be addressed when treating shoulder impingement?
9. Briefly describe the history of a rotator cuff tear.
10. How does an athlete develop bursitis in the shoulder?
11. What is myositis ossificans and how can you prevent its development?
12. How may an athlete develop biceps tenosynovitis?

REFERENCES

1. Andrews J, Wilk K: *The athlete's shoulder,* New York, 1994, Churchill Livingston.
2. Bach B, VanFleet T, Novak P: Acromioclavicular joint injuries: controversies in treatment, *Physician Sportsmed* 20(12):87, 1992.
3. Botte MJ, Abrams RA: Recognition and treatment of shoulder bursitis, *Sports Med Dig* 14:81, 1992.

4. Craig E: Fractures of the clavicle. In Rockwood C, Masten F: *The shoulder*, Philadelphia, 1990, WB Saunders.

5. Di Giovine NM, Pink M: Pitching injuries, *Sports Med Digest* 14:1, 1992.

6. Gross ML et al: Overworked shoulders, *Physician Sportsmed* 22:81, 1994.

7. Irrgang J, Whitney S, Harner C: Nonoperative treatment of rotator cuff injuries in throwing athletes, *J Sport Rehab* 1(3):197, 1992.

8. Masten F, Thomas S, Rockwood C: Glenohumeral instability. In Rockwood C, Masten F: *The shoulder*, Philadelphia, 1990, WB Saunders.

9. Masten F, Arntz C: Subacromial impingement. In Rockwood C, Masten F: *The shoulder*, Philadelphia, 1990, WB Saunders.

10. Norris T: History and physical examination of the shoulder. In Nicholas JA, Hershman EB, editors: *The upper extremity in sports medicine*, St Louis, 1995, Mosby.

11. Pagnani M, Warren R: Instability of the shoulder. In Nicholas JA, Hershman EB, editors: *The upper extremity in sports medicine*, St Louis, 1995, Mosby.

12. Sawa T: An alternate conservative management of shoulder dislocations and subluxations, *J Ath Train* 27(4):366, 1992.

13. Warner JJP et al: Patterns of flexibility, laxity, and strength in normal shoulders and shoulders with instability and impingement, *Am J Sports Med* 18:366, 1990.

14. Watson, K: Impingement and rotator cuff lesions. In Nicholas JA, Hershman EB, editors: *The upper extremity in sports medicine*, St Louis, 1995, Mosby.

ANNOTATED BIBLIOGRAPHY

Andrews J, Wilk K: *The athlete's shoulder*, New York, 1994, Churchill Livingston.

   Concentrates of both conservative and surgical treatment of shoulder injuries occurring specifically in the athletic population.

Cailliet R: *Shoulder pain*, ed 3, Philadelphia, 1991, FA Davis.

   Excellent coverage of the fundamental principles for assessing and treating shoulder pain syndromes.

Hawkins RJ, editor: *Basic science and clinical application in the athlete's shoulder. Clinics in sports medicine*, vol 10, no 4, Philadelphia, 1991, WB Saunders.

   Detailed monograph dedicated to all aspects of the shoulder in sports.

Rockwood C, Masten F: *The shoulder*, Philadelphia, 1990, WB Saunders.

   Complete two-volume set that covers every subject relative to the shoulder complex.

WEB SITES

Cramer First Aider: http://www.ccsd.k12.wy.us/CCHS_web/sptmed/fstaider.htm

World Ortho: http://www.worldortho.com

   Use the search engine in this site to locate relevant information.

Wheeless' Textbook of Orthopaedics: http://www.medmedia.com/med.htm

   An excellent page for injuries, anatomy, and x rays.

Karolinska Institute Library: Musculoskeletal Disease: http://www.mic.ki.se/Disease/c5.htm

American Orthopaedic Society for Sports Medicine: http://www.sportsmed.org

MedFacts Sports Doc: http://www.medfacts.com

The Elbow, Forearm, Wrist, and Hand

When you finish this chapter you will be able to:

- Identify common elbow, forearm, wrist, and hand injuries.
- Provide immediate care of elbow, forearm, wrist, and hand injuries.

The portion of the upper limb consisting of the elbow, forearm, wrist, and hand is second only to the lower limb in the number of sports injuries incurred. Because of the way it is used and its relative exposure, the upper limb is highly prone to numerous acute and overuse conditions.

THE ELBOW JOINT

Although not as complicated as the knee or shoulder, the elbow still ranks as one of the more complex joints in the human body.

Anatomy

Bones

The three bones that comprise the elbow are the humerus, the radius, and the ulna (Figures 19-1 through 19-3). The elbow joint allows for flexion and extension. The radioulnar joint, which allows for forearm pronation and supination, is formed by the annular ligament and the head of the radius resting close to the rounded end of the humerus (capitulum).

Musculature

An intricate network of muscles, nerves, and blood vessels serves to allow for very complicated movement patterns (Figures 19-4 and 19-5).

Assessing Elbow Injuries

History

As with all sports injuries, the coach must first understand how the injury occurred. The following questions will aid in evaluation of the elbow:

- Is the pain or discomfort caused by a direct trauma such as falling on an outstretched arm or landing on the tip of a bent elbow?
- Can the problem be attributed to sudden overextension of the elbow or to repeated overuse of a throwing-type motion?

The location and duration should be ascertained. Like shoulder pain, elbow pain or discomfort may be from internal organ dysfunction or referred from a nerve root irritation or nerve impingement.

- Are there movements or positions of the arm that increase or decrease the pain?
- Has a previous elbow injury been diagnosed or treated?
- Is there a feeling of locking or a grating during movement?

NOTE: Elbow pain may not be directly associated with an elbow injury but rather may be referred pain from the neck or shoulder.

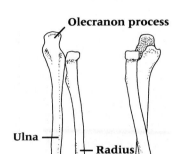

POSTERIOR ANTERIOR (pronated)

Figure 19-1

Bones of the elbow

Observation

The athlete's elbow should be observed for obvious deformities and swelling. The following should be observed:

1. The carrying angle, flexion, and extensibility of the elbow should be observed.

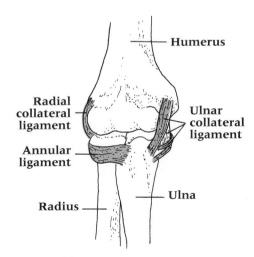

Figure 19-2

Bones and ligaments of the elbow

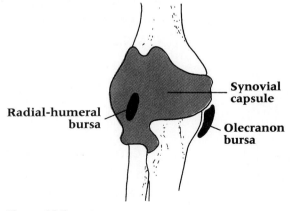

Figure 19-3

Synovium and bursae of the elbow

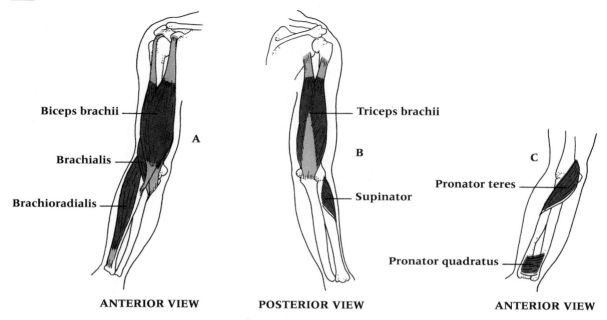

ANTERIOR VIEW   POSTERIOR VIEW   ANTERIOR VIEW

Figure 19-4

Muscles of the elbow joint:
A, Anterior view. B, Posterior
view. C, Forearm pronators.

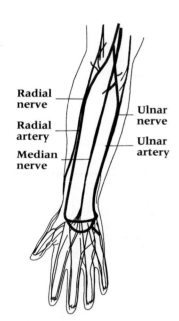

Figure 19-5

Arteries and nerves supplying
the elbow joint, wrist, and
hand

2. If the carrying angle is abnormally increased or abnormally decreased, an injury may be present.
3. A carrying angle that is too great or too little may indicate a bony or growth plate fracture.
4. The athlete is next observed for the extent of elbow flexion and extension. The elbows are compared (Figure 19-6). A decrease in normal flexion (Figure 19-7), an inability to extend fully, or a beyond-normal extension may be a cause of joint problems (Figure 19-8).
5. Next, the elbow is bent to a 45-degree angle and observed from the rear to determine whether the two epicondyles and olecranon process form an **isosceles triangle** (Figure 19-9).

Palpation

Bony palpation   Pain sites and deformities are determined through careful palpation of the epicondyles, olecranon process, distal aspect of the humerus, and proximal aspect of the ulna (Figure 19-10).

Soft-tissue palpation   Soft tissue includes the muscles and muscle tendons, joint capsule, and ligaments surrounding the joint.

Circulatory Assessment

With an elbow injury, a pulse routinely should be taken at the brachial artery and at the radial artery at the wrist.

Functional Assessment

The joint and the muscles are evaluated for pain sites and weakness through passive, active, and resistive motions consisting of elbow flexion

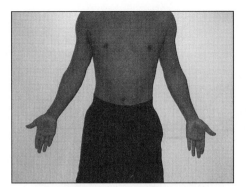

Figure 19-6

Testing for elbow carrying
angle and the extent of
cubitus valgus and cubitus
varus

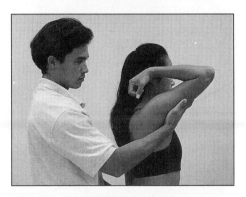

Figure 19-7

Testing for elbow flexion and
extension

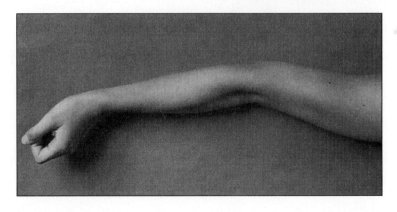

Figure 19-8

Observing elbow
hyperextension

and extension (Figure 19-11) and forearm pronation and supination
(Figure 19-12). Range of motion is particularly noted in passive and active pronation and supination (Figure 19-13).

Prevention of Elbow Injuries

As with injury prevention in other areas of the body, elbow injury prevention requires year-round conditioning consisting of strength, endurance, and flexibility activities. Because of the elbow's sensitivity to
overuse problems, it is essential that sport specific techniques be carefully
carried out.[6]

> **isosceles triangle**
> Triangle with two sides
> equal in length.

Recognition and
Management of Specific
Injuries and Conditions

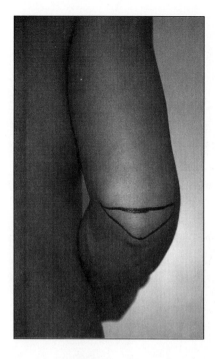

Figure 19-9

Determining whether the
lateral and medial
epicondyles, along with the
olecranon process, form an
isosceles triangle

Figure 19-10

Typical pain sites in the
elbow region

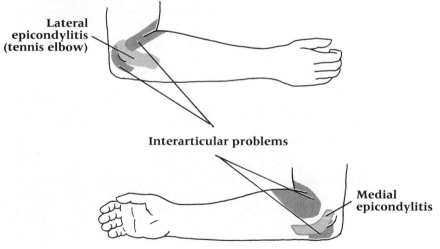

Lateral
epicondylitis
(tennis elbow)

Interarticular problems

Medial
epicondylitis

Injuries to the Elbow Region

The two most common
mechanisms of elbow injury:
Throwing
Falling on the outstretched
hand

The elbow is subject to injury in sports because of its broad range of motion, weak lateral bone arrangement, and relative exposure to soft tissue
damage in the vicinity of the joint.[2] Many sports place excessive stress on
the elbow joint. Extreme locking of the elbow in gymnastics or using implements such as racquets, golf clubs, and javelins can cause injuries. The
throwing mechanism in baseball pitching can injure the elbow during
both the acceleration and follow-through phases.[3]

Figure 19-11

Functional evaluation includes performing passive resistance flexion and extension to determine joint restrictions and pain sites.

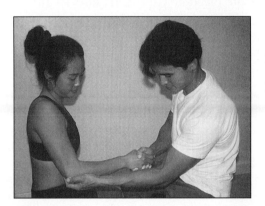

Figure 19-12

Elbow evaluation includes performing passive, active, and resistive forearm pronation and supination.

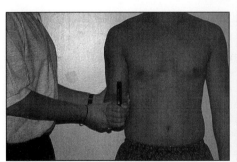
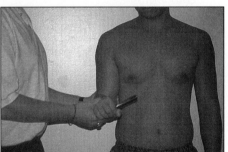
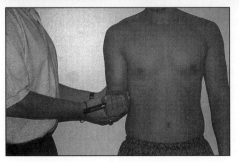

Figure 19-13

The range of motion of the forearm pronation and supination is routinely observed in athletes with elbow problems.

Contusions

Because of its lack of padding and its general vulnerability, the elbow often becomes contused in collision and contact sports.

Cause of injury   Bone bruises arise from a deep penetration or a succession of blows to the sharp projections of the elbow.

Signs of injury   A contusion of the elbow may swell rapidly after an irritation of the olecranon bursa or the synovial membrane.

Care   Elbow contusions should be treated immediately with cold and pressure for at least twenty-four hours. If the injury is severe, the athlete should be referred immediately to a physician for x-ray examination.

Olecranon Bursitis

The olecranon bursa (Figure 19-14), lying between the end of the olecranon process and the skin, is the most frequently injured bursa in the elbow.

Cause of injury   The superficial location of the olecranon bursa makes it prone to acute or chronic injury, particularly as the result of direct blows.

Signs of injury   The inflamed bursa produces pain, marked swelling, and point tenderness. Occasionally, swelling will appear almost spontaneously and without the usual pain and heat.

Care   If the condition is acute, a cold compress should be applied for at least one hour. Chronic olecranon bursitis requires a program of superficial therapy. In some cases aspiration by a physician will hasten healing. Although seldom serious, olecranon bursitis can be annoying and should be well protected by padding while the athlete is engaged in competition.

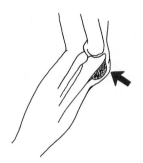

Figure 19-14

Olecranon bursitis

Elbow Strains

Cause of injury   The acute cause of muscle strain associated with the elbow joint is usually excessive resistive motion, such as a fall on the outstretched hand with the elbow in extension that forces the joint into hyperextension. Repeated microtears causing chronic injury will be discussed under *epicondylitis.*

Signs of injury   The athlete complains during active or resistive movement. There is usually a point tenderness in the muscle, tendon, or lower part of the muscle belly.

Care   Immediate care includes RICE and sling support for the more severe cases. Follow-up care may include cryotherapy, ultrasound, and rehabilitative exercises. Conditions that cause moderate to severe loss of elbow function should routinely be referred for x-ray examination. It is important to rule out the possibility of an avulsion or growth plate fracture.

Sprains

Cause of injury   Sprains to the elbow are usually caused by hyperextension or a force that bends or twists the lower arm outward.

Signs of injury   The athlete complains of pain and the inability to throw or grasp an object. There is a point tenderness over the medial elbow ligaments.

Care   Immediate care for elbow sprain consists of cold and a pressure bandage for at least twenty-four hours with sling support fixed at 90 degrees of flexion. Like fractures and dislocations, elbow sprains also may result in abnormal bone proliferation if given too vigorous a treatment or if exercised too soon. A coach's main concern should be to gently aid the elbow in regaining a full range of motion and then, when the time is right, to commence active exercises until full mobility and strength have returned.

Epicondylitis

Cause of injury   Epicondylitis is a chronic condition that may affect athletes who execute repeated forearm flexion and extension movements such as are performed in tennis, pitching, golf, javelin throwing, and fencing. The elbow is particularly predisposed to mechanical trauma in the activities of throwing and striking. Epicondylitis is also called tennis elbow, pitcher's elbow, or golfer's elbow.

Epicondylitis occurs from small microtears at these sites of muscle attachment; these microtears result from repeated forceful wrist flexion or extension (Figure 19-15).[9]

Signs of condition   Epicondylitis is an inflammation of the muscular attachments of either the long extensor muscles of the wrist and fingers at the lateral epicondyle of the humerus or of the long flexor

Common sports injuries that are forms of epicondylitis:
Pitcher's elbow
Tennis elbow
Javelin thrower's elbow
Golfer's elbow

Figure 19-15

Repeated overhand throwing actions can cause epicondylitis.

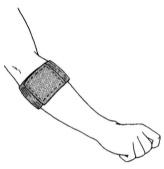

Figure 19-16

Counterforce brace for
treatment of elbow and
epicondylitis

muscles of the wrist and fingers at the medial epicondyle of the humerus.
Regardless of the sport or exact location of the injury, the symptoms and
signs of epicondylitis are similar. Pain around the epicondyles of the
humerus is produced during forceful wrist flexion or extension. The pain
may be centered at the epicondyle, or it may radiate down the arm. There
is usually point tenderness and, in some cases, mild swelling. Passive
movement of the wrist into extension or flexion seldom elicits pain, although active movement does.[13]

Care Conservative management of moderate-to-severe epicondylitis usually includes use of a sling, rest, and a variety of therapeutic modalities. A counterforce brace may be worn to relieve stress of movement
(Figure 19-16). The counterforce should only be used by individuals who
have been diagnosed with epicondylitis. It should never be used by children or adolescents who have been diagnosed with a growth plate problem or by an individual with an elbow instability.

Elbow Osteochondritis Dissecans

Although osteochondritis dissecans is more common in knees it also can
occur in elbows.

Cause of injury The cause of osteochondritis dissecans is unknown;
however, impairment of the blood supply can lead to fragmentation and
separation of a portion of the articular cartilage and bone, creating loose
bodies within the joint.[7]

Signs of injury The adolescent athlete usually complains of sudden
pain and locking of the elbow joint. Range of motion returns slowly over
a few days. Swelling, pain, and crepitation also may occur.

Care Repeated episodes of locking may warrant surgical removal of
the loose bodies. If they are not removed, traumatic arthritis can eventually occur.

Ulnar Nerve Injuries

Athletes with a pronounced
cubitus valgus are prone to
injuring the ulnar nerve.

Because of the exposed position of the medial humeral condyle, the ulnar nerve is subject to a variety of problems. The athlete with a pronounced outward angle of the elbow may develop a nerve friction problem. The ulnar nerve can also become recurrently dislocated because of
a structural deformity or can become impinged by a ligament during
flexion-type activities.

Rather than being painful, ulnar nerve injuries usually respond with
a paresthesia to the fourth and fifth fingers. The athlete complains of
burning and tingling in the fourth and fifth fingers.

Care The management of ulnar nerve injuries is conservative; aggravation of the nerve, such as placing direct pressure on it, is avoided.
When stress on the nerve cannot be avoided, surgery may be performed
to transpose it anteriorly to the elbow.

Dislocation of the Elbow

Cause of injury Dislocation of the elbow has a high incidence in
sports activity and most often is caused either by a fall on the out-

Critical Thinking Exercise

A female javelin thrower
complains of pain on the
medial aspect of her elbow that
is also referred distally to the
forearm. The athlete senses an
intermittent numbness, a
burning sensation, and tingling
in the fingers.

? What condition does this
athlete have, and how could it
have occurred?

Figure 19-17

A fall on the outstretched
hand can produce an elbow
dislocation and/or fracture.

stretched hand with the elbow in a position of hyperextension or by a severe twist while the elbow is in a flexed position (Figure19-17).[8]

Signs of injury   The bones of the forearm (ulna and radius) may be
displaced backward, forward, or laterally. The appearance of the most
common dislocation is a deformity of the olecranon process wherein it
extends backward, well beyond its normal alignment with the upper
arm.

Elbow dislocations involve rupturing and tearing of most of the stabilizing ligamentous tissue accompanied by profuse internal bleeding and
subsequent swelling. There is severe pain and disability. The complications of such a trauma may include injury to the major nerves and blood
vessels.[1]

Care   The primary responsibility is to provide the athlete with a
sling and to refer the athlete immediately to a physician for reduction, or
setting. Reduction must be performed as soon as possible to prevent muscle spasm and prolonged derangement of soft tissue. In most cases the
physician will administer an anesthetic before reduction to relax the
muscles. After reduction, the physician often will immobilize the elbow
in a position of flexion and apply a sling suspension, which should be
used for approximately three weeks. A dislocated elbow, like a fracture,
may also have possible neurovascular problems.[8]

Neurovascular problems are a
possibility when an elbow is
dislocated or fractured.

Fractures of the Elbow

Cause of injury   An elbow fracture can occur in almost any sports
event and is usually caused by a fall on the outstretched hand or the
flexed elbow or by a direct blow to the elbow. Children and young athletes have a much higher rate of this injury than do adults. A fracture can
take place in any one or more of the bones that compose the elbow. A fall
on the outstretched hand quite often fractures the humerus above the
condyles. The bones of the forearm or wrist also may be the recipients of
trauma that produces a fracture.

Signs of injury   An elbow fracture may or may not result in visible
deformity. There usually will be hemorrhage, swelling, and muscle spasm
in the injured area.

Volkmann's contracture is a
major complication of a
serious elbow injury.

Care   Because of the seriousness of an elbow fracture, careful immediate care must be rendered. Following the application of cold and a sling support, the athlete must be referred immediately for medical attention. A fractured elbow is associated with rapid swelling that may cause a condition called Volksmann's contracture, an extremely serious and often irreversible condition.

Volkmann's Contracture

Cause of injury   It is essential that athletes sustaining a serious elbow injury have the circulation monitored often throughout the day and night. Swelling, muscle spasm, or a bone displacement can put pressure on the brachial artery and inhibit blood circulation to the forearm, wrist, and hand. Such inhibition of circulation can lead to muscle contracture and permanent muscle paralysis.[12]

Sign of injury   The first indication of this problem is pain in the forearm that becomes progressively greater when the fingers of the affected arm are passively extended.

Care   Volkmann's contracture is a major problem requiring immediate referral for emergency treatment. The coach must remember that with this injury, time is of the essence.

THE FOREARM

Anatomy

Bones

The bones of the forearm are the ulna and the radius. The ulna, which may be thought of as a direct extension of the humerus, is long, straight, and larger at its upper end than at its lower end. The radius, considered an extension of the hand, is thicker at its lower end than at its upper end.

Joints

The forearm has three articulations: the superior, middle, and distal radioulnar joints.

Musculature

The forearm muscles consist of flexors and pronators, positioned anteriorly and attached to the medial elbow, and of extensors and supinators, which lie posteriorly and are attached to the lateral elbow (Figure 19-18). The flexors of the wrist and fingers are separated into superficial muscles and deep muscles.

Blood Circulation and Nerves

The major blood supply stems from the brachial artery, which divides into the radial and ulnar artery in the forearm. Except for the flexor carpi ulnaris and half of the flexor digitorum profundus, most of the flexor muscles of the forearm are supplied by the median nerve. The majority of the extensor muscles are controlled by the radial nerve.

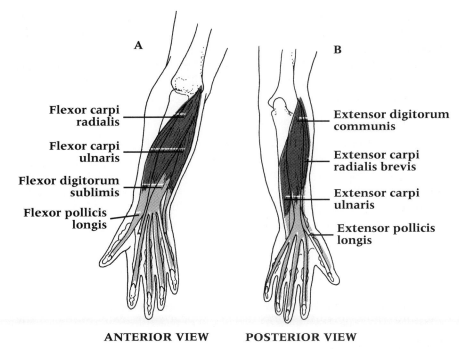

Flexor carpi
radialis

Flexor carpi
ulnaris

Flexor digitorum
sublimis

Flexor pollicis
longis

Extensor digitorum
communis

Extensor carpi
radialis brevis

Extensor carpi
ulnaris

Extensor pollicis
longis

ANTERIOR VIEW   **POSTERIOR VIEW**

Figure 19-18

Muscles of the forearm: A,
Anterior view. B, Posterior
view.

Assessing Forearm Injuries

Sports injuries for the forearm are easily detectable because of the
amount of exposure of both the ulna and the radius to sports stress.
Recognition of an injury is accomplished mainly through observation of
the range of motion present and of visible deviations and through the use
of palpation. As with all limb injuries, the coach should compare the injured forearm with the uninjured one as to movement and appearance.

Injuries to the Forearm

Lying between the elbow joint and the wrist and hand, the forearm is indirectly influenced by injuries due to overuse as well as by direct external injuries.

Contusion

Cause of injury   The forearm is constantly exposed to bruising in contact sports such as football. The ulnar side receives the majority of blows in
arm blocks and consequently the greater amount of bruising. Bruises to
this area may be classified as acute or chronic. The acute contusion can, on
rare occasions, result in a fracture. The chronic contusion develops from
repeated blows to the forearm with attendant multiple irritations.

Signs of injury   Most often muscles or bones develop varying degrees of pain, swelling, and accumulation of blood (hematoma). Extensive scar tissue may replace the hematoma, and in some cases, a bony callus replaces the scar tissue.

Recognition and
Management of Specific
Injuries and Conditions

Forearm splints, like
shinsplints, commonly occur
early and late in the sports
season.

Care   Care of the contused forearm requires proper attention in the acute stages by application of RICE for twenty minutes every 1½ waking hour, followed the next day by cold and exercise. Protection of the forearm is important for athletes who are prone to this condition. The best protection consists of a full-length sponge rubber pad for the forearm early in the season.

Forearm Splint and Other Strains

Forearm strain occurs in a variety of sports; most such injuries come from repeated static contractions.

Cause of injury   Forearm splints occur most often in gymnastics. The reason for this problem is probably static muscle contractions of the forearm, such as those that occur when an athlete performs on the side horse. Constant static muscle contraction causes minute tears in the deep connective tissues of the forearm.

Signs of injury   The main symptom of forearm splints is a dull ache of the extensor muscles crossing the back of the forearm. Muscle weakness may accompany the dull ache. Palpation reveals an irritation of the deep tissue between the muscles. The cause of this condition is uncertain; like shinsplints, forearm splints usually appear either early or late in the season, indicating poor conditioning or chronic fatigue.

Care   Care of forearm splints is symptomatic. If the problem occurs early in the season, the athlete should concentrate on increasing the strength of the forearm through resistance exercises; if it arises late in the season, emphasis should be placed on rest, cold, or heat and on use of a supportive wrap during activity.

Fractures

Fractures of the forearm (Figure 19-19) are particularly common among active children and youths.

Figure 19-19

A, Fracture of the radius and
ulna. B, Compound fracture
of the ulna.

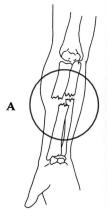

A

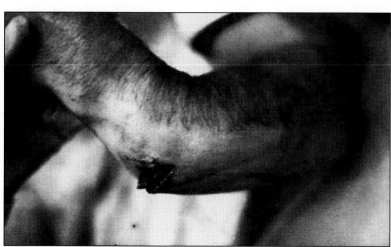

B

Cause of injury Forearm fractures occur as the result of a blow or a fall on the outstretched hand. Fractures to the ulna or the radius singly are much rarer than simultaneous fractures to both.

Signs of injury The break usually presents all the features of a long-bone fracture: pain, swelling, deformity, and a false joint.[4] The older the athlete, the greater the danger is of extensive damage to soft tissue and the greater the possibility is of paralysis from Volkmann's contractures.

Care To prevent complications, a cold pack must be applied immediately to the fracture site, the arm splinted and put in a sling, and the athlete referred to a physician. The athlete will usually be incapacitated for about eight weeks.

Colles' Fracture

Colles' fracture (Figure 19-20), among the most common forearm fractures, involves the lower (distal) end of the radius.[10]

Cause of injury The cause of a Colles' fracture is usually a fall on the outstretched hand, forcing the forearm backward and upward into hyperextension.

Signs of injury In most cases there is a visible deformity to the wrist. Sometimes no deformity is present, and the injury may be passed off as a bad sprain—to the detriment of the athlete. Bleeding is quite profuse in this area, with the accumulated fluids causing extensive swelling in the wrist and, if unchecked, in the fingers and forearm. Ligamentous tissue is usually unharmed, but tendons may be torn away from their attachment, and there may possibly be median nerve damage.

Care The main responsibility is to apply a cold compress, splint the wrist, put the limb in a sling, and then refer the athlete to a physician for x-ray examination and immobilization. Lacking complications, Colles' fracture will keep an athlete out of sports for one to two months.

THE WRIST AND HAND

Anatomy

Bones

The wrist is formed by the union of the distal aspect of the radius and the articular disk of the ulna with three of the four proximal (of the eight diversely shaped) carpal bones (Figure 19-21). The hand is comprised of five metacarpal bones that join with the wrist bones above and the five fingers below.

Musculature

The wrist and hand are a complex of extrinsic and intrinsic muscles.

Assessment of the Wrist and Hand

History

As is done for other conditions, the evaluator asks about the location and type of pain:

Figure 19-20

Common appearance of the forearm in Colles' fracture.

19-2

Critical Thinking Exercise

A young athlete falls off the parallel bars onto his outstretched left hand, forcing the wrist into hyperextension. There is a visible deformity to the wrist.

? Describe the deformity presented and the actions that should be taken by the coach.

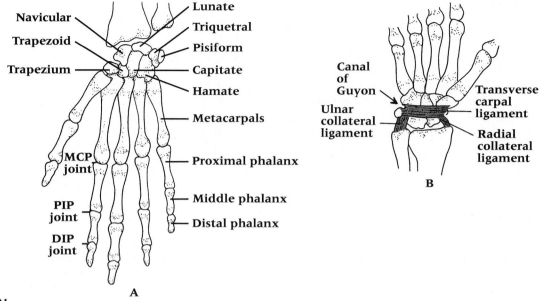

Figure 19-21

A, Bones of the wrist and hand. B, Ligaments of the wrist.

- What increases or decreases the pain?
- Has there been a history of trauma or overuse?
- What therapy or medications, if any, have been given?

Observations

The athlete is observed for arm and hand asymmetries. Hand usage such as writing or unbuttoning a shirt is also noted. The general attitude of the hand is observed (Figure 19-22). When the athlete is asked to open and close the hand, the coach notes whether this movement can be performed fully and rhythmically.

Figure 19-22

General normal attitudes of the hand

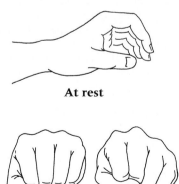

Palpation

Bony palpation   The bones of the wrist and hand regions are palpated for pain and defects.

Soft-tissue palpation   Following palpation of bones, soft tissue is palpated for pain and defects.

Circulatory and Neurological Assessment

The hands should be inspected to determine whether circulation is impeded. The hands should be felt for their temperature. A cold hand or portion of a hand is a sign of decreased circulation. Pinching the fingernails can indicate circulatory problems. Pinching will blanch the nail, and on release, there should be rapid return of a pink color.[14]

Wrist Injuries

Strains and Sprains

It is often very difficult to distinguish between injury to the muscle tendons crossing the wrist joint and to the supporting structure of the carpal region. Therefore, emphasis will be placed on the condition of wrist sprains, whereas strains will be considered in the discussion of the hand.

Cause of injury   A sprain is by far the most common wrist injury and in most cases is the most poorly managed injury in sports. It can arise from any abnormal forced movement of the wrist. Falling on the hyperextended wrist is the most common cause, but violent flexion or torsion can also tear supporting tissue (Figure 19-23). Because the main support of the wrist is derived from posterior and anterior ligaments that carry the major nutrient vessels to the carpal bones, repeated sprains may disrupt the blood supply and consequently the nutrition to the carpal bones.

Signs of injury   The sprained wrist may be differentiated from the carpal navicular fracture by recognition of the generalized swelling, tenderness, inability to flex the wrist, and absence of appreciable pain or irritation over the navicular bone.

Care   All athletes having severe sprains should be referred to a physician for x-ray examination to determine possible fractures. Mild and moderate sprains should be given cold therapy and compression for at least twenty-four to forty-eight hours.

Overuse Wrist Injuries

Cause of injury   The coach should be aware that athletes who engage in repetitive wrist motions can sustain a number of different types of overuse injuries. These injuries may be due to an inflammation of wrist tendons and/or a synovial sheath.

Signs of injury   The athlete may voice a variety of complaints to the coach, such as numbness and/or tingling in the fingers, thumb, or palm of the hand. There also may be weakness in the use of the hand.

Care   Initially the coach should have the athlete avoid activities that aggravate the condition. Immediate medical referral is necessary to rule

Sprains are the most common wrist injury in sports and often the worst managed.

Figure 19-23

Wrist injuries commonly
occur from falls on the
outstretched hand or from
repeated flexion, extension,
lateral, or rotary movements.

out a fracture or serious nerve injury. In some cases immobilization may
be required.

Dislocations

Dislocations of the wrist are relatively infrequent in sports activity.

Cause of injury   Most dislocations occur from a forceful hyperextension of the wrist as a result of a fall on the outstretched hand. Of those
dislocations that do happen, the bones that could be involved are the dis-

tal ends of the radius and ulna (Figure 19-24) and a carpal bone, the lunate being the most commonly affected.

Signs of injury The primary signs of this condition are pain, swelling, and difficulty in executing wrist and finger flexion. There also may be numbness or even paralysis of the flexor muscles because of lunate pressure on the median nerve.

Care This condition should be treated as acute, and the athlete sent to a physician. If it is not recognized early enough, bone deterioration may occur, requiring surgical removal.

Fractures

Fractures of the wrist commonly occur to the distal ends of the radius and ulna and to the carpal bones; the carpal navicular bone is most commonly affected; the hamate bone is affected less often.

Scaphoid Fracture

The scaphoid bone is the most frequently fractured of the carpal bones.[5]

Cause of injury The usual cause of the scaphoid fracture is a force on the outstretched hand, which compresses the scaphoid bone between the radius and the second row of carpal bones.[4]

Signs of injury The coach should be aware that this fracture often displays the same signs as a severe sprain. The signs of a recent schaphoid fracture include swelling in the area of the carpal bones, severe point tenderness of the navicular bone in the anatomical snuffbox (Figure 19-25), and navicular pain that is elicited by upward pressure exerted on the long axis of the thumb and by radial flexion.

Care Initially RICE and immobilization are carried out. Once the injury is determined to be a scaphoid fracture, complete immobilization is not carried out. Without proper splinting, the scaphoid fracture often fails to heal because of an inadequate supply of blood; thus, degeneration and **necrosis** (bone death) occur. Even after proper splinting, the navicular fractures may not heal and may have to be surgically repaired.

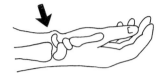

Figure 19-24

Dislocation of the wrist

necrosis (nekro sis)
Death of tissue.

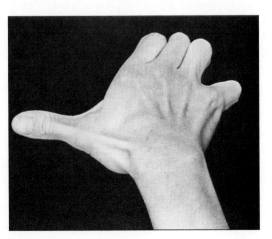

Figure 19-25

Anatomical snuffbox formed by extensor tendons of the thumb

Figure 19-26

Wrist ganglion

It is important to elevate the
hand for the first forty-eight
hours after injury to prevent
swelling in the fingers.

Wrist Ganglion of the Tendon Sheath

Cause of injury   The wrist ganglion (Figure 19-26) is often seen in sports. It is considered by many to be a herniation of the joint capsule or of the synovial sheath of a tendon; other authorities believe it to be a cystic structure. It usually appears slowly after a wrist strain and contains a clear, mucous fluid. The ganglion most often appears on the back of the wrist but can appear at any tendinous point in the wrist or hand.

Signs of injury   As the ganglion increases in size, it may be accompanied by a mild pressure discomfort.

Care   An old method of treatment was to break down the swelling by means of finger pressure and then apply a felt pressure pad for a period to encourage healing. A newer approach combines drawing the fluid off with a hypodermic needle, using chemical cauterization, and subsequently applying a pressure pad. Neither the old nor the new method prevents the ganglion from recurring. Surgical removal is the best method available.

Injuries to the Hand

Injuries to the hand occur frequently in sports, yet the injured hand is probably the most poorly managed of all body areas.

Contusions and Pressure Injuries of the Hand and Phalange

Cause of injury   The hand and phalanges have irregular bony structure and little protective fat and muscle padding, making them prone to bruising in sports.

Signs of injury   This condition is easily identified from the history of trauma and the pain and swelling of soft tissues.

Care   Cold, compression, and elevation should be applied immediately for forty-eight hours to avoid swelling. Although soreness is still present, protection should be given by a sponge rubber pad.

Bruised Fingernail

Cause of injury   A particularly common contusion of the finger is bruising of the distal phalanx, or fingertip, with seepage of blood underneath the nail.

Signs of injury   A bruised fingernail leading to an accumulation of blood is an extremely painful condition.

Care   The athlete should place the finger in ice water until the hemorrhage ceases. The accumulation of blood under the nail is then released by the athletic trainer or physician.

Tendon Conditions

Tendon injuries are common among athletes. Like many other hand injuries that occur in sports, tendon injuries are characteristically neglected.

Tenosynovitis

Cause of injury   The tendons of the wrist and hand can sustain irritation from repeated movement that results in tenosynovitis.

Signs of injury   The athlete will experience an inflammation of the tendon sheath that results in swelling, crepitation, and painful movement. Most commonly affected are the extensor tendons of the wrist.

Care   Tenosynovitis of the tendons of the hand requires referral to a physician for possible splinting and for antiinflammatory drugs.

Jammed Fingers

The jamming of a finger or thumb can lead to a variety of injuries that should never be trivialized. Mallet finger, boutonnière deformities, sprains, dislocations, and fractures represent this mechanism of injury.[11]

Mallet Finger

The mallet finger is common in sports, particularly in baseball and basketball.

Cause of injury   Mallet finger is caused by a blow from a thrown ball that strikes the tip of the finger, completely tearing the extensor tendon from its insertion along with a piece of bone.

Signs of injury   The athlete, unable to extend the finger, carries it at about a 30-degree angle. There is also point tenderness at the site of the injury, and the pulled-away bone chip often can be felt (Figure 19-27). Pain, swelling, and discoloration from internal hemorrhage are present.

Care   The distal phalanx should be splinted immediately in a position of extension, cold should be applied to the area, and the athlete should be referred to a physician. Most physicians will splint the mallet finger into extension or hyperextension and the proximal phalanx into flexion for six to eight weeks.

Sprains, Dislocations, and Fractures

The phalanges, particularly the thumbs, are prone to sprains caused by a blow delivered to the tip or by violent twisting. The mechanism of injury is similar to that of fractures and dislocations. The sprain, however, mainly affects the capsular, ligamentous, and tendinous tissues. Recognition is accomplished primarily through the history and the sprain symptoms: pain, marked swelling, and bleeding.

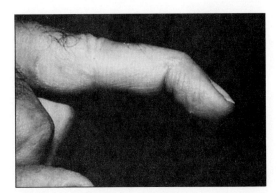

Figure 19-27

Mallet finger

Collateral Ligament Sprain

A collateral ligament sprain of a finger is very common in sports such as basketball, volleyball, and football.

Cause of injury   A common cause of collateral sprains is an axial force to the tip of the finger, producing the jammed effect.

Signs of injury   Severe point tenderness exists at the joint site, especially in the region of the collateral ligaments. There may be a lateral or medial joint instability when the joint is in 150 degrees of flexion.

Care   Care of a collateral sprain includes ice packs for the acute stage, x-ray examinations, and splinting. (See Figure 11-53 for special thumb taping.)

Dislocations of the Phalanges

Dislocations of the phalanges (Figure 19-28) occur frequently in sports and are caused mainly by a blow to the tip of the finger by a ball (Figure 19-29).

Cause of injury   The force of injury is usually directed upward from the palmar side, displacing either the first or second joint dorsally. The resultant problem is primarily a tearing of the supporting capsular tissue, accompanied by hemorrhaging. However, there may be a rupture of the flexor or extensor tendon and chip fractures in and around the dislocated joint.

Care   Reduction of the dislocated thumb should be performed by a physician. To ensure the most complete healing of the dislocated finger joints, splinting should be maintained for about three weeks in 30 degrees of flexion because an inadequate immobilization can cause an unstable joint and/or excessive scar tissue and possibly a permanent deformity.

Special consideration must be given to dislocations of the thumb and second or third joints of the fingers. A properly functioning thumb is necessary for hand dexterity; consequently, *any injury to the thumb should be considered serious.* Thumb dislocations occur frequently at the second joint, resulting from a sharp blow to its tip with the trauma forcing the thumb into hyperextension and dislocating the second joint downward. Any dis-

Figure 19-28

Compound dislocation of the thumb

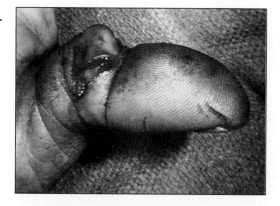

Figure 19-29

Sports such as baseball can
produce finger injuries.

location of the third joint of the finger can lead to complications and requires the immediate care of an orthopedist. *All hand dislocations must be
x-rayed to rule out fracture.*

Fractures of the Hand

Fractures of the hand can occur in a number of sports activities, especially
those that involve collisions. The mechanism that produces strains,
sprains, and dislocations can cause fractures of the metacarpal bones and
phalanges.

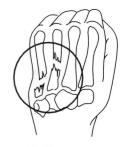

Fractures of the Metacarpal Bones

Fractures of the metacarpal bones (Figure 19-30) are common in contact
sports.

Figure 19-30

Fractures of the metacarpals

Cause of injury   Metacarpal fractures usually arise from striking an
object with the fist or from having the hand stepped on.

Signs of injury   There is often pain, deformity, swelling, and abnormal mobility. In some cases, no deformity occurs and palpation fails to
distinguish between a severe contusion and a fracture. In this situation
digital pressure should be placed on the knuckles and the long axes of the
metacarpal bones. Pressure often will reveal pain at the fracture site.

Care   After the fracture is located, the hand should be splinted over
a gauze roll splint, cold and pressure applied, and the athlete referred to
a physician.

19-3

Critical Thinking Exercise

A football player gets into a
fistfight on the field and injures
his right hand.

? What type of injury should
be suspected by the coach?

Fractures of the Phalanges

Fractures of the phalanges are among the most common fractures in
sports.

Cause of injury   Phalange fractures can occur from a variety of actions: The fingers are stepped on, hit by a ball, or twisted.

Signs of injury   The athlete complains of pain and swelling in a finger. Tenderness is felt at the point of fracture.

Care   The finger suspected of fracture should be splinted in flexion around a gauze roll or a curved splint to avoid full extension. Flexion splinting reduces the deformity by relaxing the flexor tendons. Fracture of the end phalanx is less complicated than fracture of the middle or third phalanx.

SUMMARY

- The upper limb, including the elbow, forearm, wrist, and hand, is second to the lower limb in the incidence of sports injuries.

- The elbow is anatomically one of the more complex joints in the human body.

- The elbow joint allows the movements of flexion and extension, and the radioulnar joint allows forearm pronation and supination.

- The major sports injuries of the elbow are contusions, strains, sprains, and dislocations.

- The chronic strain that produces pitcher's, tennis, javelin thrower's or golfer's elbow is more formally known as epicondylitis.

- The forearm is composed of two bones, the ulna and the radius, as well as associated soft tissue.

- Sports injuries to the forearm region commonly consist of contusions, chronic forearm splints, acute strains, and fractures.

- Injuries to the wrist usually occur as the result of a fall or repeated movements of flexion, extension, and rotation.

- Common wrist injuries are sprains, lunate carpal dislocation, scaphoid carpal fracture, and hamate fracture.

- Injuries to the hand occur frequently in sports activities.

- Common injuries to the hand include those caused by contusions and chronic pressure, by tendons receiving sustained irritation, which leads to tenosynovitis, and by tendon avulsions. Sprains, dislocations, and fractures of the fingers are also common.

Solutions to Critical Thinking E x e r c i s e s

19-1 This javelin thrower has sustained a cubital tunnel syndrome. Because of a pronounced elbow cubitus valgus, the ulnar recurrently subluxates. Because of ligamentous laxity, there is nerve impingement and compression.

19-2 This injury is a Colles' fracture, which is caused by the fracture displacement of the distal radius. The coach applies an ice compress, a splint, and a sling. The athlete is then referred to a physician for an x ray and definitive treatment.

19-3 The coach should suspect a fracture of a metacarpal bone. The injury may appear as an angular or rotational deformity. RICE and analgesics are given along with an x-ray examination. The injury is splinted for about four weeks, and early ROM exercises are prescribed.

REVIEW QUESTIONS AND CLASS ACTIVITIES

1. What are the bony and soft-tissue structures at the elbow? Why is a serious injury so devastating to the hand and wrist?
2. What are some common injuries of the elbow and what immediate care should be given?
3. How is a dislocation of the elbow immediately managed?
4. What are the common injuries of the forearm? What causes them, and what immediate care should be given?
5. What common injuries may occur to the wrist and hand? Which injuries may lead to serious complications?
6. How does the thumb differ, in terms of function, from the other digits?
7. Discuss the different finger injuries that can happen to an athlete. How are they managed? Discuss the pros and cons of reducing a dislocated finger.

REFERENCES

1. Allman FL, Carlson CA: Rehabilitation of elbow injuries. In Nicholas JA, Hershman EB, editors: *The upper extremity in sports medicine,* St Louis, 1995, Mosby–Year Book.
2. Andrews JR, Whiteside JA: Common elbow problems in the athlete, *J Orthop Sports Phys Ther* 17:289, 1993.
3. Bennett JB, Tullos HS: Acute injuries to the elbow. In Nicholas JA, Hershman EB, editors: *The upper extremity in sports medicine,* St Louis, 1995, Mosby–Year Book.
4. Brown DE et al: *Orthopedic secrets,* Philadelphia, 1995, Hanley & Belfus.
5. Gutierrez G: Office management of scaphoid fractures. *Physician Sportsmed* 24:60, August 1996.
6. Halperin BC: Elbow and arm injuries. In Birrer RB, editor: *Sports medicine for primary care physicians.* Boca Raton, Fla., 1994, CRC Press.
7. Harding WG III: Use and misuse of the tennis elbow strap, *Physician Sportsmed* 20:65, 1992.
8. Hoffman DF: Elbow dislocations, *Physician Sportsmed* 21:56, 1993.
9. Kiefhaber TR et al: Upper extremity tendinitis and overuse syndrome in the athlete, *Clin Sports Med* 11, 1993.
10. Mirabello ST et al: The wrist field evaluation and treatment, *Clin Sports Med* 11, 1993.
11. Nathan R: The jammed finger, *Sports Med Dig* 14:1, 1992.
12. Nirschl RP, Kraushaar BS: Assessment and treatment: guidelines for elbow injuries, *Physician Sportsmed* 24:43, May 1996.
13. Parks JC: Overuse injuries of the elbow. In Nicholas JA, Hershman EB, editors: *The upper extremity in sports medicine,* St Louis, 1995, Mosby–Year Book.
14. Weinstein SM, Herring SA: Nerve problems and compartment syndromes in the hand, wrist, and forearm, *Clin Sports Med* 11, 1993.

ANNOTATED BIBLIOGRAPHY

Chan KM, ed. *Sports injuries of the hand and upper extremity,* New York, 1995, Churchill Livingston.

Covers basic orthopedic principles and introduces recent literature on the care of upper extremity injuries.

Morray BF, ed: *The elbow and its disorders,* ed 2, Philadelphia, 1993, WB Saunders.

A definitive text on biomechanics, diagnosis, and medical and surgical mechanics of the injured elbow.

Plancher KD, editor: *The athletic elbow and wrist. Clinics in sports medicine,* Parts 1 and 2, vols 14 and 15 (2). Philadelphia, 1995 and 1996, Saunders.

An in-depth monograph covering the most common injuries to the elbow and wrist.

Strickland JW, Rettig AC: *Hand injuries in athletics,* Philadelphia, 1992, WB Saunders.

Covers the basic management of major hand injuries incurred in sports.

WEB SITES

Cramer First Aider: http://www.ccsd. k12.wy.us/CCHS_web/sptmed/ fstaider.htm

World Ortho: http://www.worldortho. com

Use the search engine in this site to locate relevant information.

Wheeless' Textbook of Orthopaedics: http://www.medmedia.com/med/ htm

An excellent page for injuries, anatomy, and x rays.

Karolinska Institute Library: Musculoskeletal Disease: http://www.mic. ki.se/Disease/c5.htm

American Orthopaedic Society for Sports Medicine: http://www.sportsmed.org

MedFacts Sports Doc: http://www. medfacts.com

The Spine

When you finish this chapter you will be able to:

- Describe the anatomy of the cervical, thoracic, and lumbar spine.
- Explain how the nerve roots from the spinal cord combine to form specific peripheral nerves.
- Describe measures to prevent injury to the spine.
- Describe a process to assess injuries of the cervical and lumbar spine.
- Identify specific injuries that can occur to the various regions of the spine.

Regions of the spinal column:
Cervical
Thoracic
Lumbar
Sacrum
Coccyx

Movements of the vertebral column:
Flexion
Extension
Lateral flexion
Rotation

The spine is one of the most complex regions of the body. It contains a multitude of bones, joints, ligaments, and muscles, all of which are collectively involved in spinal movement. The relationship of the spinal cord and the peripheral nerves and their proximity to the vertebral column adds to the complexity of this region. Injury to the cervical spine has potentially life-threatening implications. Low back pain is one of the most common ailments known to humans. Thus some understanding of the anatomy, assessment techniques, and specific injuries of the spine are all essential for the coach.

ANATOMY

Bones of the Vertebral Column

The spine, or vertebral column, is composed of thirty-three individual bones called *vertebrae*. Twenty-four are classified as movable, or true, and nine are classified as immovable, or false. The movable vertebrae are the cervical vertebrae, thoracic vertebrae, and lumbar vertebrae. The false vertebrae, which are fixed by fusion, form the sacrum and the coccyx. The design of the spine allows a high degree of flexibility forward and laterally and limited mobility backward. Rotation around a central axis in the areas of the neck and the lower back is also permitted.

The Cervical Spine

Because of the vulnerability of the cervical spine to sports injuries, coaches should have a general knowledge of the cervical spine anatomy

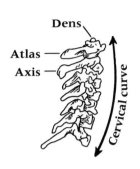

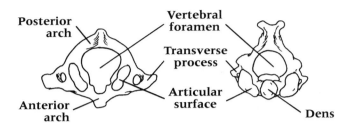

ATLAS
First cervical vertebra

AXIS
Second cervical vertebra

Figure 20-1

Anatomy of the cervical spine, atlas, and axis

and its susceptibility to sports injuries.[1,4] The cervical spine consists of seven vertebrae, with the first two differing from the other true vertebrae (Figure 20-1). These first two are called the atlas and the axis, respectively, and they function together to support the head on the spinal column and to permit cervical rotation.

The Thoracic Spine

The thoracic spine consists of twelve vertebrae (Figure 20-2). Thoracic vertebrae have long transverse processes and prominent but thin spinous processes. Thoracic vertebrae 1 through 10 articulate with the ribs. There is very little movement in the thoracic vertebrae.

The Lumbar Spine

The lumbar spine is composed of five vertebrae (Figure 20-3). They are the major support of the low back and are the largest and thickest of the vertebrae, with large spinous and transverse processes. Movement occurs in all the lumbar vertebrae; however, there is much less flexion than extension. Rotation is important in the lumbar region.

The Sacrum

The sacrum is formed by the fusion of five vertebrae and, with the two hip bones, constitutes the pelvis (Figure 20-4). The sacrum articulates with the ilium to form the sacroiliac joints. During both sitting and standing the body's weight is transmitted through these joints. A complex of ligaments serves to make these joints very stable.

The Coccyx

The coccyx, or tailbone, is the most inferior part of the vertebral column and consists of four or more fused vertebrae (Figure 20-4). The gluteus maximus muscle attaches to the coccyx posteriorly.

Intervertebral Articulations and Disks

Intervertebral articulations are between vertebral bodies. Between each of the cervical, thoracic, and lumbar vertebrae lie fibrocartilaginous intervertebral disks (Figure 20-5). Each disk is composed of the annulus

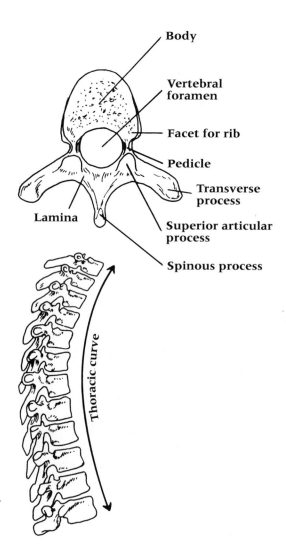

Figure 20-2

Anatomy of the thoracic
spine and vertebrae

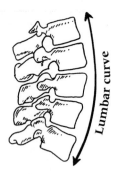

Figure 20-3

Anatomy of the lumbar spine
and vertebrae

fibrosus and the nucleus pulposus. The annulus fibrosus forms the periphery of the intervertebral disk and is composed of strong, fibrous tissue. In the center is the semifluid nucleus pulposus, compressed under pressure. The disks act as important shock absorbers for the spine.

Stabilizing Ligaments

The major ligaments that join the various vertebral parts are the anterior longitudinal, the posterior longitudinal, and the supraspinous (Figure 20-6). The interspinous, supraspinous, and intertransverse ligaments stabilize the transverse and spinous processes, extending between adjacent vertebrae. The sacroiliac joint is maintained by the extremely strong dorsal sacral ligaments. The sacrotuberous and the sacrospinous ligaments maintain the position of the sacrum relative to the ischium.

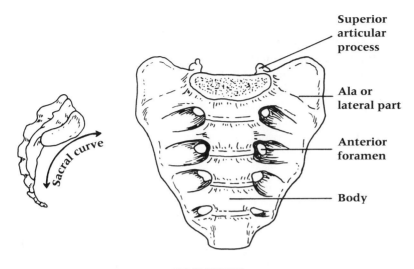

Superior
articular
process

Ala or
lateral part

Anterior
foramen

Body

Sacral curve

Figure 20-4

Anatomy of the sacrum and
coccyx

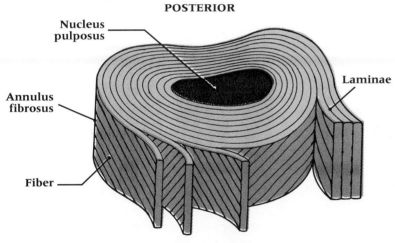

POSTERIOR

Nucleus
pulposus

Laminae

Annulus
fibrosus

Fiber

ANTERIOR

Figure 20-5

Intervertebral disk

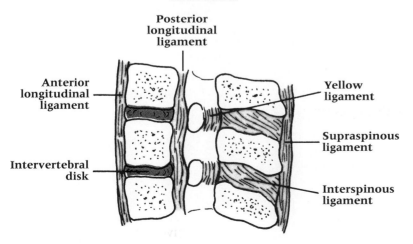

Posterior
longitudinal
ligament

Anterior
longitudinal
ligament

Yellow
ligament

Intervertebral
disk

Supraspinous
ligament

Interspinous
ligament

Figure 20-6

Major ligaments of the
lumbar spine

Muscles of the Spine

The muscles that extend the spine and rotate the vertebral column can be classified as either superficial or deep (Figure 20-7). The superficial muscles, or erector spinae, extend from the vertebrae to ribs. The erector spinae is a group of paired muscles that is made up of three columns, or bands: the longissimus group, the iliocostalis group, and the spinalis group. Each of these groups is further divided into regions: the cervicis region in the neck, the thoracis region in the middle back, and the lumborum region in the low back. Generally the erector spinae muscles extend the spine.

The deep muscles extend from one vertebrae to another. The deep muscles include the interspinales, multifidus, rotatores, thoracis, and the semispinalis cervicis. These muscles extend and rotate the spine.

Spinal Cord and Spinal Nerves

The spinal cord is that portion of the central nervous system that is contained within the vertebral canal of the spinal column. It extends from

Figure 20-7

Deep and superficial muscles of the spine

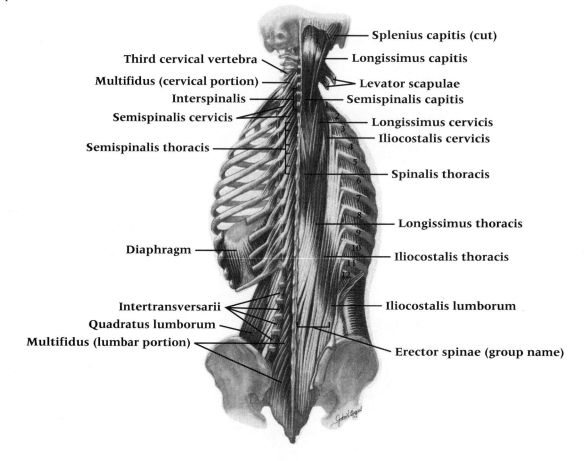

Splenius capitis (cut)
Longissimus capitis
Third cervical vertebra
Multifidus (cervical portion)
Levator scapulae
Interspinalis
Semispinalis capitis
Semispinalis cervicis
Longissimus cervicis
Iliocostalis cervicis
Semispinalis thoracis
Spinalis thoracis
Longissimus thoracis
Diaphragm
Iliocostalis thoracis
Intertransversarii
Iliocostalis lumborum
Quadratus lumborum
Multifidus (lumbar portion)
Erector spinae (group name)

the cranium to the first or second lumbar vertebra. The lumbar roots and the sacral nerves form a horselike tail called the cauda equina.

Thirty-one pairs of spinal nerves extend from the sides of the spinal cord: 8 cervical, 12 thoracic, 5 lumbar, 5 sacral, and 1 coccygeal (Figure 20-8).

PREVENTING INJURIES TO THE SPINE

Cervical Spine

Acute traumatic injuries to the spine can be potentially life threatening, particularly if the cervical region of the spinal cord is involved. Thus the athlete must do everything possible to minimize the chance of injury. Strengthening the musculature of the neck is critical. The neck muscles can function to protect the cervical spine by resisting excessive hyperflexion, hyperextension, or rotational forces. During participation the athlete should be in a constant state of readiness to "bull" the neck when making contact with an opponent. This protection is accomplished by elevating both shoulders and isometrically cocontracting the muscles surrounding the neck. Protective cervical collars can also help limit movement of the cervical spine. Athletes with long, weak necks are especially at risk. Tackle football players and wrestlers must have highly stable necks. Specific strengthening exercises are essential for the development of stability. A variety of different exercises that incorporate isotonic, isometric, or isokinetic contractions can be used.

In addition to strong muscles, the athlete's neck should have a full range of motion. Ideally the athlete should be able to place the chin on the chest and to extend the head back until the face is parallel with the ceiling. There should be at least 40 to 45 degrees of lateral flexion and enough rotation to allow the chin to reach a level even with the tip of the shoulder. Flexibility is increased through stretching exercises and

Long-necked football players and wrestlers are at risk and need to establish neck stability through strengthening exercises.

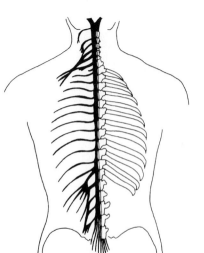

Figure 20-8

Relationship of cord and spinal nerves to the vertebral column

strength exercises that are in full range of motion. Where flexibility is restricted, manual static stretching can be beneficial.

Athletes involved in collision sports—in particular football and rugby, which involve tackling an opponent—must be taught and required to use techniques that reduce the likelihood of cervical injury. The head, especially one in a helmet, should not be used as a weapon. Football helmets do not protect players against neck injury. In the illegal spearing situation, the athlete uses the helmet as a weapon by striking the opponent with its top. Most serious cervical injuries in football result from deliberate axial loading while spearing.[13] Coaches cannot stress enough to the athlete the importance of using appropriate tackling techniques. In other sports, such as diving, wrestling, and bouncing on a trampoline, the athlete's neck can be flexed at the time of contact. Energy of the forward-moving body mass cannot be fully absorbed, and fracture or dislocation or both can occur. Diving into shallow water causes many catastrophic neck injuries. Many of the same forces are applied in wrestling. In such trauma, paraplegia, quadriplegia, or death can result.

Lumbar Spine

Low back pain is caused by many factors, many of which can be prevented by using proper body mechanics when sitting, lying, standing, or bending. (See the accompanying Focus Box.)

Coaches need to be aware of any postural anomalies that the athletes possess. With this knowledge, a coach can establish individual corrective programs. Basic conditioning should include an emphasis on trunk flexibility. Every effort should be made to produce maximum range of motion in rotation and in both lateral and forward flexion. Both strength and flexibility should be developed in the spinal extensors (erector spinae). Abdominal strength is essential to ensure proper postural alignment.

In weightlifters, the chance of injury to the lumbar spine can be minimized by using proper lifting techniques. Incorporating appropriate breathing techniques that involve inhaling and exhaling deeply during lifting can help stabilize the spine. Weight belts can also help stabilize the lumbar spine. Spotters can greatly enhance safety by helping lift and lower the weight.

ASSESSMENT OF THE SPINE

Assessment of injuries to the spine is somewhat more complex than assessment of the joints of the extremities because of the number of articulations involved in spinal movement.[11,12] It is also true that injury to the spine, or in particular the spinal cord, may have life-threatening or life-altering implications. Thus the coach must be able to rule out spinal injury by asking the appropriate questions.[1]

History

The most critical part of the evaluation is to rule out the possibility of spinal cord injury.[4] Questions that address this possibility should first establish the mechanism of injury.

20-1 *Focus Box*

Recommended Postures and Practices for Preventing Low Back Pain

Sitting

1. Do not sit for long periods.
2. Avoid sitting forward on a chair with back arched.
3. Sit on a firm, straight-backed chair.
4. The low back should be slightly rounded or positioned firmly against the back of the chair.
5. The feet should be flat on the floor with knees above the level of the hips (if unable to adequately raise the knees, the feet should be placed on a stool).
6. Avoid sitting with legs straight and raised on a stool.

Standing

1. If standing for long periods:
   a. Shift position from one foot to the other.
   b. Place one foot on a stool.
2. Stand tall, flatten low back, and relax knees.
3. Avoid arching back.

Lifting and carrying

1. To pick up an object:
   a. Bend at knees and not the waist.
   b. Do not twist to pick up an object—face it squarely.
   c. Tuck in buttocks and tighten abdomen.
2. To carry an object:
   a. Hold object close to body.
   b. Hold object at waist level.
   c. Do not carry object on one side of the body—if it must be carried unbalanced, change from one side to the other.

Sleeping

1. Do not stay in one position too long.
2. The bed should be flat and firm yet comfortable.
3. Do not sleep on the abdomen.
4. Do not sleep on the back with legs fully extended.
5. If sleeping on the back, a pillow should be placed under the knees.
6. Ideally, sleep on the side with the knees drawn up.
7. Arms should never be extended overhead.
8. The least strain on the back is in the fully recumbent position with the hips and knees at angles of 90 degrees. In the case of a chronic or a subacute low back condition, a firm mattress will afford better rest and relaxation of the lower back. Placing a ¾-inch plywood board underneath the mattress gives a firm, stable surface for the injured back. Sleeping on a water bed will often relieve low back pain. The value of a water bed is that it supports the body curves equally, decreasing abnormal pressures to any one body area.

- What do you think happened?
- Did you hit someone with or land directly on the top of your head?
- Were you knocked out or unconscious? Anytime an impact is sufficient to cause unconsciousness, the potential for injury to the spine exists.
- Do you have any pain in your neck?
- Do you have tingling, numbness, or burning in your shoulders, arms, or hands?
- Do you have equal muscle strength in both hands?
- Are you able to move your ankles and toes? Any sensory or motor changes bilaterally may indicate some spinal cord injury.

A yes response to any of these questions will necessitate extreme caution when moving the athlete. In cases of suspected cervical spine injury, if the coach is going to make a mistake, the error should be made in being overly cautious. Emergency care of the athlete with suspected cervical spine injury was discussed in detail in Chapter 7.

Once cervical spine injury has been ruled out, other general questions may provide some indication as to the nature of the problem.

- Where is the pain located?
- What kind of pain do you have?
- What were you doing when the pain began?
- Were you standing, sitting, bending, or twisting?
- Did the pain begin immediately?
- How long have you had this pain?
- Do certain movements or positions cause more pain?
- Can you assume a position that gets rid of the pain?
- Is there any tingling or numbness in the arms or legs?
- Is there any pain in the buttocks or the back of the legs?
- Have you ever had any back pain before?
- What position do you usually sleep in? How do you prefer to sit?

It is important to remember that pain in the back may be caused by many different conditions. The source may be musculoskeletal or visceral, or it may be referred.

Observation

Observing the posture and movement capabilities of the athlete during the evaluation can help clarify the nature and extent of the injury. General observations relative to posture include the following:

- Is the athlete willing to move the head and neck freely?
- Are the shoulders level and symmetrical?
- Is the head tilted to one side?

- Is one scapula lower or more prominent than the other?
- Is the trunk bent or curved to one side?
- Is the space between the body and arm greater on one side?
- Is one hip more prominent than the other?
- Are the hips tilted to one side?
- Are the ribs more pronounced on one side?
- Does one arm hang longer than the other?
- Does one arm hang farther forward than the other?
- Is one patella lower than the other?

Palpation

Palpation should be performed with the athlete lying prone and the spine as straight as possible. The head and neck should be slightly flexed. In cases of low back pain, a pillow placed under the hips might make the athlete more comfortable. The spinous processes and transverse process of each vertebrae along with the sacrum and coccyx should be palpated for spots of tenderness or increases in pain. The musculature on each side of the spine should also be palpated for tenderness or guarding. Palpation should progress from proximal to distal. It should be remembered that referred pain can produce tender areas away from the site of injury.

Special Tests

Special tests for the lumbar spine should be performed in standing, sitting, supine, side-lying, and prone positions.[6] Special tests include testing both the cervical and lumbar spines in forward bending, backward bending, side bending, and rotation. Any increase in pain or restriction in movement would indicate the existence of some condition or injury that should be referred for further evaluation.[6]

Straight Leg Raises

Straight leg raising applies pressure to the sacroiliac joint and may indicate either a problem in the sciatic nerve, the sacroiliac joint, or the lumbar spine (Figure 20-9).

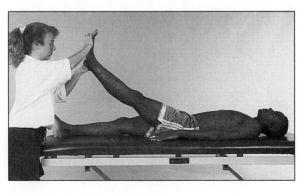

Figure 20-9

Straight leg raising test

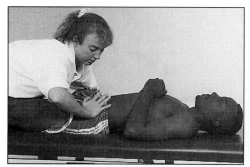

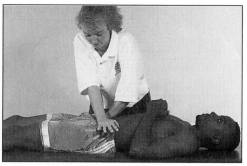

A

B

Figure 20-10

A, Sacral compression. B, Sacral distraction

Compression and Distraction Tests

Sacroiliac compression and distraction tests are useful in determining if there is a problem in the sacroiliac joint (Figure 20-10).

RECOGNITION AND MANAGEMENT OF CERVICAL SPINE INJURIES AND CONDITIONS

Because the neck is so mobile, it is extremely vulnerable to a wide range of sports injuries.[18] Although relatively uncommon, severe sports injury to the neck can produce catastrophic impairment of the spinal cord (Figure 20-11). The neck is also prone to subtle injuries stemming from stress, tension, and postural malalignments.

Figure 20-11

The possibility of cervical neck injury is always present in sport.

Cervical Fractures

Cause of injury   Fortunately, the incidence of neck fracture is relatively uncommon in athletics. Nevertheless, the coach must constantly be prepared to handle such a situation should it arise. **Axial loading** of the cervical vertebra from a force to the top of the head combined with flexion of the neck can result in an anterior compression fracture or possibly a dislocation.[14] If the head is also rotated when making contact, a dislocation may occur along with the fracture. Those sports having the highest incidence of neck fractures are gymnastics, ice hockey, diving, football, and rugby.[15]

Signs of injury   The athlete may have one or more of the following signs of cervical fracture: neck point tenderness and restricted movement, cervical muscle spasm, cervical pain and pain in the chest and extremities, numbness in trunk and/or limbs, weakness or paralysis in limbs and/or trunk, a loss of bladder and/or bowel control.

Care   An unconscious athlete should be treated as if a serious neck injury is present until this possibility is ruled out by the physician. Extreme caution must be used in moving the athlete.[1] The coach must always be aware that an athlete can sustain a catastrophic spinal injury from improper handling and transportation (see Chapter 7 for a detailed description of the emergency care of spinal injuries).

> **axial loading**
> A blow to the top of the athlete's head while in flexion.

Cervical Dislocations

Cause of injury   Cervical dislocations are not common, but they do occur much more frequently in sports than do fractures. Dislocations usually result from violent flexion and rotation of the head, as would occur in pool diving accidents.

Signs of injury   For the most part, a cervical dislocation produces many of the same signs as a fracture. Both can result in considerable pain, numbness, and muscle weakness or paralysis. The most easily discernible difference is the position of the neck in a dislocation: a unilateral dislocation causes the neck to be tilted toward the dislocated side with extreme muscle tightness on the elongated side and a relaxed muscle state on the tilted side.

Care   Since a dislocation of a cervical vertebrae has a greater likelihood of causing injury to the spinal cord, even greater care must be exercised when moving the patient. The procedures described in Chapter 7 should be applied to cervical dislocations.

> A unilateral cervical dislocation can cause the neck to tilt toward the dislocated side, with tight muscles on the elongated side and relaxed muscles on the tilted side.

Acute Muscle Strains of the Neck and Upper Back

Cause of injury   In a strain of the neck or upper back, the athlete has usually turned the head suddenly or has forced flexion, extension, or rotation. Muscles involved are typically the upper trapezius, sternocleidomastoid, the scalenes on the front of the neck, and the splenius capitis and cervicis.

Signs of injury   Localized pain, point tenderness, and restricted

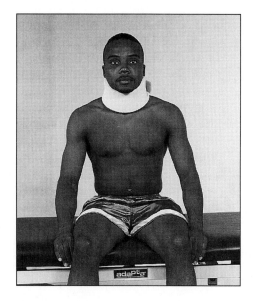

Figure 20-12

Wearing a soft cervical collar
helps reduce pain and spasm
in an athlete with an injured
neck.

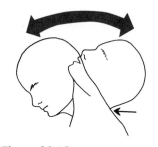

Figure 20-13

Whiplash injury

motion are present. Muscle guarding resulting from pain is common, and there is a reluctance to move the neck in any direction.

Care   Care usually includes use of RICE immediately after the strain occurs and use of a cervical collar (Figure 20-12). Follow-up management may include range of motion exercises followed by isometric progressing followed by full-range isotonic strengthening exercises in addition to cold or superficial heat and analgesic medications as prescribed by the physician.

Cervical Sprain (Whiplash)

Cause of injury   A cervical sprain can occur from the same mechanism as the strain but usually results from a more violent motion. More commonly, a cervical sprain occurs when the head snaps suddenly, such as when the athlete is tackled or blocked while unprepared (Figure 20-13). Frequently muscle strains occur with ligament sprains. A sprain of the neck produces tears in the major supporting tissue of the anterior or posterior longitudinal ligaments, the interspinous ligament, or the supraspinous ligament.

Signs of injury   The sprain displays all the signs of the strained neck but the symptoms persist longer. There may also be tenderness over the transverse and spinous processes that serve as sites of attachment for the ligaments. Pain may not be experienced initially but always appears the day after the trauma.

Care   As soon as possible, the athlete should have a physician evaluation to rule out the possibility of fracture, dislocation, or disk injury. A soft cervical collar may be applied to reduce muscle spasm. RICE is used for forty-eight to seventy-two hours while the injury is in the acute stage of healing. In an athlete with a severe injury, the physician may prescribe two to three days of bed rest along with analgesics and antiinflammation agents. Therapy might include cold or heat and massage. Mechanical traction may also be prescribed to relieve pain and muscle spasm.

Acute Torticollis (Wryneck)

Cause of injury   Acute torticollis is a very common condition, more frequently called wryneck or stiffneck. The athlete usually complains of pain on one side of the neck when awakening. Wryneck happens when a small piece of synovial membrane lining the joint capsule is impinged or trapped between the cervical vertebrae. This problem can also occasionally follow exposure to a cold draft of air or holding the head in an unusual position over a period of time.

Signs of injury   During inspection, there is palpable point tenderness and muscle spasm. Head movement is restricted to the side opposite the irritation with marked muscle guarding. X-ray examination will rule out a more serious injury.

Care   Cold or heat and massage may be used to modulate pain in an attempt to break a pain-spasm-pain cycle. Gentle traction, rotation, and lateral bending, first in the pain-free direction then in the direction of pain, can help reduce the guarding. The athlete may find it helpful to wear a soft cervical collar for comfort (see Figure 20-12). This muscle guarding will generally last for two to three days, during which the athlete progressively regains motion.

Pinched Nerve (Brachial Plexus Injury)

Cause of injury   A pinched nerve resulting from stretching or compression of the brachial plexus is the most common of all cervical neurological injuries in the athlete.[10] Other terms commonly used to indicate this condition are stinger or burner.[16] The primary mechanism of injury is the stretching of the brachial plexus of nerves when the neck is forced laterally to the opposite side while the shoulder is depressed, as would occur with a shoulder block in football.

Signs of injury   The athlete complains of a burning sensation, numbness and tingling, and pain extending from the shoulder down to the hand, with some loss of function of the arm and hand that lasts for several minutes. Rarely, symptoms may persist for several days. Neck range of motion is usually normal. Repeated brachial plexus nerve stretch injuries may result in permanent damage.[9]

Care   Once the symptoms have completely resolved and there are no associated neurological symptoms, the athlete may return to full activity. Thereafter the athlete should begin strengthening and stretching exercises for the neck musculature. A football player should be fitted with shoulder pads and a cervical neck roll to limit neck range of motion during impact.

RECOGNITION AND MANAGEMENT OF LUMBAR SPINE INJURIES AND CONDITIONS

Low Back Pain

Low back pain is one of the most common and disabling ailments known to humans. In sports, back problems are common and are most often the result of either congenital anomalies, mechanical back defects caused mainly by faulty posture, or trauma to the back including sprains, strains, or contusions.

With repeated episodes of injury, the athlete may develop recurrent or chronic low back pain. Gradually this problem could lead to muscular weakness and impairment of sensation and reflex responses. The older the athlete, the more prone he or she is to developing chronic low back pain. The incidence of this condition at the high school level is low, but it becomes progressively greater with increasing age.

The athlete, like everyone else in the population, can prevent low back pain by avoiding unnecessary stresses and strains associated with standing, sitting, lying, working, or exercising. Care should be taken to avoid postures and positions that can cause injuries (see the Focus Box on page 449).

Lumbar Vertebrae Fracture and Dislocation

Cause of injury   Fractures in the lumbar region of the vertebral column are not serious in terms of bone injury, but they pose dangers when related to spinal cord damage. Lumbar vertebrae fractures of the greatest concern in sports are compression fractures and fractures of the transverse and spinous processes.

The compression fracture may occur as a result of hyperflexion of the trunk. Falling from a height and landing on the feet or buttocks may also produce a compression fracture. Fractures of the transverse and spinous processes result most often from a kick or other direct impact to the back. Dislocations of the lumbar vertebrae in sports are rare, occurring only when there is an associated fracture.

Signs of injury   Recognition of the compression fracture is difficult without an x-ray examination. A basic evaluation may be made with a knowledge of the history and point tenderness over the affected vertebrae. Fractures of the transverse and spinous processes may be directly palpable. There will be point tenderness and some localized swelling along with muscle guarding to protect the area.

Care   If the symptoms and signs associated with a fracture are present, the injured athlete should be x-rayed. Transporting and moving the athlete should be done on a spine board as described in Chapter 7 in an effort to minimize movement of the fractured segment.

Low Back Muscle Strains

Cause of injury   There are two mechanisms of the typical low back strain in sports activities.[3] The first happens from a sudden extension, usually in combination with trunk rotation. The second is the chronic strain commonly associated with faulty posture.

Signs of injury   Evaluation should be performed immediately after injury to rule out the possibility of fracture. Discomfort in the low back may be diffused or localized in one area. Pain will be present on active extension and with passive flexion.

Care   Initially, cold packs and/or ice massage should be used to decrease muscle spasm. An elastic wrap or an abdominal support corset-type brace will help compress the area (Figure 20-14). A graduated program of stretching and strengthening begins slowly during the acute stage. Injuries of moderate-to-severe intensity may require complete bed rest to help break the pain–muscle spasm cycle.

Lumbar Sprains

Cause of injury   Sprains may occur in any of the ligaments in the lumbar spine. The most common sprain occurs when the athlete is bending forward and twisting while lifting or moving some object. Lumbar sprain can occur with a single episode or with chronic repetitive stress that becomes progressively worse with activity.

Signs of injury   The pain is localized and is located just lateral to the spinous process. Pain becomes sharper with certain movements or postures, and the athlete will limit movement in painful ranges. Flexion, extension, and rotational movements of the vertebrae can increase pain.

Care   Initial treatment should include RICE to reduce pain. Strengthening exercises for abdominals and back extensors as well as stretching in all directions should be limited to a pain-free range. An abdominal brace or support should be worn to limit movement during early

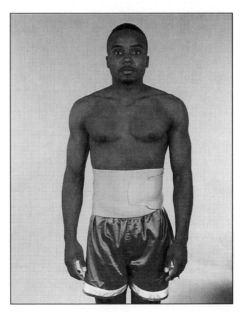

Figure 20-14

An abdominal brace helps support the lumbar area.

return to activity. As with sprains to other joints in the body, some time will be required for healing.

Back Contusions

Cause of injury   Back contusions rank third to strains and sprains in incidence. Because of its surface area, the back is quite vulnerable to bruises in sports. Football produces the greatest number of these injuries. A significant impact to the back could cause serious injury to the kidneys. Contusion of the back must be distinguished from a vertebral fracture. In some instances this distinction is possible only through an x-ray examination.

Signs of injury   The bruise causes local pain, muscle spasm, and point tenderness. A swollen, discolored area may be visible also.

Care   Cold and pressure should be applied immediately for approximately seventy-two hours or longer along with rest. Ice massage combined with gradual stretching benefits soft-tissue contusion in the region of the low back. Recovery usually ranges from two days to two weeks.

Sciatica

Cause of injury   The term *sciatica* has been incorrectly used as a general term to describe all low back pain without reference to exact causes. **Sciatica** is an inflammatory condition of the sciatic nerve that can accompany recurrent or chronic low back pain. This nerve is particularly vulnerable to torsion or direct blows that tend to impose abnormal stretching and pressure on it as it emerges from the spine.[5]

Signs of injury   Sciatica may begin either abruptly or gradually. It produces a sharp shooting pain that follows the nerve pathway along the posterior and medial thigh. There may also be some tingling and numbness along its path. The nerve may be extremely sensitive to palpation. Straight leg raising usually intensifies the pain.

Care   In the acute stage, rest is essential. The cause of the inflammation must be identified and treated. If there is a disk protrusion, lumbar traction may be appropriate. Since recovery from sciatia usually occurs within two to three weeks, surgery should be delayed to see if symptoms resolve. Oral antiinflammatory medication may help reduce inflammation.

Herniated Lumbar Disk

Cause of injury   The mechanism of a disk injury is the same as that of the lumbar sprain—forward bending and twisting that places abnormal strain on the lumbar region. This movement produces herniation or bulging of the nucleus pulposus of a disk on a nerve root (Figure 20-15).[8] The pain associated with disk herniation is substantial. The disk most often injured lies between the L4 and the L5 vertebrae.

Signs of injury   A herniated lumbar disk usually creates centrally located pain that radiates on one side to the buttocks and down the back of the leg or pain that spreads across the back. Symptoms are worse on ris-

sciatica (sigh **at** tika)
Inflammatory condition of the sciatic nerve; commonly associated with peripheral nerve root compression.

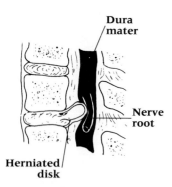

Figure 20-15

Intervertebral disk syndrome

ing in the morning. Onset may be sudden or gradual, with pain increasing after the athlete sits and then tries to resume activity. Posture will exhibit a slight forward bend with side bending away from the side of pain. Straight leg raising increases pain.

Care   Initially, rest and ice should be used to help modulate pain. Backward bending or extension makes the athlete more comfortable. As pain and posture return to normal, back extensor and abdominal strengthening should be used. Sometimes the symptoms will resolve with time. But signs of nerve damage may necessitate surgery.

Spondylolysis and Spondylolisthesis

Cause of condition   Spondylolysis refers to a degeneration of the vertebrae and, more commonly, a defect in the articular processes of the vertebrae (Figure 20-16A).[17] It is often attributed to a congenital weakness with the defect occurring as a stress fracture. It is more common among boys.[7] Sports movements that characteristically hyperextend the spine, such as arching back in gymnastics, lifting weights, blocking in football, serving in tennis, spiking in volleyball, and using the butterfly stroke in swimming, are most likely to cause this condition.[17]

Spondylolisthesis is a complication of spondylolysis often resulting in hypermobility of a vertebral segment.[5] Spondylolisthesis has the highest incidence with L5 slipping on S1 (Figure 20-16B). A direct blow or sudden twist or chronic low back strain may cause the defective vertebra to displace itself forward on the sacrum.

Signs of condition   The athlete complains of persistent aching pain or stiffness across the low back, with increased pain after, not usually

Spondylolisthesis is considered to be a complication of a spondylolysis.

Figure 20-16

A, Spondylolysis. B, Spondylolisthesis

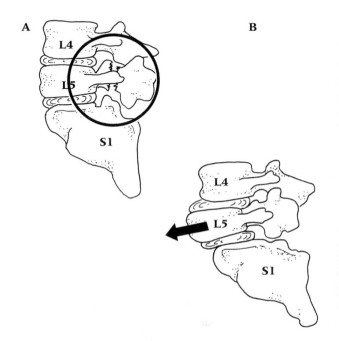

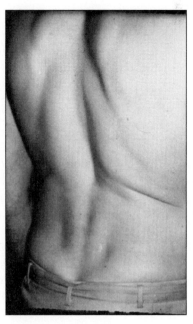

20-2

Critical Thinking E x e r c i s e

A gymnast constantly hyperextends her low back. She complains of stiffness and persistent aching pain across the low back with increased pain after but not during practice. The athlete feels that she needs to change positions frequently or self-manipulate her low back to reduce the pain. She is beginning to develop pain in her buttock and some muscle weakness in her leg.

? What type of injury should the coach suspect? Can anything be done about it?

during, physical activity. The athlete feels the need to change positions frequently or "pop" the low back to reduce the pain. There may be tenderness localized to one segment.

Care Initially, bracing and occasionally bed rest for one to three days will help to reduce pain. The major focus in rehabilitation should be directed toward exercises that control or stabilize the hypermobile segment. Progressive trunk-strengthening exercises, especially through the midrange, should be incorporated. Braces are most helpful during high-level activities. It may be necessary for the athlete to avoid vigorous activity.

SACROILIAC JOINT DYSFUNCTION

The sacroiliac is the junction formed by the ilium and the sacrum, and it is fortified by strong ligaments that allow little motion to take place. Since the sacroiliac joint is a synovial joint, disorders can include sprain, inflammation, hypermobility, and hypomobility.[2]

Sacroiliac Sprain

Cause of injury A sprain of the sacroiliac joint may result from twisting with both feet on the ground, stumbling forward, falling backward, stepping too far down and landing heavily on one leg, or forward bending with the knees locked during lifting.[12]

Signs of injury A sprain of the sacroiliac joint may have palpable pain and tenderness directly over the joint with some associated muscle guarding. Hip levels may appear to be asymmetrical.

Care Ice can be used to reduce pain. A supportive brace is also helpful in an acute sprain. Strengthening exercises should be incorporated to improve stability to a hypermobile joint.

Coccyx Injuries

Cause of injury Coccygeal injuries in sports are prevalent and occur primarily from direct impact, which may result from forcibly sitting down, falling, or being kicked by an opponent. Injuries to the coccyx may include sprains, contusions, or fractures.

Signs of injury Pain in the coccygeal region is often prolonged and at times chronic. There is tenderness over the bone, and the athlete will have difficulty sitting.

Care Treatment consists of analgesics and a ring seat to relieve the pressure on the coccyx while sitting. It should be noted that pain from a fractured coccyx may last for many months. Once a coccygeal injury has healed, the athlete should be protected against reinjury by appropriately applied padding.

SUMMARY

- The spine, or vertebral column, is composed of thirty-three individual vertebrae. The design of the spine allows for flexion, extension, lateral flexion, and rotation. The movable vertebrae are separated by intervertebral disks, and position is maintained by a series of muscular and ligamentous supports. The spine can be divided into three different regions: the cervical, thoracic, and lumbar regions. The sacrum and coccyx are fused vertebrae within the vertebral column.

- The spinal cord is that portion of the central nervous system that is contained within the vertebral canal of the spinal column. Thirty-one pairs of spinal nerves extend from the sides of the spinal cord.

- Acute traumatic injuries to the spine can be potentially life threatening, particularly if the cervical region of the spinal cord is involved. Thus the athlete must do everything possible to minimize injury. Strengthening of the musculature of the neck is critical. In addition to strong muscles, the athlete's neck should have a full range of motion. Athletes involved in collision sports must be taught and required to use techniques that reduce the likelihood of cervical injury.

- Low back pain is one of the most common and disabling ailments known to humans. The athlete, like everyone else in the population, can prevent low back pain by avoiding unnecessary stresses and strains associated with standing, sitting, lying, working, or exercising. Care should be taken to avoid postures and positions that can cause injuries.

- The most critical part of assessment of the spine is to rule out the possibility of spinal cord injury. Observing the posture and movement capabilities of the athlete during the evaluation can help clarify the nature and extent of the injury.

- Because the cervical and lumbar regions of the spine are so mobile, they are extremely vulnerable to a wide range of sports injuries, including fractures, dislocations, strains, sprains, contusions, lesions of the intervertebral disks, herniations, injuries to spinal nerves, and degenerative conditions.

Solutions to Critical Thinking Exercises

20-1 Given this set of existing conditions, the athletic trainer should have the athlete engage in extension exercises to strengthen the back extensors, stretch the abdominals, and reduce the pressure on the intervertebral disks.

20-2 The gymnast likely has a spondylolisthesis that has resulted in hypermobility of a vertebral segment.

Initially, rest will help to reduce pain. The major focus in rehabilitation should be directed toward exercises that control or stabilize the hypermobile segment. Progressive trunk-strengthening exercises, especially to the abdominal muscles through the midrange, should be incorporated. A brace can be helpful during practice.

REVIEW QUESTIONS

1. Identify the various regions of the spine.
2. What is the relationship between the spinal cord and the nerve roots?
3. Discuss the various considerations in prevention of cervical injuries.
4. Describe the special tests used in evaluating the lumbar and sacroiliac portions of the spine.

5. What can be done to minimize the incidence of low back pain?
6. Describe the mechanism of injury for a herniated disk.
7. How does a spondylolysis become a spondylolisthesis?
8. What is the usual mechanism for injury to the sacroiliac joint?

REFERENCES

1. Anderson C: Neck injuries, backboard, bench, or return to play, *Physician Sportsmed* 21(8):23, 1993.
2. Cibulka M: The treatment of the sacroiliac joint component to low back pain, *Phys Ther* 72(12):917, 1992.
3. DeRosa C, Poterfield J: A physical therapy model for the treatment of low back pain, *Phys Ther* 72(4):261, 1992.
4. Fourre M: On-site management of cervical spine injuries, *Physician Sportsmed* 19:4, 1991.
5. Herring S, Weinstein S: Assessment and neurological management of athletic low back injury. In Nicholas J, Herschman E: *The lower extremity and spine in sports medicine,* St Louis, 1995, Mosby.
6. Hooker D: Back rehabilitation. In Prentice W: *Rehabilitation techniques in sports medicine,* Dubuque, Iowa, 1998, WC Brown/McGraw-Hill.
7. Johnson R: Low back pain in sports: managing spondylolysis in young athletes, *Physician Sportsmed* 21(4):53, 1993.
8. Lord M, Carson W: Management of herniated lumbar disks in the athlete, *Sports Med Digest* 16:1, 1994.
9. Markey K, Benedetto M, Curl W: Upper trunk and brachial plexopathy, *Am J Sports Med,* 21(5):650, 1993.
10. Rapport L, O'Leary P, Cammisa F: Diagnosis and treatment of cervical spine injuries. In Nicholas J, Herschman E: *The lower extremity and spine in sports medicine,* St Louis, 1995, Mosby.
11. Rodriquez J: Clinical examination and documentation. In Hochschuler S, Cotler H, Guyer R: *Rehabilitation of the spine: science and practice,* St Louis, 1993, Mosby.
12. Saunders D: *Evaluation, treatment, and prevention of musculoskeletal disorders,* Bloomington, Minn, 1985, Educational Opportunities.
13. Storey MD: Anterior neck trauma, *Physician Sportsmed* 17(9):85, 1993.
14. Torg JS et al: The axial load teardrop fracture, *Am J Sports Med* 19(4):355, 1991.
15. Torg J, Fay C: Cervical spinal stenosis with cord neurapraxia and transcient quadriplegia. In Torg J: *Athletic injuries to the head, neck, and face,* St Louis, 1991, Mosby.
16. Vereschagin KS et al: Burners, *Physician Sportsmed* 1(9):96, 1991.
17. Weber MD, Woodall WR: Spondylogenic disorders in gymnasts, *JOSPT* 14(1):6, 1991.
18. Wilkerson JE, Maroon JC: Cervical spine injuries in athletes, *Physician Sportsmed* 18(3):57, 1990.

ANNOTATED BIBLIOGRAPHY

Hochschuler S, Cotler H, Guyer R: *Rehabilitation of the spine: science and practice,* St Louis, 1993, Mosby.

A comprehensive text that focuses on all aspects of treatment and rehabilitation of the spine. Injuries that are specific to individual sports are discussed.

Nicholas J, Herschman E: *The lower extremity and spine in sports medicine,* St Louis, 1995, Mosby.

This two-volume text discusses all aspects of injury to the extremities and the spine. The section on evaluation and treatment of spinal conditions is concise but thorough.

Torg JS, editor: *Head and neck injuries.*

Clinics in sports medicine, vol 6, no 1, Philadelphia, 1991, WB Saunders.

In-depth coverage of head and neck injuries stemming from sports activities.

White A, Schofferman J: *Spine care:* *diagnosis and conservative treatment,* vol. 1, St Louis, 1995, Mosby.

A two-volume set that looks at both conservative and surgical management of back injuries.

WEB SITES

World Ortho: http://www.worldortho.com

Use the search engine in this site to locate relevant information.

Wheeless' Textbook of Orthopaedics: http://www.medmedia.com/med/htm

An excellent page for injuries, anatomy, and x rays.

Karolinska Institute Library: Musculoskeletal Disease: http://www.mic.ki.se/Disease/c5.htm

American Orthopaedic Society for Sports Medicine: http://www.sports-med.org

Spinal Cord 101: http://www.goes.com/billr/html/_spinal_cord_101.html

The Cleveland Clinic Foundation: Spinal Cord Trauma: http://www.anes.ccf.org:8080/PILOT/NEURO/sci.htm

The Thorax and Abdomen

When you finish this chapter you will be able to:

- Describe the anatomy of the thorax and abdomen.
- Identify the location and function of the heart and lungs.
- Identify the location and function of the abdominal viscera.
- Describe the techniques for assessing thoracic and abdominal injuries.
- Identify various injuries to the structures of the thorax.
- Describe various injuries and conditions in structures of the abdomen.

his chapter covers major sports injuries to the thorax and abdomen. In an athletic environment, injuries to the thorax and abdomen have a lower incidence than injuries to the extremities. However, unlike the musculoskeletal injuries to the extremities discussed to this point, injuries to the heart, lungs, and abdominal viscera can be potentially serious and even life threatening if not recognized and managed appropriately. It is imperative for the coach to be familiar with anatomy and the more common injuries seen in the abdomen and thorax (Figure 21-1).

Figure 21-1

Collision sports can produce serious trunk injuries.

ANATOMY OF THE THORAX

The thorax is that portion of the body commonly known as the chest, which lies between the base of the neck and the diaphragm. It is contained within the thoracic vertebrae and the twelve pairs of ribs that give it its shape (Figure 21-2). Its main function is to protect the vital respiratory and circulatory organs and to assist the lungs in inspiration and expiration during the breathing process.[13]

The ribs are flat bones that are attached to the thoracic vertebrae in the back and to the sternum in the front. The upper seven ribs are called sternal or true ribs, and each rib is joined to the sternum by a separate costal cartilage. The eighth, ninth, and tenth ribs (false ribs) have cartilages that join each other and the seventh rib before uniting with the sternum. The eleventh and twelfth ribs (floating ribs) remain unattached to the sternum but do have muscle attachments. The intercostal muscles, which lie between the ribs, and the diaphragm muscle, which separates the thoracic cavity, from the abdominal cavity, function in inspiration and expiration (Figure 21-3).

ANATOMY OF THE ABDOMEN

The abdominal cavity lies between the diaphragm and the pelvis and is bounded by the margin of the lower ribs, the abdominal muscles, and the vertebral column. The abdominal muscles—the rectus abdominis, the external and internal obliques, and the transverse abdominis—collectively produce trunk flexion and rotation, but more important, they function to protect the underlying abdominal viscera (Figure 21-4).[13]

The thoracic cage protects the heart and lungs.

Figure 21-2

The thoracic cage

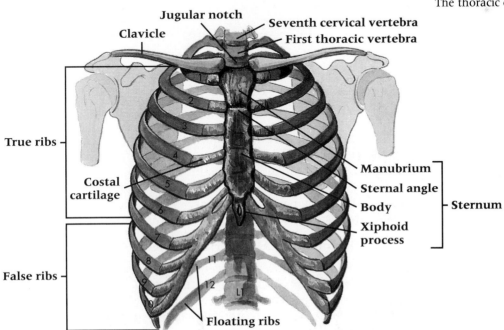

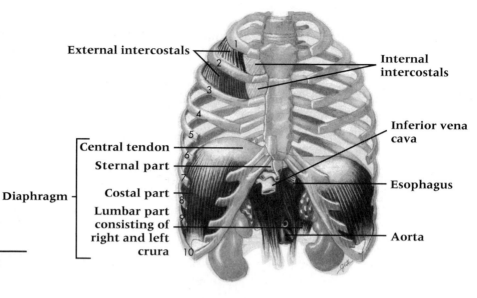

External intercostals

**Internal
intercostals**

**Inferior vena
cava**

Central tendon

Sternal part

Esophagus

Diaphragm

Costal part

**Lumbar part
consisting of
right and left
crura**

Aorta

Figure 21-3

Anatomy of the thoracic
muscles

Figure 21-4

The abdominal musculature

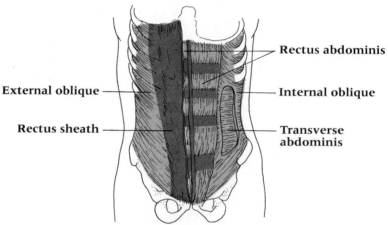

Rectus abdominis

External oblique

Internal oblique

Rectus sheath

**Transverse
abdominis**

Solid internal organs are
more at jeopardy from an
injury than are hollow
organs.

Abdominal viscera are part of
the urinary, digestive,
reproductive, and lymphatic
systems.

The abdominal viscera are composed of both hollow and solid organs.
The solid organs are the kidneys, spleen, liver, pancreas, and adrenal
glands. The hollow organs include the stomach, intestines, gallbladder,
and urinary bladder (Figure 21-5). Organs in the abdominal cavity may
be classified as being part of the urinary system, the digestive system, the
reproductive system, or the lymphatic system.[13]

PREVENTING INJURIES TO THE THORAX AND ABDOMEN

Injuries to the thorax may be prevented by wearing appropriate protective equipment, particularly in collision sport activities. In football, for
example, shoulder pads are usually designed to extend to at least below
the level of the sternum. Rib protectors may be worn to cover the entire
thoracic cage if necessary (Figure 21-6).

The muscles of the abdomen should be strengthened to provide pro-

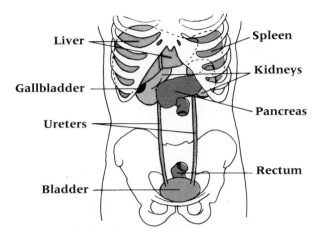

Liver — Spleen — Kidneys — Gallbladder — Pancreas — Ureters — Rectum — Bladder

Figure 21-5

Abdominal viscera

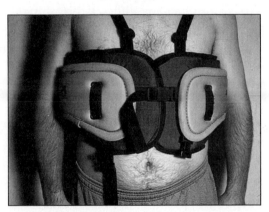

Figure 21-6

Protective rib belt

tection to the underlying viscera. A consistent regimen of sit-up exercises done in various positions can markedly increase the strength and size of the abdominal musculature.

Making sure that the hollow organs, in particular the stomach and bladder, are emptied prior to competition can reduce the chance of injury to those structures. Meals should be eaten at least three to four hours prior to competition to allow foods to clear the stomach. Urination immediately prior to stepping onto the field or court will protect the bladder from injury.

ASSESSMENT OF THE THORAX AND ABDOMEN

Injuries to the thorax and abdomen can produce potentially life-threatening situations. An injury that may seem to be relatively insignificant at first may rapidly develop into one that requires immediate and appropriate medical attention. Thus, for the coach evaluating an injury, the initial primary survey should focus on those signs and symptoms that indicate some life-threatening condition. The injured athlete should be continually monitored by the coach to identify any disruption of normal breathing or circulation or any indication of internal hemorrhage that could precipitate shock.

History

The questions asked to determine a history in the case of thoracic and abdominal injuries are somewhat different than those questions pertinent to musculoskeletal injuries of the extremities.[12] The primary mechanism of injury should be determined first.

- What happened to cause this injury?
- Was there direct contact or a direct blow?
- What position were you in?
- What type of pain is there? (sharp, dull, localized, etc.)
- Was there immediate or gradual pain?
- Do you feel any pain other than in the area where the injury occurred?
- Have you had any difficulty breathing?
- Are certain positions more comfortable than others?
- Do you feel faint, lightheaded, or nauseous?
- Do you feel any pain in your chest?
- Did you hear or feel a pop or crack in your chest?
- Have you had any muscle spasms?
- Have you noticed any blood in your urine?
- Is there any difficulty or pain in urinating?
- Was the bladder full or empty?
- How long has it been since you have eaten?

Observation

If the athlete is observed immediately following injury, check for normal breathing and respiratory patterns.

- Most important, is the athlete breathing at all?
- Is the athlete having difficulty breathing deeply, or is the athlete struggling to catch the breath?
- Does breathing cause pain?
- Is the athlete holding the chest wall?
- Is there symmetry in movement of the chest during breathing?
- If the wind was knocked out, did normal breathing return rapidly or was there prolonged difficulty? This difficulty may indicate a more severe injury.
- What is the body position of the athlete?
- Is there protrusion or swelling of any portion of the abdomen? This may indicate internal bleeding.
- Does the thorax appear to be symmetrical? Rib fractures can cause one side to appear different.
- Are the abdominal muscles tight and guarding?
- Is the athlete holding or splinting a specific part of the abdomen?

It is important to monitor vital signs, including pulse, respiration, and blood pressure. A rapid, weak pulse and/or a significant drop in blood pressure is an indication of some potentially serious internal injury often involving loss of blood.

Palpation

Thorax

The hands should first be placed on either side of the chest wall to check for symmetry in chest wall movement during deep inspiration and expiration and to begin to isolate areas of tenderness (Figure 21-7). Once a tender area is identified, the coach should palpate along the rib and in the space between the ribs to locate a specific point of tenderness.

Abdomen

To palpate the abdominal structures, the athlete should be supine with the arms at the side and the abdominal muscles relaxed (Figure 21-8). Uninjured areas should be palpated first with the tips of the fingers to feel for any tightness or rigidity. An athlete with an abdominal injury will voluntarily contract the abdominal muscles to guard or protect the

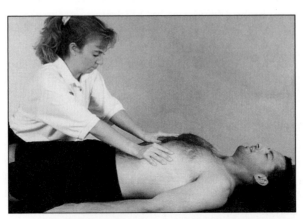

Figure 21-7

Checking asymmetry of chest wall during breathing

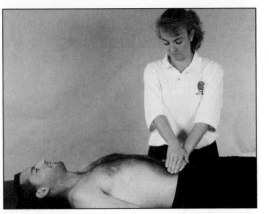

Figure 21-8

Palpating the abdomen for guarding or rigidity

tender area. If there is bleeding or irritation inside the abdominal cavity, the abdomen will exhibit what is referred to as boardlike rigidity and cannot be voluntarily relaxed. Pressure on the abdominal organs may elicit referred pain in predictable patterns away from the source.

RECOGNITION AND MANAGEMENT OF THORACIC INJURIES

Rib Contusions

Cause of injury A blow to the rib cage can contuse intercostal muscles between the ribs or, if severe enough, produce a fracture. Because the intercostal muscles are essential for breathing, when they are bruised, both expiration and inspiration become very painful.

Signs of injury Characteristically the pain is sharp during breathing, there is point tenderness, and pain is elicited when the rib cage is compressed. X-ray examination should be routine in such an injury.

Care RICE and antiinflammatory agents are commonly used. As with most rib injuries, contusions to the thorax are self-limiting, responding best to rest and cessation of sports activities.

Rib Fractures

Cause of injury Rib fractures are not uncommon in sports and have their highest incidence in collision sports, particularly in wrestling and football.[10] Fractures can be caused either by direct impact, as by a kick, or by compression of the rib cage, as may occur in football or wrestling. Ribs 5 through 9 are the most commonly fractured. There is always the possibility that a rib fracture can cause damage to or puncture the underlying lung.

Signs of injury The rib fracture is usually quite easily detected. The athlete complains of having severe pain during inspiration and point tenderness with sharp pain during palpation.

Care The athlete should be referred to the team physician for x-ray examination if there is any indication of fracture. The rib fracture is usually managed with support and rest. Simple fractures heal within three to four weeks. A rib brace can offer the athlete some rib cage stabilization and comfort (Figure 21-9).

Costal Cartilage Injury

Cause of injury Costal cartilage injuries have a higher incidence than do fractures. This injury can occur from a direct blow to the thorax or indirectly from a sudden twist or a fall on a ball, compressing the rib cage. A costal cartilage injury displays signs similar to the rib fracture, with the exception that pain is localized in the junction of the rib cartilage and rib (Figure 21-10).

Signs of injury The athlete complains of sharp pain during sudden movement of the trunk and of difficulty in breathing deeply. Palpation reveals point tenderness with swelling. In some cases there is a rib deformity and a complaint that the rib makes a crepitus noise as it moves in and out of place.

Care As with a rib fracture, the costal cartilage injury is managed

A rib fracture may be indicated by a severe, sharp pain during breathing.

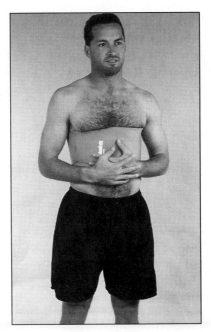

Figure 21-9

A commercial rib brace can provide moderate support to the thorax.

by rest and immobilization by rib brace. Healing takes anywhere from one to two months, precluding any sports activities until the athlete is symptom free.

Intercostal Muscle Injuries

Cause of injury   The muscles of the thorax are all subject to contusions and strains in sports. The intercostals are especially vulnerable. Traumatic injuries occur most often from direct blows or sudden torsion of the athlete's trunk.

Signs of injury   Like other muscle strains, pain occurs on active motion. However, injuries to muscles in this region are particularly painful during inspiration and expiration, laughing, coughing, or sneezing.

Care   Care requires immediate application of cold and compression for approximately one hour. After hemorrhaging has been controlled, immobilization should be used to make the athlete more comfortable (see Figure 21-9).

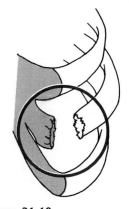

Figure 21-10

Costal cartilage injury

Injuries to the Lungs

Cause of injury   Fortunately, injuries to the lungs resulting from sports trauma are rare.[16] However, because of the seriousness of this type of injury, the coach must be able to recognize the basic signs. The most serious of the conditions are pneumothorax, tension pneumothorax, hemothorax, and traumatic asphyxia.

Pneumothorax is a condition in which the pleural cavity surrounding the lung becomes filled with air that has entered through an opening in the chest (Figure 21-11A).[14] As the pleural cavity fills with air, the lung on that side collapses.

Lung injuries can result in:
Pneumothorax
Tension pneumothorax
Hemothorax
Traumatic asphyxia

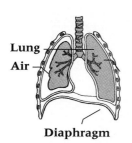
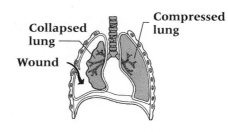
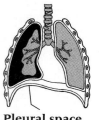

A. Pneumothorax   **B. Tension pneumothorax**   **C. Hemothorax**

Figure 21-11

A, Pneumothorax. B, Tension pneumothorax. C, Hemothorax.

A *tension pneumothorax* occurs when the pleural cavity on one side fills with air and displaces the lung and the heart toward the opposite side, thus compressing the opposite lung (Figure 21-11B).

Hemothorax is the presence of blood within the pleural cavity (Figure 21-11C). It results from the tearing or puncturing of the lung or pleural tissue, involving the blood vessels in the area.

Traumatic asphyxia occurs as the result of a violent blow to or a compression of the rib cage, causing a cessation of breathing.[6] A condition of this type demands immediate mouth-to-mouth resuscitation and medical attention.

Signs of injury   Signs may include breathing difficulty or shortness of breath; chest pain on the side of the injury; coughed up blood; cyanosis (bluish skin); and, potentially, shock. With a total collapse of the lung, medical attention is required immediately.

Care   Each of these conditions is a medical emergency requiring immediate physician attention. Thus, the athlete must be transported to the emergency room as quickly as possible.

Sudden Death Syndrome in Athletes

Common causes of sudden death syndrome:
Hypertrophic cardiomyopathy
Anomalous origin of the coronary artery
Marfan's syndrome

Cause of condition   The most common cause of exercise-induced sudden death in an athlete is some congenital cardiovascular abnormality.[1] The three most prevalent conditions are hypertrophic cardiomyopathy, anomalous origin of the coronary artery, and Marfan's syndrome.[7]

Signs of condition   Common symptoms and signs associated with cardiac causes of sudden death may include chest pain or discomfort during exertion, heart palpitations or flutters, syncope, nausea, profuse sweating, heart murmurs, shortness of breath, general malaise, and fever.[2]

Care   This condition is a life-threatening emergency situation that requires immediate access of the rescue squad.[8] The coach should be prepared to perform CPR until the rescue squad arrives (see Chapter 7).

Breast Problems

Cause of injury   Violent up-and-down and lateral movements of the breasts, such as are encountered in running and jumping, can bruise and strain the breast, especially in large-breasted women. Constant uncontrolled movements of the breast over a period of time can stretch the Cooper's ligament, which supports the breast at the chest wall, leading to premature sagging of the breasts (see Figure 6-15). Runner's nipples, in which the shirt rubs the nipples and causes an abrasion, can be prevented by placing an adhesive bandage over each nipple before participation. Bicyclist's nipples can also occur as the result of a combination of cold and evaporation of sweat, causing the nipples to become painful. Wearing a windbreaker can prevent this problem.[5]

Care Wearing a well-designed bra that has minimum elasticity and allows little vertical or horizontal breast movement is most desirable (see Figure 6-14).[5] Breast injuries usually occur during physical contact with either an opponent or equipment. In sports such as fencing or field hockey, female athletes should protect themselves by wearing plastic cup protectors.

RECOGNITION AND MANAGEMENT OF ABDOMINAL INJURIES

Although abdominal injuries comprise only about 10 percent of sports injuries, they can require long recovery periods and can be life threatening.[4] The abdominal area is particularly vulnerable to injury in all contact sports. A blow can produce superficial or even deep internal injuries, depending on its location and intensity.[4] In internal injuries of the abdomen that occur in sports, the solid organs are most often affected. Strong abdominal muscles give good protection when they are tensed, but when relaxed, the underlying organs may be easily injured. It is very important to protect the trunk region properly against the traumatic forces of collision sports. Good conditioning is essential, as is the use of proper protective equipment and the application of safety rules.

Injuries to the Abdominal Wall

Cause of injury Abdominal muscle strains occur with sudden twisting of the trunk or reaching overhead. The rectus abdominus is the most commonly strained abdominal muscle. Potentially these types of injuries can be very incapacitating.

Contusions to the abdominal wall occur because of compressive forces. Although not very common, when they do happen, they are more likely to occur in collision sports such as football or ice hockey; however, any sports implement or high-velocity projectile can cause injury. Hockey goalies and baseball catchers would be vulnerable to injury without their protective torso pads. The extent and type of injury varies depending on whether the force is blunt or penetrating.

Signs of injury An abdominal muscle strain or contusion of the rectus abdominis muscle can be very disabling. A severe blow may cause a hematoma that develops under the fascial tissue surrounding this muscle. The pressure that results from hemorrhage causes pain and tightness in the region of the injury.

Care Initially, ice and an elastic compression wrap should be used. The coach should also look for signs of possible internal injury. Treatment

Recognition and
Management of Specific
Injuries and Conditions

Inguinal hernias occur in
males; femoral hernias occur
in females.

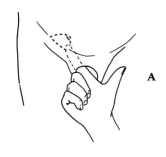

Figure 21-12

A, Inguinal hernia. B,
Femoral hernia

should be conservative, and exercise should be kept within pain-free
limits.

Hernia

Cause of injury The term *hernia* refers to the protrusion of abdominal viscera through a portion of the abdominal wall. Hernias resulting
from sports most often occur in the groin area. Inguinal hernias (Figure
21-12A), which occur in men (more than 75%), and femoral hernias
(Figure 21-12B), most often occurring in women, are the most prevalent
types. The inguinal hernia results from an abnormal enlargement of the
opening of the inguinal canal through which the vessels and nerves of
the male reproductive system pass. In contrast, the femoral hernia arises
in the canal that transports the vessels and nerves that go to the thigh and
lower limb.[9]

When intraabdominal tension is produced in these areas, muscles
produce contraction around these canal openings. If the muscles fail to
react, abdominal contents may be pushed through the opening.

Signs of injury A hernia may be recognized by the following: previous history of a blow or strain to the groin area that has produced pain
and prolonged discomfort; superficial protrusion in the groin area that is
increased by coughing; or reported feeling of weakness and pulling sensation in the groin area.

Care Most physicians think that any athlete who has a hernia
should be prohibited from engaging in hard physical activity until surgical repair has been made. Mechanical devices, designed to prevent her-
nial protrusion, are for the most part unsuitable in sports because of the
friction and irritation they produce. Exercise has been thought by many
to be beneficial to a mild hernia, but such is not the case. Exercise will
not affect the stretched inguinal or femoral canals positively.

Blow to the Solar Plexus

Cause of injury A blow to the middle portion of the abdomen, or
solar plexus, produces a transitory paralysis of the diaphragm (wind
knocked out). There should always be some concern that a blow hard
enough to knock out the wind could also cause internal organ injury.

Signs of injury Paralysis of the diaphragm stops respiration and
leads to anoxia. When the athlete is unable to inhale, short-term panic
may result. These symptoms are usually transitory. It is necessary to allay
such fears and instill confidence in the athlete.

Care In dealing with an athlete who has had the wind knocked out
of him or her, the coach should adhere to the following procedures: help
the athlete overcome apprehension by talking in a confident manner;
loosen the athlete's belt and the clothing around the abdomen; have the
athlete bend the knees; and encourage the athlete to relax by initiating
short inspirations and long expirations.

Because of the fear of not being able to breathe, the athlete may hyperventilate. Hyperventilation is an increased rate of ventilation that results in increased levels of oxygen. It causes a variety of physical reactions

such as dizziness, a lump in the throat, pounding heart, or fainting. The coach should have the athlete breath slowly into a paper bag to increase levels of carbon dioxide.

Stitch in the Side

Cause of injury   A stitch in the side is the name given an idiopathic condition that occurs in some athletes. The cause is obscure, although several hypotheses have been advanced. Among these causes are the following: constipation, intestinal gas, overeating, diaphragmatic spasm as a result of poor conditioning, lack of visceral support because of weak abdominal muscles, distended spleen, breathing techniques that lead to a lack of oxygen in the diaphragm, and ischemia of either the diaphragm or the intercostal muscles.

Signs of injury   A stitch in the side is a cramplike pain that develops on either the left or right costal border during hard physical activity. Sports that involve running apparently produce this condition.

Care   Immediate care of a stitch in the side demands relaxation of the spasm, for which two methods have proved beneficial. First, the athlete is instructed to stretch the arm on the affected side as high as possible. If this is inadequate, flexing the trunk forward on the thighs may prove of some benefit.

Athletes with recurrent abdominal spasms may need special study. Identification of poor eating habits, poor elimination habits, or an inadequate athletic training program may explain the athlete's particular problem. A stitch in the side, although not considered serious, may require further evaluation by a physician if abdominal pains persist.

Injury of the Spleen

Cause of injury   Injuries to the spleen are uncommon but occur most often because of a fall or a direct blow to the left upper quadrant of the abdomen when some existing medical condition has caused enlargement of the spleen. Infectious mononucleosis is the most likely cause of spleen enlargement.

Signs of injury   The gross indications of a ruptured spleen must be recognized so that an immediate medical referral can be made. Indications include a history of a severe blow to the abdomen and possibly signs of shock, abdominal rigidity, nausea, and vomiting. There may be a reflex pain occurring approximately thirty minutes after injury, called Kehr's sign, which radiates to the left shoulder and one third of the way down the left arm.[11] A ruptured spleen can hemorrhage profusely into the abdominal cavity, causing the athlete to die of internal bleeding days or weeks after the injury.

Care   Conservative nonoperative treatment is recommended initially along with a week of hospitalization.[11] At three weeks, the athlete can engage in light conditioning activities and at four weeks can fully return to activity as long as no symptoms appear. If surgical repair is necessary, the athlete will require three months to recover, whereas removal of the spleen will require six months before the athlete can return to activity.

A blow to the solar plexus can lead to transitory paralysis of the diaphragm and to unconsciousness.

21-2

Critical Thinking Exercise

A cross country runner complains of a recurring stitch in the side. She has a cramplike pain that develops on the left costal angle during a hard run. She indicates that when she stops running the cramp disappears but seems to come back if she starts to run again.

? What can the coach recommend to help this runner alleviate this problem?

Infectious mononucleosis can cause spleen enlargement.

Athletes who complain of external pain in the shoulders, trunk, or pelvis after a severe blow to the abdomen or back may be describing referred pain from an injury to an internal organ.

Recognition and
Management of Specific
Injuries and Conditions

21-3

Critical Thinking Exercise

A football receiver jumps to catch a high pass thrown over the middle. A defensive back hits the receiver in the low back. The athlete does not seem to have a specific injury. After the game he notices blood in his urine and becomes worried.

? Is blood in the urine a cause for concern, and what should the coach do to manage it?

Kidney and bladder contusions can cause hematuria.

Hepatitis can cause enlargement of the liver.

21-4

Critical Thinking Exercise

A soccer player is kicked in the abdomen above the umbilicus. Initially she had the wind knocked out of her. Now, she is complaining of pain and her abdomen is tight on palpation.

? What should the coach be most concerned about, and what organs may potentially be involved?

Appendicitis is often mistaken for a common gastric problem.

Kidney Contusion

Cause of injury   The kidneys are seemingly well protected within the abdominal cavity. However, on occasion, contusions and even ruptures of these organs occur. The kidney may be susceptible to injury because of its normal distention by blood. An external force applied to the back of the athlete will cause abnormal extension of an engorged kidney, resulting in injury.[3]

Signs of injury   An athlete who has received a contusion of the kidney may display signs of shock, nausea, vomiting, rigidity of the back muscles, and hematuria (blood in the urine). As with injuries to other internal organs, kidney injury may cause referred pain. Pain may radiate forward around the trunk into the lower abdominal region.

Care   Any athlete who reports having received a severe blow to the abdomen or back region should be instructed to urinate two or three times and to look for the appearance of blood in the urine. If there is any sign of hematuria, immediate referral to a physician must be made.[15] Medical care of the contused kidney usually consists of a twenty-four-hour hospital observation, with a gradual increase of fluid intake. If the hemorrhage fails to stop, surgery may be indicated. Controllable contusions usually require two weeks of bed rest and close surveillance after activity is resumed. In questionable cases, complete withdrawal from one active playing season may be required.

Liver Contusion

Cause of injury   In sports activities, liver injury is relatively infrequent. A hard blow to the right side of the rib cage can tear or seriously contuse the liver, especially if it has been enlarged as a result of some disease such as hepatitis.

Signs of injury   Liver injury can cause hemorrhage and shock, requiring immediate surgical intervention. Liver injury commonly produces a referred pain that is just below the right scapula, right shoulder, substernal area, and on occasion, the anterior left side of the chest.

Care   A liver contusion requires immediate referral to a physician for diagnosis and treatment.

Appendicitis

Cause of injury   Inflammation of the appendix can be chronic or acute. It is caused by a variety of factors, for example, a fecal obstruction. Its highest incidence is in males between the ages of fifteen and twenty-five. Appendicitis can be mistaken for a common gastric complaint. In its early stages, the appendix becomes red and swollen; in later stages it may become gangrenous, rupturing into the bowels and causing peritonitis.[15] Bacterial infection is a complication of rupture of the inflamed appendix.

Signs of injury   The athlete may complain of a mild-to-severe pain in the lower abdomen, associated with nausea, vomiting, and a low-grade fever ranging from 99° to 100° F (37° to 38° C). Later, the cramps may localize into a pain in the lower right side, and palpation may reveal abdominal rigidity and tenderness at a point between the anterior superior spine of the ilium and the umbilicus (McBurney's point).[15]

Care Surgical removal of the inflamed appendix is often necessary. If the bowel is not obstructed, there is no need to rush surgery. However, an obstructed bowel with an acute rupture is a life-threatening condition.

Injuries to the Bladder

Cause of injury On rare occasions a blunt force to the lower abdominal region may injure the urinary bladder that is distended by urine. The appearance of red blood cells within the urine (hematuria) is often associated with contusion of the bladder during running and has been referred to as a "runner's bladder."[17]

Signs of injury With any impact to the abdominal region, the possibility of internal damage must be considered, and after such trauma the athlete should be instructed to check periodically for blood in the urine. Bladder injury commonly causes referred pain to the lower trunk, including the upper thigh anteriorly. With a bladder rupture, the athlete will be unable to urinate.

Scrotal/Testicular Contusion

Cause of injury As the result of their considerable sensitivity and particular vulnerability, the scrotum and the testicles may sustain a contusion that causes a very painful, nauseating, and disabling condition.

Signs of injury As is characteristic of any contusion or bruise, there is hemorrhage, fluid effusion, and muscle spasm, the degree of which depends on the intensity of the impact to the tissue.

Care Immediately following a testicular contusion, the athlete is placed on his side and instructed to flex his thighs to his chest (Figure 21-13). As the pain diminishes, a cold pack is applied to the scrotum.

Injuries to the reproductive organs in sports are much more likely to occur in the male because the male genitalia is more exposed.

Figure 24-13

Body position following scrotum contusion

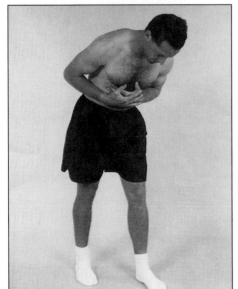

A

B

C

Increasing or unresolved pain after fifteen to twenty minutes requires prompt referral to a physician for evaluation.

Gynecological Injuries

In general the female reproductive organs have a low incidence of injury in sports. By far the most common gynecologic injury in the female athlete involves a contusion to the external genitalia, or vulva, which includes the labia, clitoris, and the vestibule of the vagina. A hematoma results from the contusion, which most often occurs with a direct impact to this area. A contusion of this area may also injure the pubis symphasis, producing ostitis pubis.

SUMMARY

- The thorax is that portion of the body commonly known as the chest, which lies between the base of the neck and the diaphragm. Its main functions are to protect the vital respiratory and circulatory organs and to assist the lungs in inspiration and expiration during the breathing process. Within the thoracic cage lie the lungs and the heart.

- The abdominal cavity lies between the diaphragm and the bones of the pelvis and is bounded by the margin of the lower ribs, the abdominal muscles, and the vertebral column. The abdominal viscera are composed of both hollow and solid organs. Organs in the abdominal cavity may be classified as being part of the urinary system, the digestive system, the reproductive system, or the lymphatic system.

- Injuries to the heart, lungs, and abdominal viscera can be potentially serious and even life threatening if not recognized and managed appropriately.

- For the coach evaluating an injury to the abdomen or thorax, the initial primary survey should focus on those signs and symptoms that indicate some life-threatening condition. Asking pertinent questions, observing body positioning, and palpation of the injured structures are critical in assessing the nature of the injury.

- Rib fractures and contusions, costal border injuries, muscle strains, and breast injuries are all common injuries to the chest wall.

- Injuries involving the lungs include pneumothorax, tension pneumothorax, hemothorax, and traumatic asphyxia.

- The most common cause of exercise-induced sudden death is some congenital cardiovascular abnormality. The three most prevalent conditions are hypertrophic cardiomyopathy, anomalous origin of the coronary artery, and Marfan's syndrome.

- Injuries to the abdominal wall include muscle strains, getting the wind knocked out, and the development of an inguinal or femoral hernia.

- With any injury to the abdominal region, internal injury to the abdominal viscera must be considered. Injuries to the liver, spleen, and kidneys are among the more common athletic injuries associated with the abdominal viscera.

- Injuries to the reproductive organs in sports are much more likely to occur in the male because the male genitalia is more exposed.

Solutions to Critical Thinking Exercises

21-1 Most often an athlete with a hernia will have some previous history of a blow or strain to the groin area that has produced pain and prolonged discomfort. There may be a superficial protrusion in the groin area that is increased by coughing, or the athlete may have a feeling of weakness and a pulling sensation in the groin area. An inguinal hernia results from an abnormal enlargement of the opening of the inguinal canal through which the abdominal contents may be pushed.

21-2 The coach should try to modify this athlete's eating habits, which might be producing constipation or gas. Cramps can be caused by improper breathing techniques that may cause a lack of oxygen in the diaphragm and ischemia of either the diaphragm or the intercostal muscles. Cramps may also be caused by a diaphragmatic spasm that results from poor conditioning or a lack of visceral support because of weak abdominal muscles.

Athletes with recurrent abdominal spasms should have further evaluation by a physician if the abdominal pains persist.

21-3 Anytime blood appears in the urine there is cause for concern. In this case it is likely that the kidneys have been contused and the blood that appears in the urine will disappear over the next couple of days. Nevertheless, the athlete should be referred to the team physician for diagnosis.

21-4 The coach should be concerned about the possibility of injury to an organ that can potentially lead to internal blood loss and eventually result in shock. It is possible that the spleen, liver, stomach, small intestine, pancreas, or gall bladder may all be injured. It is also possible that there may be a contusion to the muscles of the abdominal wall that is causing muscle guarding.

REVIEW QUESTIONS AND CLASS ACTIVITIES

1. Describe the anatomy of the thorax.
2. Differentiate among rib contusions, rib fractures, and costal border injuries.
3. Compare the signs of pneumothorax, tension pneumothorax, hemothorax, and traumatic asphyxia.
4. Identify the possible causes of sudden death syndrome among athletes.
5. List the abdominal viscera and other structures associated with the urinary system, the digestive system, the lymphatic system, and the reproductive system.
6. What muscles protect the abdominal viscera?
7. What conditions of the abdominal viscera produce pain in the abdominal region?
8. Contrast the signs of a ruptured spleen with signs of a severely contused kidney.
9. How do you manage an athlete who has had his or her wind knocked out?
10. Distinguish an inguinal hernia or a femoral hernia from a groin strain.
11. Describe the signs of a stitch in the side.

REFERENCES

1. Allison T: Counseling athletes at risk for sudden death, *Physician Sportsmed* 20(6):140, 1992.
2. Falsetti H: Sudden death syndrome, *Training and Conditioning* 5(3):24, 1995.
3. Freitas JE: Renal imaging following blunt trauma, *Pays Sports Ed* 17(12):59, 1989.
4. Haycock CE: How I manage abdominal injuries, *Physician Sportsmed* 14(6):86, 1986.
5. Haycock CE: How I manage breast problems in athletes, *Physician Sportsmed* 15(3):89, 1987.
6. Lee M, Wong S, Chu J: Traumatic asphyxia, *Ann Thoracic Surg* 51(1):86, 1991.
7. Maron B: Hypertrophic cardiomyopathy in athletes: catching a killer, *Physician Sportsmed* 21(9):83, 1993.
8. Maron B, Liviu C, Kaplan J, Mueller F: Blunt trauma to the chest leading to sudden death from cardiac arrest during sports activities, *New England J Med* 333(6):337, 1995.
9. McCarthy P: Hernias in athletes: what you need to know, *Physician Sportsmed* 18(5):115, 1990.
10. Miles J, Barrett G: Rib fractures in athletes, *Sports Med* 12(1):66, 1991.
11. Morden R, Berman B, Nagle C: Spleen injury in sports: avoiding splenectomy, *Physician Sportsmed* 20(4):126, 1992.
12. Reid D: *Sports injury assessment,* New York, 1992, Churchill and Livingstone.
13. Seeley R, Stephens T, Tate P: *Anatomy and physiology,* ed 3, St Louis, 1995, Mosby.
14. Simoneaux S, Murphy B, Tehranzadeh J: Spontaneous pneumothorax in a weight lifter, *Am J Sports Med* 18(6):647, 1990.
15. *Tabor's cyclopedic medical dictionary,* Philadelphia, 1993, FA Davis.
16. Wagner R, Sidhu G, Radcliffe W: Pulmonary contusion in contact sports, *Physician Sportsmed* 20(2):126, 1992.
17. York J: Bladder trauma from jogging, *Physician Sportsmed* 18(9):116, 1990.

ANNOTATED BIBLIOGRAPHY

Tabor's cyclopedic medical dictionary, Philadelphia, 1993, FA Davis.

Despite the dictionary format, this is an excellent guide for the athletic trainer who is searching for clear, concise descriptions of various injuries and illnesses accompanied by brief recommendations for management and treatment.

Seeley R, Stephens T, Tate P: *Anatomy and physiology,* ed 3, St Louis, 1995, Mosby.

This text clarifies anatomy of the various systems of the abdomen and thorax and also provides clinical correlations for specific injuries and illnesses.

WEB SITES

Acute Appendicitis: http://www.healthanswers.com/database/ami/converted/000256.html

Anatomy of the Human Body: http://rpiwww.nidacc.tmc.edu/mmlearn/anatomy.html

Chest Trauma: http://www.madsci.com/manu/trau_che.htm#30

National Heart, Lung, and Blood Institute: http://www.nhlbi.nib.gov/nhlbi/nhlbi.htm

The Head and Face

When you finish this chapter you will be able to:

- Describe major sports injuries to the head and face.
- Provide emergency care when appropriate and make informed medical referrals for head and face injuries.

S ports injuries to the head could be life threatening, whereas facial injuries could lead to disfigurement.

THE HEAD

Head injuries occur from direct and blunt forces to the skull. It is estimated that 30,000 to 40,000 major head injuries are reported and occasionally a death occurs during sport-related activities each year.[22]

Anatomy

Bones

The brain is housed in a skull composed of a series of bones joined together by sutures. The skull's thickness varies in different locations, being the thinnest over the temporal regions (Figure 22-1).

Scalp

The scalp is the soft-tissue covering of the skull. It is composed of skin and various types of connective tissue.[22]

Brain

The *brain* is the part of the central nervous system that is contained within the bony cavity of the cranium and is divided into four sections: the cerebrum, the cerebellum, the pons, and the medulla.

Surrounding the spinal cord and the brain are the meninges, which

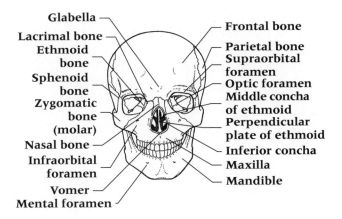

Glabella
Lacrimal bone
Ethmoid bone
Sphenoid bone
Zygomatic bone (molar)
Nasal bone
Infraorbital foramen
Vomer
Mental foramen

Frontal bone
Parietal bone
Supraorbital foramen
Optic foramen
Middle concha of ethmoid
Perpendicular plate of ethmoid
Inferior concha
Maxilla
Mandible

Figure 22-1

Bones of the skull

are the three membranes that protect the brain and the spinal cord. Outermost is the dura mater, a dense, fibrous, and inelastic sheath that encloses the brain and cord. A layer of fat that contains the vital arteries and veins separates this membrane from the bony wall, forming a space. The arachnoid is the second membrane and is extremely delicate. The space between the arachnoid and the third membrane, the pia mater, helps to contain the spinal fluid (Figure 22-2).

HEAD INJURIES

The head can sustain a variety of injuries in sports. Major types of injuries include trauma to the scalp, skull fractures, and brain injuries.

Brain Injuries

Closed head injuries are common problems in contact and collision sports. They can create medical, neurological, and psychological consequences.[12] Despite its considerable protection, the brain is subject to traumatic injury, and many head injuries that are incurred in sports have serious consequences (Figure 22-3).

The brain is one of the most vascular organs in the body. A constant supply of oxygen and blood to the brain is vital and critical to its survival. In the United States 7.5 million head injuries occur annually.[4]

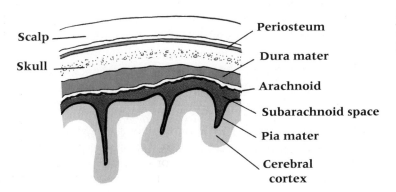

Scalp
Skull

Periosteum
Dura mater
Arachnoid
Subarachnoid space
Pia mater
Cerebral cortex

Figure 22-2

Cross section of the head and brain

Figure 22-3

Many head injuries incurred
in sports have serious
consequences.

Most traumas of the head result from direct or indirect blows and
may be classified as concussion injuries. Literally, *concussion* means an ag-
itation or a shaking from being hit, and *cerebral concussion* refers to the ag-
itation of the brain by either a direct or an indirect blow (Figure 22-4).
The indirect concussion most often comes from either a violent fall, in
which sitting down transmits a jarring effect through the vertebral column to the brain, or a blow to the chin. In most cases of cerebral concussion, there is a short period of unconsciousness having mild to severe
results.[4]

Most authorities agree that unconsciousness results from a lack of
oxygen to the brain resulting from the constriction of blood vessels. Depending on the force of the blow and the athlete's ability to withstand
such a blow, varying degrees of cerebral hemorrhage, edema, and tissue
tearing may occur.

Because of the fluid suspension of the brain, a blow to the head can
effect an injury to the brain either at the point of contact or on the opposite side. After the head is struck, the brain continues to move in the
fluid and may be contused against the opposite side. This action causes a
contrecoup brain injury.

On-the-Field Evaluation and Emergency Care

When an athletic trainer or other medical/emergency personnel is not
present, the coach is responsible for the emergency care of the athlete
having a possibly serious brain injury. *Cases of serious head injury almost always represent a life-threatening situation that requires that the athlete be admit-
ted to a hospital within a crucial thirty-minute period.*

All unconscious athletes
should be handled as if they
have a serious neck injury.

When called upon, the coach must have the basic knowledge to
recognize and interpret the major signs of brain injury. Priority first
aid for any head injury must always deal with the possibility of a life-
threatening condition such as an impaired airway or hemorrhage.[14]

Figure 22-4

Sports that use implements
can lead to serious head
injuries.

When an athlete is unconscious, a neck injury is always assumed. Before moving the athlete, the coach's on-the-field evaluation should include the following:

1. Look for the possibility of airway obstruction.[24] If breathing is obstructed, perform the following:
   a. The face mask is removed by cutting it away from the helmet while leaving the helmet in place.
   b. The athlete's head and neck are stabilized.
   c. The athlete's jaw is brought forward to clear the air passage (do not hyperextend the neck).
   d. The pulse is taken: If absent, cardiopulmonary resuscitation (CPR) is given; if present, oxygen may be given (see Chapter 7).
2. Make a quick observation of the following physical signs of concussion and/or skull fracture:
   a. Is the face color red or pale?
   b. Is the skin cool or moist?
   c. Is the pulse, if present, strong and slow or rapid and weak?
   d. Is breathing, if present, deep or shallow?
   e. Are the pupils dilated or unequal?
   f. Does the head show a swelling or deformity over the area of injury?

TABLE 22-1 Symptoms of cerebral concussion

Symptoms	Grade 1	Grade 2	Grade 3	Grade 4
Disorientation	+	+	++	+++
Dizziness		+	++	+++
Retrograde amnesia		+	++	+++
Posttraumatic amnesia			++	+++
Headache			+/++	+++
Loss of consciousness			+/++	+++
Problems in concentrating		+	++	+++
Tinnitus		+	++	+++
Balance problems		+	++	+++
Automatism			+/++	+++
Pupillary discrepancies			+/++	+++

+ Mild.
++ Moderate.
+++ Severe.

TABLE 22-2 Severity of concussion

Grade 1	Short period of confusion No loss of consciousness Concussion symptoms on examination resolve in *less* than 15 minutes
Grade 2	Short period of confusion No loss of consciousness Concussion symptoms on examination resolve in *more* than 15 minutes
Grade 3	Loss of consciousness

The athlete is then removed carefully from the playing site on a spine board as per Chapter 7, Emergency Situations and Injury Assessment. Athletes with distinct clinical signs should routinely be sent to the hospital for definitive care. The coach must also note that an initially mild concussion can deteriorate to a higher grade (see Table 22-1 and 22-2).

Additional Evaluation

Once the athlete regains consciousness, determining the status of the athlete's mental orientation and memory is imperative.[14] The coach can ask the athlete the following questions:

- Which team did we play last week?
- Who won the game last week?
- Who scored the last goal?
- What is today's date?

22-1

Critical Thinking Exercise

A football player sustains a cerebral concussion during a game.

? How should the coach determine the athlete's level of orientation and memory?

Testing Eye Signs

Because of the direct connection between the eye and the brain, pupillary discrepancies provide important information. The athlete should be observed and tested for the following:

- *Dilated and/or irregular pupils.* Checking pupil sizes may be particularly difficult at night and under artificial lights. To ensure accuracy, the athlete's pupil size should be compared with that of an official or another player. It should be remembered, however, that some individuals normally have pupils that differ in size.
- *Blurred vision.* Blurred vision is determined by difficulty or inability to read a game program or the score board.
- *Inability of the pupils to accommodate rapidly to light variance.* Eye accommodation should be tested by covering one eye with a hand. The covered eye normally will dilate, whereas the uncovered pupil will remain the same. When the hand is removed, the previously covered pupil normally will accommodate readily to the light. A slowly accommodating pupil may be an indicator of cerebral injury.
- *Inability of eyes to track smoothly.* The athlete is asked to hold the head in a neutral position, eyes looking straight ahead. The athlete is then asked to follow the top of a pen or pencil, first up as far as possible, then down as far as possible. The eyes are observed for smooth movement and any signs of pain. Next, the tip of the pen or pencil is slowly moved from left to right to determine whether the eyes follow the tip smoothly across the midline of the face or whether they make involuntary movements. A constant involuntary back and forth, up and down, or rotary movement of the eyeball indicates possible cerebral involvement.

Checking for eye signs can yield important information about possible brain injury.

Testing Balance

If the athlete can stand, the degree of unsteadiness must be noted. A brain concussion of grade 2 or more can produce balance difficulties. To test for balance, the athlete is told to stand tall with the feet together, arms at sides, eyes closed. A positive sign is one in which the athlete begins to sway, cannot keep eyes closed, or obviously loses balance. Having the athlete attempt to stand on one foot is also a good indicator of balance.

Concussion

Although the incidence of serious head injuries from football has decreased in recent years when compared with catastrophic neck injuries, the occurrence of football head injuries is of major concern. Every coach and athletic trainer must be able to recognize the signs of serious head injury to act appropriately.

Concussion of the brain results from a blow to the head or fall on the end of the spine with force transmitted upward. These forces can cause a variety of problems with consciousness (Table 22-3).

TABLE 22-3 Cerebral concussion related to consciousness and amnesia

Grade	Symptoms
1	No amnesia and normal consciousness
2	Confusion and amnesia → Normal consciousness with posttraumatic amnesia
3	Confusion and amnesia → Normal consciousness with posttraumatic amnesia and retrograde amnesia
4	Coma (paralytic) → Confusion and amnesia
5	Coma → Coma vigil
6	Death

Grade 1 (Mild) Concussion

Grade 1 concussions are minimum in intensity and represent the most common type in sports. In general the athlete becomes dazed and disoriented but does not lose memory (amnesia), especially in remembering recent events and learning new information, or have other signs associated with a more serious condition. There may also be a mild unsteadiness in gait. This injury is known as being "dinged" or having one's "bell rung." This athlete is completely lucid in five to fifteen minutes.

An athlete who has been dinged requires immediate rest and careful observation. If after a sufficient period the athlete has no headache, dizziness, or impaired concentration—if the athlete is oriented to person, place, and time and has full recall of events that occurred just before the injury—the athletic trainer or physician may make the decision to allow the athlete to return to the sport.

posttraumatic amnesia
Inability of athlete to recall
events since injury.

Grade 2 (Moderate) Concussion

A grade 2, or moderate, concussion is characterized by unconsciousness lasting less than five minutes. After consciousness has returned, the athlete experiences minor confusion that is caused by **posttraumatic amnesia.** Posttraumatic amnesia is reflected by the inability of the athlete to recall events that have occurred since the time of injury. There is also unsteadiness, ringing in the ears (tinnitus), and perhaps minor dizziness. A dull headache may also follow.

The initial management of this injury should be the same as for a grade 3 concussion. With this degree of injury, the athlete must be removed from the sport and given an evaluation by a neurologist at a medical facility.

$\boxed{22\text{-}1}$ **Focus Box**

Conditions Indicating the Possibility of Increasing Brain Pressure[24]

- Headache
- Nausea and vomiting
- Unequal pupils
- Disorientation
- Progressive or sudden impairment of consciousness
- Gradual increase in blood pressure
- Decrease in pulse rate

Grade 3 (Severe) Concussion

A grade 3 concussion consists of the athlete being unconscious for at least five minutes or more. The initial management for this degree of injury is the same as for a suspected neck fracture. The athlete should be transported on a fracture board with the head and neck immobilized to a hospital with neurological facilities. All severe concussions must be checked for a possible skull fracture and internal bleeding. See the accompanying Focus Box.

Coaches must realize that an emergency situation is present whenever an athlete experiences a loss of consciousness for more than several minutes or exhibits a deteriorating neurological state. This situation demands immediate medical intervention.

Second-Impact Syndrome

The second-impact syndrome occurs when an athlete receives a second brain concussion, even if minimal, before an initial concussion has fully been cleared.[9] As a result the brain rapidly swells, causing a herniation of brain tissue. Within fifteen seconds to several minutes, the athlete collapses and sustains respirator failure and possibly death.[3]

Postconcussion Problems

The postconcussion problem is one of the most poorly understood conditions following head trauma.

An athlete with postconcussion problems will have numerous complaints, such as impaired memory, lack of concentration, tension and irritability, lightheadedness, fatigue, depression, or visual disturbances.[12] Any athlete displaying these problems should immediately be referred for a detailed neurological examination.

Secondary Conditions Associated with Brain Concussion

In addition to the initial injury to the brain, many secondary conditions can also arise following head trauma. Some of the prevalent ones are brain swelling, postinjury epilepsy and seizures, and posttraumatic headaches.

Secondary brain injury conditions include the following:
Cerebral hyperemia
Cerebral edema
Cerebral seizure
Migraine headache

Brain swelling (cerebral edema)   Brain swelling, or cerebral edema, is a localized swelling at the injury site. Within a twelve-hour period the athlete may begin to develop swelling, which causes headache and, on occasion, seizures.[10] Cerebral edema may last as long as two weeks and is not related to the intensity of trauma.

Seizures   Seizures can occur immediately after brain trauma. They have a higher incidence when the brain has actually been contused or when there is internal bleeding. For athletes having a epileptic seizure, the coach should follow the procedures found in Chapter 23.

Headaches   Headaches, which may range from mild to severe, may follow a single or repeated head injury (Figure 22-5). Headaches stem from physical effort. Following a head injury, an athlete may experience tension, migraine, or cluster-type headaches.[4]

A tension headache is associated with abnormal contraction of the muscles in the neck and scalp. A migraine headache is a disorder charac-

Figure 22-5

Repeated blows to the head may predispose athletes to headaches.

terized by recurrent attacks of severe headache with sudden onset, with or without visual or gastrointestinal problems. The athlete who has a history of repeated minor blows to the head such as those that may occur in soccer or who has sustained a major brain injury may, over a period of time, develop migraine headaches. The exact cause is unknown, but it is believed by many to be a vascular disorder. The characteristic flashes of light, blindness in half the field of vision, and numbness are thought to be caused by blood vessel constriction. The headache is often accompanied by nausea and vomiting.[8]

Returning to Competition after Concussion

Coaches must deal with the question of whether an athlete who has been knocked out several times should continue in the sport. The team physician must be the final authority on whether an athlete continues to participate in a collision sport after a head injury. Each athlete must be evaluated individually.[2] One serious concussion may warrant exclusion from the sport; on the other hand, a number of minor episodes may not. The physician who makes this decision must ensure that the athlete meets the following criteria:

Following a cerebral injury, an athlete must be free of symptoms and signs before returning to competition.

- Is normal neurologically
- Is normal in all vasomotor functions
- Is free of headaches
- Is free of seizures and has a normal electroencephalogram
- Is free of lightheadedness when suddenly changing body positions

NOTE: *The coach must make sure that the athlete has written documentation for the return to competition.*[23]

Intracranial Hemorrhage

A blow to the head can cause intracranial bleeding. It may arise from rupture of a blood vessel's aneurysm or from the tearing of a sinus separating the two brain hemispheres (Figure 22-6). Venous bleeding may be slow and insidious, whereas arterial hemorrhage may be evident in a few hours. In the beginning the athlete may be quite alert and lucid, with few or none of the symptoms of serious head injury, and then gradually display severe head pains, dizziness, nausea, inequality of pupil size, or sleepiness. Later stages of cerebral hemorrhage are characterized by deteriorating consciousness, neck rigidity, depression of pulse and respiration, and convulsions—a life-and-death situation.

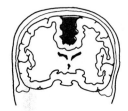

Figure 22-6

Intracranial hemorrhage

The three major types of intracranial hemorrhage are
Epidural
Subdural
Intracerebral

Skull Fracture

Any time an athlete sustains a severe blow to the unprotected head, a skull fracture should be suspected. Skull fractures can be difficult to ascertain. Swelling of the scalp may mask a skull depression or deformity. Until more obvious signs caused by intracranial bleeding present themselves, the skull fracture, even after an x-ray examination has been conducted, can be missed.[15]

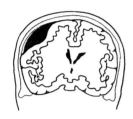

Figure 22-7

Epidural bleeding

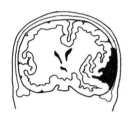

Figure 22-8

Subdural bleeding

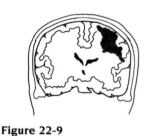

Figure 22-9

Intracerebral bleeding

22-2

Critical Thinking Exercise

A football player receives a grade 2 concussion. It is his second concussion this season.

? What guidelines should be followed regarding his return to play?

Internal Hemorrhage of the Brain

When the head receives a major concussive force, tissue bruising and/or tearing of blood vessels can occur.

A blow to the head can cause a tear in one of the arteries in the dural membrane that covers the brain (Figure 22-7). The tear can result from a skull fracture or sudden shift of the brain. Because of arterial blood pressure, blood accumulation and the creation of a hematoma are extremely fast. Often in only ten to twenty minutes the athlete goes from appearing all right to having major signs of serious head injury.[11]

Another common cause of internal hemorrhage is the contrecoup mechanism, in which the skull decelerates suddenly and the brain keeps moving, tearing blood vessels[21] (Figure 22-8). Because of lower blood pressure, veins are the primary type of blood vessels involved in this injury. Hemorrhage is slow, and signs of brain injury may not appear for many hours. Thus athletes who have sustained a hard blow to the head must be carefully observed for a twenty-four-hour period for signs of pressure buildup within the skull.[23]

Bleeding can occur within the brain itself. Most commonly it results from a compressive force to the brain (Figure 22-9). Deterioration of neurological function occurs rapidly, requiring immediate hospitalization.[16]

The coach must be aware that even a mild head concussion could result in delayed bleeding that may not reveal itself for several months (Table 22-4).

SCALP INJURIES

As soft tissue, the scalp can receive a variety of traumas such as lacerations, abrasions, contusions, and bruises. The cause of scalp injury is usually blunt or penetrating trauma. A scalp injury could exist along with a skull fracture and/or serious brain injury. Lacerations should be referred to a physician for suturing.

THE FACE

Anatomy

The facial skin covers primarily bone with very little protective muscle, fascia, or fat (Figure 22-10).

Facial Injuries

Serious injuries to the face have been reduced significantly from the past because athletes are now required to wear proper protection in high-risk sports. The most prevalent cause of facial injury is a direct blow that injures soft and bony tissue. Very common are skin abrasions, lacerations, and contusions; less common are fractures (Figure 22-11).

Facial Fractures/Dislocations

Coaches must assume that any major blow to the facial area could cause a fracture. Most fractures stem from collision-type sports. The most common sites for fractures are the angular areas of the face that have little

TABLE 22-4 Guidelines for return to activity after concussion

Grade	First Concussion	Second Concussion	Third Concussion
1 (mild)	Return to play if asymptomatic*	Return to play in 2 wks if asymptomatic for 1 wk	Terminate season; may return to play next season if asymptomatic
2 (moderate)	Return to play if asymptomatic for 1 wk	1 mo minimum restriction; may then return to play if asymptomatic for 1 wk; consider terminating season	Terminate season; may return to play next year if asymptomatic
3 (severe)	1 mo minimum restriction; may then return to play if asymptomatic for 1 wk	Terminate season; may return to play next year if asymptomatic	

*No headache or dizziness; no impaired orientation, concentration, or memory during rest or exertion.

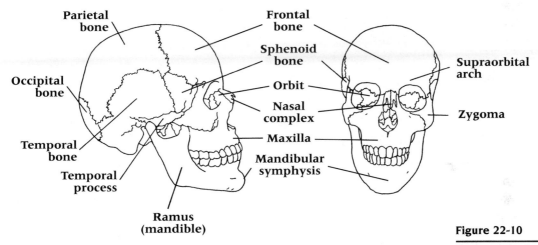

Figure 22-10

Bones of the face

padding, such as the lower jaw (Figure 22-12). The main indications of a fractured lower jaw are deformity, loss of normal **occlusion** of the teeth, pain when biting down, bleeding around the teeth, and lower lip numbness. As with most injuries of this type, cold packs should be applied to the side of the face, and the athlete should be immediately referred to a physician.

Jaw Dislocations

A dislocation of the jaw, or *lower jaw luxation*, involves the temporo-mandibular joint. This area has all the features of a hinge and gliding articulation. Because of its wide range of movement and the inequity of size between the two pieces, the jaw is somewhat prone to dislocation. The mechanism of injury in dislocations is usually a side blow to the open mouth of the athlete, which forces the mandibular condyle forward out of the temporal fossa.

The major signs of the dislocated jaw are a locked-open position, with

> **occlusion (akloo shun)**
> The way the teeth line up. Malocclusion means that the upper and lower teeth do not line up.

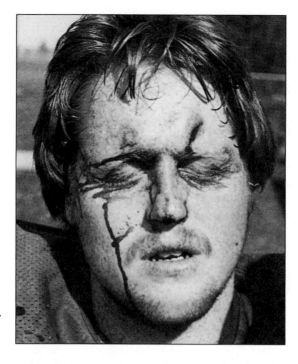

Figure 22-11

Facial lacerations can be a
medical emergency.

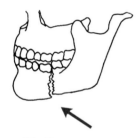

Figure 22-12

Lower jaw fracture

jaw movement being almost impossible, and/or an overriding malocclusion of the teeth. The coach must immediately refer this athlete for medical attention.

Cheekbone Fracture

A fracture of the cheekbone represents the third most common facial fracture. Because of its nearness to the eye orbit, visual problems may also occur.

An obvious deformity occurs in the cheek region, or a bony discrepancy can be felt during palpation. There is usually a nosebleed, and the athlete commonly complains of seeing double.

Dental Injuries

The tooth is a composite of mineral salts, of which calcium and phosphorus are most abundant. That portion protruding from the gum, called the *crown*, is covered by the hardest substance within the body, the enamel. The portion that extends into the alveolar bone of the mouth is called the *root* and is covered by a thin, bony substance known as *cementum*. Underneath the enamel and cementum lies the bulk of the tooth, a hard material known as *dentin*. Within the dentin is a central canal and chamber containing the *pulp,* a substance composed of nerves, lymphatics, and blood vessels that supply the entire tooth (Figure 22-13).[13]

With the use of face guards and properly fitting mouth guards, most dental injuries can be prevented. Mouth protectors need to be mandated in all sports that produce mouth injuries (for example, wrestling, rugby,

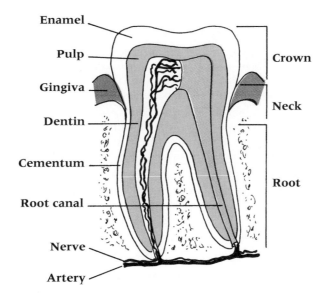

Enamel

Pulp

Gingiva

Dentin

Cementum

Root canal

Nerve

Artery

Crown

Neck

Root

Figure 22-13

Normal tooth anatomy

soccer, basketball, gymnastics, racquetball, lacrosse, field hockey, martial arts, and skiing). Any blow to the upper or lower jaw can potentially injure the teeth. Injuries to the tooth below the gum line may repair themselves because of the abundant blood supply.[17] However, fractures of the tooth below the gum line may not heal if there is an injury to the tooth pulp. A tooth could sustain a mild blow, which may not be obvious, that disrupts its blood and nerve supply.[19]

Fractured Tooth

Fracture of the crown of the tooth is an enamel fracture and can usually be repaired by smoothing, capping, or even removing the entire tooth. In contrast, fractures that involve the dentin, which expose the pulp, may predispose the tooth to infection and tooth death (Figure 22-14).

Teeth in which the enamel or dentin is chipped fail to rejuvenate

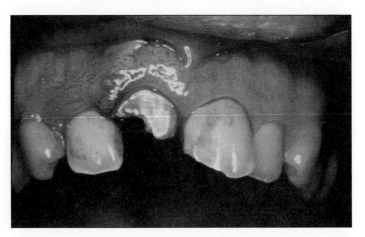

Figure 22-14

Tooth fractures exposing pulp predisposes the tooth to infection and perhaps death.

A tooth that has been
completely dislocated intact
should be rinsed off with
water and replaced in the
socket.

because they lack a direct blood supply. They can be capped for the sake
of appearance.

Partially or Completely Dislocated Tooth

A tooth that has been knocked crooked should be manually realigned to
a normal position as soon as possible. One that has been totally knocked
out should be cleaned with water and replaced in the tooth socket, if possible. If repositioning the dislocated tooth is difficult, the athlete should
keep it under the tongue until the dentist can replace it. If this is inconvenient, a dislodged tooth can also be kept in a glass of water. If a completely dislodged tooth is out of the mouth for more than 30 minutes, the
chances of saving it are very tenuous; therefore the athlete should immediately be sent to the dentist for splinting.

Nasal Injuries

Nasal Fractures and Cartilage Separation

A fracture of the nose is one of the most common fractures of the face. It
appears frequently as a separation of the frontal processes of the maxilla,
a separation of the lateral cartilages, or a combination of the two (Figure
22-15).[20]

The force of the blow to the nose may either come from the side or
from a straight frontal force. A lateral force causes greater deformity than
a straight-on blow. In nasal fractures hemorrhage is profuse because of
laceration of the mucous lining. Swelling is immediate. Deformity is usu-

Figure 22-15

A serious nose fracture may
be a medical emergency.

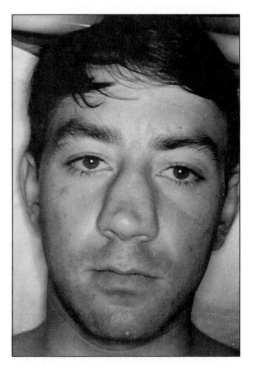

22-2 **Focus Box**

Nose Splinting

The following procedure is used for nose splinting.

MATERIALS NEEDED: Two pieces of gauze, each 2 inches (5 cm) long and rolled to the size of a pencil, three strips of 1½-inch (3.75 cm) tape, cut approximately 4 inches (10 cm) long; and clear tape adherent.

POSITION OF THE ATHLETE: The athlete lies supine on the athletic training table.

PROCEDURE:

1. The rolled pieces of gauze are placed on either side of the athlete's nose.
2. Gently but firmly, 4-inch (10 cm) lengths of tape are laid over the gauze rolls.

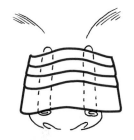

Figure 22-16

Splinting the fractured nose

ally present if the nose has received a lateral blow. Gentle palpation may reveal abnormal mobility and may elicit a grating sound (crepitus).

The coach should attempt to control the bleeding and then refer the athlete to a physician for x-ray examination and reduction of the fracture. Simple and uncomplicated fractures of the nose will not hinder or be unsafe for the athlete, and he or she will be able to return to competition within a few days. Adequate protection can be provided through splinting (see the accompanying Focus Box and Figure 22-16).

Nasal Septal Injuries

A major nasal injury can occur to the septum. The septal injury, like the fracture, is caused by compression or trauma to the side of the nose. This injury commonly produces bleeding and nasal pain.

Nosebleed

Nosebleeds in sports are usually the result of direct blows that cause varying degrees of contusion to the septum (Figure 22-17). Hemorrhages arise most often from the highly vascular anterior aspect of the nasal septum. In most situations, the nosebleed presents only a minor problem and stops spontaneously after a short period of time.[5]

Care The care of the athlete with an acute nosebleed is as follows:

1. The athlete sits upright.
2. A cold compress is placed over the nose and the ipsilateral carotid artery.
3. The athlete applies finger pressure to the affected nostril for five minutes.

If these steps fail to stop the bleeding within five minutes, more extensive measures should be taken.[5] After bleeding has ceased, the athlete may resume activity but should be reminded not to blow the nose under any circumstances for at least two hours after the initial insult.

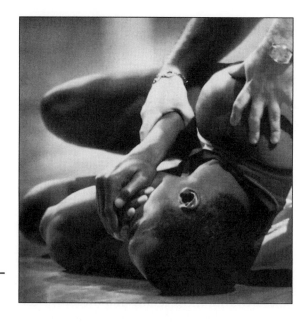

Figure 22-17

Nasal trauma is common in
contact and collision sports.

Foreign Body in the Nose

During participation, the athlete may have an insect or debris lodge in a
nostril; if the object is large enough, the mucous lining of the nose will
react by becoming inflamed and swollen. In most cases the foreign body
will become dislodged if the nose is gently blown while the unaffected
side is pinched shut. Probing and blowing the nose violently will only
cause additional irritation.[6]

Ear Injuries

Figure 22-18

Ear anatomy: A, External ear.
B, Inner ear.

The ear (Figure 22-18) is responsible for the sense of hearing and equilibrium. It is composed of three parts: the external ear; the middle ear
(tympanic membrane) lying just inside the skull; and the internal ear

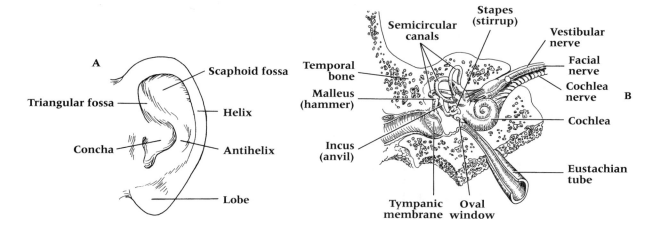

(labyrinth), which is formed, in part, by the temporal bone of the skull. The middle ear and internal ear are structured to transport auditory impulses to the brain. Aiding the organs of hearing and equalizing pressure between the middle and the internal ear is the eustachian tube, a canal that joins the nose and the middle ear.[6]

Sports injuries to the ear occur most often to the external portion. The external ear is separated into the auricle (pinna) and the external auditory canal (meatus). The auricle, which is shaped like a shell, collects and directs waves of sound into the auditory canal. It is composed of flexible yellow cartilage, muscles, and fat padding and is covered by a closely adhering, thin layer of skin. Most of the blood vessels and nerves of the auricle turn around its borders, with just a few penetrating the cartilage proper.

Cauliflower Ear

Contusions, wrenching, or extreme friction of the ear can lead to hematoma auris, commonly known as a cauliflower ear (Figure 22-19).[9]

This condition usually occurs from repeated injury to the ear and is seen most frequently in boxers and wrestlers. Recently, however, it has been held to a minimum because of the protective measures that have been initiated.[7]

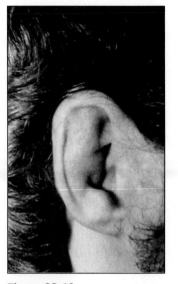

Figure 22-19

Cauliflower ear

In a cauliflower ear, trauma may tear the overlying tissue away from the cartilaginous plate, resulting in hemorrhage and fluid accumulation. A hematoma usually forms before the limited circulation can absorb the fluid. If the hematoma goes unattended, a sequence of coagulation, organization, and fibrosis results in a keloid that appears elevated, rounded, white, nodular, and firm, resembling a cauliflower. Once developed, the keloid can be removed only through surgery. To prevent this disfiguring condition from arising, some friction-proofing agent such as petroleum jelly should be applied to the ears of athletes susceptible to this condition. These athletes should also routinely wear ear guards in practice and in competition.[18]

If an ear becomes "hot" because of excessive rubbing or twisting, the coach should immediately apply a cold pack to reduce bleeding. Once swelling is present in the ear, special care should be taken to prevent the blood from solidifying; a cold pack should be placed immediately over the ear and held tightly by an elastic bandage for at least twenty minutes. If the swelling is still present at the end of this time, aspiration by a physician is required.

Foreign Body in the Ear

The ears offer an opening, as do the nose and eyes, in which objects can become caught. Usually these objects are pieces of debris or flying insects. They can be dislodged by having the athlete tilt the head to one side. If removal is difficult, syringing the ear with a solution of lukewarm water may remove the object. Care should be exercised to avoid striking the eardrum with the direct stream of water.

Eye Injuries

Eye injuries account for approximately 1 percent of all sports injuries.[1] In the United States, baseball has the highest incidence of eye injuries. According to the National Society to Prevent Blindness, there are an estimated 40,000 annual sports-related eye injuries, many of which lead to permanent damage.[27]

Eye Anatomy

The eye has many anatomical protective devices. It is firmly retained within an oval socket formed by the bones of the head. A cushion of soft fatty tissue surrounds it, and a thin skin flap (the eyelid), which functions by reflex action, covers the eye for protection. Foreign particles are prevented from entering the eye by the lashes and eyebrows, which act as a filtering system. A soft mucous lining that covers the inner conjunctiva transports and spreads tears, which are secreted by many accessory lacrimal glands. A larger lubricating organ is located above the eye and secretes heavy quantities of fluid through the lacrimal duct to help wash away foreign particles. The eye proper is well protected by the sclera, a tough white outer layer possessing a transparent center portion called the *cornea* (Figure 22-20).

Evaluation of Eye Injuries

It is essential that any eye injury be evaluated immediately. The first concern is to understand the mechanism of the injury and to ascertain whether there is a related condition to the head, face, or neck.

Proper care of eye injuries is essential. The coach must use extreme caution in handling eye injuries. If the eye injury appears to be serious, the athlete should be immediately referred to a hospital and/or an ophthalmologist (see the accompanying Focus Box).[25] Ideally, the athlete with a serious eye injury should be transported to the hospital by ambulance in a recumbent position. Both eyes must be covered during trans-

Extreme care must be taken with a serious eye injury; the athlete must be transported in a recumbent position with both eyes covered.

Figure 22-20

Eye anatomy

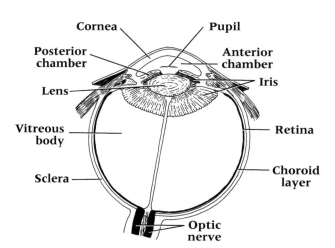

22-3 **Focus Box**

Symptoms Indicating the Possibility of Serious Eye Injury

- Blurred vision that does not clear with blinking
- Loss of all or part of the visual field
- Pain that is sharp, stabbing, or throbbing
- Double vision after injury

port. At no time should pressure be applied to the eye. In the case of surrounding soft-tissue injury, a cold compress can be applied for thirty to sixty minutes to control hemorrhage (Figure 22-21).

The Black Eye

Although well protected, the eye may be bruised during sports activity. The severity of eye injuries varies from a mild bruise to an extremely serious condition affecting vision to the fracturing of the orbital cavity. Fortunately, most of the eye injuries sustained in sports are mild. A blow to the eye may initially injure the surrounding tissue and produce bleeding into the tissue spaces. If the hemorrhage goes unchecked, the result may be a classic black eye.

Care of an eye contusion requires cold application for at least half an hour, plus a twenty-four-hour rest period if the athlete has distorted vision. Under no circumstances should an athlete blow the nose following an acute eye injury. To do so might increase hemorrhaging.[26]

Foreign Body in the Eye

Foreign bodies in the eye are a frequent occurrence in sports and are potentially dangerous. A foreign object produces considerable pain and disability. No attempt should be made to rub out the body or to remove it with the fingers. Have the athlete close the eye until the initial pain has

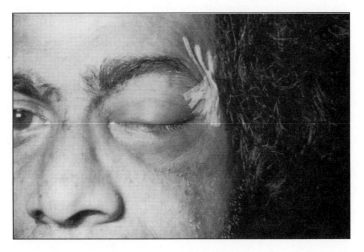

Figure 22-21

A serious eye injury should be treated as a major medical emergency.

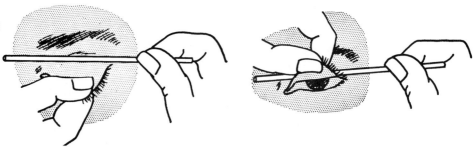

Figure 22-22

Removing a foreign object
from the eye

subsided and then attempt to determine if the object is in the vicinity of
the upper or lower lid. Foreign bodies in the lower lid are relatively easy
to remove by depressing the tissue and then wiping it with a sterile cotton applicator. Foreign bodies in the area of the upper lid are usually
much more difficult to localize. Two methods may be used. The first technique, which is quite simple, is performed as follows: gently pull the upper eyelid over the lower lid, as the subject looks downward. This causes
tears to be produced, which may flush the object down on to the lower
lid. If this method is unsuccessful, the second technique, shown in Figure
22-22, should be used.

Corneal Abrasions

Rubbing an eye with a
foreign object in it will often
scratch the cornea.

An athlete who gets a foreign object in his or her eye will usually try to
rub it away. In doing so, the cornea can become abraded. The athlete will
complain of severe pain and watering of the eye, **photophobia,** and
spasm of the eyelid. The eye should be patched, and the athlete should
be sent to a physician. Corneal abrasion is diagnosed through application
of a fluorescein strip to the abraded area, which stains it a bright green.[26]

photophobia
An intense intolerance of
light.

Hyphema

A blunt blow to the anterior aspect of the eye can produce a hyphema,
which is a collection of blood within the anterior chamber. The blood set-
tles inferiorly or may fill the entire chamber. Vision is partially or completely blocked. The coach must be aware that a hyphema is a major eye
injury that can lead to serious problems of the lens, choroid, or retina.

Rupture of the Globe

A blow to the eye by an object smaller than the eye orbit produces extreme pressure that can rupture the globe. A golf ball or racquetball fits
this category; larger objects such as a tennis ball or a fist will often fracture the bony orbit before the eye is overly compressed. Even if it does
not cause rupture, such a force can cause internal injury that may ultimately lead to blindness.

Blowout Fracture

A blow to the face that strikes the eye and orbital ridge can cause what is
commonly called a *blowout fracture of the orbit.* Because of the sudden in-

Figure 22-23

A blow to the eye can cause
the retina to become
detached.

crease in internal pressure of the eye, the very thin bone located in the inferior aspect of the orbit can fracture. Hemorrhage occurs around the inferior margins of the eye. The athlete commonly complains of double vision and pain when moving the eye. With such symptoms and signs, immediate referral to a physician is necessary.

Retinal Detachment

A blow to the athlete's eye can partially or completely separate the retina from its underlying retinal pigment epithelium. Retinal detachment is more common among athletes who have myopia (nearsightedness). Detachment is painless; however, early signs include seeing specks floating before the eye, flashes of light, or blurred vision. As the detachment progresses, the athlete complains of a "curtain" falling over the field of vision. Any athlete with symptoms of detachment must be immediately referred to an ophthalmologist (Figure 22-23).

SUMMARY

- Brain injuries, which can be life threatening, often result from direct or indirect blows that can be classified as cerebral concussion injuries.
- Depending on the severity of the concussion, the athlete may display signs of disorientation, dizziness, amnesia, headache, loss of consciousness, problems in concentrating, ear ringing, balance problems, or pupillary discrepancies.
- A serious head injury can be life threatening, requiring hospitalization within a crucial thirty-minute period. If a coach is without medical assistance he or she must make an on-the-field evaluation without moving the athlete. Cardiopulmonary function is determined as well as other physical signs. If the athlete is unconscious, the situation is

handled as if there is a serious neck injury. The coach may also be required to assess the athlete's grade of concussion through mental orientation and memory procedures as well as simple eye and balance testing.

- Concussion can be graded in three levels: grades 1, 2, and 3, or mild, moderate, and severe. Grade 1 refers to a transient confusion with no loss of consciousness; concussion symptoms or mental status abnormalities resolve in less than fifteen minutes. Grade 2 refers to transient confusion with no loss of consciousness; concussion symptoms or mental status abnormalities resolve in more than fifteen minutes. Grade 3 refers to a loss of consciousness.

- Second-impact syndrome, even if only minimal, can be fatal if an athlete has not been cleared from a previous concussion. Even a mild concussion can produce postconcussion problems with memory, concentration, irritability, depression, fatigue, and vision.

- Concussion can cause secondary conditions such as brain swelling, seizures, and headaches. A major direct or indirect force to the head can cause a number of potentially fatal conditions such as skull fracture and/or internal bleeding within the skull. An athlete may not return to competition unless he or she is completely free of symptoms as certified by a physician.

- The face is subject to many different types of traumatic sports injuries. The most common are facial wounds, with lacerations ranking at the top.

- Less common, but usually more serious, are injuries such as jaw fractures and dislocations, dental injuries, and nasal injuries.

- A potentially disfiguring ear injury is hematoma auris, or cauliflower ear.

- The eye is also at risk; therefore it is essential that the eye be protected against fast-moving projectiles.

Solutions to Critical Thinking Exercises

22-1 The coach asks the athlete questions that are related to recently acquired information. Examples are the current date, name of last week's opponent, who won the game, and who scored this game's last goal.

22-2 The athlete should be out of play for at least one month. After this period he may return to play if asymptomatic for one week. The physician may consider terminating the athlete for the rest of the season.

REVIEW QUESTIONS AND CLASS ACTIVITIES

1. Pair off with another student, with one of you acting as the coach or athletic trainer and the other as the injured athlete. The athlete simulates concussions of various grades. The coach or athletic trainer assesses the athlete, attempting to determine the grade of concussion.
2. List the on-site evaluation steps that should be taken when a brain injury occurs.

3. Demonstrate the following procedures in evaluating a cerebral injury—questioning the athlete, testing eye signs, and testing balance.
4. Describe the immediate care procedures that should be performed when a tooth is fractured and when it is dislocated.
5. Describe the procedures that should be performed for an athlete with a nosebleed.
6. How can a cauliflower ear be prevented?
7. The eye can sustain an extremely serious injury during some sports activities. What are the major indicators of a possibly serious eye injury?

REFERENCES

1. American Academy of Ophthalmology-master@aao.org and www.nbc.com
2. Berkow R, editor: *The Merck manual*, ed 16, Rayway, NJ, 1992, Merck.
3. Cantu RC, Voy R: Second impact syndrome, *Physician Sportsmed* 23:27, June 1995.
4. Cantu RC: Reflections on head injuries in sport and the concussion controversy, *Clinics J Sport Med* 7:83, April 1997.
5. Davidson TM, Davidson D: Immediate management of epistaxis, *Physician Sportsmed* 24:74, August 1996.
6. Davidson TM, Neuman TR: Managing inflammatory ear conditions, *Physician Sportsmed* 22(8):56, 1994.
7. Davidson TM, Neuman TR: Managing ear trauma, *Physician Sportsmed* 22(7):27, 1994.
8. Diamond S: Managing migraines in active people, *Physician Sportsmed* 24:41, December 1996.
9. Diamond S: Treating athletes who have posttraumatic headaches, *Physician Sportsmed* 20:167, 1992.
10. Dimeff RJ: Activity related headache, *Clin Sports Med* 11:339, 1992.
11. Gennarelli TA, Torg JS: Closed head injuries. In Torg JS, Shephard RJ, editors: *Current therapy in sports medicine*, St Louis, 1995, Mosby.
12. Henderson JM: Head injuries in sports, *Sports Med Digest* 15(9):1, 1993.
13. Kumamoto DP et al: Oral trauma, *Physician Sportsmed* 23 (5):53, 1995.
14. Maddocks DL: The assessment of orientation following concussion in athletes, *Clinics J Sports Med* 5(1):32, 1995.
15. Mac Afee KA II: Immediate care of facial trauma, *Physician Sportsmed* 20:331, 1992.
16. Maroon JC et al: Assessing closed head injuries, *Physician Sportsmed* 4:37, 1992.
17. Pashby RC, Pashby TJ: Ocular injuries. In Torg JS, Shephard RJ, editors: *Current therapy in sports medicine*, St Louis, 1995, Mosby.
18. Putukian M, Echemendia RJ: Managing successive minor head injuries, *Physician Sportsmed* 24(11) November 1996.
19. Robinson T et al: Ear injuries. In Birrer RB, editor: *Sports medicine for the primary care physician*, ed 2, Boca Raton, Fla, 1995, CRC Press.
20. Robinson T, Greenberg MD: Nasal injuries. In Birrer RB, editor: *Sports medicine for the primary care physician*, ed 2, Boca Raton, Fla, 1995, CRC Press.
21. Roob JD et al: Delayed presentation of subdural hematoma, *Physician Sportsmed* 21:61, 1993.
22. Roos R: Guidelines for managing concussion in sports: a persistent headache, *Physician Sportsmed* 24(10), October 1996.
23. Schuller DE, Mountain RE: Auricular injury. In Torg JS, Shephard RJ, editors: *Current therapy in sports medicine*, St Louis, 1995, Mosby.

24. Shell D et al: Can subdural hematoma result from repeated minor head injury? *Physician Sportsmed* 21:75, 1993.

25. Torg JS: Emergency management of head and cervical spine injuries. In Torg JS, Shephard RJ, editors: *Current therapy in sports medicine,* St Louis, 1995, Mosby.

26. Zagelbaum BM, Hochman MA: Examining a "red" eye, *Physician Sportsmed* 23:56, December 1995.

27. Zagelbaum BM: Sports-related eye trauma, *Physician Sportsmed* 21:25, 1993.

ANNOTATED BIBLIOGRAPHY

Fadale PD, Hulstyn MJ, editors: *Primary care of the injured athlete, Part I, Clinics in sports medicine,* vol 16, no 3, Philadelphia, July 1997, Saunders.

Two chapters on head and facial sports injuries provide an excellent overview of these problems.

Lehman LB, Ravich SJ: Close head injuries in athletes, *Clin Sports Med* 9:485, 1990.

A concise description of cerebral injuries common in sports.

Torg JS, ed: Head and neck injuries, *Clin Sports Med* 6:720, 1987.

In-depth coverage of head and neck injuries stemming from sports activities. The mechanisms of these injuries are discussed as well as their prevention, initial treatment, and rehabilitation.

WEB SITES

Cramer First Aider: http://www.ccsd.k12.wy.us/CCHS_web/sptmed/fstaider.htm

World Ortho: http://www.worldortho.com
Use the search engine in this site to locate relevant information.

Wheeless' Textbook of Orthopaedics: http://www.medmedia.com/med.htm
An excellent page for injury, anatomy, and x-ray information.

Karolinska Institute Library: Musculoskeletal Disease: http://www.mic.ki.se/Disease/c5.htm

American Orthopaedic Society for Sports Medicine: http://www.sportsmed.org

American Academy of Ophthalmology: http://www.master@aao.org and http://www.nbc.com

Additional Health Concerns

When you finish this chapter you will be able to:

- Explain the causes, preventions, and care of the most common skin infections in sports.
- Describe respiratory tract illnesses common to athletes.
- Identify disorders of the gastrointestinal tract.
- Describe how to avoid problems with the diabetic athlete.
- Describe the dangers that hypertension presents to an athlete.
- Describe the adverse effects that various anemias have on the athlete.
- Explain what a coach should do with an athlete who is having a grand mal seizure.
- Identify contagious viral diseases that may be seen in athletes.
- Contrast the different sexually transmitted diseases that athletes may have.
- Explain the concerns of the female athlete in terms of menstruation, osteoporosis, and reproduction.
- Explain the many concerns inherent in medical and nonmedical drug use among athletes.

In addition to the many injuries that have been discussed in previous chapters, there are a variety of additional health-related conditions that can potentially affect the athlete. Like everyone else, athletes inevitably become ill. When illnesses occur, it becomes incumbent on the coach to recognize these conditions and to follow up with appropriate care. With the illnesses and conditions discussed in this chapter, appropriate care often means referring the athlete to a physician to provide medical care that is beyond the scope of the coach and, in many instances, beyond that of the athletic trainer. The information provided in this chapter serves as a reference for the coach in making appropriate decisions regarding care of the sick athlete.

SKIN INFECTIONS

The skin is the largest organ of the human body. It is composed of three layers—epidermis, dermis, and subcutis. The most common skin infections in sports are caused by viruses, bacteria, and fungi.[24] The accompanying Focus Box lists the most common skin infections.[29]

Viral Infections

A virus is the smallest of the microorganisms that can live only inside a cell. When the virus enters a cell it may immediately trigger a disease (in-

Herpes is a common virus that attacks the skin of athletes.

23-1 **Focus Box**

Common Viral, Bacterial, and Fungal Skin Infections Found in Athletes

Viral infections
- herpes simplex type 1—cold sore, fever blister
- herpes simplex type 2—genital herpes
- herpes gladiatorum (back or shoulders)
- herpes zoster

Bacterial infections
- staphylococcus
  - boils
- streptococcus
  - impetigo
  - infected hair follicles
  - infected sweat glands

Fungal infections
- ringworm (tinea)
  - tinea capitis (head)
  - tinea corporis (body)
  - tinea unguium (toenails and fingernails)
  - tinea cruris (jock rash)
  - tinea pedis (athlete's foot)

fluenza) or it can remain dormant for years (herpes). A virus can damage the host cell by blocking its normal function and using the metabolism of the host cell for its own reproduction. Eventually the virus destroys the host cell and progressively invades other cells.

Viral infections most likely to affect the skin are herpes simplex and herpes zoster.

Herpes

Cause of condition Herpes simplex is a viral infection that results in a skin eruption of vesicles that tend to recur in the same place, usually at sites at which mucous membranes join the skin. Herpes simplex is further classified as either type 1 or type 2. Type 1 occurs as a cold sore or fever blister around the lips and type 2 usually occurs around the genitals and is classified as a sexually transmitted disease (Figure 23-1).

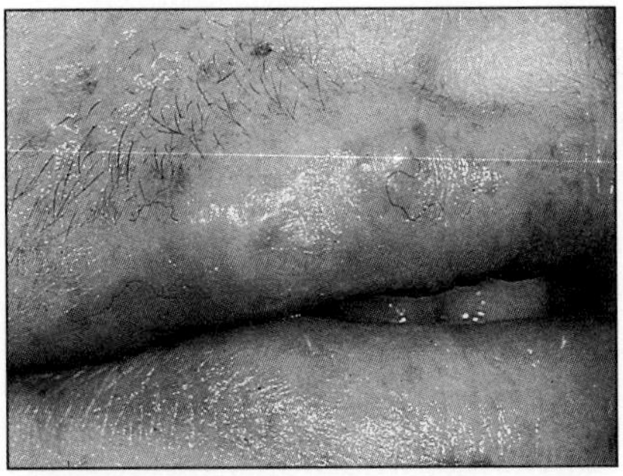

Figure 23-1

Herpes simplex type 1

Herpes simplex that appears on the back or shoulders is called *herpes glad-iatorum* and occurs most often in wrestlers.

Herpes zoster appears in a specific pattern on the body in an area that is innervated by a specific nerve root. It may appear on the face or anywhere on the trunk. Herpes zoster is the chicken pox virus that has remained dormant for many years. It is most likely to appear when the immune system is compromised.

Symptoms of condition   Athletes about to experience an outbreak of herpes will usually feel a tingling, itching soreness immediately before a small area of redness appears. The athlete will also report feeling ill, particularly with first episode outbreaks. These symptoms are followed by the appearance of painful, fluid-filled vesicles that take on a crusty appearance. These vesicles usually heal in about ten days.

Care   It is important to take universal precautions when dealing with the herpes virus. Herpes may spread by contact with the fluid inside the vesicles. Outbreaks of herpes must run their course. Acyclovir, an over-the-counter medication taken orally and applied topically, has been effective in treating the symptoms. However, athletes must realize that the virus is not destroyed and that the herpes will probably reappear in the same area.

Bacterial Infections

Cause of condition   Bacteria are one-celled plantlike microorganisms that are capable of multiplying in an environment that supports their reproduction. Bacteria that cause disease are called pathogens. Millions of nonpathogenic bacteria normally live on the skin and mucous membranes of the body. Development of a disease involves entry of the bacterial pathogen into a host, growth of bacteria and production of toxic substances, and the response of the host to fight that infection. Many different types of bacterial pathogens can produce infection in the body. The two types of bacteria most likely to infect the skin are *streptococcus* (strep) and *staphyloccus* (staph).

Symptoms of condition   The symptoms of localized infection are similar to the signs of inflammation, including tenderness, warmth, redness, and swelling. Pus may form in an infected area from either staph or strep.

Care   Bacterial infections should be treated with specific antibiotic medications that inhibit the growth and proliferation of a particular bacteria. The area should also be treated with warm compresses. If an open, pus-filled lesion develops, it should be drained. Every precaution should be taken to minimize the spread of infection as well as transmission to another person.

Fungal Infections

Causes of condition   The most common fungal infection found in athletes is *ringworm*. Ringworm fungi are the cause of most skin, nail, and hair fungal infections. Ringworm can be found all over the body and is

23-1

Critical Thinking Exercise

Fungus infections (ringworm) are commonly found among athletes. Fungi tend to grow in a warm, moist, dark environment.

? What are the symptoms and signs of the fungal infection tinea pedis, and how is this problem best prevented?

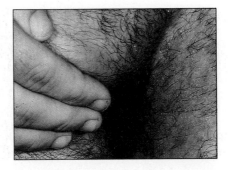

Figure 23-2

Tinea of the groin

more appropriately referred to by the term *tinea* plus the Latin term for whatever body part is effected. The two most common sites for ringworm are in the groin (tinea cruris) and in the foot (tinea pedis).

Symptoms of tinea of the groin (tinea cruris)   Tinea of the groin (tinea cruris), more commonly called jock rash, appears as a bilateral and often symmetrical brownish or reddish lesion resembling the outline of a butterfly in the groin area (Figure 23-2).

The athlete complains of mild to moderate itching, which can lead to scratching and the possibility of a secondary bacterial infection.

Care   Coaches must be able to identify lesions of tinea cruris and treat them accordingly. Conditions of this type must be treated until cured (Figure 23-3). Infection not responding to normal management must be referred to the team physician. Most ringworm infections will respond to the many nonprescription medications that are available as aerosol sprays, liquids, powders, or ointments. Powder, because of its absorbent qualities, should be the only medication vehicle used in the groin area. Medications that are irritating or tend to mask the symptoms of a groin infection must be avoided.

Symptoms of athlete's foot (tinea pedis)   The foot is the area of the body most commonly infected by dermatophytes, usually by tinea pedis, or athlete's foot. The fungus is usually found in the space between the third and fourth digits and in the plantar surface of the arch. The same organism attacks toenails. This fungus causes scaling and thickening of the soles. The athlete wearing shoes that are enclosed will sweat, encouraging fungal growth. However, the likelihood of getting athlete's foot is based mainly on the athlete's individual susceptibility. Other conditions that may be thought to be athlete's foot include a dermatitis caused by allergy or an eczema-type skin infection.

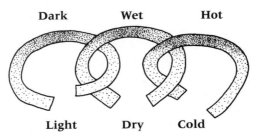

Figure 23-3

When managing a fungal infection, it is essential to break the chain of infection in one or more ways: Dark-light, wet-dry, hot-cold.

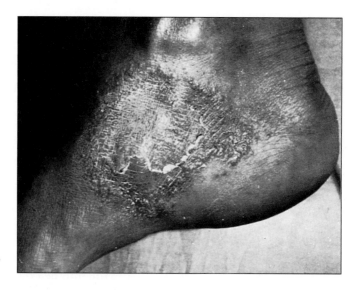

Figure 23-4

Athlete's foot (tinea pedis)

Athlete's foot can reveal itself in many ways but appears most often as an extreme itching on the soles of the feet and between and on top of the toes. It appears as a rash, with small pimples or minute blisters that break and exude a yellowish serum (Figure 23-4). Scratching because of itchiness can cause the tissue to become inflamed and infected, manifesting a red, white, or gray scaling of the affected area.[23]

Care   Griseofulvin is the most effective medication for management for tinea pedis. Of major importance is good foot hygiene. Topical medications used for tinea corporis can be beneficial. (See the accompanying Focus Box.)[30]

RESPIRATORY CONDITIONS

The respiratory tract is an organ system through which various communicable diseases can be transmitted.[22] It is commonly the port of entry for acute infectious diseases that are spread from person to person or by direct contact. Some of the more prevalent conditions affecting athletes are the common cold, sore throat, asthma, hay fever, and air pollution.

The Common Cold

Cause of condition   Upper respiratory tract infections, especially colds and associated conditions, are common in the sports program and can play havoc with entire teams. The common cold is attributed to a filterable virus, which produces an infection of the upper respiratory tract of a susceptible individual.[4] The susceptible person is believed to be one who has, singly or in combination, any of the following characteristics:

- Physical debilitation from overwork or lack of sleep
- Chronic inflammation from a local infection
- Inflammation of the nasal mucosa from an allergy

Basic Care of Athlete's Foot

- Keep the feet as dry as possible through frequent use of talcum powder.
- Wear clean white socks to avoid reinfection, changing them daily.
- Use a standard fungicide for specific medication. Over-the-counter medications such as Desenex and Tinactin are useful in the early stages of the infection. For stubborn cases see the team physician; a dermatologist may need to make a culture from foot scrapings to determine the best combatant to be used.

The best cure for athlete's foot is prevention. To keep the condition from spreading to other athletes, the following steps should be faithfully followed by individuals in the sports program:

- Powder the feet daily.
- Dry the feet thoroughly, especially between and under the toes, after every shower.
- Keep sports shoes and street shoes dry by dusting them with powder daily.
- Wear clean sports socks and street socks daily.
- Clean and disinfect the shower and dressing rooms daily.

- Inflammation of the nasal mucosa from breathing foreign substances such as dust
- Sensitivity to stress

Symptoms of condition The onset of the common cold is usually rapid; symptoms vary among individuals. The typical effects are a general feeling of **malaise** with an accompanying headache, sneezing, and nasal discharge. Some individuals may register a fever of 100° to 102° F (38° to 39° C) and have chills. Various aches and pains may also accompany the symptoms. The nasal discharge starts as a watery secretion and gradually becomes thick and discolored from the inflammation.[4]

Care Care of the cold is usually symptomatic, with emphasis on isolation, bed rest, and light eating. Medications include aspirin for relieving general discomfort, rhinitis tablets for drying the secreting mucosa, and nasal drops to relieve nasal congestion. If a cough is present, various syrups may be given to afford relief. The athlete should avoid intense training while experiencing a severe respiratory infection. Intense training can suppress the immune system.[4]

Sinusitis

Cause of condition Sinusitis is an inflammation of the nasal sinuses. Sinusitis can stem from an upper respiratory infection caused by a variety of bacteria. As a result, nasal mucous membranes swell and block the sinuses. A painful pressure occurs from an accumulation of mucus.[4]

Symptoms of condition The skin area over the sinus may be

malaise (muh **laze**)
Discomfort and uneasiness caused by an illness.

swollen and painful to the touch. The athlete may experience a headache and a feeling of being out of sorts.

Care   If an infection is present, antibiotics may be warranted. Nasal vasoconstrictors may be helpful in nasal drainage.

Sore Throat (Pharyngitis)

Cause of condition   A sore throat, or pharyngitis, usually is the result of postnasal drip associated with a common cold or sinusitis. It may also be an indication of a more serious condition, including either viral or bacterial infection.

Symptoms of condition   Frequently the condition starts as a dryness in the throat and progresses to soreness with pain and swelling. It is sometimes accompanied by a headache, a fever of 101° to 102° F (38° to 39° C), chills, coughing, and a general feeling of fatigue. On examination the throat may appear dark red and swollen, and mucous membranes may be coated.

Care   In most cases bed rest is considered the best treatment, combined with symptomatic medications such as aspirin and a hot saltwater gargle. Antibiotics may be prescribed by a physician if other measures are inadequate.

Influenza

Cause of condition   Influenza, or the flu, is one of the most persistent and debilitating diseases. It usually occurs in various forms as an annual epidemic, causing severe illness among the populace.[21]

Influenza is caused by a virus that enters the tissue's cell through its genetic material. Within the tissue, the virus multiplies and is released from the cell by a budding process and is spread throughout the body. Not all athletes need influenza vaccines; however, athletes engaging in winter sports, basketball, wrestling, and swimming may require them.[12]

Symptoms of condition   The athlete with the flu will have the following symptoms: fever, cough, headache, malaise, and inflamed respiratory mucous membranes with coryza. It should be noted that certain viruses can increase the body's core temperature. Flu generally has an incubation period of forty-eight hours and comes on suddenly, accompanied by chills and a fever of 102° to 103° F (39° to 39.5° C), which develops over a twenty-four-hour period. The athlete complains of a headache and general aches and pains—mainly in the back and legs. The headache increases in intensity, along with photophobia and aching at the back of the skull. There is often sore throat, burning in the chest, and in the beginning, a nonproductive cough, which later may develop into bronchitis. The skin is flushed, and the eyes are inflamed and watery. The acute stage of the disease usually lasts up to five days. Weakness, sweating, and fatigue may persist for many days.

Care   Flu prevention includes staying away from infected persons, maintaining good resistance through healthy living, and annual vaccines. If the flu is uncomplicated, its management consists of bed rest. During

23-2

Critical Thinking Exercise

A swimmer complains of fever, cough, headache, malaise, aching in the back and neck, and a sore throat.

?   What is probably wrong with this athlete, and how could it be managed?

the acute stage, the temperature often returns to normal. Symptomatic care such as aspirin, steam inhalation, cough medicines, and gargles may be given.

Seasonal Allergies (Rhinitis)

Cause of condition   Hay fever is an acute seasonal allergic condition that results from airborne pollens. Hay fever can occur during the spring as a reaction to tree pollens such as oak, elm, maple, alder, birch, and cottonwood. During the summer, grass and weed pollens can be the culprits. In the fall, ragweed pollen is the prevalent cause. Airborne fungal spores also have been known to cause hay fever.

Symptoms of condition   In the early stages, the athlete's eyes, throat, mouth, and nose begin to itch, followed by watering of the eyes, sneezing, and a clear, watery, nasal discharge. The athlete may complain of a sinus-type headache, emotional irritability, difficulty in sleeping, red and swollen eyes and nasal mucous membranes, and a wheezing cough. It should be noted that other common adverse allergic conditions are asthma, anaphylaxis, urticaria, angioedema, and **rhinitis.**[5]

Care   Most athletes obtain relief from hay fever through over-the-counter oral antihistamines. To avoid the problem of sedation stemming from these drugs, the athlete may ingest a decongestant during the day and a long-reacting antihistamine before going to bed.

> **rhinitis** (rye **nye** tis)
> Inflammation of the nasal mucous lining.

Acute Bronchitis

Cause of condition   Bronchitis is an inflammation of the mucous membranes of the bronchial tubes. It occurs in both acute and chronic forms. Bronchitis in an athlete is more likely to be in the acute form. Acute bronchitis usually occurs as an infectious winter disease that follows a common cold or other viral infection of the upper respiratory region. Secondary to this inflammation is a bacterial infection that may follow overexposure to air pollution. Fatigue, malnutrition, and/or chills could be predisposing factors.

Symptoms of condition   The symptoms of an athlete with acute bronchitis usually start with an upper respiratory tract infection, nasal inflammation and profuse discharge, slight fever, sore throat, and back and muscle pains. A cough signals the beginning of bronchitis. In the beginning, the cough is dry, but in a few hours or days, a clear mucous secretion begins, becoming yellowish, indicating an infection. In most cases, the fever lasts three to five days, and the cough lasts two to three weeks or longer. The athlete may wheeze and rale when auscultation of the chest is performed. Pneumonia could complicate bronchitis.

Care   To avoid bronchitis, an athlete should not sleep in an area that is extremely cold or exercise in extremely cold air without wearing a face mask to warm inhaled air. Management of acute bronchitis involves rest until fever subsides, drinking three to four glasses of water per day, and ingesting an antifever medication, a cough suppressor, and using an antibiotic (when severe lung infection is present) daily.

Bronchial Asthma

Cause of condition   As one of the most common respiratory diseases, bronchial asthma can be produced from a number of stressors, such as a viral respiratory tract infection, emotional upset, changes in barometric pressure or temperature, exercise, inhalation of a noxious odor, or exposure to a specific allergen.[19]

Symptoms of condition   Bronchial asthma is characterized by a spasm of the bronchial smooth muscles, edema, and inflammation of the mucous lining. In addition to asthma's narrowing of the airway, copious amounts of mucus are produced. Difficulty in breathing may cause the athlete to hyperventilate, resulting in dizziness. The attack may begin with coughing, wheezing, shortness of breath, and fatigue (see the accompanying Focus Box).

23-3 ▷ *Focus Box*

Management of the Acute Asthmatic Attack

Athletes who have a history of asthma usually know how to care for themselves when an attack occurs. However, the athletic trainer must be aware of what to look for and what to do if called on.

Early symptoms and signs

- Anxious appearance
- Sweating and paleness
- Flared nostrils
- Breathing with pursed lips
- Fast breathing
- Vomiting
- Hunched-over body posture
- Physical fatigue unrelated to activity
- Indentation in the notch below the Adam's apple
- Sinking in of rib spaces as the athlete inhales
- Coughing for no apparent reason
- Excess throat clearing
- Irregular, labored breathing or wheezing

Actions to take

- Attempt to relax and reassure the athlete.
- If medication has been cleared by the team physician, have the athlete use it.
- Encourage the athlete to drink water.
- Have the athlete perform controlled breathing along with relaxation exercises.
- If an environmental factor triggering the attack is known, remove it or the athlete from the area.
- If these procedures do not help, immediate medical attention may be necessary.

Care Prevention should include efforts to identify and control the causative factors. Acute attacks can be managed by using physician-prescribed medications administered through inhalers. Relief from an inhaler usually occurs in a matter of minutes. If breathing difficulty persists, the athlete should be taken to an emergency care facility.

Exercise-Induced Asthma (EIA)

Cause of condition Exercise-induced asthma (EIA) is also known as exercise-induced bronchial obstruction. It is a disease that occurs almost exclusively in asthmatic persons. An asthmatic attack can be stimulated by exercise in some individuals and can be provoked in others, only on rare occasions, during moderate exercise.[31] The exact cause of EIA is not clear. Loss of heat and water causes the greatest loss of airway reactivity. Eating certain foods such as shrimp, celery, and peanuts can cause EIA. Sinusitis can also trigger an attack in an individual with chronic asthma.[2]

Symptoms of condition The athlete with EIA may show signs of swelling of the face, swelling of the palms and soles of the feet, chest tightness, shortness of breath, coughing, nausea, hypertension, diarrhea, fatigue, itching, respiratory stridor (high-pitched noise on respiration), headaches, and redness of the skin.[24,32]

Care Long, continuous running causes the most severe bronchospasm. Swimming is the least bronchospasm producing, which may be because of the moist, warm air environment. A regular exercise program can benefit asthmatics and nonasthmatics. Fewer symptoms occur with short, intense work followed by rest than occur with sustained exercise. There should be a gradual warm-up and cooldown. The duration of exercise should build slowly to thirty to forty minutes four or five times a week. Exercise intensity and loading also should be graduated slowly. An example would be ten to thirty seconds of work followed by thirty to ninety seconds of rest. Many athletes with chronic asthma and/or EIA use the inhaled bronchodilator. Metered-dose inhalers are preferred for administration. It has also been found that prophylactic use of the bronchodilator fifteen minutes before exercise delays the symptoms by two to four hours.[2] Asthmatic athletes who receive medication for their condition should make sure that what they take is legal for competition.

The athlete undergoing a sudden asthma attack should:
Be relaxed and reassured
Use a previously specified medication
Drink water
Perform controlled breathing
Be removed from what might be triggering the attack

GASTROINTESTINAL DISORDERS

Like any other individual, the athlete may develop various complaints associated with the digestive system. The athlete may display various disorders of the gastrointestinal tract as a result of poor eating habits or the stress related to competition. The responsibility of the coach in such cases is to recognize the more severe conditions so that early referrals to a physician can be made.[22]

A balanced diet is as important as brushing the teeth in preventing gum disease.

Indigestion

Cause of condition Indigestion (dyspepsia) can be caused by any number of conditions, including food idiosyncrasies, emotional stress prior to competition, esophageal and stomach spasms, and/or inflammation of the mucous lining of the esophagus and stomach.

Symptoms of condition   Indigestion can cause sour stomach, nausea, and flatulence (gas).

Care   Care of acute dyspepsia involves the elimination of irritating foods from the diet, development of regular eating habits, and avoidance of anxieties that may lead to gastric distress.

Vomiting

Cause of condition   Vomiting results from some type of irritation, most often in the stomach, that stimulates the vomiting center in the brain to cause a series of forceful contractions of the diaphragm and abdominal muscles, compressing the stomach and forcefully expelling the contents.[12]

Care   Antinausea medications should be administered. Fluids to prevent dehydration should be administered by mouth if possible. If vomiting persists, fluids and electrolytes must be administered intravenously.

Diarrhea

Indigestion, vomiting,
diarrhea, and constipation
are common problems in the
athlete.

Cause of condition   Diarrhea can be caused by problems in diet, inflammation of the intestinal lining, gastrointestinal infection, ingestion of certain drugs, and psychogenic factors.[4]

Symptoms of condition   Diarrhea is characterized by abdominal cramps, nausea, and possibly vomiting coupled with frequent elimination of stools. Extreme weakness caused by fluid dehydration is usually present. The cause of diarrhea is often difficult to establish.

Care   Less severe cases can be cared for by omitting foods that cause irritation, eating bland food until symptoms have ceased, and using over-the-counter medications to control intestinal activity.

Constipation

Cause of condition   Constipation can be caused by insufficient moisture in the feces, causing it to be hard and dry, lack of sufficient roughage and bulk in the diet, poor bowel habits, nervousness and anxiety, or overuse of laxatives and enemas.[4]

Symptoms of condition   There is occasional intense cramping and pain in the lower abdomen, with difficulty eliminating hard-packed stools.

Care   Athletes can eliminate constipation by eating cereals, fruits, vegetables, and fats that stimulate bowel movement. Laxatives or enemas should be avoided unless their use has been prescribed by a physician.

Food Poisoning

Cause of condition   Food poisoning (gastroenteritis), which may range from mild to severe, results from infectious organisms (bacteria) that enter the body in either food or drink. Foods become contaminated by improper food refrigeration or from an infected food handler.

Symptoms of condition   Infection results in nausea, vomiting, cramps, and diarrhea that usually subside in three to six hours.

Care   Management requires rapid replacement of lost fluids and electrolytes, which in severe cases may need to be replaced intravenously. If tolerated, light fluids or foods such as clear, strained broth, bouillon, or bland cereals may be given.

Gastrointestinal Bleeding

Cause of condition   Gastrointestinal bleeding that is reflected in bloody stools can be caused by gastritis, iron-deficiency anemia, ingestion of aspirin or other antiinflammatory agents, colitis, or even stress and bowel irritation. Distance runners often have blood in their stools during and following a race.

Care   Athletes with gastrointestinal bleeding must be referred immediately to a physician.[12]

OTHER CONDITIONS THAT CAN AFFECT THE ATHLETE

Infectious Mononucleosis

Cause of condition   Infectious mononucleosis is an acute viral disease that affects mainly young adults and children. It has major significance to athletes because it can produce severe fatigue and raise the risk of spleen rupture.[7] Incubation is four to six weeks. The virus is carried in the throat and transmitted to another person by saliva. It has been called the kissing disease.[7]

Symptoms of condition   The disease usually starts with a three to five-day period of headache, fatigue, loss of appetite, and general muscle ache. From the fifth to the fifteenth day, there is fever, swollen lymph glands, and a sore throat.[8] By the second week, 50 to 70 percent of those infected will have an enlarged spleen, 10 to 15 percent will have jaundice, and 5 to 15 percent will have a skin rash, a pinkish flush to the cheeks, and puffy eyelids.[7]

Care   Care of mononucleosis is supportive and symptomatic. In many cases the athlete with this disease may resume easy training in three weeks after the onset of illness if: (1) the spleen is not markedly enlarged or painful; (2) the athlete is without a fever; (3) liver function tests are normal; and (4) the sore throat and any other complications have been resolved.

Anemia in Athletes

Iron-Deficiency Anemia

Cause of condition   Iron deficiency is the most common form of true anemia among athletes.[14] It occurs as the result of low levels of **hemoglobin** (the oxygen-carrying molecules in blood) and also of red blood cells (hematocrit). For men, iron deficiency is usually caused by blood loss in the gastrointestinal tract. For women, the most common causes are menstruation and not taking in enough iron in the diet. Athletes who are vegetarians might lack iron.

hemoglobin
Molecules that carry oxygen in blood.

Symptoms of condition   In the first stages of iron deficiency, the athlete's performance begins to decline. The athlete may complain of feeling tired and lethargic. During training there may also be complaints of muscle fatigue and nausea. Athletes with mild iron-deficiency anemia may display some mild impairment in their maximum performance.

Care   The athlete with symptoms of anemia should be sent to a physician for blood work to determine the level of hemoglobin and the hematocrit.[13] It is important to differentiate anemia from mononucleosis because symptoms are similar. Some ways that athletes can manage iron deficiency are: (1) follow a proper diet, including more red meat or dark chicken; (2) avoid coffee or tea, which hampers iron absorption from grains; (3) ingest vitamin C sources, which enhance iron absorption; and (4) take an iron supplement.

Sickle-Cell Anemia

Cause of condition   Sickle-cell anemia is a chronic hereditary anemia. The red blood cell with an abnormal sickle shape has less potential for transporting oxygen and is more fragile than normal cells. A sickle cell's life span is 15 to 25 days, compared to the 120-day life span of a normal red cell; this short life of the sickle cell can produce severe anemia in individuals with acute sickle-cell anemia. Approximately 35 percent of the black population in the United States has this condition; 8 to 13 percent are not anemic but carry this trait in their genes (sicklemia).[17] The person with the sickle-cell trait may participate in sports and never encounter problems until symptoms are brought on by some unusual circumstance.[6]

Symptoms of condition   An athlete may never experience any complications from having the sickle-cell trait. However, a sickle-cell crisis can be brought on by exposure to high altitudes or by elevated body temperature. Crisis symptoms include fever, severe fatigue, skin pallor, muscle weakness, and severe pain in the limbs and abdomen. Abdominal pain in the right upper quadrant is somewhat common. The athlete may also experience headache and convulsions.[17]

Care   Treatment of a sickle-cell crisis is usually symptomatic. The physician may elect to give anticoagulants and analgesics for pain.

Diabetes Mellitus

Cause of condition   Diabetes mellitus is a complex hereditary or developmental disease involving some imbalance between blood sugar and the hormone insulin, which is produced by the pancreas. Decreased effectiveness of insulin or an insufficient amount is responsible for most cases of diabetes. Until recently diabetics were usually discouraged from or forbidden competitive sports participation. Today an ever-increasing number of diabetics are active sports participants, functioning effectively in almost all sports. Because the key to the control of diabetes is the control of blood sugar, the insulin-dependent athlete must constantly juggle food intake, insulin, and exercise to maintain the blood sugar in its proper range if he or she is to perform to maximum. Diet, exercise, and insulin are the major factors in the everyday lifestyle of the diabetic athlete, who out of necessity must develop an ordered and specific living pattern to cope with the demands of daily existence and strenuous physical activity.[8]

Diabetic athletes engaging in vigorous physical activity should eat before exercising and, if the exercise is protracted, should have hourly glucose supplementation. As a rule the insulin dosage is not changed, but food intake is increased. The response of diabetics varies among individuals and depends on many variables. Although there are some hazards, with proper medical evaluation and planning by a consultant in metabolic diseases, diabetics can feel free to engage in most physical activities.[30]

Problems in the diabetic athlete will result either in insulin shock, in which there is too little blood sugar relative to insulin, or in diabetic coma, in which there is too much blood sugar and not enough insulin. Those who work with athletes who have diabetes mellitus must be aware of the major symptoms of diabetic coma and insulin shock and of the proper actions to take when either one occurs.[25]

Symptoms of insulin shock Insulin shock occurs when there is too little blood sugar, resulting in hypoglycemia and shock. It is characterized by physical weakness, moist and pale skin, drooping eyelids, and normal or shallow respirations.

Care for insulin shock The diabetic athlete who either forgets to eat or who engages in intense exercise and metabolizes large amounts of glycogen is more likely to experience insulin shock. To avoid this problem, the athlete must adhere to a carefully planned diet that includes a snack before exercise. The snack should contain a combination of a complex carbohydrate and a protein, for example, cheese and crackers. Activities that last for more than thirty to forty minutes should be accompanied by snacks and simple carbohydrates. Some diabetics carry with them a lump of sugar or have candy or orange juice readily available in the event that an insulin reaction seems imminent.[25,27]

Key questions to ask a diabetic athlete are:

- Have you eaten today and when?
- Have you taken your insulin today and when?

Symptoms of diabetic coma The signs of a diabetic coma include labored breathing or gasping for air, fruity-smelling breath (caused by acetone), nausea and vomiting, extreme thirst, dry mucous lining of the mouth, flushed skin, and mental confusion or unconsciousness followed by coma.

Care for diabetic coma Because the diabetic coma threatens life, early detection is essential. The only way to correct the insulin blood sugar imbalance of a diabetic coma is to inject insulin. An injection of insulin into the athlete will normally prevent coma. If the athlete does not respond within minutes following injection, emergency care is needed.

Epilepsy

Cause of condition   Epilepsy is not a disease but is a symptom manifested by a large number of underlying disorders. For some types of epilepsy there is a genetic predisposition and a low threshold to having seizures. In others, altered brain metabolism or a history of injury may be the cause.

Each person with epilepsy must be considered individually as to whether he or she should engage in competitive sports. The general recommendation is that an individual who has daily or even weekly major seizures should not participate in collision sports. This prohibition is not because a hit in the head will necessarily trigger a seizure, but because unconsciousness during participation could result in a serious injury. If the seizures are properly controlled by medication or only occur during sleep, little if any sports restriction should be imposed except for scuba diving, swimming alone, or participation in activities at some height.[4]

Symptoms of condition   **Epilepsy** is defined as "a recurrent disorder of cerebral function characterized by a sudden, brief attack of altered consciousness, motor activity, sensory phenomena, or inappropriate behavior." A seizure can range from extremely brief episodes (petit mal seizures) to major episodes (grand mal seizures), unconsciousness, and tonic-clonic muscle contractions.

Care   The athlete commonly takes an anticonvulsant medication that is specific for the type and degree of seizures that occur. On occasion an athlete may experience some undesirable side effects from drug therapy, such as drowsiness, restlessness, nystagmus, nausea, vomiting, problems with balance, skin rash, or other adverse reactions.[16]

When an athlete with epilepsy becomes aware of an impending seizure, he or she should immediately sit or lie down to avoid injury. When a seizure occurs without warning, the following steps should be taken by the coach:

- Be emotionally composed.
- If possible, cushion the athlete's fall.
- Keep the athlete away from injury-producing objects.
- Loosen restricting clothing.
- Do not try to force anything between the athlete's teeth.
- Allow the athlete to awaken normally after the seizure.

Hypertension (High Blood Pressure)

Cause of condition   Excessive pressure applied against the arterial wall while the blood circulates is known as hypertension, or high blood pressure (HBP). A normal, average pressure is 120/80 mm hg. HBP is 140/90 mm hg and over (see Table 23-1.)

Hypertension is classified as primary, or essential, and secondary. Primary hypertension accounts for 90 percent of all cases and has no disease associated with it.[1] Secondary hypertension is related to a specific under-

---

epilepsy
Recurrent paroxysmal disorder characterized by sudden attacks of altered consciousness, motor activity, sensory phenomena, or inappropriate behavior.

Individuals who have major daily or weekly seizures may be prohibited from collision sports.

TABLE 23-1 Age and blood pressure limits

Age	Upper Blood Pressure Limits at Rest*
<10	120/75 mm hg
10–12	125/80 mm hg
13–15	135/85 mm hg
16–18	140/90 mm hg
<18	140/90 mm hg

*If the upper limits of blood pressure are exceeded during three measurements, the
athlete may have hypertension.

lying cause such as a kidney disorder, overactive adrenal glands (increased blood volume), hormone-producing tumor, narrowing of the
aorta, pregnancy, or medications (oral contraceptives, cold remedies,
etc.). The presence of prolonged HBP increases the chances of coronary
artery disease, congestive heart failure, or stroke.[4]

Symptoms of condition   Primary hypertension is usually asymptomatic until complications occur.[4] Uncomplicated HBP may cause dizziness, a flushed face, headache, fatigue, epistaxis, and nervousness.

Care   The existence of HBP is not established until many pressure
readings have been taken at various times. A thorough physical examination must be conducted to ascertain the type of hypertension. Primary
hypertension can be controlled with life changes such as weight loss, salt
restriction, and aerobic exercise. In secondary hypertension, when the
underlying condition is cured, the blood pressure commonly returns to
normal. Athletes with HBP should avoid isometrics and resistive exercise
against very heavy weight.[4]

Common Contagious Viral Diseases

It is not within the scope of this text to describe in detail all the various
infectious diseases to which athletes may be prone. However, on occasion
the athlete may exhibit recognizable manifestations of such a disease; a
coach should be aware of certain signs that might indicate a contagious
viral disease (Table 23-2). When indications of a contagious disease are
present, the coach must refer the athlete to a physician without delay.

SEXUALLY TRANSMITTED DISEASES (STDS)

Sexually transmitted diseases (STDs) are of major concern in sports because many athletes are at an age during which they are more sexually
active than they will be at any other time in their life. STDs are infectious
diseases that can be contracted through sexual contact.[12] They may be
caused by bacteria or viruses. Bacterial infections such as gonorrhea,
syphilis, and chlamydia may be cured with antibiotics in the majority of
cases.[26] Serious health problems are prevented if these infections are diagnosed and treated early. Viral infections such as herpes, genital warts, and
HIV are much more difficult to treat, and in some cases no cure exists.

TABLE 23-2 Some infectious viral diseases

Disease	Sites Involved	Mode of Transmission	Incubation Period	Chief Symptoms	Duration	Period of Contagion	Treatment	Prophylaxis
Measles (rubeola)	Skin, respiratory tract, and conjunctivae	Contact or droplet	7–14 days	Appearance—like common cold with fever, cough, conjunctivitis, photophobia, and spots in throat, followed by skin rash	4–7 days after symptoms appear	Just before cold-like symptoms through approximately 1 week after rash appears	Bed rest and use of smoked glasses; symptomatic	Vaccine available
German measles (rubella)	Skin, respiratory tract, and conjunctivae	Contact or droplet	14–21 days	Cold symptoms, skin rash, and swollen lymph nodes behind ear	1–2 days	2–4 days before rash through 5 days afterward	Symptomatic	Vaccine available; gamma globulin given in post-exposure situations
Chicken pox (varicella)	Trunk; then face, neck, and limbs	Contact or droplet	14–21 days	Mild cold symptoms followed by appearance of vesicles	1–2 weeks	1 day before onset through 6 days afterward	Symptomatic	Vaccine available, including zoster immune globulin (ZIG) or varicell-zoster immune globulin (VZIG)
Mumps (epidemic parotiditis)	Salivary glands	Prolonged contact or droplet	18–21 days	Headache, drowsiness, fever, abdominal pain, pain during chewing and swallowing, swelling of neck under jaw	10 days	1 week	Symptomatic	Temporary immunization by virus vaccine
Influenza (flu)	Respiratory tract	Droplet	1–2 days	Aching of low back, generalized aching, chills, headache, fever, and bronchitis	2–5 days	2–3 days	Symptomatic	Moderate temporary protection from polyvalent influenza virus
Cold (coryza)	Respiratory tract	Droplet	12 hours to 4 days	Mild fever, headache, chills, and nasal discharge	1–2 weeks	Not clearly identified	Symptomatic	Possible help from vitamins and/or cold vaccine; avoid exposure
Infectious mononucleosis	Trunk	Contact	4–7 weeks	Sore throat, fever, skin rash, general aching, and swelling of lymph glands	3–4 weeks	Low rate	Symptomatic	None; avoid extreme fatigue

TABLE 23-3 Sexually transmitted diseases

STD	Signs	Care	Possible Problems
Chlamydia	About 75% of infected people have no symptoms. However, there may be a mild mucuslike discharge from the genitals or stinging when urinating. Also, there may be pain in the testicles (men) or abdomen (women).	Infected persons and their sexual partners must be tested and treated with antibiotics.	Painful infections of the reproductive organs, which may lead to infertility in both men and women.
Genital herpes	Sores around genitals or anus, often with small, painful blisters. Some people have no symptoms but are still infected and contagious.	Infected persons should avoid intimate sexual contact while sores persist. Acyclovir capsules or ointment may be helpful but will not cure herpes.	May contribute to cervical cancer and be transmitted to infants during childbirth.
Crab lice	Visible, blood-sucking lice in pubic hair. Causes itching. Eggs (nits) attached to hair shafts.	Treatments to kill lice. Recent sexual partners, clothing, and bed linen should be treated.	None.
Genital warts	Usually painless growths around the genitals or anus occur about 1–3 months after contact. In rare cases, growths may itch, burn, or bleed, or may not appear for years.	Chemical treatment, liquid nitrogen, laser beam, or surgery. May return after treatment.	May obstruct the urethra or complicate vaginal delivery in childbirth; may be connected to cervical cancer.
Trichomoniasis	Among women, symptoms may include a vaginal discharge, discomfort during sexual intercourse, abdominal pain, pain when urinating, and itching in the genital area. Most men have no symptoms, but some men may experience a penile discharge, painful urinating, or a "tingly" feeling in the penis.	Infected persons and their partners are treated with antibiotics.	If untreated, may lead to bladder and urethral infections in men and women.
Gonorrhea	Men may have a creamy puslike penile discharge and pain when urinating, or they may have no symptoms. Women may have vaginal discharge and pain when urinating, but often have no symptoms.	Infected persons and their sexual partners must be tested and treated with antibiotics.	If untreated, can cause arthritis, dermatitis, heart problems, and reproductive problems in both men and women. Can be transmitted to infants at birth, causing blindness.
Syphilis	Painless ulcer (chancre) at point of contact, usually penile shaft, around vaginal opening, or anus. Secondary stage may include rash or swollen lymph nodes.	Infected persons and their sexual partners must be tested and treated with antibiotics.	If untreated, may affect brain or heart, or even be fatal. Pregnant women can transmit to unborn infant.
AIDS (Acquired Immunodeficiency Syndrome)	Increased susceptibility to common infections and unusual cancers. Most people infected with the virus may show no symptoms for many years but are still contagious.	No current proven treatment. Avoid sexual contact or practice safe sex.	Full-blown AIDs almost always is fatal. Outlook for carriers of the virus is uncertain.

For more information on AIDS, see chapter 8.

STDs do not go away by themselves, although in many cases, relatively quick, painless treatments are available. No one is immune to STDs. Everyone who is sexually active can get or transmit an STD. The current trend is to emphasize prevention through safe sex practices and treatment of STDs rather than to focus on the ethics of sexual behavior. Most important, some of these diseases have the potential to cause serious, long-term health problems, even death.

Table 23-3 discusses the common STDs and their symptoms, treatment, and potential effects. It is important to keep in mind that *any* of these STDs can be transmitted through sexual contact (including vaginal and anal intercourse and oral-genital contact) with an infected partner who may or may *not* have symptoms.

SUBSTANCE ABUSE AMONG ATHLETES

There is increasing concern about the number of athletes engaging in substance abuse (see the accompanying Focus Box). Some do so in an attempt to improve performance, whereas others engage in it as a recreational pursuit. Much material has been written and discussed about the use of performance-enhancing drugs among Olympic athletes and about the widespread use of street drugs by high school, collegiate, and professional athletes. *Clearly, substance abuse has no place in the athletic population.*

Performance-Enhancing Drugs

---

doping

The administration of a drug that is designed to improve the competitor's performance.

In sports medicine, the administration of a drug that is designed to improve the competitor's performance is known as **doping.** The International Olympic Committee (IOC) defines doping as "the administration or use of substances in any form alien to the body or of physiological substances in abnormal amounts and with abnormal methods by healthy persons with the exclusive aim of attaining an artificial and unfair increase in performance in sports."

Stimulants

The intention of the athlete when he or she ingests a stimulant may be to increase alertness, to reduce fatigue, or in some instances, to increase competitiveness; ingestion can produce hostility. Some athletes respond to stimulants with a loss of judgment that may lead to personal injury or injury to others.

Amphetamines and cocaine are the psychomotor drugs most commonly used in sports. Cocaine is discussed in the section on recreational drug abuse. These drugs present an extremely difficult problem in sports because they are commonly found in cold remedies, nasal and ophthalmic decongestants, and most asthma preparations. The IOC has approved some substances to be used by asthmatics who develop exercise-induced bronchospasms. Before an athlete engages in Olympic competition, his or her team physician must notify the IOC Medical Subcommission in writing concerning drug usage.

Amphetamines Amphetamines are extremely powerful and

23-4 Focus Box

Identifying the Substance Abuser

The following are signs of drug abuse:

1. Sudden personality changes
2. Severe mood swings
3. Changing peer groups
4. Decreased interest in extracurricular and leisure activities
5. Worsening grades
6. Disregard for household chores and curfews
7. Feeling of depression most of the time
8. Breakdown in personal hygiene habits
9. Increased sleep and decreased eating
10. Clothes and skin smell of alcohol or marijuana
11. Sudden weight loss
12. Lying, cheating, stealing, etc.
13. Arrests for drunk driving or for possessing illegal substances
14. Truancies from school
15. Loses or changes jobs frequently
16. Becomes defensive at the mention of drugs or alcohol
17. Increased isolation (spends time in room)
18. Family relationship deteriorates
19. Drug paraphernalia (needles, empty bottles, etc.) found
20. Others make observations about negative behavior
21. Shows signs of intoxication
22. Constantly misses appointments
23. Falls asleep in class or at work
24. Has financial problems
25. Misses assignments or deadlines
26. Diminished productivity

dangerous drugs. They may be injected, inhaled, or taken as tablets. Amphetamines are among the most abused of the drugs used for enhancing sports performance. In ordinary doses, amphetamines can produce an increased sense of well-being and heightened mental activity—until fatigue sets in (from lack of sleep), accompanied by nervousness, insomnia, and anorexia. In high doses, amphetamines reduce mental activity and impair performance of complicated motor skills. The athlete's behavior may become irrational. The chronic user may get hung up, or in other words, become stuck, in a repetitive behavioral sequence. This behavior may last for hours, becoming increasingly more irrational. The long-term, or even short-term, use of amphetamines can lead to amphetamine psychosis, manifested by auditory and visual hallucinations and paranoid delusions.

TABLE 23-4 Examples of caffeine-containing products

Product	Dose
Coffee (1 cup)	100 mg
Diet Coke (12 oz)	45.6 mg
Diet Pepsi (12 oz)	36.0 mg
No-Doz (1)	100.0 mg
Anacin (1)	32.0 mg
Excedrin (1)	65.0 mg
Midol (1)	32.4 mg

Physiologically, high doses of amphetamines can cause abnormal pupillary dilation, increased blood pressure, and hyperthermia.

Athletes believe that amphetamines improve sports performance by promoting quickness and endurance, delaying fatigue, and increasing confidence, thereby causing increased aggressiveness. Studies indicate that there is no improvement in performance, but there is an increased risk of injury, exhaustion, and circulation collapse.

Caffeine Caffeine is found in coffee, tea, cocoa, and cola, and is readily absorbed into the body (Table 23-4). It is a central nervous system stimulant and diuretic and also stimulates gastric secretion. One cup of coffee can contain from 100 to 150 mg of caffeine. In moderation, caffeine results in wakefulness and mental alertness. In larger amounts and in individuals who ingest caffeine daily, it raises blood pressure, and decreases and then increases the heart rate. It affects coordination, sleep, mood, behavior, and thinking processes. In terms of exercise and sports performance, caffeine is controversial. Like amphetamines, caffeine can affect some athletes by acting as an ergogenic aid during prolonged exercise. A habitual user of caffeine who suddenly stops may experience withdrawal, including headache, drowsiness, lethargy, rhinorrhea, irritability, nervousness, depression, and loss of interest in work. Caffeine also acts as a diuretic when hydration may be important.

Narcotic Analgesic Drugs

Narcotic analgesic drugs are derived directly or indirectly from opium. Morphine and codeine (methylmorphine) are examples of substances made from opium. Narcotic analgesics are used for the management of moderate-to-severe pain. They have been banned by the IOC because of the high risk of physical and psychological dependency and because of many other problems stemming from their use. Slight-to-moderate pain can be effectively dealt with by drugs other than narcotics.

Beta Blockers

Medically, beta blockers are used for hypertension and heart disease. In sports, beta blockers have been used by athletes who require steadiness, whose signs of nervousness must be in control while engaging in sports such as target shooting, sailing, archery, fencing, ski jumping, and luge. Beta blockers relax the blood vessels. This relaxation, in turn, slows heart rate and decreases cardiac output. Therapeutically, beta blockers are used for a variety of cardiac diseases as well as for treating hypertension.

Diuretics

Diuretics are used for a variety of cardiovascular and respiratory conditions (e.g., hypertension) in which elimination of fluids from tissues is necessary. Sports participants have misused diuretics mainly in two ways: to reduce body weight quickly or to decrease a drug's concentration in the urine (increasing its excretion to avoid the detection of drug misuse). In both cases, there are ethical and health grounds for banning certain classes of diuretics from use during Olympic competition.

Anabolic Steroids and Human Growth Hormone

Two substance classes related to the increase of muscle build, strength, power, and growth are anabolic steroids and human growth hormone (HGH). Both are abused during sports participation.

Anabolic steroids   Androgenic hormones are products of the male testes. Of these hormones, testosterone is the principal one; it possesses the ability to function androgenically (the ability to stimulate male characteristics) and anabolically (the ability to, through an improved protein assimilation, increase muscle mass and weight, general growth, bone maturation, and virility). When prescribed by a physician to improve certain physiological conditions, these drugs have value. In 1984, the American College of Sports Medicine (ACSM) reported that anabolic androgenic steroids taken with an adequate diet could contribute to an increase in body weight and, with a heavy resistance program, to a significant gain in strength. However, in sports, anabolic steroids constitute a major threat to the health of the athlete (see the accompanying Focus Box). Anabolic steroids present an ethical dilemma for the sports world. It is estimated that more than a million young male and female athletes are taking them, with most being purchased through the black market. It is estimated that 6.5 percent of male and 1.4 percent of female high school students take or have taken anabolic steroids. Also an estimated 2 to 20 percent of male intercollegiate athletes take anabolic steroids.

If these drugs are given to the prepubertal boy, a most certain hazard is a decrease in his ultimate height because of the cessation of long bone growth. Acne, hirsutism, a deepening of the voice in the prepubescent boy, and in some cases, a swelling of the breasts, called gynecomastia, are among other androgen effects. The ingestion of steroids by females can result in **hirsutism** and in a deepening of the voice because of vocal cord alteration. When the dosage is halted, the hirsutism may cease, but the change in the vocal cords is irreversible. As the duration and dosage increase, the possibility of producing androgen effects also increases. Because self-administered overdosage seems to be the pattern of those who

hirsutism (her soot ism**)**
Excessive hair growth and/or the presence of hair in unusual places.

23-5 > **Focus Box**

Examples of Deleterious Effects of Anabolic Steroids

- *Teens*—premature closure of long bones, acne, hirsutism, voice deepening, enlarged mammary glands (gynecomastia) of the male
- *Men*—male-pattern baldness, acne, voice deepening, mood swings, aggressive behavior, decreased high-density lipoprotein, increased cholesterol, reduction in size of testicle, reduced testosterone production, changes in libido
- *Women*—female-pattern baldness, acne, voice deepening (irreversible), increased facial hair, enlarged clitoris (irreversible), increased libido, menstrual irregularities, increased aggression, decreased body fat, increased appetite, decreased breast size
- *Abuse*—may lead to liver tumors and cancer, heart disease, and hypertension

use steroids, the preceding statement is most significant. Abuse of these drugs may also lead to cancer of the liver and prostate glands as well as to heart disease.

Anabolic steroids are most abused in sports that involve strength. Power lifting, the throwing events in track and field, and American football are some of the sports in which the use of anabolic steroids is a serious problem. Because female athletes are developing the attitude of "win at all costs," their abuse of anabolic steroids is also becoming a major health concern.

Human growth hormone   Human growth hormone (HGH) is a hormone produced by the pituitary gland. It is released into circulation in a pulsating manner. This release can vary with a person's age and developmental period. A lack of HGH can result in dwarfism. In the past, HGH was in limited supply because it was extracted from cadavers. Now, however, it can be made synthetically and is more available.

Experiments indicate that HGH can increase muscle mass, skin thickness, connective tissues in muscle, and organ weight and can produce lax muscles and ligaments during rapid growth phases. It also increases body length and weight and decreases body fat percentage.

The use of HGH by athletes throughout the world is on the increase because it is more difficult to detect in urine than anabolic steroids are. There is currently a lack of concrete information about the effects of HGH on the athlete who does not have a growth problem. It is known that an overabundance of HGH in the body can lead to premature closure of long-bone growth sites or, conversely, can cause acromegaly, a condition that produces elongation and enlargement of bones of the extremities and thickening of bones and soft tissues of the face. Also associated with acromegaly is diabetes mellitus, cardiovascular disease, goiter, menstrual disorders, decreased sexual desire, and impotence. It decreases the life span by up to twenty years. Like anabolic steroids, HGH presents a serious problem for the sports world. At this time there is no proof that an increase of HGH combined with weight training contributes to strength and muscle hypertrophy.

Other Drugs Subject to IOC Restriction

The IOC indicates that although it does not expressly prohibit alcohol, blood alcohol levels may be determined at the request of the committee. Local anesthetics that are injected (excluding cocaine) are permitted. Corticosteroids have been abused because of their ability to produce euphoria and certain side effects. They are, therefore, banned during the Olympic Games except for topical use or for inhalation therapy and intraarticular injections.

Blood Reinjection (Blood Doping, Blood Packing, and Blood Boosting)

Endurance, acclimatization, and altitude make increased metabolic demands on the body, which responds by increasing blood volume and red blood cells to meet the increased aerobic demands.[11]

Recently researchers have replicated these physiological responses by removing 900 ml of blood, storing it, and reinfusing it after six weeks. The reason for waiting at least six weeks before reinfusion is it takes that long for the athlete's body to reestablish a normal hemoglobin and red blood cell concentration. Using this method, endurance performance has been significantly improved. From the standpoint of scientific research, such experimentation has merit and is of interest. However, not only is use of such methods in competition unethical, but when conducted by nonmedical personnel, it could prove to be dangerous, especially when a matched donor is used.

> Not only is the use of blood reinjection in competition unethical, but when conducted by nonmedical personnel, it could prove dangerous.

There are serious risks with transfusing blood and related blood products. The risks include allergic reactions, kidney damage (if the wrong type of blood is used), fever, jaundice, the possibility of transmitting infectious diseases (viral hepatitis or AIDS), or blood overload, resulting in circulatory and metabolic shock.

Recreational Drug Abuse

Just like it has become a part of the general world, recreational drug use has become a part of the world of sports. Reasons for using these substances may include desire to experiment, to temporarily escape from problems, or to just be part of a group (peer pressure). For some, recreational drug use leads to abuse and dependence. There are two general aspects of dependence: psychological and physical. Psychological dependence is the drive to repeat the ingestion of a drug to produce pleasure or to avoid discomfort. Physical dependence is the state of drug adaptation that manifests itself as the development of tolerance and, when the drug is removed, causes a withdrawal syndrome. Tolerance of a drug is the need to increase the dosage to create the effect that was obtained previously by smaller amounts. The withdrawal syndrome consists of an unpleasant physiological reaction when the drug is abruptly stopped. Some drugs that are abused by the athlete overlap with those thought to enhance performance. Examples include amphetamines and cocaine. Tobacco (nicotine), alcohol, cocaine, and marijuana are the most abused recreational drugs. The coach might also come in contact with abuse by athletes of barbiturates, nonbarbiturate sedatives, psychotomimetic drugs, or different inhalants.

Tobacco

A number of current problems are related to tobacco and sports. They can be divided into two headings: cigarette smoking and the use of smokeless tobacco.

Cigarette smoking　On the basis of various investigations into the relationship between smoking and performance, the following conclusions can be drawn:

- Individuals vary in sensitivity to tobacco, and relatively high sensitivity may seriously affect performance. Because more than one-third of men studied indicate tobacco sensitivity, it may be wise to prohibit smoking by athletes.
- Tobacco smoke has been associated with as many as 4,700 different chemicals, many of which are toxic.
- As few as ten inhalations of cigarette smoke cause an average maximum decrease in airway conductance of 50 percent. This decrease occurs as well in nonsmokers who inhale secondhand smoke.
- Smoking reduces the oxygen-carrying capacity of the blood. A smoker's blood carries five to ten times more carbon monoxide than normal; thus the red blood cells are prevented from picking up sufficient oxygen to meet the demands of the body's tissues. The carbon monoxide also tends to make arterial walls more permeable to fatty substances, a factor in atherosclerosis.
- Smoking aggravates and accelerates the heart muscle cells through overstimulation of the sympathetic nervous system.
- Total lung capacity and maximum breathing capacity are significantly decreased in heavy smokers; this is important to the athlete, because both changes would impair the capacity to take in oxygen and make it readily available for body use.
- Smoking decreases pulmonary diffusing capacity.
- After smoking, an accelerated thrombolic tendency is evidenced.
- Smoking is a carcinogenic factor in lung cancer and is a contributing factor to heart disease.

The addictive chemical of tobacco is nicotine, which is one of the most toxic drugs. When ingested, nicotine causes blood pressure elevation, increased bowel activity, and an antidiuretic action. Moderate tolerance and physical dependence occur. It also has been noted that passive inhalation of cigarette smoke can reduce maximum aerobic power and endurance capacity.

Use of smokeless tobacco   It is estimated that 36 percent of athletes use smokeless tobacco, which comes in three forms: loose-leaf, moist or dry powder (snuff), and compressed.[28] The tobacco is placed between the cheek and the gum, where it is sucked and chewed. Aesthetically, this is an unsavory habit during which an athlete is continually spitting into a container. Besides the unpleasant appearance, the use of smokeless tobacco proposes an extremely serious health risk. Smokeless tobacco causes bad breath, stained teeth, tooth sensitivity to heat and cold, cavities, gum recession, tooth bone loss, leukoplakia, and oral and throat cancer. Aggressive oral and throat cancer and periodontal destruction (with tooth loss) have been associated with this habit. The major substance injested is nitrosonornicotine, which is the drug responsible for this habit's addictiveness. This chemical makes smokeless tobacco a more addictive habit than smoking is. Smokeless tobacco increases heart rate but does not affect reaction time, movement time, or total response time among athletes or nonathletes.[10]

Coaches, athletic trainers, and professional athletes themselves must avoid the use of smokeless tobacco to present a positive role model.[10]

Alcohol

Alcohol is the number one abused drug in the United States. Alcohol is absorbed directly into the bloodstream through the small intestine. It accumulates in the blood because alcohol absorption is faster than its oxidation. It acts as a central nervous system depressant, producing sedation and tranquility. Characteristically, alcohol consumption, at any time and in any amount, does not improve mental or physical abilities and should be completely avoided by athletes. Alcohol consumption on a large scale can lead to a moderate degree of tolerance. Alcohol has no place in sports participation.

> Alcohol consumption, at any time or in any amount, does not improve mental or physical abilities and should be avoided by athletes.

Cocaine

Cocaine, sometimes called "coke," "snow," "toot," "happy dust," and "white girl," is a powerful central nervous system stimulant as well as a local anesthetic and vasoconstrictor. Besides being a banned performance enhancer, cocaine is one of the most abused recreational drugs. It can be inhaled, smoked, or injected (intravenously, subcutaneously, or intramuscularly).

In high doses cocaine, which is found in the leaves of the coca bush, causes a sense of excitement and euphoria. On occasion it also produces hallucinations. When applied locally to the skin, cocaine acts as an anesthetic; however, when taken into the body through inhalation, snorting, or injection, it acts on the central nervous system.

Crack   Crack, a highly purified form of cocaine, is smoked and is known to produce a virtually instantaneous high. Habitual use of cocaine will not lead to physical tolerance or dependence but will cause psychological dependence and addiction. When cocaine is used recreationally, the athlete feels alert, self-satisfied, and powerful. Heavy usage can produce paranoid delusions and violent behavior. Overuse can lead to overstimulation of the sympathetic nervous system and can cause tachycardia, hypertension, extra heartbeats, coronary vasoconstriction, strokes, pulmonary edema, aortic rupture, and sudden death.

Marijuana

Marijuana is another one of the most abused drugs in Western society. It is more commonly called "grass," "weed," "pot," "dope," or "hemp." The marijuana cigarette is called a "joint," "j," "number," "reefer," or "root." Marijuana is not a harmless drug. The components of marijuana smoke are similar to those of tobacco smoke and the same cellular changes are observed in the user.

Continued use leads to respiratory diseases such as asthma and bronchitis and to a decrease in vital capacity of 15 to 40 percent (certainly detrimental to physical performance). Among other deleterious effects are lowered sperm counts and testosterone levels. Evidence of interference with the functioning of the immune system and cellular metabolism has also been found. The most consistent sign of this interference is an increase in pulse rate, which averages close to 20 percent higher during exercise and is a definite factor in limiting performance. Some decrease in leg, hand, and finger strength has been found at higher dosages. Like tobacco, marijuana must be considered carcinogenic.

Psychological effects such as a diminution of self-awareness and judgment, a slowdown of thinking, and a shorter attention span appear early in the use of the drug. Postmortem examinations of habitual users reveal not only cerebral atrophy but alterations of anatomical structures, which suggest irreversible brain damage. Marijuana also contains unique substances (cannabinoids) that are stored, in much the same manner as are fat cells, throughout the body and in the brain tissues for weeks and even months. These stored quantities result in a cumulative deleterious effect on the habitual user.

A drug such as marijuana has no place in sports. Claims for its use are unsubstantiated, and the harmful effects, both immediate and long-term, are too significant to permit indulgence at any time.

MENSTRUAL IRREGULARITIES AND THE FEMALE REPRODUCTIVE SYSTEM

Because women in the United States participate more in sports and are training harder than ever before in history, the question arises as to what impact these factors have on menstruation and reproduction.[9]

During the prepubertal period, girls are the equal of, and are often superior to, boys of the same age in activities requiring speed, strength, and endurance. The difference between males and females is not readily ap-

During the prepubertal period, girls are the equal of, and are often superior to, boys of the same age in activities requiring speed, strength, and endurance.

parent until after puberty. At puberty the gulf begins to widen, with males exhibiting a slow, gradual increase in strength, speed, and endurance.

Menarche, the onset of the menses, normally occurs between the tenth and the seventeenth year, and the majority of girls enter it between thirteen and fifteen years of age. There is some indication that strenuous training and competition may delay the onset of menarche. The greatest delay is related to the higher caliber competition. The late-maturing girl commonly has longer legs, narrower hips, and less adiposity and body weight for her height, all of which are more conducive to sports.[3]

As interest and participation in girls' and women's sports grow, the various myths that have surrounded female participation and the effects of participation on menarche, menstruation, and childbirth are gradually being dispelled. The effects of sustained and strenuous training and competition on the menstrual cycle and the effects of menstruation on performance, however, still cannot be fully explained.

The onset of menarche may be delayed by strenuous training and competition.

Menstrual Irregularities

Menarche may be delayed in highly physically active women. **Amenorrhea** (absence of menses) and *oligomenorrhea* (diminished flow) have been common in professional female ballet dancers, gymnasts, and long-distance runners.[15] Runners who decrease training, because of an injury for example, often report a return of regular menses. Weight gain together with less intense exercise also is reported to reverse amenorrhea and oligomenorrhea. Because these irregularities may or may not be normal aspects of thinness and hard physical training, it is advisable that a physician be consulted. To date, there is no indication that these conditions will adversely affect reproduction. Almost any type of menstrual disorder can be caused by overly stressful and demanding sports activity—amenorrhea, dysmenorrhea, menorrhagia (excessive menstruation), oligomenorrhea, polymenorrhea (abnormal frequent menstruation), irregular periods, or any combination of these.[3]

> **amenorrhea**
> (amen oh **ree** ah)
> Absence or suppression of menstruation.

Dysmenorrhea

Dysmenorrhea (painful menstruation) apparently is prevalent among more active women; however, it is inconclusive whether specific sports participation can alleviate or produce dysmenorrhea. For women with moderate-to-severe dysmenorrhea, gynecological consultation is warranted to rule out a pathological condition.

Dysmenorrhea is caused by ischemia (a lack of normal blood flow to the pelvic organs) or by a possible hormonal imbalance. This syndrome, which is identified by cramps, nausea, lower abdominal pain, headache, and, on occasion, emotional lability, is the most common menstrual disorder. Physicians usually prescribe mild-to-vigorous exercises that help ameliorate dysmenorrhea. Physicians also generally advise a continuance of the usual sports participation during the menstrual period, provided the performance level of the individual does not drop below her customary level of ability. Among athletes, swimmers have the highest incidence of

Women who have moderate-to-severe dysmenorrhea require examination by a physician.

dysmenorrhea; it occurs most often, quite probably, as the result of strenuous sports participation during the menses. Generally, oligomenorrhea, amenorrhea, and irregular or scanty flow are more common in sports that require strenuous exertion over a long period of time. A great deal of variability exists among female athletes with regard to the menstrual pattern and its effect on physical performance. Each individual must learn to make adjustments to her lifestyle that will permit her to function effectively and efficiently with a minimum of discomfort or restriction.

The Female Athlete Triad

23-3

Critical Thinking Exercise

A female athlete has been diagnosed as having both an eating disorder and amenorrhea.

? Why may these two medical disorders eventually be associated with osteoporosis?

The relationship of three medical disorders has been termed the female athlete triad. The triad consists of disordered eating, amenorrhea, and osteoporosis, a bone disease marked by softening and decreased density.[28] The young female athlete, driven to excel in her chosen sport and pressured to fit a specific athletic image in order to reach her goals, is at risk for the development of disordered patterns of eating that may lead to menstrual dysfunction and subsequent premature osteoporosis. This triad has the potential for serious illness and death.[20]

Contraceptives and Reproduction

Female athletes have been known to take extra oral contraceptive pills to delay menstruation during competition. This practice is not recommended because the pills should be taken no more than twenty-one days, followed by a seven-day break. Side effects range from nausea, vomiting, fluid retention, and amenorrhea to the extreme effects of hypertension and double vision. Some oral contraceptives make women hypersensitive to the sun. Any use of oral contraceptives related to physical performance should be under the express direction and control of a physician. However, oral contraceptive use is acceptable for females with no medical problems who have coitus at least twice a week. The new low-dose preparations, containing less than 50 mg of estrogen, add negligible risks to the healthy woman.[18]

During pregnancy, athletes exhibit high levels of muscle tonicity. Women who suffer from a chronic disability after childbirth usually have a record of little or no physical exercise in the decade immediately preceding pregnancy. Generally, competition may be engaged in well into the third month of pregnancy unless bleeding or cramps are present and can frequently be continued until the seventh month if no handicapping or physiological complications arise. Such activity may make pregnancy, childbirth, and postparturition less stressful. Many athletes do not continue beyond the third month because of a drop in their performance that can result from a number of reasons, some related to their pregnancy, others perhaps psychological. It is during the first three months of pregnancy that the dangers of disturbing the pregnancy are greatest. After that period there is less danger to the mother and fetus because the pregnancy is stabilized. There is no indication that mild-to-moderate exercise during pregnancy is harmful to fetal growth and development or causes reduced fetal mass, increased perinatal or neonatal mortality, or physical or mental retardation.[18] It has been found, however, that extreme exercise may lower birth weight.

Many athletes compete during pregnancy with no ill effects. Most physicians, although advocating moderate activity during this period, believe that especially vigorous performance, particularly in activities in which there may be severe body contact or heavy jarring or falls, should be avoided.

SUMMARY

- The most common skin infections in athletes are caused by viruses, bacteria, and fungi. Viral infections include herpes simplex (e.g., the cold sore) and herpes zoster. The two most common types of bacterial infections are streptococcus and staphyloccus. Ringworm, or tinea, is the fungus infection commonly attacking all areas of the body; tinea pedis (athlete's foot) is the most common.

- The common cold, sinusitis, sore throat, hay fever, and asthma are respiratory tract illnesses that can adversely affect the athlete. Asthma can be chronic (e.g., bronchial) or induced by physical activity. Care of the athlete who is having an acute asthmatic attack requires understanding the early symptoms and signs and responding accordingly.

- A number of conditions of the digestive system, such as diarrhea, vomiting, constipation, and gastroenteritis, commonly affect the athletic population.

- Anemia is a problem for some athletes. Iron-deficiency anemia is a condition found most often in women. In an athlete with iron-deficiency anemia, the red blood cells are either too small or too large and hemoglobin is decreased. The athlete with sickle-cell anemia may have an adverse reaction at high altitudes at which the sickle-shaped red blood cell is unable to transport oxygen adequately.

- Diabetes mellitus is a complex hereditary or developmental disease of carbohydrate metabolism. Decreased effectiveness of insulin or an insufficient amount of insulin is responsible for most cases of diabetes. The diabetic athlete must carefully monitor his or her energy output to ensure a balance of food intake and the burning of sugars via insulin. If this balance is not maintained, diabetic coma or insulin shock may result.

- Epilepsy is defined as "a recurrent paroxysmal disorder of cerebral function characterized by sudden, brief attacks of altered consciousness, motor activity, sensory phenomena, or inappropriate behavior." A coach must recognize that an athlete is going into seizure and be able to provide proper immediate care.

- The athlete with high blood pressure may have to be carefully monitored by the physician. Hypertension may require the avoidance of heavy resistive activities.

- Because communicable viral diseases such as German measles, mumps, and infectious mononucleosis can infect many athletes on a team, early recognition is necessary. When such a disease is suspected, the athlete should be isolated from other athletes and immediately referred to a physician for diagnosis.

- Sexually transmitted disease has its highest incidence among younger, sexually active persons. Because most athletes are in this high-risk age group, coaches should be concerned about the spread of these diseases. Suggestions to avoid these infections are safe sex, which involves the use of a condom or the elimination of multiple partners, and complete abstinence from sexual intercourse.

- A major problem in sports participation is the extensive use of performance aids, consisting of drugs and blood doping. Certain performance-enhancing drugs, including stimulants, narcotic analgesics, diuretics, anabolic steroids, and human growth hormone, have been banned. Blood doping has also been placed in the banned category.

- Another area of concern is recreational drug abuse. This abuse is worldwide. It leads to serious psychological and physical health problems. The most prevalent substances that are abused are alcohol, nicotine, cocaine, and marijuana.

Solutions to Critical Thinking Exercises

23-1 Tinea pedis causes severe itching underneath and between the toes and on the sole of the foot. A red, white, or grayish, scaling appearance may also be present. Scratching can cause infection. Generally this condition can be prevented by wearing clean, dry socks and making certain that the foot and toes are dry following bathing.

23-2 It appears that the athlete is exhibiting sign and symptoms associated with the flu. In general the flu is caused by a viral infection, and thus the illness must simply be allowed to run its course while dealing with it symptomatically.

23-3 The female athlete triad includes some form of eating disorder, amenorrhea, and osteoporosis. The eating disorder causes amenorrhea, in which menstruation stops, thus reducing the production of estrogen, which ultimately causes a loss of calcium from the bone.

REVIEW QUESTIONS AND CLASS ACTIVITIES

1. Describe the organisms underlying the common skin infections seen in athletes. Name a disease caused by each one.
2. Invite a dermatologist or other professional to speak to the class about skin conditions, skin disease, and their care. He or she may wish to discuss specific conditions that pose a serious threat to the athlete's health and to others.
3. Describe the anemias that most often affect the athlete. How should each be managed?
4. What are the most common conditions related to the digestive system?

5. What is diabetes mellitus? What is the difference between diabetic coma and insulin shock? How is each managed?

6. What is epilepsy? What should a coach do for the athlete during a seizure? After it?

7. What is hypertension and how should it be addressed in athletics?

8. In a sports setting, what would be the indication that an athlete has a contagious disease?

9. Discuss some of the indicators of common sexually transmitted diseases. How can STDs be prevented?

10. Discuss the ethics of using drugs to improve sports performance.

11. How do stimulants enhance an athlete's performance? Do they, in fact, enhance it?

12. What are the deleterious effects of hormonal manipulation in sports?

13. Describe blood doping in sports. Why is it used? What are its dangers?

14. List the dangers of smokeless tobacco. List the effects of nicotine on the body.

15. Select a recreational drug to research. What are the physiological responses to it, and what dangers does it pose to the athlete?

16. How can an athlete who is abusing drugs be identified? Describe behavioral identification as well as drug testing.

17. Discuss menstrual irregularities that occur in highly active athletes. Why do they occur? How should they be managed? How do they relate to reproduction? What is the female athlete triad and how can it be prevented?

REFERENCES

1. American College of Sports Medicine: Position stand: physical activity, physical fitness, and hypertension, *Med Sci Sports Exerc* 25(10):1, 1993.

2. Bartimole J: Exercise-induced asthma: pre-treating for prevention, *NATA News* 4, 1995.

3. Benson MT, editor: *1994–95 NCAA sports medicine handbook: menstrual-cycle dysfunction*, Overland Park, Kan, 1994, National Collegiate Athletic Association.

4. Berkow R, editor: *The Merck manual*, ed 16, Rahway, NJ, 1992, Merck.

5. Blumenthal MN: Sports-aggravated allergies, *Physician Sportsmed* 18:12, 1990.

6. Eichner ER: Sickle cell trait, heroic exercise, and fatal collapse, *Physician Sportsmed* 21(7):51, 1993.

7. Eichner ER: Infectious mononucleosis: recognition and management in athletes, *Physician Sportsmed* 15:61, 1987.

8. Ekoe J-M: Overview of diabetes mellitus and exercise, *Med Sci Sports Exerc* 21; 4, 1989.

9. Furth SJ: Factors associated with menstrual irregularities and decreased bone density in female athletes, *JOSPT* 1:26, July 1995.

10. Glover ED et al: Smokeless tobacco: questions and answers, *Ath Train* 25:10, 1990.

11. Gledhill N: Blood doping and performance. In Torg JS, Welsh RP, Shephard RJ, editors: *Current therapy in sports medicine*, vol 2, Philadelphia, 1990, BC Decker.

12. Hamann B: *Disease: identification, prevention, and control*, St Louis, 1994, Mosby.

13. Harris SS: Exercise-related anemias. In Agostini R, editor: *Medical and orthopedic issues of active and athletic women*, St Louis, 1994, Mosby.

14. Harris SS: Helping active women avoid anemia, *Physician Sportsmed* 23(5):34, 1995.

15. Harter-Snow C: Athletic amenorrhea and bone health. In Agostini R, editor: *Medical and orthopedic*

issues of active and athletic women, St Louis, 1994, Mosby.

16. Howe WB: The athlete with chronic illness. In Birrer RB, editor: *Sports medicine for the primary care physician,* ed 2, Boca Raton, Fla, 1994, CRC Press.

17. Jones JD, Kleiner DM: Awareness and identification of athletes with sickle cell disorders at historically black colleges and universities, *Jr. Ath. Tr.* 31:220, July–Sept 1996.

18. LeBrun CM: Effects of the menstrual cycle and birth control pills on athletic performance. In Agostini R, editor: *Medical and orthopedic issues of active and athletic women,* St Louis, 1994, Mosby.

19. Mahler DA: Exercise-induced asthma, *Med Sci Sports Exerc,* 25(5):554, 1993.

20. Nattiv A, Lynch L: The female athlete triad, *Physician Sportsmed* 22(1):60, 1994.

21. Partin N: Prevention and control of influenza, *NATA News,* 23, Mar 1993.

22. Primos WA: Sports and exercise during acute illness, *Physician Sportsmed* 24:44, Jan 1996.

23. Ramsey ML: Skin care for active people, *Physician Sportsmed* 25:131, Mar 1997.

24. Rupp NT: Diagnosis and management of exercise-induced asthma, *Physician Sportsmed* 24:77, Jan 1996.

25. Robbins DC, Carleton S: Managing the diabetic athlete, *Physician Sportsmed* 17(12):45, 1989.

26. Ryan SW: Managing urinary tract and vaginal infections, *Physician Sportsmed* 24:101, July 1996.

27. Sports medicine digest: Diabetes 18:109–120 Oct. 1996. Lippincott-Raven, MD.

28. Smith AD: The female athlete triad, *Physician Sportsmed* 24:67, July 1996.

29. Stiene HA: Management of infections in athletes, *Sports Med Digest* 14:1, 1992.

30. Taunton JE, McCargarl EL: Staying active with diabetes, Physician Sportsmed 23(3):55, 1995.

31. Terrel T et al: Identifying exercise allergies, *Physician Sportsmed* 24:76, Nov 1996.

32. Virant FS: Exercise-induced bronchospasm: epidemiology, pathology, and therapy, *Med Sci Sports Exerc* 24:851, 1992.

ANNOTATED BIBLIOGRAPHY

Berkow R, editor: *The Merck manual,* ed 16, Rahway, NJ, 1992, Merck.

   One of the classic medical references available to health care professionals. It covers most medical conditions.

Tabor's Cyclopedic Medical Dictionary, Philadelphia, 1993, FA Davis.

   Despite the fact that this text appears in dictionary format, there is a wealth of valuable information on various health conditions contained in this volume.

Hamann B: *Diseases: identification, prevention, and control,* St Louis, 1994, Mosby.

   An excellent reference guide for the health professional on the most common human diseases.

WEB SITES

Cramer First Aider: http://www.ccsd.k12.wy.us/CCHS_web/sptmed/fstaider.htm

Yahoo Search Engine for Diseases and Conditions: http://www.yahoo.com/Health/Diseases_and_Conditions

Young Athletes

When you finish this chapter you will be able to:

- Explain the impact that sports has on young athletes.
- Describe the advantages and disadvantages of training and conditioning of young athletes.
- Explain the pros and cons of children competing in organized sports.
- Explain the need for better trained coaches and for the certification of coaches.
- Describe the child's potential for injury in sports activities.

Sports can promote:
Responsible social behaviors
Greater academic success
Confidence in physical abilities
Appreciation of health and fitness
Positive ethical behaviors

Many parents and health professionals question the value of sports for the immature child.

U nder the best of circumstances, sports programs for young participants promote responsible social behaviors, greater academic success, confidence in their physical abilities, an appreciation of personal health and fitness, and the development of strong social bonds. Sports, when specifically planned for, can provide a venue for the learning of positive ethical behaviors.

CULTURAL TRENDS

Organized competitive sports in North America continue to grow at a high rate even though there is some concern by parents, educational professionals, and some physicians. In 1974 the American Academy of Pediatrics adopted a position stand against organized competitive athletics for children under the age of fourteen, primarily due to excessive emotional and physical stress that might be placed on the growing child. It is obvious that this stand has not been accepted by most individuals in our society, especially those who are deeply involved with youth sports.[4]

Parents and professionals in the areas of education, psychology, and medicine have long questioned whether vigorous physical training and competition are advisable for the immature child. Increasingly, children are engaging in intense programs of training that may require many hours of daily commitment extending over many years. Swimmers may practice two hours, two times a day, covering 6,000 to 10,000 meters each session; gymnasts may practice three to five hours per day; and runners may cover as many as seventy miles each week.

TABLE 24-1 Estimated number of youth enrolled in specific categories of youth sports.[3]

Activities	Estimated number of participants
Agency-sponsored sports (Little League baseball, Pop Warner football)	22 million
Club sports (Fee-based services such as gymnastics, ice skating, and swimming)	2.4 million
Recreational sports programs (Everyone Plays, sponsored by recreational departments)	14.5 million
Intramural sports (in middle, junior, senior high schools)	10.5 million
Interscholastic sports (in middle, junior, senior high schools)	7.5 million

The number of youth between five and seventeen years of age in the United States engaging in youth sports is estimated at more than 46 million. The National Youth Sports Foundation estimates that between 20 and 30 million U.S. children are in organized out-of-school sports with another 25 million participating in competitive school sports (Table 24-1).

Forty-six million youth between the ages of five and seventeen engage in sports.

PHYSICAL IMMATURITY AND THE PROPER MATCHING OF ATHLETES

Many professionals concerned with the well-being of young athletes believe that highly competitive sports, especially collision-type sports, place great stresses on immature skeletal structures. The skeleton is not completely mature until early adulthood. An example of this point is that the femur does not reach full maturity until approximately nine years of age. The main concern of individuals against highly competitive contact or collision sports is that injuries could cause an immature cessation of growth in a particular bone. With this concern in mind, the following activities should be performed with caution:

24-1

Critical Thinking Exercise

The estimated number of youth sport participants between five and seventeen years of age in the United States is more than 46 million.

? What are the predominant injuries sustained by this age group?

- Falling, jumping, and landing with straight legs
- Excessive stress to the shoulder and elbow from repeated hard throwing motions
- Long duration exercise involving weight bearing, such as long distance running
- Heavy weight lifting

All youth sports participants should be matched by physical maturation, weight, size, and skill levels. Of major importance is that a physical examination should be given before the child enters organized competitive sports.[2]

Young athletes should be matched by:
Physical maturation
Weight
Size
Skill level
Extent of experience in the sport

Loose-jointed children appear to be more susceptible to injuries in contact and collision sports and should be directed to other sports until their bodies can withstand the rigors of falling and of physical contact. In contrast the child whose muscular system is very tight is more prone to muscle strains with an increased risk of injury to extremities and spinal region.[4]

PHYSICAL CONDITIONING AND TRAINING

According to current data, youngsters adapt well to the same type of training routines used to train the mature athlete.[8] Coaches and parents should note, however, that children do not relate to the same motivation to work as adults do. Until about twelve years of age, children are not usually aware of the different levels of effort that they can expend and do not understand that they can increase their ability in the sport by increasing their effort.

Extreme training intensity can increase a child's chance of sustaining an overuse injury. Even though Wolff's law is at work when the growing child is experiencing intensive physical training, close supervision must be taken by coaches to avoid a risk of injury. (See Figure 24-1.)

GENDER CONSIDERATIONS

There is no need to separate preadolescent girls and boys in competitive sports.

The American Academy of Pediatrics also indicates that there is no physical reason to separate preadolescent girls and boys by gender in recreational or competitive sports activities. Separation of genders should oc-

Fig. 24-1

Unsupervised play is generally more dangerous than organized sports activities are.

cur in collision-type sports once boys have attained greater muscle mass in proportion to their body weight.

PSYCHOLOGICAL AND LEARNING CONCERNS

Of even more concern than the physical aspects of sports are the psychological stresses that may be placed on children by overzealous parents and coaches. Children must not be considered to be miniature adults. Although children can mimic adult skills, they often cannot understand sports concepts such as playing fair unless specifically taught.

Children usually are eager to please adults, making them vulnerable to coercion and manipulation. A coach must use a positive approach by giving children frequent encouragement with positive reinforcements followed by corrective feedback. With this method the young athlete has the opportunity to develop a sense of self-worth and positive self-esteem.

Not all children are equal in ability. Some children respond well to competition, others respond poorly, as usually demonstrated by their level of performance. A child must be shown that there are benefits in experiencing a loss and that trying to the best of his or her ability is the most important factor in competition. Parents and coaches must realize that children are not good at making performance corrections unless instructions are given instantly at the time of the situation. In other words, half-time performance suggestions given a half-hour later may have little effect on the child.

Enjoyment of an activity, rather than winning at all costs, should be the focus of a child's training, conditioning, and competition. Too often parents who were fine athletes or who wanted to be great athletes coerce their young children to the point of anxiety and a dislike for the sport.

Sports should allow boys and girls to develop positive self-esteem.

COACHING QUALIFICATIONS

No federal laws require coaching education at any level of competition. Currently, the way to become trained as a coach in the United States is to complete a university degree program, a National Body of Sports certification program, and/or a youth sports coaching education program.[5] Up until 1996 no coaching standards had been developed.[6] The National Association for Sport and Physical Education (NASPE) is now in the process of developing an accreditation program. The United States Olympic Committee (USOC) has mandated that all coaches participating under the governance of USOC receive certification in the safety training course developed by the American Red Cross/USOC.[8]

Often coaches of youth sports have little or no background in providing safe and positive sports experiences. It is estimated that 2.5 million volunteer coaches lack formal preparation.[3] Every youth sport coach should be certified and dedicated to the highest ideals of coaching. One organization that promotes such ideals is the National Youth Sports Coaches Association (NYSCA).[5] Currently the NYSCA has a membership of more than 143,000 which serves more than 2 million boys and girls in the United States. This association offers three levels of certifications

Youth coach sports must be
certified and educated in:
Techniques of coaching
Supervising conditioning
Sport safety
First aid
Child development

10 percent of youth in
organized sports will sustain
an injury.

consisting of the fundamentals of coaching, first aid and safety, and common sports injuries; it also offers instruction in the psychological aspects of losing and in discipline. All youth sport coaches must also have a good understanding of normal child development—physical, emotional, and psychological.

INCIDENCE OF INJURIES IN YOUTH SPORTS

Of the 30 million young athletes involved in organized sports in the United States, 10 percent will sustain a sports-related injury. Each year more than 775,000 young athletes under the age of fifteen are treated in hospital emergency rooms for sports-related injuries, reports the National Electronic Injury Surveillance of the U.S. Consumer Product Safety Commission. Table 24-2 shows the number of sports-related injuries involving children between the ages of eight and fourteen years of age.[1]

INJURY CONCERNS

The coach and parent must realize why the young athlete is vulnerable to sports injuries. Three sites on the long bones characterize a child's growth. These sites are at the ends of the bones, which include the joint surfaces, the growth plates, and the sites of major muscle-tendon insertions. Because this growth tissue is cartilage, it is softer than mature cartilage and bone, and it has a greater chance of injury. As previously discussed, (see page 543) contact sports are of particular concern for growth plate injuries. In noncontact sports such as throwing sports, gymnastics, or distance running, high-velocity trauma is not likely, but intense repetitive training can produce recurrent microtraumas.

Many pediatric physicians are concerned about these repeated microtraumas that can occur to the young athlete over a period of time. Such small traumas can compound and produce chronic and, in some cases, degenerative conditions within the immature musculoskeletal system.

Children are susceptible to many of the same sport injuries that the physically mature athlete is, including joint sprains, muscle and tendon strains, and skeletal fractures. In addition, children can sustain a pulling away of soft tissue from bones (avulsion).[2]

TABLE 24-2 Incidence of sports injuries in young athletes[3]

	Organized Activities	Unorganized/ Informal Activities
Football	61,139	117,057
Basketball	55,869	165,355
Baseball	53,112	115,978
Soccer	28,165	40,978
Gymnastics	13,588	21,183
Volleyball	7,530	14,688

SPORTS INJURY PREVENTION

The simplest way to prevent serious sports injuries in the young athlete is to give close attention to the complaints of pain and/or dysfunction, especially about the major joints. With early first aid and treatment and with proper rest, healing is enhanced.[4]

Many injuries can be prevented when children are matched to the sport instead of the sport to the child. The physical matchup is important to the child's safety, but a proper emotional matchup is also important. In other words, the child should want to play the sport and at the same time have the type of personality that fits the sport.

Another way to reduce children's sports injuries is to assess the rules and tactics of the game. Every organized sport in the United States was initially designed to be played by the older and more mature athlete. Good examples of positive changes are the Little League pitchers' limit of six innings per week and the Pop Warner football limit of cross-body blocking and spearing.[3]

It is now evident that children are capable of cardiovascular training similar to that of adults with little risk of injury.[7] In addition, weight training can strengthen bones, joints, and ligaments and thereby decrease trauma to the musculoskeletal system, if the weight training is properly performed and supervised.

The role of protective equipment in preventing injury in the young has frequently been overemphasized. It is faulty thinking that youngsters who use protective equipment are safely protected, when participating in adult-style games.

Young athletes must practice good basic health principles. They must avoid rapid weight loss in order to wrestle at a lower weight or in order to increase performance in gymnastics or diving. Excessive concern with thinness can lead to anorexia and/or bulimia.

> 24-2
>
> **Critical Thinking** Exercise
>
> Young athletes can be characterized as physically immature.
>
> ? What implications does this have for the prevention of injuries?

> Youth athletes must practice good hygiene and other health habits.

SUMMARY

- The extent to which young athletes train and compete must be carefully monitored to avoid physical and emotional injuries.

- The estimated number of youth engaging in some sport in the United States is 46 million.

- A major concern to some parents and professionals is the stress placed on the young body from intense sports competition and training.

- All youth sport participants should be matched by physical maturation, weight, size, skill level, and experience.

- Young athletes can positively respond to some types of conditioning exercises, if the exercises are properly supervised and conducted.

- Activities such as falling, jumping, landing on straight legs, repeated hard throwing motions, running very long distances and, lifting heavy weights may produce injuries to the immature musculoskeletal system.

- Children are not miniature adults; coaching must be based on their emotional and cognitive level.
- Separation of genders in sport activities needs to occur only when boys have attained greater mass in proportion to their body weight.
- Enjoyment of an activity, rather than winning at all costs, must be stressed to children as the most important factor in sports participation.
- An overzealous coach can cause the young athlete great emotional stress.
- Coaches participating in youth sports must be trained in techniques and skills, safety and injury prevention, first aid, and growth and development.
- Coaches should be certified.
- Each year more than 775,000 young athletes under fifteen years of age are treated for sports-related injuries.
- Young athletes are prone to the same injuries that the mature athlete is, but they must also contend with injuries to their skeletal growth centers.
- Injuries to young athletes can be avoided through proper conditioning and supervision, proper matching, use of proper equipment, and competing under appropriate rules of competition.
- Young athletes must be encouraged to practice good health habits.

Solutions to Critical Thinking Exercises

24-1 Injuries are predominantly to lower and upper limbs, respectively.

24-2 All athletes must be matched according to maturation and size.

REVIEW QUESTIONS AND CLASS ACTIVITIES

1. Discuss the advantages and disadvantages of training and conditioning the physically immature athlete.
2. Discuss the pros and cons of the young athlete engaging in intense competition.
3. Observe a Little League or Pop Warner game, assessing the coaches' activities and conduct that might be harmful to the children.
4. Develop a conditioning and training program for young athletes engaging in tackle football, taking into consideration their immature physical and emotional nature.

REFERENCES

1. American Academy of Orthopedic Surgeons, P.O. Box 1998, Des Plaines, Illinois 60017.
2. Arnheim D, Prentice B: *Principles of athletic training*, ed 9, Dubuque, Iowa, 1997, Brown & Benchmark.
3. Carnegie Corporation of New York, 437 Madison Ave, New York NY 10022.
4. Micheli U: Safe state, injury prevention in Massachusetts. Presentation by Massachusetts Dept. of

Public Health, Bureau of Family and Community Health, Division of Prevention, Injury Prevention and Control Program, Boston, September 18, 1996.

5. National Youth Sports Safety Foundation, 333 Longwood Ave, Suite 202, Boston MA 02115.

6. National Association for Sports and Physical Education (NASPE), 1900 Association Dr., Reston VA 22091.

7. Prentice W: *Fitness for college and college life,* ed 5, St Louis, 1997, Mosby.

8. United States Olympic Committee (USOC), National Governing Bodies of Sports, One Olympic Plaza, Colorado Springs, CO 80909.

ANNOTATED BIBLIOGRAPHY

Duff, JF: *Youth sports: A medical handbook for parents and coaches,* New York, 1992, Collier Books.

Designed to bring a medical understanding of sports injuries to both the parent and coach.

Flegel, M: *Sport first aid.* Champaign, Ill, 1996, Human Kinetics.

Provides excellent coverage of the immediate care of sports injuries.

Michelli U, Jenkins MD: *Sportwise: an essential guide for young athletes, parents and coaches.* Boston, 1990, Houghton Mifflin.

Addresses sports injuries and their prevention and care.

Sidelines, National Youth Sports Safety Foundation, 333 Longwood Ave, Suite 202, Boston MA 02115.

Low-cost fact sheets on coaching topics and selected sports injuries.

Sullivan JA: *Pediatric athlete.* Des Plaines, Ill, American Academy of Orthopedic Surgeons.

WEB SITES

World Ortho: http://www.worldortho.com

Use the search engine in this site to locate relevant information.

Wheeless' Textbook of Orthopaedics: http://www.medmedia.com/med.htm

An excellent page for injuries, anatomy, and x rays.

Recognition of the Athletic Trainer as an Allied Health Professional

In June 1991 the American Medical Association officially recognized athletic training as an allied health profession. The primary purpose of this recognition was for accrediting educational programs. The AMA's Committee on Allied Health Education and Accreditation (CAHEA) was charged with the responsibility of developing essentials and guidelines for academic programs to use in preparation of individuals for initial entry into the profession through the Joint Review Committee on Athletic Training (JRC-AT). As of 1993, all entry-level athletic training education programs became subject to the CAHEA accreditation process.[1]

In June 1994 CAHEA was dissolved and was replaced immediately by the Commission on Accreditation of Allied Health Education Programs (CAAHEP). Currently seventeen professional review committees are sponsored by the forty-nine separate organizations that make up CAAHEP. The NATA is one of those organizations. CAAHEP is recognized as an accreditation agency for allied health education programs by the U.S. Department of Education. Entry-level college and university based athletic training education programs at both the undergraduate and graduate level that were at one time approved by the NATA and subsequently by CAHEA must now be accredited by CAAHEP. The JRC-AT currently comprises representatives from the NATA, the American Academy of Pediatrics, the American Association for Sports Medicine, and the American Academy of Family Practice.

The effects of CAAHEP accreditation are not limited to the educational aspects. In the future, this recognition may affect regulatory legislation, the practice of athletic training in nontraditional settings, and insurance considerations. This recognition will continue to be a positive step in the development of the athletic training profession.

1. Committee on Allied Health Education and Accreditation: *Essentials and guidelines for an accredited educational program for athletic trainers,* Chicago, 1992, American Medical Association.

Employment Settings for the Athletic Trainer

SECONDARY SCHOOLS

It would be ideal to have certified athletic trainers serve every secondary school in the United States.[1] Many of the physical problems that occur later from improperly managed sports injuries could be avoided initially if proper care from an athletic trainer had been provided. Many times a coach does all of his or her own athletic training, although in some cases, a coach is assigned additional athletic training responsibilities and is assisted by a student athletic trainer. If a secondary school hires an athletic trainer, it is commonly in a faculty-trainer capacity. This individual is usually employed as a teacher in one of the school's classroom disciplines and performs athletic training duties on a part-time or extracurricular basis.[2] In this instance, compensation usually is on the basis of released time from teaching and/or a stipend as a coach.[3]

Another means of obtaining high school or community college athletic training coverage is by using a certified graduate student from a nearby college or university. The graduate student receives a graduate assistantship with a stipend paid by the secondary school or community college. In this situation both the graduate student and the school benefit.[4] However, this practice may prevent a school from employing an athletic trainer on a full-time basis.

SCHOOL DISTRICTS

Some school districts have found it effective to employ a centrally placed certified athletic trainer. In this case the athletic trainer, who may be full- or part-time, is a nonteacher who serves a number of schools. The advantage is savings; the disadvantage is that one individual cannot provide the level of service usually required by a typical school.

COLLEGES OR UNIVERSITIES

At the college or university level, the athletic training position varies considerably from institution to institution. In smaller institutions, the athletic trainer may be a half-time professor in physical education and a half-time athletic trainer. In some cases, if the athletic trainer is a physical therapist rather than a teacher, he or she may spend part of the time in the school health center and part of the time in athletic training. Increasingly at the college level, athletic training services are being offered to members of the general student body who participate in intramural and club sports. In most colleges and universities the athletic trainer is full-time, does not teach, works in the department of athletics, and is paid by the state or from student union or alumni funds.

PROFESSIONAL TEAMS

The athletic trainer for professional sports teams usually performs specific team training duties for six months out of the year; the other six months are spent in off-season conditioning and individual rehabilitation. The athletic trainer working with a professional team is involved with only one sport and is paid according to contract, much like a player. Playoff and championship money could add substantially to the yearly income.

SPORTS MEDICINE CLINICS

For years, sports medicine clinics have been considered a nontraditional setting for employment as an athletic trainer. Today, more athletic trainers are employed in sports medicine clinics than in any other employment setting. The role of the athletic trainer can vary greatly from one clinic to the next. Most clinical athletic trainers see patients with sports-related injuries during the morning hours in the clinic. In the afternoons, trainers' services are contracted out to local high schools or small colleges for game and/or practice coverage. For the most part, private clinics have well-equipped facilities in which to work, and salaries for their trainers are generally somewhat higher than in the more traditional settings.

INDUSTRIAL SETTING

It is becoming more common for corporations or industries to employ athletic trainers to oversee fitness and injury rehabilitation programs for their employees. In addition to these responsibilities, trainers may be assigned to conduct wellness programs and provide education and individual counseling. It is likely that many job opportunities will exist for the athletic trainer in industry in the next few years.

1. Knight K: Athletic trainers for secondary schools, *Ath Train* 23(4): 313, 1988.
2. Prentice W, Mischler B: A national survey of employment opportunities for athletic trainers in the public schools, *Ath Train* 21(3):215, 1986.
3. Lephart S, Metz K: Financial and appointment trends of the athletic trainer clinician/educator, *Ath Train* 25(2):118, 1990.
4. Hossler P: How to acquire athletic trainers on the high school level, *Ath Train* 20(3):199, 1985.

Requirements for Certification as an Athletic Trainer

An athletic trainer who is certified by the NATA is a highly qualified paramedical professional educated and experienced in dealing with the injuries that occur with participation in sports. Candidates for certification are required to have an extensive background of both formal academic preparation and supervised practical experience in a clinical setting, according to CAAHEP guidelines. The guidelines listed in the following Focus Box have been established by the National Athletic Trainers' Association's Board of Certification.[1]

A-1 ⟩ **Focus Box**

NATA Certification

Purpose of certification

The National Athletic Trainers' Association Board of Certification (NATABOC) was established in 1970 to implement a program of certification for entry-level athletic trainers. The purpose of the certification program is to establish standards for entry into the profession of athletic training.

To attain certification as an athletic trainer, an applicant must fulfill the following core requirements and must either complete a CAAHEP-accredited entry-level program or an internship program.

Core requirements

Note: If one or more of the core requirements are not fulfilled at the time of application, the application will be returned.

1. The athletic training student must have a high school diploma to begin accumulating directly supervised clinical hours that are to be used to meet requirements for NATABOC certification.

2. Proof of graduation (an official transcript) at the baccalaureate level from an accredited college or university located in the United States of America. Foreign-degreed applicants who wish to credit this degree toward a bachelor's degree requirement will be evaluated, at the candidate's expense, by an independent

consultant selected by the NATABOC. Students who have begun their last semester or quarter of college are eligible to take the certification examination before graduation, provided the other core and section requirements have been fulfilled at the time of application. Verification of intent to graduate must be provided to the Board of Certification by the dean or department chairperson of the college or university the applicant is attending. Certification will not be issued until an official transcript indicating date of degree is received by the Board of Certification.

3. Proof of current American National Red Cross Standard First Aid Certification and current Basic CPR (American Red Cross or American Heart Association); EMT equivalent instead of First Aid and CPR will be accepted. Both cards must be current at the time of application.

4. At the time of application, all candidates for certification (curriculum and internship) must verify that at least 25 percent of their athletic training experience hours credited in fulfilling the certification requirements were attained in actual (on location) practice or game coverage with one or more of the following sports:

continued

NATA Certification—cont'd

football, soccer, hockey, wrestling, basketball, gymnastics, lacrosse, volleyball, and rugby.
5. Endorsement of certification application by a NATA-certified athletic trainer.
6. Subsequent passing of the certification examination (written, oral-practical, and written-simulation sections).

Section Requirements

CAAHEP *accredited program*

The candidate must graduate from an undergraduate or graduate program accredited by the Commission on Accreditation of Allied Health Education Programs (CAAHEP). Students applying to take the certification exam must complete formal instruction in the following core curriculum subject areas:

Human anatomy
Human physiology
Psychology
Kinesiology/biomechanics
Exercise physiology
Prevention of athletic injuries/illness
Evaluation of athletic injuries/ illness
First aid and emergency care
Therapeutic modalities
Therapeutic exercise
Personal community health
Nutrition
Administration of athletic training programs

It is recommended that students complete course work in physics, chemistry, pharmacology, research design, and statistics. In addition, students are required to complete a minimum of 800 clinical hours under the direct supervision of a NATA-certified athletic trainer at that college or an affiliated site. Applicants who are applying for NATA certification from a CAAHEP-accredited undergraduate or graduate program must receive their degree from that college or university.

Internship programs

If a student does not attend a CAAHEP-accredited program, he or she may still be eligible for certification by completing an internship. At the time of application, each internship candidate must present documentation of attaining at least 1,500 hours of athletic training experience under direct supervision of a NATA-certified athletic trainer. These hours must have been attained over a minimum of two calendar years and not more than five years. Of these 1,500 hours, at least 1,000 hours must be attained in a traditional athletic setting at the interscholastic, intercollegiate, or professional sports level. The additional 500 hours may be attained from an allied clinical setting and/or sport camp setting under the direct supervision of a NATA-certified athletic trainer. Each candidate must present, via official transcript, proof of completion of formal course work no more than seven years before the date of application, with at least one course in each of the following areas:

Health (i.e., nutrition, drugs/substance abuse, health education)
Human anatomy
Kinesiology/biomechanics
Human physiology
Physiology of exercise
Basic athletic training
Advanced athletic training (a course in therapeutic modalies or rehabilitation may satisfy the advanced course requirement)

Basic and advanced athletic training courses must be successfully completed in a college or university in the United States or taught by a NATA-certified athletic trainer in a foreign college or university for credit. The remaining core courses may be accepted from foreign universities as deemed acceptable by the NATABOC.

THE CERTIFICATION EXAMINATION

Once the requirements have been fulfilled, applicants are eligible to sit for the certification examination. The certification examination has been developed by the National Athletic Trainers' Association Board of Certification in conjunction with Columbia Assessment Services, Inc., and is administered four times each year at various locations throughout the United States.[1] The examination consists of three sections: a written portion, an oral-practical portion, and a written-simulation portion. The examination tests for knowledge and skill in five major domains: (1) prevention of athletic injuries; (2) recognition, evaluation, and immediate care of injuries; (3) rehabilitation and reconditioning of athletic injuries; (4) health care administration; and (5) professional development and responsibility. Successful performance on the certification examination leads to certification as an athletic trainer.

CONTINUING EDUCATION REQUIREMENTS

To ensure ongoing professional growth and involvement by the certified athletic trainer, the NATABOC has established requirements for continuing education.[2] To maintain certification, all certified trainers must document a minimum of eight CEUs attained during each three-year recertification term. CEUs may be awarded for attending symposiums, seminars, workshops, or conferences; serving as a speaker, panelist, or certification exam model; participating in the USOC program; authoring a research article in a professional journal; completing an NATA journal quiz; completing postgraduate course work; and obtaining CPR, first aid, or EMT certification. All certified athletic trainers must also demonstrate proof of CPR certification at least once during the three-year term.

1. National Athletic Trainers' Association Board of Certification, Inc.: *Study guide for the NATABOC entry-level athletic trainer certification examination,* Philadelphia, 1993, Davis.

2. National Athletic Trainers' Association Board of Certification, Inc., Continuing Education Office: *Continuing education file 1994–96,* Dallas, 1994, NATABOC.

Conversion Tables

METRIC-ENGLISH CONVERSIONS

Length

English (USA)	= Metric
inch	= 2.54 cm, 25.4 mm
foot	= 0.30 m, 30.48 cm
yard	= 0.91 m, 91.4 cm
mile (statute) (5280 ft)	= 1.61 km, 1609 cm
mile (nautical) (6077 ft, 1.15 statute mi)	= 1.85 km, 1850 m

Metric	= English (USA)
millimeter	= 0.039 in
centimeter	= 0.39 in
meter	= 3.28 ft, 39.37 in
kilometer	= 0.62 mi, 1091 yd, 3273 ft

Weight

English (USA)	= Metric
grain	= 64.80 mg
ounce	= 28.35 g
pound	= 453.60 g, 0.45 kg
ton (short—2000 lb)	= 0.91 metric ton (907 kg)

Metric	= English (USA)
milligram	= 0.002 grain (0.000035 oz)
gram	= 0.04 oz
kilogram	= 35.27 oz, 2.20 lb
metric ton (1000 kg)	= 1.10 tons

Volume

English (USA)	= Metric
cubic inch	= 16.39 cc
cubic foot	= 0.03 m^3
cubic yard	= 0.765 m^3
ounce	= 0.03 liter (3 ml)*
pint	= 0.47 liter
quart	= 0.95 liter
gallon	= 3.79 liters

Metric	= English (USA)
milliliter	= 0.03 oz
liter	= 2.12 pt
liter	= 1.06 qt
liter	= 0.27 gal

1 liter ÷ 1000 = milliliter or cubic centimeter (10^{-3} liter)
1 liter ÷ 1,000,000 = microliter (10^{-6} liter)
NOTE: 1 ml = 1cc

FAHRENHEIT-CELSIUM CONVERSION

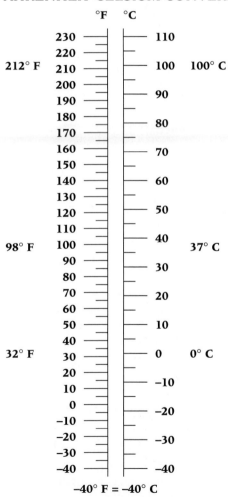

−40° F = −40° C

To convert temperature scales:
Fahrenheit to Celsius: °C = (°F − 32) × ⁵⁄₉
Celsius to Fahrenheit: °F = ⁹⁄₅(°C) + 32

Glossary

abduction A movement of a body part away from the midline of the body

accident An act that occurs by chance or without intention

accommodating resistance Form of isokinetic exercises in which speed is an element

acute injury An injury with sudden onset and short duration

ad libitum In the amount desired

adduction A movement of a body part toward the midline of the body

afferent nerve fibers Nerve fibers that carry messages toward the brain

agonist muscles Muscles directly engaged in contraction as related to muscles that relax at the same time

ambulation Move or walk from place to place

ameboid action A leukocyte moving through a capillary wall through the process of diapedisis

amenorrhea Absence or suppression of menstruation

amnesia Loss of memory

analgesia Pain inhibition

anemia Lack of iron

anesthesia Partial or complete loss of sensation

anomaly Deviation from the norm

anorexia Lack or loss of appetite; aversion to food

anorexia nervosa Eating disorder characterized by a distorted body image

anoxia Lack of oxygen

antagonist muscles Muscles that counteract the action of the agonist muscles

anterior Before or in front of

anterior cruciate ligament Stops external rotation

anteroposterior Refers to the position of front to back

anxiety A feeling of uncertainty or apprehension

apophysis A bone outgrowth to which muscles attach

arrhythmical movement Irregular movement

arthroscopic examination Viewing the inside of a joint via the arthroscope, which utilizes a small camera lens

articulation A joint

assumption of risk The individual, through expressed or implied agreement, assumes some risk or danger will be involved in a particular undertaking

asymmetries (body) A lack of symmetry of sides of the body

atrophic necrosis Death of an area due to lack of circulation

atrophy Wasting away of tissue or of an organ; diminution of the size of a body part

automatism Automatic behavior before consciousness or full awareness has been achieved following a brain concussion

avascular necrosis Death of tissue resulting from a lack of blood supply

avulsion A tearing away

axial loading A blow to the top of the athlete's head while in flexion

axilla Armpit

ballistic stretching Older stretching technique that uses repetitive bouncing motions

bandage A strip of cloth or other material used to hold a dressing in place

bilateral Pertaining to both sides

biomechanics Branch of study that applies the laws of mechanics to living organisms and biological tissues

bipedal Having two feet or moving on two feet

body composition Percent body fat plus lean body weight

bowlegged Bending outward of the lower joint

bradykinin Peptide chemical that causes pain in an injured area

bulimia Binge-purge eating disorder

bursae Pieces of synovial membrane that contain a small amount of fluid

bursitis Inflammation of a bursa, especially those bursae located between bony prominences and a muscle or tendon, such as those of the shoulder or knee

calcific tendinitis Deposition of calcium in a chronically inflamed tendon, especially the tendons of the shoulder

calisthenic Exercise involving free movement without the aid of equipment

callus New bone formation over a fracture

calorie (large) Amount of heat required to raise 1 kg of water 1° C; term used to express the fuel or energy value of food or the heat output of the organism; the amount of heat required to heat 1 lb of water to 4° F

cardiorespiratory endurance Ability to perform activities for extended periods of time

catastrophic injury A permanent injury to the spinal cord that leaves the athlete quadriplegic or paraplegic

cauterization A purposeful destruction of tissue

cerebrovascular accident Stroke

chondromalacia A degeneration of a joint's articular surface, leading to softening

chronic injury An injury with long onset and long duration

circuit training Exercise stations that consist of various combinations of weight training, flexibility, calisthenics, and aerobic exercises

circumduct Act of moving a limb such as the arm or hip in a circular motion

clavus durum Hard corn

clavus molle Soft corn

clonic muscle cramp Involuntary muscle contraction marked by alternate contraction and relaxation in rapid succession

closed fracture Fracture that does not penetrate superficial tissue

collagenous tissue The white fibrous substance composing connective tissue

collision sport Athletes use their bodies to deter or punish opponents

commission (legal liability) Performing an act outside of an individual's legal jurisdiction

communicable disease A disease that may be transmitted directly or indirectly from one individual to another

concentric (positive) contraction The muscle shortens while contracting against resistance

conduction Heating by direct contact with a hot medium

conjunctivae Mucous membrane that lines the eyes

contact sport Athletes make physical contact, but not with the intent to produce bodily injury

contrecoup brain injury After head is struck, brain continues to move within the skull and becomes injured opposite the force

convection Heating indirectly through another medium, such as air or liquid

conversion Heating by other forms of energy (e.g., electricity)

convulsions Paroxysms of involuntary muscular contractions and relaxations

core temperature Internal, or deep body, temperature monitored by cells in the hypothalamus, as opposed to shell, or peripheral, temperature, which is registered by the layer of insulation provided by the skin, subcutaneous tissues, and superficial portions of the muscle masses

corticosteroid A steroid produced by the adrenal cortex

coryza Profuse nasal discharge

counterirritant An agent that produces a mild inflammation and in turn acts as an analgesic when applied locally to the skin (e.g., liniment)

crepitus A crackling feel or sound

cryokinetics Cold application combined with exercise

cryotherapy Cold therapy

cubital fossa Triangular area on the anterior aspect of the forearm directly opposite the

elbow joint (the bend of the elbow)

cutaneous Of or pertaining to the skin

cyanosis Slightly bluish, grayish, slatelike, or dark purple discoloration of the skin due to a reduced amount of blood hemaglobin

debride Removal of dirt and dead tissue from a wound

deconditioning A state in which the athlete's body loses its competitive fitness

degeneration Deterioration of tissue

dermatome A segmental skin area innervated by various spinal cord segments

diapedisis Passage of blood cells by ameboid action through the intact capillary wall

diaphragm A musculomembranous wall separating the abdomen from the thoracic cavity

diarthrodial joint Ball and socket joint

diastolic blood pressure The residual pressure when the heart is between beats

diplopia Seeing double

dislocation A bone is forced out and stays out until surgically or manually replaced or reduced

distal Farthest away from a point of reference

doping The administration of a drug that is designed to improve the competitor's performance

dorsiflexion Bending toward the dorsum or rear, opposite of plantar flexion

dorsum The back of a body part

dressing A material, such as gauze, applied to a wound

duration Length of time that an athlete works during a bout of exercise

dysmenorrhea Painful or difficult menstruation

dyspepsia Imperfect digestion

dyspnea Difficulty in breathing

eccentric (negative) contraction The muscle lengthens while contracting against resistance

ecchymosis Black and blue skin discoloration due to hemorrhage

ectopic Located in a place different from normal

ectopic bone formation Bone formation occurring in an abnormal place

edema Swelling as a result of the collection of fluid in connective tissue

electrolyte Solution that is a conductor of electricity

electrotherapy Treating disease by electrical devices

embolus Fat or plaque that migrates through the vascular system

encephalon The brain

endurance The ability of the body to undergo prolonged activity

entrapment Organ becomes compressed by nearby tissue

epidemiological approach The study of sports injuries involving the relationship of as many injury factors as possible

epilepsy Recurrent paroxysmal disorder characterized by sudden attacks of altered consciousness, motor activity, and sensory perception

epiphysis The cartilagenous growth region of a bone

epistaxis Nosebleed

etiology Pertaining to the cause of a condition

eversion of the foot To turn the foot outward

exostoses Benign bony outgrowths that protrude from the surface of a bone and are usually capped by cartilage; callus formations

extraoral mouth guard A protective device that fits outside the mouth

extravasation Escape of a fluid from its vessels into the surrounding tissues

exudates Accumulation of a fluid in an area

fascia Fibrous membrane that covers, supports, and separates muscles

fasciitis Fascia inflammation

fibrinogen A protein present in blood plasma that is converted into a fibrin clot

fibroblast Any cell component from which fibers are developed

fibrocartilage A type of cartilage in which the matrix contains thick bundles of collagenous fibers (e.g., intervertebral disks)

fibrosis Development of excessive fibrous connective tissue; fibroid degeneration

foot pronation Combined foot movements of eversion and abduction

foot supination Combined foot movements of inversion and abduction

frequency Number of times per week that an athlete exercises

genitourinary Pertaining to the reproductive and urinary organs

genu recurvatus Hyperextension at the knee joint

genu valgum Knock knees

genu varum Bow legs

glycogen supercompensation High carbohydrate diet

hemarthrosis Blood in a joint cavity

hematoma Blood tumor

hematuria Blood in the urine

hemoglobin Molecules that carry oxygen in the blood

hemoglobinuria Hemoglobin in the urine

hemophilia A hereditary blood disease in which coagulation is greatly prolonged

hemorrhage Discharge of blood

hemothorax Bloody fluid in the pleural cavity

hirsutism Excessive hair growth and/or the presence of hair in unusual places

homeostasis Maintenance of a steady state in the body's internal environment

hyperemia An unusual amount of blood in a body part

hyperextension Extreme stretching out of a body part

hyperflexibility Flexibility beyond a joint's normal range

hyperhidrosis Excessive sweating; excessive foot perspiration

hypermobility Mobility of a joint that is extreme

hypertension High blood pressure; abnormally high tension

hypertonic Having a higher osmotic pressure than a compared solution

hypertrophy Enlargement of a part caused by an increase in the size of its cells

hyperventilation Abnormally deep breathing that is prolonged, causing a depletion of carbon dioxide, a fall in blood pressure, and fainting

hypoallergenic Low allergy producing

hypoxia Lack of an adequate amount of oxygen

idiopathic Of unknown cause

iliotibial band friction syndrome Runner's knee

injury An act that damages or hurts

innervation Nerve stimulation of a muscle

integument A covering or skin

intensity Increasing the work-load

interosseous membrane Connective tissue membrane between bones

interval training   Alternating periods of work with active recovery

intervertebral   Between two vertebrae

intramuscular bleeding   Bleeding within a muscle

intraoral mouth guard   A protective device that fits within the mouth and covers the teeth

intravenous   Substances administered to a patient via a vein

inversion of the foot   To turn the foot inward. Inner border of the foot lifts

ions   Electrically charged atoms

ipsilateral   Situated on the same side

ischemia   Local anemia

isokinetic exercise   Resistance is given at a fixed velocity of movement with accommodating resistance

isokinetic muscle resistance   Accommodating and variable resistance

isometric exercise   Contracts the muscle statically without changing its length

isometric muscle contraction   Muscle contracts statically without a change in its length

isosceles triangle   Triangle with two sides equal in length

isotonic exercise   Form of exercise that shortens and lengthens the muscle through a complete range of motion

isotonic muscle contraction   Shortens and lengthens the muscle through a complete range of motion

joint   Point at which two bones join together

joint capsule   Saclike structure that encloses the ends of bones in a diarthrodial joint

keloid   An overgrowth of collagenous scar tissue at the site of a wound of the skin

keratolytic   Pertaining to loosening the horny layer of skin

knock knee   Bending inward of the lower joint

kyphosis   Exaggeration of the normal thoracic spine

labile   Unsteady; not fixed; easily changed

lactase deficiency   Difficulty digesting dairy products

lateral   Pertaining to point of reference away from the midline of the body

liability   Legal responsibility for the harm one causes to another person

lordosis   Abnormal lumbar vertebral convexity

luxation   Total dislocation

lysis   Breakdown

macerated skin   Skin softened by soaking

malaise   Discomfort and uneasiness caused by an illness

margination   Accumulation of leukocytes on blood vessel walls at the site of injury during early stages of inflammation

mechanoreceptors   Located in muscles, tendons, ligaments, and joints; provide information on position of a joint

medial   Pertaining to point of reference closest to the midline of the body

menarche   Onset of menses

meninges   Any one of the three membranes that enclose the brain and the spinal cord, comprising the dura mater, the pia mater, and the arachnoid

menorrhagia   Abnormally heavy or long menstrual periods

metabolites   Products left after metabolism has taken place

metatarsalgia   Pain in the metatarsal

metatarsophalangeal joint   Joint at which the phalanges meet the metatarsal bones

microtrauma   Small

musculoskeletal traumas that are accumulative

mononucleosis (infectious)   A disease, usually of young adults, causing fever, sore throat, and lymph gland swelling

muscle   Tissue that when stimulated contracts and produces motion

muscle contracture   Abnormal shortening of muscle tissue in which there is a great deal of resistance to passive stretch

muscle cramps   Involuntary muscle contraction

muscle guarding   Muscle contraction in response to pain

muscular endurance   The ability to perform repetitive muscular contractions against some resistance

muscular strength   The maximum force that can be applied by a muscle during a single maximum contraction

musculoskeletal   Pertaining to muscles and the skeleton

myoglobin   A respiratory pigment in muscle tissue that is an oxygen carrier

myositis   Inflammation of muscle

myositis ossificans   Calcium deposits that result from repeated trauma

myotatic reflex   Stretch reflex

necrosis   Death of tissue

negative resistance   Slow eccentric muscle contraction against resistance with muscle lengthening

negligence   The failure to use ordinary or reasonable care

nerve entrapment   A nerve that is compressed between bone or soft tissue

neuritis   Chronic nerve irritation

neuroma   Enlargement of a nerve

NOCSAE   National Operating Committee on Standards for Athletic Equipment

noncontact sport Athletes are not involved in any physical contact

nystagmus A constant involuntary back and forth, up and down, or rotary movement of the eyeball

occlusion Alignment of the teeth; malocclusion means that the upper and lower teeth do not line up.

omission (legal) Person fails to perform a legal duty

open fracture Overlying skin has been lacerated by protruding bone fragments

orthosis Used in sports as an appliance or apparatus to support, align, prevent, or correct deformities, or to improve function of a movable body part

osteoarthritis A wearing down of hyaline cartilage

osteoblasts Bone-forming cells

osteochondral Refers to relationship of bone and cartilage

osteochondritis Inflammation of bone and cartilage

osteochondritis dissecans Fragment of cartilage and underlying bone is detached from the articular surface

osteochondrosis A disease state of a bone and its articular cartilage

osteoclasts Cells that absorb and remove osseous tissue

osteoporosis A decrease in bone density

palpate To use the hands or fingers to examine

palpation Feeling an injury with the fingers

papule Pimple

paraplegia Paralysis of lower portion of the body and of both legs

paresthesia Abnormal sensation such as numbness, prickling, and tingling

patellar tendinitis Jumper's knee

pathology Study of the nature and cause of disease

pediatrician A specialist in the treatment of children's diseases

periodization Varying training techniques during different seasons

periosteum The fibrous covering of a bone

peristalis A progressive, wavelike movement that occurs in the alimentary canal

pes planus Flat feet

phagocytosis Process of ingesting microorganisms, other cells, or foreign particles, commonly by monocytes, or white blood cells

phalanges Bones of the fingers and toes

phalanx Any one of the bones of the fingers and toes

photophobia An intense intolerance of light

plantarflexion The forepart of the foot is depressed relative to the ankle

plica A fold of tissue within the body

plyometric exercise An exercise that maximizes the myotatic, or stretch, reflex

pneumothorax A collapse of a lung due to air in the pleural cavity

point tenderness Pain is produced when the site of injury is palpated

polymers Natural or synthetic substances formed by the combination of two or more molecules of the same substance

positive resistance Slow concentric muscle contraction against resistance with muscle shortening

posterior Toward the rear or back

posterior cruciate ligament A ligament that stops internal rotation

posttraumatic amnesia Inability of athlete to recall events since injury

power Ability to accelerate a load, depending on the level of strength and velocity of a muscle contraction

primary assessment Initial first aid evaluation

prophylactic Pertaining to prevention, preservation, or protection

prophylaxis Guarding against injury or disease

proprioceptive neuromuscular facilitation (PNF) Stretching techniques that involve combinations of alternating contractions and stretches

proprioceptors Organs within the body that provide the athlete with an awareness of where the body is in space (kinesthesis)

prostaglandin Acidic lipids widely distributed in the body; in musculoskeletal conditions it is concerned with vasodilation, histaminelike effect; it is inhibited by aspirin

prothrombin Interacts with calcium to produce thrombin

proximal Nearest to the point of reference

psychogenic Of psychic origin; that which originates in the mind

psychophysiological Involving the mind and the body

psychosomatic Showing effects of mind-body relationship; physical disorder caused or influenced by the mind (i.e., by the emotions)

quadriplegia Paralysis affecting all four limbs

referred pain Pain that is felt at a point of the body other than its actual origin

regeneration   Repair, regrowth, or restoration of a part such as tissue

residual   That which remains; often used to describe a permanent condition resulting from injury or disease (e.g., a limp or a paralysis)

resorption   Act of removal by absorption

retrograde amnesia   Memory loss for events occurring immediately before trauma

revascularize   Restoration of blood circulation to an injured area

rhinitis   Inflammation of the nasal mucus lining

RICE   *R*est, *i*ce, *c*ompression, and *e*levation

rotation   Turning around an axis in an angular motion

SAID principle   *S*pecific *a*daptations to *i*mposed *d*emands

Scheuermann's disease (osteochondrosis)   A degeneration of the vertebral epiphyseal endplates

sciatica   Inflammatory condition of the sciatic nerve; commonly associated with peripheral nerve root compression

sclera   White outer coating of the eye

scoliosis   A lateral deviation curve of the spine

secondary assessment   Follow up; a more detailed examination

seizure   Sudden attack

shin splints   Medial tibial stress syndrome; anterior lower leg pain

sign   Objective evidence of an abnormal situation within the body

sling psychrometer   Instrument for establishing the wet-bulb, globe temperature index

spasm   A sudden, involuntary muscle contraction

spica   A figure-eight, with one of the two loops being larger

spondylolisthesis   Forward slipping of a vertebral body, usually a lumbar vertebrae

spondylolysis   A degeneration of the vertebrae and a defect in the pars intermedia of the articular processes of the vertebrae

sprain   Injury to a ligament that connects bone to bone

staleness   Deterioration in the usual standard of performance; chronic fatigue, apathy, loss of appetite, indigestion, weight loss, and inability to sleep or rest properly

staplylococcus   A genus of micrococci, some of which are pathogenic, causing pus and tissue destruction

static stretching   Passively stretching an antagonist muscle by placing it in a maximal stretch position and holding it there

strain   A stretch tear, or rip in the muscle or its tendon

strength   Ability of a muscular contraction to exert force to move an object (dynamic) or to perform work against a fixed object (static)

streptococcus   Oval bacteria that appear in a chain

stress   The positive and negative forces that can disrupt the body's equilibrium

stress fracture   Spot of irritation on the bone

stressor   Anything that affects the body's physiological or psychological condition

stroke volume   The heart's capacity to pump blood

subcutaneous   Beneath the skin

subluxation   A bone is forced out but goes back into place

subthreshold   Below the point at which a physiological effect begins to be produced

symptom   Subjective evidence of an abnormal situation within the body

syndrome   Group of typical symptoms or conditions that characterize an injury, a deficiency, or a disease

synergy   To work in cooperation with

synovia   A transparent lubricating fluid found in joints, bursae, and tendons

synovitis   Inflammation of a synovial membrane

synthesis   Buildup

systolic blood pressure   The pressure caused by the heart's pumping

tendinitis   Inflammation of the tendon

tendon   Tough band of connective tissue that attaches muscle to bone

tennis leg   Strain of the gastrocnemius muscle

tenosynovitis   Inflammation of a tendon and its synovial sheath

tetanus toxoid   Tetanus toxin modified to produce active immunity against *Clostridium tetani*

thrombi   Plural of thrombus

thromboplastin   Substance within the body's tissues that accelerates blood clotting

thrombus   Blood clot that blocks small blood vessels or a cavity of the heart

time-loss injuries   Injuries that require the player to suspend activity within a day of an injury's onset

tinea   Ringworm; skin fungus disease

tonic muscle cramp   Continuous muscle contraction that is long in duration

tonic muscle spasm   Rigid muscle contraction that lasts over a period of time

tonus (muscle) Residual state of muscle contraction

torque A twisting force produced by contraction of the medial femoral muscles that tends to rotate the thigh medially

torsional Rotating or twisting of a body part

tort Legal wrongs committed against another

training effect Stroke volume increases while heart rate is reduced at a given exercise load

transitory paralysis Temporary inability to move

traumatic Pertaining to the course of an injury or wound

traumatic arthritis Arthritis stemming from repeated joint injury

traumatic asphyxia Result of a violent blow to, or compression of, the rib cage, causing cessation of breathing

trigger point Area of tenderness in a tight band of muscle

valgus Bent outward

variable resistance Resistance is varied throughout the range of motion

varus Bent inward

vasoconstriction Decrease in the diameter of a blood vessel

vasodilation Increase in the diameter of a blood vessel

vasospasm Blood vessel spasm

venule Tiny vein fed by a capillary

verruca Virus causing a wart

viscera Internal organs

viscus (organs) Any internal organ enclosed within a cavity

volar Referring to the palm or the sole

water ad libitum Unlimited access to water

xerostomia Having a dry mouth

xiphoid process Smallest of three parts of the sternum

Credits

Chapter 2

Figs. 2-3, 2-4, pp. 23, 24, Courtesy, The University of North Carolina at Chapel Hill; **Fig. 2-5, p. 26,** Courtesy, D Bailey, California State University at Long Beach.

Chapter 3

Fig. 3-2, p. 37, Courtesy, The University of North Carolina at Chapel Hill.

Chapter 4

Figs. 4-3 through 4-16, Figs. 4-18 through 4-44, Figs. 4-46 through 4-59, pp. 54-92, From Prentice, WE: *Fitness for college and life,* ed. 5, Dubuque, IA: WCB/McGraw-Hill, 1997.

Chapter 5

Figs. 5-1, 5-4, pp. 101, 113, & Tables 5-1, 5-2, pp. 103, 105, From Prentice, WE: *Fitness for college and life,* ed. 5, Dubuque, IA: WCB/McGraw-Hill, 1997; **Fig. 5-2, p. 108,** From Prentice, WE: *Get fit stay fit,* Dubuque, IA: WCB/McGraw-Hill, 1996; **Fig. 5-3, p. 109,** US Dept of Agriculture/US Dept of Health & Human Services, August, 1992.

Chapter 6

Fig. 6-1, p. 129, Courtesy, Robert Freligh, California State University at Long Beach; **Figs. 6-12, 6-13, pp. 138, 139,** From Nicholas, JA, Hershman, EB: *The lower extremity and spine in sports medicine,* ed. 2, St. Louis: Mosby, 1995; **Fig. 6-14, p. 139,** Courtesy, Denise Fandel, The University of Nebraska at Omaha; **Figs. 6-19, 6-23, 6-26, 6-29 (middle), pp. 142, 146, 147, 149,** Courtesy, Mueller Sports Medicine;

Fig. 6-20, p. 142, From Prentice, WE: *Fitness for college and life,* ed. 5, Dubuque, IA: WCB/McGraw-Hill, 1997.

Chapter 7

Fig. 7-18, p. 182, Courtesy, Hartwell Medical Corporation, Carlsbad, CA.

Chapter 8

Focus box, p. 203, From Payne, WA, Hahn, DB: *Understanding your health,* ed. 5, Dubuque, IA: WCB/McGraw-Hill, 1998.

Chapter 9

Fig. 9-1, p. 213, Courtesy, Ken Bartlett, California State University at Long Beach.

Chapter 10

Table 10-1, p. 227, Modified from Berkow, R: *The Merck manual of diagnosis and therapy,* ed. 14, Rahway, NJ: Merck & Co., 1982.

Chapter 11

Fig. 11-41, p. 270, Art by Don O'Connor.

Chapter 13

Figs. 13-5, 13-6, 13-8, pp. 300-303, From Prentice, WE: *Rehabilitation techniques in sports medicine,* Dubuque, IA: WCB/McGraw-Hill, 1999.

Chapter 15

Fig. 15-7, p. 337, Courtesy, Cramer Products, Gardner, KS; **Figs. 15-17, 15-20, pp. 348,** From Williams, JGP: *Color atlas of injury in sport,* ed. 2, Chicago: Year Book Medical Publishers, 1990.

Chapter 16

Fig. 16-10C, p. 365, Courtesy, Robert Barclay and Renee Reavis Shingles, Central Michigan University.

Chapter 17

Fig. 17-8, p. 382, Courtesy, Ken Bartlett, California State University at Long Beach; **Figs. 17-10, 17-20 (right), pp. 383, 392,** From Williams, JGP: *Color atlas of injury in sport,* ed. 2, Chicago: Year Book Medical Publishers, 1990; **Fig. 17-11, p. 384,** Courtesy, Mueller Sports Medicine; **Figs. 17-15, 17-19, pp. 389, 392,** Courtesy, Robert Barclay and Renee Reavis Shingles, Central Michigan University; **Fig. 17-16, p. 389,** Courtesy BRACE International, Phoenix, AZ.

Chapter 18

Figs. 18-2, 18-5, pp. 399, 402, From Nicholas, JA, Hershman, EB: *The upper extremity in sports medicine,* ed. 2, St. Louis: Mosby, 1995; **Figs. 18-3, 18-4, pp. 400-401,** From Seeley, RR, Stephens, TD, Tate, P: *Anatomy & Physiology,* ed. 4, Dubuque, IA: WCB/McGraw-Hill, 1998 (**Fig. 18-3,** art by David Mascaro; **Fig. 18-4,** art by John V. Hagen); **Fig. 18-17, p. 411,** art by Don O'Connor.

Chapter 19

Figs. 19-6, 19-7, 19-9, 19-11, 19-12, 19-13, 19-15, pp. 419-421, 423, Courtesy Ken Bartlett, California State University at Long Beach; **Figs. 19-8, 19-27, 19-28, pp. 419, 435, 436,** From Nicholas, JA, Hershman, EB: *The upper extremity in sports medicine,* ed. 2, St. Louis: Mosby, 1995; **Fig. 19-19, p. 428,** From Booher, JM, Thibodeau, GA: *Athletic* *injury assessment,* ed. 3, Dubuque, IA: WCB/McGraw-Hill, 1994; **Fig. 19-29, p. 437,** Courtesy, Robert Barclay and Renee Reavis Shingles, Central Michigan University.

Chapter 20

Fig. 20-5, p. 445, art by Don O'Connor; **Fig. 20-7, p. 446,** From Seeley, RR, Stephens, TD, Tate, P: *Anatomy & Physiology,* ed. 4, Dubuque, IA: WCB/McGraw-Hill, 1998; **Fig. 20-16B, p. 459,** From Williams, JGP: *Color atlas of injury in sport,* ed. 2, Chicago: Year Book Medical Publishers, 1990.

Chapter 21

Figs. 21-2, 21-3, pp. 465, 466, From Seeley, RR, Stephens, TD, Tate, P: *Anatomy & Physiology,* ed. 4, Dubuque, IA: WCB/McGraw-Hill, 1998 (**Fig. 21-2,** art by David Mascaro; **Fig. 21-3,** art by John V Hagen).

Chapter 22

Fig. 22-1, p. 483, art by Don O'Connor; **Figs. 22-3, 22-22, pp. 484, 503,** Allsport; **Table 22-2, p. 486,** Adapted from Kelly, JP, Rosenbergg, JH: Diagnosis and management of concussion in sports, *Neurology* 46:575, 1997; **Table 22-3, Focus box, pp. 488-489,** Adapted from Vegso, JJ, Lehman, RC: Field evaluation and management of head and neck injuries. In Torg, JS, ed: *Head and neck injuries,* Clinics in Sports Medicine, vol 6, no 1, Philadelphia: WB Saunders, 1987; **Table 22-4, p. 493,** Adapted from Cantu, RC: Guidelines for return to contact sports after a cerebral concussion, *The Physician in Sportsmedicine* 14 (10): 79, 1986; **Figs. 22-14, 22-15, 22-19, pp. 495, 496, 499,** From Williams, JGP: *Color atlas of injury in sport,* ed. 2, Chicago: Year Book Medical Publishers, 1990; **Fig. 22-17, p. 498,** Focus on Sports; **Focus box, p. 501,** Adapted from Vinger, PF: How I manage corneal abrasions and lacerations, *The Physician in Sportsmedicine* 14 (5):170, 1986.

Chapter 23

Figs. 23-1, 23-2, pp. 509, 511, From Habif, TP: *Clinical dermatology,* ed. 3, St. Louis: Mosby, 1996; **Fig. 23-4, p. 512,** From Stewart, WD, Danto, JL, Madden, S: *Dermatology: diagnosis and treatment of cutaneous disorders,* ed. 4, St. Louis, 1978; **Table 23-3, p. 525,** Modified from American College Health Association: *Making sex safer,* Baltimore: American College Health Association, 1990.

Chapter 24

Fig. 24-1, p. 544, From Coakley, J: *Sport in society,* ed. 5, St. Louis: Mosby, 1994, photo by James Bryant.

Index